THE ENTREPRENEUR'S INTELLECTUAL PROPERTY & BUSINESS HANDBOOK

Jon M. Garon

The book offers a comprehensive guide for using a customer-focused design approach and intellectual property tools to build long-lasting, successful business enterprises. It explains the key business and legal strategies essential for start-ups and small businesses. Through examples from successful companies, lessons from failed experiments, and sample documents, it provides a roadmap for any business towards success.

The book is used by entrepreneurs, legal clinics, small business development centers, and business advisors to help entrepreneurs differentiate their products and services in a very competitive market. It emphasizes that not every business needs a patent portfolio, but every business needs to combine business strategy with intellectual property protections to build itself in a way that avoids being copied by the competition.

Manegiare Publications

Fort Lauderdale, Florida

Library of Congress Cataloging-in-Publication Data

Garon, Jon M. (Legal and business consultation), author.

The Entrepreneur's Intellectual Property & Business Handbook / Jon M. Garon.

Includes bibliographical references.

1. New business enterprises–Law and legislation–United States.

2. Intellectual property–United States.

3. High technologies industries. 4. Venture Capital. I. Title.

Published by Manegiare Publications

Printed in the United States of America 5 4 3 2 1

Preface

The Entrepreneur's Intellectual Property & Business Handbook explains the critical relationship between intellectual property and innovation in simple business language to provide advice on the financing, design, planning, legal structures, and corporate strategies used by successful start-up companies and agile businesses.

The book first focuses on the legal and business attributes of exclusivity and relevance to educate entrepreneurs on how best to build market share and maximize profitability. Using numerous examples, it helps entrepreneurs organize their business to maximize profitability.

Chapters on relevance, innovation, and design thinking focus on how to identify the opportunities for changes in processes and markets. It contrasts the market relevance of a patented medicine for a medical patient from the "social relevance" of a Barbie Doll for a child. Using simple descriptions and numerous examples, the book explains how intellectual property assets and a focus on consumer needs can build social and market relevance into products and services.

Part 2 features new chapters on franchising, financing, and privacy. These add depth to the range of business issues faced by entrepreneurs in today's rapidly changing knowledge economy. As both a guide and handbook, the text provides materials that will serve as an ongoing reference for years to come.

Part 3 of the book features the Intellectual Property Reference Guide, which carefully explains patent, copyright, trademark, publicity rights and trade secrets in the language of the entrepreneurial business. Each chapter features a foundational explanation of the intellectual property principles while addressing practical questions for business owners.

Through examples and charts, entrepreneurs can identify their own business goals to help them clarify the relationship with investors. This book provides the keys to building an economically stable business and a secure financial future. It serves as the user's manual for entrepreneurial companies seeking to be profitable, stable, and built to last.

Table of Contents

Introduction

> Build a better mousetrap and the world will beat a path to your door.
>
> - Ralph Waldo Emerson

> IP-based businesses and entrepreneurs drive more economic growth in the United States than any other single sector.
>
> - United States Patent & Trademark Office

A.   The Circuitous Sequel.

To fully understand the purpose of this book, it is helpful to put it into the context of my other writings and professional activities. I am currently Dean of Nova Southeastern University Shepard Broad College of Law. Before this I served as the director of the NKU Salmon Chase College of Law, Law + Informatics Institute; Dean of Hamline University School of Law; and Interim Dean of Hamline University Graduate School of Management. I have been a law professor and an attorney practicing in the areas of intellectual property (IP) and business law for over thirty years. As a law dean and professor, I am committed to the lawyer's obligation to make the law more accessible to the public. My goal with this book is to demystify the legal "secrets" of starting a business and to create new opportunities for anyone with the creativity and tenacity necessary to become an entrepreneur.

In 2007, I published *Own It: The Law & Business Guide to Launching a New Business through Innovation, Exclusivity, and Relevance*. This book is the second edition of *Own It*, retitled and expanded to capture the changes to the digital economy in the decade since the first edition was published. In addition to being a second edition, in some ways it is also a sequel.

In 2002, I published the *Independent Filmmaker's Law & Business Guide*, with its second edition in 2009 (and third edition coming soon). The book has been a hit among filmmakers and has assisted them to make films, create film companies, and participate in social discourse through entertainment. Since the book's publication, movies such as *The Passion of the Christ* and *Fahrenheit 9/11* have

1

demonstrated that independent films have the power to transform public discourse about important events. Since writing that book, however, I have learned a few things. First, most Americans are not filmmakers. While the audience for the book has been receptive, it is not particularly large. Second, while the book provided tools to make documentaries and films relevant to social issues, in significant ways, any book on filmmaking can have only a limited impact on society.

While my academic writing is primarily social and legal commentary, my goal with this book is to address readers directly, and in doing so, impact society in a tangible way. The most important step we can take to create a free and just society is to create economic opportunities that are universally available to each and every person. Economic security is the cornerstone of liberty.[1]

The first edition of this book, **Own It**, fulfilled that mission, so I am updating and expanding the book to continue to help provide that low-cost service. This is a book for all entrepreneurs—not just the risk takers in the film industry. However, many of the suggestions are similar because independent filmmaking is a particular form of entrepreneurship.

The Entrepreneur's IP Business Handbook is different from every other business start-up book for one simple reason. The goal is not merely to instruct new entrepreneurs on how to start a business, but to identify attributes that can lead a business from the garage to the top of the Fortune 500 list. The strategy focuses on a rule learned from independent filmmakers, authors, and musicians. This fundamental business axiom is known by every venture capital guru and dot.com success.

The central axiom of this book is exclusivity and relevance. By owning the property that provides the core asset of a business, the owner can reap the benefits, maintain healthy profit margins, and discourage competition. Through careful research and an understanding of the

---

[1] As a United States lawyer (licensed in California and New Hampshire), I simply do not have the expertise to provide the same tools to individuals in countries outside the United States. The lessons in this book, however, are not limited to U.S. citizens or to businesses operating only in the United States.

stressors that create business opportunity, entrepreneurs can identify the opportunities to build enterprises that are invaluable to their customers and protected from competition.

The new title is based on these themes. IP is essential to enable a business to have the breathing space necessary to charge a reasonable price for its services. Exclusivity is essential for profitability. But IP is wasted unless the owners place it in the heart of business operations. This book, then, highlights the integration of IP and business strategies, in a simple handbook format.

Through the legal doctrines of patent, copyright, trademark, publicity rights, and similar tools, the exclusivity once reserved for the industrial giants of the 20th century can now be used for every conceivable business. Google, Apple, Microsoft, and Intel all exist because of exclusivity; their technological inventions are patented, and their software is copyrighted. Similarly, Disney, Time Warner, and Fox derive their worth from copyrights. Nike, Mercedes, and Levi's have built empires on their most valuable assets: their names, personalities, and logos. Coca-Cola and Kentucky Fried Chicken rely on trade secrets to accomplish these goals.

But the successes are not limited to the most powerful companies. Apple is renowned for its origins in a garage. Famous Amos cookies, Mrs. Fields, Ben & Jerry's, and many others started from humble beginnings, but they built success upon the intellectual property of copyright, trademarks, patents and trade secrets, and publicity rights.

Because the relationship between the entrepreneur and the investor is critical to the success of business models built on exclusivity and relevance, the book also explores financing options and suggests how to manage the interests of the investors, the entrepreneurs, and the employees of the business. Together with some nuts-and-bolts information on the start-up phase of the business, this book will provide the keys to unlocking the American dream and building a secure financial future for every entrepreneur. The book does not offer any get-rich-quick schemes, but provides a model for building a business that will last.

4

B.   The Role of the Book.

This book is a guide to one particular aspect of creating a new enterprise. There are dozens of topics the book does not touch. There is no discussion of inventory control, double-ledger accounting, parachute colors, or the movement of cheese. Instead, it provides legal and business fundamentals. The entrepreneur must supply the business knowledge to make the book's principles useful and some business experience to know when to take risks and when to avoid them.

THIS BOOK DOES NOT CONSTITUTE THE PRACTICE OF LAW OR PROVIDE LEGAL ADVICE THAT CAN BE RELIED UPON AS AUTHORITATIVE FOR ANY PARTICULAR JURISDICTION. THIS INFORMATION IS GENERAL IN NATURE AND SHOULD BE USED ONLY IN CONJUNCTION WITH A LICENSED ATTORNEY, PROPERLY FAMILIAR WITH THE SPECIFIC LEGAL MATTER IN QUESTION.

THIS BOOK IDENTIFIES PARTICULAR INDIVIDUALS, FIRMS, AND COMPANIES. NOTHING HEREIN CONSTITUTES AN ENDORSEMENT OF THESE ENTITIES OR OF THEIR SERVICES AND CANNOT BE RELIED UPON AS THE LEGAL BASIS FOR ENGAGING SUCH SERVICES. Although many of the companies listed are the largest or most visible in their respective fields, their names are used either for illustrative purposes or to provide a starting point for the reader's own research. Conversely, the failure to appear in the book should not be deemed a negative assessment of any particular product, service, or organization.

C.   Acknowledgements.

This book was born of necessity. Not my necessity, but that of my clients and the clients at my law schools' nonprofit, small business, and entrepreneur legal clinics. Through a myriad of meetings and conversations, I learned about the barriers that kept thoughtful new business owners from succeeding. I am very grateful to those individuals for sharing their time and educating me on the needs of the entrepreneur.

This project is the result of the work supported by my colleagues at NSU Shepard Broad College of Law, NKU Salmon P. Chase College of

Law, Hamline University School of Law, Hamline University Graduate School of Management, Franklin Pierce Law Center, and the law firm of Gallagher, Callahan, and Gartrell (GCG). I particularly wish to acknowledge Donald Pfundstein, who brought the core values captured in this text to the management of GCG. Donald proved that law firm management need not always be an oxymoron.

I appreciate the efforts of many business professionals, lawyers, and other colleagues who reviewed the manuscript for this book to assure that I never ran too far off course, though the responsibility for all information in the text is solely my own. In particular, I would like to thank members of my family who read drafts of the book and provided thoughtful guidance, including Sherman Garon (obm), the business owner from whom I learned so many of these lessons; my sons Avery and Noah, who have grown of age between the editions of this book and who have provided valuable insights into entrepreneurship in a wide array of businesses; and my wife, Stacy Blumberg Garon, my constant source of inspiration, candid analysis and exceptional editing. I have benefited greatly from the advice of many other experts who reviewed my efforts and challenged my ideas, including Tom Field, Carol Honabach, Denis Malony, Susan Stephan, my research assistant Laura Haske (first edition), and my research assistant Tammy Eick (second edition).

I received a great deal of assistance on the first edition from my publisher, Carolina Academic Press, and I greatly appreciate their support in my projects, including this edition which they did not produce. They are a great asset to legal publishing, and I truly thank the friendship and assistance of Keith Sipe, Linda Lacy, and Scott Sipe.

For this edition, I have received additional assistance from many of those who helped with the first edition, particularly Stacy Blumberg Garon, Susan Stephan and Carol Honabach. Others joined in with advice and helpful suggestions, including Hannah Stephan, Alison Rosenberg, Michelle Murray, Vicenç Feliú, Steven Kass, and Christina Grimm. I am deeply indebted to everyone.

Part 1. Entrepreneurship

"Today, much confusion exists about the proper definition of entrepreneurship. Some observers use the term to refer to all small businesses; others, to all new businesses. In practice, however, a great many well-established businesses engage in highly successful entrepreneurship. The term, then, refers not to an enterprise's size or age but to a certain kind of activity. At the heart of that activity is innovation: the effort to create purposeful, focused change in an enterprise's economic or social potential."

— Peter F. Drucker, Innovation and Entrepreneurship: Practice and Principles, New York: Harper & Row (1985).

Chapter 1. Building Blocks for the Business

A.   Entrepreneurship, Intellectual Property, and the Business Start-Up.

The Entrepreneur's IP & Business Handbook identifies how the law provides different methods of protecting the outgrowth of unique ideas, how to build unique ideas into the business plan and legal structure of each company, and how to maximize the potential return from the idea. Entrepreneurs will use this book to improve each step in their business planning. Business owners will also find it serves as a valued resource as they incorporate the suggestions to differentiate their products and separate their goods from those sold by their competitors.

The chapters intersperse discussion of developing ideas into products and businesses with chapters on intellectual property because only those ideas that are eligible for some form of legal protection will serve as the basis for financing and operating the business. The handbook is designed to help the entrepreneur stay on track to develop new products and services that are structured to compete in the marketplace, enabling the inventor to obtain the financing to launch the business and the market-share needed to sustain the business.

1.   The Goals of the Entrepreneur's IP & Business Handbook Approach.

An effective business strategy provides the tools to create something about the business that makes it powerfully distinctive from any other business. This uniqueness provides for exclusive ownership. The exclusivity, in turn, allows the business to set higher prices and reduce price competition. The price protection cannot be absolute. At some point, customers are willing to accept an imperfect substitute for the product or service, but the exclusivity provides the pricing cushion needed to increase profit margins and improve business success.

For example, golfers may be willing to spend an additional $0.25 per golf ball for a ball that flies ten percent further than a conventional ball. (Experience or product testing might instead make the price difference $0.10 or $1.00—testing of the market value is essential.) If the long-ball design can be owned exclusively, then the benefit is $0.25 per unit multiplied by the total number of balls sold by the manufacturer. This can add up fast. Even better, if the long-ball becomes popular, then the benefits will include increased income for each ball sold, as well as more chances that golf stores will want to stock the long-ball. If the design cannot be owned exclusively, then the $0.25 will quickly erode as other ball manufacturers provide identical long-balls.

The golf example also highlights the need for relevance in the product design. While many variations on the golf ball have been tried by entrepreneurs, only improved performance is critical to most golfers. Colored balls, monograms, and radio-frequency identification (RFID) chips can distinguish one ball from the next. Designs that are distinctive, however, provide no market impact unless the distinctions are those relevant to consumers and are sufficiently important that they will affect consumer choice. Exclusivity without relevance leads to eccentricity. Exclusivity with relevance leads to business success.

So long as a business can create relevant, distinctive products or opportunities, then that business can capture the price difference between its unique product and other products. This is not always done through price increases. The alternative benefit is an increase in market share. Motion picture theatrical tickets are generally the same retail price for each movie exhibited in a city. Each movie is somewhat distinctive from all others, so that popularity—a simple measure of market share—

is greater for the better film. Price is held constant because of the business plan of the film exhibitors. Film exhibitors could charge a premium for the most popular of movies, but instead use a business model that makes the additional revenue by selling more tickets.

Regardless of the manner in which the distinction is utilized, the effect is to increase the revenue a company can earn through the exclusive ownership of its products and services. The World Intellectual Property Organization (WIPO) provides a wealth of free resources to businesses around the globe, encouraging them to use their intellectual property to increase wealth and value. In its introduction to the resources for small to medium-sized businesses, WIPO explains the importance of intellectual property rights as follows:

> For most small and medium-sized enterprises (SMEs), marketing products or services is a major challenge. A marketing strategy should establish a clear link between your products or services and your SME, as the producer or provider of such products or services. That is to say, customers should be able to distinguish, at a glance, between your products or services and those of your competitors and associate them with certain desired qualities.

> Intellectual property, when efficiently used, is an important tool in creating an image for your business in the minds of your current and potential customers and in positioning your business in the market. IP rights, combined with other marketing tools (such as advertisements and other sales promotion activities) are crucial for:

> - Differentiating your products and services and making them easily recognizable.

> - Promoting your products or services and creating a loyal clientele.

- Diversifying your market strategy to various target groups.

- Marketing your products or services in foreign countries.[2]

Creating a loyal clientele that values the start-up business's products over those belonging to its rivals is an essential element for business success. As described throughout the book, the combination of differentiation, which comes from exclusive ownership of some aspect of the products or services, and relevance, which is evidenced through customer loyalty, mix together for a potent business formula. Without both exclusivity and relevance, a start-up business will not succeed. Only through exclusivity and relevance can a start-up business have any opportunity to find a place in the market.

2. Identifying the Right Business to Utilize Exclusivity.

The key to success in creating distinctiveness is the ability to differentiate the entrepreneur's products or services from all other products or services which might serve as competition—as substitutes for the entrepreneur's goods or services. Some businesses without distinctive products or services become little more than self-financed, independent contractor agreements. Janitorial service companies, vending machine routes, gift shops, and corner groceries are typical start-up business opportunities, particularly within immigrant communities. Unfortunately, these businesses provide little opportunity for exclusivity and, therefore, little opportunity to create significant wealth.

The types of companies that are built on exclusivity include manufacturers of patented products; processing plants that use carefully protected trade secrets; publishers of books, film, and music, which all rely on copyrighted source material; and franchises, retail shops that sell exclusive product lines; and well-managed restaurants, which tend to rely on trademarks or publicity rights to differentiate from their competitors. These companies are successful when their business model centers on a unique idea.

---

[2] *Why is Intellectual Property Crucial for Marketing the Products or Services of Your SME?*, WORLD INTELLECTUAL PROP. ORG., http://www.wipo.int/sme/en/ip_business/marketing/marketing.htm (last visited June 26, 2018).

Even a common idea can be imbued with some exclusivity as the identity for the business grows. McDonald's and Burger King stand out from other hamburger or fast-food restaurants because of the investment and growth in the trademarks and in manufacturing processes. Molly Maid successfully franchised the simple home cleaning business by creating brand identity and loyalty.

By identifying which attributes of the business give the greatest opportunity for exclusivity, the entrepreneur can develop the business successfully. This key aspect to understanding business growth is more important than any other aspect of the enterprise—except start-up funds.

B.   Starting with a Dream.

Regardless of the type of enterprise, the starting point for any entrepreneur is a distinctive dream for the business. To be successful, the entrepreneur must create every aspect of the business in a manner that maximizes this business distinctiveness. The second essential element is that the distinctiveness must be relevant to the customer.

1.   *The Importance of Relevance.*

Being distinctive is the first step towards creating a successful start-up business, but it is insufficient without more. The second, critical step is to make the business relevant (or better yet, essential) for the customers. A relevant or essential product or service is something that the customer cannot do without. For example, automobile manufacturers cannot sell cars without tires. The tire is essential to the completion of every car. Some manufacturer must make a business selling the tires. But if the tires manufactured by different companies are not distinctive, then the auto companies buying tires can put pressure on them to lower the tire price. In contrast, if a particular tire is distinctive, then the price charged for that tire may be higher because the other tires are imperfect substitutes in the minds of consumers.

Relevance is not a legal concept. Relevance comes from knowing more about a customer's needs than the customer knows. Apple's Steve Jobs famously stated that "[a] lot of times, people don't know what they want until you show it to them."[3] That is not the same as ignoring the customer; instead it means digging past the simple answers to understand the motivations driving the customer.

Relevance comes from good industry research. Popular notions of markets are not necessarily accurate. For example, the *New York Times* bestseller list does not include the better commercial sellers such as the *New Testament* or the *Complete Works of Shakespeare*. These books outsell most books on the bestseller lists but are not listed each week because it would make the list less interesting. Similarly, favorite children's toys like crayons, modeling clay, cards, and books are seldom mentioned in the Christmas lists of top-selling toys. Good research must get beyond the "what's hot" lists to measure the real information of market trends.

2.   The Importance of Research.

Relevance also comes from identifying what customers do not yet have. The tin can was invented a full six months before the first can opener. Before that, cans were opened with a hammer and chisel. The need for a tool to open the can was obvious, although the precise nature of the necessary tool took some time to develop. The transformation from mobile phone to all-in-one pocket computer was long anticipated in science fiction, but Motorola, Palm, Blackberry, and Microsoft could not keep up with the innovations of Apple's iOS and Google's Android.

Many start-up businesses develop out of the need to solve a particular problem in industry. The typical entrepreneur creates a start-up business because a current employer cannot or will not make the changes necessary to improve the process or solve the problem. The employer is too busy producing cans to spend time or money on the can opener.

Experience in the market is a useful research tool, but it should never be the sole criterion. Creating a logical assumption that success in one area indicates success in another is a reasonable basis for identifying or growing a business. If a retail store works well in a particular neighborhood, then it is reasonable to assume that the business should

---

[3] Chunka Mui, *Five Dangerous Lessons to Learn from Steve Jobs*, FORBES (Oct. 17, 2011, 10:07 AM), https://www.forbes.com/sites/chunkamui/2011/10/17/five-dangerous-lessons-to-learn-from-steve-jobs/#25727d683a95.

work well in other, similar neighborhoods. This assumption, however, is not always correct. Additional information may be necessary to accurately predict success. For example, restaurant owners undoubtedly assume that the restaurant's success is based on the quality and type of food on the menu as well as the restaurant's ambiance. If in reality the food is bad, the selection is poor, and the environment is tasteless, the restaurant might still succeed if there is little competition and the restaurant is located in a heavily trafficked area that provides a steady supply of new customers.

Other, smaller neighborhood differences might make the assumption inaccurate. Average income levels vary among neighborhoods. The successful menu in one location might be too expensive in another. Ethnic variations among neighborhoods can also help or hurt the restaurant's ability to move from one neighborhood to the next. The number of restaurants in an area will also affect the new restaurant's success. A moderately successful restaurant might have been successful only because it was near a wildly popular competitor—which often had long waiting lines. The less popular restaurant survived as a substitute product, making money because of its neighbor. The relevance was convenience rather than food or environment. Without the proximity to its successful neighbor, the restaurant was not particularly relevant to its customers.

General industry experience can be an essential element in predicting business success, primarily because experience in a particular area will lead to asking the right questions. The more experienced restaurateur will want to know far more than annual net profits. Information on the number of seatings per evening, the balance of dine-in to take-out, the popularity of various menu items, union costs, liquor license issues, etc., all provide information about the health of a particular restaurant. An entrepreneur's industry experience cannot be underestimated as a key factor influencing success. Nonetheless, no two situations are exactly alike. Experience should not be used by itself to predict new markets. Research can help identify factors that will improve the likelihood of success and provide an important context for prior experience.

Good market research becomes critical to understanding what really matters to customers. By asking existing customers detailed questions and putting the entrepreneur in the shoes of the customer, the entrepreneur can learn a great deal. The entrepreneur should also ask for advice from people other than close friends and family. While some dreams are worth pursuing over the advice of others, they are few and far between. All business is collaborative, so it is very helpful to listen to both the encouragement and discouragement of those who will be honest with their opinions.

3.   *Adding Relevance to Distinctiveness.*

Distinctiveness can be assessed through research into the competitive market for similar products. Relevance can be assessed by studying the consumer's need. To be successful, a new business product or service must have both.

A company which provides a relevant product or service invariably struggles to maintain its profit margins against similar companies providing equivalent products or services. A company that provides a distinctive product or service risks being irrelevant if the public is uninterested. Success lies in combining relevance with distinctiveness. When a relevant product is also distinctive, the sky is the limit. A few examples may help make the point clearer.

The soft drink industry is a multi-billion dollar business. Consumers of soft drinks, therefore, have made them highly relevant. Coca-Cola's formula is distinct in flavor from its competitors and more pleasing to more consumers, so it dominates the industry. The drink is also distinctive because of the "Coke" name. Since Coke is so closely associated with the taste of this particular soft drink, even an identical product would be unable to compete. Coca-Cola's relevance comes from American consumers preferring its taste, while its distinctiveness comes from both the brand name and unique formula. Pepsi has no incentive to copy Coke's formula because that would only drive down the profits for both companies. Instead, it strives to attach its brand name to a different soft drink taste that will be equally distinctive and more relevant. If more people preferred the taste of Pepsi to Coke, Pepsi should eventually dominate the market.

In reality, the strength of the brand name may be more important than the taste because many factors other than taste go into a purchase decision by a consumer or a vendor choosing to carry Coke or Pepsi. As a result, many of the customers would remain loyal to Coke notwithstanding the public's preference for the Pepsi taste. This is why Coke retained its market despite the embarrassment of the ill-fated New

Coke product launch. Coke retained the brand name even as it lost the relevant distinctive taste. At the same time, Coke has struggled with the naming of "Coke Zero," eventually rebranding it "Coke Zero Sugar" because of the growing public dislike of sugar-filled products. Although the diet drink did not significantly change, the "Zero Sugar" name is designed to increase market awareness.

Another example can be seen every August as stores fill their aisles with back-to-school goods. Schools insist that students use folders, which makes them relevant to students. Lunch boxes are relevant because many students bring their lunch from home, and the lunch boxes can be reused daily. Typically, unadorned and inexpensive examples of both lunch boxes and school folders are available. The more expensive items, however, are those with pictures of movie characters, toys, or sports figures. Each of these is distinctive because of the unique, exclusive image used to decorate the product. The price paid for these picture lunch boxes and folders greatly exceeds the cost of printing the pictures or even the cost of licensing the pictures. The profits are much higher because the exclusive pictures make these items distinctive. Of course, children are fickle. Among the lunch boxes, relevance is based on the popularity of the displayed movie or sports figure. If the movie bombed at the box office, or if the athlete has not played due to injury (or imprisonment), those items become irrelevant and do not sell. In this case, the distinctiveness becomes a disadvantage rather than an advantage.

One subtle form of relevance is the role trademarks play in identifying the lifestyle of the consumer. Relevance derives from the brand's ability to reinforce the goals or self-image of the consumer rather than from the product itself. For example, when they were introduced, men's body sprays such as Axe Body Spray and Tag Body Spray for Men both featured advertising showing the users of these products being instantly attacked by women. In these campaigns, there was nothing subtle about the lifestyle being sold. Sports drinks, razors, facial tissues, and myriad other products are packaged as men's or women's versions when, in fact, the product is the same as the non-gendered version. But the gendered packaging signals a relevance to consumers that continues to work.

Happy Meals, play spaces, and McDonaldland characters tied McDonald's to a family experience that is not consistent with a college student's self-image. McDonald's "I'm lovin' it" campaign attempts to transition the company from its Happy Meal family market to a younger, urban, or hip crowd so that it can remain relevant to both market segments.

Levi's has had a similar problem. Levi's is a highly regarded brand name for quality jeans. Until recently the name conjured up assumptions that these jeans are Made in America and rugged rural ware. Despite this, most of Levi's jeans are manufactured outside the U.S. Levi's competitors were focused on the more popular, trendy markets where the bulk of the jean purchasing decisions were made. Levi's failed to generate a successful new identity for the suburban consumer who was the target audience for jean sales. As a result, Levi's highly recognized trademark did not relate to the core jean-purchasing market and Levi's lost market share, dropping nearly $3 billion from its top income levels. Levi's pivoted, entering a relationship with Walmart and shifting away from fashion jeans to everyday work jeans for a large part of its market segment. Although it remains a large, healthy national brand, it has shifted significantly in its position within the clothing industry as a result.

For products that are not otherwise distinctive, the relevance of the trademark comes from associating the brand with the desired lifestyle of the consumer. Companies can earn themselves market share by making their identity or lifestyle highly relevant to consumers, but this is a very expensive and often volatile undertaking. Distinctive products reduce the reliance on lifestyle, shifting the focus onto the product itself.

Perhaps the best recent example of the intersection of lifestyle and distinctiveness has come from Apple. The iPhone and iPad are highly distinctive, with proprietary music formats and features that once tied directly to Apple's Mac computer format. Apple has invested substantially in an industrial design form and marketing campaign to distinguish itself from other mobile devices. Its longstanding marketing campaign emphasizes the nontraditional and somewhat hip consumer base of Apple as opposed to the corporate consumers of the Android phones and PC computers. Apple has used its differentiation to earn twice the profit on the devices it sells in contrast to its competitors.

Under Steve Jobs, Apple products were culturally relevant. Apple's iTunes music service is the most distinctive music distribution system because of the music license provided to consumers. It negotiated terms that were more to the liking of college-age students, who comprise the bulk of consumers, than most of the other music services. Business terms provide a nontraditional, but highly effective source for distinctiveness, but a form of distinctiveness that is often temporary. By understanding the usage needs of its consumers, Apple stepped far ahead of its competition. In recent years, as the idiosyncratic leadership of Steve Jobs fades, the competitors are catching up and the distinctiveness is disappearing.

Once the entrepreneur identifies the product or service relevant to the customers, he must then strive to make it and keep it distinctive—to build that better mousetrap that will cause the world to beat a path to the business's door. The ultimate measure of distinctiveness is exclusivity. Exclusive ideas are at the heart of all new industries, start-up successes, and the brass ring every entrepreneur seeks.

C.   Ideas or Risk—the Entrepreneur's Patentable Spirit.

1.   Innovation Starts on the Outside.

The entrepreneur's task in making products and services relevant, distinctive, and exclusive is a process of fundamental change from the status quo. At the heart of entrepreneurship is the goal of being a change agent within one's field of expertise. In Peter Drucker's classic text, *Innovation and Entrepreneurship*, he quotes economists as saying "the entrepreneur upsets and disorganizes . . . his task is creative destruction."[4] He also explained that the heart of entrepreneurship "is innovation: the effort to create purposeful, focused change in an enterprise's economic or social potential."[5]

Over the years, established businesses have seen start-up competitors move from being marginalized pests to dominant forces. The railroads were powerless to stop the automakers, which could not stop the airlines. Motion picture studios acted too late to influence

---

[4] PETER F. DRUCKER, INNOVATION AND ENTREPRENEURSHIP: PRACTICE AND PRINCIPLES 26 (1993) (quoting Joseph Schumpeter and J.B. Say) (internal quotations omitted).

[5] Peter F. Drucker, *The Discipline of Innovation*, HARV. BUS. REV., Aug. 2002, at 95, 96, https://hbr.org/2002/08/the-discipline-of-innovation.

television. Radio companies participated in the development of television, but the radio stations themselves were marginalized. YouTube, Netflix, and Amazon are leading media companies, threatening broadcast networks and cable systems. Android and iOS apps are threatening to overtake Microsoft and Oracle as software companies. Tomorrow . . . is utterly unknown. What can be predicted is that entrenched companies are less able to move than the entrepreneurs who embrace change.

The failure of the entrenched companies to move with the times is not because of their unwillingness to accept risk. Many industrial giants are good at managing and participating in risk. Instead, the industry leaders struggle because one cannot be distinctive from oneself. Entrepreneurship does not come from being on the outside; but being on the inside of an industry limits the transformations and disruptions one can cause. Very few companies are willing to engage in the disruptive innovation necessary to cannibalize their own sales and risk success for the hope of staying current.

2.   *Risk-Taking is Not a Measure of Success.*

Some business books focus on the entrepreneur rather than on the business, concentrating on personality factors rather than structural business factors. While a person's willingness to accept risk might lead the entrepreneur to form a business more willingly than someone who is risk-averse, there is little practical guidance in this insight. Most start-ups fail. Many fail for lack of funding, others fail for lack of management, while still others fail for lack of business understanding. A good many start-up businesses close simply because the entrepreneur moves on to something else. One's willingness to fail or to move on is unrelated to one's ability to succeed. An entrepreneur cannot succeed if the entrepreneur never engages in the enterprise, but that willingness is unrelated to tools, funding, or market forces.

People strongly prefer not to lose something than to gain something of equal value. Decision theory and cognitive psychological studies recognize this behavior as loss aversion. Loss aversion highlights that most people are substantially less likely to seek something new than to risk losing something they already have. Entrepreneurs are likely no different than the rest of the population. If risk taking does not set the entrepreneur apart, then what does? Rather than an absence of the fear of failure, a more likely common trait is the willingness to accept the consequences of failure or success. A large company can become very entrepreneurial if the alternative is bankruptcy. But that same large company will not be able to take large risks if the consequence of success would harm substantial numbers of employees, unless the failure to try could doom the company. This is why film-based photography companies waited far too long before entering the digital film market. It is the same reason that relatively few universities are providing comprehensive online education, even as a small subset of universities are excelling within the field.

Many entrepreneurs are desperate for success, and that drive propels them to overcome the difficulties faced with new businesses. The desperate need to succeed may be driven by a financial need or by a psychological one. It might also be simply the need to change an operational step to make the existing workplace a little better. Whatever the compulsion, it is the need for success that drives entrepreneurship.

Being driven is necessary, but hardly sufficient. In art and sports, the mantra for success remains "practice, practice, practice." In business it can be restated as "watch the fundamentals." The fundamentals include researching customer needs, understanding the prices at which the customer is willing to pay for the product, carefully studying the competition, and managing finances to always have sufficient cash to meet the needs of the growing business. Without these fundamentals, no entrepreneur can survive.

3.   *The Entrepreneur Skillset.*

Much has been written regarding the mindset used by entrepreneurs. Since a mindset reflects an attitude or inclination, the public often views this as a fixed characteristic of the individual entrepreneur. A better characterization is that entrepreneurship is a set of skills that can be developed over time and improved with practice and training.

Rita Gunther McGrath and Ian MacMillan highlight the approach taken by serial entrepreneurs, including their willingness to embrace uncertainty, simplify the complex, seize opportunities quickly, and implement nonperfect solutions rather than wait for solutions that might have been better but come too late.[6] They summarize these characteristics into five traits:

Habitual entrepreneurs have five characteristics in common.

(1) They passionately seek new opportunities. . . .

(2) They pursue opportunities with enormous discipline. . . .

(3) They pursue only the very best opportunities and avoid exhausting themselves and their organizations by chasing after every option. . . .

(4) They focus on execution–specifically, adaptive execution . . . able to change directions as the real opportunity, and the best way to exploit it, evolves. . . .

(5) They engage the energies of everyone in their domain.[7]

While these five characteristics are involved with managing uncertainty, they are not specifically about risk. More generally, entrepreneurs must develop their skills of problem solving, resilience, communication, and teamwork to implement the McGrath and MacMillan approaches effectively. For the five characteristics are responses to risk more than traits or mindsets. They are about being responsive to the risks that surround business. To be successful as an entrepreneur, then, budding entrepreneurs must emphasize how to utilize their skills in recognizing and responding to novel business challenges.

The successful entrepreneur is constantly looking for new opportunities to make improvements. Once undertaken, the process of implementing improvement solutions is not casual, but systematic. Potential solutions are proposed, tested, and discarded. These efforts are not failures. Instead, they are prototypes and practice sessions. The entrepreneur learns to be resilient, accepting the dozens of false starts and incomplete solutions as necessary to the process. Resilience and

---

[6] RITA GUNTHER MCGRATH & IAN MACMILLAN, THE ENTREPRENEURIAL MINDSET 2 (2000).

[7] *Id.* at 2–3.

problem solving are entrepreneurial skills—not mindsets—that are essential to success.

And once undertaken, successful entrepreneurs become highly focused, collaborative, and iterative so that the solutions leaving the workshop work. Finally, entrepreneurs use their collaboration and team building skills to build a network of supporters that make the better mousetrap successful in the marketplace. Not every project will be a success, of course, but every success will have these attributes. And the successful entrepreneur will have developed these skills through the process.

4.   The Patent Approach for Identifying Consumer Demand.

In addition to the skills of resilience, problem solving, collaboration, and communication, the successful entrepreneur needs to understand the business fundamentals at the heart of their business and have a keen perception of the consumer's needs. To understand the needs of the business and the needs of the customer, the basic rules of patentability provide a useful framework. To borrow from the patent concepts discussed below, a new business must have the same three attributes as those needed for a patentable invention—the start-up business or innovation must be new, useful, and nonobvious to the competition. Successful entrepreneurs can both identify and satisfy the new, useful, and nonobvious needs of the consumer.

The newer or fresher the business, the less competition and the more opportunity for capturing the market.

The more useful, the more relevant and higher the demand.

The less obvious, the greater the opportunity for capturing those exclusive attributes of the business—creating the ability to own the new market.

By applying a new, useful, and nonobvious approach to satisfying consumer needs, entrepreneurs will increase their chance for success. Focusing on these attributes will transform even mundane enterprises into valuable ones. Newness and freshness can lead to innovation in restaurant menus, packaging, pricing, or service combinations.

Innovations must be tested against customer interest and demand. Just as a patent will not be issued for an innovation that serves no purpose, a new product will generate no demand if it serves no purpose or satisfies no customer need. The product's innovation must excite some population of intended consumers. This is where Steve Jobs' statement about the customer is misunderstood. Apple would not look to the customer to decide what should be new, but it worked exceptionally hard to make sure every innovation was highly relevant to its customers.

The innovation, however, must do more than merely excite consumers. The nonobvious nature of the product creates the separation between this product and the other products in the field. To have staying power, the product must be more than the next logical progression of a previous product. The competition does not stand still. Merely anticipating the next step in the product's development will be insufficient to compete with established companies. Established companies are always seeking to improve their products, iterate upgrades, and add efficiency. Established companies can build on existing product development cycles to leverage existing products, distribution channels, and relationships to keep start-up competitors from entering into the market.

If the entrepreneur's entry product is nothing more than the existing product's next logical step that "everyone" in that industry expected, then consumers are not going to leave established relationships to try the new competitor. Instead, the improvement must be at least two steps ahead, nonobvious to the competition, and not anticipated from what has come before in the field. The consumer has to be sufficiently impressed to take the risk of buying from an untested source.

The innovation must be useful to the intended customers. If the proposed product is truly new, useful, and nonobvious, then the entrepreneur has the potential to compete in the marketplace. Generally this means that there will be a positive reaction in the industry trade press, at trade shows, and in other venues which influence decision making. A positive industry response to the new product indicates that consumers will be interested. In other words, the product will be relevant.

Once the competitors see the success of this new relevant product, they will change their products to provide the same relevance to customers. To keep the lead, the entrepreneur must own some aspect of the new product so that it cannot be exactly duplicated. The harder to duplicate, the greater the opportunity for the entrepreneur to build his company and enter the market. This is the value of exclusivity.

5.   *The Personality-Based Business.*

There is another category of business that operates successfully because of the unique reputation and skill set at the heart of the company. These businesses have a uniqueness developed from the key personnel's unequaled knowledge of their customer demands or how to outperform others in the marketplace.

Examples of such businesses include the following: The master chef who provides the menu selections, recipes, and concepts to the most highly rated restaurants. The top real estate broker who provides a level of service and market expertise that is unmatched by rivals, despite all brokers having access to the same property listings. The financial manager who outperforms the markets year after year and earns a reputation for success and insight well beyond that provided elsewhere in the financial sector. And the motion picture director, who earns the "film by" credit and whose work is instantly recognized regardless of the film company producing and distributing the movie. These individuals are likely to serve as employees or independent contractors rather than be owners of their companies. Nonetheless, their acumen drives the success of the business and provides the differentiation from the competitors.

Initially, one may consider that these examples offer a different strategy than the intellectual property-based approach highlighted throughout this book. Each of these examples is "personality" driven rather than copyright or patent driven, and often these individuals do not have sufficient public reputation to truly provide a value from the marketing of their name and likeness. Instead, a combination of two attributes are essential to make such companies succeed.

The first attribute for the personality-based business is an obsessive commitment to excellence and a resilience to be the most successful. Success does not come merely from building the better mousetrap, but from building it, demonstrating it is better over and over again, and marketing the improved, better-value mousetrap to every corner of the world. Building it is never enough; it is just a start. More than other enterprises, the successful personality-based business requires the company to proselytize and market far more than others. Hedge fund managers and financiers like George Soros and Warren Buffet are far better known than most in their industry. Their fame reflects both their great economic success and their proselytization of that success on the world stage.

The second attribute for the personality-based business is the nearly unique ability to exploit market analysis to predict the right business decision. In the case of the top realtor, this is a combination of aggressively studying the real estate activity in the geographic region, the financial indicators, and the people, weather, geography, and other influences that help buyers and sellers of real estate. Plenty of people can network and make meaningful business connections, but the most successful have a better working knowledge of the market than all others around them do not. The top chef understands food, tastes, trends, and recipes at a deeper level than those of the competition. The top chef also demands an environment of excellence in the quality of the ingredients, the physical restaurant, and the customer service, so that the food experience matches the excellence of the food creation and preparation. The financier has studied the economic conditions and understands trends and data in a manner that goes beyond the short-term forecasts and readily available data relied upon by the majority of financial services companies. These companies rely on in-depth market analysis which they combine with high-quality customer service.

While this seems to be unrelated to intellectual property, in fact, market analysis is a form of trade secrets, which is at the heart of many companies' operations. Extensive market analysis, market testing, data analytics, and other techniques can sometimes formalize this process for larger enterprises, but the purpose remains the same. The entrepreneur is seeking to understand more than the rest of the competition and to use that information for the benefit of the entrepreneur's customers before everyone else catches on.

For larger companies and franchises, understanding this market segment creates an opportunity to reward those individuals who are the top performers and, in this way, to enable the company to grow successfully by promoting those employees who have the intuition, skill, and diligence to out-research or better intuit the market than the other employees.

The legal strategies for trade secret protection and the exclusivity provided by trade secrets provide an invaluable tool for companies seeking to differentiate themselves. While they may seem personality driven, they are a common segment of the intellectual property marketplace in which companies can harness that specialized knowledge to be successful.

Chapter 2. Introduction to Exclusivity

A.   Why Exclusivity Matters.

Owning the exclusive rights to a business innovation enables the entrepreneur to charge a premium for the goods or services provided. The exclusive rights prohibit competitors from offering perfect substitutes and using those identical substitutes to undercut prices. If the innovation is not exclusive, other companies will quickly enter the market to provide the same product or service. As a result, exclusivity protects business profit margins, which means that the exclusive business innovation is the most valuable item in business.

1.   *The Importance of Avoiding Becoming a Commodity.*

Most of the branding literature focuses on how companies such as Procter & Gamble, Kraft Heinz, PepsiCo, and other large manufacturers find methods to create consumer interest in their products. Most of these companies' products are commodities, protected by nothing more than brand names or trademarks. All bleach is chemically identical, so the commercial value of Clorox is in the name. Trademarks and brand management provide ways to increase consumer interest in purchasing a particular brand, but this is a tenuous advantage over competitors. In fact, many successful product brands are owned by retailers. Amazon, Target, Walmart, and even JCPenney can control the premium price differential caused by brand recognition in their own stores (as well as product placement on the store shelves).

Many products have become commodities, everything from bleach to groceries to computer chips. Commodities are products that any manufacturer can create with roughly the same attributes. Most types of produce are commodities; corn is corn no matter who grows it. Idaho has invested heavily to create the perception that potatoes might vary by state, but they certainly do not vary by farm. Wine grapes, on the other hand, are quite unique. Each vineyard's grapes have a unique flavor and are distributed separately from other vineyards. Because they are distinct, premium wine grapes generate a far greater profit or premium than other types of produce grown, cultivated and marketed in the more traditional manner.

The manufacturers of commodity products can certainly succeed in business. Commodities are essential in commerce. Commodity sellers, however, are forced to compete on price, quality, service, convenience, and delivery speed. The customers invariably demand the products be cheaper, better, and delivered faster. Every buyer demands good customer service. The competition erodes profit margins, and even a small business interruption can mean disaster for companies operating on thin profit margins. As the supplier of a commodity, customer loyalty is not tied to the need for the particular product and there are always competitors who can deliver nearly identical goods and services. To improve profit margins, increase customer loyalty, and build long term success, companies need to move beyond the commodity business by building uniqueness in their products or services.

2.   *The Ability to Control Price.*

The first benefit of being a proprietary product is the ability to set one's own product price. Many people believe that pharmaceutical companies abuse this power, but their market situation provides the textbook example of how exclusivity allows a company to set its own price. When a drug is protected by a patent, the users of that drug are forced to either purchase that particular drug or to buy some alternative that is roughly equivalent. If no substitute drug provides the same medical relief, then the pharmaceutical company can maximize its profit by setting the price of the drug as high as it wants. Because the alternative to the drug purchase may be a life or death decision, the pharmaceutical company has tremendous power over its consumers. Only the external pressures of insurance companies and public outrage can limit the pricing options of some pharmaceutical companies.

As the pharmaceutical companies are quick to point out, while the price cannot be less than the cost of manufacturing each pill, the price also needs to capture the cost of developing the drug and the costs of developing unrelated failed drugs. The price cannot be set above the price consumers (individuals and insurance companies) are willing to pay. The manufacturing costs set the lower limit; the market sets the upper limit; and the balance between the size of the market and the price per unit determines the ultimate price. In contrast, once a drug loses its patent protection (sometimes called "becoming generic"), it can be manufactured by competitors, and competition will generally drop the price much closer to the cost of manufacturing each pill. Almost all of the development costs and premium profits can only be captured during the period when the drug is protected by patents.

The market for medicine is not an entirely perfect market. The process of obtaining FDA (Food and Drug Administration) approval to manufacture a drug creates expenses, delays, and a weak form of exclusivity as well.

The drug pricing debate serves to illustrate how exclusivity—in this case patent protection—gives such dramatic power to the manufacturer. Other forms of exclusivity provide similar results. Beach property has exclusive views and, as a result, the owners of that land can command a premium price for the property.

Savvy entrepreneurs should recognize that moral or ethical decisions must also be addressed, both because it is the right thing to do and because it provides another form of differentiation from too many established, publicly traded companies. Nonetheless, the focus of the chapter is not on policies of moderating drug pricing. Certainly, fiduciary duties that companies owe to their customers should play into pricing considerations. A patent holder's monopoly over life-giving treatment should be carefully considered by start-up entrepreneurs as they implement their business strategies. But the use of such philosophical decisions may best be considered in the context of social relevance.

Unlike rare life-saving drugs, most products have substitutes. Commodities have perfect substitutes while exclusive products have imperfect substitutes. If homeowners cannot afford beachfront property on the Pacific Ocean, they can purchase lakefront property in Minnesota instead. Lakefront property is not as exclusive as its oceanfront counterpart because there is more lake frontage in the U.S. than ocean frontage. Lakefront property is an imperfect substitute for beachfront property and somewhat more available. Greater availability translates into a lower price.

Entertainment pricing has a similar pricing structure. At some level, all entertainment experiences can serve as substitutes for each other. Audiences will generally substitute one film for another film rather than paying a premium for hard-to-get movie tickets. In contrast, live music concerts are much less fungible or interchangeable, so the price of a concert ticket can be much higher. Concerts are less fungible than films because there are fewer seats available for a given artist performing on a given tour. This is particularly true if the concert is a farewell tour because the entertainment alternatives to purchasing tickets are not good substitutes. The lack of substitutes leads to higher prices. The concert album is not a substitute for the same concert, performed live. Although the music is the same, the audience values the live experience as much as the opportunity to hear the music.

Beyond the ticket prices, the price of the memorabilia is also much higher when sold at exclusive events. The memorabilia sold at the concert has many attributes of exclusivity for the attendees. First, the goods include the band's name and brand, which separates them from other tee-shirts, mugs, and other items. Second, the products sold may be unique versions of those tee-shirts and memorabilia, available only at the live show. Third, the concert-goers associate the purchase of the tee-shirts and goods with the experience of attending the event, which adds a personal value that greatly increases the desirability of the items at that moment in time. (This temporal aspect is discussed later as a form of social relevance.) As a result of these three factors, the authorized tee-shirts, posters, and memorabilia sell at a very high premium.

Imperfect substitutes limit the absolute control exclusive ownership can provide. The less perfect the substitute, the higher the product's price premium can be set. The band merchandise available at the mall is less-directly tied to the event, so it is an imperfect substitute. However, for some customers those goods are sufficient substitutes because of the price difference. (This is also true of bootleg goods sold without authorization near the concert venue.) A movie streamed at home is an imperfect substitute for the movie theater experience and concert albums are imperfect substitutes for the concert experience, but because some customers will use them as substitutes, they serve to limit the fees charged for the concert and film tickets.

Retailers have begun to learn that full retail price has been eroded by frequent sales. In the parlance of substitute products, this means that the public views the time-sensitive on-sale products as a reasonable alternative to buying the products when they are first in the stores. Some percentage of the public still wants to buy a product when it first hits the shelves, but more and more will wait, substituting the convenience of the product for the on-sale equivalent.

Under management who previously worked for Apple, JCPenney attempted to break the cycle by replacing sales and coupons with everyday prices. The experiment failed, and the management was replaced. Customers found that the coupons and sales at other retailers were a ready substitute for the JCPenney products that were no longer on sale. For the retailer that hopes to break the cycle of discounting, it needs to have little or no competition from other retailers with reasonable substitutes.

3. The Power to Own a Marketplace.

To keep the premium for their product high, manufacturers and retailers need to make their product more valuable to consumers than the substitutes. Again, the less perfect the substitute, the higher the premium that the manufacturer and retailer can charge. To make substitutes less perfect, the manufacturer must incorporate as much exclusivity as possible.

Most successful companies do not rely on one form of exclusivity alone. By combining different exclusivity strategies, a company can dominate a particular marketplace. A patented product provides twenty years of nearly absolute control, but once the patent expires, the product becomes a commodity. Trademarks last forever, but they do not stop competitors from making identical products under different names.

Taken together, however, a manufacturer that owns a patent can use that patent to create consumer awareness of the product's trade name. With a twenty-year head start, the leading trade name for a particular product retains a great deal of clout in the marketplace. Similar leverage can be used to extend the power of one patented product to other products or brands. The Intel Inside campaign was an example of extending the patents on the Intel computer chip into the brands of those manufacturers that buy Intel. The manufacturer's patent exclusivity has been extended through contract into the brand or trademark strategy of its customers. The Windows-based PCs that use Intel chips claim a market premium over their rivals.

* * *

EXAMPLE—IBM

IBM was a victim of not leveraging its patents and technical expertise. During the early history of the PC, IBM made the decision to be very efficient in purchasing the components for its IBM-XT machine from the cheapest and most efficient manufacturer, rather than use its own patented technology to build the new computer standard. IBM saved time in getting their new personal computing product to the market, but without patent exclusivity. It did not have any parts that were exclusive to IBM, nor did it have any exclusive control over Microsoft's DOS operating software. As a result, IBM was powerless to control the market, which was quickly overrun by clone computer manufacturers—all adhering to the technical specifications created, but not owned, by IBM.

* * *

The thermos provides another example. The Thermos Company invented the vacuum flask, owning the patent. Originally, the company used the term "thermos" for all its vacuum tube flasks, making the word into the generic label for such devices. As a result, when the patent ended, the company lost the exclusive rights to the term. Over the decades, however, the term thermos became more weakly associated in the public's mind with the product. Eventually, the Thermos Company was able to reclaim the right to the trademark in Thermos for all products other than the vacuum flask.

Combining various attributes of exclusivity can enable a company to dominate a particular market. While there will always be a substitute market to create competition, this is much less of a business threat than the threat posed by perfect substitutes in a commodity business.

B.   Sources of Exclusivity.

Both property rights and limitations on those rights are derived from the law. Just as the government protects the rights of landowners, the government limits the exclusive property rights to that land through zoning laws and building codes. Each area of law that provides exclusivity also includes limitations on that exclusivity. While these laws change from time to time, the central practices are as old as this country.

The first group of property rights includes real property (land and the immobile buildings on that land) and personal property or physical items other than land. The second group includes intellectual property rights, which are defined by the laws of copyright, trademark, and patent law. These two groups provide the clearest exclusivity laws but are not the only laws regarding exclusivity. In addition, the law of unfair competition and trade secret law provide limited exclusivity to items which are not publicly known. Similarly, state privacy laws protect personal information, allowing a person to control his or her identity or publicity rights. Finally, general contract law allows parties to create exclusive contracts or license agreements. These contracts can add a great deal of power to exclusive arrangements and should be part of every exclusivity strategy.

Taken together, the copyrights, trademarks, patents, publicity interest, and trade secrets create property. Contracts and license agreements can be used to protect the entrepreneur as the business develops intellectual property and works with others to maximize the value in what it has created. Like a farmer whose harvest begins from tiny seeds, the law allows the entrepreneur to plant and protect the work in order to reap the benefits of ownership.

1.   *Land.*

The exclusivity provided by land requires little explanation. The law considers every parcel of property unique and, in most cases, this is true. While the value of a parcel of land may depend on its size—ten acres should be worth ten times that of one acre—many other factors affect the value of land. The first factor is location. An acre of property in New York City or Tokyo will be far more expensive than an acre in North Dakota. Location is likely to dictate the value of land more than any other factor. A second factor is a variation on location, namely, accessibility. Land that is isolated from roads is less valuable than property with good access. A third factor is what is physically on (or under) the land. Land with water rights, minerals and mineral rights, gold, or oil, will be worth more than land without these features.

Interests in land are not necessarily limited to ownership of the property. Leases are a form of exclusive use of property for a limited time. The lessee's rights are limited by the terms of the lease, but they still afford the entrepreneur opportunities to use the property exclusively.

Technically, every parcel of land is exclusive. In practical terms, however, it is the attributes of the property that make the land unique for business purposes. In this context, "exclusive" becomes synonymous with valuable. An "exclusive" address on Rodeo Drive, Chicago's Magnificent Mile, Miami's Miracle Mile, or New York's Fifth Avenue has the most cachet of any retailer's address in America. This misuse of the term exclusive illustrates the meaning of the word. The more exclusive the property, the more sought-after and valuable it is.

On Rodeo Drive, the exclusivity comes from the location rather than the products being sold. A coffee shop moving into this type of neighborhood will expect to pay much higher rent and serve an affluent clientele. As a result, the potential to make a profit is also high.

2.   *Patents.*

Patents reflect the broadest government protection of intellectual property. A person who invents a new, useful, and nonobvious process, article of manufacture, or composition of matter, or who invents a new, useful improvement of such an invention, may obtain a utility patent. The inventor must file the patent application with the United States Patent and Trademark Office prior to any public use or sale of the invention. If the inventor publishes the invention, then the inventor has one year to file the patent. The patent will last 20 years from the date of application.

Patents provide a tremendous degree of exclusivity, or as provided by the law, "the right to exclude others from making, using, offering for sale, or selling" the invention or "importing" the invention into the United States. Patents, like other intellectual property, are territorial, meaning that the filing of a United States patent applies only within the United States. Protection for the patented invention outside the United States requires a similar filing process in each country or groups of countries that coordinate through patent treaties. In addition to the utility patent, a plant patent provides similar protection for the invention of a distinct plant variety, so long as that plant variety is produced asexually.

The federal government requires each patented invention to pass the stringent test of being new, useful, and nonobvious, and falling within the subject matter of patent law. Prior to receiving a patent, the applicant must submit a drawing and description of the invention to the Patent and Trademark Office for inspection. The government will publish the information and compare it to all known materials related to the patent, referred to as the prior art. If the prior art does not reveal that the idea had previously been used, a patent may be issued.

However, a patent may still be challenged in court or through administrative proceedings, and many patents are invalidated by competitors who can show that there was additional prior art, that the specification described in the patent was too broad, or that there is some other defect in the patent. The inventor must bear the expense of defending the patent from litigation. As a result, patents are expensive to create and maintain. Nonetheless, they provide the most exclusive form of intellectual property ownership.

* * *

EXAMPLE—Edison and the Latham Loop

Thomas Alva Edison was once a great American inventor. More than merely an inventor, however, Edison was an astute businessman who understood the power of patents. Having personally invented the light bulb and the phonograph, Edison was keen to invent the motion picture projector. His early efforts were based on the rotating disk technology of the phonograph, but these efforts led only to frustration. Meanwhile, efforts to combine the celluloid film technology of George Eastman's Kodak company with moving pictures were moving slowly along. Since 1860, inventors knew that rapidly projecting a series of still images created the illusion of movement on a screen. Unfortunately, celluloid film would rip whenever it was pulled in front of the projector window. Finally, Woodville Latham added a sprocket hole and wheel to the celluloid, timing it to the shutter on the projector. He also added a small loop of open film above and below the shutter to keep the film from ripping. Edison purchased the patent from Latham for his innovative loop—and Edison used the patented Latham Loop to control the manufacture and distribution of every movie projector in America for the next decade.

Edison exploited the law's patent protection, but he was eventually stopped because of the law's limitations on exclusivity. Edison tried to leverage his control of the film projectors to all motion picture entertainment. Edison claimed to have the right to control which companies made the film to be used with his projectors and which films were shown on his projectors. Eventually, in 1917 the U.S. Supreme Court held that the patent controlling manufacture of the projectors did not give Edison the power to limit the purchasers of his projectors from showing the films they chose.

Edison's role in developing motion picture projectors demonstrates the power of patents and the importance of understanding legal limits on exclusivity. The Latham Loop allowed Edison to control the entire motion picture projector. The law allowed the invention to be incorporated into a single product, but it limited Edison from leveraging his control of the projector into control of the filmmaking industry. Similar issues were at the heart of the antitrust litigation brought by the United States against IBM over its mainframe computer monopoly; AT&T for its control over long-distance telephone calls; and Microsoft for its integration or bundling of various software programs into its Microsoft Windows operating software.

* * *

To assist with the filing of the patent, since 1995, the Patent and Trademark Office has allowed an inventor to file a provisional application. A provisional application includes the written description of the invention, a list of the inventors, and the filing fee. Generally, the provisional application will also include drawings to support the invention. The provisional application does not require the specific claims that will be asserted in the non-provisional patent, but like the drawings, a more complete provisional application will be beneficial to provide support for the non-provisional patent application that will follow.

The provisional application is not reviewed by the Patent Office, but instead serves as an effective start date for any patent that is later approved. The provisional patent expires after twelve months, so the non-provisional patent application must follow within the year. When used to extend the period for completing the patent and managing the costs of the patent process, the provisional patent application provides a useful tool for the innovator to manage the demands of invention development and intellectual property rights protection.

Just as a patent must be issued by the United States government, each foreign country issues its own patents. Certain treaties allow companies to apply for more than one country's patent at a time, but the process for seeking international patent protection is expensive, time consuming, and time sensitive. Patenting is a process that requires careful professional legal assistance.

There is also a design patent to protect new, original, and ornamental designs. It protects the nonfunctional aesthetic aspects of products and packaging. In this way, design patents cover creative expression and are quite analogous to copyright.

Although design patent practice had become moribund for many years, Apple used design patents to protect the non-functional rounded-edge shape of its phones. In litigation against Samsung, it was this feature that led to Samsung's liability for copying the iPhone. Since then, there has been a resurgence in interest in design patents, which are particularly effective for distinctive packaging.

3.   *Copyrights.*

Copyright law provides authors with the exclusive rights to exploit their literary works. Exploitation might include computer software; words, music, and sound recordings; pantomimes and choreographic works; pictorial, graphic, and sculptural works; motion pictures and other audiovisual works; and architectural works. Books, music, dance, film, and fine art are all works of authorship.

Under modern law, an author is protected as soon as the work of authorship is "fixed in a tangible form," meaning as soon as the work is written down or recorded. The copyright lasts for 70 years beyond the life of the author. If the author is a corporation, however, the copyright instead lasts 95 years from publication or 120 years from creation, whichever is shorter.

The owner of a copyright may generally exploit the work by reproducing, distributing, publicly performing, or publicly displaying the work. Special rights exist for publicly performing digital sound recordings through a digital audio transmission.

In addition, copyright owners have the right to prepare derivative works based upon the copyrighted work. This means the copyright owner has the exclusive right to make translations of books, film adaptations of plays, or other new works based substantially on the copyrighted works. In Hollywood, the derivative rights are the exclusive rights that make books and other source material so valuable.

EXAMPLE—Ben Hur

From the beginning of the motion picture industry, courts have faced questions of whether stealing motion picture scenes from books is protected by copyright. The first important case involved *Ben Hur*, the novel by General Lew Wallace. Without permission, in 1907 the Kalem Company adapted the novel into a silent film, highlighting the now-famous chariot race. As the advertisement proclaimed, the movie was "Positively the Most Superb Moving Picture Spectacle ever Produced in America in Sixteen Magnificent Scenes."

In 1911, the U.S. Supreme Court decided the case, finding that a silent dramatization of a novel could still violate the derivative rights held exclusively by the copyright owner. The Court also ruled that the unauthorized film version of *Ben Hur* violated the copyright owner's interest in the novel. As a result, from the earliest years in Hollywood, companies have paid authors in order to own the right to utilize plays and novels as a basis for new films.

* * *

Because copyright protection is much more easily obtainable than any other form of exclusivity, it is subject to two significant limitations. First, copyright cannot extend to an idea. This idea limitation includes every procedure, process, system, method of operation, concept, principle, or discovery. While a copyrighted work may describe or illustrate the idea or process, the copyright cannot be used to stop anyone from using that idea or process. If the only way to use the process is to copy the copyrighted expression, then that expression loses its copyright protection. Protection of the expression of the idea cannot be bootstrapped to create legal exclusivity over use of the idea itself. As a result, plots cannot be protected by copyright; only the expression of the plot in a particular story receives copyright protection. Similarly, mathematical formulas, tables, and other information expressed in writing are not protected by copyright.

The second copyright limitation is known as fair use. Fair use allows otherwise unauthorized reproduction, distribution, and adaptation of works for criticism, comment, news reporting, teaching (including multiple copies for classroom use), scholarship, and research. Fair use allows reviewers and scholars to quote works; comics can create parodies of famous scenes; business competitors can show pictures of the competition's products. The fair use limitation allows copyrighted material to be used in certain situations, even when the copyright owner has not authorized the use or even has objected to the use.

Determining whether a particular copyright use falls under the fair use limitation can sometimes be difficult. The law uses four factors as a guideline, including whether the use is commercial in nature, the nature of the copyrighted work, the amount and importance of the material being used, and the effect upon the potential market or value of the copied work. Copying small amounts of another party's work to write reviews, explain the work, or publish research is generally not a problem. If the copying becomes more substantial, then it becomes more difficult and expensive to determine whether the intended use is a fair use. In such cases, the more practical business choice is to seek a license from the copyright holder for the intended use.

Copyright interests can be subdivided into an infinite number of rights. A book author may license the publication of a hardcover and paperback edition of the book to different publishers, separately license each language in which it is translated, give permission to make a parody of a particular chapter, license the rights to create a play, a movie, and a musical to different parties, and retain the right to make the book into a musical.

Because copyrights can be subdivided into so many components, careful management of the license agreements is critical. Although it is extremely easy to receive copyright protection, it takes some sophistication to manage all aspects of the copyright properly.

Finally, while the law does not require that copyrighted works be registered with the U.S. Copyright Office, there are benefits to registering. Registration provides the opportunity for the winning party in a lawsuit to recover attorneys' fees. Registration also allows the owner to seek statutory damages—a range of damage awards which may be far easier to prove than showing the actual damage or lost profit caused by copyright infringement. The forms are available on the U.S. Copyright Office website, www.copyright.gov, and are generally quite simple to complete.

4.   *Trademarks.*

Trademarks and service marks represent the third category of intellectual property. A trademark is a word, phrase, symbol, or design that identifies the source of goods associated with that mark. A service mark provides the same identification, but for services rather than for products or goods. Otherwise a service mark and a trademark are the same.

Trademarks provide exclusivity as to the source of goods and serve as the basis for brands. As discussed later, brands are much more than trademarks, but brands cannot exist without trademarks.

The origin or source of goods typically denotes a particular quality associated with the supplier of the goods, so that the consumer will trust that company. Customers prefer easily identified brands without knowing anything more about the product. As noted earlier, Clorox dominates bleach sales despite the fact that all bleaches are chemically identical. This is because the public has come to trust Clorox Bleach and the premium price they are willing to pay for the product reflects that preference. Morton Salt receives a similar benefit, as do Sun-Maid Raisins and Domino Sugar.

Trademarks provide rather narrow exclusivity. Unlike patents, which can be used to stop others from manufacturing the same goods, trademarks cannot be used to stop competing products. Any company can manufacture and sell bleach, salt, raisins, or sugar. The exclusivity is in the name. As a result, trademarks take more advertising and promoting to gain value.

* * *

EXAMPLE—Coca-Cola

Coca-Cola has become one of the most famous brands in the United States. Originally named for two of the drink's ingredients (coca and kola beans according to oft-denied legend), the company created a secret recipe to create its unique flavor. The company then marketed the drink by that name. As tastes changed, Coca-Cola adopted a second trademark for the product based on its consumer nickname "Coke." The company added Diet Coke and a host of other products under the Coca-Cola brand. At the same time, it began merchandising its trademark as a fashion item on clothes, posters, blankets, calendars, and many other products, making the trademark grow from a single item to an entire universe of products.

The growth of Coca-Cola from product to lifestyle represents the development of a trademark into a brand. The positive association consumers have with Coke creates an affinity for other Coca-Cola products. Those products, in turn, reinforce the emotional value of the Coca-Cola products rather than the actual quality of the product. The shirts, hats, and posters reinforce the lifestyle that is associated with Coke rather than reinforcing the taste or nutritional value of the product.

Trademarks differ from copyrights and patents in other important ways as well. First, trademarks have no time limit. As long as a trademark continues to be used, it is protected, even if it is used forever. Second, trademarks are protected by both state law and federal law.

Trademarks are not required to be filed with state or federal governments. Like copyrights, however, there are benefits to federal registration, including notice throughout the country that a particular mark is being used for particular goods, the availability of federal courts, the ability to file the trademark in other countries, and the ability to file the trademark with U.S. Customs Office to help stop infringing goods from being shipped into the United States.

Federally registered trademarks are typically identified through the use of the ® symbol. The ® symbol can only be used for marks that have been federally registered. The use of TM, ™, or SM is not limited and can be used by anyone who treats a mark as a trademark.

Each trademark must be identified with particular goods. The federal trademark application must carefully state which goods are identified with the trademark and provide specimens of the goods, packaging for the goods, or advertisements for the goods to show how the trademark is used in commerce. While trademark applications are often made without use of an attorney, the registration process is much more detailed than the copyright application, so hiring the help of a trained trademark attorney is often beneficial.

As trademarks have become more valuable, a category of "famous" marks has become recognized by law. As the Federal Circuit explained, "[a]chieving fame for a mark . . . often requires a very distinct mark, enormous advertising investments, and a product of lasting value."[8] In addition to Coca-Cola, Apple, and Google, which have been mentioned in the text, Kohler, Gatorade, and Nike are also marks that have been found to be famous.

Famous marks have broader legal protection than other trademarks. Famous marks are protected from "dilution" in two ways. The first is to protect from dilution by blurring, which protects the trademark holder from use of the mark in unrelated marketing channels that would tend to "blur" or reduce the unique distinguishing value of the trademark by falsely associating the famous mark with unrelated projects. The second is to protect the mark from tarnishment, which is to weaken the trademark with association of unsavory or objectionable products.

Although the legal theory for the existence of trademarks is consumer protection so that consumers know they can identify the source of goods, famous marks tend to take on the attributes of a property interest in which the law protects the investment in the mark irrespective of its use.

5.   *Publicity Rights.*

Publicity rights are primarily grounded in state law. The right of publicity may be defined as the right to control the exploitation of a person's name or likeness.[9] Not surprisingly, California and New York lead the country in the number of lawsuits regarding publicity rights and thus have the most complete set of laws on the right of publicity. California defines the protection as follows:

> Any person who knowingly uses another's name, voice, signature, photograph, or likeness, in any manner, on or in products, merchandise, or goods, or for purposes of advertising or selling, or soliciting purchases of, products, merchandise, goods or services, without such person's prior consent, or, in the case of a minor, the prior consent of his parent or legal guardian,

---

[8] Kenner Parker Toys, Inc. v. Rose Art Indus., 963 F.2d 350, 353 (Fed. Cir. 1992).

[9] Price v. Hal Roach Studios, Inc., 400 F. Supp. 836, 843 (S.D.N.Y. 1975).

shall be liable for any damages sustained by the person or persons injured as a result thereof.[10]

In New York, the formulation captures the privacy roots of the right of publicity: "A person, firm or corporation that uses for advertising purposes, or for the purposes of trade, the name, portrait or picture of any living person without having first obtained the written consent of such person, or if a minor of his or her parent or guardian, is guilty of a misdemeanor."[11]

The underlying principle of publicity rights is not complex. General Mills cannot use the likeness of any sports figure on a box of Wheaties without that person's permission. Commercial use of another person's likeness, whether flattering or not, requires the express permission of the person identified. This is because Wheaties selects sports stars to help sell boxes of cereal, and the laws require that permission be received before such commercial exploitation takes place. Some states require that the permission be provided in writing.[12] In others, the consent is not required to be in writing, but a reasonable practice would demand it, particularly for highly commercial activities such as Wheaties boxes. Along with the product's packaging, advertisements for goods or services also require permission if they use a person's name or likeness.

Publicity rights have been recognized in the majority of states, but some states have not yet addressed the issue. In addition, each state may treat the scope of publicity rights somewhat differently. Nonetheless, because they exist in so many states, publicity rights are a source of a person's exclusive control over his or her name or likeness in the use of a product or service.

Federal law provides a similar form of protection. Section 43(a) of the Lanham Act, the Federal Trademark Act, prohibits the use of any trademark or other name, word, symbol, or device to deceive the public as to affiliation, connection, or association with the source of goods. This

---

[10] CAL. CIV. CODE § 3344(a) (West 2018).

[11] N.Y. CIV. RIGHTS LAW § 50 (McKinney 2018).

[12] RESTATEMENT (THIRD) OF UNFAIR COMPETITION § 46 reporter's note, cmt. f (AM. LAW INST. 1995) (identifying Kentucky, Massachusetts, Nevada, New York, Rhode Island, Texas, Virginia, and Wisconsin as requiring written consent).

prohibition comes close to prohibiting the use of a person's name in association with goods or services unless that use is authorized and accurate. The federal law requires proof of deception, but such proof is generally available whenever someone uses another's identity to sell goods or services without that person's permission. While not technically the same as publicity rights, section 43(a) can provide similar protection. As a result, section 43(a) has the effect of expanding liability for publicity-type unfair competition claims to those parts of the country that have failed to adopt state publicity claims. It also provides federal court jurisdiction over the various identity claims.

6.   *Trade Secrets.*

Although all other forms of intellectual property focus on the public exploitation of various rights, trade secret law focuses on the non-public use of select information. Trade secrets protect valuable and secret information. The economic value derives directly from the confidential nature of the information. As discussed above, patents are granted only on the condition that the new invention is publicly disclosed. Twenty years later, once the patent expires, the entire world has the ability to make use of that invention. A trade secret, in contrast, is not publicly disclosed, and so long as its owner makes reasonable efforts to keep the information secret, then the secret can be protected forever. Kentucky Fried Chicken's secret recipe is a classic example of a business built around a trade secret.

Trade secret definitions vary somewhat in different states and with the federal government. One commonly accepted definition is that "[a] trade secret is any information that can be used in the operation of a business or other enterprise and that is sufficiently valuable and secret to afford an actual or potential economic advantage over others."[13] Examples include formulas, manufacturing processes, and business methods. If carefully managed, customer information can often be protected as trade secrets.

In 2016, Congress added trade secret protection into federal law. The federal law will grow to dominate and define all state law approaches over time. Under the federal law, a trade secret is defined as follows:

---

[13] RESTATEMENT (THIRD) OF UNFAIR COMPETITION § 39 (Am. Law Inst. 1995).

[A]ll forms and types of financial, business, scientific, technical, economic, or engineering information, including patterns, plans, compilations, program devices, formulas, designs, prototypes, methods, techniques, processes, procedures, programs, or codes, . . . if (A) the owner thereof has taken reasonable measures to keep such information secret; and (B) the information derives independent economic value, actual or potential, from not being generally known to, and not being readily ascertainable through proper means by, another person who can obtain economic value from the disclosure or use of the information.[14]

The most important aspect of trade secrets is that the information must be treated as a secret. Steps must be taken to protect the information from public disclosure. This includes limiting access to only those employees who require the information; executing and enforcing employment agreements that limit the employees from disclosing the information; limiting exposure of the information to customers or third parties; and taking other steps to keep the information private. The steps need not be perfect, but a company must make a significant effort to assure that the information is protected.

Trade secrets require an investment to maintain. Professor Tom Field explains the obligations:

[T]rade secret rights also cost virtually nothing to obtain. Maintenance, however, is a different story. Maintenance may require special personnel; employee training; restricted access to plant, equipment and documents; the need to get agreements from and to educate people with unavoidable access; and the need to monitor disclosures through publications, conferences and trade shows. The costs of such precautionary measures can be high.[15]

Despite the cost, the benefits are great. Because trade secrets can last as long as the secret is kept, some companies choose trade secrets over

---

[14] Defend Trade Secrets Act of 2016, 18 U.S.C. § 1839(3) (2018).

[15] Thomas G. Field, Jr., *Seeking Cost-Effective Patents*, IP MALL, https://www.ipmall.info/content/ip-basics-professor-emeritus-thomas-g-field-jr-seeking-cost-effective-patents (last visited July 12, 2018).

patents. In addition, many secret recipes and other formulas do not lend themselves to patent protection, so the trade secret provides the best protection available. A popular recipe can serve as the basis for a new business, so protecting the trade secrets early in development is critical to later success.

7.   *Contracts, Franchise Agreements, and Licenses.*

The last source of exclusivity comes from the private agreements between parties. Typically, these contracts do not apply to the entire world, but private agreements still provide an extremely important aspect of exclusivity protection. For example, an idea is never protected under copyright and cannot be protected under patent law unless it is turned into an invention. In contrast, however, inventors often need to raise money to develop their inventions, and writers need funds to turn story ideas into finished books or screenplays. Nondisclosure agreements provide a legally enforceable mechanism to let the inventor and the financier agree that the financier cannot use the non-public idea and provide legal recourse if a film company were to steal a writer's plot.

Other private agreements are often used to provide exclusivity. A license agreement is generally an agreement between the owner of intellectual property and a company that will pay to use the intellectual property. A software author might choose to license a new software product to a company for publishing and distribution.

If the license to use the intellectual property allows many competitors to each license the product, the license is nonexclusive. If the license to use the intellectual property allows only one company to use the product, then the license is exclusive. A novelist must grant only one film company the right to make the book into a movie, so that contract is exclusive. A playwright may hope that his play is produced in many small theatres, so every theatre in the country can be granted a nonexclusive license.

A patent to improve the sound quality in small speakers may be licensed to all cellular telephone companies, radio manufacturers, and toy companies, or it might be licensed more exclusively, so that the payment would be larger on each unit sold. Licenses can be crafted to achieve very specific results. The owner of the speaker patent may grant an exclusive license to Nokia for cellular telephones, Mattel for toys, and Phillips for radios. This makes the licenses exclusive for each product area, but otherwise nonexclusive. The playwright may limit the licenses to produce his play, so that only one theatre in each city can produce the play.

Franchise agreements represent another important category of contracts. A franchise agreement is typically a trademark license agreement, plus an agreement to coordinate advertising and a contract obligating the franchisee to follow many management rules of the business. Although franchise agreements are treated separately from other contracts by state and federal law, the franchise agreement typically represents a particular form of license agreement for trademarks, copyrighted materials (advertisements and other copy), and occasionally trade secrets.

The intellectual property tools of copyrights, trademarks, patents, publicity interest, and trade secrets provide entrepreneurs powerful tools to separate their products from other products in the marketplace. Contracts and license agreements provide additional protection and serve to extend the impact of intellectual property. The seedlings of small ideas are fertilized, nurtured, and shaped with these tools so that the entrepreneur's harvest is a bountiful one.

C.   Applied Exclusivity—Successful Start-Ups.

1.   *Patents in Practice: Bose Corporation.*

Bose Corporation speakers, world famous, high quality speakers, can best illustrate how patents can serve as the cornerstone of a business. The Bose Corporation was founded in 1964 by Dr. Amar G. Bose, who began his interest in speakers as a graduate student at the Massachusetts Institute of Technology.[16] Bose eventually earned his Ph.D. and continued his study of psychoacoustics as applied to speaker design. By 1968, Dr. Bose introduced his 901 Direct/Reflecting speaker and with the product carved an exclusive niche in the high end acoustic marketplace.

While many companies produce speakers, including high quality speakers, the ability to patent the innovations in speaker technology has

---

[16] *See Dream + Reach: The First 50 Years of Bose*, BOSE, https://www.bose.com/en_us/better_with_bose/dream_and_reach.html (last visited July 12, 2018).

allowed Bose to stay ahead of its competitors. The Bose name has become the name of its brand, synonymous with innovative, high quality sound.

2.   *Copyrights in Practice: the Walt Disney Company.*

Copyrighted works represent the primary value of publishers, motion picture companies, record companies, and education companies.

Having tried to create an animated film company in Kansas City, Walt Disney's initial efforts resulted in bankruptcy. Walt and his brother Roy, his business manager, moved to Los Angeles and started again. Disney began by selling Disney Bros. Studios animated shorts to the company that became Universal Pictures. Disney created the popular character, Oswald the Rabbit. Disney was credited as author (receiving the "by" credit); however, Universal Pictures was the copyright holder.

Disney tried to renegotiate his contract with Charles Mintz, owner of the production company distributing Disney's work. Disney then learned that Mintz had hired away some of Disney's animators and that Mintz had sold his ownership in the cartoons as part of the distribution agreement (to a company that eventually was owned by Universal Pictures). Frustrated by the loss of control over Oswald, Disney set out to create a new character over which he would have absolute control. The character of Mortimer Mouse was conceived, but Disney's wife suggested a name change, and Mickey Mouse was christened.

On November 18, 1928, Mickey Mouse debuted on the silver screen in *Steamboat Willie*. Mickey Mouse's success in *Steamboat Willie*, which surpassed the success of other animated characters like Felix the Cat and Oswald the Rabbit, has often been ascribed to the innovation of synchronizing Mickey Mouse to sound. Mickey was the first talking screen star.

By owning the copyright to Mickey Mouse, Disney was able to exploit the success of his creation into the expansion of a business. He continued to develop innovative animated films, including the first feature-length animated film, the first use of Technicolor, and the development of three-dimensional film techniques. Disney used the copyright in Mickey Mouse to build an audience and leverage resources to erect an entertainment empire that now includes the Walt Disney

Company, theme parks, ABC television, ESPN sports cable network, and many other assets.

In a final twist on the story, the Walt Disney Company reacquired the rights to Oswald the Rabbit from NBC-Universal as part of a sports licensing package. Al Michaels, the *Monday Night Football* play-by-play announcer, had originally agreed to move with the show to ESPN for its 2006 reconfiguration. When John Madden, a longtime NBC color commentator moved back to NBC for Sunday night games, Michaels asked Disney to be released from his contract. Instead, a trade was made. Michaels was released to go to NBC in exchange for the return of copyrights and contract rights in Oswald to Disney.

3.   *Trademarks in Practice: Wrigley's Gum and Coke's Bottles.*

Trademarks are everywhere. Today, kindergarten teachers remind parents that five-year-old students can recognize McDonald's Golden Arches, Target's Bullseye, and Fruit Loop's Toucan Sam as readily as they recognize the letters of the alphabet.

Modern trademarks are not particularly modern. By 1893, William Wrigley, Jr. had moved into the chewing gum business and coined the names Juicy Fruit and Wrigley's Spearmint. Those names continue to distinguish Wrigley's business.

Perhaps the most famous trademark comes from Coca-Cola. Not only is the name instantly recognized, so is the nickname, Coke, and the shape of the bottle. Although the bottle shape was federally registered as a trademark in 1960, it has been in use as a trademark since 1915 to differentiate Coke from its many competitors in the stores.[17]

For items such as soda pop and chewing gum, the flavor distinctions may be small. Trademarks allow consumers to make their choice quickly if they have a taste preference, and to choose their product based on

---

[17] *Coke Lore: Trademark Chronology*, COCA-COLA CO. (Jan. 1, 2012), https://www.coca-colacompany.com/stories/coke-lore-trademark-chronology; *125 Years of Sharing Happiness: A Short History of The Coca-Cola Company*, COCA-COLA CO., https://www.coca-colacompany.com/content/dam/journey/us/en/private/fileassets/pdf/2011/05/Coca-Cola_125_years_booklet.pdf (last visited July 12, 2018).

popularity if they do not. Retailers choose to stock well-known brands in their stores in order to create a consumer association between the retail store and high quality, well-known products.

4.   *Publicity in Practice: Paul Newman's Own.*

Acting legend Paul Newman was able to capitalize on his fame and his success as a home-brewer of salad dressings to create the brand, Newman's Own. The brand label features Newman's likeness as the image for the artwork on the dressing bottles and other products.

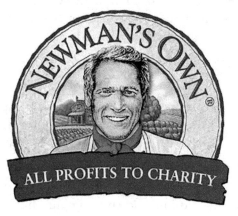

Newman created the company to generate income that he dedicates to nonprofit activities. Despite the charitable use of the net profits, the company is not a recognized charity because it makes its income in commercial rather than charitable enterprises. As a result, the company funds that are given to charities are first taxed like other corporate earnings. Nonetheless, the company claims to have donated more than $500 million dollars since the company's inception in 1982.

The use of Paul Newman's own likeness gave the company's products instant recognition on store shelves and created an image that was clearly owned by the company's founder. The company was quickly able to acquire the all-important supermarket shelf space needed to allow the premium food company to grow.

While some challenges might arise if the company were ever sold, using Newman's own name and likeness to launch his brand provided all the identity necessary for a successful launch. The famous name and face provided an instantly recognizable identity for a company and tied the social identity of the person to the goods sold.

5.   *Trade Secrets in Practice: Coca-Cola.*

According to the Coca-Cola history on its website:

Coca-Cola is the most popular and biggest-selling soft drink in history, as well as one of the most recognizable brands in the world. Created in 1886 in Atlanta, Georgia, by Dr. John S. Pemberton, Coca-Cola was first offered as a fountain beverage at Jacob's Pharmacy by mixing Coca-Cola syrup with carbonated water. Coca-Cola was patented in 1887, registered as a trademark in 1893 and by 1895 it was being sold in every state and territory in the United States. In 1899, the Coca-Cola Company began franchised bottling operations in the United States.[18]

While this history indicates the longstanding history of trademarks and the use of brands in business, the history skips one important step: the taste of Coke. While many others were able to combine carbonated water with various syrups and formulae, the special recipe was a carefully guarded secret. The lesson behind the careful trade secret of the formula became startlingly clear to the company when it tried to introduce New Coke on April 23, 1985. The attempted reformulation of the 99-year-old Coke formula resulted in an overwhelming consumer backlash that ironically served to reinvigorate the brand and breathe tremendous life into the company's flagship product.

Although the long-term results of the New Coke debacle benefited the company, the legacy reinforces the importance of the formula as Coke's most highly valued asset. Had a competitor been able to sell "Classic Cola," the precise formula abandoned by Coke, that company would likely have made a strong impact on the beverage market in the wake of New Coke.

---

[18] *Product Description*, COCA-COLA CO., https://www.coca-colacompany.com/brands/product-description (last visited July 12, 2018).

* * *

EXAMPLE—Trade Secrets in Marketing: Kentucky Fried Chicken

The famous but unknown original recipe for Kentucky Fried Chicken remains part of KFC's public brand and corporate mantra. Although no longer on its website, the company once explained this history as follows:

> For years, Colonel Harland Sanders carried the secret formula for his Kentucky Fried Chicken in his head and the spice mixture in his car. Today, the recipe is locked away in a safe in Louisville, Kentucky. Only a handful of people know that multi-million dollar recipe (and they've signed strict confidentiality contracts).
>
> The Colonel developed the formula back in the 1930s when he operated a roadside restaurant and motel in Corbin, Kentucky. His blend of 11 herbs and spices developed a loyal following of customers at the Sanders Court & Cafe. . . .
>
> Today, security precautions protecting the recipe would make even James Bond proud.
>
> One company blends a formulation that represents only part of the recipe. Another spice company blends the remainder. A computer processing system is used to safeguard and standardize the blending of the products, but neither company has the complete recipe.[19]

The explanation of the secret recipe illustrates the types of steps needed to protect valuable trade secrets as well as the marketing opportunity that can arise from creating and selling such a unique product. Trade secrets can serve as the heart of new brands, growing franchises and economic growth.

* * *

6.   Franchising in Practice: McDonald's.

One of the nation's best-recognized trademarks has been expanded throughout the nation and the world through a franchise arrangement.

---

[19] MICHAEL R. DAVIS, THE CHRISTIAN ENTREPRENEUR: HOW TO PROFIT FROM YOUR GOD-GIVEN IDEAS 57–58 (2003) (Originally found at *The Secret Recipe*, http://www.kfc.com/about/pdf/secret.pdf.).

More than 90% of the McDonald's restaurants in the U.S. are operated by franchisees. The typical franchise provides a standardized store design, access to the goods and food sold (or the recipes for freshly made products), and generally provides some amount of advertising on behalf of the franchisees. McDonald's also promises to offer assistance with "operations, training, advertising, marketing, human resources, real estate, construction, purchasing, and equipment purchasing and maintenance."[20]

McDonald's stands out among franchise operators for the level of training and operational detail, providing a comprehensive management training program for the owner-operators of the franchises, the restaurant management, and the staff. This comprehensive approach to create a common culture within the McDonald's restaurants helps guarantee that customers will have the same experience anywhere they eat, and in building that consumer promise, McDonald's adds a tremendous value for its franchisees

D.   Making a Difference with Intellectual Property.

The intellectual property described in this book will not guarantee success. Inventions fail. Patents are awarded to products that never provide a return on the investment. Thousands of copyrighted books, songs, and films are made, while only a small portion of them are profitable. However, none of the successful companies could have achieved their goals without the use of intellectual property. Owning the intellectual property will not guarantee success, but not owning the intellectual property will inevitably lead to failure.

Fans of the popular entrepreneur television show "Shark Tank" regularly hear the sharks ask whether the product is protected by patents. If there are filed utility patents, the contestant invariably moves a step closer to a deal. Without it, Kevin O'Leary will ask what is to stop a larger competitor from copying the product or business.

There is also a great deal at stake. In addition to inventing the Segway, Dean Kamen also invented the first portable infusion pump, a device for delivering insulin and other drugs for patients who required

---

[20] *Advantages of Franchising*, MCDONALD'S, https://www.mcdonalds.com/us/en-us/about-us/franchising/support-system.html (last visited July 12, 2018).

constant delivery of small doses of medication. Kamen invented the device which has transformed the lives of thousands, if not millions, of patients because his brother, the medical student, was frustrated by the challenge of administering the drugs. Today Kamen is working on inventions to radically reduce the cost and increase the availability of purified water to the world's most impoverished communities. None of these successes would be possible without following the practices outlined in this book, nor could Kamen afford to undertake the charitable activities without the income derived from his patented and commercialized products.

Intellectual property has become the ante, the necessary minimum bet an entrepreneur must make to sit at the table and play his hand. An ante does not guarantee a good hand, just an equal number of cards from the deck. Without intellectual property, one is merely a spectator. With the exclusivity afforded through intellectual property, the entrepreneur must then develop a highly relevant product for the marketplace that meets the markets' needs and adds value for the public.

E. Learning More about Intellectual Property— the IP Reference Guide.

For some readers, the lessons of intellectual property may be well known and only the business implications are new or clarified in this book. For most, however, the details of patent, trademark, copyright, trade secret, and publicity rights are not fully known. To assist with the details of intellectual property, a special reference section is reprinted in Part 3 of this book. Please refer to this section of the book to help clarify the various techniques suggested throughout the volume.

Chapter 3. Integrating Intellectual Property to Maximize Both Relevance and Exclusivity

A. Identifying Exclusivity.

As discussed earlier, a company can only protect its pricing margins if it provides an exclusive value to the marketplace. The key to developing an effective business plan is to identify the most critical aspect of the new business and use that exclusive attribute to build differentiation and value. Inventions can create patent-based businesses, while trademarks are often the only exclusivity tool available for many service companies or commodity suppliers.

The best fit is the approach that provides the greatest exclusivity for the operation of the existing business. Once the best fit is realized, the next step is to identify the opportunities to leverage that exclusivity into additional areas. As described in the four types of businesses below, all companies can create brands that are protected by trademarks, while only a select few can generate income with copyrighted works or have access to celebrity endorsements. By identifying the business's most important form of exclusivity, the entrepreneur can focus on the key assets of the new business while identifying opportunities for future growth.

B. Fit and Balance—How to Select the Correct Exclusive Elements.

For the entrepreneur, one of the most difficult steps in putting together a marketable business that will excite investors may be to understand how to select the right elements from patents, copyrights, trademarks, publicity rights, and contracts. Although the specifics for each area of exclusivity are explained in greater detail in subsequent chapters, the following illustrations of how these pieces fit together will provide the entrepreneur with a template for selecting the best business model.

The lessons described earlier suggest that a mature company employs all the techniques for exclusivity in concert. The text is copyrighted, the brand names trademarked, the inventions patented, the trade secrets carefully guarded, and the celebrity spokespersons' identities selected to enhance product relevance and recognition. For a start-up business, however, there must be some prioritization of assets. Unless the business owner is related to George Clooney or Shaquille O'Neal, there may not be sufficient funds to involve a famous superstar.

In reviewing the various types of businesses, the entrepreneur should look for the best fit. A successful company may eventually have patented products, copyrighted materials, strong trademarked brands, celebrity spokespersons, and iron-clad contracts, but this exalted status only develops over time. During the initial stages, the entrepreneur must identify which attribute is most important to the growth of the company and invest the time and effort in protecting that element first.

1.   *The Invention-Based Enterprise.*

For an inventor, patent law is available to protect new, nonobvious, and useful inventions. These can include entirely new products or undiscovered improvements. For example, if a new stuffed animal or doll had embedded voice recognition software which enabled the toy to recognize the voice of the child to whom it belonged and to respond to various family members with appropriate comments and gestures, it is likely that the toy could receive a patent (or could have before I described it in this book—now it is no longer nonobvious).

Such a mechanism could be embedded in a new line of toys or it could be added to existing products such as Care Bears and Cabbage Patch Dolls. The patent would allow the inventor to create new products, or to license that technology to others, for the twenty years of patent protection. The voice recognition interactive doll patent has exclusivity.

Another step is to pair the invention with a trademark. "Voice Recognition Interactive Doll" is not a very catchy phrase, and it is entirely descriptive of the invention. Instead, the products using the technology are known as "I Hear You" dolls. This name is suggestive of the voice recognition technology, but not descriptive of it. As a result, any product with the patented mechanism has an "I Hear You" tag and label. As the sophistication of the technology continues to improve, the "I Hear You" tag develops a following. The "I Hear You" technology may become so popular, inexpensive, or ubiquitous that soon it is added to laptop computers, cell phones and PDAs. Voice recognition for such items is not likely patentable because it has been available in some forms for several years. Nonetheless, a cell phone with the "I Hear You" tag will have a market advantage over competitors because the public recognizes the trademark.

Next, the invention should be paired with a copyrightable work. The inventor may choose not to license the invention for use with Care Bears or Cabbage Patch dolls so that the business can build an entire industry based on his doll. If the business creates its own characters for the "I Hear You" dolls, then those characters designs will be protected by copyright. With cute furry faces and oversized ears, "Eddie the Listener" and his friends are protected by copyright. The popularity caused by the technology could result in many of these characters being purchased. From their humble origins as the fur and cloth housing for the voice recognition interactive doll, these characters grow to star in television series, films, books, and video-games.

In this manner, the invention leverages both the trademark and the copyrighted materials associated with the use of the invention. It may not all come to pass. The invention may prove too expensive to sell or the audience too uninterested to buy, but this is the methodology of leveraging exclusivity in an invention from trademark and copyrighted materials.

2.   *The Copyright-Based Work.*

Every company owns copyrighted material. Brochures, websites, employment handbooks, and other documents are all protected by copyright. A copyright-based company, on the other hand, is one that generates its primary income from the sale of copyrighted works. If the company produces content that consumers will purchase independently of the other business activities, then it is in the copyright industry.

Typically, a company centered on copyrighted works would begin with a book, picture, film, musical album, or other copyrighted work. Publishers, record companies, some website companies, filmmakers, and videogame producers will begin with their copyrighted works as their primary merchandise.

For most of these companies, there is nothing to patent. The ideas in a book or film cannot be protected by the copyright, but the expression of those ideas is protected. Most authors do not also invent items at the same time.

***

EXAMPLE—From Copyrights to Patents, George Lucas truly broke the mold

Once in a great while there arises a renaissance writer-inventor. For the modern motion picture, that man was George Lucas. Lucas wrote *Star Wars*, produced the film series, directed four of the *Star Wars* films and built Industrial Light and Magic as part of his filmmaking enterprise to support *Star Wars*. Frustrated by his inability to create the special effects for the early *Star Wars* movies, he created a company that allowed him to invent the desired special effects. Lucas and Industrial Light and Magic went on to develop innovative computer technology, an award-winning sound system, and a service bureau providing the finest in the science and art of digital special effects for motion pictures.

***

Although few patents develop from copyrighted works, there are plenty of opportunities for trademarks to develop. The company that publishes the book, and the record company that produces the album, both have the opportunity to develop a name for themselves in the type of work they distribute. Companies such as Motown became known for a particular "sound"—a guarantee to audience members of the genre and quality of the music. Book publishers look for the same audience response. The genre and quality become the signature for the brand of the company, reflected in the company's trademarks. By staying focused on their style and continuing to improve the quality of their product, media companies can develop a following in the marketplace.

Such focus has the added benefit of attracting new artists. Many authors, songwriters, and filmmakers would prefer to work with a company that understands the audience than with a larger company that will not provide the focus valued by those artists. This becomes an important bargaining advantage for the independent publishers, film distributors, and record distributors.

Authors can develop a name for themselves as well. Most authors do not find tremendous success with their first book, nor do most bands top the charts with their first album. Instead, they develop a following over time. As their audience grows, the value of their name and likeness grows as well. For the most famous, they can eventually market their names independently from the books, films, or songs. Novelist Tom Clancy has developed a series of books that are written by other authors.

Finally, the works themselves may generate strong brands and additional products. George Lucas' *Star Wars* has created far more revenue in toy and merchandise sales than even its record-breaking film receipts. Characters such as James Bond, Sherlock Holmes, Lassie, and Elmo have each spun off entire cottage industries.

In contrast to the products sold through association with literary characters, many characters have been specially created to help promote sales of a particular product. The Pillsbury Doughboy, Geoffrey, the Toys-"R"-Us giraffe (which closed in 2018), the Cheerios Honey Bee, Ronald McDonald, the "silly" rabbit selling Trix, and the Lucky Charms' leprechaun are just a few of the ubiquitous marketing characters who inhabit consumer shelves. None of these characters add value to their products or change the product attributes, but each assists the sellers in retaining the attention of the public.

The copyrighted works can be leveraged to generate additional copyrighted works, trademark protected brands, and bankable fame for the authors of those works.

3. *The Trademark-Based Work and Business Branding.*

As a conceptual matter, a trademark should not be the basis of a new product. Trademarks reflect the source of goods or services, and therefore should never come first. Nonetheless, for products that would otherwise be commodities, the trademark is the brand and may become the product.

The best trademark-based business is a business that is unique but not patentable. Examples are everywhere. Starbucks has transformed the experience of buying a cup of morning coffee despite the ability of any competitor to purchase premium beans. Krispy Kreme Doughnuts' rise and fall was based on the company's high-calorie taste.

For toy companies, Frisbee stands among the most successful of companies, having "invented" a flying disc of plastic. Easy to create and replicate, this commodity toy manufacturer has created an international phenomenon. Its parent company was once Wham-O, a famous brand for goofy outdoor toys. Wham-O flew to success with the Frisbee (originally named the Pluto Flyer), only to lose focus once the company was purchased and operated as a minor division at Mattel.

Dunkin' Donuts has recently studied the experience. The company paid its regular customers to frequent Starbucks while paying Starbucks customers to dine regularly at Dunkin' Donuts. Each population was appalled by the experience enjoyed by the other group. According to the Wall Street Journal report, "Dunkin' says it found them so polarized that company researchers dubbed them "tribes" — each of whom loathed the very things that made the other tribe loyal to their coffee shop. Dunkin' fans viewed Starbucks as pretentious and trendy, while Starbucks loyalists saw Dunkin' as austere and unoriginal."[21] These two companies have each developed tremendous success by creating a very distinct brand identity that serves both to attract its core customer and repel the non-customer.

Any company that tries to corner a market with a commodity-based product may experience similar results. The brand identity must have a strong focus, and the identity being developed must resonate with a strong, particular audience. Once this step is taken, there may be opportunities to invent or acquire patented products that meet the audience's expectations for the brand. Companies such as Wham-O are constantly looking for the "next" Frisbee to continue to build the brand's recognition, while Dunkin' Donuts is trying to increase the size of its consumer base without alienating any of its loyal tribesmen.

The Wham-O example also highlights the difference between selling a trademarked product and developing a brand. The successful brand transcends any particular product to communicate attributes about the entire product line to the consumer. Thus, Wham-O, as a brand, communicates a family of outdoor toys that are fun, simple, safe, and family-oriented. Consumers can predict the attributes of a Wham-O product, even if they have not used it before, because they expect the quality and performance typical of the brand. If a company sells a number of products that have no relationship to each other, then its brand will have less impact on consumers and do less to help it sell products. Put another way, the company that respects its own brand will

---

[21] Janet Adamy, *Dunkin' Donuts Tries to Go Upscale, but Not Too Far*, WALL ST. J., Apr. 8, 2006, at A1.

be more selective in what it chooses to sell in order to maintain the trust of the public. The trademark or product name for an individual item does not have this reach.

For companies based on brand marketing, there is little extension from trademark philosophy to use of copyright for exclusivity. Strong brands that sell commodity products typically have few copyrighted works to set them apart. Starbucks' sales of music CDs from 2007-2015 was an exception to this general rule. As an exclusive retailer of certain musical works, Starbucks extended its brand, usually associated with coffee, into music merchandise by promising customers a high-quality musical experience with their favorite stars and the occasional new artist. As the music industry contracted, Starbucks served as popular outlet for music capturing its lifestyle brand promise, at least for a few years.

Unlike copyright, opportunities to connect with publicity rights are much higher. Since brand-based businesses are narrow in focus, the right spokesperson may provide a great opportunity for both that spokesperson and the company to connect with consumers. For a company like Wham-O, good spokespersons might be the reigning Freestyle Frisbee champions, and Starbucks would benefit from publicity from stars who swear by their coffee. Dunkin' Donuts would prefer NASCAR drivers or someone who better personifies the austere or homespun nature of the stores.

4.   The Publicity Rights Industry.

Publicity-based business is the least predictable of any industry. Generally, a spokesperson should have some relationship to the product. The spokesperson should be currently or recently famous for attributes respected by the public, and the public should want to associate with the lifestyle of the spokesperson, and through the spokesperson, adopt the lifestyle incorporating the product. Why George Foreman's sales pitch resonated with the public in a manner that transformed a simple, counter-top grill system into a cultural phenomenon, no one can know. His appearances were no longer newsworthy and his personal achievements were not held in terribly high regard. He is eminently likeable, but so are millions of others. His success stands out as the exception to most rules of product representation. So much for general wisdom.

Famous people are unique, which is another way of saying they have exclusivity. The reach of fame varies, including top athletes and former celebrities, including individuals such as LeBron James, Stephen Curry, Ellen DeGeneres, and Kendall Jenner. Stars who appear on late-night television have market power, as do those with active Twitter accounts and social media profiles.

Fame may propel the sales of a product, such as the Nike Air Jordan shoes and clothing. Martha Stewart created an industry of products bearing her name and approval, an affinity so strong it survived her criminal conviction. On the other hand, the product and the spokesperson may be unrelated. Pepsi rode Michael Jackson's star power to level the soft drink marketplace with Coke. Indeed, some suggest that the New Coke debacle was caused because Coca-Cola thought that Pepsi's increased market share was due to taste rather than the impact of Jackson's participation in Pepsi advertising.

Fame can most easily be transferred into brands and trademarks. Nicknames, slogans, and related titles can easily become trademarks that can eventually gain independence from the famous person who launched them.

Fame is not directly related to patents or copyrights. But like trademark-based businesses, the companies which support themselves using famous spokespersons can evolve by acquiring either copyrighted or patented works. The market and lifestyle associated with the spokesman can be used to identify patented products, entertainment content, or other goods and services to extend the marketplace supported by the famous person.

C.   Legal Limits on Exclusivity.

Just as the exclusive ownership of property is limited by laws allowing for utility companies to have easements, zoning rules that limit how the property owner uses the property, and building codes that govern how the owner can improve the property, the world of intellectual property has its equivalent in zoning rules, public easements, and building codes.

These legal limits on exclusivity are separate from the rules that define whether something can be protected by intellectual property laws. Instead, the limitations focus on balancing the power of exclusivity with the economic good that intellectual property laws were designed to promote.

The list of the six categories below highlights legal limitations on exclusivity provided by intellectual property laws. Just as with real property, laws are crafted to strike a reasonable balance between the owner's rights and the interests of the general public. Understanding these limitations helps a business determine how best to incorporate these rights into the plan for exclusivity.

1.   Fair Use.

Classic copyright fair use allows copying for such purposes as comment, criticism, research, news reporting, or education. Rather than requiring that a book critique receive permission for quoting brief passages from a book, fair use allows the critic to copy without permission. Similarly, parody sketches on *Saturday Night Live* and other shows are allowed to use copyrighted films or television shows because such parodies are a form of criticism. Fair use primarily applies to copyright, but it has also found its way into trademark law and may occasionally apply to publicity rights.

With the advent of the modern entertainment age, new forms of fair use have been recognized by the courts. The most famous was identified by the Supreme Court in *Sony v. Universal*,[22] the lawsuit that defined Sony's right to make the Betamax videotape recorder. The Supreme Court recognized that there may be a fair use in copying broadcast television shows for later viewing—known as time-shifting. This was found to be a new form of fair use.

Beginning with the Betamax, time-shifting technology revolutionized modern consumer entertainment. Courts have since acknowledged "space shifting," which made the ripping of music CDs into MP3s a legal form of fair use, so long as the person doing the ripping owns the CD being ripped.[23] This added to the public's perception that downloading content from Internet was a fair use of that content, when copied for the purpose of time shifting and space shifting. Despite feeble

---

[22] Sony Corp. of Am. v. Universal Studios, Inc., 464 U.S. 417 (1984).

[23] Recording Indus. Ass'n of Am. v. Diamond Multimedia Sys., Inc., 180 F.3d 1072 (9th Cir. 1999).

effort by YouTube and others to limit unauthorized downloading, the practice has become ubiquitous and accepted. In much the same way, expanded fair use recognition has led to an assumption (again without explicit court action) that making a backup copy of software and digital media is also fair use.

Fair use allows people to make unauthorized copies and performances of copyrighted works. The key to fair use is that it cannot replace the economic opportunity of the copyright owner. If the unauthorized use replaces the business of the copyright owner, then it will not be considered fair use. Similarly, if the business is based on encouraging copyright infringement by others or providing all the tools for copyright infringement, then that business can be liable for inducing copyright infringement by others.[24]

2.   Trademark Limits and Nominative Use.

Nominative use is a form of fair use in the trademark area. A trademark owner generally has total control over the use of the trademarks. There are many times, however, when other people, including competitors, need to refer to the product by name. This may include journalists naming the product in the news, comparative advertising, or a manufacturer showing how its product interrelates to the other product. As long as the trademark is used to identify the product, and the third party has done nothing to suggest affiliation, endorsement, or other ownership of the trademark, then the third party can use the mark.

Nominative fair use allows *Consumer Reports* and other publishers to review products. It also allows manufacturers to market improvements to other companies' products and produce comparative advertising to show how two products actually stack up against each other.

3.   Exhaustion and First Sale.

For patents, the greatest limitation on exclusivity is exhaustion, a complex rule that allows the purchase of a patented product to be free of control from the patent holder. Absent the exhaustion doctrine, a patent owner could demand additional fees from the purchasers, if those

---

[24] MGM Studios Inc. v. Grokster, Ltd., 545 U.S. 913 (2005).

purchasers resold the product or generated income from the patented product in a number of different ways. Exhaustion allows a third party to specialize in resale or servicing of the other party's patents and allows for some innovation and competition even among patented goods.

Exhaustion applies in much the same manner to trademarked works as well. This limitation allows companies specializing in the "unauthorized" servicing of another company's products to use the names of the trademarked goods, to resell trademark protected goods without permission and to be free from the trademark holder to purchase and resell products in the United States on the open market, whether from wholesalers or from eBay.

In the realm of copyright, the concept of exhaustion is known as the first sale doctrine. Again, the practice is the same. Once a copyrighted work, such as a book or DVD, is sold, any party may resell that copy of the work without the permission of the copyright owner.[25]

The exhaustion and first sale doctrines allow companies to specialize in reselling the products of other companies or serving as discounters. These rules are extremely important in limiting the restrictive power of manufacturers to over-regulate the channels of distribution for their products.

4. *Trademark Abandonment—Nonuse and Genericism.*

Although copyright and patents are both limited in time by statute, a trademark can theoretically last in perpetuity so long as it remains in use. In this context, use of a trademark "means the bona fide use of such mark made in the ordinary course of trade, and not made merely to reserve a right in a mark."[26] Instead, trademarks may lose their legal protection either from lack of use or from misuse.

---

[25] A limitation exists for certain works of fine art or visual art, because the artist retains certain rights to protect the copy of the work from alteration and to receive compensation. *See* 17 U.S.C. § 106A (2018); CAL. CIV. CODE § 3344 (West 2018).

[26] 15 U.S.C. § 1127 (2016).

A company can only protect a trademark as long as it continues to use that mark in commerce. If a trademark is abandoned, then that mark stops identifying a particular source for goods and, as a result, the mark loses its association with the good or service. Put another way, a trademark is abandoned if the company has stopped using the trademark and has no intent to resume the use of the mark. The necessary intent not to resume may be inferred from circumstances, but "nonuse for 3 consecutive years shall be prima facie evidence of abandonment."[27]

The second significant limitation on trademark is genericism, which flows from the risk that a word will move from an identifier of a particular brand of a product to the English-language word for that product. Bayer once sold the product acetylsalicylic acid under the trademark Aspirin. In the United States, no word but aspirin was ever used, so the law stripped Bayer of ownership of that word in the United States. Escalator, once the trademark of the Otis Elevator Company, entered the English lexicon in the same manner. Podcasting quickly genericized a derivation of Apple's original iPod, and Apple had to take concerted action to assure that the i-Family of names remained trademarks for the Apple product line of tablets and phones.

The genericism of a trademark is considered a form of abandonment. If the mark becomes the term for the category of products or services rather than the goods or services themselves, the mark has become generic. Genericism can be a problem when a patented product is not managed in a manner that gives it both a descriptive name and a trademark. If the product's name also describes the type of product, that particular product will become generic. If the patent protected product only exists as one product, then upon the expiration of the patent, there is a significant risk that there will be no descriptive name other than the trademark. Companies must carefully plan ahead to avoid this result by coining the description as well as the trademark.

Companies must be diligent to protect against both forms of trademark abandonment. A product cannot be retired for too long without the risk that the product's name is deemed abandoned. Conversely, companies must be diligent in assuring that the trademark names are not transformed by the public into verbs or generic terms.

---

[27] *Id.*

Kleenex, Jell-O, Post-it Notes, and Band-Aid all serve as examples of trademarks that risk becoming generic for their product categories. The owners of these marks have worked very hard to educate journalists and retailers how to properly use the trademarked name separately from the product category in which the product is sold.

5.   Antitrust.

Antitrust law is a highly complex and sophisticated area of law, but it is based on a very simple concept. Congress has declared that "[e]very contract, combination . . . or conspiracy, in restraint of trade [is] illegal."[28] This limitation applies to many different activities, including any agreement to set prices among competitors, to boycott other companies, or to allocate markets and customers. Any agreement or conspiracy to undertake these activities is illegal and may give rise to civil lawsuits and in some cases, criminal charges.

An example of an antitrust violation that relates to intellectual property is the illegal tying of one product to another. The exclusivity provided by intellectual property cannot be used as leverage for anticompetitive behavior. As a result, a company cannot require that a purchaser buy its kerosene as a condition of being allowed to buy or lease the company's patented engine. This is known as a tying relationship—tying the patented product to the commodity that is used in conjunction with the product. The manufacturer of a sophisticated product cannot bar consumers or distributors from buying accessories or replacement parts manufactured by other companies.

For patented products, this ban on tying arrangements prohibits a company from using a single patent to control a family of related products. This does not stop the companies from selling those commodities and using brands to encourage consumers to buy the "official" product.

6.   The Public Domain in Patents and Copyright.

Public domain items are those that copyright and patent law do not protect. Public domain works are often thought of as those works whose copyright or patent has expired. It also applies to those works that

---

[28] 15 U.S.C. § 1 (2018).

predate the copyright and patent laws, such as the plays of William Shakespeare and the King James Bible. The public domain serves as a meaningful check on the monopoly power of companies that control patented and copyrighted works.

The length of patent protection is fixed and therefore relatively easy to calculate. Most utility and plant patents last twenty years. There are limited extensions granted if the approval process is unusually long, but this is not terribly common. As a result, nearly all works originally patented more than twenty years ago are in the public domain. A quick search of the Patent and Trademark Office (PTO) website at www.uspto.gov will enable a savvy investor to review the patents and determine which are about to expire. Once a patent has expired, anyone can reproduce that invention without limitation. The obligation to publish the invention is the public benefit or *quid pro quo* for providing such robust legal exclusivity. After twenty years, all barriers to patented inventions fall and everyone has access to them.

To extend patents, patent holders often try to develop follow-on inventions that add new, patentable functionality to pre-existing inventions. The public is free to use the original, patented invention once it has expired, but the enhancement gives a new patent term for that version. Often, that small improvement is enough to forestall meaningful competition. As a result, some care must be given to determine that a product which is more than twenty years old has not been patented in new ways, thus extending its protection to the protected aspects of the invention.

For copyrighted works, the public domain is mercurial and difficult to follow. The length of copyright is further confused by a number of additional factors, including the year in which the work was created, the status of the author as a person or a corporation, and whether the copyright had been renewed. For example, all songs, books, or other literary works created prior to 1923 are "in the public domain," meaning all copyright protections in the United States have expired.

Public domain laws allow unlimited access to the books, music, and photographs of the nineteenth and early 20th centuries. Books by Mark Twain and stories about Sherlock Holmes can be copied because they are in the public domain. Patented inventions, with their much shorter 20-year protection, come into the market relatively quickly.

While the term for new copyrights can be clearly stated, the term for older copyrighted works depends on a series of factors, when the work was first published and whether a renewal application had been filed in a timely manner with the Copyright Office. Because of a series of changes to the Copyright Act, the duration for each copyrighted work must be individually calculated. As a result, to republish or otherwise reuse a copyrighted work, the new publisher must carefully research the copyright history. Such research can be done through the Copyright Office and can increasingly be done on line at www.copyright.gov. A summary of the copyright duration and renewal periods is reprinted in Appendix A.2.

Finally, because copyright and patent protection are specific to each country, the date at which a work falls into the public domain may vary by jurisdiction. As a result, investors and publishers must take care to assure themselves that a work is in the public domain for each jurisdiction where publication may occur.

D. Practical Limits on Exclusivity—Necessary but Not Sufficient.

Just as the previous chapter highlighted the legal limits on exclusivity, there are significant practical limits on exclusivity. These may come from technological limits, greed of those purporting to assist the entrepreneur, limits of the marketplace, or a lack of imagination. The reasons for failure of creative enterprise are as numerous as the creative activity itself. Nonetheless, the successful entrepreneur must recognize the likely cause of failure, so steps can be taken to avoid these pitfalls or change the business plan when necessary.

1. *False Promises.*

Perhaps the most obvious and pernicious danger for inventors and entrepreneurs are the companies which prey on enthusiasm and naïveté. Invention companies abound on the Internet and in late-night television advertising, but those companies make their money by charging inventors for expensive services, or by taking a large portion of the inventor's proceeds. According to Professor Tom Field, "[a]s it turns out, fewer than one in 1,000 of one large promotion firm's clients earned more money than they paid the firm."[29]

Invention companies and vanity presses often stress their large number of clients. The more important question is the results those clients have had using the services, as well as a cost comparison of those services outside the vanity arena.

The Inventors' Protection Act of 1999 created a duty for an "invention promoter" to disclose the information to customers prior to contracting for promotion services:

(1) the total number of inventions evaluated by the invention promoter for commercial potential in the past 5 years, as well as the number of those inventions that received positive evaluations, and the number of those inventions that received negative evaluations;

(2) the total number of customers who have contracted with the invention promoter in the past 5 years, not including customers who have purchased trade show services, research, advertising, or other nonmarketing services from the invention promoter, or who have defaulted in their payment to the invention promoter;

(3) the total number of customers known by the invention promoter to have received a net financial profit as a direct result of the invention promotion services provided by such invention promoter;

(4) the total number of customers known by the invention promoter to have received license agreements for their inventions as a direct result of the invention promotion services provided by such invention promoter; and

(5) the names and addresses of all previous invention promotion companies with which the invention promoter or its officers

---

[29] Thomas G. Field, Jr., *Patenting Your Idea*, IP MALL, https://www.ipmall.info/content/ip-basics-professor-emeritus-thomas-g-field-jr-patenting-your-idea (last visited July 12, 2018).

have collectively or individually been affiliated in the previous 10 years.[30]

Failure to comply with these disclosure requirements can result in actual damage or statutory damages paid to the inventor paid by the invention promotion company. In addition, the prevailing party can obtain costs and attorneys' fees.

In addition to these disclosure requirement, the Commissioner for Patents has website for invention promotion firm complaints[31] as well as to provide inventors with some introductory resources. Still, it is better to avoid being scammed in the first place. The USPTO provided some useful warning signs:

- Slick ads on radio, TV and magazines. [*These are the first "hooks."*]

- Refusal to respond to your questions in writing signed by a company official. [*Legitimate companies will provide the answers in writing.*]

- Salespersons will want money right away . . . up-front.

- You are told to describe your idea in writing, mail it to yourself and don't open the envelope. [*This is worthless advice.*]

- You are promised a patent search but no patentability opinion by a patent attorney/agent. [*This should be provided to you.*]

- You are guaranteed to get a patent or your money back. [*No one can guarantee issuance of a useful patent.*]

- You are advised to apply for a design patent. [This type of patent has limited applicability to most inventions.]

---

[30] 35 U.S.C.A. § 297 (West 2018).

[31] *Published Complaints*, U.S. PATENT & TRADEMARK OFFICE, http://www.uspto.gov/web/offices/com/iip/complaints.htm (last visited July 12, 2018).

- You can't reach salespeople or company officials without leaving many messages. [*Maybe there is no real office location or company.*]

- You are told that your idea is a "sure-fire" hit! [Probably every client of this company is told that. Be skeptical.]

- Refusal to provide client references or copies of forms and agreements for your review. [*Get at least five names to contact and show the forms to an attorney before signing.*][32]

These tips from the Patent Office provide excellent advice. The accompanying website lists the many companies which have received consumer complaints because they repeatedly take advantage of inventors.

Predatory companies steal the necessary resources for a successful business launch. This book is intended to provide entrepreneurs with the tools to avoid these companies and pursue the business launch of the entrepreneur's idea directly. For some ideas, this will greatly empower the creator. Other ideas, however, are not marketable. This book should provide the entrepreneur with the right questions to analyze the business plan so that the decision to stop pursuing an idea can be made based on the quality of the idea and its implementation.

2.   *Misreading the Market.*

Enthusiasm and naïveté lead to misreading the market, a second category of failure. Excessive exuberance for one's own invention, coupled with little understanding of its application, will lead to disappointment. Professor Field uses the "better mousetrap" story to illustrate the frailty of over-emphasizing patents in business planning.

In 1928, Chester Woolworth improved the mousetrap he had been selling through his company, the Animal Trap Company of America. His

---

[32] Office of Innovation Dev., *Protect Yourself Against Invention Promotion Scams*, U.S. PATENT & TRADEMARK OFFICE, http://www.uspto.gov/web/offices/com/iip/documents/scamprevent.pdf (last visited July 12, 2018).

patented new mousetrap increased the price from $0.05 to $0.12. Although more effective, the new trap was now too expensive to be disposable. Cleaning the traps of dead mice was much less pleasant to the consumer than disposing of the rodent—trap and all.[33] The feat of engineering was undone because Woolworth did not take into account the impact of price or the consequential changes on user behavior. This lesson from 1928 provides an introduction to UX—user design principles—that are discussed in Chapter 5.

An entrepreneur must take consumer behavior, pricing, and market impact into account. These concepts define the "relevance" of an invention or service to the public. Without relevance, even great inventions have little value.

The great Leonardo Da Vinci, for example, had designed a pyramid-shaped parachute. Da Vinci's mastery of air resistance and physics was perhaps centuries ahead of the state of the art. But the Da Vinci parachute was a mere thought exercise because there was no market for such devices. There were no airplanes to make the parachute useful. Skydiver Adrian Nicholas has since successfully used the Da Vinci design to safely land to earth from an airplane.[34] The design was accurate and could be reduced to practice using the materials available to Da Vinci, but without a demonstrated need for the invention, it did little to affect his contemporary market.

3.   *Moving Ahead of the Technology.*

The Da Vinci parachute also illustrates another common problem facing inventors. Many potential inventions need other inventions to achieve their effectiveness. Although the Da Vinci parachute does work, it is very large, rigid, and cumbersome. At nearly 200 lbs., the parachute poses a danger in the air and on the ground.

The solution to Da Vinci's parachute problem is lightweight materials. Silk was extremely expensive in the 15th century. Modern

---

[33] Field, *supra* note 29, (citing Management Institute, Boston College, Venture Capital: A Guidebook for New Enterprises 8 (U.S. Gov't Printing Office 1972)).

[34] *Online Gallery: Leonardo Da Vinci: Parachute*, BRITISH LIB., http://www.bl.uk/onlinegallery/features/leonardo/parachute.html (last visited July 12, 2018).

materials such as nylon were unavailable, as were the smelting processes for aluminum, and stronger, lightweight construction materials. Without the materials from which to shape his parachute, Da Vinci's invention was necessarily limited and impractical.

Eras of innovation are caused by scientific discoveries, new technology that frees inventors from the confines of the materials at hand. Discoveries in physics, chemistry, and medicine have led to sweeping changes in technological inventions such as transistors, microchips, or lasers. These inventions have each heralded dramatic waves of innovation because their technologies eliminated roadblocks for many inventors.

The innovator is necessarily a creature of his time, limited by the materials and mores surrounding his work. Panasonic once turned this axiom into its trademark— "Just Slightly Ahead of Our Time." While being a day late may cause the entrepreneur to be a dollar short, inventors cannot get too far ahead of the public without leaving the market behind.

E.   Conclusion—Creation is Only the First Step.

Even successfully creating a new product or service is not enough to guarantee success. The economic life of patents is far shorter than their twenty years of legal protection, and only a tiny fraction of copyrighted works continue to produce revenue at the time they fall into the public domain. According to noted technology valuation expert Gordon Smith, "[t]he average life of a U.S. patent is about five years. Two-thirds of U.S. patents have not been renewed by the 11 1/2-year stage."[35]

Anyone who sets his goal as the completion of an invention or copyrighted work will inevitably fail in the larger effort to have that work make a meaningful impact. The creative process has been analogized to the birth process. Months of gestation are merely the prelude to the

---

[35] Gordon Smith, President, AUS Consultants, Presentation at WIPO, International Workshop on Management and Commercialization of Inventions and Technology, organized in cooperation with the Mexican Institute of Industrial Property (IMPI) and the Institute of Technology and Superior Studies of Monterrey (ITESM), Monterrey (Mexico): Assessment and Valuation of Inventions and Research Results for their use and Commercialization (April 17-19, 2002), *available at* WIPO, *List of Documents on IP Valuation,* http://www.wipo.int/innovation/en/meetings/2002/inv_mty/pdf/mty02_4.pdf.

child. It is not the birth of the child, but the life that child leads as she grows into adulthood that matters. Just as the pains of pregnancy and childbirth are forgotten, the labor necessary to make the discoveries, document the processes, write the exposition, and bring the endeavor to fruition become faded memory once the author or inventor begins to expose the work to the world. The entrepreneur must look past the invention's first introduction into the market. He must find new uses, expand opportunities, and continue to create the invention, product, or service continually, making it fresh and vital season after season.

Most works are forgotten. The successful creator overcomes both the obstacles to creation and the struggles for recognition. The author, inventor, and creator are parents, nurturing the work from birth into maturity.

Chapter 4. Beyond Exclusivity—the Need for Relevance

A. Relevance—Because Exclusivity is Never Enough.

Coca-Cola's fundamental misunderstanding of the marketing for New Coke highlights a danger inherent in even the most carefully managed company: Irrelevance. Coke misjudged the customers' interests in a sweeter-tasting soda and made an unnecessary and unwanted product. Coke risked destroying the goodwill and public perception of the Coke brand because of the blunder.

Microsoft and Barnes and Noble, both mighty multinational companies, underestimated the potential of the Internet, allowing Apple and Amazon to supplant them in market share and innovation. Apple's emphasis on end-to-end product control created the opportunity for Google (now Alphabet) to create Android as a highly flexible competitor that has grown to 75% of the global mobile market. Amazon built its commercial delivery service initially with books, but it has since grown to dominate online retail and challenge Walmart and Target for retail sales across all user experiences.

The aphorism, "build a better mousetrap and the world will beat a path to your door," reflects the dual requirements of exclusivity and relevance. If the mousetrap can be reproduced in each home, then there is no need to seek out the inventor's door or buy mousetraps. If the homes have no mice, then no one will seek out even the best mousetraps.

The importance of relevance cannot be overstated. Relevance is closely tied to demand. If the new product or service is something that everyone needs, then it is much more valuable than a mere luxury item. Popular luxuries—such as tickets to a "hot" music concert or playoff event in sports—are successful because they are perceived as highly relevant. Just listen to the rhetoric used by teenagers: "I'll die if I can't go see that new band with all my friends." The teenager perceives the performance as highly relevant. The teen's perception is further shaped by her social context. While attending a concert may not have any objective relevance to a person's health or well-being, participating in the social activity can have a direct and immediate impact on the person's self-image, emotions, or social status.

1. The Interrelationship Between Exclusivity, Scarcity, and Relevance.

Relevance is based on the consumer's objective and subjective assessment of the product or service. Basic necessities are the most objectively relevant items. Air, water, food, shelter, and clothing are highly relevant to one's survival. While most Americans are fortunate enough to be able to take these items for granted, that does not make them any less relevant. The items remain highly relevant, but at the same time, these items are readily obtainable. For those living in poverty, however, these necessities can never be taken for granted and all aspects of their lives are shaped by these needs.

If a relevant item becomes scarce, then its value increases tremendously to consumers. For example, in the West, droughts and increased population have made fresh water increasingly scarce and valuable. For farmers, ownership of water rights—the exclusive access to the fresh water—is a prized possession because water is highly relevant to the success of one's crops and livestock.

Subjective relevance may be understood in the same fashion. Perrier created an international, cultural phenomenon by encouraging a social norm of purchasing bottled water instead of drinking free, fresh tap water. Increasingly, college students purchase bottled water stored at room temperature (while water fountains go unused). The campus culture that encourages the purchase of bottled water has made this activity socially relevant.

In this simple example of bottled water, the concepts of exclusivity, scarcity, and relevance can all be seen.

Exclusivity—Some legal right that gives the seller control over the good or service. There is no exclusivity if the tap water is available to everyone. If the tap water is not potable or is unavailable, then the bottlers would have exclusivity. Theoretically, different formulations that affect the water's taste create exclusivity for that taste. Such exclusivity could be based on a patented formula or an unpatented trade secret. Perrier, for example, would be more exclusive than bottled municipal water.

Scarcity—The market conditions that make a product more or less available. If safe, quality tap water exists, then there is no scarcity. If there are problems with the tap water, or the public perceives such problems, then fresh water becomes increasingly scarce. The water crisis in Flint, Michigan that began in 2014 was triggered by governmental mismanagement of the water system. It created a health danger in the city and spread distrust regarding municipal drinking water throughout the country. In a much smaller example, bars and sports venues may not provide free water, but instead require that water drinkers purchase bottled water.

Relevance—The objective and subjective need for the product. Water is essential for life and therefore always relevant. Consumers must have water; only the packaging and purification can be adjusted to change consumer purchasing. The subjective relevance of bottled water is the perception that it is "better" than tap water because of taste, convenience, or social norms. Although there generally is no differentiation between brands of bottled water, there is subjective social relevance because of the perceived lifestyle that each brand promotes.

Bottled water companies do not need to invest in creating objective relevance for their products since water is essential for life. Instead, they invest in creating a subjective preference for bottled water over tap water. They also invest in making the subjective preference specific to a particular brand.

Public concerns about the quality of tap water, particularly after the health crisis in Flint, Michigan, suggest that fresh water is scarce. As the scarcity increases (at least in consumers' minds) the bottled water becomes more relevant. Brand names provide an exclusive difference between the competing bottlers, so that the most well-respected name in water will become the most successful.

Bottled water serves as a prime example of the interaction between these concepts because water is essentially a commodity throughout the United States, not significantly superior in quality or taste to most of the free tap water available. Nonetheless, the market for bottled water continues to grow as the public becomes increasingly willing to buy the product and distrustful of municipal services.

As bottled water becomes more and more relevant in the minds of consumers, some retailers have stopped providing free tap water. Bars, movie theaters and concession stands have increasingly stopped providing free water because the public is no longer offended at being forced to purchase something that should be free.

Relevancy can transform market practices and public perception. Just as the producers of bottled water have changed the social relevance of an unnecessary commodity into a prized symbol of status, other commercial vendors, politicians, and community activists seek to shape public norms and create relevance in their message or merchandise.

2.   *Never Be a King Without a Country.*

Except in the occasional field such as the bottled water industry, the public generally expects to receive value for the money it spends. This is why products must be useful to receive a patent. An invention is not valuable unless someone can use it. If the invention has little use, it may be patentable under the law, but there will still be very few people beating that new path to the inventor's door.

For a product or service to be successful, it must satisfy some demand by the public. Absent this demand, no opportunity exists for success. This does not mean that demand must exist immediately, but among the people who know about the product or service, demand must be present.

Advertising executives suggest that in blind taste tests or product comparisons, the proposed new product should receive at least a 60% preference over the current brand leader. If the new product is less popular than the current products in the market in a blind taste test, then that product should not be marketed. The ten percent cushion is necessary to overcome the lead that the competitor has in the market.

3.   *Know Your Market Segment.*

A new invention should not be sold until there is a use for that invention. The greater the use or social relevance of the invention, the larger the potential market. More important than the size of the market is the definition of the market.

Although this approach may be unscientific, longstanding practice allows the broad markets to be carved into three segments. The first market category is known as commercial, industrial, or "business-to-business." This category represents products or services designed primarily to be used by other businesses or industries. Commercial equipment, raw materials, enterprise software, and other items the companies use in conducting their business operations fall into this category. With rare exception, the items needed by a business must provide an economic value to that business.

For example, a patent for a new industrial stapler must work better than existing staplers and be so valuable that a company is willing to replace some existing staplers, notwithstanding that they continue to operate. Put another way, for that stapler to be successful, the savings in manpower, time, and effort must exceed the value in the pre-existing stapler as well as any costs associated with training or conversion from the old stapler to the new stapler. This economic relationship is true for new computer software, industrial equipment, services, and decor.

In contrast with the commercial market, the retail, consumer, or personal market is comprised of two segments, which remain somewhat distinct despite overlap. Once characterized as necessities and luxuries, today's affluent American society renders true necessities into too small a segment to count. Nonetheless, the demarcation between needs and wants serves as a critical distinction for product design and development.

The second market category, then, is comprised of those items which are high on utility and low on social importance. Useful items often overlap with items also purchased by businesses. Cleaners, toilet paper, towels, and other necessities range from industrial quality—high on durability, low on aesthetics—to items that are barely functional but aesthetically pleasing.

The third category is comprised of those items that are socially or subjectively relevant. Electronics, toys, posters, video games, perfumes, and similar items play a large part in society's social fabric but have little or no survival value.

The distinction within the consumer market may be artificial, but it is important to make the distinction to understand the concept of relevance. Commercial customers require utility, having little need for socially or subjectively relevant equipment, except perhaps as part of their marketing strategies. In contrast, consumer items generally fall somewhere on a continuum between highly utilitarian and highly socially relevant. Truly breakthrough consumer products, however, manage to score big in both categories. While all automobiles meet similar safety requirements and efficiencies, it is a car's styling and curb appeal that determine its overall sales success. Within each market segment, there are sub-populations that share common traits and those traits help define the group's relationship to the product or service. Some populations are based on demographics, such as age, ethnicity, religious belief, geography, or languages spoken in the home. Other groups are defined by lifestyle choices such as joggers, pet owners, or science fiction fans. Still others are grouped by professional association, including doctors, lawyers, engineers, or teachers.

Entrepreneurs often focus on these sub-populations rather than the general population. The strategy makes strong business sense. The strategy reinforces the social relevance that bonds the population together. All of the demographic, lifestyle, and professional categories are merely social constructs by which people self-identify. Members of the public use these labels to declare social importance of particular constructs over other constructs. A product or service that reinforces this social relevance has an advantage in the marketplace to one that has no such attribute for that group. But that product might be less relevant to other groups. For example, bagels might be considered as a New York food or as a Jewish food, with more marketing to those markets and less marketing in other regions or to other communities. Apple computers are often considered "in" among students, musicians, and filmmakers. Apple has substantially less saturation in the business and corporate markets. Apple actually performs well among the over-55 age crowd, so it needs to address this subpopulation separately from its hipper approach.

Understanding market segmentation by the various categories in which people associate provides a focus to the development of market relevance. Once the primary market has been identified and targeted, entrepreneurs must look to bridge past the narrower audience into ever-widening markets. In this way, the opportunity for sales and growth can continue.

B.   Social Relevance—the Role of Marketing and Advertising.

Products such as the Apple iPad or Amazon Echo represent the phenomenon in which a product redefined a consumer "need" by creating a highly functional object that was socially invaluable. In both cases, competitive products quickly met or exceeded the same functionality, but the social relevance of the item allowed the companies to dominate market share.

As with the iPad or the Echo smart media system, the need for a product to be useful can be actual or subjective. Millions of little children think that a Barbie doll is an absolute necessity. Millions more are equally interested in Hot Wheels. American Girl and Build-a-Bear have transformed this desire into an immersive experience. None of these toys is essential to the child's immediate health needs, but both product lines are highly relevant to the happiness of the children and the social norms of gift-giving for birthdays, Christmas, or Chanukah.

Many other dolls, cars and other toys are less desired because they have not captured the children's imagination—or at least the attention of purchasing agents, parents or those who make the buying decision for toys. As such, these products are less socially relevant because children want the "real" present, not a generic substitute. The subjective benefits of Barbie and Hot Wheels may come from the advertising which shapes the attitudes of the children and the buyers who purchase for them.

In this way, marketing and advertising play an important but limited role in a product or service's success. As a general matter, neither marketing nor advertising can make a useless product useful. Promises of usefulness can be made, but if the promises are lies, the public will eventually uncover the truth.

1.   *Marketing and Advertising.*

Marketing and advertising serve two functions. First, they provide product promotion to inform the public that new products and services are available. The world may beat a path to find the better mousetrap, but the public must first know about the new device and where to find it. Marketing and advertising identify attributes of the new product, provide specifications, and assist purchasers in finding the product. Product promotion is essential to build a market for an audience.

Second, marketing and advertising highlight the social and subjective relevance of a product or service. Barbie, Coke, and Aquafina are "hot" because of the extensive investment in advertising to make those products seem part of our culture. Coke focuses on a hip style, so Dr. Pepper has targeted the country market. Each can be more socially relevant to a segment within the consuming public. Wrangler Jeans hopes to build market share by associating its blue jeans with NASCAR drivers.

All of these ads ignore the properties of the products themselves. Instead, they focus on the emotional or subjective impression of the relevance of the product. The ads cannot make the soda taste different than it actually tastes, but they can change the consumer's attitude towards the product.

Because so much of human perception is based on expectation, however, the marketing and advertising can play a significant role in creating social relevance for products. If the product is objectively relevant, then advertising needs to do less of the work. The subjective relevance applies both to the product category—such as water—or to the particular brand in a product category that is already relevant—such as Perrier.

In the bottled water example, the water itself is essential. Advertising and marketing serve to make bottled water subjectively relevant by emphasizing the purity of the bottled water and the potential problems with tap water. Each company's marketing also serves to make that company's product stand out as more socially relevant than its competitors. Trademarks allow the companies to have exclusive control over their brands.

As a category, toys are always socially or subjectively relevant. Within the broad category of toys, however, popularity and subjective relevance varies from season to season for different classes of toys. Some years feature classic board games while others feature electronic gadgetry. The trends are caused by the popularity of new toys and the over-exposure or staleness of older toys.

Within the vortex of these broader trends, each particular new toy struggles to gain a foothold into the market because all efforts to introduce a new toy must come from the marketing and advertising. Since no particular toy has objective relevance, a new toy's success must depend on subjective relevance.

To improve a particular toy's subjective relevance, toy manufacturers can tie a toy's social relevance to other products, particularly those from films, television shows, books, sports, or famous events. The underlying reference product creates the social context and relevance for the toy that has the potential to impact the public more profoundly than mere advertising or promotion. Toys based on these underlying products are far more likely to be perceived as "must haves" than toys based solely on the advertising of the new product, or worse, just the product itself.

A similar experience occurs in the field of pharmaceutical advertising. Advertising focuses on the lifestyle of the users rather than the details of the heavily marketed drug. Given the complexity of drugs, patients are encouraged to seek doctor assistance. But this process is slow and expensive. As a result, the advertising has a strong impact on patient behavior.

The worst consequence of the marketing phenomenon was highlighted by the failure of the Merck pharmaceutical drug, Vioxx. In addition to increasing the risk of heart attack for regular users, the drug had roughly the same effectiveness as Ibuprofen, a safer, inexpensive, over-the-counter pain killer. Vioxx should have been marketed to the small segment of the public that cannot handle the stomach upset of Ibuprofen, not as a replacement for the over-the-counter drug. Though the heavy advertising of Vioxx created a social relevance for the drug and Vioxx gained market share, its failure to limit its market to the most segment in need of the solution ultimately led to its demise

The conclusion of the Vioxx story is a strong reminder to the entrepreneur regarding the long-term strategy needed by manufacturers. Despite the initial success of Vioxx, the risks associated with the creation of an advertising campaign that exceeds the product are very high. In accord with the premise that you cannot fool all the people all the time, an advertising campaign which ignores the realities of the product will inevitably fail, often creating far more harm for the business than the temporary benefit received.

* * *

Sidebar—Knowing the audience—for whom is the product relevant?

For toys, of course, there are two different audiences that must be motivated by social relevance. The manufacturer must please both the purchaser of the product and the ultimate user or consumer of the product—the parents who purchase the toys and the children who play with them. As a result, the manufacturer must meet the subjective needs of both the adults and the children. The Parker Bros. advertising for "family game night" was geared at the adults, appealing to a general desire among adults to encourage family togetherness built over the shared experience of a classic board game, rather than the silent isolation engendered by television. The games should also have been marketed to the age-appropriate children and teens to make the campaign more effective.

Products for children, pets, and aged seniors are the most obvious examples of products with split audiences. Perhaps the largest provider of services to a split audience is a college or university. The user is the student, but the parent is an essential participating consumer. At the most mundane level, most households have a primary shopper, who buys goods for herself (most typically) as well as the rest of the household.

Historically, the marketing of medicine was subject to this split audience. Former Federal Drug Administration policies prohibited pharmaceutical companies from marketing to consumers and limited marketing to the doctors who prescribed the medications. When these rules changed, sales increased dramatically. As a result, the pharmaceutical industry now spends more on advertising than on research and development. The experience of the pharmaceutical industry suggests that markets with split audiences may not do as well as those with a single audience. An alternative lesson is that the pharmaceutical companies now market to both the doctors and the patients whereas they had previously been barred from half of the split audience.

To effectively design products, the market segments and the social relevance should be incorporated into the product design itself. In addition to the marketing of the product, there are many production decisions that will enhance relevance, and these should be identified by market segment as the product is being created and re-assessed as the product is marketed and branded.

A split audience is different from a product which has multiple markets. A manufacturer of small digital audio players may have one market in electronic devices and a second market when selling these to toy makers. These are two separate markets that both use the same product but are otherwise unrelated, so that the marketing and distribution is distinct.

∗ ∗ ∗

2.   *The Risk of Becoming a Commodity.*

In contrast to exclusivity, many products and services are commodities with little to separate one product from another. Ibuprofen is a commodity pain reliever, which is why not a single Ibuprofen company invested in an advertising campaign to show that it was more effective than Vioxx. No investment was made because a gain or benefit to the particular advertiser in excess of the cost to achieve it was unlikely.

With commodities, consumers do not receive any more benefit from one product or another. While the product category may be highly relevant to the consumer, the difference between products within the category is hard to identify. Products such as sugar, flour, salt, bleach, soaps, glassware, linens, and many other products are examples of commodities. Yes, even bottled water. Companies spend billions of dollars to create subjective relevance for commodity products. Clorox is no different from any other bleach, and the minor variations of gasoline formulas between brands rarely, if ever, affect the performance of the automobiles they fuel. In contrast, Coke and Pepsi taste different, and each manufacturer guards trade secrets to protect the formulas. The taste difference is the key source of product differentiation.

Companies such as Procter & Gamble have made a science out of differentiating commodities, but as a planning matter, this reflects one of the most difficult methods of conducting business. Successful commodity businesses typically outperform their competitors because of their distribution systems, efficiencies of scale, or cost management. In retail, the dime store industry could not compete when Sam Walton transformed his dime store into a very large, efficient version of the business. Walmart married aggressive cost management to an extremely efficient distribution system, driving K-Mart and most local dime stores out of business. Walmart is a commodity retailer which has made its identity out of price strategy. Amazon has applied the same practice to the Internet market and as it has grown, Amazon has added efficiency and scale to the price models afforded by Walmart. As these types of businesses compete, profit margins erode.

Start-up companies rarely have the distribution systems, efficiencies of scale, or cost management needed to compete against entrenched companies. The exception may be in those industries that suffer from very high "sunk costs," investment costs related to facilities and equipment that would create large losses if the company were to stop using them. Entrenched companies may be burdened by long-term overhead in capital equipment, employee pensions, and union obligations. These obstacles of entrenchment allow low cost competitors to compete effectively.

Unless the industry is burdened with tremendous sunk costs, launching a start-up business in a commodity industry is almost always fatal. As a result, the most important lesson of this book is that a new business must use the tools of exclusivity to separate its goods or services from others offered. Only then does the company have a chance to be successful. Without this, the company cannot be successful.

3.   *Relevance and Profitability.*

While relevance is key to successfully launching a new product or company, relevance itself is a relative proposition. The size of the potential market—the audience or consumer base—for the item or service offered is an important aspect of relevance success. For example, religiously affiliated products sell quite well in the United States. There is a built-in relevance for the customer, so that Christmas trees, wreaths, crucifixes, and similar items are quite popular. Churches, religious organizations, and other institutions add exclusivity to these products by tying the religious icon to the institution through trademarks and brands. For religious items affiliated with the Mormon Church, or with Jewish or Islamic faiths in the United States, the potential markets are much smaller.

The same relationship exists for all other products or services. The so-called orphan diseases are those illnesses for which the size of the population makes it unprofitable for pharmaceutical companies to commit the necessary research into combating the disease. In contrast, a medicine or medical procedure for cancer will be more profitable because the disease affects millions of people. Procedures for all terminal diseases are equally relevant to the people put at risk by those diseases as well as to the public as a whole. But the profit is greatest when the impact is on the largest population.

One simplistic formula to characterize the relationship between profit and relevance is:

Profitability = relevance * market size

As either the relevance increases or the size of the market increases, the potential for profit increases. This formula works as long as the entrepreneur can limit competition through its exclusive intellectual property ownership.

Large markets tend to attract greater competition, so one variation on this model is known as "niche marketing." A niche market is a market that is too small to support many competitors, but large enough for one or two companies to service it well. For example, the meat industry is extremely large, with companies like Hormel dominating canned meat-goods and McDonald's dominating fast-food hamburger sales. In both cases, the competition is extremely fierce, and the profit margins on the sales of items are generally quite modest. The sale of Halal and Kosher meats, meat certified as prepared under the religious disciplines of Muslims and Jews respectively, would be too small a market for either company. While the market for religiously certified foods is not large, the profit margins are better than in the general industry because the niche markets limit entrants into the markets, and there is a high level of relevance to this small market with respect to the product.

C. Shaping Relevance—Social Media and the Influence Ecosystem.

The first edition of this book was crafted to help navigate the transformation created in business by the Internet. Ten years later, a similar transformation has occurred through the rise of social media as the primary driver of consumer information and confidence. Customer ratings drive consumer trust, self-appointed connectors and influencers intermediate and shape public opinion, and brands face threats from any member of the public who happens to capture a business at the wrong moment and triggers a viral tsunami.

1. Why Many-to-Many Matters.

In the pre-Internet marketplace, radio and television were dominated by national broadcasters that commanded the substantial majority of the audience's attention. Major markets were dominated by a small number of newspapers, supplemented by national magazines. These media outlets provided a highly stable structure for the purchase of advertising. The cost for visibility in these outlets was high, leading to a powerful position for large national advertisers over new entrants and upstart competitors.

The non-paid media was managed by this small oligarchy of media outlets, and the critics, business columnists, and analysists commanded tremendous influence over the industry. The Broadway theatre market was perhaps the most extreme version of this concentration, with a single bad review able to close an otherwise promising show. *New York Times* critic Frank Rich was disparagingly nicknamed "the Butcher of Broadway," and playwright Christopher Durang once wrote that Rich "represents this Great Deaf Ear I must somehow get through to in order to reach a theater-going public."[36] In the fashion industry, that honor may have been held by American *Vogue's* Anna Wintour. Her former assistant, Lauren Weisberger, wrote *The Devil Wears Prada*, which became a *New York Times* bestseller and top grossing motion picture.

While other industries did not always have the *New York Times* or *Vogue* as the platform for the all-powerful opinion makers, most industries were shaped by powerful insiders. This structure and hierarchy added stability for entrenched businesses and created significant barriers for those storming the walls.

The Internet changed everything.

The emergence of online media companies like Mark Cuban's Broadcast.com, upstart YouTube, illegal media distributors Napster and Grokster, and open platform blogs on Blogger.com and Wordpress.com enabled the public to have free access to content coming from a virtually unlimited number of sources.

The piracy played an important role in spreading the sources of content, encouraging the public to seek more remote corners of the Internet for free, if unauthorized, broadcasts, and economically harming the incumbent media companies. The oligarchy faced direct losses from piracy and direct competition from anyone at home with a computer and an interest in uploading content.

The result was a fundamental restructuring of how the world receives its content. Although traditional media, particularly sports,

---

[36] Chip Brown, *How Frank Rich Became the Butcher of Broadway*, DEADSPIN: THE STACKS (July 13, 2017, 3:12 PM) (originally Chip Brown, *The Most Powerful Man on Broadway*, GQ, June 1990, at 172), https://thestacks.deadspin.com/how-frank-rich-became-the-butcher-of-broadway-1796376800.

continues to be created by the large film and television companies, radio struggled, and newspapers radically reduced their journalistic staffs, if they did not close entirely.

For advertising, Google, Yahoo!, and Bing delivered advertisements to increasingly segmented groups among the site users. Instead of having to spend millions of dollars to sell an ad to everyone who watches a particular television episode, an advertiser could select to spend a few dollars for each consumer who actually clicked on an advertisement. Suddenly, the interactivity of the Internet provided a mechanism for every advertiser of every size to pay for advertising on a more even playing field.

The consequence for established companies was the democratization of content, which at its best means that content on the Internet gets attention because of its popularity rather than the speaker's or seller's market share. The lack of structure means that Internet content is not necessarily so much democratized as anarchistic and chaotic. Nonetheless, the many-to-many model has eliminated the command-and-control structure that had benefited the content creators and major marketing companies in the prior century.

2.   Trust.

One of the more interesting phenomena in the transition from the broadcast/print oligarchy to the many-to-many anarchy has been the public's shift in trust from broadcasters and advertisers to the confidence in each other. Word of mouth has always been a dominant force in consumer behavior. Recognizing this, many online companies, particularly Netflix and Amazon, built business models based on the power of customer reviews. A survey from 2013 showed that 73% of the public find positive reviews make them trust a business more, while only 12% took no notice of online reviews.[37] Data from 2017 suggests the majority of consumers read Internet reviews, but the more recent survey

---

[37] Myles Anderson, *2013 Study: 79% of Consumers Trust Online Reviews as Much as Personal Recommendations*, SEARCH ENGINE LAND (June 26, 2013, 9:00 AM), https://searchengineland.com/2013-study-79-of-consumers-trust-online-reviews-as-much-as-personal-recommendations-164565.

data does not distinguish product ratings from other categories of online information.

2017 was a particularly bad year for online credibility, driven by widespread use of false news and advertisements in the 2016 presidential election. The anarchy of an unmediated media landscape opened the door for new creative artists and companies, but it also opened the door for cons, astroturfing, and widespread consumer fraud.

These behaviors have chastened the unbridled trust the public once put in online resources. Astroturfing has been a particular problem for certain rating sites and consumer marketplaces. A company commits astroturfing when it pretends the posts are coming from unbiased members of the public, when in fact the posts are coming from company employees or bloggers provided compensation for their endorsements. Yelp fought blatant astroturfing by many of its restaurants and hotels. Amazon has also undertaken many steps to stop companies from falsely posing as customers to post their own positive reviews. Consumers have come to recognize this form of astroturfing and are much more likely to trust a product with hundreds of reviews than products or services with only a few.

Despite the recent downturn in public trust of online resources, generally these sources continue to dominate how the public gets its information regarding new goods and services. Particularly given the weakening of traditional media, the public has a strong need to rely on these services. For those with strong reputations, their influence is nearly as powerful as traditional media once was.

### 3.	*Influencers, Connectors, Mavens, and More.*

There is no question that the consumer public has wrested brand control from professional media and pushed brand equity into the social media maelstrom, but what does this transformation mean and how does it actually work? Through Facebook, Twitter, LinkedIn, WhatsApp, and a multitude of social media platforms, consumers tell their stories of interactions with brands and products, show their favorite fashions and items, and comment aggressively on the paid media placed by the corporations. "Sucks" sites are dedicated to challenging and criticizing poor products and services delivered by tone-deaf companies (or employers). Videos are captured of live interactions with sales staff, how-to videos show consumers testing and demonstrating products, and hashtags are created to capture and galvanize consumer interactions.

The power of any particular meme or message grows exponentially as it is adopted by others in social media and reposted. Consider the story of the wise man and the King.[38] Challenged to a game of chess by the King, the wise man asked for a few grains of rice. Specifically, he asked for a single grain of rice on the first square, two grains on the second square, and the number of grains doubled from square to square through the 64 squares. The King was up to 1 million grains of rice by the twentieth square.

If a tweet is doubled a mere twenty times, the message will reach 1 million readers. Any social media hitting 1 million readers is likely to be picked up by other media, so the actual growth can be measured by multiplying exponential growth by exponential growth. The scale is limited because many of the messages are received by the same individuals, but even so, a powerful message can reach billions of people in a relatively short period of time.

Sometimes referred to as the "reputation economy," the ability for a meme to gain its initial traction is based on the pre-existing size of the followers for the blogger/tweeter/videographer creating the initial post as well as the power of the content. Individuals who are active in social media gain followers based on the relevance and consistency of their media over time. Some are popular because of the quality of their messages while others are good at leveraging popular media to stay active in the media space. In other words, some people are like the Kardashians and famous at being famous, while others are thought leaders and

---

[38] The wise man is sometimes explained as the Hindu Lord Krishna and the King. The total amount of rice owed was 18,000,000,000,000,000,000 grains. *See Exponential Growth and the Legend of Paal Paysam*, SINGULARITY SYMPOSIUM, http://www.singularitysymposium.com/exponential-growth.html (last visited July 12, 2018). Another variation has the King Sharim and his opponent as vizier Sissa Ben Dahir. *See Exponential Growth*, WIKIPEDIA, https://en.wikipedia.org/wiki/Exponential_growth#Rice_on_a_chessboard (last edited May 30, 2018, 6:58 AM). There are others.

communicators like Neil deGrasse Tyson, who attract a following because of the quality of the content they deliver.

A keen observer, journalist Malcolm Gladwell studied the distribution of viral word-of-mouth. Although he did not focus on the online, social media environment, the model described in his book *The Tipping Point* highlighted the interaction of three personality types that combine to spread messages.[39] Those types are connectors, mavens, and salesmen. A connector is someone who collects large networks of social connections that are actively engaged with the connector. In the context of the Internet, an effective connector is someone who has a large group of friends or followers, and those friends or followers are themselves active online and very responsive to the connector.

The maven is the subject matter expert who is willing to share knowledge and help everyone nearby. In the Internet context, a maven will make content available for free, which is accurate, informative, and easily quotable. The salesman is someone with compelling charisma who can convince those listening to believe the information and buy the story.

While the network described by Gladwell required the interaction of the three types of individuals to make a story go viral, in the online environment, the three roles can be combined and supplemented. The social media influencers may lean towards having one of Gladwell's three attributes or they may, in fact, possess all three at once.

Successful influencers require the network of followers embodied by the powerful connector. Without a dynamic network, a person cannot hope to have much influence. Successful influencers also possess a form of online charisma that makes the content compelling to watch, read, or listen to. The online salesman is mediated by technology, so the personal charisma is replaced with an online presence. For some people these are the same, but for others, these traits may be quite different. An online presence is highly artificial, so a clever online salesman can reproduce the traits needed for charismatic media even if the person has few or none of those traits.

---

[39] MALCOLM GLADWELL, THE TIPPING POINT: HOW LITTLE THINGS CAN MAKE A BIG DIFFERENCE 30–88 (2000).

Mavens, in general, are in limited supply on the Internet. The expectations for most content are not particularly high among the public, so deep knowledge and unwavering accuracy are rarely expected. For brand management, however, mavens do matter. Though not as powerful as Frank Rich or Anna Wintour, bloggers and videographers who are highly respected in their community for their knowledge tend to gain followings—and those followings tend to be more highly respected by their networks.

In a comprehensive introduction to the importance of influencers, the 2010 Conference on Corporate Communications provided this summary of the effective influencer. The Conference suggested that the effective influencers have networks with a high number of friends and followers as well as highly relevant connections, as measured by these methods:

- Viewers per month (vpm)—the number of visits to the blog per month

- Linkages—the popularity of blog post links inbound and outbound

- Post frequency—volume of posts per given time

- Media citation score—volume and level of media that cites blogger

- Industry score—number of industry guru points based on industry events such as key notes, bylines and panel participation

- Social aggregator rate—level of participation in the social Web (e.g., Twitter, other bloggers/blog communities, LinkedIn, etc.)

- Engagement index—reader response and the quantity of comments

- Subject/topic related posts—volume and velocity of subject/topic related posts

- Qualitative subject/topic related posts—qualitative review of subject/topic related posts

- Index score—identification and rank of influencer in the social Web based on above variables[40]

The list emphasizes the intersection between traditional media outlets, captured in the citation score, the maven influence captured through the industry score, and the scale of the online presence. In this way, the suggested matrix suggests that influencers are not entirely of the social media world, but actually network the social media world with the traditional media forces and the industry infrastructure.

The list, then, also provides a recipe for how to cultivate influencers—or even become an influencer. Standing in the center of social media, traditional media, and industry gatherings will give the ultimate vantage point to shape the narrative about the brands, products, and services at stake. But the competition to obtain those positions is extremely fierce. Because new media is many-to-many, there is nothing to stop new competitors from seeking to control that narrow space at the intersection of the three communities.

For the entrepreneur, the goal is to identify those influencers and build a lasting, meaningful relationship so that those influencers are supporters. The entrepreneur must do this in an environment where influencers tend to be replaced much more frequently than in the days of traditional media, and they must do so in a manner that leads to authentic support. For the entrepreneurs who can successfully engage these influencers, social media will open many doors and opportunities.

4.   *Behavioral Advertising and Public Segmentation.*

To be effective, the entrepreneur must deliver a compelling brand promise message to the most interested potential consumer. As consumers, most members of the public prefer relevant ads to ads that offer products and services of no direct interest. In traditional publishing, advertisers would purchase ads in magazines, radio programs, or television shows based on the general audience for the content. While the information would not be a perfect fit for any

---

[40] Norman Booth & Julie Ann Matic, *Mapping and Leveraging Influencers in Social Media to Shape Corporate Brand Perceptions, in* PROCEEDINGS: CONFERENCE ON CORPORATE COMMUNICATION 2010 20, (Christina M. Genest et al. eds., 2010), http://www.corporatecomm.org/cci/CCIProceedings2010.pdf#page=28.

individual listener, reader, or viewer, there would be a generalized relationship between the advertising content and the audience.

Direct mail advertising can be more narrowly targeted. Address information provides a wealth of economic correlations, so the audience can be readily segmented based on the zip code of the advertisement. This is still not particularly personalized, but it can be a much closer fit between the product and the potential customer.

One method of segmenting the public is to characterize customers in broad classifications. This may be done on the basis of geographic classes, demographic segments, lifestyle or psychographic models, or behavioral activities. Each of these classification systems helps the advertiser either focus investment on the people most likely to use a product, or shape the message about a product in a manner that communicates most effectively with that targeted segment, or both.

A second category of segmentation may be based on operational attributes. Media segmentation and distribution segmentation both are based on these distinctions. Distribution segmentation may have very pragmatic, operational considerations. Particularly for small businesses, the ability to supply local stores may result in a very different product or service model than the supply for online or national outlets. Fresh produce, for example, has a set of operational needs that cannot be duplicated nationally without a large operational network. Similarly, certain products may be sold under different trade names, packaging, and price points for one media market over another. This may, in fact, correlate with presumptions about demographic segmentations and how those segments are best reached through targeted media.

Demographic segmentation typically includes age, gender, income, housing type, accessibility needs, and education level. It need not be controversial. Clothing, for example, tends to segment based on age, with clothes and accessories for children, teens, young adults, and mature adults having different design attributes, materials, and distribution strategies. Most clothing is gender-based, though there are market opportunities to create more gender-fluid items as well. Entertainment products tend to be very segmented into demographic audiences.

Lifestyle segmentation is more controversial because the implication suggests that particular consumer attitudes, values, and beliefs will more accurately define the market population for a particular product and service. As discussed earlier, however, to effectively shape relevance of a product or service to the consumer, it is very helpful to know what motivates that consumer. The same technology or product can then be segmented and highlighted for that consumer using messaging that makes the product more relevant to the potential customer's lifestyle and beliefs. Customers, for example, want to see their own experiences reflected in the advertisements they see. Increased diversity in the casting of commercials reflects an eventual understanding that to serve a market, the advertiser must respect and engage that market.

Culture has codes. On average, opera fans are likely different from NASCAR fans. The sale of a product using a camo design will be seen very positively by hunters and pro-military customers while potentially offending those who object to hunting. Images of a product being used in an urban, hip neighborhood will engage with a different audience than showing that same product being used in a rural environment or even a suburban environment. Pick-up trucks are purchased by consumers across lifestyle segmentations, but the advertisements designed to make a truck relevant to the consumer are highly varied and delivered in a segmented manner so that different lifestyle segments find the particular truck is highly relevant to their group's lifestyle.

The entrepreneur needs to understand the segments of the audience interested in the new product or service. At the same time, however, the entrepreneur must be thoughtful not to exclude other segments of the public or run afoul of legal obligations to provide products and services in a nondiscriminatory manner.

Building on the market segmentation of psychographic, demographic, geographic, and operational models, advertisers often target even more narrowly. The two versions of this targeted advertising are known as contextual advertising and behavioral advertising. For contextual advertising, the ads are targeted based on the individual consumer's engagement with a specific company or website. For example, if a customer searches for air mattresses, then the ads selected for a website or app to be displayed to that individual will tie directly to air mattresses. The advertiser may buy the contextual advertisement to push a display ad for an air mattress. The advertiser may instead be pushing camping equipment on the inference that air mattresses are often used for camping. The contextual advertisement does not utilize any information about the consumer, only about the search terms used.

In contrast, behavioral advertisement collects personal information about the individual consumer's online activities across multiple sites. The information gathered may also include personal information about the individual's name, address, and other available information. In the context of behavioral advertising, a potential customer may have conducted a search regarding airline tickets to Boston and at a different site that person may have browsed baseball scores. The collection of those disparate pieces of information would be combined so that the advertisement displayed to the consumer would focus on Boston Red Sox tickets or restaurants near Fenway Park, the stadium for the Red Sox. If the behavioral advertising content aggregator tied the behavior into customer data, then the potential restaurant advertisements might focus on chain restaurants that the individual frequented in other cities, so that the ad displayed was for a coupon of the individual's favorite restaurant closest to Fenway Park.

Behavioral advertising is a powerful tool to segment the potential customer base into highly specific audiences. But it leads to significant privacy concerns for the public and often comes across as a creepy and stalker-like interaction between the business and the consumer. At a minimum, companies that utilize behavioral advertising have a duty to their potential customers to protect their privacy and follow the company's own privacy policy. More than this, however, the company needs to create a positive relationship between itself and its potential customer.

The issue has become more acute with the proliferation of mobile devices and the ability to track across multiple devices, including computers, phones, and wearable technologies. The FTC and advertising industry trade associations have agreed on four basic principles that apply to the minimal standards for behavioral advertisements.

- *Transparency and Consumer Control.* Everywhere information is collected, the collector of that data "should provide a clear, concise, consumer-friendly, and prominent statement that (1) data about consumers' activities online is being collected at the site for use in providing advertising about products and services tailored to individual consumers' interests, and (2) consumers can choose whether or not to have their information collected for such purpose. The website should also provide consumers with a clear, easy-to-use, and accessible method for exercising this option."[41] These policies and methods for exercising these options must be simple, easy to find, and appropriate for the device used and interface provided to the consumer.

- *Reasonable Security, and Limited Data Retention, for Consumer Data.* "Any company that collects and/or stores consumer data for behavioral advertising should provide reasonable security for that data. Consistent with data security laws and the FTC's data security enforcement actions, such protections should be based on the sensitivity of the data, the nature of a company's business operations, the types of risks a company faces, and the reasonable protections available to a company. **Companies should also retain data only as long as is necessary to fulfill a legitimate business or law enforcement need.**"[42]

- *Affirmative Express Consent for Material Changes to Existing Privacy Promises.* "[A] company must keep any promises that it makes with respect to how it will handle or protect consumer data, even if it decides to change its policies at a later date. Therefore, before a company can use *previously collected* data in a manner materially different from promises the company made when it collected the data, it should obtain affirmative express consent from affected consumers."[43] The FTC points out that this includes changes triggered by merger, bankruptcy, or other forms of reorganization.

---

[41] FED. TRADE COMM'N, FTC STAFF REPORT: SELF-REGULATORY PRINCIPLES FOR ONLINE BEHAVIORAL ADVERTISING 46 (2009), https://www.ftc.gov/sites/default/files/documents/reports/federal-trade-commission-staff-report-self-regulatory-principles-online-behavioral-advertising/p085400behavadreport.pdf.

[42] *Id.* at 46–47.

[43] *Id.* at 47.

- *Affirmative Express Consent to (or Prohibition Against) Using Sensitive Data for Behavioral Advertising.* The law has many more restrictive rules for certain types of information, including credit information, health records, data regarding children under thirteen, educational records, phone records, and many other categories. Generally speaking, these sources of market data are all "sensitive" and require more careful use. In this context, companies should obtain affirmative express consent before using any of this information for purposes of behavioral advertising.

As the mobility of markets, data, and consumers increasingly crossed international borders, changes to European laws have begun to subject U.S. companies to the much tighter data protection rules of Europe. In addition to the sensitive data examples, data gathered about European citizens in U.S. companies are arguably subject to these European privacy regulations. While those concerns might not affect a start-up business in the U.S., those concerns will impact the marketing and distribution partners used by that start-up. As a result, these four general behavioral advertising principles will likely be tightened considerably in the years to come.

5. *Marketing to the Curatorial Consumer.*

The other side of behavioral advertising is the control now held by the consumer to reshape the marketing and messaging presented by the advertiser. This effect has been described as "curatorial me," in which the nature of the audience has become social, interconnected and participatory. Today's consumer engages in products, services, and advertisements by commenting and critiquing the messaging of the advertiser through likes, tweets, posts, and videos. Every message presented by an advertiser is likely to be deconstructed and reevaluated by someone on social media.

The curatorial participant is an active partner in the promotion and dissemination of works they value. This modality builds on a tradition of fan fiction, fan clubs, community theatre, and other non-professional engagement, but has grown to a much broader scale with the explosion of social media tools. The curatorial audience participates on blogs, wikis, Facebook, YouTube, Twitter, massively multiplayer online games, and peer-to-peer networks. They engage in commerce on

Craigslist, evaluate services on Angie's List and Amazon, and redefine culture throughout cyberspace.

Curatorial audience engagement has become the predominant modality in the entertainment media, but it has moved very far beyond. Amazon owes much of its success to the consumer ratings and recommendations of its products, which has created a socially relevant, highly networked community of consumers and consumer advocates. The Department of Defense has been developing a social media advance warning system to "'develop a new science of social networks built on an emerging technology base' to help the agency keep abreast with communication technologies, namely Twitter.[44]" The Defense Department approach recognizes that the information flows "continuously over time, assembled from many small pieces, and conveyed through social networks as well as other means."[45]

The curatorial consumer should be considered an important limitation and expansion on market segmentation. The public commentary offers a check on market segmentation because consumers communicate with each other. If a razor or other consumer product is sold to "girls" in a pink package for a twenty-percent price increase over the grey version sold to the general public, that pricing disparity will be highlighted on social media—to the embarrassment of the manufacturer. Other similar stereotypes will often be targeted for ridicule.

At the same time, the curatorial consumer tends to be part of a social network comprised primarily of like-minded individuals, both psychographically and demographically. This is the echo chamber effect of social media. While the technology enables many-to-many communication, the amount of information filtered and supplied to any individual is increasingly filtered through the curation of people who are the most similar to the content consumer. Opera fans get their news,

---

[44] Chris Gayomali, *Defense Department Initiative Seeks to Analyze Social Media Patterns*, TIME TECHLAND (Aug. 2, 2011), http://techland.time.com/2011/08/02/defense-department-initiative-seeks-to-analyze-social-media-patterns/.

[45] Jaewon Yang & Jure Leskovec, *Modeling Information Diffusion in Implicit Networks*, *in* 2010 IEEE INT'L CONF. ON DATA MINING 599 (2010).

entertainment, and factual context from other opera fans and sources that cater to opera fans. NASCAR fans do the same.

The combination of behavioral advertising and the echo chamber effect means that an individual receives far less generalized, unfiltered information than under the pre-Internet, traditional media model. The very curation of the public serves to limit access to information that challenges the informational status quo or introduces new ideas, products, services, or thinking to the public.

As a result, for the entrepreneur wishing to expand the market, segmentation, and engagement with the curatorial audience requires that the story being told which makes the product highly relevant to the public be segmented and fed carefully into the various echo chambers until there is widespread acceptance. Only then will the general public approach be able to overcome the highly filtered and curated modern media landscape.

Chapter 5. Problem Solving, Design Thinking, and the Process of Lighting the Innovative Spark

A. The Opportunity for Relevance—Creating Innovation and Relieving Stressors.

1. *Finding Uniqueness Through Innovation.*

The tools of intellectual property provide a series of techniques to protect the entrepreneur's innovation. Through the lens of patent and trade secret protection, entrepreneurs often look to methods of creating uniqueness—technological innovation, invention, and discovery. Certainly, invention and discovery add great value, but they are often costly in terms of both time and expense. Publicity rights provide the easiest road to exclusivity by connecting the pre-existing fame of the celebrity to any product or service endorsed by that celebrity. For the celebrity entrepreneur, this relationship is self-evident. For other entrepreneurs, it can be achieved through a contractual relationship between the celebrity and the enterprise. Copyright and trademark can provide more indirect methods of developing uniqueness by focusing on the message associated with the product or service rather than directly on that product or service.

The five intellectual property systems provide different methods of protecting the uniqueness of a new product or service, but they only hint at the factors which foster the uniqueness. Instead, the best innovation is triggered by a perceived need. In computer software and hardware, this metaphor is often described as the "killer app," the computer application that is so important that it will trigger a new round of consumer hardware upgrades. In the early days of computing, no one anticipated that the spreadsheet programs were the killer apps that would drive thousands of companies to invest in so-called personal computers. Other killer app opportunities were identified well before they were realized. When Professor Paul Goldstein wrote of the Internet's potential Celestial Jukebox, he anticipated both the music swapping phenomenon of Napster and the universal adoration of the personal MP3 player captured by the iPod five years before their arrival.[46]

Innovation, as suggested by the killer app phenomenon, is not identifying something new, but taking something that is useful, but which has not been practical in the past, and making it widely available to the public. In some cases, the impractical is made practical through engineering or technical breakthroughs. In other cases, the technology or science for innovation has been available for years or decades, but the market had not yet matured to make use of the innovation. For example, the computer mouse predated Windows by many years, but text-based computers had no need for the mouse, so it was not used by IBM. Once the opportunity was combined with the tools to meet that opportunity, success was achieved. Often, this is not genius; it is good timing or great understanding of the needs of the marketplace.

2.   *The Seven Sources of Innovation.*

Management legend Peter Drucker identified seven key sources upon which to build the innovative company. Four of these he identified as internal to the company and three as external, belonging to broader societal changes.

Drucker identified the societal changes as:

- *Demographic* (population changes);

- *Changes in perception, mood, and meaning;*

- *New knowledge, both scientific and nonscientific.*[47]

Drucker identified the internal sources as:

- *The unexpected—the unexpected success, the unexpected failures, the unexpected outside event;*

---

[46] PAUL GOLDSTEIN, COPYRIGHT'S HIGHWAY: FROM GUTENBERG TO THE CELESTIAL JUKEBOX 197–236 (1994).

[47] DRUCKER, *supra* note 4, at 35.

- *The incongruity—between reality as it actually is and reality as it is assumed to be or as it "ought to be";*

- *Innovation based on process need;*

- *Changes in industry structure or market structure that catch everyone unawares.*[48]

For a start-up entrepreneur, all seven changes are external to the new company, but the "internal" changes are those happening with particular competitors or sectors. The external changes, in contrast, are not tied directly to any industry or sector.

Each of these sources of innovation is a stressor on the status quo. In fact, the list is not confined to these categories. Anything that creates significant stress on the status quo will create a demand to relieve the tension within the current system, and a new system which relieves the tension will eventually replace the old.

Almost all of Drucker's seven stressors are self-explanatory, but none is simple to use. Among the societal trends, a change in perception is the stressor social relevance. As new products, services, fashions, and trends become popular, they create tremendous stress on the previously popular trends. Manufacturers must retool, quickly expanding capacity to deliver new products and services while reducing output in their efforts that support the fading markets.

What Drucker refers to as new knowledge is detailed in the chapters on patents and trade secrets. Drucker suggested that new knowledge is overrated as a source of innovation, but he underestimates the power of new knowledge to beget innovation. Patents and trade secrets may be more difficult to predict than demographic trends, but each new patent brings with it the potential for innovative transformation.

Demographic change provides the best example of societal change. When Drucker first wrote *Innovation and Entrepreneurship* in 1985, the demographics focused on the baby-boom generation dominating the work force and the "baby-bust" population creating significant excess capacity in public schools and universities. Today, headlines focus on the

---

[48] *Id.*

"boomers" hitting retirement age (with the appellation 'baby' quietly deleted), while the upcoming generations have been parsed into Generation X, Generation Y, and millennials. Less frequently discussed is the emergence of Generation Z, comprised of those born mid-1990s to the early 2000s. Generation Z now makes up 25% of the U.S. population, supplanting both boomers or millennials as the population to target.

Press reports on these generations are far from complete. In addition to the children, grandchildren, and great-grandchildren of World War II veterans, there are many immigrant communities who have come into the United States during the last half century. These communities are not evenly distributed, have different educational experiences (some better, some worse) than their suburban counterparts, have different purchasing patterns, and different stressors. In addition, the urban, suburban, and rural populations have had significant population shifts. Americans move from location to location more fluidly than populations anywhere else in the world. This creates stressors on housing markets, house design, communications, relocations, and many other needs of people shifting locations. Even their reasons for moving vary: better jobs, better environment, better community, or some other opportunity.

Just as demographics are complex and constantly creating many smaller stressors—and so many opportunities for innovation—the other six identified stressors create similar complexities and opportunities.

3.   The Opportunity Not to Accept: "We have always done it that way."

If necessity is the mother of innovation, then stressors may be the elusive father. The defense to inefficiency is often the insurmountable barricade, "we have always done it that way." Drucker describes this as the "incongruity," the gap between how something actually works and how we describe it as working. If we have lived with these incongruities for any length of time, human nature allows us to shrug off these incongruities and rationalize their inevitability. As a result, old stressors require entrepreneurs to step out of the system in order to analyze it. More importantly, the entrepreneur has an opportunity to anticipate the stressors caused by new innovation and solve those problems before we have learned to live with them.

Older ongoing, systemic stressors are everywhere. For example, anyone who has worked in a large organization knows that job descriptions are written solely in the abstract. The jobs actually done are based on the strengths and weaknesses of the personnel. Good managers invariably gain responsibilities for tasks that have little to do with their job titles or reporting structures, while weak managers are cocooned like cysts with other staff bearing the responsibilities for accomplishing what those individuals fail to do. Job performance is often measured by change from year to year, rather than in terms of importance to the organizational goals, so the best managers go undervalued while the organizations reward the weak managers for even the most meager improvement. This phenomenon is not corporate incompetence. Rather, it is a natural consequence of our need to interpret the world around us as rational and for individuals to reduce their stress in the world. Without this ability to rationalize and accept the flaws and stresses in the workplace, our frustration would overtake our problem solving. Often, the only time significant staff evaluation takes place is when new management arrives. Whether through merger or reorganization, there is a brief window in which all staff are reevaluated. The downside of this external review is that it is often conducted at a time of significant upheaval to everything else in the organization and often carried out with far less knowledge than would have been available to the outgoing management.

Drucker describes the change wrought by O.M. Scott & Sons Company, when it introduced the fertilizer spreader into the business of lawn and garden fertilizers and pesticides.[49] Previously, fertilizer users struggled to evenly distribute fertilizer on their lawns. Only through time-consuming and potentially damaging trial and error could a person learn the precise concentration of the product. Scotts Miracle-Gro solved this problem, becoming the world leader in the industry, by introducing the automated spreader and eliminating consumer concerns for the use of fertilizer. While the company may suggest that its chemical compositions are different from others, the more striking improvement is the continued emphasis on removing the mixing and measurement

---

[49] *Id.* at 67.

challenges for the consumer. It has taken the spreader lesson to every aspect of its product usage model.

Similarly, Target received tremendous accolades for recognizing the historic limitations of the prescription pill bottle. By changing the shape of the bottle, Target allowed the space for labeling medications to be dramatically increased. Better labeling leads to fewer mistakes in medication and dosage—very real medical concerns. Ironically, Target has since left this market, subcontracting to CVS. CVS has not adopted Target's packaging. Like almost everyone else, it accepted the limitations in the pill bottles without challenging the way most prescription drugs were distributed. Society was used to the shape and size of the bottles. After looking at a longstanding systemic problem, Target took the step to make an improvement to the product, but despite the success in the marketplace, its successor has not maintained this advantage.

Even in the case of historic, systemic stressors, the entrepreneur who can step outside the system and identify incongruities or "work-arounds" that have been designed to accommodate the systemic flaw rather than solve the underlying problem, has the opportunity to develop a new product or method to address consumer needs related to the system. The key to innovation is to see that which is so obvious it has become invisible.

4.   *The Opportunity from the Stressors on Stressors.*

An even greater entrepreneurial opportunity lies with identifying the stressors caused by new innovation. Every change brings with it another set of problems. The Internet has increased the speed of communication, brought library resources into every home, and put the individual into the center of content selection—and even creation. On the other hand, the Internet has changed the role of public and academic libraries, it has created a need to authenticate and select written authorities from an overwhelming amount of information. It has created such a demand that consumers find home access to be insufficient, requiring the Internet to be available on devices carried in their pockets.

When the Internet was first popularized, AOL, Yahoo!, Go.com, and others focused on providing library-like organizational hierarchies to the Internet known as portals. With words rather than numbers, Yahoo! led the way in creating a Dewey Decimal System-like syntax to the Internet. Traditional media companies attempted to build portals to deliver their content and control what other content was available to the public on the Internet in the same manner that they programmed television and radio schedules before. Unlike television and radio, the Internet was not limited to a single channel or to programming time constraints. Search engines like Alta Vista and Ask Jeeves provided an alternative to the traditional structures that were not anticipated by traditional media companies.

But there were problems. The portal system was failing because traditional media companies failed to change content access from a delivery model to a consumer driven, on-demand model, and the way in which the first search engines organized Internet content was a bit raw. These stressors created the opportunity for Google to dominate the search landscape by addressing the first-generation problems and solving the stressors created by the search engines. Google's innovation in search was made to answer the inherent limitation of the portal approach to accessing Internet content.

The search engines were born of the desire to funnel from the vast body of information on the Internet that which a searcher is seeking— the truly relevant information. The first-generation search engines based their interpretation of relevance solely on the relationship between the search words and the frequency of matching content on the target sites. Therefore, by simply dumping search terms into a website's content, website owners could drastically improve their rankings. This was roughly analogous to basing search priority on the size of the ads in the Yellow Pages. Despite their shortcomings in terms of actual relevance, these search engines created the basic infrastructure that has allowed Google to lead the market in changing this structure, thereby undermining the portals and becoming a much more useful, and an overwhelmingly more popular search engine with an expanded array of web-based tools.

Search engines like Google currently use complex search algorithms when they crawl web pages looking for the websites that will best connect searchers with the most relevant content. The specifics of an algorithm change frequently, both to fine tune the ability to deliver relevant returns and to try to stay a step ahead of the website owners and consultants who try to "trick" the engines into ranking their sites artificially high. One factor in the way Google and other search engines rank sites is link popularity—how many incoming resource links a site has. Google looks at the volume of links to page as well as the quality of the page that provides the link. Links from pages that themselves have many relevant incoming links help to make the pages to which they link more likely to rank higher. If a website wants better Google rankings, it must make its content more valuable to more users and eliminate barriers to linking to that content. By aligning its criteria to the criteria of consumers, Google solved the stressors caused by the new innovation of search engines and dominated the market for relevance.

The first edition of this book stated that "[t]his process suggests, in turn, that the next generation of search engines will more carefully incorporate user data to prioritize within each search. By tracking the use made on a particular machine or user, an algorithm can incorporate the behavior pattern of the user as well as the relevance of the information based on its content or its web popularity." The product which took this advantage in the marketplace has been Facebook, which built its advertising model precisely by incorporating the user data to prioritize the advertisements being delivered to that individual and charging premium prices to advertisers that sought to target their advertisements. The technology predicted that some company would dominate that niche. Facebook's earlier flirting-app architecture provided the perfect platform to adapt in the market. Myspace nearly worked, but flirting could take better advantage of the advertising than the music-sharing nature of Myspace, relegating it to the background. Yahoo!, which had a dominant lead in online content and advertising revenue, was not designed to mine the data of their users to push content and the advertisements that accompanied the content. To the contrary, Yahoo! valued mediated content—which is much better for society—but provides less value to advertisers.

5.   *The Opportunity to See the Future.*

Google's success stems, in large part, from its founder's drive to innovate to the horizon—a Japanese phrase for far-reaching development goals. The innovation model of entrepreneurship assumes that the enterprise's goal is to solve preexisting problems of process or output. An even greater opportunity exists, however, to focus on long-term, systemic problems and system failures. By developing plans to overcome those challenges, the entrepreneur innovates to the horizon and increases the distance between his company and that of the competitors.

Most market innovations focus on the stressors that are immediate impediments to process or customer satisfaction. For established companies, a great deal of attention is required to make incremental improvements to products that will create both improved quality and a consumer perception of product freshness. Start-ups have no legacy in the marketplace, so their products and services are typically compared to the established companies, but within a few months or years, they also have their own history and incremental comparisons.

A recent study in the Journal of Marketing provides empirical data suggesting that market focus actually reduces market innovation, particularly transformative innovation.[50] The implications of this study reinforce the need for the entrepreneurs, as well as all other business leaders, to look beyond the short-term innovation when developing corporate strategies. The ability to take this long-view approach is necessarily difficult, but Drucker's list of stressors can readily be applied to the twenty-year horizon as well as the five-year strategic plan.

It is quite uncommon for start-ups to have a twenty-year scenario developed for their company. The level of speculation for the new enterprise hardly makes the exercise worthwhile. A snapshot of the marketplace developed for a five, ten and twenty-year analysis, however, may provide some valuable insights regarding the paths to follow and the paths to avoid. Such a snapshot should take the following into account:

Changes to the particular product, service and industry. The starting point for the long-view analysis should be focused on the history and trajectory of the enterprise's own products and services. But a twenty-year growth plan should be based on a twenty or thirty-year historical analysis rather than a snapshot of last year's competitors or even a five-year comparison. This retrospective analysis can then be used as a benchmark to track and compare the other factors listed below.

---

[50] Kevin Zheng Zhou, Chi Kin (Bennett) Yim & David K. Tse, *The Effects of Strategic Orientations on Technology- and Market-Based Breakthrough Innovations*, J. MKTG., Spring 2005, at 42.

The demographic trends of population size, movement and ethnic mix. Expanded immigration (both legal and illegal) are changing markets and culture throughout the United States.

The international changes in world stability and trade changes. While the past thirty years have seen the fall of the Berlin Wall and China's entry into the WTO, historical trend lines suggest both increased international trade and an inevitable balancing of world superpower domination by a single country. Presently, the East-West world dichotomy of Post-War Western domination is being challenged by a restive and reemergent Muslim world as well as an economic shift toward Asia. These changes share some common business implications, but they vary greatly in many regards. The political future has yet to be written.

Technological trends continue to impact all sectors. Gordon Moore's law regarding the doubling of computer chip transistors every two years has held since 1965 despite many scientific articles describing the physical limitations of this continued innovation.[51] Regardless of the sustainability of this particular aspect of innovation, the broader trend of technological progress is likely to continue.

Economic cycles. The U.S. economy runs through recessions and financial cycles that overlap the twenty-year approach. Universities must plan for downturns in enrollment, and companies must plan for downturns in the economy. If they fail to include these changes in their planning, they will lack the flexibility required to respond to the inevitable changes.

Changes in relevance. Products and services come and go. Fashions change. The inevitable life cycle of products, services, and social phenomena should be taken into account. The broader view that includes addressing the underlying consumer need, rather than its current mode of satisfaction, will be valuable here.

Government philosophy and regulatory environment. The regulatory environment for products, services, antitrust enforcement, and funding also follow a rough cycle based on the electorate, which inevitably decides when the leadership by one party or philosophy has

---

[51] *50 Years of Moore's Law*, INTEL, http://www.intel.com/technology/mooreslaw/index.htm (last visited July 12, 2018).

run its course. Barring assassination or criminal activity, this cycle appears to run longer than economic cycles, so the precise timing has a longer arc. Good planning should take into account the potential for the regulatory environment to change, even if predictions regarding the timing of this change will be highly speculative.

While such a detailed analysis will be difficult, it should provide invaluable information as well as a paradigm for future growth. An outgrowth of a twenty-year planning process will be a set of particularized assumptions that can serve to inform the philosophy of the company. By developing the philosophy out of the twenty-year strategy, the true core assumptions can be articulated. These, in turn, will guide the five-year strategic plan and the annual assessment measures for the growth of the company. By using this approach, the enterprise can innovate both at and beyond the minor changes essential to next year's product line, anticipating the short-term needs as incremental steps to the longer-term goals.

6.   The Need for Qualitative, Quantitative, and Comparative Analysis.

Many new companies or innovations are born from the frustration caused by the work-arounds and inefficiencies of the current product or system, so that the innovator cuts the Gordian knot. The innovator, in effect, frees the process or system from its historical constraints, or "the way it has always been done." Often, this is a form of research based on the person's longstanding personal knowledge. While this personal knowledge research often works well, an entrepreneur needs more than his own good idea or personal insight. The entrepreneur critically needs qualitative, quantitative, and comparative research.

Qualitative research should be the first step in any entrepreneurship market analysis. Entrepreneurs should listen closely to what the people on the street know about the problems and opportunities related to the new idea. Conversations with consumers, retailers, shelf stockers, equipment operators, and everyone who is involved at the hands-on level of the product or service are invaluable. Conversations with senior staff and management may help as well, but the need for innovation is often recognized much further down the corporate ladder. At universities, students and secretaries are aware of the problems in the system far earlier than deans or presidents. Auditors ask the support staff more questions than the senior management. This is not because senior management is immune from the problems—far from it. Instead, the support staff has access to sufficient details to make qualitative interpretations of the system patterns.

Qualitative analysis is holistic, impressionistic, and untidy. It may not be subject to rigorous empirical proof. But the comments and reactions of the people involved are often the most important. In his bestseller, *Blink*, Malcolm Gladwell identifies another important aspect to qualitative analysis.[52] While people may be extremely good and highly accurate in forming quick impressions, they generally cannot accurately explain their decision making. As a result, it is more important to rely on the impressions provided by these qualitative interviews than to rely on the explanations people provide to explain their impressions. If a person's initial response to "why did you think that?" is "I'm not sure," accept that answer. Any explanation thereafter is likely to have been made up and could be misleading. The inability to analyze one's impressions does not undermine the credibility of the impression. Gladwell's collection of research highlights that the accuracy of impressions is largely unrelated to the self-analysis of those impressions.

Quantitative analysis should be used to reinforce and critique the qualitative analysis. Theories should be tested systematically and outcomes should be challenged. For start-up companies, quantitative research may be expensive, but can be built into the business plan and funding strategy. Quantitative data is often available from the government and public and private universities. The available data should be incorporated into the analysis of the company. A start-up company does not have to conduct demographic studies before it launches its products, but it should use the federal census data to identify stressors that will support or undermine the launch of its product or service. Also, like all good research, the entrepreneur should invest significant time and effort to prove himself wrong. Most research is beneficial because it keeps manufacturers off the wrong paths. Like the parable of the old man in the woods, his advice may not be enough to

---

[52] MALCOM GLADWELL, BLINK: THE POWER OF THINKING WITHOUT THINKING (2005).

find the path out of the forest, but his experience (if not his wisdom) will tell the explorer which paths do not lead out.

Comparative research is a crucial step, but one that is often overlooked. Comparative research is the process of reviewing the successes of other companies in other fields to see if their innovation is adaptable to the entrepreneur's area of expertise or focus. For example, how does the suggestion from both Scotts' fertilizer spreader and Target's medicine packaging suggest new business opportunities? The most significant lesson is, if a company can maintain the product's quality, while simplifying the use, a premium price can be charged.

An example of this struggle can be seen in the field of home coffee brewing. Instant coffee is simple, quick and mess-free. Nothing can make coffee preparation simpler. Unfortunately, instant coffee does not taste like fresh ground coffee, nor does it create the gourmet experience of brewing coffee—the social relevance of selecting the beans and the sensory experience of the aroma. Keurig Green Mountain and Nescafé each solved this challenge with innovative, patented technology involving coffee pods inserted into patented machines. Keurig, in particular, saw its patented machines become the modern home standard in 2012 when the patent on the pods expired. Many of the pods sold are manufactured by Keurig Green Mountain and others license Keurig trademarks. But the availability of pods from other manufacturers greatly expanded the usefulness of the machines. This grew the shelf space for pods and further reinforced the social relevance of the Keurig coffee system.

The evolution was also described in the first edition of the book. In that edition, the yet-to-be-solved problem of high-quality, simple premium home brewing suggested the following process:

> To achieve the next step in premium home brewing, the entrepreneur must talk with coffee drinkers and home grinding customers to identify the problems or stressors to be solved. From there, the comparisons to other industries can be used to simplify the consumer's process without eliminating the benefits of that process. Careful quantitative analysis should be used to develop the potential for the market, the growth or saturation of the field and a better understanding of the price-points at which solutions will be accepted by the marketplace. The successful

entrepreneur will apply these three processes to the home brewing stressors in order to launch the next generation coffee system.

The example both mirrors many of the steps undertaken by Keurig and highlights the ability to scan any marketplace for stressors and identify opportunities for new products and services. The stressors create opportunities for entrepreneurs to provide useful market solutions. The entrepreneur does not need to be a genius nearly as much as the entrepreneur needs to understand how to identify where solutions are needed and then solve those problems with stable, somewhat exclusive business strategies.

B. Disruptive Innovation and Tsunami Stressors.

1. *Disruptive is More than Different.*

Some stressors are larger than others. In 1997, Clayton Christensen advanced the concept of "disruptive innovation," focusing on technological change that transformed business and often undermined industry incumbents in favor of start-up competitors.[53] Entrepreneurial companies have embraced both the term and the concept, but it has grown considerably to encompass virtually any incumbent market threat. Whereas sustaining technologies improve performance, increase margins, and build customer relations, disrupting technologies often start out as unusable innovations that underperform, cost too much, or focus on a different customer base. Disruptive innovations essentially redefine the value proposition for the customer, which may disintermediate the relationship between vendor and customer, opening the door to competition.

Disrupted markets are highly volatile, with corporate innovators attempting to capture the market in a pattern not unlike that of surfers competing to catch a wave. Many entrepreneurs make a run at the wave but most fall back as the successful entrant captures the dominant position and rides (or falls) based on talent and technique. Unlike open

---

[53] CLAYTON M. CHRISTENSEN, THE INNOVATOR'S DILEMMA: WHEN NEW TECHNOLOGIES CAUSE GREAT FIRMS TO FAIL viii (1997). This section is largely adapted from Jon M. Garon, *Mortgaging the Meme: Financing and Managing Disruptive Innovation*, 10 Nw. J. TECH. & INTELL. PROP. 441 (2012) (most footnotes omitted).

markets, surfers have rules of etiquette to determine who has priority. These same unwritten social and cultural rules sometimes apply to regulated markets and oligopolies as well.

A truly disruptive market is one where the existing model unravels when a competing product or service transitions the market from one business model into a substantially new model. The photographic film industry has seen such an example. Kodak and Polaroid dominated instant photography for generations. Kodak, in particular, had significant research and development in new technologies. By 1975, Kodak's engineer, Steven Sasson, had developed the charge-coupled device, which serves as the basis for the modern digital camera.[54] These efforts, however, did not match the resolution quality of photographic film, and Kodak was primarily a film company rather than an equipment manufacturer. To expand its efforts in digital cameras would generate small returns, and the success would cost them substantial losses. This is the classic dilemma leading companies are facing for truly disruptive innovations. What company wishes to invest in its own demise?

As Kodak and other existing camera and film companies watched from the sidelines, digital cameras grew to dominate the industry in part because they filled the incongruity between how the photographic experience should operate and how it actually operated. Consumers wanted to know immediately if their photographs were satisfactory, to easily share photographs, and to avoid delays in the processing. For most events, convenience was a higher priority than quality, which kept the digital market growing. At the moment digital pictures became a reasonable substitute for film-based pictures, the market became wholly disrupted and the existing markets were thrown into disarray.

The pattern is not new. IBM refused to invest meaningfully in personal computers because its mainframe computer business was too superior. By the time the convenience of personal computers for the

---

[54] *Steven Sasson*, NAT'L INVENTORS HALL OF FAME, http://www.invent.org/honor/inductees/inductee-detail/?IID=453 (last visited June 22, 2018) ("In 1974, Kodak supervisor Gareth Lloyd asked electrical engineer Steve Sasson to investigate whether charge-coupled devices could be used to create an image sensor for a camera. After a year in the laboratory, Sasson created a device that captured an image, converted it to an electronic signal, digitized the signal, and stored the image—the first digital camera.").

home and small business market became established, IBM had been sidelined. Early ship manufacturers saw little value in steam engines because they did not have the range to cross oceans. The convenience of stable power supplies was used by riverboats instead, and by the time the ocean line companies realized that improvements to the engines in riverboats provided the range needed for international voyage, the industry had moved to a different group of manufacturers.

Today, a similar transition is occurring with electric, hybrid, and gasoline engine automobiles. There are a number of companies that recognize that the convenience of electric engines will eventually compete with and then replace gasoline engines. Dominant automakers are slow to introduce these cars into the marketplace because they are not perfect substitutes for the gasoline vehicles today. But a different customer base, urban and short-distance drivers, are clamoring for the convenience and environmental benefits. Gas stations and commercial real estate developers are generally ignoring the looming crisis in their business model. By the time electric cars can compete with gasoline cars for the entire automobile market, the car manufacturers that have not invested in these disruptive innovations will be left behind.

To be successful in a disruptive market, a company has only two strategies available to it. The first strategy is to have the capital resources to lose money for many years as the technology and market mature. Rich, serial entrepreneurs can sometimes bring new markets into existence through their deep pockets and long-term vision.

The second strategy is to earn money for the disruptive, but non-competitive technology by supplying the product to a market that the existing industry does not support. Ironically, the PC provides this example. IBM characterized the PC as a toy competing in the mainframe computer market. Had it instead developed the PC as an innovative extension of its IBM Selectric typewriter, it may have understood the tremendous potential for a word processor that could store and retrieve the documents typed on the machine. Even though early PCs were little more than smart typewriters, IBM misunderstood the potential in the machines and did nothing to own the technology used to launch its fiercest competition—disrupting both IBM's lead in computing and in the office machine market.

2.   *Market Leadership Rather than Market Disruption.*

Unfortunately, the power of the term disruptive innovation has led to its overuse and misunderstanding. Any business challenge can be labeled disruptive innovation. One example of this also flows from the innovations at IBM.

IBM had been a market leader in office technology for decades when it began to develop the IBM Selectric during the 1950's. It launched in 1961, immediately exceeding its predicted output by four times its market predictions. Instead of meeting its goal of selling 20,000 units in its first year, the IBM Selectric instead sold over 80,000 units. While a tremendous hit, the Selectric failed to be a disruptive innovation because it did not change the way in which typewriters were purchased and sold, the ancillary industries associated with office supplies, or any other aspects of typing or office management. The Selectric's use of a sphere for the characters rather than a basket of moving arms made the machine faster and required it to have less maintenance. The interchangeability of the ball allowed for the user to adopt additional fonts and even mathematical symbols. But it was still just a typewriter.

Had a few different choices been made, the entire history of the technology might have changed. IBM computer scientist Bob Bemer is recognized as a pioneer in the establishment of ASCII— American Standard Code for Information Interchange—the alphabet of modern computing.

> Bemer reviewed the Selectric typewriter's specifications. To him, the Selectric would make a natural computer keyboard. He argued that the type ball should be designed to carry 64 characters required for ASCII, rather than the typewriter standard 44. That would make it relatively easy to convert the Selectric for computer input. The response, as Bemer remembers it, was dismissive. As a result, the Selectric never spoke ASCII, instead employing a unique code based on the tilt and rotate commands to the golf ball. While Bemer viewed this as his failure, engineers continued to rig Selectric typewriters to

function as the first generation of computer keyboards and input devices.[55]

Although Selectrics were sometimes rigged to be used as computer input devices, the opportunity to design them to the standard specification was lost. Had Selectrics been able to be used as both an input and printer for early PCs, then the proprietary technology of IBM would have defined the early PC age, and the conversion of thousands of businesses already owning Selectrics would have been a natural progression. Instead, the Selectric was discontinued in 1986, a victim of the PC revolution and the leadership's failure to understand how to adapt to the disruptive innovation transforming its industries.

A second example of non-disruptive industry success is the Procter & Gamble Swiffer Mop. Introduced in the late 1990's, the Swiffer underperformed on measures of durability and cleaning power when compared to conventional dry and wet mops. The ease of use, however, "convert[ed] many non-moppers and infrequent moppers into frequent floor cleaners."[56]

The introduction of the Swiffer Mop was often characterized as an example of disruptive innovation because Swiffer's convenience gained it market share even though it is not as effective as traditional mops.

The Swiffer Mop's success, however, was entirely predictable and not particularly disruptive.   At   a   time   when   products   were increasingly disposable and geared toward convenience, the Swiffer Mop followed the trend. The Swiffer Mop—which avoids the cleaning of mop heads—provides the ultimate in mopping convenience.

Procter & Gamble did not need to change its strategy of selling mops through wholesale and retail channels; it merely added another mop brand to its product array. It did not face disintermediation of its traditional distribution because of the Swiffer. The *idea* of the mop did

---

[55] *The Selectric Typewriter*, IBM 100: ICONS OF PROGRESS, http://www-03.ibm.com/ibm/history/ibm100/us/en/icons/selectric/ (last visited July 12, 2018).

[56] Jeff Lindsay & Mike Hopkins, *From Experience: Disruptive Innovation and the Need for Disruptive Intellectual Asset Strategy*, 27 J. PRODUCT INNOVATION MGMT. 283, 284 (2010).

not change. And the companies which lost market share to P&G lost market share to an existing competitor in the same market space.

3.   Market "Forking" and Self-Inflicted Disruption.

An intermediately sized form of market disruption can be predicted from a pattern common to the nature of market evolution. In many markets, manufacturers begin to differentiate themselves by adding small enhancements and features. These differentiate the products from those of the competition. Some of these improvements have no intellectual property protection, while the more valuable additions often do. For example, these improvements may be protected by patents. At other times, these changes are less significant but tie directly into the trademarks associated with the goods or the celebrity names associated with the marketing. Improvement by improvement, the profitability increases for the seller and the cost increases for the buyer.

At a certain point in the product evolution, however, these incremental improvements begin to price the product too high for a segment of the marketplace. By segmenting the market in this way, the producer of the high-cost goods creates a new market for a low-cost provider. As Christensen describes it, "[t]his follows a cycle that creates the innovators' dilemma: firms add new product/service attributes to attract the most demanding customers then these attributes are imitated by competitors, forcing innovators to add still more product/service attributes."[57] The very quality and cost create opportunities for low-cost competitors to cannibalize part of the market.

For years, U.S. automobile manufacturers understood this innovator's dilemma. Each of the big three auto companies would have brands known for different price points. Even today, GM operates Chevrolet as a lower-priced company, Buick for its middle market, and Cadillac for its upscale line. Toyota, Nissan, and Honda have luxury lines of Lexus, Infiniti, and Acura respectively to stay competitive in both the upper and lower segments of their own markets.

---

[57] CHRISTENSEN, *supra* note 53, at 105.

The innovator's dilemma has many solutions. In *The Fortune at the Bottom of the Pyramid*, C.K. Prahalad painstakingly identifies the cultural, social, and economic assumptions that shaped forty-five years of ineffectual policy regarding poverty in India.[58] Prahalad identifies the fallacy that "[t]he dominant assumption is that the poor have no purchasing power and, therefore, do not represent a viable market."[59] He documents that the poor of China and India hold tremendous purchasing power, perhaps as much as $8 trillion. Because the poor are forced to pay a premium for all the services they receive "from rice to credit" of "5 to 25 times what the rich pay for the same services," unlocking this poverty penalty would generate a huge economic opportunity.[60]

Procter & Gamble demonstrated the reality of this opportunity, using ethnographic studies to quantify that eighty percent of the public in India wash their clothes by hand.[61] Procter & Gamble redesigned a product to be less astringent on hands while still effective on clothing and priced to undercut competing products that used harsher chemicals. By formulating the product to the Indian hand-wash market, Procter & Gamble simultaneously improved service to its customers and developed a new market.

Even more interesting was the foray into this market by Intuit, makers of TurboTax.[62] Looking to develop remote tax preparation tools for the subsistence farmers of India, their first-hand experience with the farmers led Intuit to develop "Mobile Bazaar, a simple text-messaging-based marketplace connecting buyers and sellers."[63] Subscribing farmers

---

[58] C.K. PRAHALAD, THE FORTUNE AT THE BOTTOM OF THE PYRAMID: ERADICATING POVERTY THROUGH PROFITS 30 (5th rev. ed. 2010).

[59] *Id.* at 34.

[60] *Id.* at 35.

[61] *See* Bruce Brown & Scott D. Anthony, *How P&G Tripled Its Innovation Success Rate: Inside the Company's New-Growth Factory*, HARV. BUS. REV., June 2011, at 64, 69.

[62] Roger L. Martin, *The Innovation Catalysts*, HARV. BUS. REV., June 2011, at 82, 87.

[63] *Id.* at 86.

benefited because the quality of their information improved and their access to pricing data expanded. Using the simple tool, "half the farmers were able to increase their prices by more than 10% . . . [and] [w]ithin a year of launch, Mobile Bazaar had 180,000 subscribing farmers, most of them acquired by word of mouth. They report that, on average, the service boosts their prices by 16%."[64]

Intuit experienced a highly disruptive development cycle for both the company and country. It entered a market for one product but ultimately developed an entirely different product to meet a need it had not known existed. On the other hand, the product innovation of Procter & Gamble was merely incremental, not profound disruptive innovation—unless compared with forty-five years of stagnation in India and industry's systemic failure to address a market comprised of four billion poor people across the globe.[65] Both Procter & Gamble and Intuit have made a difference and expanded their business.

In this context, any effort to expand into this market is profoundly disruptive. It also serves as a stark reminder that a marketplace of four billion people with an incalculable collective bargaining power was ignored for decades. But this narrative has shifted and the race to meet these global needs has just begun. The bottom of the pyramid is replete with opportunity for entrepreneurs who can embrace profound disruptive change merely by overlooking the historical blinders created by prejudice, parochialism, and presumption.

4.   *Timing of Success in a Disrupted Market.*

Despite common misconceptions to the contrary, there is not necessarily a first-mover advantage. Timing is a critical factor, but timing merely explains why the successful entrant shaped the response of the pack. If a competitor in the market has the ability to control essential patents, hire key personnel and know-how, develop brand goodwill that shifts consumer behavior, or better predict the manifestation of the disruption, that entrepreneur will outperform the other entrants. The entrant's success drives economically inefficient competitors out of the competition and triggers a shakeout. In retrospect, that entrant is seen

---

[64] *Id.*

[65] PRAHALAD, *supra* note 58, at 27.

as having timed its entrance precisely, but in reality, it was the assets brought to bear on the disruption that shaped the timing.

This is not to say that timing does not matter. The cost of participation appears to have a saddle-curve distribution. Early entrants must bring with them the research, development, and awareness to participate, resulting in relatively high entry costs. Early entrants also face the challenge of waiting a long time before they receive any meaningful return, which reflects on both the cost of the capital investment and the political problem of assuaging investors. The late entrants are competing against an increasingly mature market, which requires greater budgets to acquire technology and larger marketing outlays to acquire market share. The well-timed entrant can reduce the overhead of participation (somewhat) by jumping in at the point that the technology is maturing but before the market is solidifying.

In addition, this timing model assumes the entrant is not affecting the shape of the innovation or the competition. To shape the development curve, an entrant must have the right assets: patents, know-how, brands, and pattern-recognition of the disruption. Moreover, all the tools for success are affected by timing. Move too early and these tools may not be ready to bring to bear; move too late and a competitor may capture these assets. Thus, understanding the pattern is an incremental tool to manage the competition, but a company must bring the right assets to the competition to be successful.

C. Design Thinking as a Process to Find Relevance.

1. *Elements of Design Thinking.*

Tim Brown, president and CEO of IDEO, utilized the term "design thinking" to capture a number of themes implied by the social relevance discussion of Chapter 4 and the stressors outlined by Peter Drucker. Brown emphasized a "human-centered, creative, iterative, and practical approach"[66] which incorporated design at all stages of the creation

---

[66] Tim Brown, *Design Thinking*, HARV. BUS. REV., June 2008, at 85, 92. *See also* HERBERT A. SIMON, THE SCIENCES OF THE ARTIFICIAL 138 (3d. ed. 1996) (recognized for his seminal work that established the design thinking study) ("in large

process rather than relegating it to the end of a stepped process of concept, specification, pricing, and prototyping.

The design thinking approach emphasizes the importance of social relevance to creative problem solving. The relevance to the consumer comes from an emotional appeal as much as from an objective need. The delight comes from the surprise that an unknown or unarticulated problem has been solved with the new product, process, or service. Solving business challenges with these goals in mind necessarily changes the way the entrepreneur treats the process and the outcomes the entrepreneur will achieve. As Brown explains:

- **Great design satisfies both our needs and our desires**—Often the emotional connection to a product or an image is what engages us in the first place. Time and again we see successful products that were not necessarily the first to market but were the first to appeal to us emotionally *and* functionally. In other words, they do the job and we love them. The iPod was not the first MP3 player, but it was the first to be delightful. Target's products appeal emotionally through design and functionally through price—simultaneously. ...

- **Taking a Systems View**—Many of the world's most successful brands create breakthrough ideas that are inspired by a deep understanding of consumers' lives and use the principles of design to innovate and build value. Sometimes innovation has to account for vast differences in cultural and socioeconomic conditions. In such cases design thinking can suggest creative alternatives. ...

- **Take a human-centered approach**—Along with business and technology considerations, innovation should factor in human behavior, needs, and preferences. Human-centered

_____

part, the proper study of mankind is the science of design, not only as the professional component of a technical education but as a core discipline for every liberally educated person").

design thinking—especially when it includes research based on direct observation—will capture unexpected insights and produce innovation that more precisely reflects what consumers want. ...[67]

Design thinking is more than merely incorporating aesthetic design as part of initial stages rather than as the end product. Brown's first step is inspiration, which can be understood to be an illustration of using Peter Drucker's stressors, Clayton Christensen's disruptions, and C.K. Prahalad's cultural disparities as motivation to make a better mousetrap.

The second step, described more fully in the next section, calls for ideation, or the team-inspired, laterally approached, narrative-inspired process of collecting, sorting, evaluating, prioritizing, and testing potential solutions to the challenge. The project team will invariably iterate between inspiration and ideation as proposals are conceived, challenged, discarded, and recycled.

Finally, in the third step, the best ideas will be prototyped and implemented, either on a trial basis or in the marketplace. The three steps (or "spaces" as Brown describes them) are fully distinct. Each of those processes will inform the other two. And so on. "Projects will loop back through these spaces—particularly the first two—more than once as ideas are refined and new directions taken."[68]

2.   *Framing the Right Question.*

The Hasso-Plattner Institute of Design at Stanford University (d.school) emphasizes a five-stage approach to the design process. In addition to the three stages listed above, it adds a different initial stage labeled "Emphasize" and recharacterizes the second stage as Define, meaning to define the problem. Ideate remains the middle step—the

---

[67] Brown, *supra* note 66, at 92.

[68] *Id.*

heart of the process—and the final stage is separated into "Prototype" and "Test."[69]

The d.school model makes the social relevance and human-centered design approach even more explicit by making listening, observing, and engaging a formal step (to the extent anything is formal). The d.school explains its approach: "As a design thinker, the problems you are trying to solve are rarely your own—they are those of a particular group of people; in order to design for them, you must gain empathy for who they are and what is important to them."[70]

The Define step helps unpack the learning that occurred during the active engagement involved in the Empathy step by requiring the design to create a "meaningful and actionable problem statement." But the designer should be very careful at this stage because the framing of the problem will shape the relevance of the solutions. An incomplete problem will leave the underlying issues unsolved; focusing on too narrow or too biased a definition of the problem will miss the great opportunities just out of reach. Take, for example, the illustration of the IBM Selectric and the IBM PC. If anyone at IBM had defined its problem as how to stay in the early PC market without cannibalizing the mainframe market, it may have answered with the Selectric. Had the question about the programming for the Selectric been framed to be the most versatile software solution, then the ASCII-compatible would have been a natural outcome. But when the question was framed by the simplest software needed to run a typewriter, the 44-key programming was adopted, and an entire marketplace was conceded by IBM.

In the practice of law, this step is known as establishing "the theory of the case." In one famous example, after nearly a century of inadequate and discriminatory education practices, then NAACP Legal Defense Fund attorney Thurgood Marshall reframed the question in *Brown v. Board of Education*. Prior to *Brown*, every discriminatory education case

---

[69] Hasso Plattner, Institute of Design at Stanford, *An Introduction to Design Thinking Process Guide*, D.SCHOOL, https://dschool-old.stanford.edu/sandbox/groups/designresources/wiki/36873/attachments/74b3d/ModeGuideBOOTCAMP2010L.pdf?sessionID=8af88fee76ecd1fb7879c915073461486c425622 (last visited July 12, 2018).

[70] *Id.* at 2.

focused on the reality that separate schools for white and non-white children could never be equal, and therefore the "separate but equal doctrine" established by the Supreme Court in 1896 was inherently discriminatory. Only by asking the right question and demonstrating the truth of the answer was Marshall able to convince all nine justices of the Supreme Court that separate but equal was a violation of the U.S. Constitution.

The lesson from *Brown*, IBM, and countless other examples is that the framing of the question is potentially more important than the solutions presented. Solutions are tested and reassessed throughout a design process. All too often, however, the definition of the problem to be addressed is established too early in the process and not challenged again. By incorporating this step into a broader, iterative step, this risk can be mitigated.

At its best, design thinking can push entrepreneurs and designers to find "multi-dimensional solutions," meaning solutions that resolve the immediate need, respond to the human-centered hunger for delight or social relevance, and also create a new opportunity that emerges from the solution rather than the problem.

3.   *Ideation.*

The middle step in every design thinking process is ideation. Ideation is the team-inspired, laterally approached, narrative-inspired process of collecting, sorting, evaluating, prioritizing, and testing potential solutions to the questions that need to be addressed. Ideation brings designers and entrepreneurs to use a wide variety of problem-solving processes to find a preferred solution.

Although the process of ideation is messy and chaotic, there are elements essential throughout the activity. A number of different strategies should be used to identify the potential solutions. Although this list suggests a structured order, effective ideation processes are not necessarily benefited from using these tools in any particular order.

- **Develop a Team**—Ideation is a messy process that involves a myriad of voices. In the typical corporate setting, there are many stakeholders who care about the final solution to the framed problem. Management, finance, marketing, engineering, human resources, and logistics departments all have perspectives on challenges that might emerge if one solution is adopted over another. As noted in the discussion on disruptive innovation, other departments and divisions within a company often block proposed solutions because the solution creates a direct competitor to the sale of existing products and services.

- Effective ideation allows the process to engage a wide, representative group of stakeholders to bring their domain expertise to the table. For at-home entrepreneurs, the process can be replicated by bringing the provisional ideas and solutions to a group of outside critics and experts. If an idea goes from the mind of the inventor directly to market, it is likely that important perspective and opportunities will be missed. Genius sometimes occurs, but by definition, it is very rare.

- **Assess the Framework**—The goals of the multi-dimensional solution should be listed explicitly for the ideation team and priorities established among the various aspects of the solution. If there are absolute parameters, those should also be made explicit. An early d.school exercise, for example, used the ideation for solving how to put a person on the moon. The survivability of the journey sets parameters and establishes speed limits for the vehicles, equipment requirements, and many other constraints. Without these constraints, the ideation process can lose focus, time, and team energy.

- **Take Stock**—Scholars studying ideation focus on a system of "convergent thinking" to determine the verifiable truth of the underlying information, accepted facts (or premises), and normative assumptions. As with the parameters, faulty assumptions and inaccurate facts can doom a product. The accuracy of the assumptions underlying the challenge must be verified. The convergent process may sometimes generate hypotheses to be tested for possible solutions, but unlike a scientific inquiry, the ideation team is not seeking a hypothesis to be proven true but a preferred solution among many alternatives.

- **Develop Tentative Strategies**—In contrast to the convergent, scientific thought process of developing testable hypotheses, the ideation team must also be able to develop any number of possible and probable solutions to the framed challenge before it. This is sometimes referred to as divergent thinking because the ideation team builds a range of possible outcomes from its set of assumptions. Most often, each tentative solution has attributes that make it preferable and other attributes that make it less desirable. That is expected; all viable solutions should be on the table. Ideation teams sometimes struggle not to hit on a quick solution rather than looking for the optimal solution.

  (Note that this is not brainstorming; there are both bad ideas and stupid questions. Solutions that violate the established parameters are not helpful. While the team can revisit the parameters; it must acknowledge that step explicitly. Change the parameters and an entirely new class of solutions may emerge. Strategies to place people on the moon using teleportation are quite efficient, but they violate a parameter of physics. Such strategies will work in a film plot but not for NASA.)

In developing the tentative strategies, team members should suggest strategies that will address various aspects of the problem. Some teams prefer that all these partial solutions be gathered before they are evaluated while other processes emphasize a more sequential approach. Research from Horst Rittel reinforced another aspect of the Aristotelian or Socratic nature of ideation, that effective ideation team dynamics are "inherently argumentative," pushing team members to challenge, reject, and reframe the recommendations.[71] Good ideation teams are not afraid to raise hard questions and argue about the viability of proposals. Team members should respect each other and understand the domain expertise brought into the group by each member, but they should not be quiet about demanding good resolutions. Without the argument and

---

[71] Clive L. Dym et al., *Engineering Design Thinking, Teaching, and Learning*, 94 J. ENGINEERING EDUC. 103, 107 (2005).

challenge, group think, fear, and institutional hierarchy will define the outcome rather than the preferred solutions.

Successful designs both meet the desired outcomes and provide some novel insight or approach to the problem. After all, obvious solutions do not need ideation teams. There are many published models for how to think about the divergent step of developing potential solutions, ranging from simple brainstorming to more structured team exercises. For example, the team approach of "SCAMPER" asks the participants to complete thought experiments following the strategies of substitute, combine, adapt, modify, put to another use, eliminate, and reverse.[72] For any product, service or process, the ideation team can use these simple exercises to re-envision and iterate from the existing strategy to a possible solution. Each of these steps, of course, should be undertaken by each team member both from the perspective of their role on the team and with their capacity to empathize and take on the mindset of the consumer.

Another well-known approach is to shift the hypothetical starting point. In perhaps the most famous thought experiment in science, the sixteen-year-old Albert Einstein asked what he would observe if he pursued a beam of light.[73] By starting his assumptions by moving outside his present world-view, he could imagine a different reality and therefore understand which solutions were viable and which solutions could not work. The simple thought experiment led Einstein to reject the theories of electromagnetism that had dominated science for half a century and led him to new approaches that developed into special relativity.

---

[72] *See SCAMPER: Improving Products and Services*, MINDTOOLS, https://www.mindtools.com/pages/article/newCT_02.htm (last visited July 12, 2018) (attributing SCAMPER to Bob Eberle).

[73] Galina Weinstein, *Einstein Chases a Light Beam*, ARXIV.ORG, https://arxiv.org/ftp/arxiv/papers/1204/1204.1833.pdf (last visited July 12, 2018). The full quote: "After ten years of reflection such a principle resulted from a paradox upon which I had already hit at the age of sixteen: If I pursue a beam of light with a velocity c (velocity of light in a vacuum), I should observe such a beam of light as an electromagnetic field at rest though spatially oscillating. There seems to be no such thing, however, neither on the basis of experience nor according to Maxwell's equations."

Ideation teams might ask themselves how their competitors would resolve the same dilemmas, attempt solutions as if from other countries, or from other industries. Organizations have many constraints in place and a simple thought exercise of asking how the solution would come from a competitor or another industry has the benefit of forcing the ideation team to make those constraints explicit. Some of those constraints may become parameters to be taken into account while others are artificial barriers that can be removed.

When looking to solve systematic challenges, design teams often use the "garden metaphor" in which the challenge is to identify the limiting resource. A garden will grow an infinite amount of food, constrained by the characteristics of the plants and space available, but further constrained by the amount of food, sunlight, and water available as well as diminished by weeds and pests. Each of these variables will cap or limit the potential of the garden. The U.S. State Department faced a similar issue when addressing concerns over the capacity of teletype machines to relay enough information during times of crisis. The solution focused on the teletype machine rather than the larger communication system. Line printers were purchased to replace the teletype machines and the output was increased by orders of magnitude. Yet the problem did not go away, since the issue was the capacity of the State Department staff to respond to the breadth and speed of crisis information. The new equipment merely highlighted the bottleneck was the ability of personnel to address the volume of data being received.[74]

In the same vein, many industries looked to the Internet as the solution to their information problems. Instead, the wealth of content on the Internet has multiplied the challenge of getting high quality, timely, accurate, and digestible information to the person in need of information. A search may result in millions of pages of information, but the searcher is highly unlikely to go more than a few pages into the search results.

Whether a team prefers brainstorming, SCAMPER, hypothetical models, garden exercises, or other systems for helping generate ideas, the goal remains to develop a multitude of possible solutions that meet the minimal needs of the framed problem. In the most formal of the

---

[74] SIMON HERBERT, THE SCIENCE OF THE ARTIFICIAL 143-44 (3d ed. 1996).

ideation processes, the ideation team will explicitly capture the untested assumptions that make certain solutions effective to be sure that those assumptions can be empirically tested to the extent possible. The "known unknowns" are captured in writing.

Integrate—Invariably, the functional parameters used to define the framed problem are reduced to the narrowest problem at hand. So, it is incumbent on the ideation team to assess the proposed solutions against the environment in which the solution is to be launched. This is the "big picture" step or long-range horizon approach. Inventors who focus on this step are sometimes credited with genius foresight, but it is merely another set of parameters that every ideation team should be taking into account.

Among the questions to be asked, here are a few:

- *Is the solution sustainable?* This returns to the question of exclusivity, because if the solution can be copied by all competitors, it will not create a long-term business advantage. If the solution pushes the pricing too far, it will result in a fork in the market, losing a segment of the market. If the resources needed for the solution are limited, the business may not be able to support and supply the solution.

- *What other departments and functions in the enterprise will be impacted by this solution?* Had the IBM Selectric division realized it could solve the PC printer problem, perhaps the Selectric would have been based on ASCII text.

- *What are the logistical opportunities and limits?* Costs for shipping are based on weight, size, and shape. Making inventions fold, telescope, or unspool may dramatically change their usability and adoptability.

- *What problems does our solution create?* Amazon replaced packing popcorn with plastic bags that are much easier for disposal. Had Amazon shipped millions of tons of packing popcorn, the success of the company would have created an environmental nightmare.

- *What else can we solve?* While secondary to the parameters of the problem, multi-dimensional strategies can bring significant success. Apple changed the user experience by approaching product packaging from the perspective of jewelry stores, making the entire experience delightful. It nearly eliminated the useless instruction manuals and challenges its engineers to build products intuitive enough to be used without manuals.

Pre-Prototype Across Stakeholders and Modalities—A good ideation team focuses on how its preferred solutions work for all the stakeholders in an enterprise (or at least as many as possible) and across the design modalities. This is a simple but important checkpoint in the ideation process to assure that each potentially viable solution can be optimized for each of the different modalities the preferred solution might address.

The stakeholder modality loops back to the same approach used to build the ideation team. Different departments and divisions within an enterprise and throughout the entire supply chain from business to end consumer each have different needs from the proposed solution. The ideation should develop a model to assess that the proposed solutions do not fail for any of the departments or divisions within the business enterprise or between the business and its supply chain to assure that the end consumer can benefit from the proposed solution.

This is not to say that every solution must be optimized for every division. In the face of disruptive challenges, old methods of operation and once-reliable products may need to be sacrificed, but those decisions should be explicit and intentional. At Apple, for example, the decision to integrate an MP3 player in the iPhone cannibalized the iPod market. The company benefited from an integrated tablet-in-a-phone concept, but the leadership understood that the trajectory of the iPod would be dramatically changed by the introduction of the iPhone. By having the stakeholders in the development process, the decision and its consequences could be understood and integrated into the business plan.

The design modalities provide a different matrix, designed to think operationally about all the human senses and experiences affected by the proposed solutions. The design modalities can be broken down into the following categories:

- *words and language*, with focus on accuracy, simplicity, reading level, and language choice;

- *static representations*, including graphics, icons, and typefaces;

- *audiovisual representations*, including sound, music, animation, and video;

- *physical objects*, including the materials, textures, scale, weight, strength, durability, and aesthetics of objects;

- *taste and smell*, when relevant, including the unintended effects on pharmaceuticals, foods, beverages, perfumes, incense, and consumer products;

- *time*, including the minimum time needed and the level of engagement for the user;

- *behavior*, including the needed and preferred actions of the user, learning curve for adoption, and accessibility; and

- *systems*, including intersection with other elements, resource demands, integration aesthetics, and integration effectiveness.

Among these many design modalities, behavior is often underestimated. Yet, if a product can capture the knowledge users have from experience with another product, such as a standardized keyboard or uniform commands in a spreadsheet, it becomes easier for those users to migrate to that competitor's product. In contrast, if a new product requires a new set of skills, it is harder for the public to switch.[75] Both ease of use and ease of adoption emphasize incremental changes to products over time. Adobe products are notoriously poor in their integration, with the user often needing to learn different techniques to use tools common to software products in the same bundle. As a result, Adobe has a fraction of the market-share it could own if the company were more effective at improving its behavioral design.

---

[75] Jon M. Garon, *Reintermediation*, 2 INT'L J. PRIV. L. 227, 234 (2009) ("Reintermediation relies upon customer affinity and behaviour of repeated reliance on a particular company to the exclusion of all other providers of that good or service. The exclusivity may have no legally enforceable parameters or it may be based on either exclusive dealing contracts or intellectual property protections.").

Assuming that the d.school design thinking five-stage model is used, prototyping is a discrete stage following ideation. Pre-prototyping, then, belongs properly in the ideation stage of the design thinking process. As noted throughout, however, these stages are non-linear and highly iterative, so this is a transitional phase before prototyping.

The pre-prototyping can be used to reduce the number of potential solutions down to the final three or four to fully prototype. The number of prototypes will vary, generally in relation to the cost in time, funds, and effort to create the prototype solution.

Taken together, these steps capture the chaos that surrounds ideation. A study on design theory summarized the goals of good ideation with these "skills often associated with good designers, namely, the ability to:

- tolerate ambiguity that shows up in viewing design as inquiry or as an iterative loop of divergent-convergent thinking;

- maintain sight of the big picture by including systems thinking and systems design;

- handle uncertainty;

- make decisions;

- think as part of a team in a social process; and

- think and communicate in the several languages of design."[76]

In practical terms, many successful entrepreneurs conflate these various steps into a working business model. Research strongly indicates three common attributes for ideation among technology entrepreneurs:

First, they all utilize complex and sophisticated social networks as sources of ideas and to test, refine, and validate trial ideas. Second, technology entrepreneurs exhibit extraordinary domain specificity by filtering ideas outside specific markets and

---

[76] Dym et al., *supra* note 71, at 104.

technologies. Finally, they actively experiment and iterate ideas rather than engage in protracted conceptual analysis.[77]

Although this research focused on technology entrepreneurs, these same three steps are equally applicable to entrepreneurs in all fields. The ability to learn from their social networks but then focus on the particular area is essential to move from good idea to specific product. The third step is also highly practical, since it is better to build and refine than to stuck in a conceptual box, unable to take the leap into experimentation.

* * *

Sidebar—Failure and Resilience.

The three-step and five-step models of design thinking both rely heavily on iteration, prototyping, testing, and refinement. Inherent in these processes is the understanding that the first version will not be a successful product, service, or design, and that through testing and conversation, something good will come out of the initial efforts. Though designers need not use the word, these early versions are essentially "failed efforts" that help propel the process towards later success.

For new innovators, it is helpful to understand that the process of failure is an expected—if not required—interim step between concept and success. Only if the innovator is sufficiently resilient and dogmatic regarding the steps beyond the early prototypes towards the eventual success, can the process succeed.

The need for resilience and the ability to "fail forward" are both necessary skills for any business owner, but they are particularly important for entrepreneurial and innovative projects.

At the same time, many commenters often refer to resilience and the ability to fail forward as personality traits or even generational traits. Entrepreneurs are often described as resilient while millennials are often chastised for not being culturally competent to overcome setbacks and failures. This suggestion, that these are traits rather than skills, misplaces the ability to learn design thinking and to contextualize setbacks.

---

[77] Robert M. Gemmell, Richard J. Boland, & David A. Kolb, *The Socio-Cognitive Dynamics of Entrepreneurial Ideation*, ENTREPRENEURSHIP, THEORY, & PRACTICE, Sept. 2012 at 1260.

Certain failures cannot be overcome. For example, Blockbuster's demise was tied to its investments in retail locations. Those locations made it highly profitable in one era and overburdened with overhead in another era. A company reliant on a patent will lose its exclusivity when the patent expires. A company built around the publicity and goodwill of its owner or of a celebrity will take a market hit if that person behaves in a criminal or immoral manner. Many, many companies fail when they run out of financing.

Many other failures are much less catastrophic but will still require the company rethink and redesign to be successful. Missing product features, excessive cost, confusing operations, and many other challenges doom products. An entrepreneur can be taught to expect these challenges and to have a plan to improve the product with each prototype or shipment. Making this strategy explicit enables the entrepreneur to be resilient and prepared to face failure. If the failures are more unexpected, then the same training will enable the entrepreneur to analogize to other forms of iterative planning and still pursue long-term success. In this way, resilience is merely a skill to be learned just like the other steps for successful business ownership and leadership.

* * *

4.   *Design Thinking's Relationship to UX (User Experience).*

As with any discipline, there is a great deal of domain jargon, and entrepreneurship is no different. The approach focusing on UX—User Experience—can be considered a component of the broader design thinking approach developing social relevance in all product and business strategies. UX tends to be used most often in the fields of computer hardware and software. The field may have been birthed from the war between the beige square boxes that defined PCs when compared to the candy-colored Macs; the black phones and tablets of Google and Microsoft compared to the pure white devices of Apple; and the general lack of aesthetic focus by any major tech company other than Apple. As Apple grew to become the most valuable company in the world, Steve Jobs' insistence on elegance and simplicity in design became noticeable.

Apple's focus on design became even more famous when Samsung leapfrogged over the dozens of phone and device manufacturers by adopting a strategy of copying Apple's proprietary design approaches.

Steve Jobs' obsession with rounded edges had resulted in both the software interface for the Mac and the shape of the iPhone. Samsung copied the patented corner design—and many other design features— to successfully reposition itself as a leader in the Android phone market. Apple won the initial lawsuit and was awarded $1 billion (which was then reduced to $399 million) in damages for the design patent violation, though even that result was ultimately overturned.[78]

The focus of UX highlights the importance of human-centered, socially relevant design thinking and the need to delight as well as to serve. In the Basics of User Experience (UX) Design, the Interaction Design Foundation suggests that UX focuses on seven factors: "1. Useful; 2. Usable; 3. Findable; 4. Credible; 5. Desirable; 6. Accessible; and 7. Valuable."[79] Some of these factors, including useful, desirable, and valuable, have been explored throughout the book as essential for relevant product development.

As used by the Interaction Design Foundation, usable focuses on the ability of the consumer to easily understand and master the interface of the product. Early MP3 manufacturers were keen to add significant functionality in their tiny machines, rendering them utterly obtuse for the user. Apple's iPod locked the machine to the computer, offloading most of the controls and making the user experience much simpler and more pleasurable.

As a category, findable is really a sub-species of usable. Still, since device navigation is so often a problem, focusing on the findability of functions and the organization of data and commands represents such a significant focus on the usability of these machines, it makes sense to treat this category separately.

Credibility or trustworthiness is an attribute of the user experience that generally lives outside the product and instead focuses on the communications, responsiveness, warranty, and reliability associated

---

[78] Samsung Elecs. Co. v. Apple Inc., 137 S. Ct. 429 (2016) (Following seven years of litigation, the parties eventually settled the dispute for an undisclosed amount and ended all patent claims against each other.)

[79] Interaction Design Foundation, *The Basics of User Experience Design* 22, https://tofasakademi.com/wp-content/uploads/2018/06/the-basics-of-ux-design.pdf (last visited July 12, 2018).

with a product or service. While the trustworthiness of a product or service is unrelated to its design, attributes such as durability and repairability can be incorporated into the design itself. All these factors are important to the overall user experience. Hype can destroy a good product. For example, a weight-loss product that allowed users to lose twenty pounds in a year would be a scientific breakthrough. But if the company tried to peddle it by promising the loss of twenty pounds in a month, the credibility of the product would be destroyed and few, if any, consumers would recognize it for the value it actually held.

Accessible is a UX factor that ties back in important ways to the design thinking step of empathy. All products should be designed to be integrated into existing accessibility tools and functional for the greatest percentage of the public. Designing products and services to take wheelchairs, limits on physical motion, hearing and sight impairments, and other such challenges should be foundational to product and service design. Accessibility challenges also represent stressors that create business opportunities for entrepreneurs who understand how to empathize and design to make their products uniquely relevant and beneficial to this population.

5.   *The Universe is Made of Stories: Crafting and Shaping Narrative.*

Independent of the formal design thinking, a successful entrepreneur must understand the importance of empathy and actively engaging with clients and the public. When looking to develop new products, services, and processes, a company's customer base will generally focus on what it hopes to get to iterate the product, usually at little or no cost.

The discussion the entrepreneur needs to have is with the non-customer, to find out from those not interested in a firm's products or services what would make that firm's competencies suddenly of interest. The customers of direct competitors will disclose useful information for modest process or product improvements, but these will not typically result in profound disruptive innovation.

The most valuable information will come from utterly disinterested individuals who had not previously considered the products or services in question. Given their lack of engagement, most of those conversations are irrelevant and the exercise is unlikely to succeed. But within the non-customer population are the members of an entrepreneur's new market.

The key is not to sift through the throngs in hopes of finding one new customer. Rather, the key is to identify what would drive new populations to goods and services that can be made profitably by the entrepreneur.

Just as "the universe . . . is made of stories, not of atoms,"[80] so is the world of business and commerce. The story defines the social narrative which provides the context for interactions. Social relevance prioritizes these interactions. Empathy makes them understandable.

Narrative is inherently social. As the public increasingly accepts a social narrative, the network effect consolidates the impact. The theory of social relevance predicts that a person is rewarded simply for adhering to the accepted narrative.[81] "All of us are prisoners of our own socialization. The lenses through which we perceive the world are colored by our own ideology, experiences, and established management practices."[82]

Culture has numerous threads, weaving narratives together. Many are surprisingly resilient to change. Education, training, media, and other tools reinforce these tropes and do little to affect them when advocates challenge particular stories or customs. The story—more than any objective truth—ultimately dominates the social narrative. The story shapes the relationships among its adherents and defines the boundaries of the shared culture.

Successful new stories have a common method for distribution and sustenance. Cultural shifts tend to come from a concerted effort of a school, group, or cult. For example, "the determining factors that influence innovation are the cognitive frames that shape what types of information are perceived relevant to the individual, and the cultural constraints that lead an individual to question if change is even

---

[80] F.S. MICHAELS, MONOCULTURE: HOW ONE STORY IS CHANGING EVERYTHING 7 (2011) (quoting poet Muriel Rukeyser) (internal quotation marks omitted).

[81] PRAHALAD, *supra* note 58, at 30.

[82] *Id.*

possible."[83] Groups often use major events as an inflection point to highlight the shift from the old meme to the new one, though the importance of the event may grow as the story is retold.

For investors, identifying goods or business models that embody this pattern will help capture the most profound disruptive innovation. Powerful stories disintermediate preexisting relationships and reintermediate them with the new narrative and new transactional relationship. It affords opportunities for horizontal growth into new markets as the meme disrupts neighboring relationships.

Events like the TED conference and the Apple Worldwide Developers Conference are not coincidental to the growth of certain technologies and platforms. By recognizing the power of the story and the role of a shared narrative—observing the rise of schools (or cults) that cohesively advocate for a particular platform or service—investors can identify the potential authors of the next social narrative and entrepreneurs can develop solutions that reinforce that narrative.

If stories, not atoms, make up the universe, then today these stories are linked by social media. Social media and other new technologies have reshaped consumer behavior, empowering the audience to share, retell and even adapt the story. The many-to-many environment pushes certain stories while retelling others. For the entrepreneur, crafting a compelling, authentic narrative is an essential first step. The story must be accurate and fully understood by everyone in the company responsible for communicating that story. Once the narrative is made public, the company must be ready to support the expansion of that story throughout the social media ecosystem and equally ready to respond to harmful distortions and intentional hijackings. If the public's acceptance of a compelling narrative is the ultimate user experience, then an effective design model must incorporate the power of the storytelling into every element of the design process.

Design thinking, to be fully successful, requires the last step of understanding the story to be communicated through the design process and how that story shapes the perception of the products, services, or

---

[83] TODDI A. STEELMAN, IMPLEMENTING INNOVATION: FOSTERING ENDURING CHANGE IN ENVIRONMENTAL AND NATURAL RESOURCE GOVERNANCE 16 (2010).

processes being developed. For all its prior success, Apple's simultaneous launch of the iPhone 8 and iPhone X hurt its narrative. The pricing and dual product launch became characterized as elitist rather than cool. The self-imposed scarcity that suggested public demand disappeared because the market was sated with two products at once. And the one-choice modality that created a story wherein Apple knew better than the public what it wanted was pierced because suddenly the consumer had choices. In one small business decision, many of the previously protected narratives were unintentionally undone.

While shaping the narrative could be considered as one of the design modalities, an entrepreneur is better served considering it independently. In many cases, the narrative can be crafted independently of the preferred design solution. Having a compelling narrative helping drive the design, however, will result in a more resilient market solution. Regardless of the sequence of development, the resulting product, service, or process must be communicated with the story and the story-telling process in place if the entrepreneur wishes the new product to be successful in the marketplace.

D.   From Problem Solving to Exclusivity.

Identifying the stressors that trigger demand for innovation provides the first step in the entrepreneurship process. The second step is to identify unique solutions to meet the needs of those stressors and their scale. Truly disruptive innovation requires much more comprehensive strategies than simple product development. The third step relies on effective design thinking and comprehensive ideation, prototyping, and testing. Even this, however, is not enough. If the solution is easily replicable by anyone in the industry, the innovator will gain little over the competition and established competitors can leverage their existing strengths to overtake the start-up company. The successful entrepreneur must complete two additional steps to be successful. The entrepreneur must create a unique, relevant solution and be able to craft a compelling story to inform the public of that solution.

Developing a unique solution is necessary for success, but insufficient. The solution must be highly relevant to consumers. If consumers do not recognize the value, the solution will not be adopted—even if it provides an overall improvement. The solution must be relevant to the decision maker. Similarly, the entrepreneur must understand how to convince the consumer of the relevance of the unique solution. The solution must fit into the narrative accepted by the consumer.

Finally then, the relevant, unique solution to the stressor will provide success for the entrepreneur only if the entrepreneur can protect it from being copied and commoditized. Only through the use of patents, trade secrets, trademarks, copyright, publicity rights, and careful contractual agreements can the entrepreneur ensure the ownership necessary to launch a successful business. Taken together, this process of moving from innovation to exclusivity will provide start-up businesses the best possible opportunity for success. Other factors such as timing, funding, and personality might impact the success or failure of the business, but this approach of moving from innovation to exclusivity is an essential ingredient without which success is not possible.

* * *

In Summary:

A start-up business can only compete if it addresses an unmet need caused by changes to demographics, attitudes, the state of knowledge, or to internal system flaws such as incongruities, unexpected outcomes, flawed processes, or other innovation.

A start-up business must address the unmet need with a unique beneficial solution to the stress on the existing marketplace.

To protect that unique aspect of the business, the company must make use of the intellectual property rules embodied in patent, copyright, trademark, contract law, trade secrets, and publicity rights.

The company must use the exclusive rights to create objective and social relevance in the company's products or services in a market large enough to sustain profitability.

The company can use marketing and branding to craft an effective story that highlights the objective benefits and enhances the subjective relevance of the product.

These steps are the prerequisites to building a successful start-up enterprise. Without completing these steps, no new company has the ability to grow beyond the individual efforts of the company's founder.

With exclusivity and relevance, a company started in a garage or basement can grow into a company like Apple, Walt Disney Co., or Newman's Own.

* * *

Chapter 6. Paying for Exclusivity: Financing and Business Structuring

A. Forming the Business.

There are three general considerations to consider in selecting the business form. These are the nature of the relationship between the controlling founders of the business, the tax consequences of the revenues from the business, and the liabilities for the conduct of the business. Most entrepreneurs want to reduce taxes, reduce liabilities in the cases of accidents and breaches of contract, and maximize their flexibility in controlling the enterprise.

For-profit business organizations tend to fall into one of five categories: Sole Proprietorships, General Partnerships, subchapter C Corporations, subchapter S Corporations, and Limited Liability Companies. Among this group, there are preferred business models and models that should be avoided.

The choice of business form becomes a process of recognizing which of the five business forms accomplish these three goals most effectively, while managing the tradeoffs among the business forms. These forms and the operational consequences of these forms are outlined by business type.

1. Sole Proprietorships.[84]

As provided under most state laws, in the absence of any legal structure, a business will be treated as either a sole proprietorship or a general partnership. A sole proprietorship is nothing more than saying that a business organizer is legally the same person as a business itself. A business may use its trade name, but all legal responsibilities rest solely on a business organizer as the owner of a business. Companies sometimes file "DBA" forms, which simply means that it has registered the trade name of the business with the state. Unlike a trademark, a DBA

---

[84] These sections are adapted from JON M. GARON, POP CULTURE BUSINESS HANDBOOK FOR CONS AND FESTIVALS (2017).

form does not confer any ownership rights or priority for the use of that business name.

A sole proprietorship means that the business owner and the business are the same legal entity for tax purposes, control purposes, and liability purposes. All costs, debts, and promises are the responsibility of the proprietor. Business income is treated as personal income and taxed accordingly. While sole proprietorships are not the ideal business model, most aspiring entrepreneurs start their business in this form.

2.   General Partnerships—The Worst Business Model in America.

A general partnership is any business organized for profit between two or more people. Like the sole proprietorship, the people who are the business owners are treated as personally responsible for all costs, debts, and promises. Like the sole proprietorship, the income is taxed as personal income. But there is one critical difference between the sole proprietorship and the general partnership: Each of the general partners is responsible for all the other general partners. So the costs, debts, and promises made by any general partner creates a liability for all of the partners. The partners rather than the business are responsible for the debts that can occur.

If one overly enthusiastic partner agrees to order 100,000 prototypes of a new product instead of 1,000, then all the general partners will be responsible to cover that cost amongst themselves. A general partnership opens each owner to the risks of loss for the business, including the bad decisions and lack of control over all the other general partners.

General partnership laws protect the public from general partnerships and provide default rules about the relationships among the general partners, but these rules are often different from the expectations of the parties. As a result, a general partnership has the worst possible rules regarding liability and control. While it treats revenue as personal income for tax purposes, which is generally the better alternative for most (but not all) entrepreneurs, the lack of liability protection and the lack of protection among the owners makes this the worst form of business any entrepreneur can operate.

An additional risk for the general partnership is the rather vague definition regarding who is a partner. A sole proprietor may inadvertently become a general partner engaging volunteers, independent contractors, or employees, unless the terms of the working agreement are clearly specified in writing. Since the legal standard is an understanding upon two or more people to engage in a business for profit, a volunteer or independent contractor may easily self-identify as a partner in the enterprise. Unless the sole proprietor takes steps to correct that misinformation with the public and with that volunteer, the assertion by that volunteer has the potential to change the legal relationship between the parties.

In practice, it may be very hard to determine who is a general partner, particularly if a business either earns a good deal of money, or worse, owes a good deal of money to its creditors. If a spouse helps out in the business during its early stage, that spouse might argue that he or she now is a general partner, which could have devastating consequences if there were to be a divorce. Instead of operating as a general partnership, business organizers should take the time and invest the effort to create a legal entity that best serves the goals of a business.

3.   Subchapter C and Subchapter S Corporations.

A corporation provides substantial benefits over the sole proprietorship and general partnership because it provides limited liability. For any owner of a company, this means that, subject to certain exceptions, the owner's risk in the company is limited to the amount of money that owner invested. Assume, for example, that a person invests $10,000 for shares in a corporation and that corporation later goes out of business owing $1 million in obligations. The investor will lose the $10,000 but not be personally responsible for the additional funds needed to make up the debt of the failing business. In contrast, the general partners would have been personally responsible to cover the debts of the corporation.

The second structural distinction between general partnerships and corporations is the separation of ownership and control. In a large, publicly traded corporation, for example, there could be many thousands of shareholders, none of whom have any control over the corporation other than to elect the corporation's board of directors. These directors operate as the management of the corporation. They, in turn, hire the executives and senior leadership who provide the day-to-day operational control of the corporation. In theory, the board of directors controls the executives of the business. In practice, the chief executive officer of a corporation collaborates with the owners of the largest shares of voting blocks in a company to control the business and its operations.

For the small business, the separation of ownership and control remains an essential aspect of its growth and development. An entrepreneur will need capital funds to invest and grow the business. For the entrepreneur, most of those investors should have only a small amount to say about the day-to-day operations of the business. Like the publicly traded companies, the entrepreneur can have the corporation issue shares of stock to those owners in exchange for ownership in the company without giving those investors operating control in the company. As a result, separation of ownership and control provides as great a reason as limited liability to incorporate.

Because the tax implications of the business structure are also very important, the IRS provides business owners with two options on how the enterprise should be taxed. The traditional model is the subchapter C corporation. The C-Corp, as a legal entity, has its net revenue taxed. Payments back to its shareholders are in the form of dividends, which are paid in after-tax dollars. The dividends are treated as a taxable income for the shareholders, so the flow of income to the owners is often described as being double-taxed.

For many corporations, however, the ability to pay reasonable salaries provides a convenient tool to offset the problems of double taxation. Moreover, the challenge of double taxation does not occur until the company is in a position that it needs to pull money out of the business and return it to the shareholders in the form of dividends. As a result, the preferred tax treatment may depend on the nature of the tax concerns for the corporation and its major shareholders.

In recognition that double-taxation is not fair for smaller companies, the tax code includes subchapter S corporations, which are treated as partnerships for purposes of certain tax laws. S corporations "pass corporate income, losses, deductions, and credits through to their shareholders for federal tax purposes. . . . This allows S corporations to avoid double taxation on the corporate income. S corporations are responsible for tax on certain built-in gains and passive income at the entity level."[85]

In many other respects, however, the S corporations remain much more like C corporations than partnerships.[86] For example, the choice whether to elect to be an S corporation is also precluded for certain types of financial businesses. S corporations can have no more than 100 shareholders and require that there is only one class of stock.

Once an S corporation elects to be treated as a partnership for tax purposes, its annual net revenue is treated as having been automatically distributed to the shareholder. The corporation owes no income tax. Instead, each of the shareholders is responsible for a proportionate share of the tax obligation. While this may reduce taxes owed in most instances, it has its own complications. For example, the tax obligation is shifted to the shareholders even if the dividend payments were not made in a particular year. This can result in shareholders owing considerable tax amounts without the cash flow to cover them.

Under state law, S corporations may also elect to be operated directly by the shareholders rather than separating the ownership from control. In the early years of a business where all the shareholders are active participants in the business, letting the shareholders operate as the directors may be a very practical model. As the world of business finance has become more complicated, however, the separation may be very useful for many companies.

Another sub-species of corporation is the social purpose corporation. Social purpose corporations are not charities, however, and they are taxed as for-profit companies. They differ from subchapter S corporations in that they specifically allow the corporate charter to include social interests to be an express component of the corporate purpose of the business, rather than the corporate purpose being limited to making profits for a return to the shareholders. They have

---

[85] *S Corporations*, IRS, https://www.irs.gov/businesses/small-businesses-self-employed/s-corporations (last reviewed or updated May 3, 2018).

[86] Martin J. McMahon, Jr. & Daniel L. Simmons, *When Subchapter S Meets Subchapter C*, 67 TAX LAW. 231 (2014), available at http://scholarship.law.ufl.edu/facultypub/621.

shareholders and may pay dividends. The benefit to business organizers is the flexibility to provide a much greater percentage of the profits to charity than the normal corporation. In this way, social purpose corporations provide a model that combines the for-profit structure of the corporation with the social purposes of the nonprofit. These exist in only a few states. They essentially allow for-profit businesses to donate most—or even all—the profits to social causes while remaining for-profit in operational structure.

Even where they do not exist, however, an explicit statement in the Articles of Incorporation and the bylaws will enable most companies to have these social purposes. They are of particular value to companies like Newman's Own, which markets traditional grocery items but provides all its net profits to charity. In a traditional company, the minority shareholders would correctly object to all of the profits going to charity as corporate waste. The most common way to solve that problem historically was not to have minority shareholders. Today, the social purpose corporation also allows such behavior.

4.   *Limited Liability Companies.*

The limited liability company (LLC) is a more recent variation of the business model, which operates as something of a hybrid between the subchapter S corporation and the general partnership. The ownership is held by members rather than shareholders. The members own membership units instead of shares or partnership interests. The LLC is managed either by its members or by managers, depending on the terms of the membership operating agreement. In an LLC, the operating agreement takes the place of both the Articles of Incorporation and the bylaws. The LLC has the ability to elect to be taxed as either a partnership or a corporation.

Unlike the corporation laws that provide shareholders the right to change from the statutory rules only in limited situations, the typical state laws governing LLCs allow the operating agreement to set out almost every term regarding the relationship among the parties. Very few rules are required under state law. LLCs are great financing vehicles for certain types of start-up enterprises and very effective at carving out the rights of different kinds of owners. With this flexibility and freedom comes a much greater need to understand and craft the organizing documents. For some entrepreneurs, the flexibility will be a great benefit, but for most, a subchapter S corporation will provide more structure while reducing the chance of something going wrong.

B.   Staffing and Starting the Business.

Although each state has its own state corporations law, most of these have similar requirements. A corporation is created by filing the Articles of Incorporation with the state, paying any required fees, and following the other steps set out in the state law. These steps usually include:

- Electing a business name and filing with the state;

- Filing the Articles of Incorporation with the state;

- Adopting bylaws, which establish the governing rules of the company;

- Electing directors;

- Accepting the resignation of the incorporator, the person who filed the Articles of Incorporation; and

- Filing any state securities documents establishing the initial ownership of shares in the company.

The LLC generally requires similar steps:

- Electing a business name and filing with the state;

- Filing the Articles of Organization with the state;

- Adopting an Operating Agreement, which establish the governing rules of the company;

- Publishing a notice of operation in those jurisdictions requiring such public notice; and

- Filing any state securities documents establishing the initial ownership of shares in the company.

Limited Liability Companies are defined by the Operating Agreement. The LLC may be managed by all its members, by owners of certain types of membership interests, or it may delegate that power to elected directors. As a result, LLCs require more attention at the outset to specify who has the power over different aspects of the business. The largest benefit is that the Operating Agreement can be tailored to the relationship of the founders of the business much more effectively than the bylaws of corporations. Findlaw lists certain key factors typical of an LLC Operating Agreement due to the mandatory provisions in state corporation statutes:

- The owners' (members') business interest in the LLC,

- The rights and responsibilities of the members,

- Regulations controlling how the business profits will be shared,

- Terms relating to the voting power of the members,

- Rules and regulations that set out how the LLC will be managed,

- Rules regarding when meetings will occur and how votes will be taken, and

- Provisions that will govern situations where a member wants to get out of the LLC, either by selling his or her interest, death or disability.[87]

In contrast, a corporation is managed by a board of directors. The duties of the board of directors are listed in the bylaws. The shareholders only vote on major changes to the company or other items specified in the bylaws. Under most state laws, the board of directors and the shareholders must each hold an annual meeting to reelect officers and directors, although these meetings can be replaced with actions taken by unanimous written consent. Corporations also typically have certain annual reporting requirements and annual fees that must be paid to remain in good standing. Provided these minimum steps are taken, the corporation remains in good standing.

Corporations do not have to be organized and operate in the same state. A corporation operating in another state is known as a foreign corporation. If business organizers believe the social purpose corporation is the best corporate form, then they can organize the

---

[87] *Forming an LLC*, FINDLAW, https://smallbusiness.findlaw.com/incorporation-and-legal-structures/forming-an-llc.html (last visited June 22, 2018).

company in a state that recognizes the social purpose corporation and file a certificate as a foreign corporation doing business in the state where a business operates.

The steps to qualify as a foreign corporation are very simple, and most companies use a low-cost service to complete the process. The ability of business entities to qualify as a foreign corporation enables an entrepreneur to select the laws of a particular state to organize the business, while still operating in the locations they choose.

The basic corporation is operated by a board of directors. The board of directors is elected annually by the shareholders or by the corporation. In small organizations, the shareholders typically elect themselves onto the board of directors, serving in both the role of owner and decision maker. A board member has no direct, individual authority over the organization. Instead, decisions are made only through votes of the board of directors acting as a single body.

If the organization is a subchapter S corporation or a member-managed LLC, then the board is replaced directly with the owners. The operating documents will state whether the board operates on a one person, one vote basis or votes based on the proportion of ownership interest.

In larger organizations, the board of directors is often comprised of some internal officers of the corporation and some outside board members. These boards are much more independent of the shareholders, bringing professional expertise to the management of the organizations. Such boards operate on a one person, one vote basis.

The day-to-day operations of the corporation are conducted by the officers of the corporation who oversee the employees and the activities of the business. Traditional corporate law identifies the president, vice president, secretary, and treasurer as the four key officers, but practice has evolved considerably. A single individual may hold more than one position. These four duties have been updated and divided.

The "president and chief executive officer" (CEO) has ultimate responsibility for all operational decisions and reports only to the board of directors. As chief executive officer, the president also convenes the board of directors and helps direct and manage the board. Occasionally, the president and chief executive officer are positions held by two separate individuals, but usually the business has only one leader who may choose to select one or both of these titles.

The "treasurer and chief financial officer" (CFO) has the responsibility for all financial reporting, budgeting, financial compliance, tax reporting, and similar functions. If the person is designated as CFO, that person will also typically be named one of the executive vice presidents.

Many organizations also utilize a "chief operating officer" (COO) who undertakes the primary responsibility for personnel, operations, marketing, sales, and other internal financial aspects of the company. For organizations with a COO, the person will often be named the vice president or one of the executive vice presidents.

The "secretary" has a unique role within the board of directors' operation. This person is responsible to assure that notices of meetings are provided to board members, minutes of meetings are properly taken, and if any actions require a state filing, that those filings are properly recorded. For larger corporations, the secretary is often a member of the legal staff or law firm. For small companies, the secretary can be any senior officer.

The titles of CEO, CFO, and COO work equally well in corporations, subchapter S corporations, and Limited Liability Companies. All other employees and departments report to supervisors who, in turn, report up through the organization's structure to one of these three positions. The CFO and COO also report directly to the CEO, and together, they report to the board of directors.

C.   Raising Debt and Equity.

For most start-up businesses, there are two primary types of funds available to help start the business until the company is generating an income: debt and equity. A debt is a loan or credit that must be repaid by the entrepreneur, while equity is payment made to the entrepreneur in exchange for ownership interests in the company.

1.   Debt.

Loans are the most common source of funds, whether from banks, credit card companies, friends, or family. The loan amount is expected to be repaid with interest by the entrepreneur at some time in the future. The loan is also known as a debt.

Generally, the debt is owed by the party signing the loan. If the company has been properly formed and the lender agrees, then only the company is liable for the debt owed on the loan. For start-up businesses, however, the lenders will often ask the entrepreneur to guarantee the loan, making the entrepreneur personally liable for the debt. This obligates the entrepreneur to repay the loan even if the company has failed and no longer has any money. In the case of a sole proprietorship or general partnership, the owner or partners are always personally responsible for the repayment of the loans.

The lender makes its money by charging interest on the loan, along with fees to enter into the agreement. Typically, the interest is fixed or based on market rates and does not relate to the success or failure of the business. For a business in trouble, the payment of the interest and repayment of the principal may be difficult. In contrast, if the business is successful, the owner keeps all profits once paying the interest and repaying the debt.

Business or commercial lenders will also require that the loan is secured. This means that the assets of the business are pledged to the lender and may be seized for sale if the loan is not paid in full. Through the process of bankruptcy, a lender can demand that its loans be paid. The secured lender receives payment in full from the sale of those assets before any other lenders or creditors can use the sale of the secured assets to satisfy other debts.

For businesses, the assets that typically secure a loan are any real property (real estate, land, houses, etc.), equipment, inventory and accounts receivable. Commercial lenders will typically try to include all the assets of the business in the list of collateral protecting a loan.

For the corporation or LLC, the debt is owed from the legal entity rather than its shareholders and members. Often, however, the lender will insist on a guarantee from the shareholders to be personally responsible to repay the interest and principal on the debt. It is an example where the legal protection of limited liability is circumvented by common business practice.

Even if there is no requirement of a guarantee, for many start-up businesses, the entrepreneur's home is used as the collateral for the loan. Instead of borrowing through the business, entrepreneurs will often take a second mortgage against the value of their homes as a fast and relatively low-cost source of funds. The risk, of course, is that if the business fails, the entrepreneur risks losing a house as well as the business. This is a risk that should not be taken lightly.

2.   Equity.

In contrast to debt, equity results from the sale of the business ownership to an investor in exchange for funds. Equity investors are not guaranteed any particular rate of return and do not have the right to repayment. In a corporation, the investors receive stock, while in an LLC they receive membership interests. Both ownership interests are securities, the offering and sale of which are regulated by both state law and federal securities law.

In a simple stock transaction, the total ownership of the company is divided into a fixed number of shares of stock. An investor is sold some of the shares, resulting in the investor owning that portion of the company. As discussed above, the rights in the stock give the investor the right to elect directors of the company and vote on key events regarding the company's future. As a result, the investor's role has much more involvement than the lender.

Equity financing reduces the financial risk of the business because the investor shares in the risk in proportion to her ownership. If the business is successful, however, the investor also shares in the success of the business in proportion to her ownership. If the business is a tremendous success, the investor will receive far more than the lender. Investing in the right business can make a person very, very rich. Investing in the wrong business will leave the investor with nothing.

3.   Managing Risks Through Exclusivity, Debt and Equity.

An entrepreneur must be able to carefully balance the risks and benefits of funds as they become available. Balancing the use of debt and equity can protect an entrepreneur both from bankruptcy and from losing ownership of the company to investors.

Assume that Addi creates a board game that can be successfully designed and manufactured for $100,000, resulting in the production of 10,000 copies of the game to be sold. As a result of a successful marketing campaign, Addi sells all 10,000 units for a gross revenue of $400,000.

Under the table below, in the first column, Addi receives a $50,000 loan; in the middle column, Addi sells 50% of the company for $50,000; in the last column Addi finances the company using personal assets.

Terms	Lender	Equity Purchaser	Entrepreneur's Own $
Owner self-funds $50,000 of cost	10% Interest	50% Purchase	Owner funds entire $100,000
Non-owner Contribution	$50,000	$50,000	$0.00
Interest	$5,000	--	--
Total cost of funds	$105,000	$100,000	$100,000
Revenue after mfg. expenses	$400,000	$400,000	$400,000
Income to non-owner	$5,000	$150,000	$0.00
Profit (loss) to Entrepreneur	$245,000	$150,000	$300,000

Next, assume Addi's games are less successful, generating a total revenue of only $50,000:

Terms	Lender	Equity Purchaser	Entrepreneur's Own $
Owner self-funds $50,000 of cost	10% Interest	50% Purchase	Owner funds entire $100,000
Non-owner Contribution	$50,000	$50,000	$0.00
Interest	$5,000	--	--
Total cost of funds	$105,000	$100,000	$100,000
Revenue after mfg. expenses	$50,000	$50,000	$50,000
Income to non-owner	$5,000	-$25,000	$0.00
Profit (loss) to Entrepreneur	-$55,000	-$25,000	-$50,000

From the chart, it begins to become clear that equity financing serves to soften the business losses as well as the profits. Debt financing maximizes the profits but places the entire cost of loss on the entrepreneur—and adds the cost of interest to boot.

When entrepreneurs add intellectual property as valuable assets to new businesses, they can put that property at risk instead of personal finances. In the following charts, rather than putting her own money into the business, Addi puts the copyright in the game's artwork, the trademark in the game's name, and the patent covering the game methodology at risk in exchange for the equity investment or as collateral for the loan. Assuming Addi does not personally guarantee the loan, the charts would instead look like this:

Terms	Lender	Equity Purchaser	Entrepreneur's Own $
Owner self-funds no cost	10% Interest	50% Purchase	Owner funds entire $100,000
Non-owner Contribution	$100,000	$100,000	$0.00
Interest	$10,000	--	--
Total cost of funds	$110,000	$100,000	$100,000
Revenue after mfg. expenses	$400,000	$400,000	$400,000
Income to non-owner	$10,000	$150,000	$0.00
Profit (loss) to Entrepreneur	$290,000	$150,000	$300,000

In this scenario, Addi would continue to make the most money if she put her own funds into the business but would also make a substantial profit with a loan or equity investment. A loan which had no risk to Addi personally maximizes the income without the risk of loss. Next, assume again that Addi's games are less successful, generating a total revenue of only $50,000:

Terms	Lender	Equity Purchaser	Entrepreneur's Own $
Owner self-funds no cost	10% Interest	50% Purchase	Owner funds entire $100,000
Non-owner Contribution	$100,000	$100,000	$0.00
Interest	$10,000	--	--
Total cost of funds	$110,000	$100,000	$100,000
Revenue after mfg. expenses	$50,000	$50,000	$50,000
Income (loss) to non-owner	-$60,000	-$25,000	$0.00
Profit (loss) to Entrepreneur	$0.00	$25,000	-$50,000

As the final chart shows, if the entrepreneur can create something of sufficient value for lenders to lend against without recourse or that investors will invest in, then the entrepreneur's risks are greatly reduced and the rewards increase. While it would be rare for a commercial bank to lend money without marketable collateral, it typically will be ready to lend against the collateral paid for with the investor's portion of funds, so the entrepreneur can mix equity investors with commercial loans to fund the business. And copyrights, trademarks, and patents can serve as collateral as well.

The second lesson from the chart is the ability of the entrepreneur to begin making a profit even though the investor has not recouped her investment. Knowing this, investors will often insist on distribution agreements that provide for recoupment prior to the payout. As with most terms, the actual payment structure is highly negotiable.

Because of the potential for the entrepreneur to begin making money well before the investor sees any return on investment, sophisticated investors make strong demands on the entrepreneurs and expect large rather than modest rewards. When entrepreneurs become owners of exclusive rights, they change their relationship with the investor, gaining a great deal of financial opportunity for themselves.

4.   *Setting Valuation and Finding Balance.*

Every business must balance the equity, debt, and assets to maintain the health of the company. While a company with no debt has no loans to repay, it also fails to use the value in its business to leverage the impact of its success. Debt financing allows the company to do more while paying only the fixed cost of the interest payments. As the United States Small Business Administration (SBA) website comments, "[i]f your firm has a high ratio of equity to debt, you should probably seek debt financing."[88]

In contrast, too much debt makes the business too risky and the cost of doing business much less flexible. In this case, the SBA suggests that "if your company has a high proportion of debt to equity, experts advise that you should increase your ownership capital (equity investment) for additional funds. This will prevent you from being over-leveraged to the point of jeopardizing your company's survival."[89]

For SBA-guaranteed loans, there is a minimum requirement that the company has 20% of the funds in the form of equity. This creates a 4:1 debt to equity ratio. For loans not guaranteed through the SBA, the ratio is likely to be 3:1 for start-up ventures and less well-established businesses or 25% equity. SBA loans also require a personal guarantee of the primary investors, shifting more of the risk back on the entrepreneur.

These ratios and balances can help entrepreneurs begin to establish the valuation for the sale of the shares or membership units.

Valuation is often arbitrary. It is not based on the value of the company today; rather, it is based on what the investor believes the opportunity to invest in the business is worth today. Typically, in a going enterprise, the valuation is based on expectations that the company will continue to operate with the same profit in the next five years as it has earned in the past five years. This expectation is wildly arbitrary, but it provides a starting point for negotiations. For new businesses, there is

---

[88] *Starting a Business*, U.S. SMALL BUS. ADMIN., https://wakizashi.www.sba.gov/starting-business/business-financials/borrowing-money-your-business (last visited July 12, 2018).

[89] *Id.*

no history and the potential for the company to gain market share cannot be known.

For a start-up business, the initial source of funds will often come from the participants who wish to own and operate the new enterprise. Each owner would contribute a specified amount of money, granting each investor ownership of a proportionate share of the organization. The founders may choose to give a different proportion of voting interest or control over company operations, depending on the other skills and attributes that each person brings to the venture. For example, if the company needs $100,000 to rent the facility, purchase initial inventory, pay staff, buy insurance, pay for marketing, and purchase supplies, then ten investors each providing $10,000 in equity would be barely sufficient to launch the business.

Assume that instead of ten equal participants, the company was organized by two individuals, each of whom could scrape together $5,000. They need an additional $90,000 to launch the new business. They have each worked for months on the project, invested many ideas using a great deal of personal knowledge, and without both of them, the company would never be possible. In this case, instead of offering new investors the same stock price the two founding organizers paid, the company can choose to issue additional stock at a much higher price. For the founders, $10,000 was worth 1000 shares. For the subsequent investors, $90,000 was worth 900 shares. The value of the share went from $10.00 per share to $100.00 per share. The total valuation of the company has been increased to $190,000. If the company can reasonably predict that it will earn somewhere between $100,000 to $500,000 in the next year, that valuation is not unreasonable. In addition, this valuation guarantees that the founding organizers together have majority control of the business ownership as well.

This stark change in valuation is not uncommon for start-ups. The early investors are investing in the value of the organization. Ultimately, valuation is defined by what an actual investor is willing to pay. As long as the ownership by the founders is fully disclosed, there is nothing wrong with the great difference in financing opportunities between the two situations.

B.   Sources of Capital or Equity.[90]

Capital investments reflect the range of equity investments available for business funding. The central attribute of capital investment is that the investor pays for ownership of the company. As reflected in the charts above, the equity owners share in the success and failure of the company in proportion to their investment.

In each of these areas, it is particularly important to consult with a lawyer competent in securities law. The sale of any equity interest is a sale of securities regulated by both federal and state law. The use of securities to compensate employees may also be controlled by employment laws and have tax consequences for both the employee and employer. Unfortunately, in the eyes of the law, there is no such thing as a small business.

1.   Introduction to Securities Regulation—Hire a Lawyer.

The difference in valuation should help to explain why both state and federal law regulate the sale of securities so closely. There are many opportunities for information to be hidden from investors or to otherwise take advantage of investors. Securities laws apply to shares in a corporation and membership interests in an LLC as well as certain types of investment contracts and other financial products.

The issuance of securities has very significant legal consequences as well as tax ramifications. This is the area of the business that requires the greatest amount of legal advice. This book will provide only a brief introduction because an entrepreneur should not issue securities without the help of an attorney familiar with both state laws and federal laws regarding the sale of securities.

Each state has its own securities regulations, which are complemented by federal laws. The state laws generally focus on the fairness of the offering, while the federal laws focus on the accuracy of the disclosure. Both sets of laws have exemptions from regulatory review for certain types of transactions.

---

[90] These sections are adapted from JON M. GARON, POP CULTURE BUSINESS HANDBOOK FOR CONS AND FESTIVALS (2017).

Under the federal securities laws, a person or entity that wishes to sell securities must first register with the Securities and Exchange Commission unless that seller qualifies for an exemption provided under the law. State laws vary significantly from federal laws, and state laws vary considerably from state to state. What they have in common is that the exemptions are based on the number of people buying the securities, the relation of those people to the seller, and the sophistication of the buyers.

For example, in broad terms, the issuance to the founders of a business who actively manage the business are likely exempt from both federal and state regulatory review, because the managing founders are insiders with better access to information than anything the government can provide. The stock interests granted to founders and insiders are also often issued very casually. They are typically few in number, very close in relation to the seller, and have a sophistication based on their personal involvement. Taken as a whole, the governmental interest is not significant.

At the same time, however, the general rules regarding anti-fraud rules continue to apply to all offerings of securities even if those offerings occur under an exemption from state and federal registration. The most important of these is rule 10b-5, which serves as a catch-all to make the fraudulent sale or trading of securities illegal:

It shall be unlawful for any person, directly or indirectly, by the use of any means or instrumentality of interstate commerce, or of the mails or of any facility of any national securities exchange,

(a) To employ any device, scheme, or artifice to defraud,

(b) To make any untrue statement of a material fact or to omit to state a material fact necessary in order to make the statements made, in the light of the circumstances under which they were made, not misleading, or

(c) To engage in any act, practice, or course of business which operates or would operate as a fraud or deceit upon any person, in connection with the purchase or sale of any security.[91]

The breadth of this law applies to almost every transaction. Even so, most states have versions of this law as part of the state statute. The rule also allows for civil liability for individuals who were defrauded through a securities transaction. As a result, all statements made by entrepreneurs must be carefully framed and documented to assure that the business financing is not based on fraud or excessive puffery.

The remaining introduction to the key securities offering exemptions are discussed in Chapter 10. In addition, however, an entrepreneur should understand that none of these exemptions is simple, and the issuer or seller of securities must be very careful about every aspect of the process. The sale of securities should only be done with the assistance of attorneys sophisticated in the nature of the federal and relevant state laws.

Even with the exemptions, there are usually requirements to file certain notices with the SEC and to file and pay fees at the state level. Therefore, all the steps to issue the securities needed to sell the company require at least some attention to both the state and federal laws.

As described in the next section, however, the new form of crowd financing may provide a low-cost alternative to issuing small amounts of stock. The use of crowd financing platforms may prove beneficial even for simple issuances to friends and family.

2.   *Crowdfunding,   Crowdsourcing,   and   Crowd Financing.*

With the growth of social media on the Internet, a new phenomenon developed, connecting the public with causes, companies, and opportunities. The power of the crowd takes on many forms, and some of these resource opportunities can provide a great benefit to the financing and resourcing of the business. These include Crowdfunding, Crowdsourcing, and Crowd Financing.

Crowdfunding—Crowdfunding provides an excellent method of financing the early stages of a business. At its heart, crowdfunding allows members of the public to financially support a for-profit enterprise by

---

[91] 17 C.F.R. § 240.10b-5 (West 2017).

either donating money to that business or buying the goods and services to be offered by that company well before those goods and services are available in the marketplace. Nonprofit organizations have always been able to benefit from these types of public support, and the modern crowdfunding platforms support both nonprofit and for-profit organizations equally well.

The offers and exchanges are conducted through third-party platforms such as Kickstarter, Indiegogo, or one of many others. In a typical example, a band, film company, or game company will put together a Kickstarter campaign explaining what the upcoming new project is likely to contain. The company will offer various premiums in exchange for the buyer's willingness to buy the work in advance of its having been created. This pre-sale of the work helps the company fund the project without going into debt, assists in gauging audience interest in the project, and frees the company from traditional financing sources that are often more controlling of the company's output.

Crowdfunding for a new product or service can work extremely well. The campaign must provide the information about the product and the design team, generating excitement about why the public should be interested in getting involved on the ground floor. For a business, crowdfunding provides early access to wholesalers and retailers interested in the product as well as direct sales to the public.

All the proceeds from crowdfunding are income. None of this form of funding impacts the equity ownership of the business. The cash generated by the crowdfund helps establish that the business has sufficient resources to seek bank loans such as those guaranteed by the Small Business Administration discussed below.

Crowdsourcing—Crowdsourcing is the flip-side of crowdfunding. It is the use of a crowdfunding style platform or campaign to obtain the goods, services, and support needed to run a new business or service. At one level, it may be little more than a call for volunteers. At another level, however, it can be used to solicit donations of time and work to help launch the company. Crowdsourcing is primarily effective for nonprofits and has modest value for for-profit business activities that are creative or highly social. For example, a microbrewery might find volunteers willing to donate time to help refurbish a location or even local musicians to serve as entertainment to help launch the company. Some artists might donate time and artwork to assist with the business launch as well. Similarly, a for-profit company looking to sell adaptability products for those with physical disabilities might find some donors dedicated to the cause despite the for-profit nature of the company. But crowdsourcing is a difficult strategy for most for-profit enterprises.

Crowd Financing—Crowd financing is the most recent addition into the online world. The reluctance of the SEC to provide the rules needed to make it operational delayed the start of crowd financing until 2015. Unlike crowdfunding, which generates income for the business through sales, crowd financing sells ownership interests in the company to the public as a means of raising capital. As such, crowd financing represents a significant exception to the registration requirements discussed above.

Crowd financing allows a company to list itself on an approved web portal. The portal serves a function similar to that of a stock exchange. Any person meeting the eligibility criteria can purchase stock in the listed company and invest as an owner of the enterprise. Unlike the traditional stock exchange, however, these investments do not have an active market, so the securities may not be as easy to sell.

Still, the registration on these crowd financing websites are far easier than traditional sales of public securities. For companies with a large community of friends and family willing to invest and only modest financial needs, the use of a crowd financing platform might be a practical solution to the legal requirements to sell the securities. Because these are public sales of securities, however, there are many regulations, including limitations on the resale of the stock during the first year of ownership.

These provisions highlight the primary opportunities and limitations on the issuer. Additional details are described in Chapter 10 on sales of securities.

3.   *Friends, Family, and Participants.*

Though most small business statistics are necessarily suspect, it is generally accepted that the most common form of business investments are investments by family and friends. Investments by friends and family have the benefit of demonstrating faith in the entrepreneur and generally low costs in arranging the transaction. Unfortunately, the low-cost arrangements can mean that the documents are unclear or non-existent. In addition, friends may not have sufficient access to business information to be able to purchase stock from the company without significant public disclosures. For friends and family, the use of a crowd-financing platform may provide the needed legal disclosures to enable the entrepreneur to comply with securities laws at a relatively low cost.

A second common source of equity investors is business participants and employees. Securities laws generally provide exceptions to registration for those individuals materially involved with the company. In addition, if the start-up costs are sufficiently low, a company may find that it can fund itself by reducing its salary obligations through the distribution of stock or LLC membership interests.

An employee-financing arrangement may be particularly beneficial if the employees are providing expensive or highly unique services. For example, the software programmers necessary to start a new company may be compensated far too highly to be hired by a start-up, but that same start-up can acquire the necessary services though the payment of stock. (Companies also employ a variation of this model by agreeing to pay key employees a percentage of profits from the sale of a particular product. A comic book illustrator may be paid based on the profits of the sale of each issue illustrated by the artist. In such a case, the cost of production is deferred, but no equity in the company is sold.)

4.   *Federal and State Grants through Grants.gov.*

For the right business or idea, state and federal government agencies do actually give money away. Many programs are open to for-profit companies in addition to nonprofit organizations. The federal government has become increasingly efficient in making these funds available. Twenty-six agencies provide financial grant opportunities through a single web portal. Beginning in November 2003, Congress required that all competitive grant opportunities be posted through the website, https://www.grants.gov/. The website boasts over 1,000 competitive grant opportunities and $500,000 billion spent annually.

There are, of course, many complexities to receiving business grants through governmental agencies. The grants are highly competitive, and the procurement process requires that the enterprise closely monitor its compliance with all applicable state and federal laws, including mundane obligations involving employment practices, OSHA health and safety regulations, and any relevant disclosure requirements. When the federal government is a party to any contract, there may be unique rights held by the U.S. government that would not be held by a commercial entity. For example, the U.S. government has certain contractual termination rights that are specified by federal law and which preempt any contract provisions to the contrary. As a result, entering into business with the government requires a great deal of due diligence. Done properly, however, it creates a great financial opportunity for the business involved. No company should ignore the potential start-up support this resource provides.

5.   *Angel Investors and Venture Capital Funds.*

Angel investors are the first group of investors who have no relationship with the company or its owners. Angel investors get their name from their ability to swoop into a desperate situation and save the business life of the struggling entrepreneur. They are corporate guardian angels who typically invest only long enough for the company to secure a more stable funding source. The term has been used for generations on Broadway to refer to the investors in legitimate theatre—the riskiest of commercial art forms.

Angel investors are typically very rich individuals who enjoy the risks and rewards of helping inventors and entrepreneurs launch new ventures. As financial thrill-seekers, they often bring a great deal of business experience and personal attention to the projects. They also tend to secure the subsequent rounds of funding on behalf of the business, protecting their financial interests and their personal pride.

Venture capital is the best-known form of business start-up financing. Venture capital funds range from thousands to hundreds of millions of dollars. The fund manager has money available to invest in businesses that she expects will be ready to enter the marketplace in a relatively short time period. Venture capital funds provide large investments to bring inventions to market, to launch business plans, and to provide the final lift-off into the marketplace.

A venture fund offers high risk investments to a pool of investors, which the fund manager spreads over a sufficiently large number of business opportunities to distribute the common risk of failure against the potential for overwhelming success. The occasional "home run" compensates the investors for the many strike-outs typical in start-up, high-risk venture financing.

For venture capital funds and certain businesses, the home run comes from the sale of the company's securities to the public through an initial public offering or IPO. An IPO allows a company to receive funds from the public in exchange for purchasing a non-controlling interest in the business. The higher the sales price, the more the theoretical worth of the company.

In addition, by registering the securities privately owned by the entrepreneur and the venture fund with the Securities and Exchange Commission, those shares of stock can also be publicly traded at the same value as the stock newly sold by the company to the public. The value of this newly tradable stock may turn a struggling entrepreneur into a multi-millionaire in the course of the stock's first day of trading. As discussed below, for some entrepreneurs this may be the ultimate goal, while for others, the potential for an IPO or sale of the company serves as nothing but a distraction from the business at hand.

C.   Sources of Loans or Debt Financing.

Debt financing has two significant advantages over the sale of a company's ownership interests. First, the entrepreneur does not lose any control of the business to investors. Banks and other lenders may ask questions, causing a certain level of intrusion, but this is much less significant than the role available to even "silent" partners.

Second, lending is much less expensive than securities financing because it does not include the high costs associated with the legal documentation, qualification of investors, and other securities obligations. Despite common frustrations over banking fees and mountains of paperwork, a loan is vastly simpler than the sale of stock to investors or the public. As a result, for companies which can raise twenty to twenty-five percent of the start-up capital themselves, moving to debt financing may be a logical first step in the launching of the business. Nonetheless, because such loans are often personally guaranteed by the business owners, debt financing entails a degree of risk of loss that is reduced through equity investment.

Many businesses manage their debt using credit cards. The extremely high interest rates and personal guarantees from most credit cards make this strategy a poor business decision that should be avoided. Instead, the various strategies listed below should be used to manage the cost of funds and avoid the convenience and high costs of credit cards.

1.   *Home Loans.*

Debt financing follows a path similar to that of capital finance. Most requests start at home. Many entrepreneurs use the equity in their homes as collateral for secured loans on their primary residence. Home loans generally fall into two categories: a home equity line of credit or a home equity loan. In both cases, the amount of the loan must be less than the equity in the home, which is the difference between the market value of the home and the owner's mortgage or other debt tied to the property.

The line of credit provides a flexible account with a maximum amount that can be borrowed, so the entrepreneur need not use all the available funds at once. This reduces the costs of carrying a larger loan than one needs. On the other hand, these tend to have variable rates of interest, raising concerns that the interest rates can spike.

The home equity loan is a loan of a fixed amount. Generally, these use a fixed rate of return, though they can use variable rates as well, depending on the bank and the product.

Taking a home loan for a high-risk venture would be a dangerous personal decision for most entrepreneurs. Unfortunately, since lenders tend to demand personal guarantees for start-up business loans, the risk is not significantly worse than other loans. At a minimum, entrepreneurs should carefully consider the cost of paying the interest and principal on the loan and proceed only if he can repay the loan even if the business is a complete failure.

2.   *Friends and Family.*

Personal loans are not uncommon for start-up businesses. Generally, they are nothing more than oral agreements in which the parents of the entrepreneur provide some money in exchange for vague promises that "I'll repay this as soon as I can." With family, these are often considered 'gifts' that the lender expects never to be repaid.

The process of formalizing these relations may be more trouble than it is worth. At a minimum, however, the entrepreneur should specify the expectations of the loan with some written document. While a contract or note would be preferable, even a receipt letter would go a long way to avoid the problem of disputes. For example, one such letter could include the following:

[Date]

[Name]

[Address]

Dear Mom,

Thank you very much for the non-recourse loan of $5,000 last night, which I plan to use for the start of my new boutique. This letter will confirm the terms of that loan as we discussed them. As I said last night, all the money will be used for the business. Among other things, your loan will help me buy merchandise and begin advertising.

Just as I explained when you provided me the loan, I intend to repay you the entire amount of the loan plus 5% interest. I hope to repay you over the next three years—beginning the first payment a year from now, but if you need the money earlier, I will repay it within a month of your asking. I also appreciate that you will only ask for the money from the money I make in the boutique.

If I misunderstood any of the terms of the loan, please let me know immediately. Your confidence in me and in the boutique means a great deal to me. Thank you for your generosity and your faith.

Love,

[signature]

Admittedly, this letter leaves much to be desired. Still, it serves to clarify the financial transaction and will serve as a clear reminder of the actual terms long after the exact memories of the offered loan are forgotten. As such, it will discourage disputes more than resolve them—an extremely important part of managing a business.

To be effective, the letter should be dated and signed. As this example does, the letter should state that it reflects the oral understanding between the parties. It should be sent very soon after the loan is offered (or received) so that it is contemporary with the funds, rather than drafted months or years later, once the parties are in the middle of a dispute. The letter may seem awkward, an unduly formal way to speak to one's mother (or aunt or friend), but the letter achieves a number of very important goals.

First, the letter clarifies that the funds were not a gift or an equity investment. It binds the recipient to understand the loan obligations, and it clarifies to the lender that no ownership interest in the company is conveyed as a result of the loan.

Second, the letter identifies the exact amount of the loan, the interest payment due and the payment schedule. These are the same terms any commercial loan would require. The purpose again is to set the rules of the relationship in place. Because the letter allows the lender to call the loan on thirty days' notice, it is drafted as a demand loan. By omitting the phrase "but if you need the money earlier I will repay it within a month of your asking," the demand nature of the loan can be removed.

Third, the letter establishes the loan as a "non-recourse" loan both because it describes the loan as non-recourse in the first sentence and because it explains the term with the phrase "you will only ask for the money from the money I make in the boutique."

The letter is not intended to serve as a legal contract. Rather, it is evidence of an oral agreement and contemporary understanding of the parties. It captures the essential terms of a loan agreement in three simple paragraphs rather than the two pages of formal text used by banks and commercial lenders. While any of these key terms can be adjusted, each of these terms should be addressed in such a letter.

In managing a start-up business, a little goes a long way. A simple letter like this provides much of the same protection as does a properly drafted and complex loan agreement. While it would be better to have a lawyer draft the loan agreements, the letter sent by the entrepreneur achieves many of the same goals at little cost. For family and close friends, this may be enough. As the complexity of the transaction increases, however, or the relationship moves beyond family, more formal documents are increasingly important to protect the entrepreneur from misunderstandings.

3.   SBA Guaranteed Loans.

The SBA does not provide direct loans to small businesses. Instead, it works with local banks and other lenders to guarantee loans to small businesses. The basic 7(a) SBA Loan Guaranty provides lenders with funds that can increase the amount borrowed against the company's equity and limit the maximum interest rate charged for the loan. It provides lower cost funds for purchase of real property, equipment, debt refinancing, and business acquisitions. The loans may be as large as $5 million.

In addition, the SBA has other programs which may be available, depending on the nature of the start-up business. The SBA offers the Certified Development Company (CDC)—504 Loan Program to provide long-term, fixed-rate financing to small businesses to acquire real estate or machinery or equipment for expansion or modernization. The loans cover the "brick and mortar" costs of buildings and equipment. To be eligible, the entrepreneur must provide a minimum contribution of 10% of the necessary amount, along with a combination of private-lender and CDC financing. "504 Loans are typically structured with SBA providing 40% of the total project costs, a participating lender covering up to 50% of the total project costs, and the borrower contributing 10% of the project costs."[92]

For companies interested in international trade, there are two programs available. The Export Working Capital Program (EWCP) provides short-term working capital to exporters. The International Trade Loan Program is "designed to help small businesses enter and expand into international markets and, when adversely affected by import competition, make the investments necessary to better compete."[93] For eligibility in the International Trade Loan Program, the business "must establish that the loan will significantly expand or develop an export market, is currently adversely affected by import

---

[92] Office of Fin. Assistance, *Resources*, U.S. SMALL BUS. ADMIN., https://www.sba.gov/offices/headquarters/ofa/resources/4049 (last visited July 12, 2018).

[93] Office of Int'l Trade, *Resources*, U.S. SMALL BUS. ADMIN., https://www.sba.gov/offices/headquarters/oit/resources/14832 (last visited July 12, 2018).

competition, will upgrade equipment or facilities to improve competitive position, or must be able to provide a business plan that reasonably projects export sales sufficient to cover the loan." While this covers a wide range of businesses, it is not a good fit for every company. In addition, the SBA has additional requirements that further limit eligibility.

The SBA-guaranteed loans are not the only loans available from commercial banks, savings banks, and commercial lenders. These banks may have other products that might serve the particular entrepreneur's needs more precisely than the SBA-guaranteed loan. The key benefit of the SBA loan program is some protection from interest rate expenses. The lending rules and other limitations, however, may make other programs more attractive to the entrepreneur, depending on the business.

4.   *Microloans.*

Microloans are another SBA initiative. Instead of commercial or savings banks, the SBA provides funds to nonprofit community-based lenders. These nonprofit organizations provide up to $50,000 in funds for start-up small businesses. The SBA reports the average loan size is approximately $13,000.

The loans come with some significant strings attached. As the SBA explains, "[e]ach intermediary is required to provide business-based training and technical assistance to its micro-borrowers. Individuals and small businesses applying for microloan financing may be required to fulfill training and/or planning requirements before a loan application is considered."[94] This training, however, should prove a second advantage rather than a disadvantage of the program. The training provides both practical skills and a support network for the start-up business.

5.   *Other Lenders.*

In addition to commercial banks and savings banks, there are other institutional lenders that should be considered. Credit unions are organized for the benefit of their members, often labor groups or

---

[94] *Guide to SBA Programs*, U.S. SMALL BUS. ADMIN., https://www.sba.gov/sites/default/files/articles/SBA%20101.pdf (updated February 2013) (last visited July 12, 2018).

corporations. These can provide very competitive lending rates and very liberal membership requirements. Some insurance companies provide commercial loans as part of their services.

Commercial finance companies and consumer finance companies provide another source of funds, but tend to be expensive. They are less heavily regulated than banks and tend to charge higher rates than commercial or savings banks for similar services. Because of the lower regulation, they are able to provide loans on weaker capital and on less secure credit history, but they charge a significantly higher amount to offset the risk associated with these investments. Typically, businesses use them when commercial banks are not willing to provide the loans.

While many are legitimate businesses, the risks associated with these companies are higher. The entrepreneur should work very diligently to learn that a particular lender has a solid track record with its customers, and that all the terms of the transaction are clearly disclosed well in advance of the funding, so that they may be reviewed by an attorney. An unscrupulous lender can destroy a business faster than almost anyone, so the cost of reviewing the transaction is a small investment to pay to protect the company's future.

6. *Seller Financing: Vendors and Customers.*

In addition to the formal lender relationships, there are some situations when the start-up entrepreneur will be "paid" to conduct the business. On the purchase of a small business, for example, the seller may be willing to accept a note rather than a direct payment. Known as seller financing, the seller of a business may agree to receive a fixed monthly amount for a period of years to reflect the value of the business plus the interest on that amount of money. While the ultimate price will be higher than a straight purchase of the business, it allows an entrepreneur to buy the company for far less up-front capital than would otherwise be required.

Similarly, commercial vendors may sell major purchases on credit, financing the cost of the item with its own financing package. Automotive sellers regularly provide financing alongside the car sales. Boeing regularly finances the sales of its commercial jets so that the airlines can manage to finance the upgrade of their fleets.

In addition, some large customers will work with their vendors to invest in plants or equipment as part of a transaction to guarantee the access to the vendor's products. For example, a manufacturer may finance the machines needed by its parts supplier when the parts supplier uses those machines to produce critical parts for the manufacturer. This guarantees that the parts will be available and probably decrease the long-term price of those goods. While this may be a successful arrangement for both parties, it clearly provides an advantage to the financing partner and may be less preferential than other financing options.

7.   *Managing Debt.*

Whatever the source of the debt financing, it is critical that the costs of the debt be built into the operation of the company. Debt is neither bad nor good. The key is to understand the relationship between the debt and the operations of the company. A simple model will highlight this relationship.

Assume, for example, that a company invests $100,000 to generate a gross profit of $120,000. The $100,000 is used for the raw materials to make the product, the advertising, the staff, to pay the entrepreneur a salary, and to cover all other costs associated with the operation. The net profit is $20,000, reflecting a 20% return on investment. If the interest rates are 5-8%, then an investment that makes 20% has a solid margin.

In managing the debt, the entrepreneur must decide if increasing the amount of money to spend on the business will result in the same return on investment, a higher rate of return, or a lower rate of return. If the loan will drop the rate of return on the additional money below the interest rate, then the entrepreneur should not take out the loan. If the rate of return stays the same or increases, then the debt will only increase the profit. Unfortunately, these decisions are based on assumptions about the economy, the product, the clients, and many other factors outside the entrepreneur's control. As a result, the entrepreneur must also take the risk of being wrong into account when determining the true cost of the loan. The entrepreneur should be cautious and not rely on risky or overly optimistic assumptions.

In some cases, the funds can be used in small amounts to assess the impact of the additional loans. For example, increasing advertising and marketing may be somewhat proportional to sales. In other situations, however, the funds will be used for new equipment or facilities. Once a large piece of equipment is purchased, the costs of that purchase must be managed, whether the machine operates at 10% of capacity or 110% of capacity. Managing the debt is to understand those variables and make the best judgment about how the business can absorb the interest expenses and repay the loans, given the potential benefit and potential risks of the loan. Since all business involves risk, the best the entrepreneur can do is be as knowledgeable about the risks as possible.

Chapter 7. Application of Start-Up Financing to Intellectual Property

A.   Reflecting Value in Intangibles—Proving the Worth of Intellectual Property.

One of the more challenging aspects of developing a company based on intellectual property assets is the challenge in valuing those assets for the purpose of both lenders and investors. As a general matter, the intellectual property assets created by a company are not reflected as having value on the company's books. As the WIPO primer on intellectual property for small business explains, "[t]he practice of extending loans secured solely by [intellectual property] assets is not very common; in fact, it is practiced more by venture capitalists than by banks."[95] Despite these accounting barriers, investors and lenders increasingly have come to value the potential of these assets.

WIPO has an extensive library of resources on valuation that can help the entrepreneur understand the complex financial models used by investors and lenders.[96] By understanding the basics of intellectual property valuation, the entrepreneur can communicate the true value of these assets to those willing to finance the start-up.

1.   *Value and Valuation.*

The value of valuation is self-evident. As soon as an inventor can put an accurate price tag on an invention, the invention can be used as an asset to promote investment, secure loans, and increase the worth of the company owning that invention. Unrealized worth does not help the inventor or the business owner—it is as if it does not exist. WIPO suggests that the ability to value the intellectual property independently

---

[95] Small & Medium-sized Enter. Div., *Intellectual Property for Business* 16 WORLD INTELL. PROP. ORG., http://www.wipo.int/export/sites/www/sme/en/ip_business/pdf/ip_business.pdf.

[96] *List of Documents on IP Valuation*, WORLD INTELLECTUAL PROP. ORG., http://www.wipo.int/sme/en/documents/valuationdocs/index.htm (last visited July 12, 2018).

from the business best establishes the commercial value of the intellectual property assets. Unfortunately, while true, this advice may be of little assistance. For the start-up, the intellectual property assets may be the only significant assets held by the company. Still, the intellectual property assets of the company add to the overall value of the business and may tip the balance for lenders or investors.

For the entrepreneur, the more one can do to formally or informally create a valuation of the intellectual property, the greater the chances that investors and lenders will recognize the value in the company. This value and valuation may not be based on the same accounting rules used for creating the corporate balance sheet that recognize or ignore asset values. Just as accounting rules depreciate property based on accounting tables rather than the attributes of the property, these rules value intellectual property in an artificial and generally unhelpful manner.

2.   *The Predictable Lifespan of IP Assets.*

Skilled lenders and investors will look past mechanistic accounting practices to seek real worth. In his paper, *Assessment and Valuation of Inventions and Research Results for their use and Commercialization,*[97] noted valuation expert Gordon Smith[98] explained the meaning of value:

> Value is the representation of all future benefits of ownership, compressed into a single payment. Therefore, value is continually changing as the future benefits increase or decrease, either with the passage of time or with changing perceptions of what the future will bring. Value does not exist in the abstract and must be addressed within the context of time, place, potential owners and potential uses . . . *Market value is defined as the present value of the future economic benefits of ownership.*[99]

Smith is saying that the intellectual property should be valued as equal in worth to the income it will generate throughout its lifetime of use or exploitation. Such a value makes a great deal of sense, but Smith

---

[97] Smith, *supra* note 35.

[98] President, AUS Consultants, Moorestown, New Jersey, United States of America.

[99] Smith, *supra* note 35.

also recognizes that the passage of time and changing perceptions will always affect that lifetime of income, making such a valuation hard to calculate.

In 1926, the copyright in silent films were considered highly valuable, but within two years, the invention of the "talkie" or sound motion picture rendered them increasingly worthless. A decade later, films were generally thought to have a five-year life span because that was the maximum usefulness of the shows. Most movies were exhibited in major markets in their first year. They moved to smaller and smaller towns in the following years. After five years, there were no markets left to show the movies. In consequence, many copyrights were allowed to expire because their owners did not anticipate the future revenue that would arise first from broadcast television and later, VHS tapes, DVDs, and Internet downloads. In both cases, the intellectual property owners did not—and could not—fully anticipate the value of the intellectual property over its lifespan because changes in technology rendered attempts to predict the future laughable.

As a result, the estimate of present value of future economic benefits is fraught with uncertainty. The longer the lifespan one tries to predict, the less certain the prediction becomes. The practical valuation of intellectual property takes these risks into account. As Smith explains,

> [w]e must . . . be concerned with the economic life of the intellectual property, or the period during which the intellectual property can be expected to afford its owner an economic benefit. . . . Technology moves on; in some sectors such as the semiconductor industry, the technology is obsolete before a patent application can be prosecuted . . .

> We must also realize that the decline in value of most intellectual property over time is not linear, so the economic benefit may vary greatly from year to year.[100]

These lessons are important for the entrepreneur to understand so that the new product or service is neither oversold nor undersold. Underselling the value of the intellectual property may result in the entrepreneur giving away too much of the company's value to investors,

---

[100] *Id.* (citations omitted).

while overselling the intellectual property may result in discouraging any investment at all. If entrepreneurs want to show the potential to investors of a new product, they will increase credibility by separating the potential for revenue over the first five years from the remainder of the lifespan of the product. While the longer lifespan may be highly valuable, the predictability is significantly lower than during the first five years.

Similarly, the investor must realize that the "cost approach" to valuing the intellectual property based on the investment in that property is largely irrelevant as a measure of anything other than the risk undertaken by the parties. As Smith points out, "[t]he cost of developing technology is seldom relevant to its value. Think of the important inventions that have been made as a result of fortuitous insight, and the costly research projects that have ended in failure."[101] The costs associated with developing the business may be important to the participants, but they do little to provide meaningful information regarding the true market value of the intellectual property.

3.   *Methods of Valuation.*

Economic analysts point to a number of different valuation methods for placing a price tag on intellectual property and inventions. These generally reflect the cost of development, the market price for the intellectual property, and the economic impact of the intellectual property.[102] As noted above, the cost of development provides little useful data for new inventions or start-up businesses. The cost of development will tell the entrepreneur what is needed to get off the ground but will say little about either the short term or long term value of the asset.

Market rates are the best predictor of a property's worth. To assess the market value of an intellectual property asset, one merely need compare the new item to the transactions for similar items in the

---

[101] *Id.*

[102] Nick Bertolotti, Partner, Arthur Anderson, London, Presentation at the WIPO National Seminar on the Valuation of Industrial Property Assets: The Valuation of Intellectual Property (Nov. 26–27, 1996), available at http://www.wipo.int/sme/en/documents/valuationdocs/ip_bj_96_7.pdf.

marketplace. Simple as this sounds, its application is highly unpredictable. In the motion picture business, for example, the copyrights of films are the intellectual property asset bought and sold. These products are actively traded by a small group of companies who understand every manner of exploiting these rights. Nonetheless, no one can predict whether a $300 million film will be a smash hit, a flop, or merely break even.

The industry compensates for this by each large company producing enough movies to create an average rate of return for each studio's films. Small companies that produce only one or two films a year never develop the size to manage this process. Nonetheless, to the extent that an entrepreneur can learn the value of the market and understand the transactions, the more likely he can be successful at providing some parameters on the value of the start-up.

A word of caution is necessary here. When working with independent filmmakers, it is common for them to compare their film with the occasional success, such as *Night of the Living Dead, Blair Witch Project, Fahrenheit 9/11, My Big Fat Greek Wedding,* or *An Inconvenient Truth*—all independent films of smash hit return on investment. But the market is not defined by the occasional success. Roughly three thousand independent films are screened for the Sundance Film Festival, of which fewer than a dozen are likely to receive theatrical release. The real market reflects an extremely small chance of success and is misrepresented if only the few success stories are touted.

The economic benefit approach to the property is perhaps the best method available to the start-up entrepreneur. Here, the property is based on its short-term and long-term value as a revenue center. Like the market approach, the entrepreneur should be able to determine the value of licenses used in the applicable industry. If a similar copyright or patent is worth 1% or 5% or 50% of the revenue in the market for that kind of item, then the potential for the invention has a baseline.

This is not the same as knowing what the new invention is worth. It does, however, provide investors some understanding of the range of possibilities available. When Apple released the iPod, it was unlikely that the company expected a market share in excess of 90% of the music player market. Certainly, Sony and the other manufacturers never anticipated the instant dominance created. But Apple could predict the profitability on its products at different levels of market share and use those predictions to base the scale of its investment.

4.   *Applying Valuation to Help "Sell" the Start-Up.*

For the entrepreneur of a start-up business relying on intellectual property, no valuation method will provide any guaranteed return because the risks and unknowns are too great. Nonetheless, the entrepreneur should carefully identify all the intellectual property assets, including the trade secrets and licensed trademarks in addition to the copyrights, trademarks, and patents owned exclusively by the company. Each should be compared to the greatest extent possible with those of the competition.

The five-year income that can reasonably be expected to be generated from each of these assets should be listed on a table, with an explanation regarding the assumptions made to calculate those figures. A similar table of longer-term income can also be included, though it should be noted as speculative. Among the many considerations, the following are the most significant:

- Identify the costs of development; create a careful budget of the development costs in stages so that the investors' funds are released as milestones are achieved.

- Identify the actual market for licensing similar intellectual property rights; investigate the range of royalty rates and payments for the particular type of property.

- Identify the markets to be initially targeted with the inventions or intellectual property; track patterns of new entrants into those markets or into similar markets.

- Identify any production savings or incremental benefits anticipated to be achieved through use of the inventions or intellectual property.

- Carefully document the sources for these projections to the greatest extent possible so that the research can be verified by the investors and lenders.

- Carefully document all the intellectual property involved in the business, looking past a patent to include know-how,

> trade secrets, trademarks, and copyrights; similarly look past copyrights in a literary work to include characters, trademarks, and potential publicity rights.

Understandably, a long list of assumptions and carefully researched market data proves nothing unless the invention works, the trademarks reflect good customer value, or the copyrights generate demand. But the effort will make the entrepreneur much more knowledgeable of the industry and better prepared to work with investors. The documentation will also provide some assurance to the investors and lenders that the company knows how to conduct itself. While still highly speculative, it moves the valuation from mere guesswork to a working hypothesis.

Savvy investors will expect no more from the start-up entrepreneur. Even Gordon Smith acknowledges the fundamental difficulty in applying valuation strategies to start-up technologies:

> We are often told that the income approach is impossible to use for early-stage technology because the necessary economic benefit forecasts are too difficult to make. Forecasts are difficult, to be sure, but if the income approach is abandoned there is no valuation method available, and estimating value becomes an unsupported speculation.[103]

For the entrepreneur, these speculations may be essential to communicate with potential investors, customers, and others engaged in helping the start-up. Despite the speculative nature of the methodology, the entrepreneur can gain credibility by attempting some approximation of valuation, provided the entrepreneur carefully shows his work. In this way, any assumptions are made explicit to the investors, and the investors can discuss and assess these assumptions directly.

A secondary benefit is that the careful valuation exercises provide the entrepreneur some credibility when talking with investors, lenders, and others. Unsupported claims carry no weight. Comparable data, risk factors and other benchmarks will help both parties grapple with valuing the unknown and thereby determine the value of the invention.

---

[103] SMITH, *supra* note 35.

Once a buyer and seller agree on a price, the price of that item is established. A painting may be worth $100 or $1,000,000 depending only on the mutual agreement of buyer and seller. The valuation benchmarks provide the tools needed to conduct the conversation and reduce the potential gaps between buyer and seller—or investor and entrepreneur.

Ultimately, these assumptions may be assessed by a professional intellectual property valuation company. Again, the methodologies vary considerably and there is a great deal of imprecision in the process, so the range of valuations from the professionals may be quite great. Nonetheless, the professional valuation creates another set of assumptions and predictions to use to compare to that of the entrepreneur's own work. As such, the professional valuation will complement or contrast with the entrepreneur's valuation and serve to help the parties determine value for the purposes of their transaction.

Along with the goals of the business, the valuation of the intellectual property will be of more importance to the investors and lenders than to the entrepreneur. Together with the identified goals for the business, the asset valuation will determine the interest for most investors and lenders.

B.   Identifying the Entrepreneur's Goal for the Business.

An important decision to the development of a start-up business is the purpose for launching that business in the life of the entrepreneur. The purpose will, in turn, strongly influence decisions about where to raise money to start the venture and how to organize the ownership. This short exploration of the psychology behind the entrepreneur's motivation should help predict which decisions will most likely help the business goals.

1.   The Psychology of the Start-Up.

Given the risk inherent in running one's own business, most people choose the safer road of employment. Successful entrepreneurs should have a good understanding of the motivation which encourages them to launch their ventures.

Some of the more common reasons include the following:

- Freedom from having a boss.

- Keeping the financial rewards for me rather than letting them go to my employer.

- Allowing myself to accomplish my professional goals in a manner that is not available as an employee.

- Building a family business to hand down to future generations.

- Making what I know work for me.

- Choosing the only way to make money and meet my family or other obligations.

- Owning my own business creates the best social and professional opportunities I can achieve.

- Believing in the value of my ideas and inventions.

- Finding no company who could do what I planned to do.

- Achieving my goals that have nothing to do with money.

- Making money from my hobby, passion, or vocation.

None of these reasons is better than the others, but they do suggest different goals for different entrepreneurs. As a result, the planning choices may vary depending on which reasons dominate the decision to forego the safety net of employment and jump into the shark infested start-up waters. A few examples of these reasons will help illustrate the choices.

Emilio is a first-generation U.S. immigrant.[104] Coming to the United States from Mexico City to find work, Emilio started as a busboy and worked his way up to managing restaurants. Restaurants, however, are high-risk businesses that require a great degree of capital. Instead, to launch his own business and gain financial independence, Emilio began

---

[104] Based loosely on Manny Gonzalez, owner of Manny's Tortas, which is perhaps Minnesota's best Mexican restaurant.

as a caterer, working weddings, corporate events, and other social occasions. With only the smallest of family loans, Emilio slowly expanded the number of ovens, trucks, and employees required by his business. Eventually, his specialties grew so popular that he opened two retail locations and sold his specialty products through restaurants in other locations as well. At each stage in the company's growth, Emilio ignored offers to sell his company to wholesale food distributors or to merge with larger catering companies. Instead, the mix of catering, retail, and specialty foods gave Emilio the ability to build the business, create a large work force—primarily of similarly situated immigrants—and to provide a strong economic and political presence in his community. For an entrepreneur like Emilio, the goals of creating a sustainable business that he can give to his family and improving his community are the primary motivations for the business.

Gwen is a creative artist. She is an excellent amateur photographer, designs her own clothes, and has worked as the financial analyst or comptroller for various studios and galleries. When Gwen launched her own fashion store, it was because she could not promote her own work through any other outlet. Over time, she found that her photographs and her jewelry sold better than her clothing designs. The jewelry sold internationally through her Internet website, Etsy, Amazon, and eBay. The photographs began appearing on consignment in other galleries and restaurants. Within three years, Gwen's fashion design business was a "failure" not because she did not sell any designs, but because the success of her jewelry and photographs left her too little time. Gwen was motivated to open her own business because she could not develop distribution for her work without selling it herself. By owning her own retail shop, she also learned what worked best and adjusted her business to maximize her interest and opportunities. The investors did not mind that the goods changed, so long as the revenue continued growing.

Addi patented a new board game. After realizing that the large toy companies interested in the game would pay the equivalent of $1.00 per game sold, Addi realized that a great deal more money would be made producing and selling the game herself. Addi was a retired locomotive engineer, so the time spent marketing her game also provided her the chance to be productive in retirement.

Karen worked for an automotive shop, detailing cars and motorcycles. She had developed a method that utilized specialty paints and dyes to apply a unique finish to the vehicles she prepared. Her employer was a franchised car detailing company which did not approve of her method. After encouraging her to meet with the owners in the corporate headquarters, her boss told Karen that she could no longer use her method because the headquarters had not approved its use. Karen opened a detail shop across the street from her former employer and also patented her unique process, which she was then able to license to other detail shops across the country.

Lee wrote a software program designed to improve the speed and reliability of banking transactions conducted on home computers. The software allows banks to reduce fraud and speed up the transactions for their customers. Lee hopes to acquire enough money to test the software, finalize the product, and sell it to one of the larger U.S. or international banks so that he can retire.

Emilio, Gwen, Addi, Karen and Lee reflect some of the common stories told by entrepreneurs. The stories illustrate the range of entrepreneur goals and highlight how these goals will affect the relationship between the entrepreneur and others engaged in forming the business.

2.   *Lifestyle Business to IPO.*

In business circles, the most notorious tension in business psychology is the dichotomy between the lifestyle business and the business seeking to cash out through an initial public offering (IPO). The lifestyle business is a company built to be owned throughout the professional life of the entrepreneur. In the examples above, Emilio and Gwen are operating on the lifestyle end of the continuum. Emilio's decision not to sell his specialty brands to food wholesalers is a refusal to consign the company to others, even if the financial offer is generous. In addition, the structure of Emilio's business that combines retail restaurants, wholesale and retail catering, and wholesale product sales to other restaurants improves the company's income but makes the sale of the company to any third party more difficult. Combining these three income streams reduces the kinds of companies that could benefit from a merger.

Companies that hope to be purchased or merge with other companies tend to be highly focused. A tight business focus allows potential buyers to more readily value the company and determine precisely how the target company can be integrated by the acquiring company. Without this tight focus, potential buyers will not be able to easily value and integrate the potential acquisition.

Gwen's company is also a lifestyle company. Balancing clothing design, photography, and jewelry is an extension of her personality. Except for Gwen's creativity, these fields had little in common. Nor did any of the three fields have enough to support a sale or merger. Gwen could potentially license her photographs to an art distributor or gallery management company, but that would create a new representative for the sale of her work, not a buy-out option.

In contrast to Emilio and Gwen, Lee is explicitly building his company for purposes of the IPO or sale. Whether the company becomes publicly traded because of the size of its software sales or is sold for a large amount of cash or stock from a national bank, the result is a change of control and a large, typically one-time payout for Lee.

The examples of Karen and Addi are examples that fall in the middle of the continuum between a lifestyle business and an IPO play. Both are willing to operate their businesses as long as needed and both seem to enjoy the success of their companies. But neither is primarily motivated by the independence of operating the business. Instead they are motivated by the inability to achieve their goals in other ways. For the right financial reward, it is likely that both would sell their companies or sell stock in the companies and allow professional management to step in.

The decision to launch a lifestyle business is no better or worse than the decision to launch a company that is designed to be acquired. The entrepreneur, however, must understand this decision in seeking and structuring investments so that the investor's goals and the entrepreneur's goals align properly. Since the investors have a clear understanding regarding their investments, it is the entrepreneur who must plan carefully.

3.   *The Psychology of Venture Capital.*

In contrast to the psychology of entrepreneurs, the psychology of the venture capitalist is very simple and clear. A venture capital fund is a company that has accumulated a large amount of money to invest in a start-up company early in its business cycle. The early investment generally means that the investor runs a significant risk that the company will fail, and the investment will be lost. As a result, the potential reward for the investment must be many times the size of that initial investment.

For example, if only one in five businesses is successful, then the venture fund which funds the successful companies should expect at least a five-fold return on its investment just to break even. And the venture fund does not merely hope to break even—it hopes to provide a substantial profit to its investors.

The second aspect of the venture fund's expectations is the amount of time the venture fund is willing to wait for the return. Generally, venture funds want to recoup the investment and the profit in a period from eighteen to thirty-six months. The question for the venture fund is which of its opportunities will generate the greatest annual return. For example, an investment that creates a ten-fold profit in one year would need to create a thirty-fold profit in three years for it to maintain the same annual return.

In his book, *The Startup Garden*, Tom Ehrenfeld explains the importance of understanding the psychology and motivation of the investors. "[M]ake sure that you find investors whose interests align with yours. ... And be clear with others what your long-term goals are. You don't want to surprise investors if you eschew rapid growth, or make other decisions that are consistent with your vision, yet don't reconcile with theirs."[105]

The capital fund manager wants to know the potential upside of the investment and the timeframe in which that investment will be realized. For entrepreneurs that have the potential for large returns on investment in a short period of time, venture capital may be the best way to fund their companies. For entrepreneurs that expect a longer-term return on the investment, other types of funding may be more appropriate.

4.   *Applying Funding Goals to Lifestyle Needs.*

The relationship between financing and lifestyle is very straightforward. The longer the entrepreneur desires to own the

---

[105] TOM EHRENFELD, THE STARTUP GARDEN: HOW GROWING A BUSINESS GROWS YOU 82–83 (2002).

business, the more the entrepreneur should prefer debt to equity and partners to venture capitalists.

From the examples above, Lee should seek venture capital funding because it will provide the funding necessary to launch the company quickly and will also provide connections for presenting the software to multinational banks or for launching the company into the public markets. Emilio, in contrast, should seek small SBA-guaranteed loans or lines of credit as he slowly expands his business. A restaurant owner or chef embodies the brand of most non-chain restaurants. The reputation, and therefore the trademark of the restaurant, is based on that "know-how." If the restaurant expands beyond the personal supervision of that individual, it risks losing its uniqueness, and because the restaurant business is extremely competitive, it risks losing its market edge. For restaurants, protection of reputation is more important than the speed of growth, so lines of credit allow Emilio to control the cost of debt while expanding only as needed.

Lee and Emilio reflect the extremes of entrepreneurship. Karen illustrates its center point. Her patented paint process has an immediate impact on the automotive industry and may have potential in other industries. Her decision to open a retail detail shop—across the street from her former employer—suggests both a lifestyle choice and an attempt to capture some of her former business's goodwill for her new venture.

A venture capital fund would be likely to care more about the paint technology and seek to own that rather than the individual shop. If the technology proves successful, it could launch a national chain of body paint shops, either through direct ownership or by franchising the business to individual store owners. By understanding the choices created through the business model, Karen can maximize her opportunities and put the investor's funds into the best activities.

Addi, the game designer, is similarly in the middle of the financing continuum. She can grow the company slowly as she sells the game to retailers and directly through the Internet. It may grow, but it is likely to take a great deal of time. She can sell to a large company, but her experience suggests that this will earn her the least amount of money, and she will lose control over her game.

Addi can seek loans or investment dollars to increase the marketing efforts of the game. Addi would also do well by growing the market for the game through crowdfunding. With investors, she could also decide to grow by creating other games and building a new game company with a line of products. Such a business would be unlikely to attract venture capital since the business growth would still be slow, but it could attract private investors to help her launch this effort.

To illustrate the relationship, a graph would show that the shorter the intended ownership, the more likely venture capital is appropriate and the longer the intended ownership, the more appropriate is debt financing.

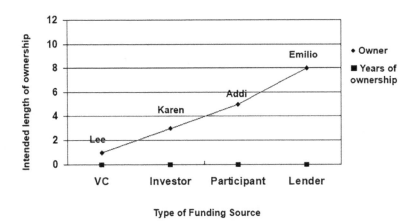

Type of Funding Source

The chart represents a simple summary of the goals of the entrepreneur and financier. Balancing the needs of the entrepreneur with the goals of the investor or lender is a necessary first step in aligning these interests and reducing conflict. A venture capital fund may seek an exit strategy of one to three years, while other investors may be more committed. Still, investors will want some liquidity and the ability to sell their interest far sooner than lenders, which may provide loans that last up to twenty or more years. As a result, the entrepreneur should align his goals with the financier by selecting the right type of financing for the company.

5.   *Scale and Profitability for the Investment.*

The second relationship of importance to the financier is the scale of profitability. The potential for profitability comes from the relationship between relevance and market size (*Profitability* = *relevance* * *market size*). The larger the market size for the product or service, the greater the potential profitability there is for the entrepreneur and investors. Lenders, of course, merely receive a return of the principal and interest, so lenders do not participate in the success potential of the enterprise.

A product that can be used by every person in the United States has more potential than a product that can be used only by children in Des Moines, Iowa. Size does matter. Food, entertainment products, and certain medicines fall into the category of potential relevance with every person in the United States. An aviation sensor has a much more limited market.

Relevance reflects the value placed upon that item by the market. One potential measure for relevance is the share of the market controlled by the seller of the product or service. Microsoft Windows computer operating software once controlled over 95% of the U.S. operating software market, making it highly relevant. Although it has lost ground to Apple, it still retains over 82% of the market. Apple, which failed to compete in that field, was successful in securing greater than a 75% market share with its iPod product (and holding a 95% market share in the first two years of its launch in 2001). In both cases, alternative products exist, but copyright and trademark keeps the competition far behind.

Price also affects profitability. Ten percent of $1.00 is a lot less than 10% of $1,000,000. An aviation sensor may be worth more than many inventions if it is worth enough for each airline to install it. Microsoft has priced Windows in such a way that it is very cost effective for computer manufacturers to include it with the computer, something that its early competitors failed to understand until it was too late.

In the first edition of the book, it was noted that Apple's iPod will have a much harder time maintaining its market share than Microsoft's Windows because competitors can use price and features to challenge iPod's relevance. This proved to be the case. Nearly two decades after the launch of the iPod, Apple continues to be the largest seller of tablets despite a dramatically more competitive marketplace. Today the iPad has roughly 25% of the market, while Amazon increased its market share to over 15% and Samsung has the third position with 14%.

The copyrighted software used by Apple gives it exclusive rights, but other software authors created their own media systems. The iTunes dominance in music did not translate to control over video, books, and newspaper distribution. Copyright provides modest exclusivity, but not the powerful monopoly of patents. By creating similar features at a lower price, Amazon has emerged as a much more powerful competitor. By managing price points, Samsung has reshaped the economic stratification of the market.

For start-up businesses relying on exclusivity, the relationship between market size, relevance, and price will inform the investor of the potential profit that an investment can bring. Early on, these projections are necessarily speculative; however, they do provide at least a benchmark for pricing the investment.

* * *

EXAMPLE—Jewel's Jewelry

Lana Jewel has worked for ten years in the fashion industry and has developed a strong reputation for her original jewelry. Some of her work has been featured in exclusive collections as well as in films. She plans to launch a collection. Each design will be protected by copyright, trademark and publicity rights in Lana Jewel's name.

Business Plan Preparation

	Mass Consumer	Department Store	Designer
Market Size	Very Large	Mid-size	Small
Relevance	Small—designer name not highly known	Medium—some recognition of designers	Large—designer well known in elite circles
Price	Lower priced goods create alternatives	Medium priced goods create alternatives	High priced goods create alternatives; exclusive pricing a plus
Material (affects price)	Glass, plastic and silver plate to reduce price	Mixed media of semi-precious materials; gold plate and silver	Semi-precious and precious stones; gold, silver, and platinum
Anticipated mark-up	25-50% markup	50-100% markup	100-500% markup
Profitability	Large market with small profit per item; most like a commodity	Good-sized market with reasonable profit on items	Small, exclusive market with excellent return on investment
Strategy	Avoid this market or cycle into it with previous designs	Good market for items less popular in exclusive shops or recycled from prior year's designs	Primary market for goods. Build reputation and trademark, which can be extended into department store
Business Plan	Do not participate in this market	Create simplified trademark to show association with exclusive shops, but distinct from those shops	Invest in trademarks, copyrights and publicity rights of name

As demonstrated from this table, a comparison of the potential for Jewel's jewelry provides a logical business strategy. The greatest profitability flows from the exclusive shops. This maximizes relevance through Lana's prior activities, highest profit per item and highest percentage return on the goods. Through copyrighted original designs and the development of both a trademark in the jewelry line, along with the publicity rights associated in Lana's name, relevance and exclusivity can be established. These can then be extended into the larger, but somewhat less profitable sector in the department store trade.

A second trademark will be created exclusively for those goods sold through department store channels (and perhaps different versions of the trademark for different department stores). In this way, the department store sales will not siphon exclusivity built through the designer shops. The copyrighted designs can be "recycled," meaning that the new designs for the designer shops can be used in the department store in the following seasons. In this way, the designer shops always receive the newest of the original designs. Combined with the most expensive materials, the designer shops will not be directly affected by the department stores, and the two markets can both be maintained.

* * *

The decisions involving lifestyle objectives and financing goals combine with decisions regarding pricing and primary markets to develop the key features of the business plan. As with the example above, the answer to these questions help outline the business plan for the company.

C.   Integrating Goals, Value, Exclusivity, and Relevance.

The successful new business integrates the four central aspects of the book's prescription—goals, value, exclusivity, and relevance—into a single business plan. The business must achieve the personal goals of the entrepreneur, the necessary returns for the financier, and the demands of the customers. These are the goals, value, and relevance, respectively. To sustain success, the entrepreneur must exclusively own an aspect of the business that protects it from allowing better-situated competitors to undercut the entrepreneur and steal the idea and market out from under the start-up. Exclusivity protects the entrepreneur and financier from becoming a commodity.

The integration of goals, value, exclusivity and relevance creates a planning matrix that will help the entrepreneur articulate the purpose for the business, raise funds, organize the business plan, and operate the company successfully. By addressing each of these four questions, the entrepreneur can plan much more effectively.

The relationship between the investor and entrepreneur is shown in this graph.

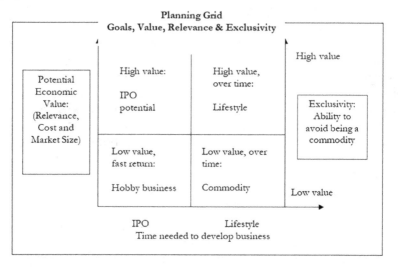

The chart reflects the interrelationship between the four planning factors. The entrepreneur must balance the goals for the business against the needs of the financier and the expectations of the market. If the business calls for a great deal of capital investment, then the resulting income stream must be sufficiently large to generate the needed return for the investor. That, in turn, requires that the potential market be large enough, the product or service relevant enough, and the methodology exclusive enough to protect the investment.

IPO and Lifestyle: If the business has high relevance and high exclusivity, then a large return on investment would dictate a large investment. A patentable automobile efficiency device that would increase the gas mileage on vehicles by 25% could be worth $100-$250 per vehicle sold (based on gas savings and pricing effects). The 2017 automotive market has the potential for 17-18 million new vehicles. That suggests a potential $1.7—$4.5 billion revenue for this device if it were added to every vehicle. The adoption rate would be based on the price and value the manufacturers would put on the additional efficiency. Such a device would be highly attractive to investors and likely to generate great interest from the automotive industry.

At a 5% increase in fuel efficiency, the value and relevance of the device would be much lower. The return on investment would still result in a successful business, but more likely over a much longer period of time. The relevance would change the adoption rate by consumers, slowing the period in time before break-even. At some point, the return would attract only investors willing to accept a much slower return on their investment.

Hobby Business: A clever toy that can be copyrighted and sell 10,000 units at a net profit of $5.00 will generate $50,000 in profit. If the investment can be made to operate this hobby for $5,000-$10,000 dollars, then this is a nice hobby business. If the investment required is much greater, however, the risk of loss will outweigh the investment. In most cases, such an example would fall into the category of "hobby business"—quick, with a low cost and modest return. If this same result would take three years rather than one to achieve, then it has a low rate of return and is unlikely to be a successful business.

In sum, the chart reflects the interrelationship between the key predictors in the start-up planning process. By balancing exclusivity, relevance, value, and the entrepreneur's goals, the nature of the business can be better understood and the business better aligned with all the parties' interests.

Chapter 8. Drafting a Business Plan with Exclusivity and Relevance

A.   Proper Uses of the Business Plan.

A useful business plan provides a blueprint for the operations, direction, and growth of a business. It explains the needs for funding, anticipates the cash flow operations of the business, highlights strategic partnerships, and serves as a proof-of-concept for key partners. The credibility of the business plan will help investors, founders, suppliers, lenders, and other key partners be able to assess the thoughtfulness and planfulness that has gone into the business. The business plan is a fifteen page calling card.

The business plan is not a "disclosure document" in the sense that it is not expected to provide the necessary warnings and disclosures regarding the risks associated with the start-up enterprise. The business plan does not have sufficient information to counsel a potential investor regarding the many risks associated with the investment or offering. That task is left to financing documents described in the next chapter. The business plan should provide a comprehensive overview of the business and the business's potential for success.

In modern business transactions, however, all the information provided by the business owner must be accurate and truthful. Although it is not a disclosure document, neither should it be an investor's sales pitch. It should be accurate and as reasonably objective as the entrepreneur can draft it. Any material mistakes in the facts must be corrected, including statements which might have been true at the time the business plan was drafted but are no longer true because circumstances have changed. One common mistake in business plans is to highlight the success of one or two similar companies without acknowledging the risks associated in the field as a whole. Further, since the sophisticated investor understands these risks, the refusal to acknowledge the risks undermines the credibility of the business plan.

The business plan can, however, contain projections based on speculation. Acknowledging that projections are based on reasonable estimates and not on historical data is acceptable. Often business plans guarantee rates of returns. Again, these are wildly speculative statements and should be more thoughtfully described. The optimistic speculations can be included, so long as the reasoning for these enthusiastic statements is carefully described and balanced with more reasonable assumptions and projections. For example, a restaurant cannot base its revenue on the potential size of the population in the city it serves. Instead, it must base its potential revenue on the number of seats available in the facility and the number of seatings the restaurant hopes to achieve. Once the business plan provides this realistic calculation, it can list the revenue based on full capacity. It should, however, also calculate revenue based on a more conservative estimate of weekly customers and include the number of patrons necessary to break even.

The tone and voice of the document should be directed toward the outside investor. While the business plan has many uses and many audiences, the focus should stay on the investor, because the investor's goals of creating a return on investment, managing risks, planning realistically and providing good value will also serve to inform all the other readers. The investor is a financially successful, sophisticated outsider. The language selected must reflect the business owner's ability to grasp complex ideas while recognizing that, to the investor, acronyms and industry jargon may have little or no meaning. So long as the document remains true to the investor, it can be used for its other essential purposes efficiently.

1.   *Creating the Plan as a Planning Device.*

Perhaps the most valuable aspect of the business plan process is the actual planning and exploration of building the business. There are many software products now available to assist entrepreneurs in the creation of their business plans. These may be particularly helpful to the extent that they ask questions of the key personnel and provide financial documents and forms.

The software products carry a significant risk, however, of oversimplifying the questions to be answered. The software should only be used to *help* write the plan rather than to write the plan. The federal Small Business Administration and the various state SBAs have links to many sample business plans that can help generate ideas for the entrepreneur's plan. Reading these plans should create questions for the entrepreneur to answer.

2.   *Building the Plan to Build the Enterprise.*

The business plan should be drafted as a collaborative exercise. Unless the company will start as a one-person operation, the entrepreneur should be discussing the sections of the business plan with the other key personnel at each stage of the development process. On many occasions, potential key personnel will read draft provisions in the business plan and withdraw from the project or renegotiate the relationship. This means the plan is working. A business is extremely vulnerable if the key personnel are not in agreement regarding their roles in the business's development.

One key use of the business plan is to build a consensus around the business, its goals, and its measures of success. If the key personnel cannot reach this consensus, the business will not succeed. In contrast, a business operating with strong internal agreement and a common vision has a much greater chance of weathering the inevitable challenges.

The drafting of the business plan will assist the entrepreneur in determining which types of financing best meet the company's strategic needs. For a lifestyle business that will generate a moderate and consistent rate of return based on ownership of tangible assets, loans appear to be a better strategic fit than investors. For a start-up venture with significant start-up expenses and a great chance of a public offering within the first three years, venture capital may be a much more attractive solution that pushes the financial risk off the entrepreneur and onto the investors. Each category of funds carries with it assumptions about goals and strategies which must be explored and developed through the drafting process.

3.   *Making the Plan Useful for Investors.*

Entrepreneurs generally assume that the primary use of the business plan is to serve as an informational calling card for prospective investors. Although this is true for the operational plan, the document has far less influence over the financing structure that may be proposed by prospective investors. Nothing in the business plan will stop a potential investor from making an offer different from the proposal put forth by the entrepreneur. Invariably, the offer (when it comes using other documents) will be treated as an invitation to negotiate. Only when there are multiple outstanding offers and a commitment to treat all investors exactly the same will the flexibility to negotiate fall away. Even in this case, the offerees may ask to negotiate. It will simply be harder for the entrepreneur to accommodate them.

In addition, as described more fully in the next section, there are strict legal limitations on the offering of business interests for sale. The business interests are a form of security and are subject to both state and federal law. As a result, the investors use the business plan to assess the logic of the business operation, the ability of the management to deliver on its promises, underlying market assumptions made by the entrepreneur, and the financial status of the proposal. Investors do not rely on the business plan to define the investment offer.

In many ways, the investors are seeking precisely the same information as are the key personnel. They want to know that the investment makes sense. For investors, the question is generally asked at two different levels. First, whether the company has a reasonable chance to deliver what it promises, and if it has taken all reasonable steps to mitigate the risks inevitably associated with the business.

Second, the business must meet the strategic financial objectives of the investor. The potential for a high rate of return and the degree of risk must be introduced. These are highly speculative aspects of the business, so they must be described in much greater detail in the financial offering documents, but the broad, general hopes of the entrepreneur must be described in the business plan and the investor must find the description credible. If the investor does not believe the entrepreneur's projections, the likelihood of any investment becomes extremely low. Similarly, the investor may wish to make a quick return, or may be willing to participate in the enterprise for a much longer period of time. The so-called exit strategy of the investor must coincide with the expectations of the entrepreneur. Closely related, the liquidity of the investment—the ability for the investor to sell his interest—must be understood on the same terms by both investor and entrepreneur. Taken together, these financial expectations must be sufficiently described in the plan, so that the investor remains interested, without providing so much detail that the plan constitutes an offer to sell securities.

- Investors will receive a return on the funds in a timeframe reasonable to the size of the investment of 6-36 months.

- Investors have confidence in the competence and leadership of the enterprise.

- Investors believe the business has meaningful growth potential which can withstand competition in the marketplace.

Finally, the investor will assess the business opportunity against other opportunities from other entrepreneurs. Here, the question is whether this business plan will better use the investor's resources in the marketplace than the other available opportunities. This comparative analysis is often referred to as the opportunity cost of the investment. The money invested in this enterprise cannot be used in other enterprises. While every investment must make financial sense, the opportunity cost and opportunity benefit for investors may be weighted heavily by non-financial factors. Among the factors motivating investors are the following:

- Investors often want to put their money to work within their community or geographic region.

- Investors often want to provide financial opportunities to those who do not traditionally have access to economic resources.

- Investors may be keen on the social benefits of the investment because of the fame or prestige of others involved.

- Investors may be interested because the investment has a secondary benefit to their other financial interests.

Investors are never interested in losing money, so these non-economic factors address the opportunity cost of the decision. Unless the business plan is financially sound, the economic reward sufficient and the goals of the investor are consistent with the goals of the entrepreneur in terms of liquidity, length of investment, and rates of return, there will be no match. In such cases, the entrepreneur is better off waiting rather than taking the money of an investor whose goals are at odds with the business plan.

4.   *Use of the Business Plan for Lenders.*

In some ways, lenders have the same interests as investors, but in many ways, their interests are much simpler. Like investors, the lenders will only lend to a company that has a management team they perceive as knowledgeable and capable of operating the business. Lenders will closely examine the viability of the company and the credibility of the company's operating plans. Unlike investors, however, the lenders are focused on whether the loan will be sufficiently risk-free so that the interest and principal will be repaid on schedule.

The answer to the lender's questions can focus on the tangible and intangible assets owned by the company, its cash flow projections, and its ability to provide guarantors in the event the new business is not successful. Lenders are less interested in the rates of return and levels of success than in having confidence that the business will be at least reasonably successful for a sufficiently long period of time to repay the loans.

For lenders, the business plan should address the "five Cs of credit," which track the risk factors assessed by lenders and bond investors.[106]

- *Cash Flow.* Is the firm's expected cash flow large enough to meet the debt payments?

- *Collateral.* If we have to foreclose on the loan, are there sufficient assets in the firm that we could sell to repay the loan?

- *Conditions.* Do the current economic conditions favor timely debt payments?

- *Course.* Is the use to which these funds will be put appropriate? Is the general strategy of this firm on course?

- *Character.* Are the people involved not only sufficiently intelligent and skilled, but also *morally inclined* to honor the repayment commitment?[107]

---

[106] ROBERT F. BRUNER ET AL., THE PORTABLE MBA 204 (4th ed. 2003).

[107] *Id.*

These five questions of character, course, conditions, collateral, and cash flow are equally important to investors, employees and the key leadership. Without entrepreneurs morally committed to those supporting the enterprise, there can be no trust or confidence. If the business strategy is not viable, there is no potential for success. And if the financial situation—including the internal cash flow and the external market conditions—are unfavorable, the chances of overcoming the hurdles of a start-up business become insurmountable. Only the collateral question is unique to lenders, because only lenders have the opportunity to recoup their investment using collateral.

5.   *What to Keep Out of the Business Plan.*

First, the business plan should have no offers to sell securities or business interests. The business plan is not an offer to sell securities or ownership in the business. It is a description of the company. It can have alternative descriptions based on different assumptions regarding funding or there can be different versions of the plan, as long as the different versions do not create any misleading information for any of the plan recipients.

Second, the business plan should contain no trade secrets. Business plans are often far less confidential than the offering documents described in the next chapter. Unless a confidentiality agreement is signed before the business plan is presented, the business plan should contain no confidential information or information that the company hopes to protect as trade secrets. Most investors will refuse to sign a nondisclosure agreement. Distributing the business plan to a group of people who have not agreed to treat the information confidentially will fail to meet the company's obligation to take reasonable steps to protect the trade secrets.

The strategic market data gathered by the entrepreneur will not be considered trade secrets unless that information was gleaned from empirical studies or nonpublic and proprietary data. Generally, the market projections will also fail to rise to trade secrets. On the other hand, if the company has developed a unique business strategy, created internal research data, or invented anything economically useful, those are trade secrets. To use trade secrets in business plans, it is sufficient to explain that the company has created a new recipe or process. Without providing details of that recipe or process, for example, the business plan can describe the available consumer data regarding the recipe or process, it can explain how the process reduces production time or increases efficiency, or it can provide other explanations regarding the way the trade secret will improve the company, without describing the new recipe or process.

The entrepreneur should err on the side of caution when writing the business plan. An interested investor will ask more questions—which can be answered after a confidentiality agreement has been signed. Details of trade secrets can be explored more fully in the disclosures of private placement memoranda, which will be offered to a much smaller set of individuals.

B.   The Key Business Plan Provisions.

The basics of the business plan will flow directly from the sections of the book on the innovation, relevance, exclusivity, participants, sources of funds, and goals for both the owners and the entity. Business analysts often suggest that the failure to adequately plan the business is a leading cause of small business failure. This, along with weak management and poor financial planning, are the leading causes of the untimely demise of most start-up companies.[108]

Weak management and poor planning are both results of an incomplete understanding of the factors that affect success and failure. The process of developing a business plan will help educate the entrepreneur on critical questions regarding the start-up enterprise, greatly improving the chances of business survival.

1.   Understanding How to Organize the Writing of the Business Plan.

The organization of the business plan should not follow the organization of the book, but instead tell the potential investor the story of the start-up and its future in a crisp, short story format. Good persuasive writing is organized backwards from thoughtful research and

---

[108] Sharif Khan, *The Chief Cause of Business Failure and Success*, SHARIF KHAN BLOG (Apr. 2, 2005, 6:22 PM),
http://www.nationalbusiness.org/NBAWEB/Newsletter2005/2029.htm.

analysis. The business plan should reflect a scientific paper far more than a mystery novel.

To prepare a well-structured business plan, the entrepreneur should take on the role of a mystery novel sleuth or scientific principal investigator. A problem is identified, the participants are slowly introduced, and the tangled web of opportunities and false leads are explored until the solution becomes clear. This is the same structure for the detective novel, the scientific breakthrough, the planning of a start-up business, and the methodology for new product development.

The documentation of the final result, however, should not follow the same steps. The story of how the solution was crafted is not a compelling story for the investor. Investors, regulators, potential employees, and business associates do not desire a leisurely exploration of the world inhabited by the entrepreneur.

Instead, the model for a business plan should be modeled after the persuasive memorandum. It must begin with a thesis or goal statement that immediately identifies the goals of the start-up business. A summary should identify the exclusivity, the uniqueness, the relevance, and the stressors related to the business. These factors are described in reverse order from their development because the author needs to convince the reader that the optimal solution has been developed.

Reversing the order allows the author to lead and persuade the potential investor regarding the path chosen. For example, there may be two or more patents that would each solve a market need in an equally successful manner. If the business plan identifies the need first, the reader may anticipate the other potential patent, a solution different than the one in the business plan. The plan thereafter will appear flawed to the reader because it does not solve the problem in the manner anticipated by the reader. Had the reader first been introduced to the business plan solution and then asked to agree that it solves the identified problem, the reader would have been less likely to speculate about alternative solutions and more likely to agree with the entrepreneur. If never thwarted, the reader is more likely to be engaged with the proposal.

The remainder of this section lists the components of the business plan in the suggested order—an order opposite of that used by the entrepreneur to create the business. These concepts are built into the traditional sections of the business plan. Business plans vary from company to company. They should be tailored to tell the persuasive story of that particular enterprise. Nonetheless, the sample plan provides a helpful suggested organization:

1. **Executive Summary**—1.1. Objectives; 1.2. Mission; 1.3. Keys to Success.
2. **Business Activities: Product & Services**—2.1. Services to be Offered; 2.2. Product Description.
3. **Market and Competitive Positioning**—3.1. Target Market; 3.2. Competitive Comparison; 3.3. Sales Literature & Advertising; 3.4 Sourcing; 3.5. Future Services.
4. **Strategy & Implementation**—4.1. Pricing Strategy; 4.2. Sales Forecast; 4.3. Strategic Alliances.
5. **Company Summary**—5.1. Company Ownership; 5.2. Start-up Summary; 5.3 Company Locations & Facilities.
6. **Management**—6.1. Organizational Structure; 6.2 Management Team; 6.3 Key Agreements; 6.4 Personnel Plan; 6.5 Decision Making Process of Management.
7. **Key Risks and Risk Mitigation Strategy**—8. Financial Plan; 8.1 Balance Sheet; 8.2 Equity Stakes; 8.3 Projected Income & Expense Report—Cash Flow and Profit and Loss.

The first four sections of the business plan emphasize the exclusivity, uniqueness, relevance, and innovation of the entrepreneur. The company and management sections focus on the personnel and decision-making processes. Marketing and market competition focus on the product's innovation and relevance, with a more general emphasis on the strategies for marketing. Finally, the financial plan provides the numbers necessary to demonstrate the plan has sufficient capital to operate, reasonable economic projections, and cash flow to allow the company to grow at a reasonable pace.

2.   *Introduction or Executive Summary—the Goal Statement or Story Lead.*

The executive summary should serve as the goals statement of the enterprise, much as a thesis statement frames the academic research paper. A second analogy is the lead paragraph of a newspaper story. It contains the entire story—who, what, when, and where plus a special emphasis on why. Appendix F provides a sample business plan. The sample included is not based on newly patented inventions, because these opportunities do not arise as frequently. Instead, the first example is based on the intersection of publicity rights and trademarks.

There are many different styles available to the business plan writer. The sample has an introduction and three short subsections: 1.1—Objectives; 1.2—Mission; and 1.3—Keys to Success. The introduction provides both the "who" and the overarching goal statement. The mission provides the "what" of the business plan, and the objectives state the immediate "where" and "how" the business will proceed. The "Keys to Success" provides a bullet-point summary of the "why," highlighting the exclusivity, relevance, and innovation that will be detailed in later portions of the business plan.

Unless the most important questions are answered on the first page of the business plan, few readers will turn to page two. Like good journalistic writing, the business plan cannot bury the lead—it must establish the strength of the business in its introductory section.

3.   *Identifying the Exclusivity Afforded by the Business to Sustain Profit and Profit Margins.*

The *"Business Activities: Products and Services"* section of the business plan emphasizes the aspects of the business plan that provide the exclusivity. The section must identify the exclusive opportunities held by the entrepreneur. An analysis of the potential patents, trademarks and trademark licensing opportunities, trade secrets, publicity rights, and copyrights will illustrate the degree to which the business opportunity is exclusive and therefore unlike any others available.

The financial section will return to this theme by showing that the competition will have less ability to undermine price margins because the exclusive ownership of the intellectual property reduces the likelihood of adequate competitive alternatives in the marketplace. These exclusive rights may not all be in place prior to fully funding the start-up business, so the business plan needs to highlight them and demonstrate the potential to use funding to obtain these interests.

In the case of the sample business in Appendix F, the exclusive elements are the publicity rights provided by adopting the bicycle design innovation of a famous cyclist. This section would also feature any patents owned or applied for, research that is promising, or other exclusive attributes of the company. The plan should highlight how this solution will work. A second aspect of the section is a plan to cross-license the trademark opportunities. Again, this utilizes an exclusive trademark licensing arrangement to provide uniqueness and increase relevance for the business's products or services.

4.   *Providing   Context—Relevance,   Stressors   and Innovation.*

The next section of the business plan puts the exclusivity into the context of the uniqueness of the solution. This aspect may be expressed through an analysis of the target audience and a competitive comparison of the marketplace. Although these sections may be quite comparable to the provisions in traditional market sections of business plans, it is important to highlight the context and the relevance of the opportunity presented by the exclusive solution through the business plan.

The *"Marketing and Competitive Positioning"* introduction provides an opportunity to contextualize the relevance of the product and identify the stressors that create the need for the new product or service. The section *"Sales Literature and Advertising"* can be used to further reinforce the stressors in the existing marketplace and how the start-up business utilizes targeted advertising and marketing literature to highlight the stressors and the solution to that tension through the start-up's goods or services.

Depending on the type of business, some plans may need to provide a much greater amount of general context. A business plan based on a medical device patent, for example, would require significant information on the Food and Drug Administration process for approving the device as well as that process' impact on the patent application. It may also be critical to discuss the extent to which federal Medicaid or Medicare would cover the device and the potential issues for health insurance. These stressors and external factors will determine the success or failure of the proposal, so each must be addressed. The demographic changes that are a key stressor for so much innovation should also be mentioned in most business plans.

Not all the stressors are under the control of the business. Nonetheless, each significant stressor should be described. In the example of a medical device business, the plan should include a statement explaining that the success or failure will be conditioned on human trials and FDA approval of the product. Sophisticated investors and lenders understand these external factors. Failure to address them suggests the entrepreneur is naïve, disingenuous, or both. A persuasive document recognizes the weaknesses in its argument and acknowledges the limitations inherent in the thesis. It argues that these weaknesses are overcome by its strengths. A document that does not acknowledge its weaknesses cannot be credible in claiming it has overcome all objections. To be persuasive, the business plan must be comprehensive and candid.

For the entrepreneur drafting a business plan, questions about the relevance of the product or service to the target market, the innovation provided to solve the stressors, and the uniqueness of the solution offered should be used as a litmus test for each of the business plan's provisions. If the business plan drifts off these central themes, it will lose its persuasive impact.

5.   Another Approach: The Patent Plan—What is New, Useful, and Nonobvious.

A patent metaphor can serve as an alternative organizing principle for the business plan. The attributes of new, useful, and nonobvious can be combined into the description of the start-up's "*Business Activities, Market Analysis,*" and "*Competitive Strategy.*" What is new is described in the business activity section because the company's innovation is the key to the plan's success. The market analysis reflects the utility of the new business. If the business is not useful, it should not be funded. If it does not increase efficiency or add social relevance for the consumer, then the business should not be launched. Finally, the nonobvious nature of the plan should be addressed.

The business plan should also explain why the model will not be immediately replicated by competitors. Unless one of the intellectual property disciplines provides exclusivity, even a successful plan will be replicated into oblivion.

C.   Rounding   Out   the   Business   Plan— Disclosures and Other Provisions.

1.   Identifying the Leadership and Key Personnel.

Identification of key personnel and providing resume information is an essential aspect of the business plan and one that many investors read first. The names of the key personnel should be in the executive summary. A delay in identifying the "cast" will leave the readers wondering if something is amiss. The placement of the key personnel provision is not critical to the success of the business plan as long as the names are listed in the introduction. For a persuasive organizational style, the personnel provision should serve as the introduction to the financial planning section unless the personnel are directly responsible for the exclusivity of the proposal.

If the business plan is built around patents held by the primary business owner or the publicity rights of the company spokesman, then that role should be mentioned in the Business Activities section immediately after the executive summary. The entire resume of that individual need not be provided at that point, merely the attributes that make the person central to the success of the venture. Of course, if every principal is famous and the real value of the venture is to bring the strongest professionals in their respective field in an effort to let them be creative and successful, then the business plan really is merely the resumes. Such models generally fail, however, so there should be innovation based on relevance and supported by exclusivity rather than mere reliance on experience. As long as the principal individuals are competent and somewhat experienced, the focus on relevance and exclusivity will keep the business on track and competitive.

2. Management Goals and Investor's Liquidity Strategy.

The business plan should also make the time commitments of the key personnel clear, as well as the expected time frame and exit strategy for the financing. Investors want liquidity and lenders want the return of their principal. Business plans are provided to lenders as well as investors; the goal is not necessarily to have a ten-fold return on investment in eighteen months, but to provide a realistic statement of the timing goals.

Unfortunately, the drafting of the business plan is often the first time the key personnel have addressed issues regarding timing and shared expectations, so it also serves a critical internal purpose of committing the participants to an explicit shared vision. Founders must invest the time and effort to come to an internal agreement about these targets to avoid conflict later in the operations of the business.

3.   Articulating the Business Operations: Getting it Done.

The next element necessary for any business plan is an explanation of what the company will do to accomplish its operational goals. A description of the start-up's capacity to deliver the goods or services is the first aspect of this section. While much of this information may be uncovered in the financial projections, the business plan must address these obligations directly.

Employment agreements that incorporate nondisclosure and noncompetition provisions are one aspect of intellectual property that helps entrepreneurs meet this goal. These contracts assist the entrepreneur in protecting business operation know-how while still expanding the staff to meet the business's growing needs.

Of course, employment contracts do not substitute for the underlying knowledge necessary for the operation to work. The entrepreneur must be able to manufacture goods, provide a service, or sell a product. Without the ability to deliver the products or services to the customers, the business cannot succeed, no matter how brilliantly conceived.

If the cost of manufacturing exceeds the anticipated revenue cost per item, the business has failed before the first investor's packet leaves the printer. If the business relies on a technology which is not available for licensing, then the project should be shelved until that technology is freely available in the public domain. These are not idle suggestions. During the height of the dot.com boom, even companies that could not answer these preliminary questions received venture capital based on the irrational exuberance of the era. That era has passed, however, and present investors and lenders expect more concrete answers.

In addition to the operations side of the equation, business plans tend to focus heavily on the marketing and sales aspects of the plan, emphasizing relevance to the target audience. Marketing sections in the business plan highlight the need for the entrepreneur to understand and carefully identify the target audience for the launch of the product or service. While it can be appropriate to expand that target audience as the product meets market success, the initial focus should emphasize the greatest market opportunity. Thereafter, continuing research should include an assessment of the consumer make-up so that the target audience can be refined to maximize efficiency and return.

The marketing plan can provide a detailed strategy for website marketing, print advertising, direct mail, radio and television advertising, product placement opportunities, trade association opportunities, and other advertising and publicity opportunities. Again, the need to identify the target audience is crucial because different target audiences are served by different media. Each market segment researches and purchases products very differently from other market segments, basing its assessment on geography, age, affinities, professions, and ethnicity. This information may inform the trademark and branding strategy as well.

D.   Anticipating Risk.

1.   *Assessing the Reasonable Range of Risks and Rewards.*

Professor William Sahlman suggests that every business plan requires "[a]n assessment of everything that can go wrong and right, and a discussion of how the entrepreneurial team can respond. . . . Risk is understood, and the team has considered ways to mitigate the impact of difficult events."[109] Financing documents absolutely require this type of disclosure to inform potential investors, with strong language, of all the significant risks involved.

Professor Sahlman's suggestion reinforces the earlier discussion that context and external factors should be fully disclosed when they might potentially undermine the strength of the business plan. A plan that does not provide a meaningful context, or that paints only the most optimistic picture, will not convince its sophisticated readers of the entrepreneur's candor or ability.

This section also creates an opportunity to address the extent to which the risks have been mitigated through the entrepreneur's careful planning. For example, in the Riders business plan provided in Appendix F, the section, *"Key Risks and Risk Mitigation Strategy"* identifies the

---

[109] William A. Sahlman, *How to Write a Great Business Plan*, *in* HARVARD BUSINESS REVIEW ON ENTREPRENEURSHIP 29, 32–33 (1997).

business's reliance on the celebrity, whose publicity rights are licensed, and the company which holds the cross-licensing trademark agreement. Acknowledging this risk does more than state the obvious; it helps the business seek ways to mitigate the risk through insurance, indemnification, and noncompetition provisions. Identifying risk factors can transform them into an opportunity to show how the risks are being effectively minimized to the greatest extent possible and calculated into the financial assumptions when the risk cannot be avoided.

2.   *Financial Information and Analysis—Avoiding Under-Funding and Reporting Cash Flow.*

One of the more common causes of small business failure is the under-funding of the enterprise. Under-funding can take a variety of forms. A few of the more common are:

- Companies can fail to anticipate the start-up overhead expenses and run out of money before the minimum equipment for manufacturing is purchased or leased.

- Companies can underestimate operating expenses such as payroll and have insufficient operating funds to continue.

- Companies can fail to incorporate reasonable and unavoidable risks, such as overtime costs, shoplifting, damaged goods and returns, late payments and non-payments ("shrinkage"), and excess stock.

- Companies can fail to pay the entrepreneur a reasonable salary, so that the success of the business requires the financial failure of its owner.

- Companies can fail to plan for the schedule of payments and the cash flow of the business.

Of the many under-funding problems, the timing of payment is perhaps the most painfully ironic cause of business failure. If a manufacturer makes a $500.00 item and sells it on a thirty-day net sales agreement, that manufacturer should receive funds within thirty days of delivery. There are two additional delays in the system. The first is the time between the receipt of the order and the time of delivery. The second is payment delay. Many customers will take closer to sixty days to pay, and some will take even longer than ninety days. As business expands, the manufacturer needs to purchase parts and materials. If the business is too successful, the cost of purchasing equipment and materials (plus meeting payroll and paying rent) might exceed the revenue actually coming in the mail each month. Although the company would be profitable at the end of the year, it will run out of operating cash because its costs to meet growing demand exceed the payment from the previous sales.

Cash flow management is critical to protect a company from these kinds of risks. There are also loans and other financial products available to help companies manage their cash flow problems, but the companies cannot use these tools unless they are carefully tracking their cash flow. Cash flow accounting provides very straightforward payments and expenses based on the hard costs of doing business.

3.   Describing the Financial Picture—Accounting Methods and Income Statements.

Income statements or profit and loss statements provide another version of this information on both a month-by-month and annual view of the costs of operating a business. For a small, start-up business, these two forms may reflect very similar data. For more sophisticated companies, categories such as depreciation must be shown as a cost in the profit and loss statement, but it is not a cash payment to be shown in the cash flow accounting. The cash flow statement and the income statement will also vary more significantly if the enterprise uses an accrual basis for its accounting rather than a cash basis.

The cash basis of accounting requires the enterprise to record income only when cash is received from customers and to record expenses only when the item has been paid for. It is the method used to balance a personal checkbook. As a business grows, however, it does not provide information about the orders booked, the obligations incurred, or other significant financial events on the horizon. As a result, businesses generally use accrual accounting to better reflect the true assets and liabilities of the ongoing enterprise.

The accrual basis of accounting requires the business to record the income at the time a sale is consummated through delivery of the product or service. The payment for the sale may be due thirty days later, but since it is earned when the sale is completed, that future payment is an asset of the business and is reflected on the income statement and balance sheet. Similarly, an expense is recognized at the time the obligation to pay the expense occurs, regardless of whether it is paid immediately or is merely a future obligation.

The accrual basis of accounting has the effect of recognizing both revenue and expenses before they are paid. This means that the timing of cash receipts is different than the timing on the income statement. It captures the accounts receivable and the accounts payable, which are significant indicators of the health of an enterprise. In addition, a good deal of attention will be focused on any difference between the accounts receivable and the "write-offs" for bad debt. If a start-up business is having difficulty collecting the payments for sales of products or services, there is a strong indicator that the company is not performing as well as the other financial indicators suggest. The entrepreneur must watch this aspect of the financial performance extremely closely and adjust the business to take this risk into account.

4. Describing the Financial Picture—Balance Sheets and Other Measures.

The balance sheet provides a snapshot of the company at a moment in time, highlighting the value of its assets and liabilities. The assets summarize all the items of value owned by the company, while the liabilities illustrate the debts or financial obligations of the company. These show the "worth" of the company at this moment in time.

The most important axiom of the balance sheet is that "a balance sheet must balance." The balance sheet allows every aspect of the business to be calculated as an asset (something of value held by the company), a liability (an obligation to be paid by the company) and equity (the value of the company held by the owners). The balance of these three measures is reflected on the balance sheet as follows:

Assets = Liabilities + Owner's Equity

The assets are the resources the company has to operate. Liabilities, such as business loans, are essential resources for a company. The corollary of the balance sheet math formula allows the owners to measure the worth of their holdings:

Owner's Equity = Assets - Liabilities

Mathematically, the two formulas represent the same information. But this variation on the formula allows the entrepreneur to understand when the ownership is worth less than the liability and when the company has provided a return to the investors.

Accounting practices, however, make the balance sheet somewhat misleading, particularly if the company has created valuable intellectual property. Patents, trademarks, copyrights, and other assets of intellectual property and goodwill do not appear on the balance sheet. Nor do the value of commitments by key personnel to stay with the enterprise. Nonetheless, the balance sheet is a necessary and helpful aspect of financial planning which lenders, investors, and management must use to assess the success and positioning of the company.

Microsoft has a number of templates for use with its products that have been created in conjunction with SCORE (Service Corps of Retired Executives), available at https://templates.office.com/. These provide an excellent set of instructions and information on how to use the various forms.

Other financial projections, including sales projections, revenue forecasts, and similar tools may be helpful in a variety of cases, but the precise tools will depend on the specifics of the products or services offered.

A statement of the equity ownership of the enterprise is also helpful to show the anticipated final ownership of the company. If the ownership changes as a result of different contingencies, then a chart showing these contingencies is useful.

5.   Another Approach: The Bell-Mason Development Framework.[110]

Another summary approach is provided by the Bell-Mason Development Framework. Created by the Bell-Mason Group, a consulting firm providing corporate strategy and consultation, the approach focuses on innovation and "venturing" for the larger traditional company. Part of their work focuses on the "innovation from within" strategy best exemplified by IBM in 1981 when it allowed a small

---

[110] *See* HEIDI MASON & TIM ROHNER, THE VENTURE IMPERATIVE: A NEW MODEL FOR CORPORATE INNOVATION 92, 96–98 (2002).

distinct team to work outside the corporate framework to create the personal computer. In doing so, IBM avoided the collapse that most of the large computer companies of the era suffered when the personal computer revolutionized the computing business model.

The Bell-Mason Development Framework provides a four-step process and twelve-point matrix for corporate analysis of a company's development strategy. A variation of that plan can easily be adapted to the exclusivity and relevance method by focusing on the twelve points of the key measures in the fourth step of corporate readiness. This chart of attributes (below) captures the twelve attributes of the Framework.

Exclusivity and Relevance	Technology	Product	Business
Production Capability	Delivery	Marketing	Sales
Management	CEO	Team	Board
Finance	Cash	Finance-ability	Control

The first row of attributes emphasizes the importance of exclusivity and relevance, the second focuses on the ability to deliver that promise through production capability, the third group of attributes assesses the competency of the entrepreneur's team and the fit of goals between the entrepreneur and the investors, while the final row emphasizes the financial ability of the venture and the need to have sufficient resources to operate.

Only when a venture has all four aspects of its operations working effectively can a start-up company succeed. The preparation of the business plan should be far more than merely a financing document. It should provide a process of assessment for each of the four aspects of the development framework.

Chapter 9. Operating a Franchise as an Alternative to Starting from Scratch

For some future business owners, the opportunity to start a business is the driving force behind their entrepreneurial zeal. The independence of business ownership and the ability to provide for themselves is a primary motivator. For a potential business owner looking for a lifestyle business, the ability to purchase a franchise license may provide all the economic and professional opportunities needed while reducing the risks of creating a new business and providing a network of support to help improve the chances of success.

Franchises are like any other business, however, which means that the potential for success and failure will be based on many factors. Some of those factors, like managerial skill, are dependent on the new business owner. Other factors, such as the location, and the employee talent pool, can be managed by the new business owner. And then there are factors like the national economy, weather, natural disasters, and other factors that are outside of any individual's control. All these factors impact the success or failure of a business, so that even the most successful franchise still includes a high degree of risk.

A.   Franchising Basics for Franchisees.

A franchise is a license or agreement to use the existing business model provided by a company, including its trademarks, recipes and other know-how, its patented products, and processes, in exchange for agreeing to pay the company for the license and to adhere to a set of rules or guidelines on how the business is expected to operate. The company selling the franchise license is the franchisor and the new business owner is the franchisee.

A franchise provides a lifestyle business opportunity for the franchisees. The franchise system—owned and operated by the franchisor—may have the combination of exclusivity and relevance to make the franchise a great national brand. Most franchises rely heavily on trademarks for their national presence. Household cleaning franchise opportunities, for example, provide little more than the power of national advertising and some management expertise. The service is a commodity. While highly relevant to its customers, any company can provide the service at rates generally controlled by wage and hour laws. Other franchise systems are based on patented inventions, trade secrets, publicity rights, or other attributes that give the system strong exclusivity. The size and marketing clout of major franchises tend to increase the social relevance of these companies through their marketing influence.

But because the exclusivity and relevance are under the control of the franchisor rather than the franchisee, the potential business owner of the franchise must be very diligent to assure that franchisees are treated with respect by the franchise, provided important legal protections under the franchise agreement, and generally demonstrate that the existing franchise owners are successful in their financial return and professional experience.

1.   *Examples of Major U.S. Franchises.*

Many of the world's fast-food restaurants and chain restaurants are operated on a franchise basis. Most McDonald's locations are owned by franchisees, as are most KFC locations, Hertz rental agencies, Great Clips, RE/MAX realtors, Pet Depot stores, and service companies like Servpro, uBreakiFix, The Maids, and Nurse Next Door Home Care Services. Entrepreneur Magazine, which annually ranks the top five hundred franchises, has over 75 different business categories. These businesses have little or nothing to do with each other except for the decision to license the right to operate the business to third parties rather than to have the company own each location.

Categories range from automotive to vending, with restaurants and fitness being the most visible to the ordinary consumer. There are also many opportunities for business services, industrial services, technology services, and other features.

Most franchises are location-based. A franchisee licenses the right to operate a retail operation in a particular area. For less established franchises, the territory might be exclusive to an entire city, while franchisees for large companies may not be able to control more than a single block. Other franchises are online services, meaning that the franchisee is essentially providing its own marketing and networking effort behind a service that is essentially identical to every other franchisee on the Internet. If the potential business owner has the marketing tools, network depth, unrelated trademarks, and publicity rights to drive traffic away from the other franchisees and towards the new franchise, then that model might work. Otherwise the franchise is a commodity service.

2.   *What Makes a Good Franchise.*

A good franchise enables a new owner to enter the franchise system and have immediate success while also having opportunities for continued growth and success for long-term franchisees. The Entrepreneur Magazine Top 500 listing uses five categories to determine its ranking. These are:

COSTS & FEES——Franchise fee; Total investment; and Royalty fees

SIZE & GROWTH—Open & operating units; Growth rate; and Closure rate

SUPPORT—Training times; Marketing support; Operational support; Franchisor infrastructure; Financing availability; and Litigation

BRAND STRENGTH—Social media; System size; Years in business; and Years franchising

FINANCIAL STRENGTH & STABILITY—Franchisor's audited financial statements[111]

Each of these categories is essential for the franchise relationship to be successful. If the franchisor is not financially healthy, it puts the business of all the franchisees at risk. The strength of the franchisor's brand and trademark penetration directly impacts the value proposition of the franchisee's customers, so that the stronger the brand, the greater the success for the franchisee.

Still, for the new franchisee, the support is perhaps the most important consideration. A good franchise is much more than a list of trademarks, recipes, and formulae. The franchisor should have learned a great many lessons regarding the best ways to attract, service, and retain

---

[111] *Franchise 500 2018*, ENTREPRENEUR, https://www.entrepreneur.com/franchise500/2018 (select "Understanding the Ranking") (last visited July 12, 2018).

its customers. Those lessons are essential for the start-up franchise to succeed. The methods of training staff, of laying out the retail space, of managing the acquisition of goods and services needed to provide service to the customers, the potential to provide internal financing, and other services will make a tremendous difference in the success of the franchise.

The franchise also needs to be a good investment. The franchise license is only one of the costs. If the franchise is for a retail operation, then the total cost of the business will include the leasehold acquisition costs, the staffing expenses, the costs of materials and inventory, and the expense of marketing. Some franchise systems aggressively market for the franchise, and the individual franchisee pays a proportionate cost back to the licensor. Other franchises provide far less marketing and brand support, so the costs of customer acquisition and retention are paid by each franchise individually.

The FTC guidance on franchise ownership also raises other important questions for the potential new business owner. These questions focus on the demand for the product or service, the competition in the industry from other companies as well as from the franchisor and other franchisees, and the potential new business owner's ability to run the business independently, particularly if the franchisor was to go out of business.[112] Most of these concerns apply to all business acquisitions and are not restricted to franchises. Nonetheless, they are essential to be addressed by the potential new franchisee.

Ultimately, what makes a good franchise is the fit between the goals of the franchisee and the operations of the franchisor. Franchises are all lifestyle business operations.

3.   *Franchisor Control and Management Expectations of the Franchisee.*

The expectation of the franchisor is that each franchise will look and feel like every other franchise in the system. This helps assure a consistent customer experience and protects the brand from dilution.

---

[112] FED. TRADE COMM'N, A CONSUMER'S GUIDE TO BUYING A FRANCHISE 5 (2015), *available at* https://www.ftc.gov/system/files/documents/plain-language/pdf-0127_buying-a-franchise.pdf.

Franchisors also do not want their franchisees to become competitors with other franchises, so assuring consistency in products and services keeps some locations from going rogue and upsetting the business.

The FDD, or FTC Franchise Disclosure Document, is discussed more fully below. One of the key provisions of the FDD and the franchise agreement is the description of the limits and expectations the franchisor will have for the franchise. As the FTC explains, the restrictions listed in the FDD and franchise agreement are designed to limit the franchisee's ability to exercise independent business judgment regarding the operation of the franchise. On the other hand, the lack of certain restrictions will mean more competition from the franchisor and other franchisees. A restriction on territory limits the scope of what the new business operator can do, but it protects that new business from direct competition as well. The list of restrictions for a franchisee typically includes the following:

- suppliers from whom you may purchase goods

- the goods or services you may offer for sale

- where and to whom you can sell goods or services

- your use of the internet to sell goods or services to customers within and outside your territory

- the right of the franchisor (or other franchisees) to use the internet to solicit customers or to sell in your territory[113]

The franchisor knows the business much more intimately than does the new franchisee. The disclosure documents provide an important tool for the franchisee to become knowledgeable about what the actual expectations will be when operating the franchise.

4.   *Franchisee Control and Management Expectations of the Franchisee.*

The best aspect of the franchise purchase opportunity is the potential for new business owners to truly understand the expectations of control and management that will be required to be successful for the

---

[113] *Id.* at 8.

new franchise. New business owners tend to overestimate their own ability and underestimate the challenges involved in starting a new business. They are faced with drafting business plans for highly skeptical investors and challenged by managing unknown risks.

For the potential franchise operator, many of those costs and risks can be calculated because they have been experienced by other franchise owners. The potential purchaser can speak with others in the franchise system to learn how much money was really invested before a return started, how high the annual returns are for various locations, how responsive the franchisor is regarding marketing and other brand challenges, where the competition really comes from, what the customer base tends to be, and a myriad of other questions that will help determine the success or failure of the new franchise.

Franchises have a higher rate of success than other new business ventures. This is not surprising, since the new franchise is not really a new business at all, but instead an extension of an already successful business. Strong marketing support and effective training can also account for a great deal of the difference in success. Financing resources may solve some of the cash-flow challenges that close fast-growing but underfunded start-ups.

More than these factors, however, the new franchise operator is in a much better position than a new business operator of an untested business venture. By aggressively researching the costs, operations, brand management, and training available to the franchise, the new franchise owner does not need to take the same blind leap of faith required of true start-up ventures. As a result, franchises provide a very practical opportunity for the potential business owner seeking a lifestyle business and an intermediate level of independence.

B. Understanding the Franchise Agreement.

1.   *Qualifying as a Franchise.*

The FTC regulates the disclosures to protect the franchisee under the "FTC Franchise Rule."[114] The franchise rule only applies to the franchise relationship, which is defined with a simple three-part test: "the

---

[114] *See* 16 C.F.R. pt. 436.

franchisor must: (1) promise to provide a trademark or other commercial symbol; (2) promise to exercise significant control or provide significant assistance in the operation of the business; and (3) require a minimum payment of at least $500 during the first six months of operations."[115]

The three-part test, rather than the label used between the parties, governs whether a franchise relationship exists that must be covered under the rule. Many "distributorships" satisfy all three categories, so those trigger the franchise regulations. As discussed below, certain trademark license agreements can be drafted in a manner that results in unintended franchises, so trademark agreements must also be crafted to avoid that unintended result.

The payment amount is quite modest, and the definition of trademark used by the FTC is quite broad, including all registered or unregistered trademarks, tradenames, and service marks. The most critical definition, then, is the significant control or assistance element of the test. To be significant, the franchisor "will exert or has the authority to exert a significant degree of control over the franchisee's method of operation, or provide significant assistance in the franchisee's method of operation" in a manner that will "relate to the franchisee's overall method of operation—not a small part of the franchisee's business."[116]

The list of significant control examples serves both to understand what typically makes a relationship fall within the legal definition of a franchise and help the franchisee understand the types of control that a franchisor may wish to exert:

- site approval for unestablished businesses;

- site design or appearance requirements;

- hours of operation;

- production techniques;

---

[115] FED. TRADE COMM'N, FRANCHISE RULE COMPLIANCE GUIDE 1 (2008), *available at* https://www.ftc.gov/system/files/documents/plain-language/bus70-franchise-rule-compliance-guide.pdf.

[116] *Id.* at 2.

- accounting practices;

- personnel policies;

- promotional campaigns requiring franchisee participation or financial contribution;

- restrictions on customers; and

- locale or area of operation.

Similarly, there are significant types of assistance that should benefit the franchisee:

- formal sales, repair, or business training programs;

- establishing accounting systems;

- furnishing management, marketing, or personnel advice;

- selecting site locations;

- furnishing systemwide networks and website; and

- furnishing a detailed operating manual.[117]

There are additional factors that sometimes come into consideration as well, including the obligation of the franchisee to provide repair services for products (except warranty work), mandatory displays for goods, comprehensive inventory controls, and other training and supervision such as on-the-job assistance with sales or repairs.

There are also exemptions to these rules for a variety of unrelated business arrangements or for franchises in excess of $1 million, presumably because the parties can negotiate those terms as highly sophisticated parties that do not need the disclosure protections provided by the FTC Franchise Rule. Similar exemptions apply to the rule for insiders of the franchisor, who have better information than can be provided in the disclosure agreement because of their relationship to the franchisor. Even then, however, the insider may wish to insist on FDD documentation even though it is not required under the law.

---

[117] *Id.* at 2–4 (*citing* Original Interpretive Guides, 44 Fed. Reg. 49,966, 49,967 (Aug. 24, 1979)).

2. *Using the Franchise Disclosure Document.*

The Franchise Rules requires that the franchisee must receive the FDD at least 14 days before the franchisor can ask the franchisee to sign the franchise agreement or pay for the license. The FDD should be both the first step and the last step in analyzing the potential to license a franchise. Certain negative information in the FDD should preclude investment in that franchise. Even if the FDD has no red flags, however, it should be reviewed very carefully after the potential buyer has met with franchise owners and conducted thorough due diligence about investing in the company.

Although franchising takes some of the risk out of launching a business, it also provides many traps for the unwary. Since so many new franchisees are not sophisticated in business, the FTC has strict rules on disclosures that must be made to potential franchise purchasers. The terms are provided in the FDD. The FTC Consumer's Guide to Buying a Franchise identifies aspects of the key provisions on which every potential franchisee should focus:

Franchisor's Background (FDD Item 1)—focuses on how long the franchising company has been in business and the general nature of the competition, licensing requirements, and other contextual information.

Business Background (FDD Item 2)—should provide similar information regarding the management of the franchisor.

Litigation History (FDD Item 3)—provides an important red flag if the franchisor or its key personnel have been involved in litigation, particularly if that litigation highlights problems between the franchisor and its franchisees.

Bankruptcy and Financial Statements (FDD Items 4 and 21)—if the franchisor has poor financials or any history of bankruptcy, the potential business owner should recognize the significant risk of losing the investment to the franchisor's creditors.

Initial and Ongoing Costs (FDD Items 5-7)—much more than the license fee for acquiring the license, these disclosures help explain the true cost of ownership, including leasehold improvements, equipment, expected salary obligations, insurance, deposits, franchise fees, required inventory, signage, advertising, royalties, business promotion expenses, licenses, equipment, leases or rentals. Any business fees not listed should become part of the potential franchisee's questionnaire to the franchisor and to other franchisees.

Supplier, Territory and Customer Restrictions (FDD Items 8 and 12)— these controls over the operation of the franchise establish the rules of the operation of the franchise, including geographic or other limitations on how and where the franchise can operate, whether other franchises (or the franchisor) can compete with the franchise, and whether there are limits on the source of supplies, materials, and goods.

Franchisor's Advertising (FDD Item 11)—outlines one of the key relationships between the franchisor and franchisee regarding the collective advertising system used by the franchise. This is one of the key benefits to being part of a franchise, but the costs can be considerable, particularly since the best locations for established franchises have likely been acquired earlier in the business's operations. The provision should help the franchisee determine how much advertising for which the franchise is responsible and the financial details of the shared advertising program. This is also a topic that should be explored in depth with existing franchisees.

Franchisor's Training (FDD Item 11)—training is another important aspect for many national franchises. Particularly for a new business owner, the national training may be essential for a successful launch of the company.

Renewal, Termination, Transfer and Dispute Resolution (FDD Item 17)—renewal and termination provisions are often among the most contentious between a disgruntled franchisee and the franchisor. If the franchisee has invested time and effort to develop a franchise, the franchisee should be protected from an arbitrary decision by the franchisor to terminate the franchise. At the same time, both parties should have the ability if the obligations under the franchise agreement have not been met. There may also be non-competition provisions incorporated into the termination provisions, limiting the franchisee's ability to remain in business without the benefit of the franchise.

Financial Performance Representations (FDD Item 19)—most franchisors provide sales and earnings information, which they can do provided there is a reasonable factual basis for those claims. These are extremely helpful, but will likely be the most optimistic version of this information that can be provided, so the franchisee should be cautious in reliance on the data.

Franchisee and Franchise System Information (FDD Item 20)—the charts provided enable the potential franchisee to see the turnover of franchises over time. Any significant turnover of franchises or any significant closures should serve as a red flag that the franchises are not sufficiently profitable to manage the ups and downs of the economy.

The FDD and the FTC Guide provide important roadmaps for the first-time franchise buyer. Current and former franchisees are another great resource to learn more about the particular franchise and the general nature of operating franchises. The roadmap provided by the FDD and the FTC Guide serve entrepreneurs well even for starting businesses that do not have franchise agreements because they highlight the operational needs of new and emerging businesses.

C.   Avoiding the Unintended Franchise.

The FTC Franchise Rule is not the only law regulating franchise relationships. Many states also have versions of disclosure laws or laws requiring fair dealing. The states with fair dealing regulations enforce state-based legal obligations on the franchisor that cannot be modified by the contractual terms. The intersection of federal law with the array of state regulations make the issuance of a franchise complex. A company should not develop a franchise system without the assistance of legal and accounting counsel experienced in the field.

1.   *State Law Concerns.*

Because most franchise regulation is designed to protect consumers and less sophisticated businesses from being taken advantage of by much more economically powerful franchisors, the laws place significant restrictions on the franchisor. If a company is not 'really' a franchisor, then these laws create surprising and unintended burdens on otherwise ordinary business transactions.

Despite specific exemptions under the Franchise Rule for trademark licensing, there is a real concern that a trademark license agreement with significant control provisions could fall within the definition of a franchise agreement. For example, in *Girl Scouts of Manitou Council, Inc. v. Girl Scouts of the United States of America Inc.*,[118] the attempt of the Girl Scouts to eliminate local councils was stopped by a federal court because the closure of the territory for the Manitou Council lost its ability to sell Girl Scout Cookies and other merchandise. The Seventh Circuit rejected arguments about free association and nonprofit status, to rely on the terms of the Wisconsin fair dealing law regarding franchises. Under Wisconsin law, the dealership statute forbids a franchisor to "terminate, cancel, fail to renew or substantially change the competitive circumstances of a dealership agreement without good cause."[119]

Different states use different terms to regulate franchise relationships. But the expansive power of the state to limit termination is a real change to a contractual relationship for parties who do not intended to be in a franchise relationship. While only minimal law governs private contracts, bona fide franchise agreements are subject to substantial disclosure requirements and restrictions on parties' business practices.

2.   Trademark Licensor's Steps to Avoid the Label Franchise.

As noted above, a franchise is typically defined by three elements: (1) the right to use another's trademark to offer, sell, or distribute goods or services; (2) significant interest or control over the licensee's business— which in some jurisdictions can be found in a prescribed marketing plan; and (3) payment of a fee such as the $500 fee recited in the FTC Franchise Rule. Under some state laws, the second element is even broader because it is described as a "community of interest" which can encapsulate an even broader version of the control test: "While federal and state jurisdictions that regulate franchises share common definitional

---

[118] 549 F.3d 1079 (7th Cir. 2008).

[119] *Id.* at 1087 (quoting WIS. STAT. § 135.03).

approaches, each jurisdiction has its own definitional subtleties and mix of exclusions and exemptions. What qualifies as a franchise under the federal franchise sales law may not qualify under state law definitions, or vice versa."[120]

If a company owns a trademark and controls how retailers, distributors, and resellers use that trademark, it is likely that the trademark element of the test will be satisfied. Authorized resellers of trademarked goods generally have the right to use another's mark to offer or sell goods in a manner that satisfies the test. Services that include requirements to wear uniforms with brands will also meet that test.

More important, to protect both the legal rights in the trademark and the consumer value in the trademark, it is essential that the trademark owners manage how trademarks are licensed and exploited. Without these protections, the trademark owner risks losing control of the trademark, problems policing the mark from unauthorized use, and loss of consumer goodwill.

At the federal level, the FTC Franchise Rule Compliance Guide provides a series of exclusions and exemptions for trademark licensors to avoid being franchises. Among the most important is the longstanding interpretation that excludes from franchises those "trademark controls designed solely to protect the trademark owner's legal ownership rights in the mark under state or federal trademark laws (such as display of the mark or right of inspection) . . ."[121] There are other exclusions for trademark licensing between the manufacturer of the goods and the trademark holder as well as for the use of trademarks on decorative items, such as soft drink logos sold on tee-shirts and drinkware.

The similarity to the state law will vary by jurisdiction, however, so these exemptions and exclusions have only limited authority. Similarly, the federal rules regarding the structure of the payment may have only limited applicability to the states.

---

[120] Rochelle Spandorf, *Structuring Licenses to Avoid the Inadvertent Franchise*, LANDSLIDE, Mar.–Apr. 2010, at 37, 38.

[121] FED. TRADE COMM'N, *supra* note 115, at 4.

3.   Strategies to Reduce the Risk of an Unintended Franchise.

The laws protecting franchisees are draconian and do not require any intent on the parties to form a franchise. Nonetheless, there are practical steps that may help to avoid the legal challenges if a non-franchise agreement becomes somewhat similar to a franchise. These strategies will not help a traditional franchisor-franchisee relationship avoid the protections of franchise law. In fact, if a franchisor were to try to disclaim a bona fide franchisor relationship using these techniques, it is likely that the strategy will result in additional liability.

First, a traditional trademark licensor should avoid confusing the relationship by steering clear of any marketing plans. Trademark licensors generally do not provide assistance, control, or guidance on the marketing of the trademarked goods and services. This does not preclude the obligation of the trademark holder to police the mark from inappropriate uses (such as using the mark on unrelated products or services), but by avoiding this control, an essential element of the test should be avoided.

Second, when selling trademarked goods to wholesalers and retailers, structure the payments so that it is not for the right to use the mark. For a company selling trademarked goods, the payment for those goods at their wholesale price will not be reconstrued as a franchise payment.

Third, while a court will interpret the relationship based on the applicability of the business relationship to the state and federal laws, a trademark license should explicitly state that no franchise relationship is created under the agreement. This is particularly helpful if the licensee is a sophisticated party. Rather than using a single sentence in the boilerplate provisions of the agreement, this disclaimer of state and federal law should be very explicit, identifying the provisions of the law that the parties understand and are not using.

Fourth, in the provisions regarding the trademark licensor's rights to police the mark, the provision should specifically state that the licensor's control over the use of the mark does not extend to other business operations. The contract may further explain the limitations on the licensor to negate any future claim that there is significant control or a community of interest between the parties.

Fifth, make the grounds for termination, modification, and revision very detailed. Most likely, the risk of a dispute arising will occur when the trademark licensor attempts to end the relationship. If the rights to terminate the relationship are very clear and the contract is closely followed, then it is less likely the terminated party will sue. It is also less likely that the state will step in to invoke a franchise law remedy.

Finally, use an expansive mediation and arbitration clause that covers any and all disputes between the parties to improve the likelihood that the conflict can be resolved without resort to litigation. Mediation allows the parties to arrange efforts to work out the conflict without a third party deciding the outcome. If that process fails, then the arbitration process will allow for a process that is likely more flexible, less expensive, and more responsive to the actual dispute.

These strategies are most effective at making the true relationship between the parties easier to understand so that honest disagreements do not result in such litigation. They will not always work; some lawyers and some business people will use any technical basis for achieving their goals, but most lawyers and business people will not resort to technical tricks to make unfounded claims. They are designed to encourage honesty and integrity in the pursuit of these claims.

D. Becoming a Franchisor.

Although the approach to franchising is generally to protect the naïve new business owner from being overwhelmed by the obligations of a new business, there are considerable benefits to owning and operating a franchise as well. It is a very common, popular, and profitable method for building a national or even global brand.

1. What Makes a Great Franchise.

The same attributes that make a franchise a good investment for the franchisee generally make for the most successful franchisors. Strong financial health, well-recognized trademarks, excellent training and operational support, clearly demarked territories so competition among franchisees is minimized, and other attributes are equally important for both franchisee and franchisor.

The franchisor is highly dependent on the skill and effectiveness of the franchisees, so careful selection and extensive training also protect the franchise from weak stores and poor customer service. In the world of social media, the brand of the entire franchise system can be damaged by a single interaction between a store manager and a customer.

Some business types lend themselves to stronger franchise systems than others. Franchising is necessarily a territorial activity, so restaurants, pre-schools, real estate agencies, and retail outlets that are based on geographic territory are more likely to work well as franchises than online stores that leave each franchisee competing with all other franchisees.

At the same time, a strong national brand has benefits for each of the individual locations. The customer wants the same level of product quality and service at every location. Customers do not want to think about whether the shop they are in is operated as a company store, a franchisor-owned outlet, or a franchise. National—or at least regional—advertising is important to help drive traffic. The ability to supply each franchisee with the needed goods in a timely and cost-effective manner is essential for both the franchisor and the franchisee.

If the franchises operate as retail stores, then typically, higher profit margins on the goods would make those stores more valuable. The public is highly sensitive to price, however, so volume may be much more important than price margins. This is why the franchise industry is dominated by fast-food restaurants. Although these have low margins on the food they sell, they have high volume, great efficiency, and good returns on investment.

Like any business, the nature of the competition and the commoditization matter greatly. If a hot new product is available in a region that cannot be duplicated by the competition, then the franchisor may have a premium opportunity. For example, assume a newly founded electric car company were to begin offering a line of cars and motorcycles. The company is named for Lewis Latimer, the son of African slaves who escaped to Massachusetts. He represents a strong historical example since his electric light bulb filament improvements were sufficiently more effective and less expensive than the design by Edison that they led to the widespread commercial adoption of the light bulb.

The Latimer Automotive Company owns a myriad of patents on its battery and power consumption technology. But it is competing with Toyota, Honda, and Tesla for market share. If the car is a commercial success, franchised dealerships could earn $5,000-$10,000 per vehicle.

There is excitement in the marketplace and a price premium on the Latimer designs. The franchisor can increase its revenue by licensing franchises in the top 200 U.S markets, but if it does, then the pressure to deliver enough cars is magnified considerably. Failure to meet market demands for the cars could put the franchisees out of business, resulting in devastating litigation for the manufacturer. Without the dealerships, however, the manufacturer has a much harder time getting the public an opportunity to see the vehicles and commit to the brand. To balance these concerns, Latimer elects to license only a few dealerships in key territories so that the company can manage the availability of inventory with the power of having retail locations.

2.   Putting Exclusivity and Relevance into the Franchise.

New franchises often begin as extensions of existing businesses that wish to expand. This approach gives the franchisors time to develop the intellectual property essential to build the franchise package. For example, a food truck or restaurant business may grow into a franchise by developing a very popular group of recipes, a pricing strategy that makes the food highly sought-after by the public, a trademark that can be protected nationally, trade dress that makes the look and feel of the business highly iconic, funding to make the transition, and the management team able to lead multiple locations with the training, service, and support needed to run a large-scale enterprise. Each of these elements is critical.

- *Trade Secrets and Know-How*—a very popular group of recipes is a form of trade secret or know-how that makes the franchised company stand apart from the competition. Restaurants are in a highly competitive market and open and close very quickly. Understanding how to make fresh ingredients come alive for repeat customers is the essential know-how of successful restaurants. Other businesses achieve their value proposition in slightly different ways, but the know-how is essential to make the franchisee want to invest in the franchise.

- *Pricing Strategies*—franchise operations are less unique than many other forms of business, so they are generally much more price sensitive than companies reliant on patents as the source of their exclusivity. As a result, the right balance of revenue and volume are essential to the long-term success of a franchisee and the overall franchise system.

- *National Trademark*—many local stores and restaurants use names highly similar to one another. But as a company grows from a single location into a national franchisor, it must invest in a unique name that will not result in trademark disputes as it grows. The cost to establish a trademark is much lower than the cost to rename and rebrand a company once it has lost a lawsuit over the rights to its name.

- *Trade Dress*—trade dress refers to the look and feel of the business, including its color schemes, typefaces, artwork, furniture, decorations, and even architecture. If truly unique, a company can protect itself from being copied by other competitors. More importantly, the consistent trade dress provides a strong signal to the customer that each franchise location operates according to the same playbook as every other franchise and the experience in the store will be consistent from location to location. Some companies, such as coffee shops, can build a brand based on the uniqueness of each location. For certain businesses, this anti-standardization can work as a customer signature, but unless carefully managed, it simply results in customer confusion and dissatisfaction.

- *Invention and Innovation*—the strongest franchises established themselves through game-changing invention and innovation. McDonald's was famous for simplifying the menu, redesigning the steps to make an order, and changing the time it took to order a fast-food meal. The innovation and inventions of the process for making food gave it a significant advantage over the competition that launched the enterprise ahead of all competitors. Retailer franchises that secure exclusive rights to sought-after brands gain market share over similar stores without those brands. While patents provided the strongest version of this separation, process innovations and other inventions can separate the franchise opportunity from the rest of the marketplace.

3.   *Understanding   the   Considerations   Before   Franchising.*

Once a business owner has decided to consider becoming a franchisor, the work has only begun. In addition to the conceptual idea behind creating the franchise system, there are a myriad of details that the franchisor must establish.

The franchisor should spend as much time and effort identifying the ideal franchise locations and terms as was suggested for the franchisee. The success of the franchise is dependent on having each franchise be a financial and professional success. Selecting the locations is very important. One of the benefits to multiple locations is the efficiency of the advertising and marketing. For example, assume the franchise sells unique packing and moving materials. Customers are unlikely to travel more than 30 minutes to get these materials (and most would not go nearly that far). Rather than providing a franchise in a single large metropolitan market like Chicago, Miami, or Dallas, the company would be better off putting the franchises in key traffic areas all within one of those cities. The retailer gets a smaller area of exclusivity, but the advertising dollars go much further.

- *Networking*—the franchisor should spend a great deal of time learning from other franchisors and franchisees. There are many lessons to be learned in the business from both sides of it. Networking, attending national franchise conferences, and learning the best practices will repay the time and effort many times over.

- *Funding*—each of the steps needed to grow from local company to national franchisor adds cost to the business. The upgrades in trademark and trade dress, the legal requirements to prepare the FDD and agreements with the franchisees, the costs of selling the franchises, the expanded advertising budgets, and other expenses associated with a much larger operation will need financing to get started. While this may be a worthwhile investment, the start-up costs are significant and the consequences of meeting those expenses could result in significant liability.

- *Management Team*—the ability to address all the legal, business, and operational needs of a franchise are significantly different than running the business itself. The management team must be able to train and delegate new employees and franchisees to undertake the roles that management previously had. Managing managers is a different experience than managing front-line employees. Developing training materials for multiple locations is different than helping train new employees. Each of these steps require additional skill sets for the key management.

- *Legal and Accounting Team*—the development of a franchise system is complicated because of the intersection of state and federal law. The activity is highly regulated by some states, and there are many pitfalls for those companies that treat the process casually. The legal team must address the rules in each state where the franchisor plans to conduct business and adjust some of the documentation accordingly. A strong team can open the business to many new opportunities, while an inexperienced team could struggle to address these demands.

There are many other considerations in addition to this short list. Nonetheless, this provides a brief checklist for the questions a small business owner must ask before moving from one or two locations into a regional or national franchise system.

4.   *Thinking Like a Franchisee.*

Only after the business owners have studied other franchise operations should they begin to quantify all the operational steps of the potential franchise. Many processes and assumptions will be noticed only after the business owners have spent time asking about similar issues in other companies' operations. The ability to compare and contrast the experience will make the details shine out.

Similarly, the ability to understand the characteristics that will make a successful franchisee will become more apparent after networking with franchise owners and franchise operators. Having the funds needed to acquire the franchise is necessary, but it is not sufficient to mean the potential franchisee will be the right fit. Successful franchisees need a great deal of independence and drive as well as a willingness to follow instructions and work within a system. Capturing that balance will make for a much stronger franchise owner. The franchisees must also be good problem solvers, excellent communicators, and patient trainers. Finally, the franchisee must know the market in which they plan to operate, so they can build business, work with the local community, and establish a presence within their territory.

A potential franchisor, then, should be studying the lessons for the successful franchisee in an effort to deliver the best possible franchise relationship for the franchisees. The success of the franchisor is dependent on the success of the franchisees. The pricing, legal relationship, products and services offered, locations selected, training, operational support, and other details of the relationship must support both the franchisor and the franchisee. Some of these choices will increase the cost for the franchisor, but most will not. Most of these considerations are designed to enable the franchisor to make thoughtful decisions regarding its operations so that both the franchise system and all of its participants can be successful year after year.

Chapter 10. Documenting the Limited Liability Company

Although Chapter 6 provided an overview of a variety of business forms, for most small businesses, the LLC provides the best choice in terms of limiting liability, providing partnership-like tax benefits, and allowing for management provisions that are narrowly tailored to the objectives of the participants.

Subchapter S corporations have the same potential tax structure as the LLC and allow for the shareholders to also be managers, but the corporate laws in most states have many provisions and requirements that business owners find difficult to follow or that are contrary to the goals of their business. Because corporate laws have changed very slowly over time, they are not as relevant or flexible as the LLC alternative.

Each state has its own laws governing LLCs, and different states have different requirements regarding the minimum number of members, the types of businesses which cannot use the LLC form, public notice for formation, and other details. Because the sale of LLC interests is a form of securities sales, it will be important to consult an attorney during the business formation. Despite the variations among the states, this chapter provides a common roadmap for starting the new business venture.

A. Articles of Organization.

The Articles of Organization for an LLC provide very little information for the state or the parties. This simple form is free to download from a website at the Secretary of State's office. The Articles of Organization is a simple document, often one page in length, designed to name the company and identify the agent for service of process within the state.

For example, the California LLC Articles of Organization form contains the following questions:

- the name of the limited liability company,

- the address of the company or its registered agent,

- the date of scheduled dissolution if it is anything less than perpetual,

- an election regarding the management by members or by managers,

- the names of the initial members or managers, and

- a place to attach additional pages.

These provisions, along with the signature of the registered agent and the filing fee, are all that are necessary to form an LLC. Like corporate filings, the name of the LLC cannot be confusing with any existing business within the state, and it cannot be misleading. Different states regulate the use of specific words in names. For example, it is common that the word "bank" cannot be used unless the entity has met state banking requirements.

The filing of the Articles of Organization and the payment of the state filing fees are sufficient to begin the operation of the LLC. In most states, if not all, a written Operating Agreement is not required. Nonetheless, as is evident from the list of topics covered in the Articles of Organization, all the critical rules regarding the operation of the business are missing from the Articles of Organization. Unlike corporations, there are very few legal rules governing the management of the LLC in the absence of the Operating Agreement. As a result, the Operating Agreement is an essential part of the enterprise's plan and should be fully completed prior to the filing of the Articles of Organization.

The choice to attach the Operating Agreement to the Articles of Organization has the effect of publishing the document as a public record, which may be available online for anyone to access. While this is often not a problem, for many business owners, privacy considerations may dictate avoiding publication. The benefit of publication is that any future purchaser of LLC interests is aware of the Operating Agreement and cannot claim ignorance because it is a publicly available agreement.

B.   The Operating Agreement.

1.   *The Role of the Operating Agreement.*

The Operating Agreement serves as the equivalent of an LLC's bylaws, providing the rules for all ownership transfer, voting rights, business activities, management structure, management authority, and any other questions important to the success of the business.

In the absence of an Operating Agreement, state law provides the rules under which the business is conducted. Because LLCs are a much more recent legal development than corporations, there are far greater variations in the laws from state to state and many fewer legal cases explaining these laws. The effect is to make any disputes that arise under LLCs much harder to solve than corporation disputes—but only if there is no Operating Agreement to provide governing rules.

In contrast, a well-drafted Operating Agreement provides the answers to the situations which arise within the LLC, greatly reducing the potential for confusion and dispute to arise as well as discouraging lawsuits among LLC members. This requires that the LLC include provisions regarding personnel, financial, and operational aspects of the enterprise.

Because the laws vary greatly from state to state, and because there is no single right way to draft an LLC, this chapter will describe the key provisions and decisions the entrepreneur must make regarding the Operating Agreement. Printers, websites, and software companies often sell "standardized" Operating Agreements, but like state default laws, these documents should be avoided because they are unlikely to address the situations to be faced by the start-up company. Proper legal advice is essential to maximize opportunity for business success.

2.   *Member and Manager Authority.*

As an introductory explanation, members are the owners of the LLC, while managers have the right, power, and duty to conduct the business of the LLC. "Ownership" in this case means that the member has both an equity interest in the LLC and the authority to vote on limited aspects of the LLC. In the typical LLC, managers are also members, having both the ownership interest and the business authority. However, members can employ managers who have no ownership interests.

The managers work together as the officers and directors of the LLC, depending on the LLC provisions. In the start-up business, the entrepreneur may be the only manager, or there may be more than one manager. In companies based on inventors, the inventor, key investor, and chief business executive may serve as the managers together.

One of the primary benefits of the Operating Agreement is the ability to draft the management clauses to give different managers different powers. In the case of an inventor-based company, for example, the LLC could provide that the inventor is a manager with primary responsibility for product research and development, while the business executive is the manager with primary responsibility for all marketing and financial decisions. The key investor under this hypothetical is a manager but has no duties. The voting rights of the managers could be distributed at 35% to the inventor, 35% to the business executive, and 30% to the investor—meaning that so long as the inventor and business executive are in agreement, the investor would not affect decisions, but if they disagreed, the investor had the voting power to break a tie. Such a model can be used to overcome many business roadblocks and is much more easily achieved using the Operating Agreement of the LLC. Corporate law is not as flexible. In the LLC, the parties may vary the ownership rights and voting rights as needed to meet the expectations of the parties.

The LLC can also specify the extent to which managers can act with individual authority as officers and the extent to which they must act as a group with formal meetings. The need to formalize the operation will be a function of the size of the management team and the degree to which there is disagreement and poor communication among the group.

In a manager-run LLC, members generally vote on only a few key decisions. They can vote to dissolve the LLC, replace the managers if the managers have resigned, amend the Operating Agreement, raise additional capital investments, and admit additional members. Most or all of the operational decisions are left to the managers.

For smaller companies, the managers can be eliminated entirely, and the members can serve as member-managers. Over time, however, ownership is often transferred. Original owners die so that ownership interests transfer by will, managers retire, and a variety of other life-cycle changes occur. As a result, it may be preferable to plan ahead with separate provisions in the LLC for members and managers, even if initially there are no members who are not also managers.

Setting up the decision-making authority of the managers and members is the most crucial aspect of the LLC. This is where the primary disputes are likely to develop, and because of the limits placed on the members, these provisions are most important to the non-manager members.

3.   *Membership Authority to Elect and Remove Managers.*

Another important provision related to authority flows from the ability of the members to remove the managers of the LLC. Ultimately the members, as owners of the company, have the legal right to remove the managers. The LLC will provide rules for exercising this power. Members generally vote based on their membership interests rather than the number of members. This voting is the same as the corporation model of "one share, one vote," designed to protect the ownership interests tied directly to the proportionality of ownership. But unlike subchapter S corporations, the LLC can have different classes of voting units, so the one unit, one vote approach can be adjusted as needed by the parties.

Membership power to elect and remove managers can vary depending on the need for independent managers or membership control. At one extreme, a simple majority vote of the membership interests, excluding the manager's interests, may remove managers without cause. Such a provision would provide strong membership oversight of the managers. More commonly, however, managers draft the LLC to severely limit the members' ability to remove managers. In these Operating Agreements, the members may be required to prove that the managers acted improperly.

Alternatively, the Operating Agreement may require that a high percentage of the members vote in favor of removal. To avoid the tremendous difficulties of establishing appropriate standards and methods of determining when a manager has acted improperly, the super-majority voting provision, which requires a high percentage of membership voting interests to remove the managers, may be more practical.

State law will generally provide the ultimate limit on managers. Regardless of the LLC provisions, a manager who has breached the duty of loyalty to the company by stealing from the company or committing fraud can be terminated by the membership for cause. Theft and fraud are extreme examples of impropriety, however, so the LLC should always provide the members with some ability to remove managers when the conduct can be proven to be improper.

4.   *Variations on Ownership and Authority.*

The flexibility provided by the LLC allows the participants to tailor the LLC to the needs of the participants. One common concern for the start-up business is that the entrepreneur may not have the ability to run or grow the business. The entrepreneur, in contrast, is fearful that venture capitalists or investors will want to use their ownership interests to wrest decision-making from the original team.

The LLC can be drafted to address this tension. One potential solution is to provide certain categories of decisions to remain solely within the authority of the entrepreneur-managers, while other decisions, such as those on financial issues or marketing, are expanded to include the investor-managers.

Another potential solution is to base the decision-making authority on the financial success or failure of the enterprise. If the value of the investor's ownership drops to a certain level or drops a certain percentage from year to year, then the investors are provided additional voting rights. Under a variation of this approach, the investors might receive their full manager voting rights only after a certain amount of time has elapsed. Combinations of these approaches allow flexibility and creativity in addressing the interests and concerns of the participants.

In addition to provisions allocating decision-making authority, it is important to include provisions that allow for mechanisms to approve transactions between the LLC and its members or managers. These transactions must be carefully assessed and approved to avoid self-dealing and arrangements that disadvantage members, but they must be available to the LLC because often the only business opportunities available to a start-up enterprise are from those who have a stake in its success. Often, the Operating Agreement will provide for creation of a special committee of people with no financial stake in the transaction who can serve to review all the information and make a recommendation to accept or reject the transaction.

5.   *Allocation of Profits and Losses.*

The next most important aspect of the LLC's Operating Agreement is its ability to determine how profits and losses are distributed. In some cases, every member is treated precisely the same, while in other situations, the manager-members will receive profit distributions only after the non-manager-members have recouped their investments or achieved some other measure of financial reward.

The LLC excels in its ability to distribute profits in a variety of ways, allowing investors who are taking financial risk to receive profit distributions with priority over those members who received ownership in exchange for intellectual property assets, or who are also receiving salary payments. This is a common practice in many start-up companies, providing an incentive to the investor for assuming the financial risk and the lack of liquidity.

The drafting of these distribution and capital account provisions are quite complex. The goal is to reflect the agreement among the parties regarding the allocation of both profits and losses. To avoid unintended tax consequences, the Operating Agreement provisions must be drafted by an experienced tax attorney, particularly since the tax provisions change quite frequently. Despite the complexity of the drafting, investors are quite attracted by this incentive. Such provisions may make the difference between funding and failure.

6.   *Annual Reporting Requirements and Annual Membership Meetings.*

The Operating Agreement will specify the extent to which the LLC must provide an annual written report to the members, whether such a report will be audited, and the nature of the financial reporting. At a minimum, enough information must be provided to allow the members to complete their personal tax forms. Other financial reporting will generally focus more on balance sheets and income statement information. For example:

> The Manager shall furnish the Members with a balance sheet and an income statement prepared by the Manager as soon as is reasonably practicable after the end of each fiscal year of the Company. The financial statements of the Company need not be audited by independent public accountants; provided, if audited financial statements are so obtained, the Company will forward a copy of such financial statements to each Member.

One of the less attractive aspects of corporations is the common state law requirement of an annual corporate meeting of the shareholders. Given how little the shareholders have to vote on, the expense and distraction of these meetings usually outweighs the benefits of the gathering. Oftentimes, small businesses fail to meet this obligation, putting their business activities at risk of legal attack. In LLCs, members do not automatically get a right to an annual meeting, so the Operating Agreement can specify whether or not such events will take place. For example, rather than having an annual meeting automatically, the Operating Agreement could specify that an annual meeting would be called only if some percentage (*e.g.*, 25%) of the members request such a meeting in writing within 90 days of the scheduled date of the meeting. Since the Operating Agreement should already provide for special meetings called by the managers or by a percentage of the members, creating an optional annual meeting should cause few problems.

7.   *Ownership Transferability.*

Like closely held corporations, there are stringent restrictions on the transferability of LLC membership interests, and these restrictions must be incorporated into the language of the LLC. Most of these restrictions are required by state and federal securities laws. The LLC could be in trouble if a member sold her membership interest to someone who was not qualified to enter into the transaction, or if the information provided during the transaction was insufficient. The business itself could be jeopardized by such a sale, so the Operating Agreement will prohibit that transfer and give the LLC authority to ignore the attempted transfer. For example, most Operating Agreements will include the following language as a legend on the first page of the agreement or as a provision within the agreement, to protect the business from improper transfers:

NO UNITS REPRESENTED BY THIS AGREEMENT HAVE BEEN REGISTERED UNDER THE SECURITIES ACT OF 1933, AS AMENDED (THE "1933 ACT"), OR QUALIFIED UNDER ANY STATE SECURITIES LAW, IN RELIANCE UPON EXEMPTIONS FOR SALES NOT INVOLVING ANY PUBLIC OFFERING AND UPON THE REPRESENTATION THAT SUCH UNITS WILL NOT BE TRANSFERRED UNLESS AN OPINION OF COUNSEL OR OTHER EVIDENCE SATISFACTORY TO THE

MANAGER IS SUPPLIED TO THE EFFECT THAT REGISTRATION IS NOT REQUIRED.

Other ownership transfer restrictions focus on the LLC's interest in having a cohesive group of members. The members are typically a small group that have come together to finance the LLC. There may be reasons to include or exclude potential investors, and the Operating Agreement can use appropriate criteria to assure that the members are beneficial to the LLC because of their creditworthiness, business experience, or other directly relevant criteria.

The ownership restrictions may also provide an initial period in which the purchaser cannot voluntarily offer the membership interest for sale. This creates an unambiguous limitation on the membership of the LLC. This restriction may not be appropriate for entities seeking quick public offerings, but it may be useful for the business with long-term, family-owned enterprise goals.

Finally, managers are commonly assigned the final authority to approve the transfer of membership interests. Since the managers have control of the members' right to transfer ownership, managers could use this power to interfere with member supervision of management. As a result, a conflict of interest exists. This power must be expressly stated in the Operating Agreement so that the members waive any potential conflict of interest. The managers' authority regarding transfers may be a key aspect of protecting the entrepreneur from losing control of the business. As long as investors are made aware of the limitation in advance, the provision should be enforceable when utilized in good faith and for the benefit of the business.

* * *

Sidebar—Ownership of the exclusive interests.

One potential concern regarding the structure of the LLC for the inventor-entrepreneur is the ownership of the intellectual property interest assigned to the LLC. Refusing to transfer the intellectual property ownership is often fatal to the business formation, but inventors are concerned that if the company fails, the ownership of the patents or copyrights will be effectively tied up indefinitely.

Some forms of protection are available through the LLC. One possible approach is to provide that upon dissolution of the LLC, the intellectual property transferred to the LLC by the inventor must be distributed back to the inventor as part of the LLC liquidation. A second approach could provide that the LLC receives an exclusive license to utilize the intellectual property until such time as certain thresholds are met—thresholds based on the passage of time, payments to the inventor, sales by the LLC, funding for the LLC or whatever seems appropriate to the transaction. The LLC and license agreement obligate the inventor to convert the license into a sale at the time the threshold is met. This provides more protection to the investor and avoids possible complications that might arise in a bankruptcy. However, this option also weakens the LLC's ownership of the invention so that investments and bank financing might be harder to obtain.

Closely related to the question of ownership is the question of control. Perhaps the most deep-seated fear of inventors is that the invention is going to be secretly purchased for the purpose of keeping it off the market. For example, the Electric Vehicle Company of the late 19th century acquired the Selden gasoline vehicle patent in an attempt to thwart the electric car's competitors.[122]

Nonetheless, inventors want assurances and contractual guarantees that their inventions will not languish and will not be shelved. For reasonable inventors, provisions that create meaningful reversion rights or other safeguards should be sufficient. If these are insufficient to satisfy the inventor, most investors and business executives will simply stay away.

✳ ✳ ✳

8.   Registration of Member Securities if the Company Goes Public.

For entities formed with a plan to eventually be made available through public offerings, there is sometimes reluctance to use the LLC because the business will need to become a corporation at some point

---

[122] See John Rae, The Electric Vehicle Company: A Monopoly that Missed, STANFORD, http://web.stanford.edu/dept/SUL/library/extra4/sloan/EVonline/rae.htm (last visited July 12, 2018). Associate MIT professor John Rae has published an interesting history on this era in monopolization efforts in the early automotive industry. Similarly, an apocryphal story suggests that the first seat belt patents were purchased by Detroit automakers to keep them off the market. Instead, the first seat belts were patented in 1907, so the lapse of 49 years cannot be explained by efforts to warehouse the lap belt patent. In 1956, Ford finally offered the first U.S. seat belt, beginning the modern move towards passenger safety. The lack of safety features lasted decades after the lapse of the patent.

to allow for a public offering. A simple provision in the LLC will protect this interest and assure members that their ownership interests will transfer into registrable shares of stock at the time of the public offering. Here is an example of appropriate language:

Registration. If at any time the Company or its successor corporation shall of its own volition register any securities on Form S-1 or Form S-18 under the Securities Act, the Company will give at least sixty (60) day's prior written notice of the registration to the Members and provide an exchange rate for the Member Owner Interest into the securities to be registered. Upon request of any Member or Members, the securities of such Member or Members shall be included in the registration, at the cost and expense of the Company; provided, however, that the Company's underwriters do not object to the inclusion of those securities in the registration statement. The Company agrees to use its best efforts, at its expense, to register or qualify the securities covered by the registration statement under other securities or blue sky laws of such jurisdiction as each holder shall reasonably request. In connection with any registration statement to be filed pursuant to this paragraph, the primary responsibility for preparing and filing the registration statement shall be that of the Company, but the Members and shareholders whose shares are being registered shall furnish all information to the Company, in writing, that it reasonably requests to assist in the preparation of the registration statement.

This paragraph provides a basis for members to receive publicly tradable stock once the IPO is successful. Even if the company is unlikely to go public any time soon, it is prudent to put the language in the agreement—just in case.

9. Other Housekeeping and Non-Controversial Provisions of the LLC.

In addition to the more interesting aspects of the LLC, there are many provisions that are necessary to operate the business that will generally go unnoticed by anyone other than the entity's accountant or attorney.

These provisions include the following:

- Name of the LLC

- Address and state of formation

- Address of place of business

- Authority to file additional forms with the state

- Admission of initial Managers and Members

- Purposes of the LLC (which often includes "to conduct any lawful business" but it can be much narrower to control the activities of the Managers)

- Powers, duties, and limitations of Managers

- Powers, duties, and limitations of Members

- Capital contributions and advances

- Right of Managers to also be Members

- Allocation of profits and losses

- Profit or financial distributions by the company

- Withdrawal, removal, and addition of Managers

- Transfers of interest and admission of Members

- Power to amend the Operating Agreement

- Fiscal year, insurance, books, and records

- Indemnification of Managers

- Dissolution and liquidation

- Representations made by Members regarding their investment

- Spousal consent to the Operating Agreement (necessary to restrict the spouse's ownership interest and transfer restrictions)

- Power of attorney for Managers (to act on behalf of Members)

- Acknowledgements by Members of securities laws obligations

While many of the LLC provisions are standardized, each has legal and financial significance. An entrepreneur should never rely on a "standardized" form to draft such a complex legal document, and an investor should never sign such a document without careful scrutiny. Unless the investor has participated in many such transactions, the investor should consult with an attorney before signing such an agreement.

The attorney should ensure that the investor understands the implications of the agreement. This helps both the investor and entrepreneur avoid future misunderstandings. Skipping this step can create far more harm than good, and any problems identified by the lawyer can be resolved far more easily before money has exchanged hands and production has started than months into a complex transaction.

Entrepreneurs and LLC managers should encourage their potential members to seek legal advice. This creates a foundation of full disclosure and trust, rather than speed and ignorance.

C.   Raising Investor Capital.

The sales of LLC membership interests are governed by state and federal securities laws. These are strictly enforced regulations on how an offer to sell the membership interest can be made, the information or disclosures which must be provided to the potential investor, the qualifications of those potential investors, and the high level of accuracy required in the offer.

This section provides an introduction to this highly complex area of law. No entrepreneur should ever offer to sell securities without carefully discussing the transaction with an attorney and providing the necessary documentation for the transaction. However, an understanding of the nature of securities obligations and the strategies to minimize costs associated with raising capital should inform the entrepreneur in how to develop funding. With this information, the enterprise should be able to identify reasonable potential funding sources and eliminate those which are too expensive to pursue.

1.   *Compliance with Federal Securities Laws.*

Regardless of the nature of the transaction, the offer to sell securities is governed by federal law under the Securities Act of 1933, the Securities and Exchange Act of 1934, and the laws of almost every state. Broadly speaking, the federal government regulates the information provided to prospective purchasers of the securities, while the states also have the legal authority to approve or disapprove the value of the transaction.

Compliance with the federal laws can be quite expensive. The details required for a full disclosure, sufficient to allow a company to sell stock to the public, can easily exceed $1 million in legal and accounting fees. The recurring costs for maintaining a company's status of a public company has been suggested to be in excess of $1.5 million.[123] For situations where the securities are being made available to a small number of individuals, there are exemptions from the federal disclosure laws that allow the company offering the securities to provide much less disclosure or avoid any disclosure.

The exemptions reducing or waiving federal disclosure requirements do not waive federal anti-fraud provisions. As a result, even if no disclosure is required, the enterprise offering the securities must make no false statement of material fact or omit any material facts that would make the information disclosed inaccurate.

The company selling securities must be able to assure that it has made no material misstatements in its offer. The only way to meet this standard is to provide all information in writing. This protects the entrepreneur because the written information can be checked for accuracy and verified. It also helps avoid disputes which might arise if the business is less than successful. The written offering document contains the promises and expectations of the parties, so a disgruntled investor cannot claim he received promises that were not in the offering document—particularly if the offering document and the written

---

[123] *See* PWC, Strategy&, *Considering an IPO?: The Costs of Going and Being Public May Surprise You* 4 (2012), *available at*
https://www.strategyand.pwc.com/media/file/Strategyand_Considering-an-IPO.pdf.

agreement state that no oral promises were made, and that the purchaser will rely exclusively on the written materials provided.

2. Insider and Intrastate Exemptions from Federal Disclosure Requirements.

There are a number of different exemptions from federal disclosure requirements depending on the nature of the offering recipients, the geographic scope of the offering, and the amount of money to be raised. Comparing these different choices provides some strategic information to the entrepreneur that can be used to develop a funding strategy. Each potential federal exemption carries restrictions on the sources of funds or size of the offering. As the financial needs of the enterprise become clearer, the particular funding choices narrow.

The insider exemption under Section 4(a)(2). Federal law assumes that a senior leader in an organization has sufficient access to financial and business information that the person does not need the protection of the federal disclosure laws. The federal statute incorporates this exclusion for any transaction not involving public offering. Through court interpretation, offers to corporate leadership necessarily do not involve public offerings. The scope of this exemption, however, may be quite limited. It does not even extend to all employees, only to those employees who are in a sufficiently high position to have access to adequate information on which to base a purchase decision. As a result, the entrepreneur should use it only for the top leadership.

> Section 4(a)(2) of the Securities Act exempts from registration transactions by an issuer not involving any public offering. ...
> To qualify for this exemption, which is sometimes referred to as the "private placement" exemption, the purchasers of the securities must:
>
> - either have enough knowledge and experience in finance and business matters to be "sophisticated investors" (able to evaluate the risks and merits of the investment), or be able to bear the investment's economic risk; and
>
> - have access to the type of information normally provided in a prospectus for a registered securities offering.

In general, public advertising of the offering, and general solicitation of investors, is incompatible with the private placement exemption.

The precise limits of the private placement exemption are not defined by rule. As the number of purchasers increases and their relationship to the company and its management becomes more remote, it is more difficult to show that the offering qualifies for this exemption.[124]

Intrastate offerings. The next exemption applies to offerings that occur exclusively within a state. In this situation, the federal law essentially defers to the state as the primary regulator of the offering. As a result, the state disclosure and filing requirements are more significant for these types of offerings.

To be an intrastate offering, the enterprise must be organized in that particular state and conduct a substantial part of its business there, meaning it must have a significant presence in terms of operations. The securities must be offered, sold, and kept in the state of the offering following the transaction. For small offerings, this may be the easiest way to avoid federal disclosure requirements.

The intrastate offering exemption does not limit the size of the offering or the number of purchasers. A company must determine the residence of each offeree and purchaser. If any of the securities are offered or sold to even one out-of-state person, the exemption may be lost. Without the exemption, the company would be in violation of the Securities Act if the offering does not qualify for another exemption.

Rule 147 is considered a "safe harbor" under Section 3(a)(11), providing objective standards that a company can rely on to meet the requirements of that exemption. Rule 147, as amended, has the following requirements:

- the company must be organized in the state where it offers and sells securities

---

[124] *Private placements - Rule 506(b)*, U.S. SEC. & EXCH. COMM'N, https://www.sec.gov/smallbusiness/exemptofferings/rule506b (last modified Dec. 4, 2017).

- the company must have its "principal place of business" in-state and satisfy at least one "doing business" requirement that demonstrates the in-state nature of the company's business

- offers and sales of securities can only be made to in-state residents or persons who the company reasonably believes are in-state residents and

- the company obtains a written representation from each purchaser providing the residency of that purchaser

Securities purchased in an offering under Rule 147 limit resales to persons residing within the state of the offering for a period of six months from the date of the sale by the issuer to the purchaser. In addition, a company must comply with state securities laws and regulations in the states in which securities are offered or sold.

Rule 147A is an intrastate offering exemption adopted by the Commission in October 2016. Rule 147A is substantially identical to Rule 147 except that Rule 147A:

- allows offers to be accessible to out-of-state residents, so long as sales are only made to in-state residents and

- permits a company to be incorporated or organized out-of-state, so long as the company has its "principal place of business" in-state and satisfies at least one "doing business" requirement that demonstrates the in-state nature of the company's business.[125]

3.   *Regulation D Offerings and Accredited Investors.*

The Regulation D offerings are segregated based on the size of the offering sought. There are separate rules for offerings less than $5 million where the company complies with state securities disclosure laws (Rule 504), provides a general solicitation which is limited to accredited investors (Rule 506(c)), or provides a private placement of securities of any amount of money to an unlimited number of accredited investors

---

[125] *Id.*

and no more than 35 non-accredited investors (Rule 506(b)). These offerings sometimes overlap with other offering exemptions, and the regulations do not require that the offeror select one set of rules or another. This serves as something of a safety net for those offers which fail to meet the technical requirements of one regulation, because they may still have met the exemption of a different regulation or statutory provision.

While there is no registration requirement, companies offering securities under Regulation D must still file a simple Form D to provide certain information publicly, such as the names and addresses of the company's promoters, executive officers, and directors as well as basic details about the offering.

All of these exemptions are available for securities issued by the enterprise, not the purchasers of the enterprise. The entrepreneur cannot sell his own interests using these rules; only the business itself can use these exemptions. As the amount of money increases, the amount of information which must be disclosed also increases.

One of the more important definitions for these offerings are the "accredited investors," because there is no numerical limit on the number of accredited investors under federal law for offerings under Rule 506. Rule 401 provides the following definition for accredited investors of natural persons (as opposed to business entities of various types):

- Any director, executive officer, or general partner of the issuer of the securities being offered or sold, or any director, executive officer, or general partner of a general partner of that issuer;

- Any natural person whose individual net worth, or joint net worth with that person's spouse, at the time of his purchase exceeds $1,000,000, excluding the net value of the person's primary residence;

- Any natural person who had an individual income in excess of $200,000 in each of the two most recent years or joint income with that person's spouse in excess of $300,000 in each of those years and has a reasonable expectation of reaching the same income level in the current year.[126]

Another group of exemptions apply under Reg. D. These have also been expanded to make access to capital easier. Under rule 504, a company may raise up to $5 million in a 12-month period. There is a form that must be filed to comply with this rule, but it a simple disclosure form rather than the much more expansive public disclosure document. In raising the funds that can be raised under this exemption to $5 million from the previous $1 million limit, the SEC also repealed rule 505, which had restricted the securities being sold to accredited investors plus no more than 35 non-accredited but sophisticated investors.

For Rule 506 offerings, an unlimited number of accredited investors can participate. In addition, the issuer can offer up to 35 sophisticated investors as well. The rule provides that "[e]ach purchaser who is not an accredited investor either alone or with his purchaser representative(s) has such knowledge and experience in financial and business matters that he is capable of evaluating the merits and risks of the prospective investment, or the issuer reasonably believes immediately prior to making any sale that such purchaser comes within this description."[127]

Under Rule 506(b), a business can sell to an unlimited number of accredited investors and up to 35 other persons while raising an unlimited amount of money. There are a number of additional restrictions:

- The issuer can make no general solicitation or advertising to market the securities.

- The securities may not be sold to more than 35 non-accredited investors (all non-accredited investors, either alone or with a purchaser representative, must meet the legal

---

[126] Office of Inv'r Educ. & Advocacy, *Accredited Investors*, U.S. SEC. & EXCH. COMM'N, http://www.sec.gov/answers/accred.htm (last modified Nov. 27, 2017).

[127] 17 C.F.R. § 230.506(b)(2)(ii) (West 2017).

standard of having sufficient knowledge and experience in financial and business matters to be capable of evaluating the merits and risks of the prospective investment).

- If non-accredited investors are participating in the offering, the company conducting the offering (i) must give any non-accredited investors disclosure documents that generally contain the same type of information as provided in registered offerings (the company is not required to provide specified disclosure documents to accredited investors, but, if it does provide information to accredited investors, it must also make this information available to the non-accredited investors as well); (ii) must give any non-accredited investors financial statement information specified in Rule 506; and (iii) should be available to answer questions from prospective purchasers who are non-accredited investors.

- The issuer must inform the purchasers in a Rule 506(b) offering receive "restricted securities."[128]

Through the use of a Private Placement Memorandum, the offeror can raise funds by disclosing sufficient information about the business, the use of proceeds of the offer, and the risks associated with the offer. While these disclosures are more detailed than the information provided in the business plan, they are far less complex than public registration documents.

4.   *Regulation A and A+.*

In 2015, the SEC expanded the ability to complete mid-sized public offerings under Regulation A, substantially revising the potential for access to public securities markets for companies. Under the revised Regulation A and A+ rules, companies can issue up to $50,000,000 in a twelve-month period. There are restrictions regarding the issuer's eligibility and requirements for both disclosures and ongoing reporting. As such, this is a category of public offering that is less expensive and

---

[128] Office of Inv'r Educ. & Advocacy, *Private placements - Rule 506(b)*, U.S. SEC. & EXCH. COMM'N,

https://www.sec.gov/smallbusiness/exemptofferings/rule506b (last modified Dec. 4, 2017).

extensive than a full S-1 registration but still takes considerably more time and effort than a private placement offering under Regulation D.

Tier 1 offerings are limited to $20,000,000 while Tier 2 offerings are limited to $50,000,000. Both allow a portion of the issuance to be from affiliated security-holders, enabling the early investors to sell their interests at the time of the issuance. Issuers are able to provide the SEC drafts of the offering documents for non-public review and to solicit offers. Tier 1 offerings, with their more limited disclosure, will typically be required to be filed with the states in those states where the securities are issued.

Tier 2 offerings have more restrictive federal obligations including qualification, but as a result, these should exempt the offeror from needing state qualification. "The offering circular will contain important information such as information about the offering and the securities offered, risks of the investment, use of proceeds, any selling shareholders, the company's business, management, performance, plans and financial statements. Financial statements disclosed in a Tier 2 offering have to be audited by an independent accountant."[129]

One other distinction applies to non-accredited investors. While non-accredited investors are not limited under the Tier 1 offerings, for the Tier 2 offerings, individual investors can invest no more than 10% of the annual incomes or total net worth of the investor and the investor's spouse (exclusive of the primary residence).

If a business intends to issue securities that will be offered and are purchased exclusively within a single state, then the federal law provides exemptions from registration for that offering. To meet this exemption, the issuing organization must operate carefully to meet all the regulatory definitions and assure that all stock will only be issued to residents residing entirely in the same state as the issuing entity. Under rule 147A, there is even some flexibility in this requirement, permitting the company to be organized outside the jurisdiction, such as Delaware, but otherwise still sell stock to the residents of the state where the business primarily operated.

---

[129] *Investor Bulletin: Regulation A*, U.S. SEC. & EXCH. COMM'N (July 8, 2015), https://www.sec.gov/oiea/investor-alerts-bulletins/ib_regulationa.html.

A second federal exemption is available to an offering limited to the senior leadership of the issuing entity. This exemption recognizes that the people receiving the stock are all in a position to know the company well and evaluate it based on their roles and responsibilities. (It is the basis for the example of the so-called founder's exemption discussed previously.) Merely having a senior title is insufficient. Each individual must be personally involved in the operations of the company for this exemption to be available.

5.   Crowd Financing Using Securities and SAFE Investment Products.

When the start-up community clamored for crowdfunding to be added to federal securities exemptions, the SEC was highly reluctant to comply. There were concerns that the lack of sophistication of the purchasers could lead to substantial fraud and the naïveté of the offerors would result in a very high-risk market for investors ill-prepared for such a market. Despite the concerns, Congress bowed to the public pressure, adding securities-based crowdfunding to the 2012 JOBS Act. To distinguish between traditional crowdfunding, which is conducted through donations, or the pre-sale of goods and services, the use of these securities should properly be labeled crowd financing.

The resulting exemption is much less helpful than the changes to Regulation A and Regulation D. Nonetheless, crowd financing does provide an alternative for small offerings. The issuer may raise up to $1.07 million (adjusted annually for inflation) in a twelve-month period, across all crowdfunding platforms. To retain the funds, the issuer must meet the stated minimum goal, but there is ample room for an issuer to set a low minimum and accept funds above that amount, if the structure is fully disclosed. There is also a one-year holding period for the purchasers of the securities, but these securities are also likely not to have significant secondary markets.

The limitations on the investors are much more stringent than other offerings and do not exempt accredited investors. As a result, funding through accredited investors may be better using Regulation D or another exemption. To participate in a crowdfunding securities offering, the issuer must offer the securities through an SEC-registered broker-dealer or an SEC-registered funding portal, which typically charge 5%

commission for the transaction. At the time of this writing, FINRA, the leading national securities association, lists 41 portals that it regulates.

Investors through crowd financing platforms have significant limitations on the amount they can invest during any twelve-month period, covering all offers.

- If either of an investor's annual income or net worth is less than $107,000, then the investor's investment limit is the greater of $2,200 or 5% of the lesser of the investor's annual income or the investor's net worth.

- If both annual income and net worth are equal to or more than $107,000, then the investor's limit is 10% of the lesser of their annual income or net worth.

- During the 12-month period, the aggregate amount of securities sold to an investor through all Regulation Crowdfunding offerings may not exceed $107,000, regardless of the investor's annual income or net worth.

- Spouses are allowed to calculate their net worth and annual income jointly.[130]

There are many other reporting requirements and restrictions on sales. The regulations are not intended to encourage usage, and the impact has been exceedingly modest. In the early period of crowdfunding studied, the level of success was not significant.

In a preliminary report tracking the offering in 2016, only 28 offerings reported success out of 163 unique offerings. Since this was relatively early after the portals began offerings, some of the offerings were still open and had not yet reported success or failure. Of these, the

---

[130] *Regulation Crowdfunding: A Small Entity Compliance Guide for Issuers* (reformatted), U.S. SEC. EXCH. COMM'N,
https://www.sec.gov/info/smallbus/secg/rccomplianceguide-051316.htm (last modified Apr. 5, 2017).

median raised was $53,000 and mean raised was $110,000, suggesting a very few highly valuable issuances among the 28 successful offers.[131]

6.   *Disclosure Documentation Through the Private Placement Memorandum.*

As used for Rule 506 sales of securities, the Private Placement Memorandum (PPM) sets forth the nature of the company, the offering, the use of the funds, the risks associated with the investment, and financial information regarding the transaction. Generally speaking, entrepreneurs do not like the PPM because, unlike the business plan, it is often rather pessimistic. Whereas the risk discussion in the business plan focuses on the risks that the business can anticipate, the PPM is a giant warning label to be affixed to the securities, telling investors as many things as the lawyers can imagine that could ruin the investment.

Like product warning labels, the disclosures are designed to protect the business by showing that the investor had been told of every eventuality. As such, they are very useful documents even when state and federal securities laws do not require the disclosure, because the PPM puts the potential investor on notice in writing. Since smart investors know these risks anyway, the document helps inoculate the relationship for problems that might emerge later.

The table of contents for a PPM may look something like the following:

- Investment Summary

- Special Note Regarding Forward-Looking Statements (warning that any statements regarding the future are speculative and should not be relied upon)

- Use of Proceeds (describing how the funds will be spent)

- Business

- Management

---

[131] Vladimir Ivanov & Anzhela Knyazeva, *U.S. securities-based crowdfunding under Title III of the JOBS Act* 5–6 (Feb. 28, 2017), *available at* https://www.sec.gov/dera/staff-papers/white-papers/RegCF_WhitePaper.pdf.

- Risk Factors

- Conflicts of Interest

- Fiduciary Duty of Management

- Management Compensation

- Federal Tax Aspects

- ERISA Considerations

- Terms of the Placement

- Plan of Distribution

- Allocations and Distributions

- Summary of Certain Provisions of the Company's Limited Liability Company Agreement

- Reports to LLC Members

The most important aspect of the PPM is providing up-to-date, accurate information regarding the business and the risks associated with the business. While the commitment to provide accurate and honest information is one that most entrepreneurs would welcome, the need to keep the information accurate often means regular updating of the information provided to potential investors of any changes in the business information throughout the lifespan of the offering.

Specific provisions set the time frame of the offering, the minimum and maximum amount of money sought during the offering, and how that money will be used. Changes to the PPM must be provided to all the recipients of the PPM, and if significant changes occur before the offering is closed, there may be an obligation to permit those who received older and now inaccurate information to choose to remain or withdraw. This is particularly true if an offer originally made only to accredited investors has been expanded to include sophisticated investors, meaning the PPM would have to be re-drafted to comply with Rule 506.

The PPM is closely linked with the Operating Agreement of the LLC. Each of the Operating Agreement provisions in the LLC limiting the authority of the members' voting rights and financial returns should be described in the PPM. This assures that the members have sufficient notice of all the material facts affecting the value of their potential purchase. Simply attaching the LLC Operating Agreement may not be sufficient, so the PPM serves to summarize the Operating Agreement provisions. Similarly, any provisions that give managers the authority to conduct business and the ability to enter into transactions with the enterprise should be disclosed in the PPM in addition to being authorized in the Operating Agreement.

Although the PPM is a complex legal document, the text regarding the business, the management, and the use of proceeds should begin with the entrepreneur. The lawyers will add to that language and assist with the disclosure of information, but the entrepreneur is responsible for describing the business and the use of the proceeds. The entrepreneur and the senior business leadership are all responsible for the accuracy of any statements made to potential investors on behalf of the enterprise, so they must be diligent in policing the accuracy of the statements.

D.   Founders' Agreements and Other Significant Start-up Agreements.

1.   *Founders' Agreements.*

Founders' agreements are akin to antenuptial agreements among the betrothed. The partners to a new business enterprise join the business with great ambitions, hope for professional bliss, and denial of the many conflicts that may be lurking just below the surface. The founding participants in a business often want to avoid these conflicts by hoping that success will make the problems fade into the background, but invariably, the tensions of the start-up process will exacerbate the tensions and often doom the business.

To avoid this, the parties need a founders' agreement to establish key issues that will help define the terms of the LLC's Operating Agreement and create the roadmap for the emerging company. Founders should not rely on the founders' agreement too long, since it has the legal potential to become a general partnership agreement—even if it expressly disclaims this relationship.

Each founders' agreement will be tailored to the particular transaction, but most will cover the following key items:

Name of Enterprise—although the initial business name does not necessarily have much to do with the business success, it is often the topic most discussed by the parties. The name may not be the tradename later selected. After all, Subway is owned and franchised by Doctor's Associates Inc.

Mission, Vision, and Executive Summary of Business Plan—the founders should be able to commit to the business plan. Since many of the projections and details of the business plan will evolve over time, incorporating an understanding and commitment to the mission, vision, and executive summary should provide enough of a common commitment to the business to align the founders without bogging them down in details.

Roles and Responsibilities of Each Founder—founders are generally personally involved in the start-up process for the company. Frustrations quickly develop among founders if one or another is not carrying the person's weight. Having the duties specified will make this process much easier for the parties to understand and meet their obligations.

Ownership, Contribution, and Vesting—founders tend to get preferential treatment in the ownership of the company (at least until venture capital is raised and the ownership is restructured). These expectations must be spelled out very clearly for each founder, including the obligation to contribute cash, contribute sweat-equity, contribute intellectual property assets, or other contributions, the percentage of founders' interest each will receive, and the schedule to receive that amount. Particularly if sweat equity is being used by a founder to buy in, the vesting of interest should occur over time, as the work is completed.

Exclusivity and Non-Competition Expectations—as founders, there is usually no money yet. Unless all the parties are spending 100% of their time on the business, the founders may still be working at their day jobs. Particularly if there are aspects of the day jobs that may compete with the start-up, the level of exclusivity and the expectations regarding the current positions must be specified.

Interim Authority—although the company is likely not yet formed, the agreement should specify who can act on behalf of the business to be formed and how decision making is likely to be conducted. These provisions will likely become the same or similar as those in the Operating Agreement, once it is complete.

Intellectual Property Contributions and Retention—the intellectual property needed to found the company may predate the company as assets created and owned by individual founders. The contribution must be specified, as mentioned earlier, but there must also be an express understanding about maintaining the intellectual property and owning the rights in the event that the business is not formed, or it fails. These reversionary rights may be very valuable, and an understanding of the consequence of failure is important to all the participants. Like other provisions, these clauses should translate directly into the Operating Agreement, subject to any necessary modification caused by the difference in funding of the formed LLC.

Term and Termination—the founders' agreement should be a relatively short-lived agreement that is incorporated into the LLC. If the founders' agreement lingers too long, the relationship can readily be understood to be a general partnership, which should be avoided if possible. The founders should give themselves a reasonable but short period to either form the LLC or move on. The document should make clear what happens if the LLC is not formed or if the agreement is terminated for any other reasons.

These are not difficult provisions to understand, but they force the founders to address the key concerns regarding the enterprise. The outline should enable the founders to understand the goals and operations of the business. Together with the business plan, the agreement to sign a binding contract on these terms will help solidify the expectations of the participants and help assure that the enterprise is off to a strong start.

2.   *Other Planning Documents.*

As discussed in the chapters on intellectual property, the enterprise should insist on confidentiality agreements before disclosing any information regarding the business that could be part of its unique strategy or trade secrets. The confidentiality agreement (also known as a nondisclosure agreement or NDA) provided in Appendix B provides a template for the agreement. The template serves to protect discussion about the developing start-up with potential employees, investors, and others who need to know the details of the unique assets of the company.

Employment agreements should include confidentiality provisions and grant the business the necessary publicity rights to incorporate the identity information of the founders in the company's materials. This information is used heavily in the business plan, PPM, and other public documents. While it is generally assumed that the company has the right to describe its employees in an accurate manner, the contractual provisions assist in this and allow the enterprise to use this information in marketing materials as well.

License agreements, leases, and any other significant commercial agreements should be available to the potential investors, either as appendices to the business plan and PPM, or upon request. The existence of these agreements and the terms of these agreements may provide a great deal of legitimacy to a start-up company, so they should be made available to educate and support the decisions of the investors.

Part 2. Technology, Change, and the New Entrepreneur

Chapter 11. The Internet, E-Commerce, and the New Sales Paradigm

No text written on entrepreneurship and innovation in the first quarter of the 21st century would be complete without a separate chapter dedicated to the changes wrought by the Internet and the continuing transformation as Internet-enabled devices expand interconnectivity into mobile devices, commercial equipment, and consumer products. In the first edition, the book suggested that "there may be less revolutionary change than first met the eye." As smartphones propel Apple to be the most highly capitalized company in the world and suburban malls begin to fail under the pressure of online shopping, the transformation continues.

The first edition was not entirely wrong. It continued: Despite the boom in dot.com companies at the end of the 20th century and the crash caused by the capital overinvestment, businesses have incorporated the Internet into every aspect of commercial transactions. The question for entrepreneurs is not the existence or impact of the Internet, but the changes it continues to bring and the aspects of business that it leaves generally untouched.

With the second edition of the book, the realization is that there no longer are any businesses untouched by the suite of technologies involving the Internet, RFID chips, wireless connectivity, or other forms of connectedness. These, in turn, have fueled an explosion in data that empowers the fields of data analytics, machine learning, and artificial intelligence. The automobile that was once sold based on its color scheme and tailfins now features self-parking options, self-driving possibilities, and unlimited connectivity. There is no going back to brick and mortar.

A.   The Critical Elements for the Information Enterprise.

Information, like any other type of property, has value to the extent that it meets the standards of relevance to the recipient. Relevance may be based in part on exclusivity, but it is also based on the reliability, resilience, and security of the information. Particularly when the information is data rather than entertainment content, these features will determine the success or failure of the enterprise. Without all three elements of validity—reliability, resilience, and security—the information will be suspect.

1.   *Reliability as Verification of the Information.*

Reliability is a measure of the trustworthiness of the source of information. For scientific information, the academic industry relies upon the peer-review process to review and verify the information before publishing findings. This process of verification assures scientific journal readers that the published information is reliable. Retractions, or other challenges to published data, undermine both the reliability of the data and the entire verification process.

Reliability may come from the independence of the verifying source or from the proximity of the source. Product specification information, for example, will likely be treated as more reliable if it comes directly from the manufacturer, because the likelihood of error is reduced. If there are incentives for the business to be untruthful, then independent review from outside organizations, governmental agencies, or other independent sources are often deemed more reliable.

Reliability is a critical concern on the Internet because there is no publishing process. Anyone can publish a blog, edit Wikipedia, or add other types of content. A reputation system by the vote of readers may help for content that does not have a strong editorial or peer-review process, but such votes will tend to emphasize popularity rather than accuracy. As a result, there will remain a strong need for independently verified information.

* * *

Sidebar—Russian Bots and the Disinformation Crisis.

The growth of social media platforms as the primary medium through which news and information are published and distributed has had a disturbing impact on the ability of the public to use source of information as a surrogate for reliability. Instead of getting news from newspapers, radio, or television, the public increasingly sees those mass-media outlets as feeders for social media content promoted based on popularity rather than reliability. This resulted in a massive public fraud in the U.S. presidential 2016 election.

In February 2017, the FBI brought a wide-ranging criminal indictment against an organization known as the Internet Research Agency, an organization operated by Russian intelligence and funded through Russian government operations. The indictment alleged a campaign by which Russian operatives invested tens of millions of dollars in websites, astroturfing activities, paid advertisements on Facebook and other social media outlets, computer networks, cryptocurrency accounts, and sophisticated data analytics. The $100,000 in Facebook ads that tipped investigators to the attack on U.S. elections was the tip of a very sophisticated cyber-iceberg.

At the heart of the operation was a strategy to flood U.S. social media with false and highly inflammatory information that would drive those who generally held moderate political opinions to more extreme versions of those opinions. Based on the operational approach, the goal was not apparently to shift the electorate to the right or to the left. Instead the goal was to shift the electorate away from the center, and in that effort the goal was accomplished quite effectively. The Internet Research Agency created many versions of ads and posts that were critical of some candidates and laudatory of others. Most of the claims were false and overblown. But using sophisticated data analytics, the Internet Research Agency would use its bots to promote different extreme positions. The public would react, often with revulsion or exasperation that the other party could say such things. And post-by-post, wedge-by-wedge, these false statements would lessen the ability of politically-interested individuals to engage with members of the opposite party.

It cannot be established whether this process changed the outcome of the election or the subsequent difficulty Congress has witnessed in the increasingly divided populace. It may have occurred precisely when the politics were pushing in these directions anyway. But the intentional falsity of the content highlights the inability of the public to discriminate between authentic information, inaccurate but well-intended publications, and intentional lies.

The Internet Research Agency reflects the best example of what happens when reliability fails. Instead of basing reliability on the historical accuracy of a source or a process of content vetting, the public has increasingly relied on social media platforms and the popularity of content to establish reliability. Popularity has no direct relation to accuracy and the result was that highly interesting but intentionally false information was regularly shared by the public and promoted as truthful.

***

2. *Resilience of Source and Durability of Information.*

Resilience of source means the source of the content will remain available for a reasonable period of time. Given the large numbers of websites that are created and forgotten, URLs which become broken links, or web pages that are orphaned as the architecture and content of websites are updated, it seems that much of the information on the Internet is almost ephemeral. In contrast, libraries provide an expensive, but critical, service of adding permanence to knowledge. They achieve this by building and cataloging a collection of materials and serving as conservators of the physical manuscripts on which the content is stored. Libraries and academics require permanence of information. The Internet poses a serious problem for academic libraries and institutions that require permanence rather than transitory existence.

Resilience and reliability are also tied together because information that disappears from the Internet can no longer be verified and is no longer deemed reliable. Business, consumer, and student users of the Internet require at least resilient storage of the content provided through the Internet. Ephemeral sites can do more harm than good, leading readers to unsupportable conclusions and down blind alleys.

Resilience of access has also become a problem. As the public relies increasingly on search as the method for navigation on the Internet, the constant addition of new content, new device modes, and new pages can make it increasingly difficult to return to content. It is still hosted somewhere, but it is buried in a digital haystack that makes it impractical to access.

The need for resilience is at once both a stressor, calling out for innovation and business solutions, as well as a flaw inherent in the communications model of the Internet. Proprietary services like Lexis-Nexis and Westlaw provide comprehensive text-based databases that are expensive to maintain, but they provide the resilience necessary to be used as primary search tools. Industry and law rely very heavily on these databases for published information in electronic form, but being proprietary, they are private subscription systems. Because of their proprietary nature, government agencies and others with public duties towards content dissemination increasingly rely on Internet-based resources. These have the benefit of being open and publicly available. Unfortunately, open systems often have weak infrastructure. This, in turn, increases risks regarding the data resilience and reliability. In consequence, as the volume of data has increased, and the data have increasingly been made publicly available, the security of that infrastructure has weakened.

Because the need for resilience is an obvious stressor, companies and academic institutions should be working to create the resilience necessary to bring an increasing amount of Internet content into the realm of sustainable content. Sadly, little has been accomplished in the decade between book editions. A secondary lesson from this need suggests that enterprises publishing content on the Internet should take great care to provide resilience in their own websites.

3.   *Security of Data and Information.*

Security for data means that the integrity of the information cannot be readily compromised, creating a presumption of accuracy. Whether or not actual breaches in security have occurred, there is an inevitable loss of confidence in data that is at risk of security breakdowns.

Lapses in security can come from hackers, software malfunctions that inaccurately index data, human error, human misconduct, or other external forces that alter, destroy, corrupt or improperly disclose the data. The most common security focus is on hackers, spyware, and attacks on the integrity of information from the outside.

These are significant threats that must be taken seriously. Acts of extortion, in which an attacker encrypts the data of the target and requires payment to return access to the information, are now commonplace. A variation on this extortion occurs when the hacker threatens to release sensitive health, financial, or personal information publicly in an effort to destroy the reputation of the company with the public. Many companies bow to these forms of extortion.

Software, hardware, and other countermeasures should be deployed to protect the integrity of information and data from outside threats. Encryption should be used for any sensitive data. Well-designed data systems should store copies of nearly up-to-date data in a system that cannot be encrypted by the same attack that crippled the primary site. There are a multitude of resources to help a company reduce the risks of an outside attack and to respond efficiently when that breach inevitably occurs.

Security lapses, however, are just as likely to come from within an entity. Security problems may be caused by the owners of the information. This can occur when confidential and proprietary data is stolen or left on unsecured equipment. Security problems may be caused by the businesses which manage data when personnel have access to content that they are not trained to handle and have no reason to access. Security problems may be caused from insufficient attention to equipment, software, and environmental factors.

Enterprises have an obligation to diligently review and assess their procedures, personnel, and equipment to protect the integrity of their information. The failure to do so can compromise the validity of the organization's entire data pool. Since many companies no longer have independent paper records as independent sources of validity, the destruction of the data pool can mean the destruction of the business itself.

4.   *Reach and the Accessibility of Information.*

The greatest change to the information economy comes from the consumer's ability to access any information provided on the Internet. For the content provider, the reach of the enterprise's message is almost limitless. In traditional terms, reach of content was the size of the market that received the corporate message. A ten-second television spot during the Super Bowl maximized the reach by targeting one of the widest mass audiences available.

Theoretically, the Internet makes the reach of all content universal, but this ignores the problem of clutter on the Web. Reach becomes a measure of the population accessing the business's message. Most information can no longer be found unless the consumer already has very specific details about the information sought. Search engines on most corporate websites provide a narrow haystack in which to search for the needles of wisdom, but even these are sometime a struggle. Google and other search engines on the Internet perform an astounding task, returning pages of relevant content. The people searching, however, are unlikely to read past the first few pages of hits, making the vast majority of responses effectively invisible and certainly underutilized.

The portal systems, which were once the media companies' attempt to provide ownership and taxonomy to the Internet, collapsed under the weight of the effort. Creating the Internet's Dewey Decimal System is a daunting task given the amount and variety of available information. The task becomes impossible when the information changes, disappears, or becomes corrupt.

As a result, businesses struggle for reach of their content, even on the Internet. Today's strategy focuses on paid links at the top of the search results, paid advertising on television, websites, blogs, sponsored videos, mobile ads, game inserts, and other media. Companies sponsor all manner of online content in an attempt to drive traffic to the enterprise's message and information.

The need for reach has only increased the need for advertising and marketing. The information revolution has expanded the need for consumers' attention, with no signs of slowing in the near future. New technology in the form of blogs, RSS feeds, podcasts and videocasts, and listservs, expand reach and make content easier for consumers to find. These technologies have the unintended consequence of adding clutter to the Internet, further reducing the efficiency for finding new and useful content on the Web.

Internet media strategies are trying to clear through the clutter. Presently, these are focusing on social networks and affinity groups. Using these technologies, consumers identify self-identified similar individuals to see what choices those people are making. In all their many permutations, these trends allow Internet sites to harness the statistical ability to track website interactions to provide information on social relevance to others using the website.

5.   *Timeliness and Instant Convenience.*

While the use of the Internet suggests instant communication, another aspect of information's value comes from its timeliness. Traditional libraries struggle between operating a physical collection of materials that can be browsed immediately for check-out, in contrast with their vastly larger database of cataloged content which can often be requested for pick-up on a twenty-four hour hold. Ignoring the benefits of browsing the shelves, most patrons still prefer to have the book available on demand rather than after a day's wait.

Timeliness also reflects the marketing competition that once existed between Blockbuster and Netflix, the mail-based video rental store. Blockbuster touted the immediate availability of the titles in each of its physical locations. Netflix competed by emphasizing the depth of its collection and criticizing video rental stores' problems of being out-of-stock on popular titles. Then Netflix flipped the competition by offering its services as an on-demand streaming service. Suddenly the convenience of the video store became an antiquated model. And even though Netflix struggles with access to the top hit movies due to its competition with the Hollywood studios, its instant access business model quickly drove Blockbuster into bankruptcy.

Philip Evans and Thomas Wurster describe this phenomenon as "currency" and point to the high value of instantaneous market quotes for Wall Street market makers.[132] Timeliness is equally important for assembly line materials as it is for information. Just-in-time purchasing strategies emphasize the critical importance of having all materials available at the time they are needed while avoiding the costs of warehousing and managing materials. Blockbuster thought it understood the convenience model for business, but instant is far more powerful than nearby.

Just-in-time strategies are equally important for content as for product materials. Information that comes too late to be used cannot be helpful and delays in gathering information can be costly. Collecting and storing data has warehousing and managing costs just like those costs

---

[132] PHILIP EVANS & THOMAS S. WURSTER, BLOWN TO BITS: HOW THE NEW ECONOMICS OF INFORMATION TRANSFORMS STRATEGY 25 (2000).

associated with physical materials. Consumers rebel at even adding the step of signing in to websites that host relevant content because it slows down the retrieval process.

Effective logic and labeling of navigation flows are another variation of the just-in-time model. Although the longstanding "rule" that public information should be found within three clicks of the home page has been dispelled through empirical studies, there is a high correlation between the willingness of a user to continue clicking and the certainty that the clicks will result in the anticipated goal. While fewer clicks are helpful, clear navigation and understandable structure is even more critical. Consumers expect a nearly instant return on their effort, so poor navigation or unneeded interference will discourage customer engagement.

6.   *Richness and Customization.*

Richness measures the amount of information made available in any communication. The more information delivered, the richer the content. In-home product demonstrations are the richest source of content because they communicate an almost unlimited amount of information to the consumer.

Truly rich communication is more than just in-depth. Richness comes from the ability to customize the information to the needs of each recipient and allow the recipient to directly participate in the information process. All education provides generally rich content, but the seminar class is much richer than the introductory psychology courses often offered to hundreds of college freshmen at a time. In the computer setting, the computer game may provide a much richer experience, because of its interactivity, than even a book.

Most computer games lack substantial informational content, but educational games and simulations still hold tremendous promise. For example, a virtual chemistry course could provide the same textual information as the student's chemistry book, while creating simulations in which the student selects the chemicals, conducts the experiments, and participates in the processes. It is likely that the student's recollection and understanding of the chemistry "game" would be more profound than the reading from the text, and it would better supplement the limited classroom lab time.

One of the best examples of integration of richness, timeliness, and reach is Khan Academy. Initially launched by Salman "Sal" Khan to tutor his extended family in math, Khan Academy transformed from online videos to a learning platform dedicated to the fundamentals of richness, timeliness, and reach. The richness in the content is provided by thousands of volunteers who help make K-12 educational content models covering most subjects taught around the globe. Over thirty different languages are supported. Targeted learning paths are provided for the ACT, SAT, GMAT, LSAT, and other standardized tests.

The site features instant access to thousands of lessons. More importantly, the lessons are not passive lectures or reading assignments. Students can take quizzes and tests, have those tests scored instantly, and receive effective feedback on the skills and knowledge that the student needs to focus on next. This engaged activity integrated with instant feedback maximizes the learning process. In addition, the reach of Khan Academy is worldwide, with many primary languages and content geared to students in North America, Europe, Asia, the Middle East, Africa, and virtually every other part of the globe. Through its integration of richness, timeliness, and reach, Khan Academy embodies the best the Internet has to offer.

7.   *The Information Marketplace.*

Without rich, reliable content, the entrepreneur of the information-based company has nothing to offer. With quality content, the next challenge is to be noticed through the myriad of traditional media, Internet, and other techniques. Many of these information techniques have remained the same, while a few are unique to the information marketplace.

- Television advertising

- Radio advertising

- Print magazine and newspaper advertising

- Print magazine and newspaper content

- E-mail newsletters and advertising

- Website advertising

- Blogs and video channels

- Postings to social media, newsgroups, Usenet sites, community boards, and similar spaces

- Social networking

- Management of multiple websites cross-linking and promoting the content at each site

- Direct mail advertising

- Billboards

- Wireless marketing, broadcasting in hotspot zones

- Sponsorships of websites, charities, and public events

- Sponsorship of mobile devices and geo-cached public locations

In *Blown to Bits*, Evans and Wurster suggest that, historically, the relationship between richness and reach has been a direct, inverse relationship.[133] They explained that published books had a richness to their content, but they did not have the circulation or reach of the television commercial, since books are typically read by thousands while television commercials are viewed by millions. University courses were even richer than the books used to teach, but reached even fewer pupils. Particularly if the cost and medium were held constant, this inverse relationship appeared consistent. The Internet and other low-cost distribution media changed this formula. The disintermediation caused by new technology unlocks the relationship between richness of content and its potential reach.

The ability to expand richness without sacrificing reach affects consumers and businesses in a number of ways. As Internet commerce transformed business, many successful companies focused on process innovation to "replace the middleman." For example, used car purchasing and consumer lending are two industries where the profit margins are rapidly dropping. Realtors have come to rely on sites like Zillow for home pricing and availability information. The number of travel agencies dropped considerably, while those that remain provide

---

[133] *Id.* at 24.

specialized customer service. Companies focusing on process innovation have largely eliminated companies that relied on market inefficiencies for their profits.

The relationship between richness and reach has been largely eliminated on the Internet and through other computer technologies. All content is distributed through the Internet at a cost limited to that of server space and bandwidth. While not zero, the cost is negligible for any particular transaction.

Richness of content is greatly enhanced by the ability of the customer to customize or interact with the content. The success of the door-to-door demonstration was the ability to answer the homeowner's questions rather than the comprehensiveness of the sales pitch. Consumers and researchers want their questions answered more than they want to know that all possible information has been made available. The car demo websites were effective because consumers could customize the cars being offered and focus on the details of interest to the purchaser. They also connected the consumer directly to the dealership and solved the problem of closing the transaction.

Early adopters of product CDs and websites focused on richness without remembering to address issues of reliability, resiliency, and security. Consumers were frustrated by the changing location of information, the changes in the content, and the concerns about security regarding the personal information requested on those websites.

While richness is no longer an obstacle to customer relations, the other aspects of successful content maintenance and customer relations have not been fully resolved. The best Internet and technology companies focus on each of these elements of data, gaining a commercial advantage in the process. Amazon, for example, has excellent data resilience for its customers, so re-orders are easy, returns are understood, and information from other customers is quickly updated. While Walmart is a larger retailer and moving into the online market business, it does not have the same attention to the data ecosystem, and the customer experience suffers as a result.

Beyond these issues, perhaps the greatest challenge to information producers continues to be the cost of reach. No longer tied to richness or resilience, Internet clutter and widespread competition continues to create high costs to attract and retain customers. Content and data producers need to reach the intended audiences to be successful, so the competition focuses initially on the reach of the message, more than its content.

* * *

Sidebar—Information Management for the Successful New Business.

The successful information-based company will pay close attention to each of the six attributes of quality information.

- The reach of the content must be sufficient so the consumer can find the information, whether through traditional advertising or social networking.

- To be rich, the content must provide a wealth of usable, customizable information that addresses the questions likely to be asked by consumers so it will be considered useful.

- To remain valuable, however, the content must be secure, so that the user has no fears that the data has been compromised or that the source of the data will compromise the user's computers.

- To be useful, the information must be timely and accessible at the time the consumer needs to find the information.

- The information must be resilient, available each time the consumer returns to the source of the content.

- The information must be reliable—vetted and accurate so that it can be cited as a source or relied upon.

Taken together, the modern enterprise must constantly struggle to expand its reach to the marketplace with increasingly rich, reliable content. The public has developed high expectations of security and reliability of content and content providers. Entrepreneurs today must enter the market meeting these expectations if they hope to succeed.

* * *

B.   The Small Differences and Large Similarities to the Old Sales Paradigm.

1.   *Universality of Access.*

As a new technology, the public's Internet access increased more rapidly than radio, television, or any form of entertainment medium. Used at home, work, public libraries, and academic institutions, the availability of Internet use is bordering on universal.

By the end of 2017, more than half the world's population had secure access to the Internet. In North America, this number is estimated to be 95% of the population, while Europe has over 85% of the public using the Internet. Asia, which reflects 55% of the world's population, has a 48% Internet saturation rate. Although Africa has the lowest usage rate, it still has over 35% of the population online.[134] Added to these data, the penetration of smartphone use has accelerated mobile Internet access in many areas of the world where traditional computer and other infrastructure has not been developed.

2.   *Removal of Geographic Barriers for Content.*

The ubiquity of the Internet and access to mobile Internet devices have significantly reduced geographic barriers. Transactions supported on the Internet can occur with equal efficiency between people on the same block as between people across the continent, or even around the globe. This elimination of geographic barriers has had an unanticipated impact on regionally-recognized trademarks. The geographic separations, which once kept consumers from being confused as to origin of goods and services, no longer serve to define markets. Jazz clubs, summer camps, restaurants, and other businesses that promote themselves on the Internet have found themselves litigating trademark ownership and priority.

The removal of geographic barriers to the online experience does not translate into the removal of geographic barriers to the shipping of goods. The cost of shipping is based on the speed of delivery, weight, distance, customs, legal barriers, and need for special handling.

---

[134] Statistics compiled at https://www.internetworldstats.com/stats.htm derived from sources including data published by Nielsen Online, by the International Telecommunications Union, by GfK, and by local ICT Regulators.

Information, software, and digital content have close to no distribution expense or time delay, while coal, fresh produce, and grains receive only modest benefit from the improvements in Internet communication.

Over time, larger Internet-based companies have recognized that there are efficiencies by moving distribution centers across the country and the globe based on the logistical issues involved with the creation and storage of goods, movement and customs, and other physical considerations. Companies that can offer the economic efficiency of an online service and the scale to amortize the cost for multiple distribution sites can gain significant process advantages over both traditional brick-and-mortar operations and single-site online competitors.

3.   *Time and Its Influence on Communication.*

The Internet experience has no direct relation to time. New content is constantly appearing. Pages refresh data almost continually. The 24/7 nature of the Internet creates a constant need to feed the content and keep information current. In many ways, Internet updates simply capture the productivity of existing content as it is being created and distributed. Social media, blogs, and podcasts may be the leading edge on new content sources. As the traditional media companies are transitioning to the Internet, media of all forms are beginning to evolve. Even so, the golden age of Internet content has not yet arrived.

On the other hand, real-time communication using the Internet is no different than the telephone. To the extent that the time zones affect the availability of personnel, those time zone differences must be taken into account. Conversely, for the enterprise that wishes to create human support on the Internet, either the staff must increasingly work multiple shifts, or the staff must be distributed among multiple time zones, so that each staff location is time-zone appropriate.

The consequence of this has been the "flattening" of the world. Call centers providing U.S. corporations with live telephone service and call center support have become a key part of Indian business growth. The cost savings to telecommunications allows for this shift in time and space from U.S. workers to Indian workers. In some cases, U.S. companies use the call centers to augment the staff hours available in particular time zones, while in other cases the call centers operate 24 hours daily—all overseas.

This flattening, however, may soon end. An increasingly viable alternative to global call centers is the use of artificial intelligence based chatbots. Though not fully deployed across all industries, these chatbots have moved out of the beta stage and into meaningful operations for some companies.

4.   The Same Consumers, Only Smarter and More Comfortable.

What has changed the least following the introduction of the Web has been the consumer. While the Internet may have changed aspects of consumer behavior, it is critical to remember that the customer has not significantly changed in that time. Admittedly, younger consumers tend to adapt to technology faster than older consumers, and content preferences have changed, but the factors driving customer choice— relevance, cost, convenience, and trust—have remained the same.

Both business customers and individual consumers use the Internet to gain knowledge about products and services. Businesses that once made unsupported promises, relying on the lack of client knowledge, have been forced to stop this practice or adopt other methods to achieve this goal. For example, price guarantees were once a popular sales pitch. Companies that made price guarantees could predict the rather small percentage of consumers who would challenge the price guarantee based on the difficulty of researching and establishing the price differential. With a quick Internet search, however, price disparities are documented in writing. For a time, companies circumvented the price guarantee enforcement by offering goods with unique product numbers. In this way, MegaStore would carry the 3250 model of a product that was labeled 3270 with its competitor, SuperStore. This allowed the store to avoid its price guarantee. Manufacturer websites arm the customer with the comparison information, so the fraudulent nature of this practice has been exposed and largely eliminated.

The value added reseller (VAR)—the specialty retailer that prices products at a premium to allow the retailer to pay for better knowledge and service—has always struggled with the free rider problem. Customers use the reseller for research and then purchase from a lower priced competitor. The Internet has provided another independent source of information. Initially, this was seen as highly damaging to the

VAR, reducing the customer base and supporting the low-service retailer.

In response, the VAR began serving as a source of online information in order to build brand recognition and loyalty. The VAR emphasized post-purchase support, which is unique to those service providers and lacking from most discounters. For the VAR that understands the implications of the Internet business environment, the business model continues to prove successful.

The low-price leader can continue to differentiate itself from the VAR. For these companies, price sensitivity is the primary driving force for their customers. Even price sensitivity, however, is secondary to satisfaction and trust. For example, in the battle of the mass-market retail giants Target and Walmart, Walmart competes using lower prices while Target promotes higher customer satisfaction by emphasizing an experience of cleaner stores, less cluttered aisles, and a more generous return policy. Customers with higher incomes choose to forego Walmart's lower prices for Target's preferred shopping experience. The same remains true in every consumer transaction. Customers put great emphasis on the satisfaction of the experience in choosing where to conduct business. Because of this strategy, a 2013 Target data breach that affected 40 million customers during the holiday shopping period cost Target a 10% loss of customers in the months initially following the breach. Target's customers were paying a premium for high quality and high trust. The breach violated that social contract.

One unanticipated aspect of the Internet has been the rapid growth of reported trustworthiness ratings. Sometimes known as "reputation systems," they are described as "interactive word-of-mouth networks that assist people in making decisions about which users to trust, or to compare their opinions with the opinions expressed by others."[135]

Comparison shopping sites provide customer satisfaction ratings regarding the quality of vendors on the issues of trust—accuracy, delivery, and return policies. These ratings profoundly impact the ability of a company to expand its customer base. Similarly, the postings,

---

[135] V. Kumar, *Researching International Markets: Philosophical and Methodological Issues*, *in* THE SAGE HANDBOOK OF INTERNATIONAL MARKETING 127 (Masaaki Kotabe & Kristiaan Helsen, eds. 2009).

comments, and customer ratings on the sales websites have a similar impact, building consumer confidence regarding particular purchases.

By 2004, 26% of adults had been rating products online, meaning that within the first decade of online commerce, 33 million users had begun to understand the power of the digital word-of-mouth.[136] Customer ratings provide a level of public confidence in highly rated commercial sites. Consequently, low ratings are harmful to the public's impression of the company.

Customer ratings have also served to increase consumer and business comfort in online transactions. Despite concerns of data privacy and risks associated with online theft, the public continues to expand the use of the Internet for consumer and business transactions. As a result, as long as trust is maintained, then the cost savings, convenience, and relevance of the product or service will dictate the consumer's decision to purchase online or through other venues. E-commerce simply has become commerce.

C.   Understanding Disintermediation.

Radio Shack; Blockbuster Video; Toys-R-Us; Bebe; Bon-Ton Stores; The Limited; Maplin (UK); Borders bookstores; Circuit City; HMV (UK); and many more famous brands are gone as a result of competition with Internet retail. Eastman Kodak and Polaroid are vastly smaller licensing entities because they could not adjust to digital photography. What went wrong? These companies could not understand the changing circumstances in their business model, particularly the competition from companies that could provide similar goods at better costs or with greater convenience. In each case, the strategic advantage that kept these companies in business was eliminated by changes in market and consumer behavior triggered by new technologies.

1.   *The Blown to Bits Phenomenon.*

Most of the examples listed above are retail operations or brands closely associated with a retail presence. Retail requires rich interactions

---

[136] Paul Hitlin & Lee Rainie, Pew Internet & American Life Project, *Pew Internet Project Data Memo* (Oct. 2004) http://www.pewinternet.org/files/old-media/Files/Reports/2004/PIP_Datamemo_Reputation.pdf.pdf.

between the seller and the buyer. But new technologies changed how that rich interaction can be delivered.

Perhaps the most important aspect of the unbundling of distribution systems was captured by Philip Evans and Thomas Wurster of the Boston Consulting Group in their October 1997 Harvard Business Review article entitled, *Strategy and the New Economics of Information*[137] and subsequent book *Blown to Bits*.[138] They studied how the Internet's informational flow fundamentally reshaped the relationships between consumers and retailers as well as the relationship among businesses. Though the book may have overstated the transformative power of the Internet, it accurately articulated the nature, if not the scope, of this transformation.

The Blown to Bits phenomenon captures the unbundling of information through its delivery mechanism. Known as disintermediation, the phenomenon can be simplified to mean the removal of the middleman, but it has a more profound impact. Disintermediation is the process of eliminating steps in the communication and response process because of new efficiencies in the process. The original example was the demise of the Encyclopedia Britannica and its World Book annual supplements. All aspiring parents felt compelled to purchase the expensive encyclopedia set with its annual updates to educate their children. Microsoft released Encarta, a CD-based encyclopedia that sold for a fraction of the cost. The efficiency of the CD eliminated the small army of door-to-door encyclopedia salesmen. Then Wikipedia was founded, providing a free service on the Internet that was richer than Encarta, so that product also disappeared. In each case the richness of the content was improved while the reach expanded. CDs were available to millions of people who could not afford an encyclopedia set. Wikipedia reached billions of users through a multiplicity of languages, reliance on only the Internet, and elimination of cost.

A modern example of disintermediation comes from the increased use of RFID tags on goods shipped to retailers. The RFID-tagged

---

[137] Philip B. Evans & Thomas S. Wurster, *Strategy and the New Economics of Information*, HARV. BUS. REV., Sept.–Oct. 1997, at 71.

[138] EVANS & WURSTER, *supra* note 132, at 24–25.

products can be electronically tracked while being shipped. The tags are used to monitor the stocks of retailers. This process, in turn, allows manufacturers to track the precise location of all shipments. The need to warehouse products and better regulate the amount of goods being shipped on a daily basis is minimized. Walmart uses a similar process to control shipments to its distribution centers, resulting in loading-dock-to-loading-dock distribution that eliminates the cost and delay of warehousing products.

Another example of the potential for disintermediation can be found in printing technology. As digital printing is making the ability to produce books one by one, a new book distribution paradigm has developed. Book orders can be processed at the time of the order, the book printed, packaged, and shipped with no warehousing, book overruns, or stocking process. Amazon's CreateSpace provides this service for books, CDs, and DVDs, and has reshaped the nature of publishing retail in the process.

Rather than make information free, disintermediation frees information from any particular medium or delivery mode. As a corollary, the medium previously used to distribute the information may become irrelevant. Although Amazon sells millions of books, CDs, and DVDs, it sells millions more in digital form. Apple's iTunes and stores have done the same.

The corollary of this phenomenon has been captured by Chris Anderson, editor of Wired Magazine. In a series of articles and a book entitled *The Long Tail*, Anderson explains how disintermediation of the publishing world has been replaced with the social networking and direct researching of consumers in the seemingly unlimited selections of retailers like Amazon, Netflix, and iTunes. The theory behind the Long Tail is that niche markets will enable content creators to find their audiences once the hit-making publishers are removed from the business model.

With the disintermediation of entertainment, the critics and marketers will lose control of the public's tastes, to be replaced by affinity groups. Smaller niche markets will be sufficient to support the creation and distribution of content—as well as other products and services— because the direct ability of the public to find goods of interest will allow producers to meet these demands. Boutiques will not be as frequent on the local corner, but boutique sellers will serve global markets, freed from the costs of mediated distribution channels.

There are many examples of artists and authors who are very popular for a small segment of the public. At the same time, however, the unmetered nature of Internet platforms makes it very difficult for the public to find niche artists. It happens, but national marketing campaigns have a very powerful influence on consumer behavior that makes the long tail very thin and wispy.

2.   *The Limits of Disintermediation.*

While disintermediation may unbundle content from any particular medium, it is still not entirely free. Accurate information remains costly to produce and valuable while exclusive. Even when publicly available, it attracts consumers who will pay for access to the information. And even if consumers will not pay for the content directly, advertisers are often willing to pay to have their sales information provided to consumers at the same time.

Information may want to be freed from its medium, but only so that it can be provided to the public in multiple formats and in a manner that maximizes the value of the content rather than the value of the distribution channel. *Blown to Bits* highlighted this aspect of disintermediation using the death of the print encyclopedia. The demise of the print encyclopedia did not devalue the content of these compendiums. Instead, educators today are trying to find new ways to teach students to utilize properly edited, fact-checked sources.

Disintermediation may throw out the distribution system, but it does not eliminate the need for the content or the value of an editorial process. In the rare example of Wikipedia, the global social network of volunteer editors helps assure high quality content. Unfortunately, on many Internet sites, there is not a sufficient fact-checking system to assure that same quality.

Using the lesson of disintermediation, enterprises must treat information separately from the medium in which it is housed. Analysts sometimes refer to the metaphor of the wine and the bottle, suggesting that consumers pay for the bottle rather than the wine. But of course, even when the wine remains in its initial vats, it has value, regardless of the bottle. Consumers pay for the convenience of the bottle separately from the wine, but each has its price.

Information, whether in the form of business data, software, or entertainment content, has a production cost. This overhead must be recouped to allow the business using the data to survive. Even if the cost of distribution is reduced to almost nothing through the Internet, the production costs remain. Disintermediation does not provide meaningful cost savings or alternative business solutions to the production side of information, so it cannot free information. The best that disintermediation can do is to unlink content from particular distribution models and free the content to be linked to multiple models. Further, the lesson of *The Long Tail* reinforces the uncoupling of the content from the medium so that the content can be provided to the market in multiple formats, responsive to the niches as they develop.

3.   *The Newspaper Legacy and the Lesson for the Entrepreneur.*

Disintermediation in the newspaper industry highlights the economic challenges for other industries facing disintermediation. News wires are the ideal content source for the Internet because they update constantly. Stories post the number of minutes since they were last updated. This constant updating has rendered the daily newspaper's timeliness merely quaint, a relic of a bygone era.

Newspapers continue to serve a small part of the information marketplace, but it is an increasingly small part built more around the social custom of reading at the breakfast table rather than relevance and need. Everything available in the newspaper is also available on the Internet. The consumer could have read the content of the paper before it ever hits the front porch, but the remaining subscribers are willing to pay for the physical format of the newspaper. Even without print, if the advertising revenue generated online is greater than the cost of content creation, then the paper remains financially solvent. The online advertising enables the newspaper to maintain a physical paper so long as the subscription revenue exceeds the printing and delivery cost.

Today, most newspapers have limited their free views to generate additional revenue through subscription online access. This further reinforces the value of the content. But they serve a fraction of the audience they once served. Still, for some consumers, high quality, unique content, protected through copyright and made relevant to its target audience because of its timeliness and its relevance to the business community, can retain profit margins in both the traditional economy mode of print delivery and the digital economy.

The transition for entrepreneurs will be much like that of the newspapers. The costs of production must be separated from the costs of distribution, so that distribution can be analyzed separately in each market and segmented for each potential customer base. Each step in the production and distribution process should have its pricing reviewed regularly to assure that the costs are not based on historical practices developed at a time when the distribution costs were much higher.

4.   *The Components of Information Pricing.*

The lesson of the newspaper is that informational content has many different audiences and revenue streams. Newsstand purchasers pay a premium for the ability to purchase the paper only when the headline makes the paper interesting. Print subscribers pay less per paper, but more in the aggregate, with typically different rates for daily, Sunday only, or combination packages. Online paying subscribers pay a much lower amount, but they continue to pay for the service. Free online papers dominate the field, but have not replaced the *Wall Street Journal*, the *New York Times*, and a few other pay subscription newspapers that have unique content not otherwise available. Free online papers earn revenue through advertising, both the ads placed in conjunction with the newspaper content and those ads that the readers click on. Finally, headline aggregator websites link to the newspaper headlines, generating advertising revenue of their own while helping the newspapers extend their reach.

Newspaper content pricing must be designed to separate each market from the price competition of the other markets. If the newsstand price was less than the cost of the subscription, people would drop their subscriptions in place of occasional purchases. Even though the customer is paying primarily for the benefit of home delivery, there are only a few subscribers willing to pay a premium for that service. While the percentage of adults willing to pay for this print subscription may be shrinking, the market still exists.

Even among entirely digital content, the struggle continues. Amazon, Netflix, Google, Redbox, Apple, Pandora, and Spotify provide examples in the marketplace of the effort to distinguish pricing channels for content. "Ownership" of a download has a premium value that is priced much higher than a temporary download provided as part of a subscription service. Streaming of music is essentially free to the consumer, supported only by advertising. To give the consumer the power to edit the streaming content lists, the consumer is expected to subscribe at a premium price. Less than 10% of the public will pay this fee. Google has struggled to sell either its pay music service or its pay video service, a victim of its own free content.

The elements that are typically manipulated by the content retailer include the following:

- *Quality of the content*—the quality comes first for all but the most casual of consumer engagement. This is why the public will ignore the massive amount of free content to purchase (or pirate) commercial content.

- *Timeliness of the content*—new releases can be sold at a premium (whether to paying consumers or in the form of heightened ad rates).

- *Exclusivity as a source of the content*—being the only source for popular content drives audience behavior. HBO's use of *Game of Thrones* and *Westworld* have propped up weak movie purchases while Netflix original series have strengthened its market hold.

- *Depth of content*—the Long Tail is certainly a selling point for consumers who believe they want to find the hard-to-find content, even if the behavior of those consumers suggests they mainly consume the most heavily advertised content.

- *Convenience of access to the content*—user interface (sometimes referred to as UX) dominates the value consumers put on the experience accessing content. This creates a challenge for providers, given the many machines and devices on which a platform must operate, but it will often be the deciding factor for consumer behavior.

- *Interactivity and feedback*—consumers want to be involved with the content, even if it only to like, share, comment, or look up ancillary information. Members of the public believe they can multitask effectively (despite cognitive studies which suggest the contrary) and want to be entertained while they are being entertained, educated, or engaged.

5. The Need for Mediation and Service.

The last lesson of the Internet newspaper example flows from the local newspaper's resilience. The readership remains interested in local issues, whether it is the local police beat, high school sports scores, or human-interest stories. While international, national, and business coverage can be the same in any city, the teacher of the year should come from the local kindergarten, and the gardening tips should be based on the particular climate of the neighborhood.

Like the need for local newspapers, the need for mediation and service has not been displaced by the Internet. To the extent that mediation means customer-centered service, consumers and the business enterprises have never stopped wanting or supporting it. Mediation and service can be provided by both human support and sophisticated technology. Companies are racing after artificial intelligence to expand this service. The value will be measured by customer satisfaction.

Perhaps the company that best exemplifies service-oriented technology is Amazon.com. A leader in online sales, Amazon has undertaken a number of innovations to provide personalized service to its customers. Through four different forms of service mediation, Amazon puts human and technological support into product purchasing. First, through the use of sophisticated data management, a regular user's home page will highlight new products that are the kind often browsed by that patron. Second, when a customer looks at a book title, the computer provides the purchase patterns of similar readers. This advice is often more helpful than the information available from book store clerks—even those knowledgeable in the subject.

Third, Amazon allows readers to post their own recommendations, so human-edited suggestions are available to patrons who prefer the editorial comments of live readers. Fourth, Amazon allows affinity websites from nonprofit organizations to aggregate books and suggestions, driving traffic to the Amazon website, while highlighting the company's charitable nature. The idyllic time spent in the local bookstore, perusing the shelves and receiving sage advice, is closely mimicked through the commercial website on a scale that can serve millions rather than dozens of customers.

Other companies have made considerable efforts to provide real-time support. Pop-up windows allow phone contact or text contact with support personnel. Once provided by live staff, these services are increasingly driven by artificial intelligence software products. As the products improve, the ability to recognize that the service is provided by a machine is becoming much harder for the average consumer, and the consistency of the experience generally results in improved service for the public. Whether provided by humans, machines, or a combination, these service opportunities illustrate that the need for service and mediation of information did not end with the computer, it merely changed forms.

The difference between mediation before and after the rise of the modern technology is this: Before the Internet, the mere access to information required mediation. Today, computers can communicate directly without human oversight. Now, mediation is limited to those instances where the information must be assessed or used by the human—and even this is changing.

For modern businesses, it takes both good customer service and sophisticated data management to be successful. Walmart employees knew that Florida storms would affect their customers' purchasing patterns, but it was careful data analysis that showed how the sale of PopTarts spiked before each hurricane. In retrospect, it seems obvious that a sweet, easy-to-carry breakfast product in a water-proof package would be a popular emergency item. The combination of trend data and store service allowed Walmart to promote PopTarts before the storm. The need for service never ends.

Chapter 12.   Business Models of the Digital Economy

A.   The Real Revolution—Smart Business.

As early as 1993, Harvard Business Review asked "What's So New About the New Economy?"[139] To give the question context, at that time, the Mosaic/Netscape graphical Internet browser responsible for opening the Internet to commercial activity was still in beta and not released officially until 1994. Despite this, the article noted a business environment that was struggling: "Across the corporate landscape, in every industry and at every level, managers are struggling to adapt to unfamiliar circumstances and new strains of competition."[140]

In the magazine issue dedicated to answering the question, Harvard Business Review editor Alan Webber described elements of the shift, including the move from mass production to flexible production, from a manufacturing economy to an information economy, and towards an integration of manufacturing, service, and retail functionality.

What stood at the center of this quarter century of economic transformation has been the role of information throughout the economic lifecycle of all business processes. The 1993 article highlighted the front edge of this transformation that has engulfed the world's economic development.

1.   *Understanding the Customer.*

Deep knowledge of customer behaviors can now be gleaned from easy-to-conduct surveys and correlated with shopping, purchasing, and consumption activities. A/B testing can provide real-time data about what works in the marketplace. Just-in-time tracking of goods using bar codes has been augmented with RFID chips, enabling companies to track products. Similar tracking using blockchain technologies will allow

---

[139] Alan M. Webber, *What's So New About the New Economy?*, HARV. BUS. REV., Jan. 1993, at 24, https://hbr.org/1993/01/whats-so-new-about-the-new-economy. (Author Alan Webber went on to become the cofounding editor of Fast Company.)

[140] *Id.*

the companies to pinpoint an individual item and know its entire history. Customer feedback is now almost standard on most online market platforms. The many-to-many media model assures that companies have access to a tremendous amount of feedback on their products, services, and operations.

As noted in Chapter 5, businesses can purchase or create tracking data to know the attributes of the individuals or businesses that make up the customer base so that communications and services are closely tracked to the specific demographic, geographic, and sociographic needs. Tracking the goods and services provided also gives very important information about how the customers interact with the products and services sold.

The best companies use these data to reconceive the value proposition for their customers. Gillette was once known for giving away its razors and selling its razor blades. This strategy was based on a simple insight into consumers' behavior. The Massachusetts Institute of Technology (MIT) similarly recognized that it could give away its course content because it was in the business of selling accredited academic degrees. It does not matter who attends MIT's online courses, since its business would remain in high demand for those people who needed to earn a degree from the university.

A company can use a variety of technologies—including face-to-face conversations—to gather this information and integrate it into models that will maximize value for the customer. By maximizing the customer's value, the company will have made the product the most relevant to the customer and improved the likelihood of an ongoing business relationship.

In addition, as efficiencies have been unleashed in the marketplace, the public's patience has disappeared. Customers will look at a service line in a fast food restaurant and pull out the app on their phone rather than wait the additional ninety seconds to order in-person. The just-in-time economy of instant downloads, cars-on-demand, and delivery services have reshaped the public's expectations regarding the service they expect. For companies operating in the new economy, staying put means falling quickly behind. Every customer interaction needs to be reassessed to determine if it can be simplified, automated, or improved.

2. Understanding the Process.

Nimble manufacturing and automation has reduced workforces while improving production quality and safety. These upfront investments reduce overall costs of production and enable manufacturers to dramatically increase the ability to manufacture materials and goods to meet present orders without needing to stockpile unsold product. More precise testing assures greater quality control and a much higher level of accuracy in the manufacturing process.

Surprisingly, despite widespread automation and the increased use of robotics, the U.S. manufacturing sector has actually increased in size, adding roughly 1 million jobs in the last decade. The reversal is due, in part, to the reduced costs of automation, which tends to democratize access to automated equipment and processes. 3D printing, laser cutters, and other technologies are also allowing for low-volume, highly specialized manufacturing to occur using efficient technologies. The tools allow for cheaper prototyping which opens one aspect of business and allows for much greater individualization of manufacturing for another category of businesses.

Automated manufacturing reduces waste, improves safety, and adds flexibility to the unit costs of goods manufactured. Automation is particularly beneficial to protect employees from dangerous working conditions. At the same time, use of data analytics can capture information about the manufacturing, distribution, and sales process to further refine the desirability of products and improve their quality, safety, and demand.

3. Understanding the Value of Knowledge.

The modern economy is based on knowledge. The ability to create complex computer code, to manage databases, to provide cybersecurity, and the problem-solving ability to apply these skills in a thoughtful, systematic basis sell at a tremendous premium in today's economy. The best knowledge workers command premium salaries, stock options, and supportive employment environments.

Many of the early employees in Silicon Valley became millionaires as their companies went public, and more than a few have become billionaires. Thousands of others have moved west in hope of the same payday. Universities are rapidly developing programs to keep pace with computer science training, including specialties in areas such as cloud computing, machine learning, computational media, and artificial intelligence. This transformation was highlighted by Peter Drucker in his book, *Post-Capitalist Society*, in which he argued that unlike the prior age in which the traditional factors of production were labor, land, and capital, in the modern economy, knowledge is more than a fourth factor, it is "the only meaningful resource."[141] This is not a Silicon Valley phenomenon. "In fact, whichever traditional industries managed to grow during the past forty-years did so because they restructured themselves around knowledge and information."[142]

Drucker also understood another transformation of the modern economy; namely, the need for loyalty to be earned by the enterprise using something other than a paycheck. The undifferentiated resource of low-skilled labor has been reclassified as human resources to reflect this transformation. Humans with needed skills, knowledge, and social traits command a high premium for their services. The best companies of this century attract those employees through a commitment both to the employee's well-being and to customer's satisfaction. Being part of a company that matters helps attract and retain the highest quality workforce.

The risks of globalization and losses of jobs to low-wage markets is offset by the value of highly skilled workers with excellent problem solving and communication skills. This does not mean that the United States has any particular advantage in the global economy. It merely highlights that all countries across the globe will be competing to train their workforces within the global competitive knowledge economy.

B.   Models of the Information Economy.

There are many companies that have helped define the transformation of the economy and rebuild U.S. leadership after decades in which manufacturing and service leadership were ceded to Japan and other Asian companies. None of these are "great" companies in a moral sense; but each has tremendous reach and positive attributes, while at

---

[141] *Id.* (quoting PETER F. DRUCKER, POST-CAPITALIST SOCIETY 42 (1993)).

[142] PETER F. DRUCKER, POST-CAPITALIST SOCIETY 182 (1993).

the same time they may sometimes engage in practices that raise significant political, social, and moral concerns.

Among the companies discussed is Google, which was founded with the motto and corporate policy: "Don't be evil." By 2015, the company had amended the simple admonition to: "Do the right thing," and in 2018, even that corporate policy has been withdrawn. (Google has also been restructured so that the corporate parent is now called Alphabet.) One can only speculate about the policy debates that surrounded a decision to remove "Don't be evil" and "Do the right thing" from a policy manual. For most entrepreneurs, the better strategy would be to continue to adhere to such policies.

As start-ups, each of these companies strove to make the world a better place, so there may be a different lesson to learn. It may be that any enterprise risks losing its ethical compass if it grows too large— whether business, government, or nonprofit. Alternatively, it may be that the demands on the largest enterprises cannot be met and in failing to meet unreachable expectations, these enterprises cannot help but disappoint. It is safe to say, however, that the public eventually discovers unethical policies, and the long-term consequences of such conduct can be devastating to the enterprise.

With that caveat, these five companies reflect important aspects of the transformation in the economy and technology driving the change. Although selected for their individual roles in the transformation of the information economy, each of these companies is also a leader in machine learning and artificial intelligence. Indicative of their position in the information economy, they are now in an arms race to deliver the most helpful, thoughtful, and functional artificial intelligence engagement service on the market in hopes to leapfrog the others and dominate the coming decades of information intelligence and economic growth.

1. *Microsoft.*

Though often overshadowed by its flashier rivals, Microsoft is more directly responsible for the modern economic revolution than any other company. Founded by Bill Gates and Paul Allen in 1975, the pair started with a focus on BASIC interpreters for the Altair 8800. When the IBM PC was being developed, IBM engineers refused to participate in the hobbyist enterprise. Instead, the engineers turned to outside vendors for operating software. IBM licensed both CP/M and DOS to run on the machine, but Gates allowed DOS to be sold for $75 per machine instead of the much higher price of CP/M. Not surprisingly, customers chose the cheaper operating system and MS-DOS quickly gained dominance on the IBM PC and then on all the other PC machines. Microsoft quickly leveraged its success with the operating system to create Office, a suite of products driven by the word processor Word and the spreadsheet program Excel.

Despite the longstanding public rivalry with Apple, Microsoft developed Apple's spreadsheet programs, invested in Apple, and kept developing products for Apple, which helped Apple survive many bushes with bankruptcy. Microsoft's success has created numerous antitrust challenges, and its efforts to support Apple were due in part to its strategic need to have a viable competitor in the marketplace.

Unlike all other computer companies, Microsoft has remained dominant and profitable throughout the decades, moving more slowly than its competitors in areas such as the Internet and mobile, but relentlessly iterating its products and services to remain competitive in almost every modern computer market. It continues to dominate in computer operating software based on the lead it first took in 1980; dominates in business services; and remains competitive in gaming, artificial intelligence, and many other sectors.

There are lessons that can be learned from Microsoft:

- *Respect your customer*—As an enterprise company, Microsoft understands that a workforce does not want to be disrupted through retraining every time a product is updated. By building on the knowledge and skills developed from the prior products, Microsoft created a highly dedicated customer base. The customers might not be emotionally loyal to Windows, but they are very reluctant to switch to something else. This respect has built relations that have lasted for generations of users.

- *Be relentless with improvement*—Microsoft has not dominated every market it entered and has often started with underperforming products, but its commitment to its installed customer base has been ongoing efforts to achieve success. The initial Windows product was a failure. Not until version 3.1 did the company have its breakthrough moment. The ongoing commitment, however, allowed it to dominate that market as well.

- *Value partnerships and remain relevant*—Microsoft is a pioneer in new technologies and as such it invests in technologies that do not all find a home in the market. For example, although its mobile devices struggled with failures—like the Zune music player—its mobile and phone patents were foundational to the Android operating system and earned the company a royalty on each handset. As a result, Microsoft is nearly as great a beneficiary of the Android market as is Google, its owner. Microsoft's open architecture has enable it to remain more profitable and more relevant in more segments of the computing, entertainment, and communications industries than any other corporation.

2. *Apple.*

Founded by Steve Jobs, Steve Wozniak, and Ronald Wayne in April 1976 to build and sell a hobby computer designed by Wozniak, the combination of Wozniak's engineering genius and Jobs' relentless creativeness destructiveness enabled the small Apple Computer to transform itself into the largest consumer electronics company in the world. There are many lessons that entrepreneurs can learn from Apple's tumultuous history. These are perhaps the four most important of them:

- *Understand your customer*—Using the trademark and brand "Think Different," Apple captured the counter-culture ethos of the early hobbyists and anti-corporate aesthetic to make a product that worked for business while creating a personal statement for its users. Jobs famously rejected asking customers what they wanted, but he deeply valued understanding his customers' emotional responses to the new technologies, color schemes, user designs, wants, and dreams. Apple repeated this with the Apple 2, Mac, iPod, iPhone, and iTunes, dominating generations of innovation.

- *Understand that disruption is inevitable*—Apple embraced the lessons of Clayton Christensen regarding disruptive innovation with a healthy disrespect of entrenched technologies and legacy systems. In part, this was an ethos to "not be Microsoft." Despite this, Apple was a beneficiary of Microsoft's dismantling of IBM's computer industry dominance. As time went on, however, Microsoft, Sun, and other multinational companies became more conservative and protective of their existing products. Jobs exulted in the lesson he taught Xerox, buying access to its prototype mouse and converting a forgotten technology into an essential computer accessory. Apple understood that laptops would replace desktops and that iPhones would replace iPods. By embracing obsolescence, Apple assured itself that as markets faced challengers, the primary challenger would be itself.

- *Understand your role*—Despite its competition with Microsoft, Apple shifted from a technology company into a consumer electronics company early in its history. With this shift came a foundational difference in its product development philosophy. Apple focuses on a very few products that rarely require new technology. Instead, Apple focuses on near perfection regarding the consumer experience with the product. The shape of the window on a Mac received much more attention than that of the window on a Windows machine. The command wheel on the iPod represented one of the best engineering feats in computing history. Apple purchased the hard drives, screens, and batteries from other manufacturers, but it understood how to make the device usable and elegant better than all the other competitors in the field.

- *Leverage your strengths*—Apple's commitment to a closed architecture enabled it to integrate its products and services more tightly than any other company. At its simplest, this meant it had no obligation to invest in supporting hundreds of third-party products, simplifying product development. Equally important, this enabled Apple to leverage the value of one product for another. The iPod worked better than all other music players because most of the functionality was shifted to the iTunes player that was required to make the device work. iTunes was initially available only for Mac computers. The iPod marketing budget came from the Mac computer account, enabling Apple to spend hundreds of millions of dollars more to support the iPod than Sony, Rio, Microsoft, or others could spend. And with the addition of the iTunes store, this leverage extended to marketing campaigns featuring Bob Dylan, Bono, and other famous artists. Sony, for example, had the same suite of machines and music, but it lacked a culture of integrating operating divisions. In the end, the company that invented portable music lost its market to a minor computer company.

These Apple strategies often came with significant internal cost to the Apple management teams and its engineers. Steve Jobs was famously uncharitable and often heartless in his personal dealings. His management failings resulted in his being fired from his own company and destroying the company that followed. The recognition of these institutional strategies should not be equated with a management approach that should never be emulated or even tolerated. That Steve Jobs was successful in his third act should likely be attributed to a management team that worked relentlessly to compensate for his personal limitations and a design team that was the strongest in the 21st century.

3.   *Google.*

If the small computer revolution was dominated by Microsoft and Apple, then the Internet was utterly disrupted by a simple innovation from two Stanford students, Sergey Brin and Larry Page. While still students, they developed a program called "Backrub" to rank web pages based on the number of links a page received rather than through word counts or portal hierarchies. The company received financing to go commercial in 1998 at a time when millions of new web pages were being added to the Internet.

Google is predominantly an advertising company. In exchange for providing the search results, it sells advertising to be placed at the top and sides of the page. Although Google has grown to deliver a multitude of ad-based products and services, it derives virtually all its revenue through the sale of advertising. Even though Google has many strategic initiatives including Nest, Waymo autonomous vehicles, and countless others, less than 4% of revenues and profits are attributable to non-advertising revenue.

Google's business strategy is not particularly new. Broadcast radio and television also used advertising as their revenue model, selling ad space and creating media content to host the ads. Google's business model differs from the traditional media because traditional media created its own content, while Google exploited the content of the many-to-many media stream to provide websites, news feeds, and eventually audio and video content through YouTube, packaging third-party content and selling the associated advertising.

The Google business model is the ultimate in the consumer interface. At its heart, Google is a service, connecting the content provided by the public on the Internet to those same users of the Internet in a highly convenient, easy to use manner paid for through targeted advertising. Google uses all the behavioral advertising techniques described throughout this book to track the behavior of virtually every online citizen, connecting their search, Gmail content, viewership activities, and other movements to create a detailed pattern of behavior, psychology, and conduct.

Google has created the world's largest content repository. It utilized the Google Book Search Project, which scanned the university libraries to make academic research easier, as a way of deepening its language database and improving its translation services. These, in turn, drive ever more traffic to Google's pages and enhance the value of Google's advertising revenue. The Android mobile platform creates a system that provides Google the ability to capture revenue streams for 75% of mobile devices. The intersection of the myriad of Google tools enable it nearly to monopolize online advertising revenue.

There are lessons that can be learned from Google:

- *Understand your customer*—Google may understand its customers better than any company in the world, given the data set it has about its users. While this raises ongoing privacy concerns, Google manages this exceptionally well by exploiting this information primarily to improve its services and by giving those services to the public for free. Free is good; free is welcome; and the public rarely asks who really pays for free.

- *Understand your employees*—Google has set new standards for employment of the creative class, providing food, transportation, telecommuting, recreation, pets, and other amenities to its employees so the stress of a grueling and intensive work environment is offset with fun and comradery. Google also incorporates a policy to allow its employees to direct up to 20% of their time on their own side-projects, empowering the creativity of their employees to express themselves and try new ideas. It also provides generous parental leave and on-site child care. As a result, Google regularly wins Fortune's Best Companies to Work For award.

- *Have a moral business plan*—Google's chief purpose is the laudatory and unattainable goal "to organize the world's information and make it universally accessible and useful." That mission has a purpose well beyond the actual business of selling advertising. The deep moral vision enables employees to care about the corporate success. This is reflected by over 73% of Google's employees who find their jobs to be meaningful, according to PayScale.

Despite growing privacy concerns over the conduct of Google, Facebook, and other companies, Google has avoided the embarrassing disclosures about resale of customer data that have plagued Facebook. Consumers like free services, and Google has done an excellent job at delivering free tools in a way that makes the loss of privacy appear a reasonable tradeoff.

4.   *Amazon.*

Exemplifying and dominating the retail industry is Amazon. Founded as an online bookstore in 1994 by Jeff Bezos, Amazon has grown to be the second largest online retailer, trailing only Alibaba in China. It is also the second largest retailer in the U.S., trailing only Walmart. Amazon built its business model by harnessing the social impact of customer ratings.

Bezos spent a year building Amazon with the stated goal embodying a singular vision: "To be the world's most consumer-centric company, where customers can come to find anything they want to buy online." It chose books over CDs because there were millions available to sell and an incredibly poor concentration among book retailers at the time of Amazon's launch.

Amazon understood that the online version of the best local book store was one in which the salesforce was highly knowledgeable; where other customers provided their own helpful opinions; where the store could offer any book in print (and most out of print books as well); and where the shopping process to select among a million books was simple and intuitive. No bricks-and-mortar bookstore could make all those promises, so Amazon quickly had the market to itself.

Bezos built a company intended to last and grow. For many years, Wall Street criticized Amazon for its very low profitability. Bezos invested revenue in expansion and improvement, first adding music, then seasonal goods, toys, and eventually products in nearly every product segment.

There are lessons that can be learned from Amazon:

- *Engage your customer*—In capturing the best of the local bookstore experience, Amazon integrated customer reviews and ratings more deeply than any other online business. Unlike mere ratings, detailed reviews from verified consumers create a high degree of trust for the other shoppers online. Trust is a virtuous cycle, leading consumers to be willing to take risks on products they might not otherwise purchase because of the trust built up in the platform.

- *Engage your potential competition*—Amazon has created a middle path between the open platforms of Google and Microsoft versus the walled garden offered by Apple, with a marketplace that empowers small businesses and bookstores to use Amazon as the vehicle to reach the public. In creating a global marketplace for smaller vendors, Amazon has also claimed the moral high ground over Walmart, which is often criticized for putting local retailers out of business when it moves into rural areas. Thousands of companies use Amazon for their marketing and fulfillment, allowing them to stay relevant in the fiercely competitive online economy.

- *Have a moral, long-term business vision*—Amazon's vision includes two discrete goals: "to be the world's most consumer-centric company," and to have a catalog so large that "customers can find anything." To have a consumer experience that is better than any other, is often associated with expensive and elite retail. And the size of the virtual catalog is often associated with giant warehouse stores, which are not generally known for their customer experience. Combining these two goals into a single experience has the effect of democratizing service while expanding opportunity. Although the vision may seem simplistic at first, it actually embodies a profound shift in the world of retail. As has been demonstrated, it is the most disruptive vision of any of the listed companies.

- *Reinvest*—Amazon regularly ignored Wall Street's demands for profitability and spent its income on its expansion and improvement. Understanding the benefits of scale and capitalizing on the lead it had as an online retailer, Amazon took a long-term approach to corporate growth that has now paid off very handsomely. Companies that are more beholden to financial leverage do not have the ability to leave the funds in the business for the long game. Those that do, tend to do much better than their competitors.

5.   *Khan Academy.*

The final example is Khan Academy. Sal Khan founded the nonprofit Khan Academy as an outgrowth of the tutoring he was doing for his younger cousins. The tutoring started with phone calls and video chats, but as the demand grew, Khan switched to YouTube videos, opening the lessons to members of the general public. Demand grew, and Khan left his position at a hedge fund to run the business full time. The effort gained the notice of Bill Gates from Microsoft and shortly thereafter, from Google.

Like Wikipedia many other free, nonprofit resources on the Internet, Khan Academy provides videos, tutorials, and lessons across a wide range of subjects. What makes Khan Academy stand out are its mission, strategy, and tactics. The mission is deeply moral, expansive, and aspirational: to provide "a free, world-class education for anyone, anywhere." It moves beyond the informational tools of Wikipedia and YouTube because it creates and hosts thousands of individual lessons that comprise the bulk of the kindergarten through twelfth grade curricula in the United States and for many other countries. It offers its materials in many languages, and provides these services entirely for free, creating a powerful supplement for underfunded school systems across the country and the world.

The organizational basis for the programs emphasize a personalized learning and competency model that is widely praised by cognitive scientists but often difficult to implement in existing school systems. The content becomes a supplement to the classroom experience, allowing students to learn and practice the areas in which they might be falling behind in school. The software also helps motivate the students with badges and a gamified interface.

Finally, through strategic partnerships, Khan Academy has brought content from the Advanced Placement curriculum, the SAT, MCAT, and LSAT to the public for free. These training tools help provide access to those students who do not have the economic resources or geographical opportunities to have the study aids essential for these highly competitive standardized admissions tests.

There are critical lessons from Khan Academy:

- *Just get started*—The early Khan Academy videos were rudimentary. But slick production values have not been shown to improve student learning. Providing the consumer needed lessons was more important than waiting to be funded. Particularly in the nonprofit sector, funding rarely comes before production.

- *Consider the nonprofit model*—Khan Academy receives significant competition from for-profit test preparation companies, and higher education includes both for-profit and nonprofit entities. The mission statement of Khan Academy, Wikipedia, and Google are remarkably similar, and online search is probably not improved through the inclusion of advertising.

- *Have a charitable, long-term purpose*—Effective nonprofits must be attuned to their long-term, moral, or charitable purpose. Like the vision of the for-profit enterprise, the chartable purpose should align the interests of the donors, the volunteers, and the benefactors of the organization. When these groups have inconsistent expectations, the charity tends to struggle with focus and purpose.

- *Build partnerships*—Khan Academy is not the only nonprofit educational enterprise on the Internet, but its relationship with the top national testing agencies guarantees a credibility and relevance that other charities will not have. The greater the relational network, the stronger the nonprofit's influence and credibility.

- *Embrace the power of the Internet*—Khan Academy also stands out from other online nonprofit educational resources by embracing the ability to deliver content on mobile devices, in many languages, with in-depth feedback, and through a predictive model that provides each student the lessons on which he or she needs to work to address the skill deficits diagnosed by the student's practice experience.

Khan Academy is not as far along with artificial intelligence as Microsoft, Apple, Google, and Amazon, but it is testing tools for natural language essay grading; algorithms for expanding how it predicts which lessons should be provided after a student gets feedback on the current modules; and careful research on the effectiveness of the modules on the partner standardized tests. Hopefully studies will also be undertaken to validate the usage for classroom supplements as well. (Though admittedly, that would be beneficial for every book adopted by school districts, and that validation is also missing.)

Khan Academy is not as far along as the for-profit examples, but its potential impact on the future of education is far greater than any of the others. Increasing the math literacy of the public, the language skills, critical thinking skills, and problem-solving abilities will be essential for the information economy workforce. Given the ever-changing needs for the jobs of the future, Khan Academy and its competitors are the most important companies to emerge in the 21st century.

6.   *Honorable Mentions.*

There are many companies that could have been discussed in addition to the five companies listed above. Among the notable mentions are the following:

- Netflix, which has been nearly as disruptive to broadcast and cable as Amazon has been for retail;

- PayPal, which simplified financial services;

- Wikipedia, which provides the most comprehensive and global collection of the world's information in a curated and educational format;

- eBay, which created online auctions;

- Uber and Lyft, which have transformed the personal transportation business through their sharing approach to underutilized vehicles;

- Zillow, which has transitioned from competitor with realtors to an essential service of everyone in residential real estate;

- Airbnb, which leads the market of short-term housing rentals that barely existed before the introduction of the app; or

- Aggregator sites like Travelocity, Priceline, Hotwire, and Hotels.com.

C.   Other Talked About Economies.

There are many other emerging economies, which will likely take center stage for the third edition of this text in the years to come. Some of these are fundamental trends, while others may be passing fads. A few of these are introduced to be sure they are considered in the development of any business model for a start-up or repurposed enterprise.

1.   *Mobile Economy.*

The transition to mobile devices, primarily phones and tablets, has become the vehicle for trillions of dollars in transactions, and yet it accounts for less than 5% of economic volume. Nonetheless, mobile has already become a primary driver for behavioral changes for both consumers and workers. Companies like Uber, games like Ingress and Pokémon Go, traffic flow analysis of people and vehicles, and many other activities are unique to mobile.

According to Anindya Ghose, author of *TAP*,[143] the mobile economy is more than the movement of technology from laptop to computer. Instead, mobile creates a new platform for monetizing customer behavior and addressing societal needs. At its heart, mobile creates a new modality for the consumer and the employee based on the person's location. The device also captures the time of the interaction. Mobility also has some intersection with weather, particularly in increasingly extreme or unexpected weather patterns. Ghose's other categories of mobile data include saliency (another term for relevance), crowdedness, trajectory, social dynamics, and technical mix.

Using data analytics, mobile devices provide tremendous information about the user. The trajectory, for example, provides the owner of the wireless network real-time data of all the people in the shopping mall, airport, or sports arena regarding the physical movement and flow of the individual. Such data is very helpful to improve security, but it can also be used to push discounts to the customer's phone as the person nears the store.

More will be coming. Networked phones may also become versions of audio sensors to track gunshots and explosion audio data, and to track crowd responses, leading to better responses to emergency situations. The variety of input sensors on mobile devices can create tracking and patterning information that goes well beyond the consumer's interaction with particular device functions—providing not only new avenues to data tracking and personal security, but also opening new risks to cyber attacks, physical threats, and intrusions into personal liberty. The cat-and-mouse game of liberty, privacy, and security risks will itself spawn another growth industry.

In the near future, integrated with augmented reality, the phone will provide just-in-time information that offers a much deeper

---

[143] *See generally*, ANINDYA GHOSE, TAP: UNLOCKING THE MOBILE ECONOMY (2017).

understanding about the environment surrounding the user. This can go well beyond commercial advertisements to include history information about public spaces, improved traffic information, and deep contextual information to create learning opportunities at museums, galleries, libraries, and schools. Malls, which are currently struggling to compete with online sales, may utilize the mobile information to redesign the customer experience in the facilities to improve the experience for customers moving through the location, making the walks more engaging and redesigning the store placement and other interactions in a manner that makes the experience more effective for the consumer.

2.   App Stores.

Apps on mobile devices are a discrete marketplace from the mobile devices themselves. The mobile phone experience is moderated primarily through the apps on the phones, which are provided almost exclusively by either the Apple App Store or the Google Play Store. Microsoft has a nascent presence, as do some device retailers like Amazon, and cellular network carriers like Verizon, Sprint, and T-Mobile. Globally there are many additional app stores, particularly in China; and there is an expanding proliferation of app availability in channels outside Apple's and Google's control.

For the consumer, apps tend to fall into three categories. Some apps are software applications paid for by the customer. The app is purchased and available to use on the mobile device without additional charge. At the other pricing extreme, some apps are entirely free to use, and the app publisher generates revenue through advertisements posted within the app. In between these two models is the "freemium" model, in which apps are provided without charge, and then the user can increase the functionality or reduce the advertising content by paying for additional services, add-ons, or in-app services. Game apps frequently use the freemium model by encouraging the purchase of in-game assets to advance in the game. Each of these revenue models works for a variety of applications, and the particular mix of paid, freemium, and advertising-based revenue is nearly independent of industry or functionality.

For the publisher of apps, the policies of the app hosting platform impose significant additional expectations and obligations. Each of the app platforms assesses the proposed apps to assure that the new app meets its contractual obligations. This may include age ratings to assure that adult content is not distributed to minors; privacy disclosures, so that the app's use of the device's other data is disclosed to the user; functionality compliance, so the app meets the technical specifications for the device; and many other requirements. Not surprisingly, the requirements on the Apple platform are much more stringent than on the open platform supported by Android.

As noted by the FTC, "some apps access only the data they need to function; others access data that's not related to the purpose of the app." Slowly, public pressure is building on the app platforms to police the collection of customer data not relevant to the use of the app. Regulations outside of the United States including the European Union's General Data Protection Regulation (GDPR), often prohibit the collection of this data, and the extraterritoriality of these rules is adding to pressure on U.S. companies to self-police and protect the public from these data intrusions.

There is an additional layer of regulation in the U.S. to protect children under thirteen from the collection and use of personal information. These regulations have been updated to protect these minors from manipulation by marketing companies and other targeted, predatory use of their personal data. The FTC is primarily responsible for the creation and enforcement of these policies.

Generally speaking, the revenue-sharing model which has emerged with Apple and Google gives 30% of the app's revenue to the platform host and leaves 70% for the app developer. Whether the 30% overhead is a reasonable fee is highly dependent on the business model of the app developer. But merely qualifying an app for the app store is not a business model or strategic plan. There are well over three million apps in the Apple App Store and nearly as many for Android.

Given the scale of the competition, customers are unlikely to find a new company's app through browsing or searching the app store. Instead, an entrepreneur must understand the cost of acquisition for a new customer and the cost to retain that customer each month or year. This may come from advertising; bundling with other apps and services; partnerships with non-app business activities; nonprofit sponsorships; or other forms of promotion and integration. Without a user acquisition strategy, however, the launch of a new app has the same statistical advantages of funding the company as a trip to Vegas.

3.   *Sharing Economy.*

As often used, the sharing economy is a catch-all for a number of modern, economic interactions that have always existed in society but operate efficiently through the mediation of mobile technology. The idea behind a sharing economy is that underutilized infrastructure can be bartered or time-shared in a manner that allows the owner to recoup costs or earn a profit. The phenomenon is best highlighted by Uber, Lyft, and Airbnb.

For example, many automobiles sit unused most of the day and night. Under the Uber/Lyft model, these cars can be repurposed by enabling their owners to become part-time chauffeurs, using personally owned cars to replace the need for others to buy cars. Overall, car purchasing would go down and efficiency of the auto purchases would increase. Under the model, the preferred operational approach would be to conduct this with self-driving vehicles, so the role of the car owner as chauffer could be eliminated. Other car companies such as Zipcar and Car2Go provide short-use car rental services in urban markets through centrally owned cars while providing the customer the ability to drive a car.

Municipalities also have been doing this for a long time. Public transportation is actually a function of the sharing economy, as are bike rental services in downtown and tourist districts. Whether the focus on the consumer's purchase of the capital equipment makes this a new phenomenon is a debate best left to economists.

Vacation rentals, in the form of timeshares, have also been in the market for decades. They also provide something of a warning story. The rental of timeshares provides significant convenience to travelers who want an experience outside of standard hotel accommodations. But the fractional ownership of timeshares often leaves the owners with an unmarketable asset and unanticipated maintenance expenses. The secondary market for timeshares suggests that most consumer-entrepreneurs lose money, time, and vacation freedom through these systems.

Similarly, the misconduct rife within Uber has cast a shadow over the sharing economy it promoted. The consumer ownership of cars and apartment units avoids the regulations designed to protect the public from unsafe conditions in public accommodation and transportation. Perhaps the inroads of the sharing economy suggest the need for revisions to the regulations on these public accommodations, but the emerging privacy, safety, and security issues surrounding these operations suggests that these opportunities may have unintended consequences.

4. *Gig Economy.*

If the book reflects some skepticism with the sharing economy, it reflects outright contempt for the so-called "gig economy." In the gig economy, creative knowledge-based workers and others have the ability to move from project to project, independent of direct employment supervision, to maximize their remuneration and personal autonomy. In the old economy, those people were known as independent contractors, and they have always played an important role in society. Most commercially successful artists, authors, filmmakers, and entrepreneurs are independent contractors, who work in their own companies and contract with other enterprises when the economics justify the relationship.

But most people in the gig economy do not have the creative output to command the incomes needed to justify nontraditional employment. Instead, these individuals are essentially the piece-meal workforce of the 19th century—paid to drive cars, sew clothes, write software code, sell goods, pick fields, and provide menial labor just as the underpaid immigrant workforce has done in every era of exploitation.

For employers, gig employees are an excellent choice: employees have no rights to continuous employment; no right to minimum wage; no rights to health care contributions; and no right to receive an employer portion of their taxes. At the same time, gig employers have no duties to protect employees from harassment or dangerous working conditions and theoretically no obligation to respect child labor laws. But if the success of the modern economy is dependent on stripping its workers of protections from employer predation, then it is a disheartening return to the world that existed before unions and OSHA regulations. This is not the progress promised by Silicon Valley, and the public must look beyond the rhetoric to the harmful strategies involved in stripping workers of their minimal employment rights.

5.   *Reputation Economy.*

In contrast to the weak promises of the sharing economy and false promises of the gig economy, the reputation economy provides an interesting new approach to public protections. Like the other innovations, the concept is not new, but the use of technology can propel it in powerful ways.

The paradigmatic reputation economy model is found within academic publishing. By using peer review, academic publications assure that the quality of an academic paper has been vetted by peers capable of assessing its claims and methodology in a manner that generally assures high standards of accuracy. Like any system, peer-reviewed academic journals are not perfect. The reputation of an author's university affiliation and past publications may sway the reviewers towards a more positive or more negative impression, and the general competition for academic publications tends to somewhat distort the publication process. These contaminants to an ideal system, however, are found in almost all exchange models, and are likely less problematic in academic publishing than in most fields.

The commercial equivalent of peer reputation are customer reviews found on Amazon, Netflix, Yelp, and many other commercial sites. The consumer ratings and reviews, when aggregated over a sufficiently large population, can provide a highly valid predictor of the quality of goods and services available from vendors. Variations like Rate My Professor attempt to provide similar information to students as consumers of educational services. Stack Exchange and helpfulness reviews tend to push such helpful and usable information to the top of search results. Similarly, as concerns grow over truthfulness in online media, public accuracy and objectivity ratings—rather than popularity ratings—should help push better content through social media platforms.

The reputational economy already has direct economic impact in online transactions. Riders on Lyft rate the quality of the driver, which incentivizes customer service. The satisfaction scores for fulfillment services on Amazon help identify those vendors that provide high quality customer service and meet expectations over those that do not.

Of course, there are dangers within the reputation economy as well. Implicit bias and explicit racism may result in women and minorities finding that these technologies replicate the biases existing in traditional economy. Studies and safeguards should be developed to assure that as these tools are used to supplement objective tools for employment decisions or contracting decisions, these tools are also assessed to assure fairness and accuracy. For example, when deploying software to allow Uber drivers to rate customers and improve customer behavior, there appears to have been no consideration for the risk of driver red-lining to avoid customers in urban neighborhoods or more explicitly discriminating on racial, gender, or other bases. With better planning, however, these challenges can be addressed and the power of the reputation economy to improve quality and service, while highlighting those best examples in the economy, has great potential.

6. Artificial Intelligence, Big Data, Analytics, Informatics, and Machine Learning.

Perhaps the greatest change on the horizon is the emergence of artificial intelligence and its corollary fields of big data, analytics, informatics, and machine learning. While each of these could be treated as a discrete field, they overlap in their economic consequences and can be treated as a common transformation in the future of the economy.

These technologies combine to offer a future world in which many routine processes and services are offered directly by computers, mobile devices, and robots rather than by humans. Currently or in the near future, these technologies will enable chatbots to carry on conversations with millions of consumers simultaneously to help solve most customer service questions, offer students course selection advice, and transact business. The robotic versions will run check-out counters, take restaurant orders, help tailor clothing, and teach in all levels of education. Already, essays submitted on the GRE are partially evaluated by software rather than human readers.

While the technology will be highly disruptive in education and throughout the workforce, projections and past history suggest that the transformation will also create new categories of employment and redirect many positions in new ways. These will require new technologies, training, and strategies. Individual employees may find themselves with great new opportunities or with skill sets made redundant and unwanted.

The disruption is likely to be fierce. The silver lining is that the disruption will create many stressors for which entrepreneurial solutions will be essential.

Chapter 13.   Beyond the New Economy: The Other Technology Revolution

While this book refers to the Internet as perhaps the most significant technological change in the 21st century, computer technology, microbiology, and many other fields have undergone similar explosions in innovation.

A.   The Unlimited Array of Innovation.

A look at the database of the National Inventor's Hall of Fame includes a wide array of inventions and their life-changing impact. These include Seymour Cray's Supercomputer; Gordon Gould's lasers; Bryan B. Molloy's Prozac; Baruch S. Blumberg's vaccine for Hepatitis B; Raymond V. Damadian's magnetic resonance imaging (MRI) scanner; James Fergason's Liquid Crystal Display; Donald B. Keck's Optical Fibers; Willem J. Kolff's Artificial Heart; and Stephanie Louise Kwolek's Kevlar. This is a small illustration of a list that has changed the face of medicine, technology, communications, and society.

Other inventions on the list are more complex but equally critical. Kary Mullis' Polymerase Chain Reactions to amplify DNA sequences have led to a host of medical breakthroughs in science, medicine, and criminology. Robert N. Noyce's Integrated Circuit led to the computer revolution that opened the door for most of the inventions described elsewhere in the book.

The contributions of inventors are not necessarily linear, nor does the attribution tell the whole story. Theodore Harold Maiman is also credited for lasers, and there are many instances of inventors having added different contributions in collaboration or in competition that are necessary until the marketplace can take advantage of the innovation.

B.   On the Drawing Boards.

Today, new work is being developed in areas of nanotechnology, pharmaceuticals, and genetics which may have the same revolutionary impact as that of the inventors discussed above. Others such as Dean Kamen are returning to older theories such as the Stirling engine to provide very low-cost power or purified water. The low-cost device has the potential to transform entire nations. Introducing low-cost water purification into regions that have little access to electricity or clean water has the potential to dramatically reduce disease and transform the quality of life. Work being done with polymers is hoped to be able to release the fuel potential of soybeans and other renewable sources to eliminate our dependence on fossil fuels. Nanotube technology has a similar potential to unleash solar energy and build new materials of unimaginable tensile strength. These technologies and inventions will, in turn, release a new wave of inventions and stressors that will continue to transform industry and potentially improve the quality of life for all humanity.

The commercial space industry is being made real by Elon Musk's SpaceX, Richard Branson's Virgin Galactic, new ventures Ad Astra Rocket Company, Xcor Aerospace, and other smaller enterprises joining stalwarts like Boeing and Airbus to build more efficient reusable vehicles, develop potential for mining operations, and add low-orbit routes to terrestrial travel. Some of the engineering successes are beginning to result in commercially viable initiatives.

1.   *Wearable Tech.*

At a more practical level, there are many products that are in development and soon to be in the marketplace. Among those, wearable tech will mature as the next step in interactivity. A fully successful wearable device will include goggles or glasses to see the images, immersive virtual reality and augmented reality interaction, wireless network capacity, and input devices using a combination of voice, gesture, and text. All of the elements for this device are under development, but the actual product is not yet fully realized.

The first generation of wearable tech has already entered the marketplace. Apple has taken the lead with the Apple Watch, surpassing Fitbit as the largest supplier of mobile, wearable devices. These machines typically rely on the mobile connectivity of the wearer's smartphone, though other manufacturers are incorporating cellular phone functionality directly into the watch, bringing the Dick Tracy moment truly to life.

Companies are working on wearable clothing to provide kinesthetic feedback for directions, improved health monitoring on jewelry, social networking feedback to share information among participants on wearable devices, including augmented reality glasses, and increasingly secure payment platforms built into glasses, jewelry, or other devices.

For medical and disability accommodation, the potential is even greater. Improved monitoring of insulin, heart rate, and other health indicators is already on the market. Devices to assist with mobility, balance, and motor coordination are coming available. These tools have the power to transform the lives of those who need them.

2.   *Biometrics.*

Improved technology, sensors, connectivity, and machine learning have empowered a renaissance in biometric recognition. Systems exist that rely on facial recognition, fingerprint recognition, voice recognition, palm print recognition, ocular print recognition, and even others. The quality of facial recognition from photographs and live images has brought crowd scanning software into reality. Even passport control may be replaced with simple facial recognition scans.

Biometric device improvements have also greatly reduced the ease of spoofing, whereby an imposter can fool a fingerprint reader with false prints, use a photograph to create a false identity, or wear a baseball cap to confound a reader. Improvements in software and hardware are helping with this problem. In the field, the use of multi-factor authentication works even better. Over time, that multi-factor authentication might include a body recognition at one control point and facial recognition later in the funnel.

Biometric scanning has a host of commercial benefits in terms of crowd flow, payment systems, risk management, education, and convenience features. It also has an increasing role in policing and security. There are, of course, significant privacy concerns. These are magnified if the government can use these technologies to track individuals in the public sphere without due process protections. The law has not caught up with the technology and its potential for abuse. Nonetheless, the commercial, educational, and practical potential will drive ongoing development.

The ability to eliminate devices may be the only reason wearable tech might be limited. For example, a biometric-enabled payment system could have the wearer of glasses look into a machine. The reader would identify the person through facial or ocular recognition. Whereas the design for such a system might have once required a card reader or perhaps a digital handshake provided by the customer's glasses to select the correct account and confirm receipts, the biometric reader and pre-selections on an app can now accomplish such tasks.

3.   *Internet of Things.*

Many of the innovations emphasized in the first edition of the book featured Internet-enabled businesses and technologies. Perhaps the greatest trend in the following decade has been the movement off the computer and into networked devices and machines. The Internet of Things (IoT) represents the largest expansion in this direction. IoT devices are those devices that use a variety of technologies to enable the device to be connected through the Internet as an appliance.

The term appliance may be literal for coffee makers, washers, dryers, and refrigerators that use Internet connectivity to enable remote programming, reordering of filters and other replaceable parts, to monitor functionality and order repairs, or serve other functions. More broadly, the term appliance simply separates computers, tablets, and phones that can be used as input and retrieval devices for generalized Internet content with other Internet-connected devices which communicate using the same technologies as the Internet but do not have input and retrieval functions.

Of course, these are general categories. A refrigerator remains a household appliance and remains one even if it is equipped with an Android tablet display in the door. Some IoT devices operate on mobile-to-mobile networks using other protocols. General Motors and Toyota, for example, are developing and implementing technologies that enable cars to communicate directly to create a collision avoidance network.[144]

The most staggering aspect of IoT is scale. IoT's value is predicted to exceed $6 trillion by 2025, including the sale of the machines, the

---

[144] Chris Neiger, *6 Internet of Things Facts to Make Investors Sit Up and Take Notice*, MOTLEY FOOL (June 9, 2018, 1:00PM), https://www.fool.com/investing/2018/06/09/6-internet-of-things-facts-to-make-you-sit-up-and.aspx.

revenue generated through the technology, and the cost savings.[145] Geometric growth in the number of connected devices will result in an expansion of 15 billion devices connected in 2015 to increase to over 200 billion by 2020.[146] Large products like airplanes can include thousands of IoT sensors and devices within a single aircraft. This enables real-time reporting of performance data and safety updates for the wings, engine, and fuel supply. Farm equipment, vehicles, and even an individual's plants and animals are connected through the IoT networks.

Similarly, the RFID product tags can be used for far more than merely tracking the shipment of products and will invariably be incorporated into many other products. For toys, the technology will allow action figures or dolls to recognize each other and interact based on which other dolls are within range. The technology would also be adaptable to security systems, fire alarms, or even gym and bike locks.

The IoT infrastructure has similar cybersecurity concerns as the rest of the information economy, but it has one additional risk factor. Unlike computers that are increasingly pushed to update their software, the public is unlikely to update firmware on its appliances. The risk from a widespread breach into 200 billion devices could be devastating to the critical national infrastructure, banking sector, or other systems. As a result, the rapid expansion of IoT will also require a foundational rethinking of data hygiene in coming years.

C.   From Innovation to Start-Up: Making the Invention Commercial.

In addition to the breakthroughs of the scientists and inventors of the 20th and 21st centuries, entrepreneurs provide another essential role in making the inventions practical. In bringing an invention from the laboratory to the market shelf, there are many decision points and processes which must be crafted to allow the product to succeed. Great chemistry that is too unstable or that requires too high a temperature or energy cost will not result in new commercial products. Dean Kamen's innovation in the Stirling engine is not to build a new invention but

---

[145] *Id.*

[146] *Id.* (*quoting* Intel).

rather to make a 19th century invention practical using 21st century materials and processing.

Innovations in light bulbs, plastics, and food additives come from the invention of new products and the development of new methods of manufacturing. Other than Henry Ford's assembly line, there have been very few individuals recognized for adding to the efficiency of manufacturing, but the savings of even a few cents per unit may mean the difference between a product being viable or not.

Process innovation is one of the key stressors that entrepreneurs can seek to solve. The solutions can often create entire industries. The Internet and its disintermediation of media products does not suggest that processes are disintermediated in other fields. The U.S. Post Office, for example, has lost first class mail to the growth of e-mail. Instead, online retailers have made the U.S. Post Office very successful in the home delivery of retail packages. So long as the inventor's creativity is matched with the entrepreneur's knowledge of how to bring the product to market, opportunities for innovation are available in every field imaginable.

The Internet serves as a great illustration of technological and social change, but it is only one among many of the changes reshaping the world around us. New inventions can be extended into an unlimited range of products and services.

D.   The Business Model Lesson: Exclusivity and Relevance in the New Economy Business Models.

Whether the business is an entirely disintermediated amalgam of outsourced contracts, or a restaurant keeping a single web page available to show the menu and driving directions, each business model must provide relevance to its target audience. If the business's web content is sufficiently relevant, then Google will list it more prominently because others on the Internet are already linking to the website.

The domain name provides one simple form of exclusivity. Every web page has a unique number that allows computers to navigate and find the correct page. Because the numerical system is too difficult for humans to read, Internet designers added domain names to go along with the numbers, and these names must be unique.

In addition to the domain name, the content on each web page is likely to be protected by copyright, which allows the owner of a particular site to stop others from copying the text for their own sites. Links, in contrast, do not copy the text, so they are unlikely to create copyright problems for either party. Using trademarks on the website is another way to further differentiate one site from the next.

Through the domain name, copyrighted text, and use of trademarks, some exclusive material is likely used on every existing website. Together with the relevance of the content, this exclusivity will improve the effectiveness and success of the business.

In fields dominated by strong industry leaders, the entrepreneur will struggle to develop relevance unless the business model resolves significant stressors and generates great relevance. In contrast, patents may even be available for new business models that solve a problem in a truly new, useful, and nonobvious fashion. Patents on processes can extend even to business methods, so the development of these new websites can occasionally lead to patent-protected business models.

The business embracing new technologies must identify each opportunity for exclusivity in the business plan. The enterprise must look closely at the market to determine the relevance of the new product or service and how that product or service ties into the business model. The entrepreneur must identify the problem and solve it in a manner that appeals to consumers. Finally, the entrepreneur must ensure that the solution adopted is one that is difficult for competitors to replicate. If the entrepreneur meets those four goals, then the business will be successful. Without these steps, the business will be short-lived.

What the innovation companies truly have in common is the rapidity of change. Stressors are being introduced as fast as the solutions to the previous problems. The lack of reflection time creates new opportunities to solve the next wave of changes and system inefficiencies. Entrepreneurs should be prepared to step into this gap to be successful.

Chapter 14. Exclusivity, Relevance, and Innovation: Industry Examples and Approaches

This chapter provides a series of examples which highlight how intellectual property assets have enhanced relevance and created exclusivity in a wide array of well-known businesses. In each case, the illustration tends to oversimplify the many decisions, large and small, which have allowed those companies to be successful and competitive. The illustration of McDonald's, for example, focuses on the use of trademarks to build its awareness and business. This is at the heart of McDonald's success, but McDonald's is also one of the great process innovators in retail product distribution. Every aspect of McDonald's process is analyzed for maximum efficiency and cost-effectiveness. The lead it gets from its trademarks provides only a slim margin with which it can move ahead in an extremely competitive field. That slim edge, however, is enough to keep McDonald's the best business model in fast-food.

A. Exclusivity in Retail: the Restaurant Business.

Since the restaurant business is a highly competitive sector with high risks, a large failure rate, and a product difficult to customize, it seems appropriate that restaurants provide the leading examples in how best to apply trademarks, copyrights, trade secrets, and publicity rights to create relevance and exclusivity as a way to gain market share and financial success.

1. Trademarks and Mascots.

As the introduction to the chapter suggests, McDonald's stands apart as a trailblazer in a number of methods related to trademarks and brands, as well as in process innovation and entrepreneurship. It remains number one in sales volume as well. Starbucks is number two, followed by Subway, KFC, Domino's Pizza, Burger King, and Pizza Hut.

McDonald's created a unique brand by creating iconic images to get its stores noticed. The Golden Arches began as an architectural feature of the stores in the early 1960s. These were neon yellow parabolic arches on each end of the building. In 1968, the company translated the parabolas into an "M" indicative of the company name and adopted the modern graphical design as its trademark. The symbol has become so internationally famous that the only McDonald's arches logo not colored yellow is on the store in Sedona, Arizona. The zoning rules for the city did not permit the bright yellow to interfere with town aesthetic. Instead, the store selected a turquoise color, which has turned the small McDonald's franchise into a tourist destination. Another story often tied to the Golden Arches was the analysis by design consultant Louis Cheskin, who saw in the Golden Arches a graphic evocation of breasts. The rounded parabolic shape of the "M" went from an alphabetical allusion to a Freudian appeal regarding the primal need to be nurtured. Whether the logo has this effect has not been tested.

McDonald's also created a family-friendly clown trademark. The first Ronald McDonald appeared in 1963, played by a young Willard Scott. As a pioneer of character-based marketing, the Ronald McDonald character has kept McDonald's restaurants more visible in advertising than any of its rivals. The character was never allowed to stagnate, but received constant but small modifications to keep him and his companions up to date with the current animation and style. McDonald's ran into legal problems when it redesigned the McDonaldland characters to emulate the popular H.R. Pufnstuf television show.[147] Despite losing a copyright dispute, McDonald's succeeded in keeping the characters fresh and current. In recent years, however, advertising directed to children has been disliked by the public, and Ronald's role in television advertising has largely dropped.

In addition to the athletic Ronald, McDonald's seeks to segment its market with its "I'm lovin' it" marketing campaign, which emphasizes the happening lifestyle of its consumers and the centrality of McDonald's food in their lifestyle. These campaigns highlight the importance of making one's product relevant to the target audience. Every consumer in America knows McDonald's. The goal of the new campaign is to make consumers view eating at McDonald's as part of their lifestyle choice.

Like the "You deserve a break today" campaign of an earlier generation, the focus of the jingle and the imagery emphasizes the

---

[147] *See* Sid & Marty Kofft Television Prod., Inc. v. McDonald's Corp., 562 F.2d 1157 (9th Cir. 1977).

relevance of the McDonald's fast-food experience to the consumer. Each ad focuses directly on the need for relevance.

2. Patents and Technology in Food Distribution.

Again, McDonald's serves as part of the history lesson on leveraging exclusivity. In this case, the leverage was the intersection of patented inventions and franchise agreements. The launch of the modern McDonald's came from Ray Kroc's initial investment in the exclusive franchise rights to the "Multimixer," a patented five-spindled milkshake maker. The single McDonald's restaurant, owned by Dick and Mac McDonald, was running eight of the Multimixers. Kroc felt he could deliver eight of his Multimixers to each store, so he entered into a franchise agreement with the McDonald brothers to franchise the restaurants. Armed with the rights to the Multimixer and the restaurant, he began opening restaurants, buying out Dick and Mac in 1961, seven years after first selling his Multimixers.

Perhaps the most current example of technology and fast-food can be found in the competing methods of fast-food payment. Sonic restaurants, the leading drive-in restaurant chain, has installed a wireless network of card readers to allow credit card customers to pay at the sign and significantly reduce the time the car hop needs to spend on each transaction. The technology adds efficiency and convenience for the consumer.

3. Trade Secrets and Special Recipes.

The special recipe used by KFC (formerly Kentucky Fried Chicken) and the formula used by Coca-Cola for its Coca-Cola Classic have both been mentioned earlier, but both provide classic examples of the importance of trade secrets in the restaurant business. At the more mundane level, the secret recipes held by each chef gives that individual chef his edge in the highly competitive business for supremacy among top-rated restaurants.

Restaurateurs Georges Perrier, owner of Le Bec Fin, and Howard Wean, manager for Steven Starr's restaurants, were quoted during a program for Penn State students: "To be part of the 10 to 15 percent of restaurateurs and chefs who make it through to the first year after opening a restaurant, they said there are five important things you need to have: a concept or a clear positioning statement, a designer, a manager and lastly the chef . . . ."[148] The concept and clear positioning statement focuses the business plan on relevance and efficiency, the manager ensures that there is a significant focus on the task at hand. The designer and the chef are charged with creating the unique and secret food and ambiance that combine to create a restaurant's essence. Through careful and highly secret innovation in these two areas, great restaurants can differentiate themselves from their competitors.

4.   Publicity-Based Businesses and the Great Chef.

A natural extension of the trade secrets available to the great chefs is the ability to market the chef as a distinct, unique feature. For example, the best-known chef among a broad segment of the public today is Gordon Ramsay. He has held as many as 15 Michelin stars, run an eclectic array of restaurants, hosted multiple television shows, and published successful cookbooks.

Each of these ventures is promoted and maintained by the publicity rights in the owner/chef who created the empire. Through the use of his name at each stage of his businesses, Gordon Ramsay has leveraged his presence to open new markets and continue to build the brand.

Gordon Ramsay is certainly not alone. James Beard and Paul Prudhomme pioneered the business model. In recent years they have been eclipsed by Bobby Flay, Rachael Ray, Paula Deen and others. They built many restaurants and world class reputations as chefs, cookbook authors, and industry leaders.

Julia Child was perhaps known in more homes at the height of her success, though she did not extend her fame to as many businesses. Emeril Lagasse of Emeril's Restaurant followed in Child's footsteps, as have many of the stars of the Cooking Channel. These television stars combine their skills with their personality to reach out to consumers through the intimacy of the medium. Finally, there is Martha Stewart. Stewart focused on the publishing empire for her success and then branched out into the food preparation and television fields.

---

[148] Kimi de Freytas, *Top City Restaurateurs Divulge Trade Secrets*, DAILY PENNSYLVANIAN (Feb. 10, 2005, 5:00 AM), http://www.thedp.com/article/2005/02/top_city_restaurateurs_divulge_trade_secrets.

B.   Exclusivity in Retail: Brand Stores and Exclusive Offers.

1.   *Walmart, Target, and Amazon: Branding, Relevance, and Exclusivity.*

The demise of K-Mart came about as a result of the rivalry between retail giants Target and Walmart. Each of these two retail giants recognized the competitive, cut-throat marketplace and the need to supply product exclusivity and social relevance to their customers. The problem was that the three companies all sold many of the same commodities to the same people. In a straight price war, all three companies would lose.

Walmart took the commodity challenge head on. It declared itself the "low price leader" and emphasized its ability to beat the competitors on price alone. It achieved these prices through extreme process efficiency and through labor practices that have resulted in lawsuits that continue as of the publication of this book. In a three-way price war, Walmart was likely to win, but perhaps at a cost that could have destroyed the company.

Target chose to fight the battle on a different front. Rather than focus exclusively on price, it developed the slogan, "expect more, pay less," suggesting that it might not offer the lowest price, but that it provided better value than the competition. It targeted slightly more expensive goods; emphasized private-label products that were exclusive to Target; priced its commodities based on the store's proximity to Walmart or K-Mart; and invested heavily in the cleanliness and convenience of its stores to improve the satisfaction or social relevance to the consumer. Target knew that its intended audience was slightly better off than Walmart's customer base, and Target's customers would pay a small premium for quality, good service and convenience.

Amazon has further disrupted the businesses of both Walmart and Target, with Target being the larger loser of the two. Just as Walmart emphasized price and Target emphasized value, Amazon focused on convenience. With free shipping for Amazon Prime customers, highly competitive pricing, and 24/7 to-the-door-delivery, Amazon leapfrogged Target to become the second largest retailer after Walmart.

Within the facilities, Walmart emphasized price and range of products, stuffing its stores so that its customers need shop nowhere else. Target added store lights, expanded its checkout lines to improve the customer experience, and focused on specialty product lines exclusive to the chain. Walmart increased its loyalty; Target increased its uniqueness; Amazon increased its convenience and customer satisfaction; and K-Mart was left with neither a strategy nor a customer base.

The winners in this battle emphasized the relevance of their strategies to their key customers. They differentiated themselves from one another, leaving K-Mart as the weak competitor without a market share.

Both Walmart and Target use their market power to develop a large number of private-label products, which are products sold under brands wholly owned by the retailer. These products were designed by the retailers with the strategic objective of the chain at the forefront. In recent years, Amazon has followed suit with its own growing list of house brands as well. Each chain uses these goods to emphasize its pricing, quality, and packaging strategy to maximize customer interest. In this way, each chain reinforced its business model by creating exclusive products and packages designed for its own customers.

2.   *Best Buy's Four Flicks and Apple's Beatles Box Set.*

Another version of retail exclusivity was built on The Rolling Stones' copyrighted concert film *Four Flicks*. In November 2003, the decades-old rock band signed an exclusive deal with Best Buy to release its concert DVD. Best Buy paid a significant premium and featured The Rolling Stones and its music in its holiday advertising. The pairing paid off handsomely for the band and the retailer.

Coming at the time of holiday sales, the exclusive distribution of the concert DVD boxed set brought a significant amount of traffic to Best Buy and away from both the smaller record and video stores and the large box-store rivals, Walmart and Target. Despite complaints from smaller retailers, the success of the alliance will likely be repeated from time to time, when the exclusivity benefits both the artist and the retailer. Best Buy had previously launched exclusive arrangements with the Eagles, U2, and John Mellencamp.

In 2010, Apple did something similar when it finally moved the Beatles to digital, arranging for "The Beatles Boxed Set"—which was a digital download without a box—to be sold for $149. Steve Jobs personally curated the collection of albums, songs, and other material that went into the project. It may have been more of a personal triumph for Jobs than a marketing bonanza, but it highlighted the power of exclusive contracting among powerful brand owners.

3.   Tea Source—the Shop Around the Corner Rides the Long Tail.

At the other extreme from Target, Walmart, and Best Buy are the single store retail outlets. In today's market, operating a single retail store is an uphill battle. Location and convenience matter a great deal to customers, so the lack of stores creates some problems. In addition, the size of the store limits the negotiating leverage for exclusive relationships and other advantages.

While nothing can make these impediments go away, there are business models that suggest a successful approach. A company serving a niche market may satisfy the long tail created through national marketing of local goods. The Internet creates an opportunity for a company to build a small community around its products, reaching well beyond its geographic location. If it can tap into the affinities of social networks, the community will spread the gospel of the company throughout the community and build awareness at a surprisingly low cost to the entrepreneur.

A St. Paul, Minnesota retailer, TeaSource,[149] provides an example of this model in practice (although it has grown to three Minnesota locations). TeaSource sells teas. Not teas and coffee, just teas. TeaSource boasts exclusivity through its product line. It features a large number of tea flavors grown or blended exclusively for the store. Of course, the exclusivity may be only in the U.S., but that is sufficient for most retailers' marketing purposes.

The store developed its primary success from walk-in business and referrals. The wide range of teas and the quality of selection provides a

---

[149] TEASOURCE, https://www.teasource.com/ (last visited July 12, 2018).

very small but successful business model. In 2015 it was voted best tea business at the World Tea Expo.

Today's shop around the corner, however, has neither the money to advertise competitively nor the location to demand a sufficiently loyal following to stay afloat. TeaSource recognizes this. It has a catalog, which supplements its store front, and a website to supplement the catalog. Rather than spending significant amounts on advertising, it provides good coupons in its catalog for its customers who are successful in referring new customers.

Building on this "viral marketing" model, the store uses its locations to build credibility with the locals, who serve as the primary promoters on the Internet. This creates a national and even international marketplace for this single, small store. The Internet business and loyal local following provide the necessary leverage to arrange a few exclusive deals with tea growers across the globe. Although only a few of the products are exclusive to TeaSource, they are sufficient to give the little shop the edge it needs.

4.   *Selling to the People: The Infomercial.*

Since the 1970's, entrepreneurs had another method of getting their unique products directly into the hands of the consumer: through the infomercial. Although sponsored television had existed since the earliest days of TV broadcast, the FCC did not lift the prohibition on long-form advertising content for television until 1984.[150] In the infomercial, a fifteen-minute to hour-long program would feature product demonstrations and testimonials to encourage the public to get this product. Typically, the product was exclusive to the infomercial and not sold in stores or other distribution channels.

Ron Popeil, founder of Ronco, was among the most successful of those entrepreneurs. He created a wide range of products, including the

---

[150] *See* Revision of Programming and Commercialization, Policies, Ascertainment Requirements, and Program Log Requirements for Commercial Television Stations, 98 F.C.C.2d 1075 (1984) (rescinding the FCC's policy banning program-length television commercials). *See also* Deregulation of Radio, 84 F.C.C.2d 968, 1007 (1981) (rescinding the FCC's policy banning program-length radio commercials); ENFORCEMENT POLICY STATEMENT ON DECEPTIVELY FORMATTED ADVERTISEMENTS, 20160513A NYCBAR 53.

Showtime Rotisserie, the Ronco Spray Gun with its proprietary soap pellets, and a spray-on hair thickener marketed exclusively for men. His infomercials and catalog sales exceeded $2 billion in revenue before sliding into bankruptcy in 2018.

Ronco epitomized the success of low-technology patented products. Some of his patented products were odd. Some of the products were different than those on the market because of unique features rather than patented improvements.

The success of infomercials spawned many imitators and led to the launch of cable channels dedicated to commercial product sales. HSN and QVC operate full-time product distribution channels. Infomercials provide a rich opportunity for direct sales by entrepreneurs, but this medium has been challenged by online distribution channels in recent years.

For example, due to the softening of the revenue for the cable marketing channels, Liberty Interactive, the owner of QVC, was able to acquire total control of HSN in 2017. Competition among the cable operators increased costs and lowered net profits. By combining the two primary cable product channels, the multichannel distributor will remain a powerful competitor to Amazon, Target, and Walmart as one of the world's largest retailers. HSN and QVC together generate over $14 billion in sales. Liberty Interactive also operates a large suite of online retail sites to complement the television merchandising.

The infomercial has become the primary form of marketing for athletic equipment and an effective outlet for apparel, jewelry, electronics, and small home appliances. It may be that television sales are better suited to low-technology innovation, or it may be the unique relationship between the TV viewer and the marketing vendor. For infomercials, better mousetraps are not as important as plastic containers that close tightly and store easily in the kitchen cabinets. A consumer may not focus on this enough to make a special trip to the store, but if the commercial comes on while the viewer is cooking in the kitchen, a customer is born. Good return policies and quick transaction support create the value needed to keep consumers returning.

C.   Social Entrepreneurship, Public Benefit, and the Exclusivity through Purpose.

In the United States there has been the development of a relatively new category of for-profit enterprise that focuses on a public good that occurs directly as a consequence of the company's operation. Unlike a tax exempt, nonprofit charity which can have no shareholders, the public benefit corporation allows for shareholders and profits, but it also allows management great flexibility in transferring the profits of the enterprise to the charitable purpose identified in the organizational documents of the company.

In Colorado, for example, a public benefit is defined as "one or more positive effects or reduction of negative effects on one or more categories of persons, entities, communities, or interests other than shareholders in their capacities as shareholders, including effects of an artistic, charitable, cultural, economic, educational, environmental, literary, medical, religious, scientific, or technological nature."[151]

A growing number of states are adding statutes to give corporate management the power to expend resources on these charitable activities. Companies where ownership and management are integrated can always make these arrangements, provided there is not dissension among the owners.

Newman's Own has served as such a company for decades. It includes "all profits to charities" in its marketing. While it makes good sauces and dressings, it is in the business to raise funds for other charities. Another example is TOMS Shoes, which donates a pair of shoes to an African charity for every pair it sells. Bixbee backpacks follows a similar model for its goods as does Bombas, which donates a pair of socks to a homeless shelter for every pair purchased.

The category gains a great deal of attention, but it is an uneasy mix of services that fall uncomfortably between true nonprofit organizations that address social and cultural needs and for-profits that provide goods

---

[151] COLO. RES. STAT. § 7-101-503(2) (West 2018). *See Business FAQs: Public Benefit Corporations*, COLO. SEC'Y OF STATE, https://www.sos.state.co.us/pubs/business/FAQs/pbc.html (last visited July 9, 2018).

and services for a fee. Target, for example, has long committed to provide 5% back to the local public schools in the communities it serves. It is a reason some people choose Target over Walmart. But it remains a profit-seeking publicly traded enterprise.

Newman's Own has a level of commitment that makes the company a nonprofit in purpose even as it remains a taxable entity in operation.

Another variation on social entrepreneurship is to focus on addressing matters of public concern and social welfare through the types of products and services developed. Examples may include "Fair Trade" shops that assure working wages are paid at all steps in the manufacturing process, that products are sourced only from areas with meaningful environmental policies, and that recyclable materials are used to minimize waste. Companies that do well by doing good will tend to resonate with the public, provided the commitment is real and the effects are both substantial and verifiable.

D. Exclusivity in Manufacturing and Service.

Manufacturing is the most common realm for process innovation and efficiency goals. Patents allow manufacturers to maintain extended exclusivity in their products. Trade secrets protect the methods of creating the products and the inside know-how on the best way to get the job done. Copyright is useful to protect the text of the manuals, brochures, and other printed materials, diagrams, and tools that assist with the products. Finally, trademarks provide companies the tools to build product lines and create a strong presence among the purchasers regarding the company's products and services.

Service companies have no tangible products, so they have far fewer of the manufacturer's tools available to build patent exclusivity. They must rely almost exclusively on trademarks to generate relevance, but they can also use copyrights and trade secrets to augment their core services.

1. Exclusivity through Licensing.

In licensing a patented new invention, the license to exploit the patent may be exclusive or non-exclusive. A non-exclusive license provides the party receiving the license (the licensee) with the permission needed to use the patent, but it does not stop the party licensing the patent (the licensor) from giving the same permission to multiple parties.

An exclusive license grants permission to use the patent to only one party. The scope of the exclusive license, however, can vary dramatically. Often exclusive licenses are restricted by geography, time, and type of usage.

For example, assume an inventor creates a newly patented voice recognition device. The software algorithms are sufficient to satisfy the patent requirements that the software is both new and nonobvious. The inventor sells the patent to MicroVoice, Inc., a software manufacturer, in exchange for a payment and royalty. MicroVoice purchased the software in order to use it with its own operating software. That transaction is a sale. While MicroVoice will have a duty to track the sales of the product and pay the royalty to the inventor, all other ownership decisions and control over the patent are now held by MicroVoice.

The following year, MicroVoice is approached by Cuddly Toys, Inc. to use the software in its plush toys. The teddy bears and other Cuddly Toys products listen to their owners, responding to identified words with appropriate pre-recorded responses. Cuddly Toys acquires licenses for use of the MicroVoice software for its toys. Because Cuddly Toys does not wish to compete with any other toy companies for this special kind of toy, it seeks an exclusive license from MicroVoice.

Exclusivity is not all-or-nothing. Instead, exclusivity is carefully defined for each transaction. Absent any other consideration, the greater the amount of exclusivity, the greater the cost of the license. Cuddly Toys wants sufficient exclusivity to eliminate competition, but still desires to keep the cost of the license manageable. Cuddly Toys should not pay for exclusive rights it does not hope to use. As a result, the negotiated license agreement may provide that Cuddly Toys will have the exclusive right to use the patented software in plush toys for a period of five years. MicroVoice could then license the patent to Mattel, Inc. for use in a new line of Hot Wheels toy car garages and Barbie salons. If Cuddly Toys did not want this type of competition, then it would have to purchase the exclusive license to cover all toys rather than merely plush toys. The length of the initial license will also affect the annual cost of the license, with longer licenses generally costing less per year.

2.   Creating New Products.

James Dyson has become legendary, particularly in Europe, with continual inventions and improvements in vacuum cleaner design. His original 1993 bagless vacuum cleaner resulted in patent infringement claims against Amway, which allegedly negotiated to purchase the patent in bad faith and then manufactured without consent, as well as with Hoover UK, which refused to license the patents and instead infringed them.

Dyson proved successful first in the two patent disputes and then in the marketplace. Each new product is the beneficiary of an increasing number of patents. The company remains family-owned in Britain, and in 2018 Dyson was listed as the 12th richest British citizen, according to the Sunday Times in Britain.[152]

Electrolux has had a more difficult history. Also starting as a vacuum cleaner company, the Swedish consumer equipment giant has been struggling of late and losing some market share to its rivals. In response, the company has focused on efficiencies and increased its emphasis on research and development to build the next generation of products that can sustain it against the fierce competition from smaller rivals like Dyson and larger competitors like Whirlpool. Led by the new Pronto vacuum, new designs in ovens and washing machines, Electrolux hopes to have repositioned itself through new technologies to stay competitive in these fierce consumer product segments.

3.   Trumpeting   Recognition,   Awareness,   and Relevance.

The insurance industry is highly regulated, selling products that are much more like services. These companies are generally known for their staid, traditional stature. Prudential's former slogan, "Get a piece of the rock," captured the essence of the industry and made those in the business feel secure. The trouble was that the approach did not provide relevance to the public. While the existing client base might have found some assurance from the message, such messages did little to motivate consumers' purchasing decisions.

American Family Life Assurance Company (AFLAC) had similar problems. The company had little name recognition. Its acronym, AFLAC, was far from a household word. Then Dan Amos, company CEO, broke the mold and allowed the company to be represented by a

---

[152] Robert Watts, *The Rich List*, SUNDAY TIMES, May 13, 2018.

duck. The AFLAC commercials featured a frustrated duck trumpeting out the company name. This strategy increased the company's name recognition to over 90% of consumers. A second wave of commercials used the duck but focused on illustrating the benefit behind AFLAC's supplemental medical insurance. While the first campaign might have provided a bit more focus on relevance, the two-step process transformed AFLAC from an unknown entity to a household name. The company used this public awareness to increase the relevance of its services.

Companies use ducks and other creatures to support their campaigns. Commercials featuring the Geico gecko have actually featured the talking lizard explaining why his presence in the ads helps engender trust by the public.

4.   *Extending Innovation to Brand Enhancement.*

The 3M Company stands out as a corporate innovator, developing products from sophisticated medical equipment and military technology to Scotchgard and Post-it Notes. The Post-it Notes story has become famous as a failed experiment. An attempt to make a stronger glue resulted in a weak formula that was fully removable. From there, the simple yellow square tab of paper was born.

And growth continued after its birth. The patented technology once provided exclusivity, but that source disappeared when the semi-permanent adhesive entered the public domain. Instead, 3M has extended the reach of the product to a wide range of interesting services, including semi-sticky photograph paper and colorful children's stick-um books. The Post-it brand knows no boundaries because of the innovation that has gone towards extending the brand across multiple sectors.

5.   *Athlete Endorsements: From My Field to Yours.*

Sports figures loom large in product support. The current pitchman leader is Shaquille O'Neal, who commands a wide range of endorsements and an annual salary that may be twice his former NBA salary. Although LeBron James has become a top endorsement earner with estimates above $45 million, O'Neal continues to beat James off the court. Tiger Woods, who has had more surgeries than titles in recent years, is still reported to have earned $65 million in his 2017 endorsement compensation.

Other examples include Michael Jordan's endorsements with Nike, Hanes, Gatorade, and Upper Deck, as well as Serena Williams' endorsement of Puma tennis shoes, and thousands of others. As mentioned earlier in the book, George Foreman took his fading fame to an entirely new profession with the expansion of cooking products. Magic Johnson extended his fame and endorsement prowess to become a principal owner of his chain of California movie theaters.

The product support for manufactured goods provides instant credibility to those products and affords attention far past the paid ad exposure. Whether it is apparel that the athlete is seen wearing, mentions in sports pages, or enhanced attention from retailers, the effect is significant. There are Federal Trade Commission rules that require the endorsements to be truthful, particularly regarding the celebrity endorser's use of the product.[153] For the right fit of personality, endorsements can lift a commodity to the top of the market.

Athletes popular in the local sports market can also achieve similar success. Miami Dolphins Coach Don Shula has created a successful national chain of restaurants that began in Florida and the South. Chicago Bears Coach Mike Ditka did the same, starting in Chicago. Football's defensive linemen and other less glamorous skill players often find themselves popular with local car dealerships. At a certain scale, the fame of the individual can be tied to the reach of the audience, benefiting both the athlete and the manufacturer or retailer.

E.   Exclusivity in the New Economy: Software Strategies.

1.   Building Friends in Software Gaming.

Software companies are built on copyright exclusivity. Copyright allows the author of the software to have exclusive rights over the expression created, which in the case of code means the precise programming language. However, the ideas or objectives of the software

---

[153] Guidelines Concerning Use of Endorsement and Testimonials in Advertising, 16 C.F.R. §§ 255.0–255.5 (2018).

are not protected. Microsoft owns the copyright to Word, but it does not own the idea of word processing.

Copyright may create a strong barrier against copying, but it provides only modest protection from legitimate competition. The challenge for software companies is to create works that are sufficiently unique. Only the most unique software can separate itself from other copyrighted works.

Computer games provide the most obvious form of protection. Electronic Arts, the owner of The Sims, Madden Football, and many other titles, has found that the best way to protect copyright and build relevance is to add more and more exclusivity to the mix. Electronic Arts has extended copyrights, trademarks, and publicity rights to separate its titles from those of its competitors. For example, it brands its sports games with popular athletes and coaches in the titles of the games. "Madden Football" builds a stronger presence than "Pro Football" could provide. The publicity rights also extend beyond the packaging into the games themselves, with the names, images, and voices of the celebrities serving as elements of the games.

Electronic Arts also uses team building in its other products. It regularly licenses signature music for its games from well-known popular bands, and it had a three-game deal with leading motion picture producer and director Steven Spielberg to design three new titles. In its sports division, it regularly licenses exclusive rights with professional sports leagues. By tying its software to the trademarks, publicity rights, and copyrights of other leaders in their respective fields, Electronic Arts has propelled itself to the top of the market.

2. *Bundling to Overcome Compatibility Learning Curve Barriers.*

Consumers have somewhat odd behavior when it comes to computers. They regularly buy expensive new machines because the incessant software upgrades demand more productivity than their hardware can deliver. At the same time, they are a bit reluctant to spend money on new software and generally rely on whatever software comes bundled with their machines.

For the software company fortunate enough to sign a bundling arrangement with a hardware manufacturer, the pre-loaded software on shipped computers provides a tremendous boost towards dominating that product segment. The fees paid by computer manufacturers to software companies tend to be low as a result, since the computer manufacturer also knows that the delivery of the software is an extremely effective method to develop market share. Despite potentially low payments, this strategy has helped Microsoft and others gain and sustain market share.

A second bundling strategy is used by smaller software companies and those writing for a niche market. Software products are bundled into suites that share a common user interface. Microsoft pioneered this strategy as well, and many others have followed. Bundling provides three key benefits to consumers, and as a result, improves sales. First, a bundled product is likely to be, or at least appear to be, a more cost-effective purchase for the consumer than a stand-alone product and a more efficient delivery method for the manufacturer. Although the development costs for each component of the bundled package may remain the same or actually increase, the costs associated with packaging, marketing, and distribution are the same whether there is one product or ten in the package. Reducing these distribution and packaging costs may be enough to make the bundled product more cost effective.

Second, consumers are appropriately concerned with software compatibility. A bundled product is presumably well integrated, so that all compatibility problems have been eliminated. There is also a presumption that the larger products have greater quality control, so that the purchaser will have less technical difficulty. The corollary of this presumption is that software compatibility problems will destroy the marketability of a software product and should be eliminated at all costs.

Third, consumers are frustrated by the need to continually learn new software navigation, new keystrokes, and different interfaces. The consumer will likely stay with the tools offered in the bundle, even if they really only like one of the bundled products, because of the shared interface. Although Microsoft Office provides the best example, Roxio has created a suite of tools for CD and DVD creation, and Adobe's Creative Suite combines Photoshop, InDesign, Illustrator, GoLive, Acrobat, and many other products. Although Adobe has not fully integrated its user interfaces across its various products, each product is, by itself, an extremely complex bundle of tools and programs, providing the best example of the suite model.

3.   *The Open Source Dilemma.*

Perhaps the best suite on the market today is the Google Chrome suite of tools for Internet browsing and e-mail. Google's domination of search and its suite of free products have led to Chrome's having 67% of all browsing, compared to Apple Safari's 5.5% and Microsoft's 11% split between Internet Explorer and Edge. Firefox is comparable in usage to Microsoft. Google's dominance and free distribution have also led to success for products like G-mail and Google Drive.

Firefox is an open source product, as was the initial version of Chrome. Open source software remains protected by copyright. The copyright license allows copying without charge and adaptation or alteration to the software as long as the changes are then subject to the terms of the original open source software license. Copyright provides the legal protection necessary to stop companies from using open source software to produce proprietary products. Open source differs from public domain products, because once in the public domain, anyone can change the content. This includes changing the content in such a manner that it becomes exclusively owned by the person making the changes.

Open source software has an inherent limitation in its commercialization. A legitimate open source company cannot make revenue from the adaptation of the software. There is no exclusivity for the author of open source software. In the case of Chrome, for example, Google provided the public a free version of the software but incorporates proprietary updates into the version it provides.

At the operating system level, Linux is perhaps the best known open source software, but most users need much more assistance than is available from the free version of Linux. To meet this need, Red Hat created a strong service model to provide enterprise solutions for Linux adopters.

Red Hat has built a subscription model around the free product, presumably selling not the software but the services associated with the support for that software. If companies hope to use the subscription support model based on open source software, they must provide relevant service for a product that they do not exclusively control or provide. Process innovation and the elimination of stressors create opportunities for exclusivity through servicing, developing trade secrets in know-how, building brand reputation and trademarks, and potentially, promoting publicity rights. However, copyright and patent exclusivity are foreclosed by the nature of open source software licenses.

4. Software Patents.

In addition to the inherent ability to copyright software, some innovations rise to the level of patentability. Mathematical algorithms are not protected by patent, but there are many processes that are patentable. Patents have been issued to Unisys for computer graphics which overlapped with CompuServe's GIF format, for encryption, computer style sheets, and for many more seemingly mundane features.

As an industry, the bulk of academic and empirical literature tends to reject the efficacy of software patents. Research suggests that the competitive need for innovation and service is not further promoted by the potential for patent protection. Having acknowledged this, the availability of patents to differentiate an entrepreneur's business and the risk that another company or enterprise has patented an innovation under development are both important considerations which must be taken into account.

Finally, there may be the truly novel extension of software that is so far beyond the state of the industry that patents are appropriate. Dan Bricklin and Bob Frankston invented VisiCalc as the first spreadsheet, before software patenting was available.[154] That product was later sold to Lotus to create Lotus 1-2-3, a product that revolutionized PC sales and fueled the PC revolution. The authors of this revolution did not receive nearly the financial reward earned by less creative business owners. If there is a defense for software patents, the ability to have rewarded this caliber of innovation may be its best support.

F. Exclusivity in the New Economy: Internet Businesses.

1. The Content Model of Website Business.

The Internet is primarily a medium. Like radio and television, the Internet provides a distribution structure for companies to distribute content to the public. Of course, the Internet is much more than this,

---

[154] *See* Dan Bricklin, *Patenting VisiCalc*, http://www.bricklin.com/patenting.htm (last visited July 12, 2018).

but terms of traffic and usage, this remains one of its key functions. Chapter 4 highlights the most fundamental difference involving the many-to-many, disintermediated model of social media content. Nonetheless, the Internet serves as a rich media platform.

Traditionally, there have been four types of media companies, and the content side of the Internet has these same options. Websites are not as separate as the pre-Internet media, so the typical website may include aspects from each of the four revenue models. An understanding of the four discrete revenue models will help the entrepreneur develop a more refined content strategy for each aspect of a web-based business.

(1) Public performances, concerts and interactive festivals.

The first type of medium includes those that sell the opportunity to enjoy a public performance of the content. Motion picture houses, Broadway theaters, and concert halls provide these opportunities to attend the public performance of the content. While the public performance aspect of traditional film and concerts can be expanded to include interaction, the models remain the same. The audience comes together to experience the performance and, in many cases, to participate in the performance at some level.

At the moment, the Internet equivalent of this model is focused on the interactive sites, particularly the "MMORPG" or massive multi-player online role-playing games. The phenomenon of the Renaissance Festival is perhaps the best analogy to the interactive gaming experience. Audience members mingle in the fantasy world, participating in the day-to-day life created by the performers. Online role-playing games include Everquest II, Unification Wars, Star Wars Galaxies, and World of Warcraft. Like the traditional public performance model, these rely on participants paying to attend or join. The benefit of interaction further engages the audience and helps maintain player membership.

(2) Sale of private copies for personal ownership and use.

The second revenue stream flows from the sale of private copies of works to individuals for their personal ownership or private use. This includes the sales of books, music, movies, television episodes, and videogames to consumers for their permanent ownership.

In each case, the consumer purchases a copy of the work which can be read, played, or used at home, but which cannot be used to broadcast or publicly perform the work.

Sidebar—Microsoft v. Google: Google's free services.

Google must also be mentioned in this section for dumping free tools onto the marketplace to thwart Microsoft. These products are not open source. They are proprietary code but are being made available as free services to the public. In some cases, they are extensions of the Google search engine software and are cleanly bundled with Google's core applications. The desktop search feature fits nicely in this category.

Google has made company purchases and developed products that do not fit neatly into its core service. G-mail, the Google e-mail feature, straddles the line. E-mail is not directly tied to web browsing, but Google uses data mining tools to analyze the de-identified content in the email messages to target advertising and develop advertising relevance data. As a result, the users of G-mail are providing valuable market information and research for Google. Products such as Picasa, a photograph organization tool, and Writely, an online word processing product, have little to do with Google's own business. They serve little purpose other than to target core Microsoft products and services.

Perhaps the best small software company strategy is to design a product that does something better than one of Microsoft's core services and hope that Google will buy it to further frustrate Microsoft. Like the Walmart v. Target battle, third-party vendors with insufficient resources and market focus will likely be eliminated. If the elimination comes through a profitable buy out, however, many entrepreneurs might consider that a success.

* * *

The warnings at the start of films advising that the content is for private viewing reflects this distinction that the purchaser of a download or DVD does not acquire permission to rebroadcast that movie to a general audience.

(3) Broadcast radio and television.

The third type of medium is provided by the broadcasters, those on radio and television. The classic over-the-air media of terrestrial television and AM and FM radio provide free content supported by intermittent paid advertising. In publishing, weekly neighborhood newspapers followed the same model by using the advertising to provide the newspapers free of charge.

On the Internet, this model has been duplicated. Streaming music and video is the equivalent of terrestrial broadcasting. Both provide free content supported by advertising. In some cases, the advertising is also part of the broadcast; while in others, the advertising is contained in separate windows or boxes on the website. Most broadcasters have some web presence as well.

(4) Integration of advertising and subscriptions.

The fourth model combines consumer subscription prices and advertising support. The newspaper championed this model, which is also used by magazines and comic books. In recent years, cable television and satellite radio have also incorporated this model into parts of their business.

The model may be further separated by identifying companies that pay to carry someone else's content. Cable companies, for example, receive a subscription fee from consumers to carry the signals of television stations. In some cases, a small portion of that consumer fee is paid to the broadcaster, but more often the broadcaster continues to rely on revenue from advertising, while the cable operator depends on subscription revenue.

Through some combination of these four revenue models, all websites relying on public performance, distribution, or display of content can find financial returns. The content is all protected by copyright and, thus, is exclusive.

Most websites re-broadcast or re-distribute content created and owned by third parties. This makes exclusivity and relevance harder to obtain. Some of the film sites may enter into exclusive distribution agreements when they launch new films. Few of the music sites are presently able to do so. The best the websites can provide is strong editorial selection, so that the site provides a branding to the content, which in turn increases the site's relevance to its target audience. Although this focus narrows the interested audience range, it intensifies the importance of that site to its key consumers.

2.   *The Disintermediation & Service Model for the Web.*

The second significant category of websites is booking agents and shopping aggregators of various kinds. These include travel sites, e-loans, realtor services and others. Agency services work particularly well on the Internet because they combine the best aspects of disintermediation and service.

Successful agencies mediate the price, availability, and service information from many providers in the marketplace. Each website has replaced hundreds of small businesses which once provided this mediation, but these companies still act as "middlemen" in the transaction. Whether the market is plane fares, hotel rooms, insurance products, loans, event tickets, or housing, the database tools and sophisticated algorithms can outperform brokers and agents with ease. This has led to a dramatic decline in the personal service industry.

The limited mediation provided by these websites is fine for topics such as price and availability, but it is less helpful regarding quality features. Because there are only a small number of competitors in the airline industry, quality assessments may be less important. But for hotels, the difference in quality between offerings can be quite dramatic. Through research methods, surveys, and customer feedback, each website can develop strong predictors regarding the quality of the hotels or other services provided. Again, this broad-based information net has proven more reliable than the limited amount of information available to pre-Internet brokers and agents.

3.   *Connecting Catalogs, Retail and Infomercials.*

The third general category of Internet business is the extension of the brick-and-mortar industry to the Internet. Companies vary widely on the extent to which they replicate their retail store on the Internet. Almost every catalog company that existed before the Internet and survived its launch has a strong web presence. Leading retailers such as Target, Walmart, and Best Buy must also maintain a strong Internet presence in addition to their retail locations.

Other competitors use the Internet as little more than a store locator or a place to post their weekly newspaper insert. For these companies, Internet presence is primarily defensive. It does little to further their core business, but merely maintains name recognition. Unlike companies such as TeaSource, described above, which maximize their business through a strong web presence, companies that ignore the potential for word-of-mouth and viral advertising leave this aspect of their business to atrophy as consumers are drawn to competitors' information and resources.

4.   *Individual Artisans.*

Perhaps the people best served by websites on the Internet are individual artisans who can connect directly with their previous buyers to announce shows and tours, hopefully spurring on their loyal followers to promote their art and handicraft to other buyers.

Art and handicraft collectors are generally proud of their finds and prefer to promote, rather than hoard, the information. A website can build a word-of-mouth community around the artist, building a permanent presence that would never have been available twenty years earlier. Artisans represent the best opportunity described through the long tail phenomenon. The works from artists around the globe can be shipped to clients anywhere. The trip of a lifetime can lead to annual pilgrimages to the website of the distant artisans, and an ongoing collection of these products.

Individual artisans also reflect what is best about the Internet. They capture the disaggregated aspect of the information. Just as portals were made obsolete by search engines, the individual artist can choose to eliminate galleries, agents, or brokers by selling directly to the public. If the artist still chooses to use an agent or broker, it is only because the professional adds value to the artist's career and opportunities. The disaggregation of artist from gallery remains one of the more significant trends on the near horizon.

5.   *The Future Remains Unpredictable.*

In the first edition of the book, this section was dedicated to the following business analysis: Pets.com—the Worst Model Ever. Pets.com is no longer a separate business, so in that sense the prediction was accurate. But Amazon, PetSmart, Petco, and others have managed to make good of the business mocked when run by Pets.com. Here was the original explanation:

The last Internet company example should serve as a reminder of what the Internet cannot do. The Internet is best at transferring content, not bulky commodities. Unless the transaction involves purely digital content, transaction costs will be involved. Also, the Internet has not supplanted all brick-and-mortar competition in any field. For almost every task, some form of the pre-Internet business method remains.

Given these realities, the history of Pets.com emphasizes what the Internet cannot do. This highly valued, publicly traded company created an Internet pet store. Of course, the pets themselves could hardly be shipped by UPS or Federal Express, so Pets.com was limited to pet supplies and products. Any pet owner knows that the most commonly purchased pet product is food. In fact, more pet food is purchased annually in the United States than baby food. However, pet food can be heavy and expensive to ship.

Pets.com should serve as a reminder to every entrepreneur. Just because a business can operate in a particular manner does not mean that it can do so profitably. Profits flow from providing relevance to the customer. The Internet never replaced the need for common sense.

The executives at the publicly traded Pets.com missed the simple lessons of Internet business. They established a business to sell products like fish tank rocks and pet food—heavy commodities with only small price margins. No imaginable online business plan to ship dog food can beat Walmart's efficiency.

Why was this statement inaccurate? It was correct that Pets.com could not be an online pet shipping business, nor could it make a profit shipping high-cost goods nationally. But the statements assumed that the goods shipped were coming from a single location and shipping costs would be exorbitant. When the shipping is attached to a national chain of retail outlets or warehouse system, then the costs of moving goods drops significantly. The statement also ignored the high profit margins for food supplements, pet toys, and food for small animals, fish, and birds that can be distributed nationally at a huge profit.

While the sale of software downloads has the highest profit margin, the physical distribution of profitable goods can be very profitable.

When commodity goods are used to maintain strong customer relations, then the costs of those goods may be a worthwhile expense to keep customer loyalty and retain the rest of the customer's patronage.

So Pets.com might not have been the worst online company ever. It just launched before there was a sufficient network of distribution and profitable, additional products to make the plan viable. And in this there are two lessons. First, that the future remains very hard to predict. And second, that in business, timing is everything.

Chapter 15. Fundamentals of Privacy and Cybersecurity

A.   Introduction.

In today's business environment, cyber security and privacy are so essential for the operation of a business that every new company must understand its privacy obligations as part of its starting structure. This section outlines the basics of how a company goes about establishing basic privacy protocols, training its staff to think of privacy first, and arranging to make its privacy and security a foundational component of its corporate planning period.

1.   *Privacy Rules Establish Company Obligations.*

In the pre-technological age, privacy was simply defined as "the right to be let alone." As intrusive technologies emerged, state laws were developed to protect individuals from unwanted intrusions. Fast exposure cameras, radio, and even silent films disturbed the public's expectation of privacy and triggered the first wave of privacy regulations.

More than a century later, a similar debate continues. At its heart, the focus remains on the rights of the government to collect information about its citizens and the rules under which private enterprises can collect information about their customers and others. Although this book does not address the role of the government in collecting private information for purposes of law enforcement, the policy debates shape the rules for private companies.

Many of the rules involving privacy assume some model of consent or contractual relationship. But with click-thru check-the-box contracts and opt-out provisions that assume consent unless the customer objects, the reality of these contracts is often called into question. As used here, the focus on privacy is what the company is permitted to do with the information it collects. The answer to that question shapes which information is collected, how it is stored, when it is exploited, and whether it is sold.

Every business has certain obligations to respect the privacy of its customers. There are state and federal regulations that govern what information must be kept private. In some industries these rules are very exacting, while in other industries there are few specific guidelines. In the United States, we refer to the rules as "sectoral privacy." This means that there are additional privacy obligations for industries or sectors such as finance, health care, education, video rentals, library lending, and for businesses involving minors under the age of 13.

Beyond the federal rules, there are also many states with laws that require additional protection. Since most companies operate via the Internet in all jurisdictions, every company must pay attention to the more restrictive rules in states like California and Massachusetts. These states require that a company post a privacy policy on the business website and then adhere to the terms of the posted policy.

Beyond the legal obligations, there is also the duty that the company owes to its customers to assure that the customers' transaction information is not misused. Customers are often willing to share a great deal of personal information, including their name and address, their credit information, their billing information, their shopping patterns, and even their family relations. But they will only do this if they think that the information is being used to help them receive better service from the company. If the company resells the information to third parties without providing better service, then the customers will turn away. It is in the best interest of the company to provide high quality service, including effective protection of private information and financial information.

2.   *Security Practices Assure Data Reliability and Resilience.*

Data security is an essential aspect of any data collection system. As noted in Chapter 11, for data to be useful, it must be reliable, resilient, and secure. Reliability requires verifiability; resilience requires permanence; and security requires protection from all unauthorized changes. If data is not secure, then the business owning the data cannot know for certain that the information has remained reliable and resilient. Security is at the heart of all data systems.

Although privacy and security go hand in hand, a useful way to distinguish between the two concepts is to consider who is taking advantage of the data. Security protections for a data system assure that only authorized users have access to the system while privacy protections assure that the data is used only in the manner authorized. Privacy cannot exist without security. In every business today, customers expect vendors to keep their information safe and not to have their financial information misused.

Information security is formally defined as "[t]he protection of information and information systems from unauthorized access, use, disclosure, disruption, modification, or destruction in order to provide confidentiality, integrity, and availability."[155] Information security encompasses people, processes, and technologies. It concentrates on how to protect:

- *Confidentiality*—protecting information from unauthorized access and disclosure. For example, what would happen to your company if customer information such as usernames, passwords, or credit card information was stolen?

- *Integrity*—protecting information from unauthorized modification. For example, what if your payroll information or a proposed product design was changed?

- *Availability*—preventing disruption in how you access information. For example, what if you couldn't log in to your bank account or access your customer's information, or your customers couldn't access you?[156]

In addition to adhering to the state and federal rules mandating security, there is also the obligation to keep payment card information (PCI) secure to avoid risks of credit fraud and other financial misconduct. The PCI rules are dictated by an association of the credit card companies and serve as conditions to be able to accept credit as part of the consumer transactions. The PCI standards provide thoughtful and reasonable security steps. Companies that do not follow those standards

---

[155] William C. Barker, *Guideline for Identifying an Information System as a National Security System*, COMPUTER SECURITY DIVISION INFORMATION TECHNOLOGY LABORATORY, NATIONAL INSTITUTE OF STANDARDS AND TECHNOLOGY (NIST) SPECIAL PUBLICATION 800-59, 1 (Aug. 2003) (citing 44 U.S.C., Sec. 3542 (b)(1)).

[156] Celia Paulsen & Patricia Toth, *Small Business Information Security: The Fundamentals* 2 NATIONAL INSTITUTE OF STANDARDS AND TECHNOLOGY (2016), https://doi.org/10.6028/NIST.IR.7621r1.

are more likely to face legal and financial consequences in the event of a data breach.

3.   *Privacy and Security Require Policies, Practices, and Technologies.*

In the United States, privacy and security of personal health information are held to the most rigorous form of legal data protection. In the regulations that protect this information, the rules are categorized into administrative, physical, and technical safeguards to protect patient confidentiality and assure the integrity and security of the protected health information. Although not every company need apply the detailed approach required under these HIPAA guidelines, the structure creates an excellent blueprint for any organization's data protection management.

The three categories of privacy and security protection can be better understood as policies, practices, and technologies needed to protect and secure the business information. And these same approaches apply equally well to trade secret protection as they do to customer information.

- *Policies*—Privacy and information security begin with a series of corporate policies that dictate what information is treated as secure and how the organization will go about providing that security. In highly regulated industries, the board of directors is assigned legal responsibility to assure that these policies are enacted, followed, and updated. The policies help outline which information is collected, who has access to protected information, how the information is stored, how long it is retained, what protocols exist in the case of a data breach, and how to respond to a crisis. Without effective operating policies to protect information, no system can be secure.

- Practices—The weakest link in most security systems is the human factor. Employees do not always follow the written policies, they are not trained or forget to follow their training, they violate the corporate policies both willfully and negligently, they take shortcuts, and they make mistakes. To minimize the risk associated with human error and lack of information, every organization must have a training program in place as well as a system to audit the actual compliance of the employees and retrain those who make mistakes. No system is effective unless the employees understand and comply with the requirements of the system.

- Technologies—In most cybersecurity implementations, the technology comes last. This is to help organizations understand that the encryption software, antivirus tools, and data intrusion protections will not work unless the technology is used to enforce appropriate data hygiene policies and operational practices that enforce real data protection. The technologies include both physical safeguards, like locking the servers in areas where they cannot be stolen or accessed by unauthorized personnel, and software safeguards such as encryption, firewalls, antivirus protections, back-up systems, traffic logs, and other steps.

An alternative categorization defines six elements within the security matrix: Privacy, Cybersecurity, Physical Security, Personnel Security, Operational Security, and Contingency Planning with Disaster Recovery.[157] While most companies focus on cybersecurity, the security associated with personnel is probably the greatest concern for the small business and the area which requires the greatest attention.

B.   Privacy Policies.

1.   *Understanding Privacy Policies.*

A company's privacy policy provides a written, published set of rules from the company about the information it collects, the parties with which it shares the data, and how customers can go about having their information corrected or removed. If only it were that simple.

Privacy policies were intended to provide this kind of information. As originally conceived, the first wave of published policies were merely published statements explaining what information was collected and how it was shared. As consumers challenged some of these policies, however, companies moved to incorporate these policies into "clickwrap" agreements that limited access to apps and websites to those

---

[157] *Id.* at 3.

customers who affirmatively agreed to the terms in the privacy statements and other terms of use. These statements are rarely read and are poorly understood. For example, a 2008 study suggested that the average consumer would require 244 hours to simply read the privacy policies presented each year.[158] Since that time, the number of policies and their complexity has greatly expanded, making the problem even worse.

Despite the frustrations for the public, policies that limit data collection or data sharing can be strategically beneficial for companies. Customers are much more concerned about data exploitation on adult-content sites and as a result, these customers review the privacy policies much more intensively. Similarly, parents of young children are much more sensitive about and protective of their children's data than they are of their own, so sites which cater to children's content have both federal laws and customer expectations to drive higher enforcement of privacy rules.

2.   *Requirements under California and European Rules.*

Although the federal government has no generalized data privacy policy requirement, this gap was filled by the state of California and followed by a few additional states. In 2004, California created the California Online Privacy Protection Act (CalOPPA), which originally applied to the operator of a commercial website but has since been expanded to include any online service, mobile service, or app that collects personally identifiable information about California residents. Although it is limited to residents of California, unless a business can geographically preclude Californians from accessing the site, the law will apply to that business.

As legally defined, "personally identifiable information" refers to details collected on the Internet about an individual consumer, including an individual's first and last name, a physical street address, an email address, a telephone number, a Social Security

---

[158] Aleecia M. McDonald & Lorrie Faith Cranor, *The Cost of Reading Privacy Policies*, I/S: J. L. & POL. INFO. SYS. 541, 560 (2008), http://moritzlaw.osu.edu/students/groups/is/files/2012/02/Cranor_Formatted_Final.pdf.

number, or any other information that permits a specific individual to be contacted physically or online. The term extends to details such as a person's birthday, height, weight or hair color that are collected online and stored by an operator in personally identifiable form. ...

CalOPPA also requires website operators to adhere to their stated privacy policy. As May 2014 guidance from the California Attorney General's Office says, "It requires them to say what they do and do what they say—to conspicuously post a privacy policy and to comply with it."

To be considered in compliance with CalOPPA, the website's privacy policy must contain the following:

- A list of the categories of personally identifiable information the operator collects;

- A list of the categories of third parties with whom the operator may share such personally identifiable information;

- A description of the process (if any) by which the consumer can review and request changes to his or her personally identifiable information as collected by the operator;

- A description of the process by which the operator notifies consumers of material changes to the operator's privacy policy;

- Disclosures for websites and online services' tracking of visitors, defined ... as "the monitoring of an individual across multiple websites to build a profile of behavior and interests"; and

- The effective date of the privacy policy.[159]

Failure to comply with the privacy policy was a violation of the statute. Other states including Pennsylvania and Nebraska added similar

---

[159] Education Foundation, *California Online Privacy Protection Act (CalOPPA)*, CONSUMER FED'N OF CAL., https://consumercal.org/about-cfc/cfc-education-foundation/california-online-privacy-protection-act-caloppa-3/ (updated July 29, 2015).

laws that made it a violation to post false privacy policies or fail to adhere to the posted policy.

Beginning in 2020, a much more stringent California law is scheduled to go into effect. Under the California Consumer Privacy Act, individuals can ask to see what information about them has been collected and request that the data be deleted. The law protects these consumers, requiring that the companies continue to provide the same level of service to these customers as the customers who consent to having their data exploited.

The California statute is similar to the European GDPR (General Data Protection Regulation). Although that is a law outside the United States, it has significant extra-territorial effect because it covers American companies that store European customer data. The scope of the regulation impacts universities with foreign and visiting students, health care organizations with European patients, and businesses that can offer information, sell goods, or provide services to European customers.

Like the California Consumer Privacy Act, the GDPR requires that members of the public can ask to review the information collected about them and can have that information deleted. Under both systems, companies have a much greater obligation to explain why information is collected, how it is used, and with whom it is shared.

The GDPR goes further than the California law, however, because it includes substantial fines for noncompliance, with fines that may be as high as 4% of a company's global revenue. The European jurisdictions have national data protection regulators who have been given investigatory authority under the regulations, with the power to impose fines and take additional actions.

For companies in the United States, the combination of the new California laws and new European reach of external regulation are requiring a much higher level of management over the collection and resale of customer data than has existed prior to 2018.

3.   Enforcement Policies of the FTC.

The FTC has only general authority to enforce privacy, but it has very broad authority under Section 5 of the Federal Trade Commission Act to bring enforcement actions against "unfair or deceptive acts or practices." As understood by the FTC, the failure of a company to adhere to its posted privacy policy amounts to such an unfair and deceptive practice. Known as a "notice and consent" strategy, the FTC does not generally dictate the content of the policy but does require that it be provided to the public and followed.

For example, a company could choose to have a policy that says "we collect information only to process your commercial transactions. We do not sell or share that information. And we eliminate all customer records more than six months old." That policy would provide great assurance that customer data was not being sold to advertisers or others. Another company could have a policy which says "we collect all information you share with us and track your visits using cookies. We sell that information to anyone who wishes to purchase it." That policy would also be permitted under the FTC regulations. It is clear regarding the scope of the private information collected and sold.

Even notice and consent can be misleading. In practice, the FTC has limited authority to require posted privacy policies. But it does not need such a policy, since California, Delaware, and other states make the disclosures of the company policies a requirement to do business online. But once there is a posted policy, the FTC can take steps to assure compliance. As a result, through years of ongoing enforcement, the FTC has established itself as the primary driver of regulation by companies who overstep their posted privacy policies.

4. How Not to Violate Privacy Policies.

For the entrepreneur, the admonitions to create readable, usable privacy policies may appear a far cry from advice to create exclusivity, relevance, and sustainability in products and services. But the failure to adhere to a company's policies can doom the enterprise and result in both the loss of business and regulatory actions.

Most companies do not set out to violate their privacy policies. Instead, breaches occur because companies make one or more common missteps. First, some companies do not update their privacy policy to reflect changes in operations. As companies grow, they often expand their advertising and partnership strategies. These new vendors may start helping with the website and in doing so add data collection tools, availing themselves of the data as part of the relationship. This is a form of data sharing with a third party that should be part of the privacy policy, and if it was not, the relationship will violate the posted privacy policy. Second, some companies' business expands to include services often used by minors under thirteen or touching on financial services, credit, health care, or other areas governed by specific federal laws and regulations. As a company changes its services, it must update the privacy policy.

Third, small and start-up companies often acquire or are acquired by other enterprises. These mergers and restructurings often change the operations and in doing so the posted privacy policies must be taken into account. A similar problem may occur if a company's customer information is sold as part of a bankruptcy proceeding.

Fourth, many violations of privacy policies stem from failures to protect the data and information from breaches triggered by outside intruders or internal employees. Both forms of data breach, discussed in the next section, trigger a failure to comply with the privacy policy and also require that a company to publicly disclose the breach to its affected customers and often to state and federal law enforcement.

C.   Security Fundamentals.

1.   *Understanding Risk.*

The comprehensive NIST (National Institute of Standards and Technology) publication on "Small Business Information Security" provides a wealth of helpful information.[160] It reinforces the need for small businesses to plan for security.

> Because small businesses typically don't have the resources to invest in information security the way larger businesses can, many cyber criminals view them as soft targets. … It is important to note that criminals aren't always after profit. Some may attack your business out of revenge (e.g. for firing them or somebody they know), or for the thrill of causing havoc. Similarly, not all events that affect the confidentiality, availability, or integrity of your information (called "information security events") are

---

[160] *See* Paulsen & Toth, *supra* note 156.

caused by criminals. Environmental events such as fires or floods, for example, can severely damage computer systems.[161]

A business must understand that the risks come from the criminals or "hostile actors" that may include both outside criminals and hackers and inside disgruntled employees, careless employees, and employees planning to compete with the business. A second category of risk comes from the failure of the business resources such as the equipment, vendors, supply chains, or other operational disruptions. And finally, the small business is at risk from environmental factors such as fire, flood, storm, power outages, riots, and other natural or man-made disasters.

Not all risks are created equally. All Florida companies must have contingency plans in the case of hurricanes, while all Minnesota companies must plan to withstand blizzards. The risk of a blizzard in Florida or Georgia is quite low. Conversely, the chance that some employees will be upset and pose a risk to the business data is quite predictable. Even divorce is statistically predictable.

For a small company, it is a simple process to look at the scope of possible risks and the impact of those risks to assess what risks must be actively managed and which risks can be more generally monitored. Importantly, the risk assessment plan needs to be updated regularly. As the company grows, it may be relying much more heavily on outside vendors, changing the nature of the risk related to those vendors' failure. Risk assessment is an ongoing process.

NIST provides a chart to weigh the costs related to the breach, disclosure or destruction of the company's information, including the cost of breaching confidentiality, the cost to re-verify the information, the business loss caused by interruption of access to the information, legal expenses, data breach notification expenses, additional fines and penalties, public relations damage, and finally, the cost to repair the damage and return to the status quo. These costs add up.

2. *Safeguarding Business Information.*

Once a company has inventoried and weighed its threats along with the costs associated with those threats, it needs to inventory its

---

[161] *Id.* at 4.

informational assets. This includes an understanding of the types of information collected by the company. Customer files, financial records, trade secrets, production know-how, and many other valuable categories of data and information need to be identified. Only through the identification of these assets can the company take the steps needed to protect them.

The identification extends beyond the categories of information to the physical and network access points to the information. Corporate know-how and trade secrets should be kept in locked files. All data directories should be segmented so that only those employees who need access to particular databases or files have access to those files. Controls should be put in place so that information is not generally shared across the company, no matter how small.

There are many simple steps to help assure the physical safety of information and data:

- *Maintain all systems*—computers need to be updated constantly to have the latest patches. All equipment must be current enough to accept regular updating of patches and new programming.

- *Integrate firewalls*—small companies must work with a vendor well-versed in how to establish both hardware and software firewalls to thwart data security attacks on the computer systems. All default passwords must be changed when first introduced and updated regularly. This also applies to all networks and access points.

- *Use web and email filters*—malware, malicious websites, and other traps must be managed through aggressive software designed to protect the company from intrusion.

- *Encrypt sensitive information*—encryption systems are becoming much more common and easier to use. All protected information must be encrypted both while stored (at rest), while in transit, and in use. The adoption of encryption will greatly reduce the liabilities associated with data breach because the information stolen cannot be readily accessed.

- *Inventory and protect all devices*—each machine with access to the information must be monitored to be sure that older devices do not inadvertently compromise the system. This includes assuring that older machines, including digital photocopiers, are properly erased so the data is not accidently made public.

- *Maintain physical control of the environment*—all equipment, including servers, desktops, laptops, routers, network devices, and other equipment must be protected from theft or tampering at all times. Many credit card machines have been physically compromised as a way for credit card thieves to steal information. Other such devices have been used to create back doors on credit card systems used by retailers.

- *Back-up information offsite*—onsite back-up systems do not provide any protection from fire or other natural disasters. Information should be secured in geographically remote locations. Use of cloud-based technologies can overcome even regional power outages and other disasters. These large systems often provide much greater security than a small company can otherwise afford, at a price scaled to the data storage volume.

If the facility has cleaning crews, shared working space, or other reasons that unauthorized persons can get physical access, then additional steps need to be taken to lock all the equipment. Other important hygiene steps include assuring that passwords are not written next to devices; controlling home access to sensitive information; limiting the ability to put unauthorized software on company equipment; and many other common-sense steps.

3. Employee Risks.

Employees, independent contractors, vendors, and interns pose the greatest risk relative to loss of business data, far greater than outside hackers. And hackers are a real and continuous threat. Unless properly selected, trained, and supervised, the employees (including the others mentioned) will violate the privacy and security policies adopted by the company, ignore the lessons established at training, and take actions that are not permitted.

Examples of employee failure or misconduct have cause a myriad of data breaches and thefts. Employees have used passwords improperly to snoop through IRS, hospital, pharmacy, and small business customer information, thereby getting these enterprises into trouble for violations of privacy policies. Employees have made personal duplicates of nude photographs developed at photography studios, violating the strict privacy protections the companies provided to their customers. Employees have added software, enabling hackers to penetrate systems. Employees have clicked on infected emails, unwittingly launching cyberattacks.

Employees have logged into the customer lists and copied them to use in planned new businesses competing with their soon-to-be former employer. Employees have changed student grades. Employees have erased the hard drives and back-up drives of their former employer. Employees have changed the passwords of the computer system to shut down their former employer. Employees have stolen the company servers when leaving the company. And there are many, many more acts of theft and destruction recorded every day.

To avoid these risks, even the smallest company should conduct background checks on its prospective employees, limit access to computer systems so that each employee can access only the minimal amount of information needed for the employee to do the job, publish understandable policies so their employees are made aware of the security expectations, conduct regular trainings so the employees are practiced in data hygiene and safety, and regularly update these steps for both new and continuing employees.

4.   *Vendors.*

Although vendors present the same types of risks as do the company's employees, vendors are under less control and supervision. As a result, sound risk management requires additional diligence for vendors. Many companies have been subject to data breaches triggered by consultants who gave themselves access and then failed to properly return systems to their secure status. Vendors often ask for sensitive data to test new systems, but the vendors may not be fully informed of the privacy policy and the vendors may not offer the same level of data hygiene as the employees.

Vendors should be provided the minimum access needed to provide the service conducted. Whenever possible, vendors should be provided sample data rather than actual customer data of any kind. Vendors should also verify that they have an obligation to certify the return or destruction of all data at the end of the project and payment should be withheld until there is proof that the data protection steps have been undertaken. Although this risk cannot be fully eliminated, it should be highlighted and managed to the greatest extent possible.

D.   Managing and Surviving Disaster.

Managing a significant data breach or natural disaster depends entirely on the planning that occurred before the attack began. If all the information is stored on the entrepreneur's laptop hard drive, then the theft of the laptop could end the business.

If an unencrypted laptop was stolen containing personally identifiable information, then the business will likely need to contact the customers and the attorneys general in all the states which had any of the customers. Considering the legal fees, mailing fees, costs of providing free credit monitoring, and potential state fines in multiple jurisdictions, the cost of a data breach can run hundreds of dollars for each customer in the data set. According to the Ponemon Institute, for 2017 the average cost was $141 per record and the average breach cost $3.62 million.[162] If instead, the laptop was fully encrypted, then there may not be any obligation to report the loss of the laptop. Survival turns on planning.

In addition to the steps described in the earlier section, a company of any size should have a disaster plan in place. The disaster team will test that the offsite back-up system will load and operate on a regular basis. It will work with any cloud providers to test shutting down the primary company systems and operating from other systems.

A thorough system test will also be sure that the risk of a ransomware attack does not propagate to the back-up records. In a ransomware attack, a hacker encrypts all the company's files, sends out malware to

---

[162] Larry Ponemon, *2017 Ponemon Institute Cost of a Data Breach Study*, SECURITYINTELLIGENCE (July 26, 2017), https://securityintelligence.com/media/2017-ponemon-institute-cost-of-a-data-breach-study/.

encrypt all connected systems, and then blackmails the victim by refusing to decrypt the information without a ransom payment. If a system is not properly configured, then the information on the back-up systems can be encrypted simultaneously with the primary system, rendering it useless.

The disaster plan should also include the steps to take in advance of a natural disaster. To the extent possible, machines should be disconnected from power and networks, and they should be stored in waterproof, physically resilient storage facilities. In the case of floods, this also means high off the floor in rooms without windows.

Assuming the back-up system works appropriately, then the next step in the recovery is to work with the company's other disaster recovery team members. Every company should have a management telephone tree, identifying the various senior leadership team members and how to reach them in the case of an emergency. That team may include outside IT vendors, legal counsel, and communications specialists. Each of these outside vendors has an important role in getting the company back on its feet.

There may also be key suppliers and customers that need to be contacted, and that information must be kept available in a form that will be accessible if the company's systems are compromised. This usually means that some documents are kept as hard-copy files at the business owner's home.

Depending on the nature of the breach or intrusion, local or federal law enforcement should be contacted. Again, it is much better for the company to have collected this information in advance of any incidents rather than having to figure out where to turn once the emergency occurs.

Finally, the company will likely have some insurance, so contact with the company's insurance agent will be important and generally helpful. Cybersecurity insurance has grown into a significant business for many insurance companies, but the nature and scope of these policies varies greatly. The business should work with its broker to understand what types of risks are insured and how to go about establishing assistance for recovery and the steps for claims.

Although bad things happen to good companies, those businesses which took steps to anticipate and minimize the impact of disaster will be well situated to respond to those pressures with a well-communicating team that is following a concrete and comprehensive disaster plan. Tested back-up systems, phone trees, communication plans, and mitigation strategies can all be assessed, refined, and kept current provided the team prepares in advance for the likely potential disasters.

Part 3. Intellectual Property Reference Guide

A.   Introduction.

The purpose of this book has been to highlight successful strategies to help entrepreneurs achieve their goals. While the book may suggest a variety of business opportunities, the innovation and perseverance must come from the entrepreneur. The first step towards success is the ability to see that a problem can be fixed, that there must be a better way, or that something which works well in another entirely different context might work to solve the problem at hand.

Only when entrepreneurs recognize the need for solutions can they begin to craft them. Sometimes the solution is patentable, sometimes it can be protected by a trade secret, and sometimes the law provides no absolute exclusivity. Without patents or trade secrets, entrepreneurs must rely on trademarks, copyrights, and occasionally the power of celebrity to add publicity's value to the enterprise.

For the successful enterprise, trademarks can make even the most common of commodities stand out from the crowd. Sometimes copyrights and publicity rights are all that are needed to make the mundane special enough to capture the marketplace.

Trademark, copyright, and publicity rights help build relevance to the consumer. The entrepreneur must know his market and provide the solution that the customer wants. The entrepreneur must solve the right problem in the right way, or even a patented solution will have no value.

If the entrepreneur has solved the problem with the right solution, then the entrepreneur must still struggle through the process of building the business in the right way, to protect his interests, respect his investors and finance his enterprise. All of this is necessary so that the business solution has a chance to compete in the marketplace.

The method described in this book serves as an outline on how to build that business. Through frank and candid conversations with potential investors, both entrepreneur and investor will know what to expect before the LLC is structured. By applying the lessons in this book, both the entrepreneur and the investor will be better protected by the business decisions they make. From formation to financing, every aspect of the company should be designed to maximize the potential for success and align the interests of the entrepreneur with the entity being formed.

The true measure of the strategies provided may be the ability to encourage visionaries willing to risk their pride to achieve independence and success. This book shares the secrets of success: the need for exclusivity, the importance of relevance, and the power of innovation. Hopefully, the book has provided enough examples, suggestions, and tips to open the world of entrepreneurship for every hard-working visionary and give each the tools for success.

B.   How to Use with the Reference Guide.

The intellectual property reference guide should be used by all entrepreneurs who need a greater understanding of the types of intellectual property described throughout the book. While the guide does not replace the need to consult with an intellectual property attorney, it should simplify the meetings with those attorneys and explain the basics regarding the types of protection available for different types of inventions, ideas, drawing, and brands.

Each of the chapters begins with an explanatory summary showing the subject matter or type of property covered by the law, the methods to obtain legal protection, and the parameters of the legal protection available.

The choice regarding which intellectual property protection to use does not need to be an either/or choice. An innovative child's toy, for example, may have a patentable mechanism, artwork that can be copyrighted, titles and logos that will become trademarks, and a development process that includes trade secrets. A contract with a famous person can result in the toy incorporating the publicity rights of the spokesperson featured on the packaging, and sales licenses can be drafted to give exclusive rights to another company so that it can develop the software or gaming systems that incorporate the key features of the toy. As a result, every conceivable aspect of intellectual property can be part of an idea's development.

Following the Reference Guide are a series of sample agreements that help illustrate how to use these intellectual property rights in business. Taken together, the contracts and the Reference Guide should enable the entrepreneur to maximize the relevance and exclusivity of new products, services, and business opportunities.

Chapter 16.   Patents and Patent Law

A.   Attributes of Utility Patents.

Utility Patents—Summary

Subject Matter: Inventions or discoveries of any new and useful process, act or method, machine, manufacture, or composition of matter, or any new and useful improvement thereof.

Method Acquired: Applied for by the inventor, joint inventors, or the enterprise to the PTO. The employer usually acquires through written employment agreement. In addition, an employee "employed to invent" does so for the benefit of the employer, who will own the patent.

Term: 20 years from the date on which the application for the patent was filed.

Time Needed to Acquire: A patent application is generally published 18 months following the filing. The time for the issuance of the patent may be much longer.

Renewals: Renewal not required, but payment of "maintenance" fee is required. Maintenance fees are due at 3 ½, 7 ½ and 11 ½ years from the date the patent is granted, due during a six-month period preceding each period.

Federal Government Office and Website: United States Patent and Trademark Office www.uspto.gov.

Applicable Law: U.S. Patent Act, 35 U.S.C. §1 et. seq.

Transfer: Fully transferable, through a signed writing. It should be recorded with the PTO within three months of execution.

Property Excluded from Protection: Laws of nature; physical phenomena; abstract ideas; works of authorship; choreography and other processes involving human movement; and any machine or process that is not new or nonobvious.

B.   Patents Explained.

The basic law of patents appears to be quite simple. "Whoever invents or discovers any new and useful process, machine, manufacture, or composition of matter, or any new and useful improvement thereof, may obtain a patent therefor, subject to the conditions and requirements of this title."[163] As the introduction to the patent section of the Patent and Trademark Office—Inventor's Website explains:

> A patent is a property right granted by the Government of the United States of America to an inventor "to exclude others from making, using, offering for sale, or selling the invention throughout the United States or importing the invention into the United States" for a limited time in exchange for public disclosure of the invention when the patent is granted.[164]

1.   *Subject Matter of Utility Patents and Plant Patents.*

Inventions can include machines, chemicals, genetic inventions, compositions of matter, processes, and articles of manufacture of various kinds. Asexually reproducing plants are covered by plant patents. Since plant patents have the same general properties as utility patents, the following discussion will be limited to utility patents. The law excludes the patenting of inventions exclusively for nuclear material or atomic weapons.

As explained by the PTO, "Interpretations of the statute by the courts have defined the limits of the field of subject matter that can be patented, thus it has been held that the laws of nature, physical phenomena, and abstract ideas are not patentable subject matter."[165] In the same vein, a patent can only be granted once an idea has been transformed into an actual machine, manufacture, or composition, rather

---

[163] 35 U.S.C.S. § 101 (2018).

[164] *Patent FAQs*, U.S. PATENT & TRADEMARK OFFICE, https://www.uspto.gov/help/patent-help#1900 (last visited July 9, 2018).

[165] *General Information Concerning Patents*, U.S. PATENT & TRADEMARK OFFICE (Oct. 2015), https://www.uspto.gov/patents-getting-started/general-information-concerning-patents#heading-4.

than the abstract idea itself. The prototype is not required, however, just a complete description of the item to be patented.

2.   *Subject Matter of Design Patents.*

A second category of patents is design patents, which focus on non-functional ornamentation. These patents last only fourteen years. In the first edition of this book, it stated that design patents "generally have little value in the marketplace." Since that time, however, Apple had significant success against Samsung in enforcing its design patents on the shape of the iPhone, specifically its rounded corners. Rounded corners were a design feature of Apple products going back to the earliest days of the graphical user interface. Apple's success triggered a tremendous interest in the protection of product shape, ornamentation, and packaging design.

For more ornamental design elements, copyright can provide protection for aesthetic graphical designs without the expenses of filing and maintaining a patent. Despite the renewed interest, the PTO warns that an invention assistance company who suggests a design patent for the entrepreneur may be perpetrating a scam.[166] As demonstrated by Apple, there are some effective uses for design patents, and a qualified attorney may find a design patent appropriate for a particular design and a unique competitive environment.

3.   *An Invention Must Be New.*

The initial limitation of patentability under U.S. patent law is that the invention is new. It cannot have been in public use, on sale, patented, or otherwise available to the public before the filing of the patent application. An inventor can publish or otherwise publicly disclose the invention up to one year prior to filing the application, but this creates a risk that the invention will be put to public use or sale and extinguish the patentability of the invention.

Every patent issued should be absolutely "new" for the public. For example, when Rollerblades first became popular, the company applied for a patent of its inline skates. A search of the "prior art"—the Patent Office files and relevant literature—resulted in the discovery of a 19ᵗʰ

---

[166] Office of Innovation Dev., *supra* note 32.

century patent for inline skates. Although Rollerblade had not relied on the patent, and in all likelihood the patent had long been forgotten, the existence of that old patent was sufficient to prohibit Rollerblade from obtaining a valid patent on its technology. This sets a very high bar for patentability. Fortunately, the statute specifically allows for improvements on inventions to be patented, so modifications of existing products and processes are eligible for patent protection.

4.   An Invention Must Be Useful.

The second core requirement for patent eligibility is that the patented invention be useful. This requirement precludes any attempt to patent ideas. Instead, any novel idea must be "reduced to practice" or implemented into a working invention. The patent is the end product of the idea, research, design, and implementation of the invention.

The device, in its usefulness, must do what the inventor claims it does. The patent must describe an invention that works. The classic example of the unpatentable device is the perpetual motion machine. Since such a machine cannot exist under the laws of physics, any claim to have created a perpetual motion machine will always be rejected.

Useful is not the same as marketable. There are a great many patents which are granted because the inventor achieved his goal in making the device do what the specification said the invention would do—even though no rational consumer would want the device. These "wacky patents" adorn many websites.[167] Some, however, may be less wacky than others. Only the marketplace can determine whether a functional patent is relevant to the public or doomed to adorn a wacky patent website.

---

[167] Examples of Wacky Patents include: Totally Absurd Inventions at http://www.totallyabsurd.com/; Electronic Frontier Foundation's Stupid Patent of the Month at https://www.eff.org/issues/stupid-patent-month; or Free Patents Online's Crazy Patents at http://www.freepatentsonline.com/crazy.html.

5. An Invention Must Be Nonobvious.

The statute again prescribes those inventions that cannot be patented:

A patent for a claimed invention may not be obtained ... if the differences between the claimed invention and the prior art are such that the claimed invention as a whole would have been obvious before the effective filing date of the claimed invention to a person having ordinary skill in the art to which the claimed invention pertains.[168]

The test for nonobvious has been called the most subjective aspect of the patent application, because the examiner must determine what a person with some professional experience in the field would consider obvious.[169] Consider, for example, the earlier discussion of Leonardo Da Vinci's parachute. A person with ordinary skill in the art would know that designers are on a constant quest to replace existing materials with new, stronger, and lighter materials. A patent on the use of a new, lightweight material for the parachute cloth might be obvious unless it confers an unexpected advantage and therefore, simply applying lightweight fabric to parachutes is not patentable. In contrast, if the parachute invention were to use a new system of controlled apertures (or holes) in the cloth to steer the parachute, replacing the use of cords with an electronic aperture system, it is likely that such a system is sufficiently different from the steering mechanism used in parachutes, sails, or other similar systems to satisfy the nonobvious requirement.

6. Patents are Issued to the First Inventor to File the Application.

In 2011, Congress amended the patent law with the Leahy-Smith America Invents Act (AIA). The AIA made a number of significant procedural changes to U.S. patent law. Among them, the AIA granted priority to the first inventor to file a patent on an invention. This change from the former rules that the first person to prove that he or she was

---

[168] 35 U.S.C. § 103 (West 2018).

[169] *See* Brian Farkas, *Qualifying for a Patent FAQs*, NOLO, https://www.nolo.com/legal-encyclopedia/qualifying-patent-faq.html (last visited July 9, 2018).

the inventor of a patentable invention is considered to greatly simplify the patent application process, as well as to bring the U.S. into the practice generally followed in most of the world.

As a result of this new rule, the application for a patent in the claimed invention filed prior to the date of filing by another inventor will disqualify the patent application. This has the effect of increasing pressure on inventors to move from the lab to the patent application as quickly as possible.

C.   The Patent Application.

The patent application is a very technical process. It is far more complex than any other form of intellectual property protection, requiring a significant amount of technical skill by the patent agent or patent lawyer. Unlike other forms of intellectual property, the rights provided by a patent only come into existence if the government issues the patent. The following provides a brief overview of the language of the patent application process and the key concepts used by those involved in the patenting process.

1.   *Application by the Inventor or Assignee.*

A patent application must be made by the inventor, assignee, or employer of the inventor. The process of financing the inventors or supporting their activities is not the basis for becoming an inventor. In the case of a deceased or incapacitated inventor, the legal representative of the inventor can act on the inventor's behalf.

The application is comprised of a written document providing the specifications, which is made up of the description of the invention and the claims of the invention, along with drawings in most applications, and an oath or declaration affirming the veracity of the information contained in the application. There are also filing, search, and examination fees, with discounts for small entities and even larger discounts for micro entities.

2.   *Reducing the Patent to Writing—Specification and Claims.*

The invention and its functions must be reduced to writing before the patent application can be filed. The invention must be explained in sufficient detail so that another person of reasonable skill in the field can produce the invention from the description in the patent application.

The application includes forms, filing fees, invention specifications, drawings, and claims. The specifications are the written description of the invention. These must detail the "manner and process of making and using" the invention.[170]

The claims set out the legally enforceable rights for the patent. The claims define the scope of the protection of the patent. "More than one claim may be presented provided they differ from each other. Claims may be presented in independent form (e.g. the claim stands by itself) or in dependent form, referring back to and further limiting another claim or claims in the same application. Any dependent claim that refers back to more than one other claim is considered a "multiple dependent claim.""[171]

Whether a patent will be granted is determined, in large measure, by the choice of wording of the claims. Each claim should be a single sentence, and where a claim sets forth a number of elements or steps, each element or step of the claim should be separated by a line indentation.

As these instructions make clear, the legal challenge in patent claims drafting is a rather arcane art of carefully describing complex processes—each in a single sentence. While a patent application does not have to be filed by an attorney, it is unwise to risk filing an invention without the aid of anyone other than a patent agent or patent attorney with significant experience in claims drafting.

Finally, drawings may be used, when helpful, to illustrate the claims and specifications, making clear with pictures what may be too difficult to communicate with words. Again, great care must be taken because "[t]he drawings must show every feature of the invention as specified in the claims."[172]

---

[170] *Nonprovisional (Utlitiy) Patent Application Filing Guide*, U.S. PATENT & TRADEMARK OFFICE (Jan. 2014), https://www.uspto.gov/patents-getting-started/patent-basics/types-patent-applications/nonprovisional-utility-patent.

[171] *Id.*

[172] *Id.*

3.   *Timing and Issuance.*

The patent application process presumes an eighteen-month cycle of review, but applications often take much longer. The assigned patent examiner reviews the patent application to see that the subject matter is acceptable and that the patent meets the standards of new, useful, and nonobvious. If it meets these standards, the patent will be issued, and the patent rights are enforceable for twenty years from the date of the completed application (not the date of issuance). In certain situations in which the application process has had lengthy delays, the applicant may seek an extension of the twenty-year period to recover some of the protection time lost to the application process.

Great care should be taken regarding the invention's movement toward commercialization. Changes brought by the AIA have complicated the so-called grace period. "No one should disclose or try to commercialize an invention without having discussed the situation with a specialist! U.S. law contains a one-year grace period, but if an invention is offered for sale, used or described publicly before filing an application, patentability is lost in most of the world."[173] If an inventor discloses an invention to third parties and those third parties further disclose the invention, then the inventor will now be required to prove that the third party was merely republishing the information of the inventor. This could prove very difficult in many instances. As a result, the one-year grace period should be considered a safety net rather than a planning device.

From the earliest stages of the invention, the inventor should create and maintain a notebook. The notebook is used to prove the timeline of the invention. This tool is needed to protect the invention against claims by a second inventor who might be creating the same invention. Under the previous legal rules of first-to-invent, these notebooks were essential evidence for proof of the date of invention. Under the AIA's first-to-file rules, these notebooks are less important since the timeline of the invention is no longer at stake to the same degree. There are many other

---

[173] Thomas G. Field, Jr., *Intellectual Property Some Practical and Legal Fundamentals*, 35 IDEA: J.L. & TECH. 79, 92 (1994), http://www.ipmall.info/sites/default/files/hosted_resources/IDEA/6.Field.pdf.

contexts, however, where the timeline will still matter, so the inventor notebooks should still be used.

4.   *Filing a Provisional Patent Application.*

The race to the filing office has been exacerbated by the changes of the AIA, putting even more value on the filing date of an invention. There is, however, some modicum of relief. Since 1995, inventors have been provided the opportunity to file a patent on an invention or process being developed. An inventor who has filed a provisional application must follow-up by filing a non-provisional application within one year of the initial provisional filing.

The provisional application extends the legal protection for the patent and helps the inventor know that the invention will receive protection. Inventor benefits from the provisional patent application in three ways:

- Patentability is evaluated as though filed on the provisional application filing date rather than the subsequent nonprovisional filing date.

- The resulting patent would be treated as a reference under 35 U.S.C. § 102(e) as of the provisional application filing date.

- Despite the provisional filing date, the twenty-year patent term is measured from the non-provisional application filing date.

The provisional patent application provides an inventor an alternative to the rush to the filing office. In order to take advantage of the provisional application, the inventor must be fairly close to completing the work on one of the ultimate claims. The PTO lists a number of limitations that an inventor must take into account:

- Provisional applications for patent may not be filed for design inventions.

- Provisional applications are not examined on their merits.

- Provisional applications for patent cannot claim the benefit of a previously-filed application, either foreign or domestic.

- It is recommended that the disclosure of the invention in the provisional application be as complete as possible.

- In order to obtain the benefit of the filing date of a provisional application, the claimed subject matter in the later filed nonprovisional application must have support in the provisional application.

- If there are multiple inventors, each inventor must be named in the application.

- All inventor(s) named in the provisional application must have made a contribution, either jointly or individually, to the invention disclosed in the application.

- The nonprovisional application must have at least one inventor in common with the inventor(s) named in the provisional application to claim benefit of the provisional application filing date.

- A provisional application must be entitled to a filing date and include the basic filing fee in order for a nonprovisional application to claim benefit of that provisional application.

- There is a surcharge for filing the basic filing fee or the cover sheet on a date later than filing the provisional application.

- Amendments are not permitted in provisional applications after filing, other than those to make the provisional application comply with applicable regulations.

- No information disclosure statement may be filed in a provisional application.[174]

If the description and drawings do not support the non-provisional claims, the benefits of the provisional application will be lost. Some latitude exists, however, because the drawings and descriptions need not be identical, just of sufficient to support the subject matter of the application.

---

[174] *Provisional Application for Patent*, U.S. PATENT & TRADEMARK OFFICE, http://www.uspto.gov/web/offices/pac/provapp.htm (last visited July 9, 2018).

The effect of the provisional application is to align U.S. practice with the method of filing patents elsewhere in the world. In most countries, a patent application may be made before making any disclosure or commercial use of patents. The provisional application process allows for both processes to occur in the U.S. with some slight advantages to the provisional filing method. It also allows the applicant to begin using the "Patent Pending" designation on the item.

* * *

Sidebar—Patent economics.

Patent economics are a heavily debated topic among business leaders and intellectual property academics. The AIA was adopted in response to a widespread consensus that patents were being issued too readily by the PTO, and as a result, there was a great uncertainty regarding the validity of patents when they are challenged in court. Since the adoption of the AIA, new procedures allow for additional challenges to patent validity. The result of these challenges has been to revoke a high percentage of patents that were about to be issued. These procedures serve as a second check on the patent examiner's willingness to issue a patent.

Along with the statutory changes, the U.S. Supreme Court has issued a series of rulings that have narrowed the scope of what falls within the subject matter of patents. Although articles of nature were never patentable, discoveries of how to use natural molecules had often been within the realm of patent protection. The Supreme Court has ruled against such discoveries of use of natural materials as well as the identification of DNA, however rare and unique in its properties. These changes have dramatically shifted the perspective on the eligibility for patents.

In all situations, patent litigation is very expensive, and risk-averse companies struggle to balance the need to defend their own patents, challenge the validity of other patents, and manage the costs of the patent management.

Patent critics have also focused on the monopoly power granted by patents. While in some industries, the non-patented alternative is acceptable, in areas such as medicine, there is no reasonable substitute for a life-saving drug. The patent provides the manufacturers with a guaranteed twenty-year period in which to amortize the development costs of these drugs—a cost which can be quite high. The monopoly also condemns the public to a twenty-year wait before less expensive alternatives can legally be sold in the market.

A very successful patent for a new medication may have no reasonable market alternative. Put another way, the consumer cannot turn to another product as a substitute. The pricing is also outside of any market system because of health care regulations, federal laws, and other anomalies in the medical delivery system.

Whatever the other problems associated with health care costs may be, to the extent that the costs of the drug's development are amortized during the patent term, the shorter the term, then the higher the drug expense. This suggests that shortening the patent term would only increase the cost of the drugs, but this may over-simplify the problem. The only limit on the price of a life-saving drug is the ability or willingness of the customer to pay. If no comparable drug is available, it is unlikely that market forces will lower the price. Instead, the bargaining power of the insurance companies, the drug company's discomfort at accusations of price gouging, and the fear of government intervention will control the drug's price. The price of pharmaceuticals is not limited by normal market forces. The pathology of pharmaceutical pricing may help explain how patent economics should work.

Pharmaceutical pricing is unlike the pricing for most patented machines or processes. A patented car safety device, such as Volvo's safety features, increases the cost of the car. Some customers are willing to pay for the marginal increase in safety—meaning the incremental increase in safety—afforded by the patented devices. Other drivers do not value the safety benefit as sufficiently great (or alternatively, do not value the risk of injury as sufficiently large) to justify the increased price. Other drivers, of course, might value the safety benefit, but do not have the money to make such a choice.

Airbags were an extremely popular form of passive restraint in cars, allowing those manufacturers that first adopted airbag technology to command a large price premium for those cars. Sliding seat belts were a competing form of passive restraint, but it was a technology not appreciated by most drivers. Consumer demand made airbags a standard feature on most cars, eliminating the premium that could be charged. As the premium price for airbags disappeared and the patented technology became widely available, the feature evolved into a standard item on all cars and competing passive restraint systems were dropped by all car manufacturers.

The airbag adoption illustrates the final aspect of patent economics. As a patent license becomes generally available to all competing manufacturers, the premium price for those products with the patented technology diminishes. There remains some price premium because the patented product is enhanced in some manner in comparison to similar products without the patent enhancements. But there is no competitive advantage between manufacturers, which is the source of the greater price premium.

For the patent owner, the choice is to have more units sold or to have a higher price paid for fewer units sold. The optimal licensing plan will depend on the size of the market and the size of the price premium. Because there are also significant costs associated with the adoption of new technology, it is common that the early licensees will insist on exclusivity as a condition of making the initial investments.

✳ ✳ ✳

D.   Acquiring Patents.

Patents are a form of property, and like land, a patent can be bought, sold, inherited, mortgaged, and sold in a bankruptcy auction. Patents are initially acquired through the inventor's or assignee's filing with the patent office, but once the patent is granted it can be acquired by others through some other legal transaction. Employers typically receive the patents of their employees by operation of employment law, while other transfers involve contracts, licenses, or legal transfers of ownership. Licenses are the most significant forms of ownership acquisition and transfer for the entrepreneur and start-up business.

1.   Invention.

The most obvious source of patent ownership is through the patent application process described in the preceding section. For the person who is both the entrepreneur and the inventor, the primary source of the patent is through one's own intellectual efforts and application of industry. All patents flow from some person or persons' intellectual efforts and industry, and every patent can be traced back to its inventor.

2.   Hired to Invent, Shop Rights Doctrine, and Employment Agreements.

While all patents require inventions, not all patents are the progeny of the inventor. In the more common situation, the inventor applies his effort to solve a problem identified by his employer, making the idea into a practical invention or to "reduce to practice" an idea proposed by the employer or other person.

As a general matter, when an inventor or engineer patents an invention as part of her employment, the patent is owned by the company. Known as the "hired to invent" doctrine, the patent is considered the work product of the inventor, made on behalf of the employer. Under employment law, the hired inventor's work product belongs to the employer as part of the employee's duty of loyalty to the employer. The "work-for-hire doctrine" is analogous and provides the same result in copyright law.

Patent law has a subsidiary doctrine, known as the "shop rights" doctrine, for those situations in which the employee uses the equipment and facilities of his employer outside of the regular scope of the employee's employment. In this situation, the employee has the ownership of the patent, but the company has the free use of the patent as a form of repayment for its resources. Many great inventions arose by clever engineers and scientists who used the facilities of their employers after hours on projects unrelated to the employer's business. The shop rights doctrine provided an incentive to both employer and scientist to continue the pursuit of new knowledge and industry.

These legal doctrines are applied where there is no contractual agreement between the employer and employee. Good business planning requires that specific ownership of employee-developed patents and other intellectual property be detailed in the employment agreements and personnel handbooks. The economic difference between patents developed by employees who are hired to invent and those patents that are granted to the company based on the "shop rights" doctrine could be worth millions of dollars and should not be left to chance.

For an entrepreneur who hires an engineer or other expert to develop and patent the entrepreneur's original idea, the need for a signed contract specifying the ownership of the patent and the payment obligations is critical. In such a situation, no traditional employment relationship exists. Thus, a contract is needed to specify that the idea, which should be subject to nondisclosure by the parties, originated with the entrepreneur. Additionally, the contract should include a funding plan for the engineer to develop the invention and reduce the idea to practice. The engineer would be paid for her work, either as a commissioned amount, a salary, or a portion of the future royalties generated by the patent. The engineer would be the inventor for purposes of the patent, but the contract would transfer the ownership of the patent to the entrepreneur.

While the contract could have provisions to account for many more contingencies, the nondisclosure provisions, patent ownership clauses, and compensation terms provide the core essence of these types of agreements. The "idea" would have to be respected as a trade secret by the parties. Without this contract, the rights of both the entrepreneur and the engineer would be ambiguous and likely to result in significant disputes. Even the risk of such disputes would drive away most funding opportunities for the start-up business.

3.   *Acquisition through Purchase or Licensing.*

The employment agreement is just one example of a purchase agreement, uniquely tied to the performance of the inventor. The company can also acquire the patent through a purchase or license agreement, which grants to the company either the patent or some rights to use the invention.

It may be helpful to label the purchase of the patent as a transaction in which the entire patent property ownership transfers from the first party to the second party. This transfer could be from the inventor to a manufacturer or from one manufacturer to another manufacturer. A license, in contrast, is the purchase of the right to use some aspect of the patent, but the original owner still retains some rights to the patent and remains the patent owner.

Although not technically correct, the entrepreneur may find it helpful to contrast the purchase of the entire patent with the license of various uses of a patent in planning for the business. As with all other property, the purchase cost of a patent is dependent on the scope of ownership acquired. An entrepreneur may not need to purchase everything in order to achieve the business goals, so choices regarding licenses should be made with both budgets and competition in mind.

As discussed in the prior chapter, patents are often licensed in narrow segments based on time windows, specific industries, geographic territories, and other restrictions. In making the licenses narrow, the patent holder is finding the most valuable use for each aspect of the invention and assuring that the payments are maximized in each segment. In other cases, the licensee wants to acquire all the rights to assure there is no competition, but that is an expensive proposition if the licensee cannot make money using the license in those fields.

For example, assume a company has patented a gill-like device to extract oxygen from water to make it breathable. The primary use would be to make a mouthpiece that could replace oxygen tanks for divers. The patent holder licenses the patent to a sporting goods manufacturer for use with underwater sports enthusiasts. Rather than selling the patent to that company or licensing all rights to that company, the patent holder instead limits the license to commercial manufacturing and reserves the right to manufacture or license the technology for governmental agencies, including military agencies. If the commercial licensee did not have the expertise to contract with the government and meet the demanding procurement requirements, it would likely prefer to avoid paying the additional cost of owning this market that it could not efficiently exploit. The sports diving company would pay less for the license and the licensor would earn a greater profit by creating separate, limited exclusive markets for the device.

It is interesting to note that an actual crowdfunded attempt at this technology resulted in the company refunding all its raised funding when it was disclosed that it relied on liquid oxygen to achieve its underwater results. Although gills work quite well in nature, no biomechanical devices have managed to achieve this goal, as yet, for humans.

4.   Other Transfers.

As a form of property, patents are subject to other forms of transfers, just like real estate. A patent can serve as collateral for a loan, and if the loan is foreclosed, then the patent can be foreclosed upon and sold to pay the debt. Similarly, if an inventor or other natural person dies owning a patent, that patent will be part of the estate and transferred by will or by law. The patent rights may be a significant asset for collateral in bank loans or other financing opportunities.

For the start-up business, some care should be taken regarding any agreements that may involve the use of the patents as collateral. Similarly, due care must be exercised to assign the patents to the business rather than leaving those assets in the hands of the business founders. Otherwise, if the founder dies, the company ownership and the patent may be distributed separately depending on the terms of the inventor's will, potentially destroying the value of either or both assets.

E.   Enforcement of Patent Rights.

The process of protecting one's patent rights is as complex as the process of obtaining a new patent. This brief overview provided below understates the time consuming, expensive, and highly unpredictable process of identifying infringement and bringing legal action to recover damages.

1.   Identifying Infringing Conduct.

A patent protects the patent owner from any sale, offer for sale, commercial use, or importation of an item that has the same attributes that are specified in the patent claims. The owner of a patent can stop any third party from selling the identical product even if it was invented independently, without any knowledge of the existing patent.

In addition to identical inventions, patent law provides protection from inventions that are designed around the patent. Known as the doctrine of equivalents, this rule provides that "if two devices do the same work in substantially the same way, and accomplish substantially the same result, they are the same, even though they differ in name, form or shape."[175] The doctrine of equivalents expands protection from literal infringement to a somewhat broader category of activities, enriching the value in the patent.

2.   Contacting the Infringer.

Once an infringing product has been identified, the next step is generally to contact the infringing party and attempt to arrange an agreement without a lawsuit. A "cease and desist" letter is generally sent by the patent owner's lawyer, explaining that the invention is patented by another party and demanding that the unauthorized use stop, or that the use become authorized through a licensing arrangement. If the patent owner has already provided an exclusive license to another party, the patent owner may have no choice but to sue to stop the infringement pursuant to the terms of the exclusive patent license.

The alleged infringer may respond by negotiating with the patent owner or it may challenge the claim. Generally, the challenge will take

---

[175] Graver Tank & Mfg. Co. v. Linde Air Products Co., 339 U.S. 605, 608 (1950) (*quoting* Union Paper-Bag Machine Co. v. Murphy, 97 U.S. 120, 125 (1877)).

one of two forms. The alleged infringer will claim that the patent is invalid, and therefore unenforceable, or that the patent does not cover the usage presently being made.

3.   The Litigation Process.

Either party may file a lawsuit regarding the dispute. Patent litigation is heard in federal district courts, and either party may request that the case be presented to a jury. Like other trials, a great deal of time and effort is spent in discovery, reviewing documents and evidence collected from the other party, asking written questions, taking depositions or oral testimony, and gathering experts to testify. The complexity of patent claims creates complexity in the discovery process of reviewing corporate documents and relevant potential evidence.

After the parties have engaged in a substantial part of the discovery process, the federal court will hold what is known as a *Markman* hearing, at which the federal judge or magistrate will determine how to interpret or construct the patent claims. The claim construction is not subject to jury decision, and this hearing can often determine the outcome of the dispute.

The judge or jury will then need to determine whether the patent is valid, and if it is valid, whether the use by the defendant violated the rights of the plaintiff. Since the PTO issued the patent, it is presumed to be valid. The defendant, however, can overcome this presumption with clear and convincing evidence. Although the language suggests this is a very high standard, courts tend not to defer to the PTO. As a result, despite the initial presumption of validity, many issued patents are determined to be invalid through the litigation process. But this is certainly not always the case, so these trials and their appeals to the Federal Circuit are lengthy and costly.

4.   Recovery and Damages.

If the plaintiff is successful in proving infringement, then the court typically enjoins the defendant from continuing to infringe the patent. While the Supreme Court has ruled that injunctions are not automatic, in many cases the courts will protect the patent owner with an injunction barring continued use of the patent. In addition, the plaintiff is typically entitled to a recovery based upon some calculation of what the reasonable royalty would have been for the patent had it been licensed, or for the lost profits the patent owner would have made if the infringement had not occurred. Lost profits are generally the larger amount, but they are also difficult to determine and prove. In order to recover lost profits, the patent owner must show that it could have manufactured the products itself, establish what net profits it would have made on that manufacturing, and demonstrate that there was no adequate substitute for its products to reduce the value of the claimed net profits. If the plaintiff can show that it is entitled to the profits rather than merely the royalty, it can receive the larger award.

In extraordinary cases, the court may also provide the prevailing party with costs and attorneys' fees in addition to the injunction relief and the recovery of profits or royalties. Costs and attorneys' fees are awarded at the discretion of the court and are not automatically available. In situations of willful infringement or misconduct before the PTO, the court is more likely to award attorneys' fees. In contrast, if the parties were in a legitimate fight over the meaning of a patent claim, it is far less likely that a court would award attorneys' fees. Attorneys' fees are available to the prevailing party, whether plaintiff or defendant.

5.   *Violating the Patent Rights of Others.*

The infringement of another party's patent rights may occur in one of three different ways. A company may invent something that is covered by a patent claim previously recognized by the PTO for another party, a party may utilize the published information of a patent to manufacture its own device before that patent has expired, or a party may import or purchase a product which has infringed on another's patent.

A patent is infringed whenever a new invention is identical or equivalent to the issued patent. The patent holder does not have to prove copying, and the infringer cannot claim independent creation as a defense to the infringement. It is this breadth of protection that makes the patent such a formidable right. The innocence of the infringing party may affect damage awards and the award of attorneys' fees, but it will not eliminate the infringement.

Copying the published information from the patent application is a willful infringement. This is patent piracy and will elicit no sympathy from either court or jury.

For most companies, however, the most likely cause of a cease and desist letter will be the use or importation of a patented item that was, itself, unauthorized. For example, assume a company successfully patents a new molecular compound from which a man-made thread is spun. The thread is patented in the U.S. only. After reading the patent, a manufacturer in Brazil begins manufacturing spools of this synthetic thread. The Brazilian manufacturer can lawfully produce the thread because it is not patented in that country, and it can lawfully ship the thread into other countries where no patent application was made. A U.S. clothing manufacturer imports the thread for use. Unlike the Brazilian thread manufacturer, the U.S. company importing the thread can be sued for infringement of the patent owner's exclusive rights in the United States.

Companies must be careful to review the source of goods and technology in their acquisition of source materials so that they do not inadvertently interfere with the patent rights of other companies. In addition, all contracts should contain provisions that guarantee the buyer of the seller's legitimate intellectual property in the product being sold. These contracts should also include an indemnification clause, which would pass the liability on to the seller in the event that an infringement challenge is made.

Unfortunately, the valuable property interests created by intellectual property rights also complicate the business of manufacturing products. Companies must be very proactive, using intellectual property as a corporate benefit rather than merely a compliance annoyance.

F.   The International Implications of Patent Law and Practice.

The internationalization of trade has dramatically increased the importance of international protection of intellectual property. Despite this growing trend, the laws protecting intellectual property operate nationally rather than internationally. This means that the law of each country must be applied to each particular intellectual property. Generally, the legal enforcement of those rights must occur in the courts of the country where the property is recognized.

1.   Patent Cooperation Treaty.

In the area of patent law, the Patent Cooperation Treaty (PCT) provides a collaborative system for 152 signatory countries (and more jurisdictions continue to join). This treaty is significant because it coordinates the application process. It helps reduce international application delays and simplifies the international process greatly. The United States is an active participant in the PCT, and English is one of the major treaty languages.

The PCT uses a two-step process in which the inventor files an "international" treaty application through one of the major international treaty offices, including the PTO. The PTO explains its expectation regarding the process: "In most instances a national U.S. application is filed first. An international application for the same subject matter will then be filed subsequently within the priority year provided by the Paris Convention and the priority benefit of the U.S. national application filing date will be claimed."[176]

2.   Other International Filing Options.

The PCT may also be supplemented with other international filings. "The PCT offers an alternative route to filing patent applications directly in the patent offices of those countries which are Contracting States of the PCT. It does not preclude taking advantage of the priority rights and other advantages provided under the Paris Convention and the WTO administered Agreement on Trade-Related Aspects of Intellectual Property (TRIPS Agreement)."[177]

This suggests that the U.S. inventor should file the application with the PTO and determine what advantages may exist to paying the national filing fees of each additional country. For certain inventions, the TRIPS filing process may prove best, while for smaller inventions, the decision not to apply outside the U.S. may be preferred.

---

[176] U.S. PATENT AND TRADEMARK OFFICE, MANUAL OF PATENT EXAMINING PROCEDURE § 1801 (9th ed. 2014), http://www.uspto.gov/web/offices/pac/mpep/documents/1800_1801.htm#sect18 01 (last modified Jan. 24, 2018) (section 1801 is titled Basic Patent Cooperation Treaty (PCT) Principles [R-08.2017]).

[177] Id.

3.   *Impact of International Trade.*

Patent protection remains territorial. A patent is valid only in those countries where the application and maintenance fees have been made. This means that an invention may be patented in some countries but not others. Import companies must be very careful about importing items that are protected by U.S. patents, as well as those licensed in a country that did not grant the patent (or in which no patent was sought). In these situations, the company could be violating its contract by not delivering the exclusivity promised or by infringing the rights of other parties.

The international obligations go well beyond the patent process to inform the manner in which international trade is conducted by the company and how best to target foreign opportunities in a strategic and economic manner. Treaties, tariffs, and trade agreements also affect the decision to market a patented product in each country. International trade is affected by intellectual property rights, but it is a distinct legal field. Particularly for manufactured goods, the role of patents is only a small aspect of the overall practice of international trade.

Chapter 17.   Copyrights and Copyright Law

A.   Attributes of Copyright.

Copyrights—Summary

Subject Matter: "Original works of authorship," including literary, dramatic, musical, artistic, and certain other intellectual works.

Method Acquired: Automatically acquired upon fixation of the work (paper, disk, computer memory, sculpture, etc.).

Term: Life of the author plus 70 years. Works-for-hire have a term of 95 years from publication or 120 years from creation, whichever is shorter.

Time Needed to Acquire: No waiting period. Registration with Copyright Office confers additional protections.

Renewals: None required for works created beginning 1978; renewal required for works published before 1964.

Federal Government Office and Website: Copyright Office, a division of the Library of Congress. www.copyright.gov.

Applicable Law: 1976 Copyright Act, 17 U.S.C. §101, et. sec.

Transfer: Fully transferable, exclusive transfer only in writing signed by transferring party. Registration of transfer helpful but not required.

Property Excluded from Protection: Ideas, procedures, methods, systems, processes, concepts, principles, discoveries, devices, or listings of ingredients or contents; and titles, names, short phrases and slogans; typefaces; familiar symbols or designs.

B.   Copyright Explained.

Drawing from the statutory rules that make up copyright, the Copyright Office provides this elegant working definition of copyright:

[a] form of protection provided by the laws of the United States for "original works of authorship" including literary, dramatic, musical, architectural, cartographic, choreographic, pantomimic,

pictorial, graphic, sculptural, and audiovisual creations. "Copyright" literally means the right to copy but has come to mean that body of exclusive rights granted by law to copyright owners for protection of their work. Copyright protection does not extend to any idea, procedure, process, system, title, principle, or discovery. Similarly, names, titles, short phrases, slogans, familiar symbols, mere variations of typographic ornamentation, lettering, coloring, and listings of contents or ingredients are not subject to copyright.[178]

This simple introduction captures the key attributes of copyright, providing all the information an entrepreneur needs to understand when copyright applies.

1.   *Subject Matter of Copyright.*

As described in the definition above, copyright ownership covers, with limited exceptions, "original works of authorship," including literary, dramatic, musical, architectural, cartographic, choreographic, pantomimic, pictorial, graphic, sculptural, and audiovisual creations that are protected by law as soon as the work is "fixed in any tangible medium of expression."[179]

Fixation is merely the requirement that the expression be recorded in some manner. The material can be written, recorded, videotaped, filmed, digitized or otherwise fixed in an entirely new form. Manuscripts, brochures, websites and all writings are fixed on paper or computer memory. A business presentation can be a copyrighted work if the text of the presentation is written out or if the presentation is videotaped. Absent fixation, an oral presentation will not be protected by copyright.

The originality requirement for copyright is quite modest. The primary aspect of originality is that the work must be the creative product of the author, rather than copied from another source. The ideas need

---

[178] *U.S. Copyright Office Definitions*, U.S. COPYRIGHT OFFICE, http://www.copyright.gov/help/faq/definitions.html (last visited July 10, 2018); *see* 17 U.S.C. § 101 (2018).

[179] 17 U.S.C. § 102 (2018).

not be new or original. Unoriginal works are those failing to have even a minimal level of creativity. The white pages phone book text, consisting of the names and telephone numbers of individuals in a specified geographic location in alphabetical order, allows for no creative interpretation and therefore, is not protected by copyright. Similarly, the Copyright Office suggests "standard calendars, height and weight charts, tape measures [and] rulers,"[180] as examples of works lacking in creative input.

Like patents, copyrights are treated as property and may be used to secure loans, transferred by will, or otherwise treated as property by their owners. Copyrights comprise valuable commercial assets of companies and must be cataloged and managed to maximize corporate assets.

2.   *Matters Not Protected by Copyright.*

Copyright and patent laws do not often overlap. The innovations, processes, and methods protected by patent are excluded by copyright. The statute specifically provides that "[i]n no case does copyright protection for an original work of authorship extend to any idea, procedure, process, system, method of operation, concept, principle, or discovery, regardless of the form in which it is described, explained, illustrated, or embodied in such work."[181]

The difference in the law's scope of protection between patent and copyright is directly related to the ease with which one can obtain a copyright and the difficulty one faces when applying for a patent. Since all an author has to prove for copyright protection is that he said something or created some expression in a fixed form, the law is similarly limited in its protection. The copyright provides the author exclusivity only on the expression, with no protection for the work's underlying ideas.

This inherent limitation of copyright makes copyright the wrong body of law to protect business plans, sensitive data and innovative proposals. Ideas which have been reduced to practice can be protected

---

[180] *Circular 32: Blank Forms and Other Works Not Protected by Copyright*, U.S. COPYRIGHT OFFICE, https://www.copyright.gov/circs/circ32.pdf (revised Oct. 2015).

[181] 17 U.S.C. § 102(b) (2018).

by patent law, while the confidential and valuable information in the business plans, data, and innovation should be treated and protected as trade secrets. Copyright can supplement these systems, but it is secondary.

Copyright is also kept somewhat distinct from trademark because copyright does not extend to "[t]itles, names, short phrases, and slogans; [f]amiliar symbols or designs; [m]ere variations of typographic ornamentation, lettering, or coloring; [m]ere listings of ingredients or contents."[182] Short phrases such as McDonald's "I'm lovin' it" will be protected by trademark law because the phrase helps identify the source of goods, but it cannot be protected by copyright.

Some trademarks do have copyright protection. The cartoon drawing of Mickey Mouse is a pictorial work that has also been used as the company's trademark. Copyright protects the drawing of Mickey Mouse, while trademark associates The Walt Disney Company as the source of goods bearing the Mickey Mouse logo. The usage of a drawing as a trademark will not eliminate its copyright protection, but the protection provided by copyright will be quite different than that provided by trademark.

3.   *Exclusive Rights for the Copyright Owner.*

The owner of an exclusive right in copyright has the right to reproduce the copyrighted work, publicly display the work, distribute copies of the work, publicly perform the work and prepare derivative works.[183] Only the owner of an exclusive right under copyright can authorize new copies of the work to be made and sold, authorize public performances using the copyrighted work, or authorize adaptations, translations, or other new uses of the work.

---

[182] *Circular 1: Copyright Basics*, U.S. COPYRIGHT OFFICE, https://www.copyright.gov/circs/circ01.pdf (revised Sept. 2017).

[183] 17 U.S.C. § 106 (2018). In the case of sound recordings, copyright holders also have the exclusive right to perform the work publicly by means of a digital audio transmission. *Id.*

Adaptations are known as derivative works. "A 'derivative work' is a work based upon one or more preexisting works, such as a translation, musical arrangement, dramatization, fictionalization, motion picture version, sound recording, art reproduction, abridgment, condensation, or any other form in which a work may be recast, transformed, or adapted. A work consisting of editorial revisions, annotations, elaborations, or other modifications, which, as a whole, represent an original work of authorship, is a 'derivative work.'"[184] Updated versions of software programs are derivative works of the earlier editions of those programs. A translation of a novel or website from one language to another is a derivative work. Creating a plush toy version of Mickey Mouse is a derivative work from the pictorial version. Similarly, each new Mickey Mouse film or television show is a derivative work of the copyright in the Mickey Mouse character.

4. *Transferability and Licensing of Copyright.*

The exclusive rights of the copyright owner may be sold or licensed to others. Like patents, copyrights are personal property that can be sold or licensed in whole or in part. A sale of a copyright is generally called an assignment, while a transfer of anything less than the entire copyright interest is a license of the copyright. And like patents, the license can be made exclusive based on many categories such as time, geography, or market segment.

The key to maximizing the value in a copyrighted work is that the owner of a copyright does not have to own the entire copyright but can exclusively own just a portion of the copyright. Copyright licenses generally cover a period of time far less than the term of the copyright. At the end of the license term, the copyright returns to the original copyright owner. Similarly, copyright licenses are often subdivided into very narrow product distribution channels and often divided into geographic areas as well. Further, depending on the terms of the copyright license, these rights may be further subdivided and sublicensed.

For example, assume Sue Smith owns the copyright in her novel, *Smithville*. The copyright vests in Ms. Smith as soon as she saves the text

---

[184] 17 U.S.C. § 101 (2018).

on her computer. The computer's memory is sufficient to fix the work in a tangible form, a primary requirement for copyright protection.

Ms. Smith will likely mail copies of the unpublished manuscript to potential publishers, inviting those publishers to offer to publish her work. If a publisher desires to publish *Smithville*, it will negotiate for the rights to publish the novel from Smith. Under prevailing business custom, the publisher will not purchase the copyright, but will instead acquire an exclusive right to publish the English language version of the book in the United States and Canada in hardback form. The license is limited to language, geography, and physical format. The publisher of the hardback version will also negotiate to acquire the rights to the e-book version of the work.

The license may preclude Ms. Smith from offering the paperback or trade paperback rights to any other publisher for a period of time following the publication of the hardback. In some situations, the e-book rights might be bundled with the paperback publisher instead of the hardback publisher, but in practice this is not too common.

When e-books were first emerging as a market, an e-book license would often only be for a short period, such as three years. Relatively new media formats are often licensed for shorter periods of time to test the viability of the technology and assess the value of the markets. Although this is no longer true for e-books, new technologies are always emerging, and this general practice will continue, particularly for copyright licenses.

If the publisher chose to acquire all English language publication rights in all print media, it could then sublicense the paperback rights to one publisher and the Canadian hardback and paperback distribution rights to yet another publisher. There is no limit to the number of slivers into which a copyright can be sliced.

Finally, Ms. Smith will separately negotiate various derivative rights in her novel. She may negotiate foreign language translations with different publishers located throughout the world. She will negotiate to allow her novel to be adapted into a motion picture, television show, or audio book with other companies.

In this way, the copyright in the novel can be divided into time-based licenses, geographic licenses, product-based licenses, and licenses that permit carefully described adaptations. As a negotiating strategy, the parties should only acquire the rights that have economic value to them. Buying rights one does not need adds to the expense, while licensing rights to a party that cannot exploit those rights causes a loss in revenue for the copyright owner. Some publishers want to own all rights, but they should pay a premium for that monopoly position.

* * *

Sidebar—Music copyrights and performing rights organizations.

The rules for copyright licensing in music are somewhat different than for other entertainment media and copyrighted works. Music is a complex area of copyright protection because there are separate copyrights in the composition (the lyrics and score of the music, and sometimes the arrangement as well) from the sound recording. The composition is generally fixed on sheet music, while the sound recording is fixed on a phonograph record or CD. Both the sheet music and the phonograph record have modern, digital format equivalents. The sound recording has a very limited public performance right, so that the composer receives most of the copyright protection and revenue for public performances.[185]

For business owners, an understanding of the public performance of music is helpful. Many businesses play music in their establishments and are surprised to find that much of the activity requires a public performance license. Public performances include more than live musicians. A public performance may include music piped through a stereo system, or even running a radio station or television broadcast in the establishment that can be heard by the public. Radio and television

---

[185] *See* 17 U.S.C. § 106(6) (2018) which provides that "in the case of sound recordings, [an exclusive right exists] to perform the copyrighted work publicly by means of a digital audio transmission." Section 114(d) provides an extensive definition of rules that cover when the digital audio transmission is an exclusive right of the sound recording copyright holder and when it cannot be enforced. Broadly speaking, the digital audio recording exclusivity gives the sound recording copyright holder rights to control interactive broadcasts on the Internet and some limited rights regarding the use of Internet streaming or Internet radio. The specific rules are beyond the scope of this text.

stations are licensed to broadcast for private use, and any public use of those signals requires an additional license, unless there is an exemption from the requirement.

The primary exemption was the "home style" exemption, which provided that the use of a radio or television similar to that owned by a homeowner could be used in public without any additional licensing. This protected stores from needing a public performance license for having a radio sitting on a counter or a television in the corner.

Since 1998, the Fairness in Music Licensing Act has created an additional exemption to the public performance licensing requirement. While the home style exemption has been retained, the exemption has been expanded for stores of less than 2,000 square feet and restaurants of less than 3,700 square feet. By meeting the equipment restrictions,[186] no public performance license is needed for radio or television performances.

For all other public performance, including the playing of CDs or live music in any sized venue and the playing of the radio in larger venues or with large stereo systems,[187] a public performance license is required. Since it is highly impractical to ask every composer for permission to play his or her song, music composers created performing rights societies to provide a single license to stores and restaurants for the right to play the music within their catalog. There are three major U.S. performing rights

---

[186] The restriction on home style stereo systems under the square foot restrictions are as follows:

> (I) If the performance is by audio means only, the performance is communicated by means of a total of not more than 6 loudspeakers, of which not more than 4 loudspeakers are located in any 1 room or adjoining outdoor space; or

> (II) If the performance or display is by audiovisual means, any visual portion of the performance or display is communicated by means of a total of not more than 4 audiovisual devices, of which not more than 1 audiovisual device is located in any 1 room, and no such audiovisual device has a diagonal screen size greater than 55 inches, and any audio portion of the performance or display is communicated by means of a total of not more than 6 loudspeakers, of which not more than 4 loudspeakers are located in any 1 room or adjoining outdoor space....

17 U.S.C. § 110(5)(B)(i) (2018).

[187] *See* § 110(5).

societies: American Society of Composers, Authors and Publishers (ASCAP), Broadcast Music, Inc. (BMI) and the Society of European Stage Authors and Composers, Inc. (SESAC). ASCAP and BMI together represent most publicly performed music in the United States, but each represents a different roster of composers, making the need to have both ASCAP and BMI licenses quite common. The license fees are generally based on the size of the business and its annual revenue.

Because of antitrust violations involving ASCAP and BMI dating back to the 1940's, the organizations' pricing structures are supervised by a New York Federal District Court. This supervision was put in place to protect businesses from coercion and to force the performing rights societies to defend the fairness of their pricing when faced with a legal challenge. The performing rights societies are extremely aggressive in suing those companies which fail to purchase a license, with the litigation expenses and court awards far exceeding any savings made by venues which ducked their licensing obligations.

Most bars and restaurants display stickers on their doors showing that the establishment is licensed by ASCAP, BMI, or both. Larger stores will either license through performing rights societies or purchase music specially tailored to the store's needs by background music services. These background music services license the music either through the performing rights societies or directly with the copyright holders.

* * *

5.   The Term of the U.S. Copyright and the Public Domain.

Copyrights in works created after January 1, 1978 last for 70 years after the author's death. If the author is a corporation or the work was made by an employee on a work-for-hire basis, the copyright lasts 95 years from publication or 120 years from creation, whichever is shorter. For works created prior to 1978, the length of the copyright protection depends less on the lifespan of the author and more on the date of publication. Nonetheless, the maximum length of copyright for works published before 1978 is 95 years from the year of first publication.

A work created before 1978 was also required to have its copyright renewed in its 28th year of copyright protection. Prior to 1964, the failure to renew the copyright resulted in the loss of copyright protection, leaving the work to the public domain and outside the scope of copyright protection. After 1964, the renewal was provided automatically by law. Because Congress has increased the length of copyright protection from time to time, there is no uniform length of copyright. Appendix A.2, *Copyright Timeline for Duration, Renewal & Termination*, provides a helpful chart on copyright schedules.

The length of copyright protection for each work must be carefully reviewed based on the date of publication, renewals, the nature of the authorship (by an individual, as a joint work by multiple authors, or as a work-for-hire), and the required formalities in effect at the time of publication. There is no automatic rule. Instead, a company wishing to acquire a license in a copyrighted work must review that work's copyright history.

The length and nature of copyright protection may also vary by country. There is no international standard for copyright terms or registration, so if the work will be exploited in another country, the copyright owner should review that country's copyright laws. Despite the large variations, however, international treaties make it very likely that a work copyrighted in one country will be protected in most other countries.

* * *

Copyright Term: Special Points to Remember

- **Works Published or Copyrighted Before January 1, 1964:** Works published with notice of copyright or registered in unpublished form prior to January 1, 1964, had to be renewed during the 28th year of their first term of copyright to maintain protection for a full 95-year term.

- **Works Originally Copyrighted Between January 1, 1964, and December 31, 1977:** These works are protected by copyright for the 28-year original term and the 67-year renewal term, without the need of a first term or a renewal registration.

- **Copyrights in their Second Term on January 1, 1978:** These works were automatically extended up to a maximum of 95 years, without the need for further renewal.

- **Works Already in the Public Domain:** These works cannot be protected under the 1976 law or under the amendments of 1992 and 1998. The Act provides no procedure for restoring protection for works in which copyright has been lost for any reason. [188]

* * *

6.   Fair Use.

Fair use provides the largest exception to the exclusive rights of a copyright holder. Fair use permits the reproduction, distribution, public performance, or other use of a copyrighted work without the owner's permission. The law provides that "the fair use of a copyrighted work … for purposes such as criticism, comment, news reporting, teaching (including multiple copies for classroom use), scholarship, or research, is not an infringement of copyright."[189]

Comment, criticism, and classroom use comprise the core applications for fair use, but the range of fair use applications is much broader. The 1961 Report of the Register of Copyrights on the General Revision of the U.S. Copyright Law cites examples of activities that courts have regarded as fair use:

> Quotation of excerpts in a review or criticism for purposes of illustration or comment; quotation of short passages in a scholarly or technical work, for illustration or clarification of the author's observations; use in a parody of some of the content of the work parodied; summary of an address or article, with brief quotations, in a news report; reproduction by a library of a portion of a work to replace part of a damaged copy; reproduction by a teacher or student of a small part of a work to illustrate a lesson; reproduction of a work in legislative or judicial proceedings or reports; incidental and fortuitous reproduction,

---

[188] *See Circular 15a: Duration of Copyright*, U.S. COPYRIGHT OFFICE (reviewed Aug. 2011), http://www.copyright.gov/circs/circ15a.pdf.

[189] 17 U.S.C. § 107 (2018).

in a newsreel or broadcast, of a work located at the scene of an event being reported.[190]

The primary difficulty in applying fair use is that the test for whether any particular use will be deemed a fair use is highly fact specific. In updating the Copyright Act in 1976, Congress added four factors to the historical explanation of fair use to help clarify the standard:

(1) the purpose and character of the use, including whether such use is of a commercial nature or is for nonprofit educational purposes;

(2) the nature of the copyrighted work;

(3) the amount and substantiality of the portion used in relation to the copyrighted work as a whole; and

(4) the effect of the use upon the potential market for or value of the copyrighted work.[191]

Generally, the last factor becomes the most critical in a lawsuit over the fair use of copyrighted material. If the new work tends to replace the existing work in the marketplace or creates the kind of work that the copyright owner would have created for that market, then the work will be infringing. On the other hand, if the work does not serve as a substitute for the copyrighted work, then it will be less likely to be an infringement. For example, a book review cannot generally replace the book which has been reviewed. In contrast, an abridgement of the book will replace the market for that book.

For businesses wishing to utilize the copyrighted materials of other copyright owners, they must take great care, especially if fair use is going to be the primary defense to copying. Earlier in this book, for example, a copy of the Newman's Own brand was reproduced *without* the permission of the copyright owner. Given the use of the drawing in this book, the stronger legal claim would be for copyright infringement of the drawing rather than trademark infringement for use of the trademark

---

[190] H. Comm. on the Judiciary, 87th Cong., Rep. of the Reg. of Copyrights on the General Revision of the U.S. Copyright Law 24 (Comm. Print 1961), https://www.copyright.gov/history/1961_registers_report.pdf.

[191] 17 U.S.C. § 107 (2018).

in association with this text. Trademark has a similar fair use concept, discussed further in Chapter 18.

Using the four factors listed in the law, it is likely that a court would find this book's use of the copyrighted drawing a fair use. Admittedly, looking at the first factor, this book's use of the Newman's Own drawing is of a commercial nature because this book is sold for profit. Courts look past this aspect of commercial use, however, to determine whether the usage is transformative of the copied work or merely duplicative of that work. The educational nature in this situation is significant. The use of the picture is not incidental to the book, but rather an important tool in a lesson on the nature of fair use. This book uses the image in a manner fundamentally different from the way the copyright owner uses it, so it should be deemed sufficiently transformative.

The nature of the copyrighted work is a business logo, and so the need to protect the expressive or creative work of the author or artist is less than if the drawing had been an artistic depiction. Generally, this factor protects fictional works more than fact-based works. Here, however, the reproduction of the Newman's Own logo is being used in a factual manner.

The amount of the copyrighted work taken is the entire work—the drawing as a whole. This tends to hurt any finding of fair use. This third factor would influence a court to find against fair use, but for a small work such as a logo, it may be less significant.

The most important aspect of the fair use claim is the effect on the market. Here, the effect upon the potential market or value of the logo is negligible. The book has neither a negative effect on the copyright nor changes its usage. While authors who rely on fair use to take the copyrighted material of others like to suggest that their use of the material actually helps the copyright owner, courts rarely give that argument much weight. A court would prefer that the book publisher had asked permission rather than merely claimed it had done a favor for Mr. Newman.

Not all factors of the fair use test support this book's use of the Newman's Own logo, but the negligible financial impact of the usage combined with the transformative use for comment and criticism, should support the conclusion that the use is a fair one. Nonetheless, there is a certain degree of risk associated with a reliance on fair use. A publisher does not know that the copyright owner will not object to the unauthorized use. A challenge to the use will result in legal costs and the risk of a lawsuit. For this reason, publishers are reluctant to rely on fair use and companies ought to be particularly cautious in relying on fair use for commercial activities.

Since 1994, the Supreme Court has also suggested a second test for fair use analysis that emphasizes the "transformative" nature of the unauthorized use.[192] Under this approach, the emphasis is on the extent to which the new use is made in a completely new or unexpected manner. The primary example of transformative fair use is parody, where songs or video use a prior creative work to comment on that work, and to a much lesser extent, to comment on society through a recasting of that work. Transformative fair use often is used to explain the very practical business practice of allowing and even encouraging fan fiction as an audience outlet for participating in pop culture phenomena such as *Harry Potter*, *Star Wars*, *Star Trek*, and *Game of Thrones*. Transformative use has also been applied to the transformation of works through new technologies, although in this area, the traditional four-factor test emphasizing the effect on the market provides an equally effective and often more pragmatic understanding for what new technological uses are permitted without the copyright owner's permission and which will be deemed infringing absent a license.

C.   Acquiring a Copyright.

1.   *Authorship and Joint Authors.*

Copyright law assumes that the author of a work is the copyright owner. For novelists, painters, and composers, this assumption works quite well. The economic realities are somewhat different, however, for software companies, motion picture makers, and the creators of technical journals or product manuals. For modern industry, it is less likely that a work will be created by an individual author and more likely that a work will be developed by a team of professionals in the scope of their professional endeavors. Corporate employees may be located across the globe, creating interrelated components of a single

---

[192] Campbell v. Acuff-Rose Music, 510 U.S. 569 (1994).

copyrighted work. Business contracts for copyright must take these conditions into account.

Current copyright law grants protection for the lifespan of the author plus 70 years, so the identity of the author is critical in determining the term of the copyright. If the work is anonymous or pseudonymous, then the term becomes the shorter of 95 years from first publication or 120 years from creation. If the author is later identified in Copyright Office records, the fixed term is replaced with the life-plus-seventy period.

Joint authors receive the benefit of copyright protection for seventy years following the last surviving author. A work by more than one author is described by the statute as a "joint work." "A "joint work" is a work prepared by two or more authors with the intention that their contributions be merged into inseparable or interdependent parts of a unitary whole."[193]

The key to joint authorship is the agreement between the authors, at the time the work is created, to merge their efforts into one work. Although the law does not require a signed, written agreement, such an agreement would eliminate most conflicts, which often develop years later when memories shift, and the financial consequences increase.

In addition, some courts require that each participant provide some copyrightable expression in the work, not just ideas. This requires the authors to actually write the dialogue or narration as a team, precluding the writing team in which one participant provides the ideas while the other provides the entire dialogue or narration. Other courts have rejected this rule because it could bring about the absurd result that the work was protected by copyright even though each author's contribution was insufficient to be protected. Since the threshold for copyright protection is rather low, the expression requirement is usually not too difficult to achieve. Nonetheless, each joint author should provide some expression so that any authorship ambiguity is eliminated.

2.   *Authorship as Works-Made-for-Hire.*

Most often, a work is not created by one or even two authors, but instead by a multitude of authors. Corporate brochures include text

---

[193] 17 U.S.C. § 101 (2018).

drafted by a copy writer working in conjunction with other staff members, graphic designers, photographers, and others. Most business works are created as works-made-for-hire, which vests the copyright in the employer rather than the employee.

U.S. copyright law provides two very distinct rules for work-made-for-hire (or work-for-hire). One rule regulates regular employees and the second deals with specially commissioned works. The application of the two rules does not overlap, and each should be analyzed separately.

Under the regular employee rules for work-for-hire, the copyright in a work vests in the employer when the copyrighted work is "prepared by an employee within the scope of his or her employment."[194] The law of agency applies to determine when a person is considered an employee. The factor carrying the greatest weight in this determination is the characterization of employment made by the employer. However, this factor is not dispositive. If an employer provides employment benefits, contributes the employer's portion of taxes, and withholds the employee's portion of income taxes, the hired individual will likely be found to be an employee. In addition, the employer's control of both the work and the employee will support the agency claim of employment. These areas of control may include controlling how the work is done, where the work is done, the schedule of work, and the ability to add new projects or obligations to the work.

In addition, the work must be part of the employee's regular employment. The company will own the copyright in works created by a salaried employee, like marketing materials, technical manuals, software, and the corporate website. Employers generally do not own the copyrighted works made by their employees outside of the scope of their employment. For example, if an employee works on a novel over her lunch hour every day for years, that novel will not be owned by the employer, unless the employee was employed as a novelist. Similarly, if a boiler mechanic creates a statue for his employer's building lobby, that statue would be beyond the scope of the mechanic's employment, and the copyright owned by the mechanic, not the employer. The work-for-hire employment presumption can be modified by contract, so the

---

[194] *Id.*

employer and employee can elect to change the agreement to adjust the copyright ownership.

The second category of works made for hire applies to those works which are specially commissioned. For such works, the employment status of the author is not relevant. Instead, the work must fall into one of nine categories enumerated under the law and be transferred to the acquiring party in a writing signed by both parties.

The nine categories of work that are eligible to use contracts for specially commissioned works are those used "as a contribution to a collective work, as a part of a motion picture or other audiovisual work, as a translation, as a supplementary work, as a compilation, as an instructional text, as a test, as answer material for a test, or as an atlas."[195]

---

[195] To better understand the nine categories of specially commissioned works, the statute and definitions provide additional information:

[A] "supplementary work" is a work prepared for a publication as a secondary adjunct to a work by another author for the purpose of introducing, concluding, illustrating, explaining, revising, commenting upon, or assisting in the use of the other work, such as forewords, afterwords, pictorial illustrations, maps, charts, tables, editorial notes, musical arrangements, answer material for tests, bibliographies, appendixes, and indexes; and an "instructional text" is a literary, pictorial, or graphic work prepared for publication and with the purpose of use in systematic instructional activities.

A "collective work" is a work, such as a periodical issue, anthology, or encyclopedia, in which a number of contributions, constituting separate and independent works in themselves, are assembled into a collective whole.

A "compilation" is a work formed by the collection and assembling of preexisting materials or of data that are selected, coordinated, or arranged in such a way that the resulting work as a whole constitutes an original work of authorship. The term "compilation" includes collective works.

"Audiovisual works" are works that consist of a series of related images which are intrinsically intended to be shown by the use of machines or devices such as projectors, viewers, or electronic equipment, together with accompanying sounds, if any, regardless of the nature of the material objects, such as films or tapes, in which the works are embodied.

Id.

[195] 17 U.S.C. § 203(a) (2018).

When a work is specially commissioned, the copyright vests in the employer or purchaser rather than in the employees or independent contractors. Motion pictures are prime examples of the need for specially commissioned works because the screenwriter, director, set designer, cinematographer, and even the actors might otherwise be contributing copyrighted material to the final product. The motion picture company hires parties using contracts that specify that the work is done as a specially commissioned work, so that the copyright in the movie and all elements of the movie vest exclusively in the company.

Work-for-hire is not universally recognized, so it is prudent to include a clause in the specially commissioned work agreement that states, "to the extent the transfer is not recognized by law, the employee hereby assigns any copyright ownership to the employer."

3.   Termination and Renewal.

The key difference between owning the copyright and purchasing the copyright are the length of the copyright term and the rights an author has to terminate transfers in the copyright. Throughout the history of copyright, the transfer of copyright ownership has had two different terms, allowing the copyright owner two different periods of copyright ownership rather than one continuous period of ownership. Because this approach does not apply to works-made-for-hire, corporations have much greater copyright ownership if the copyright vests in the corporation as a work-for-hire rather than through a transfer or assignment.

For copyrighted works created by an author or joint authors, copyright law provides two different mechanisms for the two-term copyright. Works created before January 1, 1978 had a renewal term for the second estate. Works created under the modern law, beginning January 1, 1978, include a termination provision regarding the transfer of any copyright interests.

For works created under the modern law, all transfers—including any "exclusive or nonexclusive grant of a transfer or license of copyright or of any right under a copyright ... otherwise than by will, is subject to termination. . . ."[196] The termination must be made by the original author, or the heirs of the author if the author is no longer living.

The termination takes place 36 to 41 years following the date of the grant, depending on when the copyright author initiates the termination.[197] The owner of the grant must have at least two years notice, and certain aspects of the rights transferred are not terminated. Most importantly, no earlier agreement not to exercise the termination can be enforced. A business acquiring copyright interests must be cautious because the rights can be shortened to 36 years. If the business is acquiring rights from another grantee, then the company must carefully check the potential that the rights acquired might be much shorter than 95 years because of termination provisions.

For works created under the 1909 Copyright Act, the copyright owner was required to renew the copyright in each published work in its 28th year or else the copyright would fall into the public domain. Under the 1909 Act, the law assumed that only valuable works would be renewed, and all other works would be allowed to fall into the public domain after 28 years. As a result, many movies, films, books, and a tremendous number of corporate documents created under this law are now in the public domain. The 1976 Copyright Act eliminated the need to register copyright renewals for all new works, effective January 1, 1978. A 1992 law further protected the copyrights for those works which required renewals, by making renewals automatic for all works first

---

[196] *Id.*

[197] The statute specifies the termination period as follows:

> Termination of the grant may be effected at any time during a period of five years beginning at the end of thirty-five years from the date of execution of the grant; or, if the grant covers the right of publication of the work, the period begins at the end of thirty-five years from the date of publication of the work under the grant or at the end of forty years from the date of execution of the grant, whichever term ends earlier.

§ 203(a)(3).

published and copyrighted between January 1, 1964, and December 31, 1977.

Because of the timing of the changes in the laws, there are no longer any copyrighted works that must be registered. All works were either renewed or have fallen into the public domain. U.S. Copyright Office Circular 15 provides detailed explanations of the effect of renewals.[198] Unlike terminations, the obligation to transfer the renewal term to the licensee of a copyright was enforceable against the copyright owner. An oddity in the application of the law, however, limited the enforcement to the author but not the heirs of the author, so a widow of an author could take the renewal term without the obligation that the author would have had, if the author was living.

Finally, in 1998, all copyrights still in force were extended by an additional twenty years. For the authors of those works that had not been otherwise terminated, the twenty-year period creates a new termination period for use by author or the author's heirs. This provision has been something of a surprise to companies that thought they were the beneficiaries of the latest twenty-year extension.

The laws and intricacies of both terminations and renewals are very technical. For a business relying on the acquisition of copyrights— particularly copyrights for works in their third decade—the company should be certain that the ownership in the copyright is consistent with the terms of the copyright licenses or transfers.

4.   Transfer, Notice, Registration, and Deposit.

When a copyright owner grants exclusive rights to another to use the copyrighted work, the assignment must be in writing, dated and signed.[199] Non-exclusive permission may be granted either orally or in writing. Copyright transfers of published works can be filed with the U.S. Copyright Office. Unpublished works must first be registered to have the transfer filed. Transfers and mortgages may also be filed in the state or territory where the work exists particularly if the work is unpublished or incomplete, so for ongoing software development and other similar

---

[198] *Circular 15: Renewal of Copyright*, U.S. COPYRIGHT OFFICE, http://www.copyright.gov/circs/circ15.pdf (revised July 2006).

[199] 17 U.S.C. § 204 (2018).

activities, filing with both the state and the Copyright Office is preferable.

Since March 1, 1989, U.S. law has not formally required an author to register the work with the Copyright Office or identify the work as copyrighted. Works published before that date had to comply with the law in effect at the time of publication. Copyright notice is still commonly used, and works that continue to meet both the notice and registration provisions are granted additional legal protections, discussed below. Copyright notice takes the following form:

1. *The symbol* © (the letter C in a circle), or the word "Copyright," or the abbreviation "Copr."; and

2. *The year of first publication.* If the work is a derivative work or a compilation incorporating previously published material, the year date of first publication of the derivative work or compilation is sufficient. Examples of derivative works are translations or dramatizations; an example of a compilation is an anthology. The year may be omitted when a pictorial, graphic, or sculptural work, with accompanying textual matter, if any, is reproduced in or on greeting cards, postcards, stationery, jewelry, dolls, toys, or useful articles; and

3. *The name of the owner of copyright in the work,* or an abbreviation by which the name can be recognized, or a generally known alternative designation of the owner.

Example: © 2004 Jane Doe[200]

The notice typically appears on the title page of books, front or back of publications, on the contributions page of anthologies, or in any other position that gives reasonable notice of the copyright. Unpublished works have never needed notice.

Registration with the Copyright Office is also no longer required upon publication. Registration with appropriate notice, however, provides certain benefits. First, registration is a requirement if the

---

[200] *Circular 3: Copyright Notice*, U.S. COPYRIGHT OFFICE, http://www.copyright.gov/circs/circ03.pdf (revised Sept. 2017).

copyright owner is ever going to defend the copyright in litigation. This means that for copyright owners who produce a lot of works, the authors will only file a registration in the event they decide they need to take an infringer to court over the work.

Second, registration of a work published with proper notice within three months of publication will enable the owner of the copyright to seek statutory damages, rather than having to calculate the actual damages, if the copyright is infringed. Registration with proper notice will also allow the prevailing party in a copyright lawsuit to seek attorneys' fees for the cost of the litigation. As a result, it is always a good idea to include proper copyright notice and register the work with the Copyright Office within three months of publication.

In addition, the law continues to require that two copies of the published work be provided to the Copyright Office for the use of the Library of Congress. This is no longer a prerequisite to obtaining copyright protection, but it remains a legal requirement for authors as a form of tax on published works which has resulted in the Library of Congress boasting the largest collection of works ever amassed in human history. Failure to participate can result in substantial fines.

D.   Enforcement of Copyright Rights.

1.   *Prima Facie Case for Copyright.*

To win a copyright action against an infringer of one's copyright, the copyright owner must be able to establish that she owns an exclusive interest in a valid copyright. For U.S. copyright owners, they must also show they have registered the copyrighted work prior to filing the lawsuit.

The copyright owner's legal claim is quite simple. She must establish that the copyrighted work was copied, meaning that the alleged copier had access to the copyrighted work and an ordinary observer would believe that the copier's work was substantially similar to the copyright owner's work. Copyright specialist David Nimmer describes this quote from *Harold Lloyd Corp. v. Witwer* (65 F.2d 1 (9th Cir. 1933)) as the "traditional" test:

> The question really involved in such comparison is to ascertain the effect of the alleged infringing play upon the public, that is, upon the average reasonable man. If an ordinary person who has

recently read the story sits through the presentation of the picture, if there had been literary piracy of the story, he should detect that fact without any aid or suggestion or critical analysis by others. The reaction of the public to the matter should be spontaneous and immediate.[201]

The "ordinary observer" test is characterized in many different ways by judges and analysts, but ultimately the decision is a factual determination made by the ordinary men and women who comprise a jury.

Courts and juries work to protect literary expression while assuring that copyright does not extend to the underlying ideas embedded in a work. Only the original expression is protected, so novelty and originality of ideas are outside the protection and separated from the text. "Boy meets girl" cannot be protected by law; only the details of a particular love story can create copyright ownership.

A more sophisticated version of the test attempts to first separate out ideas, facts, and other non-copyrighted aspects of the works. Only once these elements are filtered out of the comparison should the two works be compared. Some courts adopt this test, others adopt it selectively.

Once the copyright owner has established access to the plaintiff's copyrighted work and substantiality between the two works, the defendant will try to prove an affirmative defense to the claim of copying. For example, the defendant may acknowledge copying but claim that the copying of material was a fair use, so that no liability should apply.

2.   *Injunctions and Remedies.*

If copyright infringement is established, courts generally enjoin the defendant from further copyright violations. This will result in an immediate bar to the sale of infringing goods and a judicial order that all master copies, molds, dies, or other source materials used to make infringing copies be destroyed.

---

[201] 4 MELVILLE B. NIMMER & DAVID NIMMER, NIMMER ON COPYRIGHT, § 13.03 (2018) (quoting Harold Lloyd Corp. v. Witwer, 65 F.2d 1, 18 (9th Cir. 1933).

The copyright owner is entitled to the actual damages caused by the infringement and the profits received by the infringer, to the extent that they exceed the measure of damages. The profits are the net proceeds earned by the infringer by the sale of the infringed work, after deducting all actual expenses for preparing the work for sale.

For copyrighted works that were registered with the U.S. Copyright Office within three months of publication, the successful plaintiff may elect to receive statutory damages rather than actual damages. Statutory damages remove the difficulty of proving the precise extent of damages, an amount that is often speculative and difficult to prove. The statutory damages for a work can range from $750 to $30,000 "as the court considers just."[202] If the court determines that the infringement was "committed willfully, the court in its discretion may increase the award of statutory damages to a sum of not more than $150,000."[203] Willful infringement includes outright copying of the copyright owner's work, or ignoring a "cease and desist" letter by the copyright holder, notifying the infringer of the infringement and demanding that the unlawful activity cease.

In addition, the prevailing party in a copyright lawsuit may be awarded attorneys' fees at the discretion of the court. This applies to the successful defense of a lawsuit as well as the successful prosecution of such a claim. If an infringement is willful, it is much more likely that attorneys' fees will be awarded.

3.   *Violating the Copyrights of Others.*

For companies, copyright can be infringed in a variety of ways, so a business must be diligent to ensure its employees do not copy other companies' works. Common company copyright infringements include:

- Copying software from other companies to shorten the development cycle of products.

- Copying brochures and marketing material.

- Using photographs without reproduction permission.

---

[202] 17 U.S.C. § 504(c) (2018).

[203] *Id.*

- Posting material from the Internet to the company's website without the permission of the copyright owner.

- Copying the images or text from product packaging.

These examples are typical mistakes companies make in using copyrighted materials. Senior company officials must also do more than utilize employment handbooks prohibiting copyright violations. The company must actively review the content it creates to be sure no copyright infringement is taking place. Otherwise, the company may find itself responsible for willful infringement of another party's copyrights.

Because fair use is a vague legal rule, companies must be diligent to protect the copyrights of others when quoting material and researching. In the end, the difference between infringement and research may turn on the number of sources cited and the range of materials used. In contrast, too conservative an approach to fair use undermines the public benefits of commentary, criticism, and research that fair use was designed to provide. Companies should be mindful of industry practice and seek to model behavior after the accepted protocols in each field.

E.   The International Implications of Copyright Law and Practice.

Copyright is subject to many multilateral and bilateral treaties, which grant authors of one country protection under the laws of the other countries that are party to the treaty. There is no true international copyright. Fortunately, the United States has treaties with most countries of the world, so authors have a high degree of copyright protection, even if the specifics of that protection may vary from nation to nation.

1.   Extraterritorial Protection of U.S. Authors.

The first international copyright treaty in the world was the Berne Convention, established in 1886. The United States was unwilling to adjust its domestic laws to comply with the Berne Conventions, so it began entering into bi-lateral treaties in 1891 and promoted an alternative treaty, the Universal Copyright Convention, beginning in 1955. The United States was a latecomer to the Berne Convention, and indeed, to most of the international protection of copyright. As international trade increased, however, and goods protected by copyright became an increasingly important part of that trade, changes were made in both U.S. law and Berne treaty interpretations to allow the United States to participate. The United States joined only as of March 1989.

Through the two multi-national treaties and a number of bi-lateral treaties, U.S. copyright holders are protected if their works are infringed abroad. Despite these treaties, an action for copyright infringement often requires that the lawsuit be brought in the country where the infringement has occurred, making the enforcement of a copyright holder's rights abroad expensive to protect.

An author who is a U.S. national or domiciliary automatically receives copyright protection in all Berne Convention countries. The Berne Convention has no formalities and most member countries have no provision for notice or registration of copyrighted works. In contrast, under the Universal Copyright Convention, the pre-1989 notice should still be used. This means that the copyright symbol © (C in a circle), year of first publication and the name of the copyright proprietor should appear on the work (e.g., © 2006 Jane Doe).

Many foreign jurisdictions do not recognize the work-made-for-hire doctrine, or may not apply it to the category of specially commissioned works. Any contract providing for transfer based on a work-made-for-hire category should include an alternative clause providing for an assignment of copyright in the event that the jurisdiction does not recognize the validity of the work-made-for-hire transfer.

2.   *Exploitation of Foreign Copyrighted Works.*

Foreign authors receive similar protection for their works used in the United States to U.S. authors being used abroad. Under the Berne Convention, a Canadian, French, or other Berne national or domiciliary is entitled to full copyright protection, as if the work had been created by a U.S. author.

There is one notable distinction between U.S. and foreign works. The length of copyright protection varies from country to country. A work in the U.S. public domain may remain under copyright protection in the foreign country, while a work in the public domain in the foreign country remains under copyright in the United States. Therefore, it is important that the copyright owner's research include major international markets in addition to the U.S. status, especially when the project involves a long-running international copyright.

Chapter 18. Trademarks, Service Marks, Brands, and Trademark Law

A. Attributes of Trademarks.

Trademarks—Summary

Subject Matter: A word, phrase, symbol, or design, or a combination of such, that identifies and distinguishes the source of the goods.

Method Acquired: Through usage. ® May only be used after federal registration, but TM and SM may be used at any time.

Term: Indefinite, trademark will continue so long as usage continues.

Time Needed to Acquire: May be acquired as early as six months prior to use in commerce, but generally acquired when mark is used in conjunction with the use of goods or services.

Renewals: An Affidavit of Use ("Section 8 Affidavit") must be filed between the fifth and sixth year following initial registration, and within the year before the end of every ten-year period thereafter.

Federal Government Office and Website: United States Patent and Trademark Office: www.uspto.gov.

Applicable Law: Trademark Act of 1946, 15 U.S.C. §1051, et. sec.

Transfer: Assignable. Registration available through USPTO.

Property Excluded from Protection: No protection for inventions, ideas, or products. Limited to protect the marks when used to designate the goods and services, rather than providing exclusive ownership of the mark. Trademarks do not prevent others from making the same goods or from selling the same goods or services under a different mark.

B.   Trademarks Explained.

1.   *Subject Matter of Trademark Law.*

Trademarks are the most visible form of intellectual property used by businesses, dating back to the origins of commercial trade. In both Europe and Asia, archeologists have identified the practices of artisans, smiths, and others identifying the source of their goods with marks or engraved names. Through these marks, consumers knew who was responsible for the quality of a product. A successful vendor could expand his business through his reputation. In the alternative, the family members of a blacksmith's unfortunate customer could seek appropriate revenge if a poorly forged sword broke in battle and led to its owner's untimely demise. Throughout the law, business and this text, the word "mark" encompasses all forms of trademarks, service marks, collective marks, and certification marks.

From its origins, trademarks are fundamentally different than patents or copyrights because trademarks were conceived as protecting the public rather than the user of the trademark. Although this distinction has blurred under modern American jurisprudence, the fundamental difference in emphasis explains a great deal about the evolution of trademark law and protection.

"A trademark is a brand name. A trademark or service mark includes any word, name, symbol, device, or any combination, used or intended to be used to identify and distinguish the goods/services of one seller or provider from those of others, and to indicate the source of the goods/services."[204] A trademark is very context-specific. For example, "apple" is the generic name for a fruit but also serves as a valid trademark for a grocery store chain, a record label, and a computer manufacturer. The grocery store chain has nothing to do with the computer company, which illustrates that the scope of a trademark is shaped by public perceptions of the trademark and the scope of the company's activities.

The laws of trademark block third parties from using a trademark in a manner that interferes with the public's interest not to be confused

---

[204] *Trademark Basics*, U.S. PATENT & TRADEMARK OFFICE, https://www.uspto.gov/trademarks-getting-started/trademark-basics (last visited July 10, 2018).

regarding the source of goods or services. Trademarks differ from copyrights and patents because they are not considered personal property. For example, if a new company selected the name Apple Software, it would be likely to confuse the public, so Apple (the computer and consumer electronics company) would be successful if it were to bring a lawsuit against this new company. In contrast, if a tree nursery was to adopt the name Apple Fruit Trees, then Apple would be unlikely to prove the public was confused by the association with the word apple.

The explanation that treats trademarks as having no personal property rights tends to understate the property interests companies have in their trademarks. Changes in U.S. law that permit applications to protect trademarks before they are used, along with state and federal law protecting the trademark from dilution, disparagement, or tarnishment, all reflect the property interests held by the trademark holder. As a result, trademarks are better considered to have both property and consumer protection aspects, rather than to be wholly lumped into one category or another.

2. Sources of Legal Protection from Both State and Federal Law.

The U.S. Constitution provides federal power for copyright and patent legislation because such laws need to be uniform throughout the country. Congress, nearly a century after providing federal protection for copyright and patent legislation, provided the same protections for trademarks. The initial effort failed. In 1879, an attempt to create national trademark laws was struck down as beyond the power of Congress.[205] Congress responded by restructuring the law to focus on goods in interstate commerce, an area that it had constitutional authority to regulate. This resulted in the first successful federal law to be enacted in 1881, but which regulated only interstate use of trademarks and left states free to regulate trademarks used exclusively within a state.

The result of this trademark history is a two-tiered system of trademark protection. State law can protect trademarks used only within that state, while federal law protects the interstate use of trademarks. In

---

[205] *In re* Trade-Mark Cases, 100 U.S. 82 (1879).

recent years, however, the Internet has undermined the core of this distinction, causing geographically diverse and highly local businesses to run into customer confusion on the Internet.

In addition, because trademark protection relies primarily on the use in commerce of the trademark, actual usage is more important than registration at either the state or federal level. To assert trademark priority, a business must show it used the trademark first.

3.   *Benefits of Federal Trademark Registration.*

The registration and filing processes reinforce the central axiom that the business which first uses a trademark in commerce has priority to use that trademark and to stop others from making use of that trademark in a manner likely to confuse the public. In this way, the federal trademark system builds upon the common law and state law system to create a national clearinghouse for trademarks used in the United States.

To encourage use of the federal system, Congress has created incentives for participation in the federal regime. Federal trademark protection is preferable to state trademark protection because it has a much broader geographic scope. The USPTO lists other benefits as well:

- A legal presumption of your ownership of the mark and your exclusive right to use the mark nationwide . . . ;

- Public notice of your claim of ownership of the mark;

- Listing in the USPTO's online databases;

- The ability to record the U.S. registration with U.S. Customs and Border Protection to prevent importation of infringing foreign goods;

- The right to use the federal registration symbol "®";

- The ability to bring an action concerning the mark in federal court; and

- The use of U.S. registration as a basis to obtain registration in foreign countries.[206]

The benefits are procedural in nature. The existence of trademark protection flows from the use of a mark in commerce rather than a particular state or federal filing.

4. *A Trademark Must Be Distinctive.*

At the heart of trademark is the obligation that the trademark be distinctive. The very definition of a trademark provides that the purpose of the use of the mark is "to identify and distinguish his or her goods, including a unique product, from those manufactured or sold by others and to indicate the source of the goods, even if that source is unknown."[207]

The distinctiveness or distinguishing characteristic of the trademark must establish a one-to-one relationship between the manufacturer and the product. If two companies both use the same trademark on similar products, then the public will not know which company provided the good, and the mark cannot be used. The level of distinctiveness turns on the creativity of the mark adopted and the association made by the public.

Under longstanding law and tradition, there are "four different categories of terms with respect to trademark protection. . . . These classes are (1) generic, (2) descriptive, (3) suggestive and (4) arbitrary or fanciful."[208] Generic terms can never be trademarks, while arbitrary or fanciful marks with few exceptions can always be used as trademarks. Suggestive, arbitrary, or fanciful marks are entitled to trademark protection without direct evidence that the public associate the trademark with particular goods. For example, "squirrel" is an arbitrary name for computer software and thus would be available to use as a product name unless it is in use by another party. In contrast, "squirrel"

---

[206] *Basic Facts About Trademarks: Protecting Your Trademark, Enhancing Your Rights Through Federal Registration* 11 U.S. PATENT & TRADEMARK OFFICE (May 2016), https://www.uspto.gov/sites/default/files/documents/BasicFacts.pdf.

[207] 15 U.S.C. § 1127 (2018).

[208] Abercrombie & Fitch Co. v. Hunting World, Inc., 537 F.2d 4, 9-10 (2d Cir. 1976).

would be generic for squirrel cages, just as "software" would be generic for software. A fanciful mark is different than an arbitrary mark because it is invented by the owner. Alternatively, "squirrel" might be suggestive of a children's toy collection of plastic nuts.

As one leading court opinion observed,

> [t]he category of "suggestive" marks was spawned by the felt need to accord protection to marks that were neither exactly descriptive on the one hand nor truly fanciful on the other. . . . A term is suggestive if it requires imagination, thought and perception to reach a conclusion as to the nature of goods. A term is descriptive if it forthwith conveys an immediate idea of the ingredients, qualities or characteristics of the goods. . . .[209]

The goal of companies launching new products is to have a trademark that associates the product with the attributes that the manufacturer hopes will promote the item, making the item more relevant to consumers. Suggestive marks are often selected to reinforce the attribute that the seller is hoping to promote. For example, the trademark "Sleep Comfort" adjustable beds provides a rather descriptive appellation of the feature that such a mattress should provide. Tempur-Pedic, a registered trademark, alludes to the temperature control attribute and orthopedic benefits of the bed. The USPTO did not find the name Tempur-Pedic too descriptive for trademark registration. Another competitor, Angelbeds, uses an even more suggestive allusion to the bed's lightness of the touch.

5.   *Secondary Meaning and Acquired Distinctiveness.*

If a mark is not distinctive when first used, it may become distinctive by its association with the goods over time. Generic words, however, can never become trademarks. "Bed" could never be used as the trademark for a bed. Descriptive words, in contrast, may become distinctive through ongoing usage, if the usage is "exclusive and continuous" for a period of five years. So if only one company is using a descriptive word

---

[209] *Id.* at 10-11 (internal quotations and citations omitted).

or phrase for its product, then that company may gain trademark rights over it.

> "A term which is descriptive . . . may, through usage by one producer with reference to his product, acquire a special significance so that to the consuming public the word has come to mean that the product is produced by that particular manufacturer. . . . This is what is known as secondary meaning."

> The crux of the secondary meaning doctrine is that the mark comes to identify not only the goods but the source of those goods. To establish secondary meaning, it must be shown that the *primary* significance of the term in the minds of the consuming public is not the product but the producer (citations omitted). This may be an anonymous producer, since consumers often buy goods without knowing the personal identity or actual name of the manufacturer.[210]

To establish that a mark has acquired distinctiveness in the marketplace and is no longer merely descriptive, the business using the mark may rely on evidence of acquired distinctiveness by showing the consumer's knowledge of the mark as well as by verifying the substantially exclusive and continuous use of the mark for a period of five years. In addition, the existence of federal trademark registration of the mark for other goods sold by the business may substantiate the claim of distinctiveness.

Survey evidence, market research and consumer reaction studies may be useful in showing the acquired distinctiveness of a mark. Other factors demonstrating distinctiveness of a mark include the length of time the mark has been used, the advertising expenditures invested in promoting the mark, the care in which the words were used as a trademark, affidavits and declarations by knowledgeable individuals regarding the use of the mark, and other evidence that helps establish

---

[210] U.S. PATENT & TRADEMARK OFFICE, TRADEMARK MANUAL OF EXAMINATION PROCEDURES § 1212 (Oct. 2017), https://tmep.uspto.gov/RDMS/TMEP/current#/current/TMEP-1200d1e10316.html (quoting Ralston Purina Co. v. Thomas J. Lipton, Inc., 341 F. Supp. 129, 133 (S.D.N.Y. 1972)).

the mark's role as a unique, exclusive identifier of the goods. These rules parallel the manner in which a business should promote and manage its trademarks.

6.   *A Trademark Owner Must Be First in Priority.*

Because trademark law was historically based on actual usage, the party using the mark in association with the goods has priority over other users. But a priority does not equate to a monopoly. Businesses may often select the same marks, totally unaware of other users of the name in other markets.

To set national notice standards, the federal application process provides a single, national registry. If a company federally registers its trademark, then the entire country is put on constructive notice of the registration. With a federally registered trademark, no one can rely on their lack of knowledge about a potential competitor's use of the same trademark. The "innocent user" defense is blocked from the date of application on the federal register. As a result, the registrant of a federal trademark cannot find itself facing a claim that another company began using the trademark in another state after the date of the federal registration.

A federal trademark registration can only be made if the registration does not interfere with the rights of other trademark holders. A company cannot receive federal trademark registration for a mark that resembles another mark—whether registered or not—that is likely to cause consumer confusion, cause mistake, or otherwise deceive the public. This limitation of consumer confusion is at the heart of trademark practice.

The examination process of the federal trademark application is designed to assure the examiner that the use of the requested mark does not infringe the use of any other trademark holder, so as to eliminate the likelihood of consumer confusion.

Once a trademark is used, particularly if it is federally registered, the trademark owner has an obligation to enforce the trademark against others using the mark. In most situations, when a third party adopts aspects of a company's trademark, it is done without the company realizing the situation. Once the two companies are aware of each other, however, action must be taken. Failure to police the trademark will undermine the trademark owner's obligation to use the mark exclusively, as required by both state and federal law. If the trademark owner allows others to use the trademark without taking any action, the exclusivity is lost and the trademark rights may be destroyed.

7.   *Junior Users and Other Limitations.*

The senior user is the first business to adopt the trademark and is therefore the party with priority. A junior user is the business adopting the trademark subsequently. A junior user cannot generally gain the right to use a trademark if it knowingly adopted the trademark of another party. Instead, the law only protects the innocent junior user from losing the investment it has made in its name and the public's interest in identifying the sources of goods. This limited junior protection provides another strong incentive for the senior user to "police" the mark, being careful to let potential junior users know that the trademark is used by a senior user and that the junior use is not permitted.

> [J]unior users, parties who use a mark subsequent to another's use, may retain rights. If the use predates the senior user's [federal] registration, then the [Federal Trademark] Act provides a defense if the mark "was adopted without knowledge of the registrant's prior use and has been continuously used by such party . . . from a date prior to . . . registration of the mark . . . ."[211]

The geographic scope of the junior user's trademark is typically determined by the nature of the business practices that existed prior to the trademark dispute. In the case of Peaches Records, for example, the Louisiana record store was permitted to operate in the seven-parish region where it sold its records, while the owner of the federally registered trademark in Peaches could sell its records in stores everywhere in the United States other than those seven parishes in Louisiana. A similar dispute between New York's Patsy's Pizzeria and Patsy's Italian Restaurant suggests that the boroughs of New York are sufficiently geographically distinct as to be separated for trademark purposes.

---

[211] Peaches Entm't Corp. v. Entm't Repertoire Assocs., 62 F.3d 690, 692 (5th Cir. 1995) (quoting 15 U.S.C. § 1115(b)(5)).

In addition, the failure of the senior trademark holder to police the trademark can sometimes result in a claim of "laches," meaning that the court may choose not to allow the trademark owner to bring a claim if the claim should have been brought in a timely fashion years earlier. If the passage of time has prejudiced the junior user, and the senior user was at fault for not taking action, then the court will not allow the senior user to exercise its rights. Such a determination is at the discretion of the court, but it is a risk that the senior trademark owner should not take.

8.   *Use of Surnames.*

Although the use of surnames in business has been common throughout history, the use of a person's name is not a strong trademark strategy. The law provides that trademark registration may be denied if the mark is primarily considered merely a surname. The right to use one's surname as a trademark would preclude many others with the same name from conducting business using their own names. This restraint on a person's livelihood is highly intrusive and should occur only if the public would be greatly confused or misled by the use of a junior surname. McDonald's may be the best example of a surname that should not be used by a second individual to operate a fast-food restaurant. Few other restaurant names, however, should be owned by an individual to the exclusion of others bearing the same name.

Surnames can develop into trademarks. Names have the benefit of being arbitrary as applied to most goods. Retailers with names such as Macy's, JCPenney, Bloomingdale's, and Woolworths all bear little relation between the name and the service. To develop into trademarks, however, the demonstration of longstanding use and acquired secondary meaning must be strong enough to overcome the burden exclusivity would create for others with a similar surname.

Words that double as surnames require additional analysis. Since there are many individuals whose surnames are common words, whether spelled the same or not, the law requires that the limitation on surnames focus on those which are "primarily" surnames. King, Queen, Cotton, Wolf, Fox, Powers and Lane are examples of relatively common surnames that have obvious English language usage. For this category, the trademark office will look at whether the selection is used as a surname or as its English language meaning in determining the eligibility to receive the trademark registration. Names such as Jones, Smith,

Rodriguez, Garcia, Liu, Patel, and Eng are all very common names that have no English language usage, so they are always treated as surnames.

Because marks are looked at as a whole, a hyphenated surname such as Hewlett-Packard will be less likely to be treated as a surname. While the question remains whether the public will perceive the name as a surname, as a general statement, the public is less likely to do so. In contrast, if the person seeking to register the trademark goes by a hyphenated name, then the examiner is more likely to treat the name as merely a surname and deny registration.

9.   *Unfair Competition as a Broader Alternative.*

It is important for the trademark owner to remember that the goal of federal trademark law is primarily to protect the public from confusion and to stop fraudulent or unfair competition. Section 43(a) of the trademark law creates broad protection for registered and unregistered trademark owners alike to stop competitors from misleading the public by "palming off" one's own products as the products of another party.

(a) (1) Any person who, on or in connection with any goods or services, or any container for goods, uses in commerce any word, term, name, symbol, or device, or any combination thereof, or any false designation of origin, false or misleading description of fact, or false or misleading representation of fact, which—

(A) is likely to cause confusion, or to cause mistake, or to deceive as to the affiliation, connection, or association of such person with another person, or as to the origin, sponsorship, or approval of his or her goods, services, or commercial activities by another person, or

(B) in commercial advertising or promotion, misrepresents the nature, characteristics, qualities, or geographic origin of his or her or another person's goods, services, or commercial activities, shall be liable in a civil action by any person who believes that he or she is or is likely to be damaged by such act.[212]

The law does not restrict itself to federally registered trademarks, so legal protection can extend to surnames, nicknames, and phrases. Similarly, it extends to the goods and services themselves, as well as to the packaging and advertising of those goods and services. To maintain a legal action under §43(a), the trademark use must be false or misleading, and it must be likely to confuse or deceive the public. If these two elements can be established, then the court is likely to protect the senior user of the mark, regardless of the status of registration.

10.   Service Marks, Collective Marks, and Certification Marks.

In addition to trademarks, marks are used in a number of other situations. A service mark is a mark used for services rather than for goods, or more specifically, "to identify and distinguish the services of one person, including a unique service, from the services of others and to indicate the source of the services, even if that source is unknown."[213] Service marks have essentially the same relation to services that trademarks have to goods, and the rules are the same for both.

Certification marks range from the "union label" to approvals by Underwriters Laboratory, Better Business Bureau, or other voluntary quality assurance systems. A "certification mark" represents any mark used to "to certify regional or other origin, material, mode of manufacture, quality, accuracy, or other characteristics of such person's goods or services or that the work or labor on the goods or services was performed by members of a union or other organization."[214] The owner of the certification mark is typically a union, trade association, or certifying agency. Those owners must manage the certification mark like most trademark owners. Other certification marks are assertions of fact.

---

[212] *U.S. Trademark Law: Rules of Practice & Federal Statutes* 234 U.S. PATENT & TRADEMARK OFFICE (Jan. 1, 2018), https://www.uspto.gov/sites/default/files/documents/tmlaw.pdf; 15 U.S.C. § 1125 (2018) (referred to as § 43(a) of the Lanham Trademark Act).

[213] *Id.* at 242.

[214] 15 U.S.C. § 1127 (2018).

"Idaho Potatoes" may be used by any potato farmer in Idaho, but not by a potato farmer outside the state.

For those parties acting under the auspices of the certification mark, the mark owner will likely have contractual obligations regarding the conduct of the business and the use of the mark. Those contractual obligations or rules are controlled by the agreement between the certification mark owner and the business being certified.

A collective mark is somewhat different than the certification. A collective mark is "used by the members of a cooperative, an association, or other collective group or organization" such as fraternities, trade associations, and Indian tribes.[215] For example, North-Eastern Band of Cherokee Indians is a collective mark designating membership, as is United Way. The collective mark shows affiliation rather than approval. Chapters of loosely affiliated national organizations are the most common example of collective marks. Of course, some marks may serve both roles, acknowledging the membership in an organization that also sets high minimum competency standards.

Collective marks are a form of service mark, while certification marks may be applied to either goods or services. The rules applying to trademarks for goods apply in the same way for service marks for services.

C.   Dilution and Disparagement.

Although traditional trademark law has focused on protecting the consumer rather than the property interests of the trademark owner, the doctrines of dilution and disparagement recognize that there are property interests at issue for certain trademarks, particularly highly prominent and publicly recognized marks. As the Supreme Court has explained, "[u]nlike traditional infringement law, the prohibitions against trademark dilution are not the product of common-law development, and are not motivated by an interest in protecting consumers."[216]

---

[215] *Id.*

[216] Moseley v. V Secret Catalogue, Inc., 537 U.S. 418, 429 (2003).

1.   *Dilution.*

Certain highly renowned trademarks are so well known that the use of those trademarks in unrelated fields would tend to associate those fields with the senior user's trademark. Failure to provide legal redress in this situation could result in the "dilution" of that mark; it would become associated with a broader range of goods or services. Tiffany lamps, Rolls-Royce cars, and similar elite trademarks are the most obvious examples where this concern exists.

The consequence of protecting trademarks from dilution is to greatly expand the power of the trademark owner. Various states have protected trademarks from dilution since 1925 but only in recent times has the federal statute added dilution to the range of rights protected.

The Federal Trademark Dilution Revision Act provides –

"Subject to the principles of equity, the owner of a famous mark that is distinctive, inherently or through acquired distinctiveness, shall be entitled to an injunction against another person who, at any time after the owner's mark has become famous, commences use of a mark or trade name in commerce that is likely to cause dilution by blurring or dilution by tarnishment of the famous mark, regardless of the presence or absence of actual or likely confusion, of competition, or of actual economic injury."[217]

Federal law places a few limitations on dilution protection. First, the language of the statute itself provides three situations where the use of another company's famous trademark does not interfere with that company's rights. Those three exclusions are "Any fair use, including a nominative or descriptive fair use," "news reporting and news commentary," and "noncommercial use" of the famous mark.[218] These limitations are of a fair use and free speech nature, so they will generally be read into the law of most states as well, though the precise scope of the law's application may still vary from state to state.

---

[217] 15 U.S.C. § 1125(c)(1) (2018).

[218] 15 U.S.C. § (1125(c)(3)).

In this context, fair use is further expanded to be a use "other than as a designation of source for the person's own goods or services"[219] and to permit uses "in connection with—(i) advertising or promotion that permits consumers to compare goods or services; or (ii) identifying and parodying, criticizing, or commenting upon the famous mark owner or the goods or services of the famous mark owner."[220]

Unlike situations in which a famous trademark is parodied or referenced, the Supreme Court suggests that a direct use of a famous mark in a commercial context may be stopped on far less evidence. The Court referenced statements in the hearings on the new law that "the use of DUPONT shoes, BUICK aspirin, and KODAK pianos would be actionable under this legislation."[221] These congressional statements suggest little evidence is needed when famous marks are duplicated by unauthorized junior users. Entrepreneurs must therefore exercise caution in developing and adopting trademarks if they utilize the famous marks of other companies, even if those companies do not conduct business involving the goods or services of the entrepreneur's new business.

2. *Disparagement or Tarnishment.*

Disparagement or tarnishment represents another property-like interest in the trademark. Disparagement protection provides the trademark owner tools to stop misuse of a company's trademark in a manner that may bring the trademark into disrepute. A popular tee-shirt which showed the word "Cocaine" written in the trademarked Coca-Cola script illustrates the nature of tarnishment that companies try to stop. Toy manufactures and children's media often face unauthorized use by adult-oriented businesses trying to use the association for attention and the juxtaposition for humor, but at the expense of the family-oriented business. The law is generally quite supportive of the

---

[219] *Id.*

[220] *Id.*

[221] Moseley v. V. Secret Catalogue, Inc., 537 U.S. 418, 431 (2003) (*citing* 1012 H.R.Rep. No 104–374, p. 3 (1995).

efforts to stop these adult-only tarnishing uses. Courts are somewhat more respectful of parody and free speech concerns when the tarnishment is less salacious or the trademarks protect less wholesome goods.

Tarnishment, in turn, is defined "association arising from the similarity between a mark or trade name and a famous mark that harms the reputation of the famous mark,"[222] which allows for a legal cause of action even in the absence of "confusion, of competition, or of actual economic injury."[223]

Despite some limitations on dilution, the 2006 statute has continued to expand the power of trademark anti-tarnishment laws. Courts are highly protective of the trademark holders under the tarnishment law, much more than general dilution actions or likelihood of confusion claims for non-famous marks. As the court in *V Secret Catalogue, Inc. v. Moseley* explained, "the new Act creates a kind of rebuttable presumption, or at least a very strong inference, that a new mark used to sell sex related products is likely to tarnish a famous mark if there is a clear semantic association between the two."[224]

Blurring is a more complex analysis, much more typical of a trademark infringement action. The statute provides the following:

In determining whether a mark or trade name is likely to cause dilution by blurring, the court may consider all relevant factors, including the following:

(i) The degree of similarity between the mark or trade name and the famous mark.

(ii) The degree of inherent or acquired distinctiveness of the famous mark.

---

[222] 15 U.S.C. § 1125(c)(2)(C).

[223] 15 U.S.C. § 1125(c)(1).

[224] V Secret Catalogue, Inc. v. Moseley, 605 F.3d 382, 388 (6th Cir. 2010).

(iii) The extent to which the owner of the famous mark is engaging in substantially exclusive use of the mark.

(iv) The degree of recognition of the famous mark.

(v) Whether the user of the mark or trade name intended to create an association with the famous mark.

(vi) Any actual association between the mark or trade name and the famous mark.[225]

State laws are similar, but they vary considerably from state to state. Although state laws used to have stronger anti-dilution laws than the federal statute, recent changes have made the federal law very protective of famous marks.

Disparagement claims tend to provide a greater scope of protection for trademark owners, allowing them to stop not only the direct use of their trademarks, but also clever puns or indirect references to their marks that the federal courts would not recognize under a dilution claim. For the entrepreneur hoping to develop economic value in his own marks, the temptation to use the literary reference to another party's trademark must be carefully weighed against the cost of fighting a trademark battle, particularly if the likely outcome of such a battle will be a loss of the entrepreneur's trademark and goodwill.

D. Acquiring, Licensing, and Maintaining Trademarks.

Because many trademarks are created through usage over time, the nature and formality of trademark acquisition is somewhat different than other forms of intellectual property. In addition, because trademarks have a dual function as a property interest and a consumer protection mechanism, the rules governing their ownership and transfer are unlike most types of property.

1. Use in Commerce.

The primary method of acquiring a trademark is through using it in commerce. For federal law, this requires that the use be in interstate commerce, meaning that the goods or services are sold across state lines

---

[225] 15 U.S.C. § 1125(c)(2)(B).

or marketed to the public from out of state. Mail order and Internet sales serve this purpose well. For a restaurant seeking a service mark in its name, evidence of marketing to customers in neighboring states and the patronage by those customers is strong evidence of interstate commerce.

The nature of the evidence required to establish usage of the trademarks and service marks differs somewhat because trademark owners use the marks differently for goods than services. Evidence of use of a mark for goods in interstate commerce must appear directly on the goods, on labels, on shipping containers and packages, or on displays. When filing the trademark application, a photograph of the products bearing the trademark is acceptable rather than sending the actual product. Leaflets, brochures, publicity releases, and similar items do not provide evidence of the use of a mark with goods because they are too indirect.

Services must display the service mark in their advertising or sales literature. Signs, brochures about the service, advertisements, and even business cards and stationary may be acceptable evidence of a service mark. These items would not be accepted for evidence of a trademark for goods, but given the lack of a tangible item with which to attach the service mark, they are sufficient.

2.   *Intent to Use.*

The United States has modified federal law to permit the filing of trademark applications for trademarks that are not yet used in commerce. The policy change was made in response to growing recognition of this common practice in other countries. Because this is a significant change from prior U.S. practice, it has many limitations. The trademark applicant hoping to protect a trademark not yet in use must proceed with a great deal of care.

The intent to use application allows a company to provide a declaration that it has a bona fide intention to use the mark in commerce. This simple form, along with evidence similar to the type required for trademark use in commerce, will allow a company six months in which to begin using the trademark. This six-month period can be further extended up to three years with extension applications and filing fees.

The actual registration will not take place until after the mark has been used in commerce and the company has filed a form entitled

"Allegation of Use," which documents the use of the mark. The intent to use application has a significant advantage for the launch of a new product or service because it allows the entrepreneur to pre-clear the name of the product and avoid the expense of selecting a mark that will be opposed.

3. Elements of an Application—Specimens and Drawings.

Although the definition of a trademark includes the broadly inclusive statement that a mark may be "any word, name, symbol, or device," most trademarks are textual—typically common or proper nouns. The second largest category would be comprised of images in the form of designs, pictures, or logos. The text trademark is known as a "standard character" (formerly "typed") drawing, while a drawing including a logo or image is a "stylized or special form" drawing.

One point of confusion between the two categories is the protection of typeface or font. If the trademark owner claims the specific typeface or font is part of the trademark, then that trademark requires a stylized or special form drawing. The special form drawings can also protect the specific choice of color in the trademark, but unless this is specially applied for, the application is based on black and white trademarks only. "The application includes a statement that the mark is in standard characters and no claim is made to any particular font style, size, or color."[226] If the trademark owner wishes to make color, font, size, or image part of the trademark, then it must file the special form application.

To file the federal trademark application, the trademark owner must file an actual example of the trademark as it is actually used in commerce or intended to be used in commerce. The example is known as a "specimen" of the trademark. The specimen shows how the drawing relates to the goods or services for which the application is sought.

The specimens that may be used for the trademark application tie directly to the examples of the trademark that establish that the mark is properly used in interstate commerce. As a result, for goods, the trademark submitted should be on tags, labels, containers, or displays.

---

[226] 37 C.F.R. § 2.52(a)(1) (2018).

Given the size and dimensions of products, photographs that capture the specimen and the product are sufficient. The actual products should not be provided to the PTO. The PTO uses the specimen to determine that the trademark is actively used in commerce in conjunction with the product. Thus, invoices, announcements, order forms, bills of lading, leaflets, brochures, publicity releases, letterhead, and business cards are rejected because they fail to show this connection.

Similarly, the specimens that may be used for a service mark application tie directly to the examples of the service mark that establish the mark is properly used in interstate commerce in conjunction with the service promoted. Unlike specimens for trademarks, service marks allow a more general category of specimens, including signs, brochures about the business, advertisements, business cards, and stationary which shows the services provided. The specimen must show the relationship between the mark and the service. As the PTO explains, there must be

> some reference to the services, that is, it is not just a display of the mark itself. . . . For example, if the mark sought to be registered is 'T.MARKEY' for retail stores featuring men's sportswear, a specimen that only shows the wording 'T.MARKEY' and no other matter would not be acceptable, but a specimen that shows the wording 'T.MARKEY' on a clothing store sign would be acceptable."[227]

4.   *Acquisition Through Purchase or Licensing.*

The nature of the property interest in a trademark has a somewhat schizophrenic relationship to traditional notions of property. Trademarks are least like personal property in that they cannot merely be purchased and sold. Because marks must always relate directly to the goods or services used in commerce, they can only be transferred as part of transactions involving those goods or services.

Instead of wishing to acquire a brand name from a company, it is more likely that another company would like to associate the name with its own goods. This commonly occurs with the sale of tee-shirts bearing

---

[227] U.S. PATENT & TRADEMARK OFFICE, *supra* note 206, at 21.

company brands, but it also occurs commonly with the extension of one brand into another, corporate joint ventures, and similar transactions.

The senior trademark owner can accomplish this by licensing the mark to the goods or services of a third party if certain conditions are met regarding scope and quality control. The most important of these conditions is that the senior trademark owner continues to have a significant involvement in the control of its trademark. Among the key provisions:

- *Control of the mark itself*—so that the licensee cannot change the wording or artwork of the trademark without permission.

- *Control of the goods and services marked*—so that each product or service using the mark is approved by the senior trademark owner.

- *Quality control of the goods and services*—the right and actual practice of reviewing the goods and services on which the trademarks are used to assure that they meet the standards of the senior user.

- *Obligations to police the trademark*—so the junior trademark user and the senior trademark user each have duties to be sure no infringement or unauthorized junior use is occurring.

With a properly drafted license agreement, the licensee becomes a junior user of the senior trademark. This allows great expansion of a trademark's reach into new fields.

5.   *Benefits of Co-Branding and Licensing.*

Co-branding is a version of licensing in which the owners of each trademark enter into a cross-license agreement, so that each company is the licensee of the other company's mark for the purpose of promoting a particular good or service.

Cross licensing allows for the co-branding of cellular phones by the manufacturers and the wireless carriers, the expansion of cartoon characters into virtually every conceivable product line, the ability of diet book authors and restaurants to launch food lines, and automobile companies to sell toy versions of their vehicles.

Trademark licensing and co-branding create opportunities for entrepreneurs to jump-start into new lines of business and expand the opportunities of other companies' products. These relationships have the benefit of extending the brand reach of the senior user without distracting that company from its core competency. It provides a strategy for companies who have the potential to diversify but understand that diversification may lead to lack of focus and poor integration of business models across competing sectors. If, instead of adding new divisions, an established company can simply employ a few trademark experts to focus on brand management, new revenue can be found with far less risk.

6.   *Maintaining Trademarks.*

Trademarks are highly valuable for a corporation. For commodity products, the premium price differential demanded by brand name goods is a quantitative reflection of the market value of the trademark. A less quantifiable aspect of that value is the shelf space made available to retailers. The market presence that results in greater market share for brand name goods also reflects the economic value of the trademark.

Valuable assets must be carefully maintained. If a trademark no longer reflects the particular source of the goods, the trademark can become the generic word for that class of goods. Professor Charles McManis has written a simple seven-step process to protect trademarks from becoming generic and losing their market value.

(1) Select as fanciful or arbitrary a mark or name as possible.

(2) Register it as a federal trademark at the earliest possible time.

(3) To distinguish it in advertising that the public will recognize it as a trademark (i.e., use distinctive type face, quotation marks, etc. use the term in association with some other term which will function as a generic term and, where registered, use the symbol ®).

(4) Avoid using corruptions of the term.

(5) Use the mark on several different but related products.

(6) Engage in continuous advertising.

(7) Aggressively police the mark by challenging misuse of the mark, not only by competitors and other commercial parties, but

by the public at large. To police a mark, one may institute a media monitoring program with follow-up letters of varying degrees of forcefulness reminding editors, publishers, broadcasters and other businesses and public figures who have misused a mark or name, that it is a protected trademark. . . . .[228]

Through this seven-step process, the trademark that is carefully selected, registered, thoughtfully used, and actively protected from misuse has the potential to return value to the trademark owner for decades and perhaps even centuries.

E.   Enforcement of Trademark Rights.

1.   Enforcing Trademark Rights Before Litigation.

Most trademark enforcement does not start or end on the courthouse steps. Trademark enforcement begins with internal policing to assure that the mark is not being altered or modified by company employees, vendors, manufacturers, retailers, or others in the product distribution process. A trademark which feels stale to the employees who see it every day may be just gaining recognition by the public which has only occasional exposure to the mark. Companies must actively police themselves to avoid clever but unregistered modifications to their trademarks since material changes to the trademark will destroy the federal trademark registration.

Trademark owners must also work with newspapers, magazines, and other publishers to assure that a trademarked term is not regularly used as a generic name for the category of goods or turned into a verb regarding the use of such goods. "Xeroxing a copy" is a phrase that risks diluting the Xerox trademark for photocopiers. The trademark owner has the obligation to educate the public on this misuse. Similar, terms such as "googling" risk genericizing the Google trademark for its search engine.

For companies that believe competitors are using their trademarks improperly, the trademark owner generally begins with a "cease and desist" letter. The letter typically explains the ownership of the

---

[228] CHARLES R. MCMANIS & DAVID J. FRIEDMAN, INTELLECTUAL PROPERTY AND UNFAIR COMPETITION IN A NUTSHELL 174–75 (2013).

trademark, the misuse of the trademark and a request that the misuse stop. Before this letter is sent, however, the trademark owner should invest time and resources to investigate the competitor. A trademark search should be conducted to better understand the trademark use by that company. Copies of the infringing trademark, specimens of the trademark on a range of the competitor's goods or services, advertising, and a comprehensive collection of the competitor's trademark use should be collected. The more a trademark owner knows about the activities and use by an alleged infringer, the more effectively it can craft the cease and desist letter, and the more likely it can find a reasonable compromise to the dispute. The research helps the company explore the strength and weakness of its claim before the first shot is fired. As a result, the research may better arm the company for a future fight, or it may keep the company from entering a fight it should not fight or cannot win.

If the company's trademark covers a broad range of uses and the alleged misuse is not directly competitive, the reasonable compromise is for the two not-quite-competitors to enter into a written agreement regarding each company's use. This converts the potential infringement into a licensed activity, sets limits on the changes and results in a stronger, rather than weaker, trademark. If the parties cannot reach such an arrangement, or if the parties are actual competitors, then one of the parties must agree to stop using the infringing trademark. The owner of a trademark cannot back down once it learns of an infringement, because the knowing of the infringement and failing to take action is tantamount to granting permission for the activity, greatly weakening the trademark's scope and value. If both parties believe that they have priority to use the mark, then litigation may be the only solution to settle the priority of the trademark interests.

2.   *Elements of the Trademark Infringement Claim.*

To win a trademark action against an infringer of one's trademark, the plaintiff trademark owner must be able to establish that (1) plaintiff has a valid trademark, (2) plaintiff has priority in the use of the trademark, (3) defendant has used an identical or similar trademark, and

(4) defendant's use of the mark results in a likelihood of confusion on the part of the public.[229]

The first two elements were discussed in the previous section. Federal registration of the trademark, though not essential, makes the evidence of the first element much easier to establish. Priority requires that the plaintiff be the senior user of the trademark—the party who used it first. As described above, there is a risk that two users were both using the same mark in different geographic regions at the same time. In this case, the junior user can establish priority in its geographic reason.

The third element is a factual question regarding whether the right defendant is in the lawsuit. If the defendant never used an identical or similar mark, it should not be sued. The plaintiff must prove that the defendant used the marks in commerce.

There is usually little evidentiary doubt of this element in cases involving established businesses, but it is the critical element in the case of intellectual property counterfeiters. Counterfeiters will make goods with fake trademarks that are quite close to that of the legitimate trademark owners. They will stay one step ahead of the law and the lawful trademark owners with false names and dummy corporations, making it harder to establish who is actually responsible for the piracy.

3.   *Likelihood of Confusion.*

For lawsuits involving legitimate competitors, the likelihood of confusion element is the most complex and heavily disputed. Different courts use different formulas for their analysis of likelihood of confusion, but the formulations tend to summarize the same test:

> [T]he court is required to consider several factors when assessing whether or not there is a likelihood of confusion by the general public: the degree of similarity between the marks in appearance and suggestion; the similarity of the products for which the name is used; the area and manner of concurrent use; the degree of care likely to be exercised by consumers; the strength of the

---

[229] Nike, Inc. v. "Just Did It" Enters., 6 F.3d 1225, 1227 (7th Cir. 1993). *See also* A.J. Canfield Co. v. Vess Beverages, Inc., 796 F.2d 903, 906 (7th Cir. 1986).

complainant's mark; actual confusion; and an intent on the part of the alleged infringer to palm off his products as those of another.[230]

No one of these factors will determine whether the court will find that it is likely the public will be confused by the defendant's mark. Actual confusion is evidence of likelihood of confusion, but is neither required nor sufficient to answer the test. Instead, the courts use these factors to make a much more subjective determination. The court will find infringement if the two marks are too close to each other when used in the manner before the court.

The factors the court weighs are interrelated. A highly fanciful or arbitrary trademark is stronger whereas a descriptive mark that relies heavily on the attributes of the goods is weaker. So the strength of the trademark will actually vary depending on the particular goods in question. For example, 3M's Post-it brand for notes is not quite as strong for small notepads as it is for removable CD labels or wall charts, because the trademark is increasingly arbitrary for those goods. In a lawsuit, the nature of the goods in dispute may strengthen or weaken the mark.

The similarity of the marks is a critical feature. "Marks may be confusingly similar based on physical design, sounds, psychological, commercial, or social connotations and significance, color scheme, or linguistic characteristics.[231] If a court determines that the marks are not sufficiently similar, the plaintiff will not be able to prove its case. If the words, artwork and colors are all similar, the court is much more likely to find confusion than if only the words have some similarity.

In trademarks, spelling does not count, so "Light" and "Lite" are the same potential trademark. DreamWorks and Dreamwerks are identical for trademark purposes. Trademarks are reviewed in their totality rather than dissected when comparing them for similarity.

---

[230] *Nike, Inc.*, 6 F.3d at 1228.

[231] ARTHUR R. MILLER & MICHAEL H. DAVIS, INTELLECTUAL PROPERTY, PATENTS, TRADEMARKS, AND COPYRIGHT IN A NUTSHELL § 17.2, at 291 (6th ed. 2018).

The comparison of products or services is also critical. As discussed earlier, identical marks are often used in unrelated fields. The closer the products are to each other, the more reasonable it is to expect the public to be confused by similar trademarks.

Similarly, the nature of the intended consumers of the goods will affect the comparison. The more sophisticated the audience, the greater the trademark owner's burden of establishing the likelihood of confusion. The general public is not as attuned to details in products and services as are more specialized markets. The broad general public, therefore, is not expected to pay too much attention to the trademarks or the goods. In contrast, a more discerning clientele is more likely to understand the nuance in the products and be able to avoid confusion more readily than casual purchasers.

Famous or well-recognized trademarks also cast a larger shadow than marks that are less well-recognized by the public. If the public does not know about a trademark, it cannot be confused by seeing something similar. Put another way, the more famous the trademark, the broader an array of goods and services it can cover.

As a consequence, the strength of the mark may extend from the individual marks to the family of trademarks. Perhaps the best known example of a family of marks comes from the extension by Apple of the iPod to the iPad, iPhone, iTunes, and iOS. Similarly, McDonald's was successful in stopping the use of McBagel by a competitor because the McDonald trademark family included the well-known McMuffin, McChicken, Big Mac and the lesser known McPizza, McFeast, and McDonuts. Ken McShea's attempt to launch McBagel was barred because of the fame of McDonald's trademarks and its active policing of those marks.[232]

Finally, the intent of the alleged infringer goes to both the culpability of the defendant and the measure of damages. "Most circuits find that where a defendant adopted its mark intending to copy the plaintiff's mark and benefit from the plaintiff's reputation, the court may infer that there is in fact confusing similarity between the marks."[233] If the

---

[232] McDonald's Corp. v. McBagel's, Inc., 649 F. Supp. 1268 (S.D.N.Y. 1986).

[233] ANNE GILSON LALONDE, 5 GILSON ON TRADEMARKS § 5.09 (2018).

discovery process or the nature of the trademarks demonstrates a willful intent to model the defendant's trademark on the plaintiff, the courts often find that the defendant's actions were purposefully seeking confusion, which satisfies the likelihood of confusion standard. Intentional misconduct is much more likely to result in the defendant being enjoined from continuing the misuse of the mark and may result in an award of attorneys' fees against the defendant.

4.   *Nominative Fair Use and Collateral Use.*

When the defendant uses the plaintiff's trademark to describe the plaintiff's product rather than its own product, the courts will provide it some latitude. This is important under both free speech principles and commercial competitiveness principles. The defendant must be careful to use the mark only to the extent necessary to identify the trademark owner's products and do nothing that suggests sponsorship or endorsement of the defendant's product by the trademark holder.

Fair use allows comparative advertising, identification of the products reviewed in each issue of a consumer products magazine, and allows a certain amount of parody commercial conduct—so that the trademark owners remember not to take themselves too seriously.

Collateral use allows third parties to use a trademark to represent the accurate information about components used within the underlying products. A computer manufacturer has a legal right to identify the trademarked software sold as part of the bundled package of hardware and software shipped to the consumer. The software company cannot stop the manufacturer from including its product if the product is lawfully purchased, and it cannot object to the use of the trademark on the software itself. Collateral use is limited, however. It cannot be used to create a false impression of endorsement or mislead the public as to the association between the companies.

Collateral use also allows repair shops and reprocessors to accurately depict their business without running afoul of the trademarks owned by the companies—often companies who would prefer that no reprocessing of their products takes place. If a product is refurbished and put back into commerce, the reprocessor is not obligated to remove the trademark. Again, as with the product bundler, it cannot use the first manufacturer's trademark to mislead the public as to endorsement or association, but it can use the trademark to show the source of the original goods.

5.   *Other Defenses to Trademark Infringement.*

There are always defenses to trademark litigation, and these defenses serve as warnings to the trademark owner regarding the diligence necessary to police their trademarks. Professor McManis lists the defenses as "abandonment, loss of distinctiveness (i.e. genericide), functionality, and collateral or fair use ... and the equitable defenses of laches, estoppel, acquiescence, and unclean hands (including misuse)."[234]

If a trademark becomes generic because the term is used for a category of goods rather than for a particular manufacturer's goods, then anyone is free to use that trademark. Similarly, if the trademark owner stops using the trademark in commerce, then it may have been deemed to have abandoned the trademark, giving up its rights to stop others from using the trademark.

The equitable defenses focus on the conduct of the trademark owner and whether justice is served by enforcing the rights of that trademark owner. If the trademark owner was not diligent in pursuing the claim, then the junior user may have invested considerable time and effort in pursuing the uncontested trademark use. Courts may refuse to grant relief to a company that has failed to police its trademarks vigorously and let other competitors use the trademark to grow in the marketplace.

F.   The International Implications of Trademark Law and Practice.

Trademarks are territorial in nature, meaning that the laws of each nation govern the protection of trademarks used in that country. With the growth of international commerce, however, the ability to use the same trademarks across multiple countries is increasingly a financial imperative. To improve the consistency across nations and streamline the administrative requirements, international treaties have been developed to coordinate marks across the globe. The World Intellectual Property Organization (WIPO) is the U.N. body primarily responsible for managing these international treaties.

---

[234] MCMANIS, *supra* note 228, at 202.

1.   *The Madrid Protocol.*

Although the first of these treaties dates to 1891, relatively recent changes have made it possible for U.S. companies to gain significant benefit from these treaties. The U.S. joined the Madrid Protocol in 2003 and the European Union joined in 2004. The Madrid Protocol (or formerly "The Protocol Relating to the Madrid Agreement Concerning the International Registration of Marks") is a separate treaty from the 1891 Madrid Agreement, which the U.S. continues to refuse to join. Instead, by adhering to the Madrid Protocol, U.S. companies can gain the primary benefit of trademark protection in the Madrid Union countries with a single filing at the USPTO in English and paid with U.S. currency. Since the European Union has also recently joined, the value of this application has increased significantly.

The Madrid Union does not include Canada or Mexico, so U.S. companies operating across North America should be aware that regional applications still require additional state-by-state applications.

For the Madrid Union countries, however, the application process has never been easier. "Any trademark owner with an application filed in or a registration issued by the USPTO and who is a national of, has a domicile in, or has a real and effective industrial or commercial establishment in the United States can submit an international application through the USPTO."[235] Eligible companies must have one or more basic U.S. applications or registrations, and the owner of the international mark must be the same as the U.S. mark. The international application must include a list of goods and services that is identical to its U.S. registration or is a subset of those goods and services.

If the international application meets the USPTO requirements, the USPTO will certify the application or registration and forward the international application to the International Bureau. The International Bureau, in turn, reviews and registers the mark. It then forwards the mark to each country in the Madrid Union designated by the applicant. Although each country can object to the registration locally, they have

---

[235] *The Madrid Protocol: Frequently Asked Questions by U.S. Trademark Owners Seeking International Rights*, U.S. Patent & Trademark Office, http://www.uspto.gov/web/trademarks/madrid/madridfaqs.htm (last visited July 12, 2018).

only eighteen months to do so, and following that period, the registration is accepted. Thereafter, like the U.S. registration, the international application requires renewal and maintenance fees every ten years.

2. *Continued International Enforcement.*

Registration remains only the first step in trademark protection. With a registered trademark, the trademark holder still has the ongoing obligation to police its marks and stop infringers in each country where the mark is registered or used. As a result, the Madrid Protocol is an extremely helpful first step, but it does not eliminate the national borders for policing, enforcement, or management of the trademarks and brands.

Chapter 19.   Publicity Rights and Privacy Law

A.   Attributes of Publicity Rights.

Publicity Rights—Summary

Subject Matter: Name, nickname, likeness, biography, voice, and identity.

Method Acquired: Varies by state. In most states publicity rights are automatic, but some require actual use of rights in commerce.

Term: Throughout lifespan of person in all states where recognized. States differ on length of protection after death.

Time Needed to Acquire: No waiting period.

Renewals: Not applicable.

Federal Government Office and Website: None (some similar protection under trademark law). State law protection only.

Applicable Law: Examples of state law: Cal. Civ. Code §3344 (a) (West 2018); N.Y. Civ. Rights Law §§50-51 (McKinney 2018).

Transfer: Owner of publicity rights may license use; licenses may be transferable.

Property Excluded from Protection: Does not extend to non-commercial use of name, likeness, etc. One cannot stop news sources or unauthorized biographies, etc.

B.   Publicity Rights Explained.

Perhaps the least understood intellectual property doctrine is the law of publicity, which weaves together the broad category of state laws and federal trademark practice in the United States. Despite this highly chaotic body of law, the practice of licensing publicity rights is quite straightforward and very important for the entrepreneur. This chapter provides a comprehensive summary of the major concepts of publicity rights. Because the law is based on the laws of individual states, it is subject to significant variation from location to location. Nonetheless, a good understanding of the law is sufficient for most businesses to work around the legal gaps and derive the economic opportunities available to the entrepreneurs and celebrities alike.

The law on publicity rights owes its origins to a theory first identified by Samuel Warren and Louis Brandeis in 1890.[236] In their seminal article, they explained that an individual's protection of person and property "is a principle as old as the common law; but it has been found necessary from time to time to define anew the exact nature and extent of such protection. Political, social, and economic changes entail the recognition of new rights, and the common law, in its eternal youth, grows to meet the new demands of society."[237]

Although there were some historical discussions that suggested the property interest in one's identity could only be found if the person seeking protection had used his or her identity in commerce—analogous to trademark law, this notion has not taken hold to define most state laws. Instead, any person has a publicity right in his or her name, whether famous or not. Nonetheless, the value of publicity rights rests in their marketability. Referring to the owner of publicity rights as a "celebrity" provides a convenient way to distinguish the rights licensors from the entrepreneurs who are typically the licensee of these rights. Of course, some famous entrepreneurs such as Spago's Wolfgang Puck have merged the two, creating brand value in their own names instead of having to license the names of famous people to promote their business.

1.   Subject Matter of Publicity Rights.

At its heart, the right of publicity provides simple legal protection. "The right of publicity is simply the right of every person to control the commercial use of his or her identity."[238] The Restatement (Third) of

---

[236] Samuel D. Warren & Louis D. Brandeis, *The Right to Privacy*, 4 HARV. L. REV. 193 (1890).

[237] *Id.*

[238] J. Thomas McCarthy & Paul M. Anderson, *Protection of the Athlete's Identity: The Right of Publicity, Endorsements and Domain Names*, 11 MARQ. SPORTS L. REV. 195, 197 (2001). *See also*, 1 J. THOMAS MCCARTHY, THE RIGHTS OF PUBLICITY AND PRIVACY § 1:3 (2d ed. 2018).

Unfair Competition provides one of the simpler summaries of the law. "One who appropriates the commercial value of a person's identity by using without consent the person's name, likeness, or other indicia of identity for purposes of trade is subject to liability. . . ."[239]

The concept of identity includes name, voice, signature, photograph, or likeness. It typically extends to nicknames and associated catch phrases. For example, Johnny Carson was protected from another company using "Here's Johnny" to sell its products (portable toilets).

Properly understood, the exclusive property interests protected by publicity rights only apply to the commercial use of the celebrity's identity and do not inhibit press or noncommercial use of the name or likeness. The scope of commercial use, however, is perhaps the most controversial aspect of publicity rights. Critics of publicity rights raise concerns that publicity rights unduly infringe on the free speech rights of the public. To avoid this result, publicity rights generally do not restrict noncommercial uses of a celebrity's identity. Commercial use is one in which a good or service is sold, not an editorial or communicative service. Food, consumer electronics, automobiles, and the vast majority of products are commercial goods. While this summary is an over-simplification, it is perhaps a more commercially pragmatic approach and suffices in a majority of jurisdictions.

The items which should be exempt from the commercial products category are those which are editorial or communicative in nature. Newspapers, televisions shows, movies, music, books, games, and theater are in a very broad category of editorial or communicative services. It should be noted that a newspaper such as the *New York Times* is still sold in a tangible form for a profit. Neither the tangible nature of the newspaper nor the for-profit motive of the business eliminates its communicative role. A newspaper is free to print photographs of individuals without their permission because a free press is of much higher societal value than the property rights associated with publicity rights, and this societal value is incorporated into the First Amendment of the U.S. Constitution.

---

[239] RESTATEMENT (THIRD) OF UNFAIR COMPETITION 46 (1995).

Various states grapple to make the distinction between commercial products and communicative products or services. California law, for example, exempts newspapers and others from the restrictions of publicity rights by providing that "a use of a name, voice, signature, photograph, or likeness in connection with any news, public affairs, or sports broadcast or account, or any political campaign, shall not constitute a use for which consent is required . . . ."[240] The law also explains that the commercial nature of a work is a question of fact.

Generally speaking, newspapers, television news, television comedy shows, original paintings (as well as limited edition lithographs), and broadcasts of sporting events will not be considered commercial. Posters, coffee mugs, lunch boxes, and similar memorabilia will generally fall into the commercial category. The difference between these categories can be very subjective, however, resulting in a great deal of ambiguity and hand-wringing.

* * *

Sidebar—The commercial nature of tee-shirts.

Tee-shirts are a unique case in the debate over commercial versus communicative product. Some tee-shirts are sold as memorabilia, and therefore will be commercial, while other tee-shirts are highly editorial in their expression. In 2001, the California Supreme Court took up this debate regarding Gary Saderup's drawings of the Three Stooges on tee-shirts as well as lithographs without permission of the assignee of the publicity rights.[241] The court grappled with the meaning of the First Amendment in the context of the Three Stooges tee-shirt debate:

> But having recognized the high degree of First Amendment protection for noncommercial speech about celebrities, we need not conclude that all expression that trenches on the right of publicity receives such protection. The right of publicity, like copyright, protects a form of intellectual property that society deems to have some social utility. "Often considerable money, time and energy are needed to develop one's prominence in a

---

[240] CAL. CIV. CODE. § 3344(d) (West 2018).

[241] Comedy III Prod., Inc v. Gary Saderup, Inc., 21 P.3d 797 (Cal. 2001).

particular field. Years of labor may be required before one's skill, reputation, notoriety or virtues are sufficiently developed to permit an economic return through some medium of commercial promotion. For some, the investment may eventually create considerable commercial value in one's identity."[242]

After considerable analysis, the court came to the self-evident conclusion that the tee-shirts were unauthorized memorabilia which violated the publicity rights owned by the heirs and assignees of the Three Stooges. The practical rule which flows from these court decisions is that parody or offensive tee-shirts are communicative while respectful tee-shirts are commercial. It is hard to imagine, however, that courts and legislatures are willing to adopt the "*offensive tee-shirt* rule," so they will continue to use much longer analysis to achieve this same result.

* * *

2.   *Unfair Competition Under the Lanham Act for Rights of Publicity.*

Section 43(a) of the Lanham Act, discussed in Chapter 18, provides a general statement of liability for using any name or mark in a manner likely to cause consumer confusion.[243] The recently revised statute specifically includes the term "name," reinforcing Congress' intent to allow an individual to protect the person's name from commercial use without consent. Use of a celebrity's name on a commercial product is likely to cause confusion with the public because it states or implies sponsorship or approval of the unauthorized user's goods or services. In this way, §43(a) covers a broad range of publicity rights claims.

The largest distinction between §43(a) and publicity rights is that a state law publicity claim does not require proof of any misleading conduct or likelihood of confusion. In this way, the federal test is somewhat more demanding than the evidence of impact required in most states.

---

[242] *Id.* at 804–05 (*quoting* Lugosi v. Universal Pictures, 603 P.2d 425, 438 (1979) (Bird, dissenting)).

[243] 15 U.S.C. § 1125(a) (2018). Section 43(a) of the legislation is codified at §1125 in the United State Code.

The state and federal legal claims complement each other because each has a slightly different set of allegations. If a celebrity can establish both the unauthorized use of the identity and a likelihood of confusion regarding that use among the public, then the celebrity can choose to bring an action in state or federal court. The state court action on publicity rights would otherwise require less evidence to prove and may therefore be strategically preferable.

Lanham Act claims are so common for celebrity cases that courts have adopted a set of factors to determine the likelihood of confusion specifically for these types of claims. The eight factors are as follows:

(1) The level of recognition that the plaintiff has among the segment of the society for whom the defendant's product is intended;

(2) The relatedness of the fame or success of the plaintiff to the defendant's product;

(3) The similarity of the likeness used by the defendant to the actual plaintiff;

(4) Evidence of actual confusion;

(5) Marketing channels used;

(6) Likely degree of purchaser care;

(7) Defendant's intent on selecting the plaintiff; and

(8) Likelihood of expansion of the product lines.

Although these are all factors that are appropriate for consideration in determining the likelihood of confusion, they are not necessarily of equal importance, nor do they necessarily apply to every case.[244]

These factors parallel the likelihood of confusion factors for other trademarks, but they focus on the fame of the plaintiff and the relationship of the fame to the defendant's product. At least with regard to the famous plaintiff's complaint about the misuse of her identity for

---

[244] Downing v. Abercrombie & Fitch, 265 F.3d 994, 1007-08 (9th Cir. 2001).

the false endorsement of products, federal protection remains available under this law.

3.   *Matters not Protected by Publicity Rights.*

Publicity rights are highly circumscribed by public policy concerns for free speech. For example, the subjects of unflattering biographies have tried to claim that the books, the book covers, or the book marketing campaigns violate their publicity rights. These attempts to stifle unflattering biographies generally fail. Biographies are inherently communicative, and courts are quite mindful of the First Amendment implications of stopping the publication of a book merely because it is unflattering. If the book is sufficiently misleading as to be libelous, then the book can properly be stopped under that legal rule, but the law of libel is carefully structured to take First Amendment considerations into account.[245]

Because news reporting and other editorial activities are typically outside of the definition of commerce, publicity rights do not affect news, commentary, criticism, or other editorial uses of one's identity. The limitation is not restricted to news reporting. Films, novels, and books based on true stories do not require permission of their subjects, meaning that publicity rights need not be licensed. Having said that, there are many sound business reasons to seek a license, and the lack of publicity rights does not eliminate the need for the producers of these films and authors of these books to be mindful of defamation laws.

In much the same way, factual use of one's name cannot be used as a bar to commercial activity. While theoretically every software company should insist on obtaining a release to list its engineers' names in the programming credits, the industry custom of including these credits may create an implied license to use the names. Under this implied license, the company can reasonably expect that everyone who worked on the project has consented to have their name be listed in the credits. Had an engineer instructed the employer not to use her name or identity, however, the company could no longer rely on this implied license for listing that person's name, and it would be liable for inclusion of her name in the credits if it ignored her instructions.

---

[245] *See* New York Times Co. v. Sullivan, 376 U.S. 254 (1964).

Finally, there remains an inherent limitation because names are not unique, even among celebrities. Michael Jackson refers to both the internationally famous youngest brother of the family music group and a nationally famous radio host. Janet Jackson refers to both Michael's equally famous sister and a highly respected professor at Washburn University School of Law. Just as with the trademark laws of surnames, the laws involving publicity rights do not give a celebrity an exclusive right to his or her name to the exclusion of others with the same name.

4. *Relationship Between Publicity and Copyright.*

Copyright and publicity rights do not generally overlap. "Use in commerce" is an element of publicity rights that does not apply to copyright, so the two laws are distinct. As a result, federal copyright is rarely held to preempt state privacy or publicity law. In the most common example, a photographer is the copyright holder of the picture he takes, while the person photographed has no property interest in either the physical photograph or the copyright of the photograph. The photographer, however, cannot use his photograph on a product or service without the permission of the person photographed. The photographer can reproduce and sell an unlimited number of copies of the photograph, but if the photographer uses the picture to sell a bag of flour or a box of screws, the person in the photograph has the property interest in her image.

Publicity rights also have a very strange relationship with copyright, particularly in the context of motion picture and television production. Actors become famous for portraying characters, but the actors have no direct ownership interest in those characters. The actors begin to develop a publicity interest not just in their own identity, but in the identity of the copyrighted character owned by the motion picture or television studio.

To address this problem, Hollywood union agreements have contract terms in the standard union agreements that specifically provide that the film producers receive the publicity rights of the actors in order to create and distribute the film. The actors, in turn, retain their publicity rights for the purpose of commercial exploitation of goods other than the film and its potential sequels or remakes. While this is not theoretically necessary, the law of publicity rights has evolved awkwardly over time, so the industry has come together to clarify its policies using contracts and collectively bargained union agreements.

If the film company wants to use the actual likeness of an actor to sell action figures, then the actor must agree to enter into a new agreement with the producer—often with significant compensation for the actor. Often, the film producer will forego the actor's consent by giving the toys different faces than the actors in the movies. When Paramount Television, the producer of the hit television show *Cheers*, decided to open a series of bars modeled after the set of the show, it could not agree to terms with the actors playing Cliff and Norm. The bars were opened with animatronic mannequins that looked only vaguely like the actors playing the roles. But in the minds of the public, the actors were so closely linked with the roles of the characters that the court found there could still be a likelihood of confusion, despite the attempts to make the dolls look different than the actors.[246]

As the *Cheers* dispute illustrates, copyright and publicity rights cover very different legal interests. The copyright in the television show covers each episode. The content of the television episode should be deemed communicative and therefore only the copyright holder has a property interest in each episode of the television show. Because the scope of commercial use is somewhat unsettled, contractual agreements make this outcome part of the arrangement between producer and actor.

If the copyright holder of a television show selects a photograph of the show's cast for the advertising posters and cover of the television series DVDs, only the copyright holder has a property interest in those photographs because communicative nature of the television show extends to the marketing of that content. The actors depicted in the photograph generally will not have a claim under state rights of publicity. To reinforce this result, however, contracts are used to reinforce this understanding between the parties.

If, however, the copyright holder uses the same cast photograph used on the DVD for a lunch box, the persons depicted in the photograph have a property interest in their images for that product. The lunch box is a commercial product, and the publicity right is fully realized

---

[246] Wendt v. Host Int'l, Inc., 125 F.3d 806 (9th Cir. 1997).

because when the photograph in this example is used in a commercial manner. State court decisions explain the outcomes of their cases differently, but the most rational and consistent explanation for the various theories applied by state courts centers on the distinction between the nature of the product as either a communicative work which has no rights of publicity or a commercial product or advertisement, which does trigger the right of publicity. More importantly, if an entrepreneur adopts this set of rules, the company is likely to avoid most publicity rights disputes and maximize the opportunity to use publicity rights to help promote its products.

5.   *Other Limitations on Publicity Rights—First Amendment and Quasi Fair Use.*

Publicity rights serve as one of the few recognized limitations on free speech in the U.S. A person's right to control his identity is directly at odds with the right of another person to speak or print the identity of that person. As a result, courts struggle to find an appropriate balance between the constitutional rights of the speakers and the innate rights of the individual.

For example, when Cardtoons, L.C. began selling parody major league baseball trading cards, the players objected. Like the Wacky Packages from a generation earlier, these cards served to poke fun and parody the increasingly commercial national pastime. Trading cards are a commercial product, so the only basis for denying the Major League Baseball Players Association's requested injunction to stop the sale of the cards was fair use or First Amendment limitations on their claim.

> Cardtoons' parody trading cards receive full protection under the First Amendment. The cards provide social commentary on public figures, major league baseball players, who are involved in a significant commercial enterprise, major league baseball. While not core political speech . . . this type of commentary on an important social institution constitutes protected expression. The cards are no less protected because they provide humorous rather than serious commentary. Speech that entertains, like speech that informs, is protected by the First Amendment

because "[t]he line between the informing and the entertaining is too elusive for the protection of that basic right."[247]

The *Cardtoons* court found that because the Oklahoma statute did not allow for a fair use exception, it could not infer one from other laws such as copyright or trademark. Without a fair use exception to state publicity law, the court instead limited the application of the state publicity laws so that the laws were consistent with First Amendment protections of speech. By limiting the law, it provided Cardtoons with legal protection to continue selling its parody baseball cards.

Despite the refusal of some courts to imply fair use when it is not provided by statute, many courts recognize that fair use was a court-created doctrine for both copyright and trademark, so there is no significant barrier to courts applying fair use in cases and statutes involving publicity rights. As a result, the law of publicity rights is beginning to develop its own form of fair use.

In another sports example, the Court of Appeals for the Sixth Circuit attempted to balance the tension between free speech and publicity rights involving a series of lithographs entitled *"Masters of Augusta"* depicting Tiger Woods and other Masters champions. The court explained "[t]here is an inherent tension between the right of publicity and the right of freedom of expression under the First Amendment. This tension becomes particularly acute when the person seeking to enforce the right is a famous actor, athlete, politician, or otherwise famous person whose exploits, activities, accomplishments, and personal life are subject to constant scrutiny and comment in the public media."[248] The court looked to both First Amendment and copyright fair use analysis to shape its opinion. It relied on a California Supreme Court opinion which suggested the fair use test could be synthesized into whether the "celebrity likeness is one of the 'raw materials' from which an original work is synthesized, or whether the depiction or imitation of the celebrity is the very sum and substance of the work in question."[249] After

---

[247] Cardtoons, L.C. v. Major League Baseball Players Ass'n., 95 F.3d 959, 969 (10th Cir. 1996) (*quoting* Winters v. New York, 333 U.S. 507, 510 (1948)).

[248] ETW Corp. v. Jireh Publ'g, Inc., 332 F.3d 915, 931 (6th Cir. 2003).

[249] *Id.* at 936 (quoting Comedy III Prod., Inc., 21 P.3d at 809).

reviewing the First Amendment and fair use issues, it determined that the artist's use of Tiger Woods and the other famous golfers in the limited edition painting and lithographs was a fair use of their publicity rights.

Courts are recognizing that even commercial products may make fair use of a celebrity's identity. In some cases, these fair use rights are closely analogous to trademark fair use. For example, competitors of *"The Next Grilleration"* George Foreman Digital Grill must be able to show the product in a comparative advertisement. To the extent that Mr. Foreman is using his name as a part of the product's packaging, it must be subject to the same nominative fair use as his coined term "Grilleration." Similarly, once an authorized use of a person's identity is associated with a commercial product, then others who are retailing, marketing, and refurbishing that product all retain a fair use or collateral use of the person's identity to the extent that it is necessary to utilize the product. Of course, using the identity cannot be conducted in a manner that is misleading to the public.

Other cases emphasize the copyright aspects of fair use. The California Supreme Court, in particular, has struggled to use the copyright fair use test. It emphasized the importance of the first factor of copyright's four-prong analysis, focusing on "whether the new work merely 'supersede[s] the objects' of the original creation, or instead adds something new, with a further purpose or different character, altering the first with new expression, meaning, or message; it asks, in other words, whether and to what extent the new work is 'transformative.'"[250] The court also looked to the effect on the marketplace—"does the marketability and economic value of the challenged work derive primarily from the fame of the celebrity depicted? If this question is answered in the negative, then there would generally be no actionable right of publicity."[251]

---

[250] Comedy III Prod., Inc., 21 P.3d at 808 (*quoting* Folsom v. Marsh, 9 F. Cas. 342, 348 (CCD Mass. 1841) (No. 4,901), *in* Campbell v. Acuff-Rose Music, Inc. 510 U.S. 569, 579 (1994)). Although the court may be misguided in rejecting the entirety of the fair use analysis in favor of only two prongs, the explanation of that analysis will be better placed in another publication.

[251] Comedy III Prod., Inc., 21 P.3d at 810.

Whether the limitation is First Amendment, trademark fair use, copyright fair use, or an amalgam of the three, the goal remains to find an appropriate balance between the interests of the person whose identity is being used against another party wishing to use that person's identity in the marketplace of ideas or the marketplace of commerce. Because the law remains highly unsettled, all parties must proceed with a degree of caution.

6.   *Relation of Protection for State-Law Right.*

The publicity rights vary in scope from state to state, including whether the rights are recognized, the manner in which they are described, the range of identity interests protected and the term of the publicity rights after death. According to Professor McCarthy, "[t]oday, recognition of the rights of privacy in some form is nearly unanimous among the states, either at common law or by statute. Also, at the present time, the right of publicity has been recognized in some form at common law or by statute by half of the states."[252]

With the growth of the Internet and a new blurring of the distinctions between privacy, publicity and unfair competition, it is likely that the number of states recognizing some type of protection for their citizens will only increase. When added to the federal unfair competition protection of §43(a) and the corresponding state unfair competition law, business owners would be wise to assume that there is some identity ownership in every state.

From a business perspective, the simplest rule is to assume a national distribution of one's product or service and to take into account the most protective state's publicity rights laws when structuring transactions. Taken together, California, Indiana, Massachusetts, and New York tend to provide a national model. The economic differences are modest between highly protective states and those states that offer little protection. By applying this approach, the business is assured that it will acquire all the rights necessary to proceed. The celebrity involved is treated as if the publicity rights are fully vested property rights without

---

[252] 1 J. THOMAS MCCARTHY, THE RIGHTS OF PUBLICITY AND PRIVACY § 6:1 (2d ed. 2003).

regard to the vagaries of local laws, and the transactions can be better understood by investors and others.

7.   *Term of Publicity Rights.*

One of the more difficult issues involving publicity rights is the term of the rights.

Twenty-three states currently recognize a postmortem right either by statute or common law. These states include, among others, California, Florida, and Nevada. The duration of the right after the death of a celebrity varies, ranging from 10 years from the date of death in Washington if there was no commercial value at death, to 100 years from the date of death in Indiana and Oklahoma. California provides for the right to survive 70 years after the death of a celebrity.[253]

For example, because Marilyn Monroe's estate elected to treat her as domiciled in New York rather than California at the time of her death, New York law applies to determine whether or not her estate would be protected with postmortem publicity rights. Although Monroe, LLC and CMG Worldwide tried to assert her rights of publicity, a court applied the law of her domicile—New York— as it was established at the time of her death. Under the law of New York, no postmortem rights of publicity exist. In contrast, the singer Michael Jackson was domiciled in California when he died, so California law applies, and his estate is protected with postmortem rights. Other states, however, provide for postmortem rights in their states even though the celebrity was not a resident or domiciled. As a result, the commercial use of even dead celebrities may give rise to potential liability from unexpected places.

The states that have adopted publicity rights through the courts provide even less guidance regarding the existence of postmortem rights or their duration. Because it is clear that some states reject postmortem rights while others extend these rights for an entire century, business decisions will either be very local in nature or they will focus on the

---

[253] Erik W. Kahn & Pou-I "Bonnie" Lee, *"Delebs" and Postmortem Right of Publicity*, LANDSLIDE, Jan.-Feb. 2016, at 10, 10–11 (internal footnotes omitted).

economic value of rights for living parties with the knowledge that the rights will lose some protection after the death of the celebrity.

8.   Taxonomy of Publicity Rights Usage.[254]

There are many different points in the creative process where publicity rights may be helpful to producers or publishers of creative materials. Each use and its market should be carefully identified prior to the execution of a license agreement to assure the producer or publisher that the scope of the rights acquired is sufficient.

First, there are products focusing on the identity itself. Autobiographies, biographies, personal websites, fan websites, and infomercials typically fall into this category. Docudramas and true-life stories can fall into this category for the persons highlighted by the work. Each of these has content primarily about the celebrity or person featured.

Second, there are products where the celebrity or identity is used to endorse or promote some other product or service. This group may include products bearing celebrity names, infomercials, videogames and websites featuring celebrities, sports-based games featuring celebrity players, and the docudramas from the perspective of the minor characters to the story.

Third, there are products where the particular identity is reproduced in a manner incidental to the product: Background photographs that viewers can recognize, names used in song lyrics, personally identifiable data that can be culled from databases, and actors' images when those actors are portraying characters other than themselves (as actors rather than in their role as celebrities). These reflect the most common uses of identity interests, and for these common commercial uses, simple releases are sufficient. In practice, implied consent often suffices, though written documentation always provides greater certainty.

Each of the three categories listed above reflects the relationship of licensed identity to the creation of the product. Such usage can be categorized separately in terms of how the identity interest will be

---

[254] This section is largely taken from an earlier publication on the topic. Jon M. Garon, *Acquiring and Managing the Identity Interests for Software and Media,* 1 FLA. ENT. L. REV. 39 (2006).

developed by the producer or publisher. It should be treated distinctly from the question regarding what media will be used to reproduce, distribute, or display the final identity interests.

C.   Acquiring Publicity Rights.

Publicity rights exist for every person involved in the business, whenever a person's identity is used for commercial purposes. The entrepreneur has publicity rights that must be assigned to the business entity and may be of value as a marketing asset for the company. The company may also wish the assistance of a celebrity to promote the goods or services it markets. For this activity, the company will seek a license from the celebrity as well as some participation by that celebrity to help launch or promote the product.

1.   *General Considerations.*

The key provisions of a publicity rights agreement are similar to that of any licensing agreement, but certain provisions are more critical than others. There is no particularly right way to draft these provisions, but each plays a significant role in the legal rights acquired by the company. The terms discussed do not constitute a comprehensive publicity rights agreement. Instead, the explanation focuses on the provisions that make a publicity rights agreement somewhat different from a licensing agreement for trademarks, copyrights, or other interests.

Although states vary on requiring publicity rights to be granted in writing rather than orally or through conduct, a business should never rely on anything less than a signed writing for publicity rights, especially those that might have significant financial implications. States such as New York require a signed writing. In other situations, the inability to document the rights associated with a product will interfere with its manufacture and distribution. A signed contract will clarify a significant number of problems that may arise over time.

Companies should also be careful not to rely on releases for stock photographs without very careful review of the license agreements. At a minimum, the license agreement must specify that the photograph and the person depicted agree to the use of the image in association with the sale of a commercial product or service. The agreement must also provide that the stock photography house will indemnify the company from any loss incurred through a breach of its obligation to provide the rights. If the indemnity is limited to the value of the payment for the stock photographs, then the company should not use those photographs in any situation where the economic risk is greater than the small sum paid for the photographs. The stock photographs may be fine for the occasional brochure and other inconsequential uses, but they put more significant advertising campaigns at financial risk.

2.   Protecting the Publicity Rights of the Entrepreneur.

Publicity rights begin with the rights of the entrepreneur, the inventors or designers, and the others involved in launching the start-up business. At the inception of the business, any of the people involved might rise to become the next Steve Jobs or Bill Gates. These rights should acquired by the company early in its formation.

At the outset of a start-up enterprise, the future is bright, and the parties are optimistic. The primary assets of the company are its founders. As part of the initial phase of organization, the company should acquire the right to use the publicity rights of its founders for its commercial endeavors. In the event that the relationship among the parties begins to erode, having acquired the identity interests in advance avoids tensions over continued, factual use of the founders' names and biographies in the marketing of the start-up company.

3.   Acquisition of Celebrity Promotion through Purchase or Licensing.

The more traditional notions of publicity rights involve agreements between companies and celebrities for the endorsement of products by celebrities. Typically, these are negotiated by the celebrity's agent on his or her behalf. In addition to the financial incentives to participate, celebrities seek to be associated with products that enhance their image, provide them lifestyle opportunities (in the form of products, travel, or contacts), and provide some guaranteed economic stability in their highly volatile and often short careers. Famous television actors often have only one key role during their careers. Association with a quality product or service can keep that person in the public's eye while they work at finding an opportunity to make lightning strike a second time.

Unfortunately for both celebrities and businesses, most celebrities do not realize the ephemeral nature of fame until it is too late for it to be recovered. They—or their agents—tend to overvalue their services and importance to the companies. Strategies that rely on sharing the risks of the association, known in Hollywood as "back-end" deals, can be used to entice the celebrities to participate at costs reasonable for the company, while having economic rewards sufficient to engage the celebrity's sense of self-worth.

4.   Grant of Rights—Defining the Identity Rights to be Licensed.

The first provision is the grant of the identity rights by the celebrity—the licensor, who is granting the permission to use the name to the business—to the licensee. Based on California law, a comprehensive definition of identity rights should include "name, nicknames, likeness, voice, signature, photograph, and biographic information." The contract clause would then provide as follows:

> Licensor hereby grants to Licensee an exclusive right to use the Publicity Rights of Licensor in connection with the manufacture, sale, and distribution of the products and services listed on Appendix A to this Agreement. For purposes of this Agreement, Publicity Rights shall include, but not be limited to the name, nicknames, likeness, voice, signature, photograph, and biographic information of Licensor.

5.   Exclusivity.

As listed in the preceding paragraph, implicit within the licensor's publicity rights is a presumption that these rights should be exclusive to the company. The association between the company and the celebrity is not worth as much if the celebrity is simultaneously promoting a competitor's goods. At the same time, however, as with other licenses, a company should not purchase what it cannot exploit. Shaquille O'Neal, one of the most prolific commercial endorsers, would need to charge tens of millions of dollars annually to maintain his annual endorsement salary if one of his licensees insisted that it have exclusivity in all markets. Instead, the exclusivity is provided narrowly for each category of goods or services. His popularity likely increases his value as a product endorser for each project because of his ubiquity in all other products, but this is the rare public celebrity who can reach this stage.

Even in a narrowly drafted agreement, however, care should be taken to protect the licensee's interests. For example, in the example paragraph reproduced above, the provision could be supplemented with a separate provision that specifically states that the licensor will not endorse, promote, or be associated with any products that can be reasonably expected to compete with the products and services promoted under this agreement.

6.   Term.

The term of a publicity rights agreement has two potentially different dates. One set of dates covers the dates of use of the celebrity for advertising and promotion of the product. A second set of dates applies to the use of the publicity rights on the product itself or on the packaging. If the identity rights are used on the product or packaging, then all dates should be based on the date of manufacturing, so that once a product is produced, there is no risk that the term will expire and the products will need to be destroyed. The licensor, in contrast, will seek to base the dates on the sales of the products rather than the manufacturing. A typical compromise is to include a sell-off period of an additional six months in which the manufacturer can sell off previously manufactured licensed goods but not create any additional goods. Terms for most publicity rights transactions are short, usually one to three years' duration. The vagaries of fame make longer agreements generally unwise for the business licensing the rights.

7.   Identification and Approvals of Products or Services.

The list of products and services might be very broad, but more commonly, the association is focused on one or two products at a time. Approval rights by the celebrity licensor may range from trivial to very complex. Some require that overseas manufacturers adopt certification that child labor is not used; others insist on reviewing the quality of the products from time to time throughout manufacturing; all require approval of their name and likeness.

In situations where the celebrity retains approval rights, those rights should be focused on the development of the product. Other than issues regarding quality control, celebrities should be far less involved in controlling the distribution of the content once it is created. For example, a professional golfer may be very involved in approving the graphic images of a video game and may even demand approval over the design of the golf courses used in the game. Nonetheless, it is unlikely that the golfer will be involved in the choice of computer platform for which the game is optimized or the video-clips featured in the advertising. By separating out the creation of content from its distribution, the parties can more appropriately structure approval rights for the project.[255]

8.   *Morality Clauses.*

A morality clause reminds the parties of the valuable goodwill owned by the company and also requires that the licensor conduct himself in a manner that will not bring disrepute to the product. It may prohibit any criminal actions, professional suspensions, voluntary or involuntary drug commitments, or any acts of moral turpitude. The strongest of such clauses give the licensing business the sole discretion to determine that conduct or news reports of coverage may be damaging to the product, so the licensee may terminate the agreement. Such discretion must still be used in good faith, while a clause that merely prohibits the licensor from being convicted of a crime does little to protect the licensee, given the time it takes to obtain a criminal conviction (particularly if it is not finalized until after the appeals).

9.   *Payment and Royalties.*

Celebrity licensors are typically guaranteed a minimum annual payment. In some cases, there is an advance minimum, but more typically, the payments are based on the royalties paid monthly. If the monthly payments do not meet the annual guaranteed minimum, then there is an additional payment due at the end of the year to make up the difference between the royalties received and the minimum guaranteed. The royalty can be based on the revenue earned by the manufacturer, the suggested retail price, or the number of units sold. The guaranteed minimums may change from year to year as well.

---

[255] *Id.* at 55.

10.   No Obligation.

The corresponding aspect of guaranteed minimum is that it should replace the obligation for the company to engage in the sale of the products if it is not commercially reasonable to do so. Nonetheless, the contract must specify that the licensee is under no obligation to actually utilize the publicity rights, and it is not obligated to manufacture and sell the products in question. The risk of selling the goods may be much greater than the guaranteed minimum payment due to the celebrity. For example, assume a manufacturer has an agreement with a large retailer such as Target or Walmart for distribution of 50,000 exercise balls featuring an Olympic gold-medal-winning athlete. The license agreement guaranteed a minimum royalty of $100,000 and $4.00 per unit sold. If the retailer cancels that contract, the obligation to manufacture and find an outlet for those 50,000 exercise balls will cost the company $100,000 if it elects not to manufacture, but it could be required to pay $200,000 if it is obligated to sell the balls. Since it is unlikely any other retailer needs that volume of goods, the company could be stuck with expensive inventory as well. Therefore, it is critical that the company specify that it is not obligated to use the licensed rights or to manufacture any products under the agreement.

11.   Promotional Services.

Contracts requiring the celebrity licensor to participate in the promotion of the products or services are a smaller subset of the publicity licensing agreements. Typically, the licensor approves certain photographs in advance and has little to do with the product. In other cases, the celebrity may agree to film infomercials, participate in tours, or otherwise engage in an active promotion of the products. In this situation, the agreement must specify what the performance obligations are for the performer, provide that the licensee is obligated to pay the costs of those appearances, set the manner in which the schedule is to be agreed upon (though typically not the actual schedule), and provide for any additional compensation due for the performer during the performance. If this includes infomercial activities, the person may be required to join a television actors' union (AFTRA or SAG), and the company must be ready to pay the union minimums and otherwise meet the union obligations for employing the actor in a long-running infomercial.

12.   *Spokesman and Advertising Issues.*

A celebrity-endorsed product requires close attention to the product's development process. The endorsing celebrity will first want to know precisely what the product is. If the endorsement includes any claims, the celebrity should have confidence those claims are legitimate. The Federal Trade Commission has promulgated guidelines for advertisers to avoid committing unfair and deceptive trade practices (FTC Guides).[256]

> [A]n endorsement means any advertising message (including verbal statements, demonstrations, or depictions of the name, signature, likeness or other identifying personal characteristics of an individual or the name or seal of an organization) that consumers are likely to believe reflects the opinions, beliefs, findings, or experiences of a party other than the sponsoring advertiser.[257]

The identity release is not a waiver of the obligations under the FTC Guides. Under the FTC Guides a person endorsing a product must conduct some minimal due diligence. Notwithstanding the rights acquired under the identity licensing agreement, the parties should make every effort to assure that the endorsing party has taken reasonable efforts to substantiate any claims made.[258] "Endorsements must always reflect the honest opinions, findings, beliefs, or experience of the endorser."[259] The FTC Guides require that the statements of the

---

[256] Guides Concerning Use of Endorsements and Testimonials in Advertising, 16 C.F.R. §§ 255.0–255.5 (2018).

[257] § 255.0(b).

[258] Fed. Trade Comm'n v. Garvey, No. 00-9358 GAF (CWx), 2002 U.S. Dist. LEXIS 25725, at *20 (C.D. Cal. Nov. 25, 2002), aff'd, 383 F.3d 891 (9th Cir. 2004); Fed. Trade Comm'n v. Garvey, No. 00-9358 GAF(CXW), 2002 WL 31744639, at *7 (C.D. Cal. Nov. 25, 2002), aff'd, 383 F.3d 891 (9th Cir. 2004).

[259] 16 C.F.R. § 255.1(a).

endorsing party "reflect his [or her] good faith belief and opinions."[260] "[W]here the advertisement represents that the endorser uses the endorsed product, then the endorser must have been a bona fide user of it at the time the endorsement was given. Additionally, the advertiser may continue to run the advertisement only so long as he has good reason to believe that the endorser remains a bona fide user of the product."[261]

The ongoing obligations for the endorsement need to reflect honest opinions and experience of the celebrity endorser. This duty may be incorporated into the license agreement, but regardless of the drafting, the company is obligated to meet this test. Repudiation by the endorser will undermine the company's ability to continue to use that person to market or promote the product. This provision of the license agreement should therefore be phrased as an affirmative duty of the endorsing party, separate from the identity interests acquired elsewhere in the agreement.

D. Enforcement of Publicity and Privacy Rights.

1. *Prima Facie Case for Publicity Rights.*

Because the law varies somewhat from state to state, there is no standard prima facie case that applies in all states. The following basic elements, however, provide a reasonable checklist for most situations.

(1) Plaintiff is the owner of the publicity interest in her name, likeness or other protected right of publicity.

(2) Defendant reproduced substantially the same name and likeness of plaintiff.

(3) Defendant's use was a commercial use.

(4) Defendant's use was unauthorized.

---

[260] *Garvey*, 2002 U.S. Dist. LEXIS 25725, at *20; 2002 WL 31744639, at *7. *See* 16 C.F.R. § 255.1(c).

[261] 16 C.F.R. § 255.1(c).

Although not an element of the prima facie case, in most situations the plaintiff will also allege that (5) Plaintiff suffered economic damage as a result.

The first element is a simple assertion that this is the correct plaintiff. As with copyright and trademark claims, the plaintiff must allege and prove that it is her identity being used. In most states there is no obligation to prove that the plaintiff has made commercial use of the identity, but if the situation is that the identity rights are highly valuable, then that can certainly be added to the first allegation.

The second element again parallels copyright and trademark claims in that there must be actual use of the plaintiff's identity by the defendant for the claim to be actionable. This element is central to every publicity rights case in every jurisdiction.

The third element is that the use is a commercial use. This has no corresponding element in copyright infringement claims, only in trademark claims. As discussed earlier, this is the factual allegation that separates editorial uses from commercial activity. Technically, this is not always stated as an affirmative element to be proven by the plaintiff, but the plaintiff should be prepared to bear the burden of proving that the defendant commercially used her identity. As a practical matter, courts are extremely reluctant to interfere with First Amendment rights, so if the defendant raises a constitutional defense, then the burden shifts to the plaintiff to prove that the use was commercial. Furthermore, as a matter of public policy, businesses should be prepared to suffer a certain amount of negative comment or criticism—even if it comes in the form of Wacky Packages—so they should either be able to establish that the use is commercial or they should not seek legal redress.

The fourth element is a mere recitation that the use was made without permission. This may vary somewhat. If the state in which the lawsuit is filed requires a written release, then the allegation should specify that there is no written release or any other authorization.

2.   *Other Aspects of the Publicity Claim.*

If the plaintiff can establish that his publicity rights were reproduced for commercial purposes without authorization, there is no need to prove it caused economic harm. The damage is presumed from the conduct. Although proof of economic harm is not an element of the claim, it may be helpful, particularly if the damages go beyond the market value of the license agreement to a larger measure of damages.

Similarly, some courts discuss the intent of the defendant in the context of publicity claims. Because both defamation law and trademark law include some requirements of culpability, there seems to be emphasis on the intentional use of the publicity rights. As a practical matter, it may not be too common that a name or likeness is used without knowledge. There may be situations where the authorization was faulty, such as a failure to obtain a signed release instead of an oral release; a photograph approved for one product was accidentally used for a different product; or the wrong photograph was provided by the photographer. While the innocence of these situations may reduce the damages, they should not eliminate culpability.

A manufacturer has an affirmative duty to control the production and distribution of its product, so the failure to police the process of production, distribution, and marketing of its product should create the affirmative duty to ensure the accuracy of its use of any publicity rights. Failure to ensure against the unauthorized use of another's publicity rights is inherently (per se) negligent.

3.   *Comparison to the Section 43(a) Prima Facie Case.*

Section 43(a) of the Lanham Act provides the federal claim for unfair competition. Under this cause of action, the plaintiff must prove that the use of the publicity rights created the likelihood of confusion regarding the celebrity. The claim must be designed to stop the defendants from falsely claiming endorsements, affiliation, or sponsorship by the celebrity.

In comparison to the prima facie case for publicity rights, the analogous case for federal unfair competition under §43(a) requires proof of additional elements. The four initial elements must still be met that—

(1) Plaintiff is the owner of interest in her name, or other word, term, symbol, or device;

(2) Defendant reproduced substantially the same name and likeness of plaintiff;

(3) Defendant's use was a commercial use; and

(4) Defendant's use was unauthorized.

The three additional elements are that –

(5) Defendant's use of the name constitutes a false designation of origin for the commercial use;

(6) Defendant's use of the name is likely to cause confusion, or to cause mistake, or to deceive as to the affiliation, connection, or association of plaintiff with defendant, or as to the origin, sponsorship, or approval of plaintiff's goods, services, or commercial activities by defendant; and

(7) Defendant's infringement was intentional, willful or deliberate to gain value from the goodwill associated with plaintiff's name.

The courts have limited §43(a) to situations involving intentional misconduct, not merely negligent misrepresentation by one company about another company's goods. As a result, even in cases involving celebrity names, there remains a requirement of intentional misconduct.

For most cases today, any use of a celebrity's name creates an assumption in the public's mind that the celebrity is associating with that product. The exception would be in the case of a marketing parody, where the celebrity was mocked along with the product. If the content made clear that no association was present, then the key element of §43(a) would be avoided.

4.   *Injunctions and Remedies.*

Typically, the plaintiff in a publicity rights claim will seek an injunction to stop the conduct from continuing. Courts may order injunctions at either the preliminary hearing stage or at the end of the trial on the merits. Although injunctive relief requires demonstrable evidence that mere monetary damages are insufficient, the unique nature of publicity rights and the need of the celebrity to endorse and affirm the use creates a general expectation that injunctive remedies are necessary.

Damages may be based on the economic value of the license, but more typically, the plaintiff will seek to establish either that the defendant made windfall profits by using the unauthorized publicity rights or that the use caused damage to the plaintiff's goodwill or marketing opportunities. Since the conduct is often willful, plaintiffs can also seek punitive damages.

5. *Violating the Publicity Rights of Others.*

Most commercial enterprises can steer clear of violating the publicity rights of other parties simply by adopting policies requiring written releases for all photographs and names and enforcing this policy.

In contrast, companies involved in the sale of artwork and memorabilia will have a more difficult time assessing each product regarding its commercial or communicative use. For companies that rely on the fair use or First Amendment limitations on publicity rights to manufacture and sell products, it is extremely difficult to know precisely when a celebrity will object to the unauthorized use.

E. The International Implications of Publicity and Privacy Interests.

Publicity rights and privacy interests vary much more dramatically from country to country than do the other intellectual property interests. The international treaties generally do not reach these interests except to the extent they are covered by trademark law. Great Britain specifically rejects publicity rights,[262] while Canada does recognize a version of the right.

For international transactions, the preferred strategy is to emphasize the trademark rights associated with the identity interests. Individuals hoping to exploit their names or likenesses should seek federal trademark registration for those rights and utilize the Madrid Protocol to register the trademark in the foreign jurisdictions where protection is sought. This will help provide a better footing for international trade protection and may avoid problems of enforcement in countries that require that the publicity rights be part of the privacy rights afforded to those domiciled or resident within the jurisdiction.

Federal and international trademark registration circumvents the jurisdictional problems of international publicity rights enforcement while reinforcing the economic value of those rights.

---

[262] Cairns v. Franklin Mint Co., 24 F. Supp. 2d 1013 (C.D. Cal. 1998).

Chapter 20.   Trade Secrets and Trade Secret Law

A.   Attributes of Trade Secrets.

Trade Secrets—Summary

Subject Matter: All forms and types of financial, business, scientific, technical, economic, or engineering information, including patterns, plans, compilations, program devices, formulas, designs, prototypes, methods, techniques, processes, procedures, programs, or codes, whether tangible or intangible, and whether or how stored, compiled, or memorialized physically, electronically, graphically, photographically, or in writing if (A) the owner thereof has taken reasonable measures to keep such information secret; and (B) the information derives independent economic value, actual or potential, from not being generally known to, and not being readily ascertainable through proper means by, another person who can obtain economic value from the disclosure or use of the information.

Method Acquired: Initially, through usage, but maintained only through necessary steps to protect the secret.

Term: Indefinite, trade secret will continue so long as secret maintains economic value and secrecy.

Time Needed to Acquire: No waiting period.

Renewals: Not applicable.

Federal Government Office and Website: USPTO—Trade Secret Policy: https://www.uspto.gov/patents-getting-started/international-protection/trade-secret-policy

Applicable Law: Defend Trade Secrets Act, 18 U.S.C. § 1836 (2016); The Economic Espionage Act of 1996, 18 U.S.C. §§1831-39. Uniform Trade Secrets Act (most states).

Transfer: Fully transferable. Care must be taken not to disclose the information before the transfer is complete.

Property Excluded from Protection: Any publicly disclosed information; any information without economic value; and any information independently created.

B.   Trade Secret Law Explained.

Trade secrets play a significant role in the management of key corporate assets and can be a critical part of a business's overall intellectual property strategy. Trade secrets have significant practical limitations, however, and should generally not be the exclusive strategy used to manage intellectual property.

According to the Restatement (Third) of Unfair Competition, "[t] he protection of confidential business information dates at least to Roman law, which afforded relief against a person who induced another's employee to divulge secrets relating to the master's commercial affairs."[263] Trade secrets cover employee confidentiality agreements and agreements to safeguard commercial processes and formulas that may lie at the heart of a company's enterprise.

In 2016, Congress substantially improved the U.S. protection of trade secrets by adopting the Defend Trade Secrets Act (DSTA), which had the effect of adding federal protection for trade secrets in a form very similar to that of the uniform state law. By doing this, it created an independent legal cause of action for every trade secret case "if the trade secret is related to a product or service used in, or intended for use in, interstate or foreign commerce."[264] The use of a single federal law should also help to standardize the legal rules across jurisdictions over time.

1.   *Subject Matter of Trade Secret Protection.*

Trade secrets cover a wide variety of information, including

all forms and types of financial, business, scientific, technical, economic, or engineering information, including patterns, plans, compilations, program devices, formulas, designs, prototypes, methods, techniques, processes, procedures, programs, or codes, whether tangible or intangible, and whether or how stored,

---

[263] RESTATEMENT (THIRD) OF UNFAIR COMPETITION § 39 cmt. a (AM. LAW INST. 1995).

[264] 18 U.S.C. § 1836(b) (2018).

compiled, or memorialized physically, electronically, graphically, photographically, or in writing if (A) the owner thereof has taken reasonable measures to keep such information secret; and (B) the information derives independent economic value, actual or potential, from not being generally known to, and not being readily ascertainable through proper means by, another person who can obtain economic value from the disclosure or use of the information."[265]

The list is all-encompassing, ranging from recipes that could never be copyrighted or patented to inventions that could easily meet the patent requirements of originality, utility, and non-obviousness. Inventions, processes, and confidential pricing information are common subjects for trade secret protection, as are corporate acquisition targets and product performance data.[266]

The DTSA and the state versions in the USTA recognize that the economic value of the trade secret derives from the secrecy of the information. The secret recipes relied upon by Kentucky Fried Chicken and Coca-Cola derive their value because these recipes are not available to competitors. Trade secrets are not easily reproduced by the competitors through experimentation, reverse engineering, or other lawful means. Finally, trade secrets are protected by the company which claims the trade secrets by using reasonable efforts to protect those secrets.

Trade secrets are not property interests. Instead, a better way to characterize the law governing trade secrets is to treat the rule as a statement regarding the business norms of competition. A company has a duty not to steal the secrets of its competitors if those competitors have undertaken the steps necessary to protect their secrets. Like an academic honor code, it creates an expectation regarding the conduct that is permitted. Companies—like students—can do independent

---

[265] 18 U.S.C. § 1839(3) (2018).

[266] The Illinois definition of information, for example, provides "information, including but not limited to, technical or non-technical data, a formula, pattern, compilation, program, device, method, technique, drawing, process, financial data, or list of actual or potential customers or suppliers …." Illinois Trade Secrets Act, 765 ILL. COMP. STAT. 1065/2(d) (West 2018).

research to learn the answers, replicate findings, and solve problems already solved by others, but they will be sanctioned if they steal the information from a competitor or the test from the teacher. The company—like the teacher—must take reasonable steps to safeguard the test from inadvertent disclosure or extreme temptation.

Trade secrets serve to enforce an ethical business practice. Trade secret protection creates an obligation to conduct one's business in a good faith manner. The most important aspect of this ethical responsibility arises in the context of hiring. Employers have an obligation not to use job opportunities as a vehicle to steal a competitor's corporate files, trade secrets, or other documents and data. While the rule does not directly apply to hiring away the experience and expertise, the rule definitely covers the data and hard information that an employee carries in his briefcase rather than his head.

Trade secrets also reflect one of the key themes of the book, that exclusivity creates value. Here, exclusivity in the form of secrecy, is protected to the extent that exclusivity has an ongoing economic benefit. As a result, trade secrets are a key component of developing business know-how for the successful business. Since trade secrets exist only if a company takes reasonable steps to protect the unique, internal information it creates, only those companies that follow appropriate business practices can acquire and maintain trade secrets.

* * *

Sidebar—Noncompetition agreements.

Noncompetition agreements are often used in conjunction with trade secret protection, but they cover a different aspect of the company's trade secrets. As discussed throughout this chapter, a trade secret exists only if it remains confidential and has economic value to the business. However, the open markets of American business and the opportunity employees have to seek new employment and to compete with their former employers creates tension with the goal of protecting trade secrets.

Absent any other agreements, an employee is free to leave her job and open a company across the street from the former employer. An employee's duty to her employer ends when the employment terminates, and for an employee who is not an officer or director, the law even protects the person if she begins making plans and actively prepares for the day of departure. So long as the employee has not diverted the employer's customers or competed directly while still employed, the employee has not violated any duties to the employer.

Business owners struggle with these policies. Though sound public policy, they put employers at risk of losing valuable employees at critical times. Additionally, these policies do not protect the knowledge learned by these critical employees. This knowledge may be extremely valuable. Nothing committed to memory can be controlled by the employer. Good employees know the customers they call on, they understand the processes they use in manufacturing, and they recognize the innovations their business have use to gain market share and commercial advantage.

Since the law values the freedom to contract nearly as much as the freedom to compete, state employment laws attempt to balance the ability of the employer and its employees to enter into contracts that limit the employee's ability to compete with the employer following employment. These noncompetition agreements are limited by state law, but the scope of permitted provisions varies widely from state to state.

Noncompetition contracts provide payment or other consideration to the employee in exchange for an agreement not to compete with the company for a specified period of time and in a specified geographic range. These contracts also add a second set of confidentiality agreements, extending the time during which an employee is obligated not to divulge any trade secrets. The difference between the noncompetition provisions and the confidentiality provisions is that the noncompetition provisions can extend to the employee's craft and knowledge. By prohibiting the employee from using the skills acquired and knowledge learned on the job, the noncompetition provisions often effectively bar the person from obtaining meaningful employment.

Because the noncompetition provisions have such a detrimental effect on the ability of the former employee to gain meaningful work, courts look at four aspects of these contracts quite carefully. First, they look to see whether the agreement was really part of a meaningful financial transaction, or whether the employer forced it on the employee after employment began, when the employee had no ability to bargain over the contract. If there was no payment or value given to the employee, then the contract may not be enforceable.

Second, the court looks at the scope of the prohibition. The narrower the prohibition, the more likely the court will find that it is acceptable. An optical engineer's noncompetition agreement prohibiting her from working for the direct competitor of the former employer will be viewed more favorably than if the contract clause limits the employee from serving as any type of engineer in any company.

The third and fourth factors follow the same pattern. Courts will look at the period of the prohibition and the geographic scope to be sure that the length and physical range are both sufficiently narrow so as to allow the employee some reasonable employment. If the noncompetition agreement is too broad, then it will not be enforced.

Although these four factors tend to be used in most states, the scope of a permissible restriction will vary significantly. California laws treat most of these restrictions as against public policy while other states such as New York and Massachusetts are more likely to find these contracts enforceable.

In addition, noncompetition agreements are looked on more favorably and with greater latitude for prohibitions against the owners of companies who enter into noncompetition as part of the sale of their company. The agreement often prohibits the owner from going back into competition with the person to whom the owner just sold her business. These types of noncompetition agreements should be enforced, and courts recognize the social benefit and good faith aspect of such a prohibition.

For highly compensated individuals, the best way to maximize the noncompetition provision is to make much of the agreement an ongoing obligation. If the person is receiving a weekly or monthly payment, then the relationship is a continuing one, and employment law always enforces the rights of an employer to limit disclosures by current employees. Many so-called consulting agreements are actually forms of noncompetition agreements in which the relationship is transmuted into a continuing one in an effort to limit the ability of the consultant to compete with the former employer.

✳ ✳ ✳

2.   Trade Secrets Must Have Value Because They are Secret.

For trade secrets to rise to a level warranting protection, they must have some minimal economic value. Most client data, business processes, and price lists have economic value. Business know-how that reduces production costs or improves market competitiveness would have economic value to competitors, so these types of secrets are protected under the law. The secrecy of the information provides the business advantage, reflecting the economic value of the trade secret.

Trade secrets, however, differ from merely confidential or private data. Health and educational records, for example, are required by federal law to be kept confidential and the privacy of the personal information protected. A student's academic transcript, therefore, is a confidential record, but it is not a trade secret because it has no commercial use or value to any competitor.

3.   *Creating the Duty to Keep the Secret.*

Economically valuable information does not automatically become secret. The information can only become a trade secret if the initial owner of the information secures an obligation from others to maintain the secret. Typically, this obligation would come from a contractual agreement or be implied by the legal consequence of the relationship. For example, employees owe a duty of loyalty to their employers, so the law will imply a duty not to divulge a trade secret whether or not there is a written employment agreement or written policy requiring this duty. The duty of loyalty bars an employee from using company assets for personal gain, so the sale or misuse of trade secrets would be prohibited under this aspect of the duty of loyalty as well. To the extent the employee learned client information or other aspects of the business, however, an employer cannot stop an employee from seeking new employment, even when that employee has client information or other aspects of the business stored in her memory.

While the duty of loyalty extends to all employees of the company, the scope of the duty is broader for officers and directors. For closely held businesses, these duties of good faith and loyalty will generally extend to the managing owners as well, whether shareholders or LLC members. The parties to the business have some flexibility to heighten or lower these duties, but only within the context provided by state law.

Some courts imply the duty of good faith and fair dealing to situations involving the negotiations involving an attempted business purchase or merger. In theory, at least, trade secret disclosures made during the due diligence phase leading up to a transaction are protected by the law even if the transaction does not take place. As is always the case, such implied duties are not as easily relied upon as express, written obligations. In the case of both merger talks and employment relations, companies are much better off with written agreements regarding the duty not to disclose information. See Appendix B for a sample agreement.

Since a trade secret requires reasonable steps to protect the secrecy of the information, disclosure of the information without those protections will destroy the trade secret protection. As a result, the disclosure of a valuable trade secret before any agreement has been made between the parties renders the information fully disclosed and beyond the scope of trade secret protection. Similarly, unsolicited disclosure generally destroys the opportunity to create trade secret protection. Particularly if the trade secret is of limited originality, the duty to protect the trade secret by non-employees must be expressly made in advance of the disclosure.

4.   *Reasonable Efforts to Maintain Secrecy.*

A second element of claiming trade secret protection is the company's responsibility to undertake reasonable steps to protect the information. Companies should specify the types of records that it treats as trade secrets in its employment contracts, confidentiality agreements, and employee handbooks. If the company endeavors to protect manufacturing processes, then it must not open its process to the general public, but rather limit physical access. "Employee Only" areas of a company must actually be limited to employees with exceptions made only for carefully screened guests. All too often, employees pay little regard to posted signs limiting access. Corporate espionage agents and disgruntled former employees can often walk unchallenged through the heart of secure facilities.

Documents such as price lists, processes, new product specifications, and other reports should be marked as confidential—particularly if it is not obvious on the face of the document that the company would treat it as confidential information. File cabinets should not be accessible by employees without clearance to those files, which should be locked or restricted. Similarly, computer networks should be password protected, and information storage systems should be carefully segregated so employees have access to only the information they need. Password protocols should follow professional security guidelines. For example, companies should enforce policies so that computer passwords are changed regularly, use effective pass-phrases, and are not taped to the computer monitor or hidden under mousepads.

The secret can sometimes be widely shared. The number of individuals who share the trade secret is far less important than the fact that each person with access to the trade secret has the same affirmative duty not to disclose the information. In this way, potentially thousands of employees could know the precise chemical composition and production process for a secret manufacturing process, but as long as each of those employees was subject to the trade secret confidentiality obligations and knew that the process and chemicals were protected trade secrets, then the process would be protected. Of course, as a practical matter, the larger the number of people sharing a secret, the less likely the secret will be properly kept. Common sense is always a better source of protection than legal doctrine.

The company seeking to protect trade secrets must also address obvious risks to breakdowns in confidentiality. Confidential documents and trade secrets should be shredded rather than thrown into waste cans and recycling tubs. Once trash has been taken to the curb, the original owner loses its rights to the garbage, and no one has the right to stop others from investigating the information in the garbage. The corporate practice of "dumpster diving" has developed something of a cachet precisely because it is beyond the rules of trade secret protection or criminal conduct. What one finds in the garbage can be kept and used to commercial advantage.

Another obvious breach of confidentiality may come through the use of temporary employees and independent contractors. These individuals are not necessarily subject to the personnel handbooks, so contracts must be signed by each temporary employee or independent contractor at the start of employment, obligating that person to be bound by the same confidentiality provisions.

The protection of the trade secrets need only be reasonable, not absolute. Hidden wall safes, sleeping gas, and laser beams are not usually required. If a company has controls on its doors to keep uninvited guests out of the facility, then plans stolen through the use of helicopters and telephoto lenses can be recovered and remedies sought (if the victim can prove the thefts). The courts do not expect every company to be in the anti-espionage business, and the law will punish those companies that are caught taking extraordinary measures to steal from their competitors.

5.   *Independent Disclosure.*

Perhaps one of the more frustrating ways in which trade secrets are destroyed is through independent disclosure. Inventions and ideas tend to develop independently from unrelated sources. If a person without access to the trade secret makes that information generally known, then the information is no longer secret and cannot be protected. Patent applications may publish inventions that had been in use by competitors and protected as trade secrets. The patent application destroys the value of that trade secret, and the trade secret can then be disclosed to the patent examiner to show the "prior art" regarding the claims in the patent. Trade publications will often publish comparative corporate data that was carefully gathered and highly valuable to the company that collected the data. Once the independently authored report is out, however, the secret nature of the private report is destroyed.

In the arena of trademarks, companies are becoming increasingly savvy. Companies can track trademark filings for future products and services of competing companies. The disclosures made in the trademark registration process are public documents. Any information disclosed during the trademark application is no longer protected by trade secret. Similarly, information contained in a patent application loses its confidentiality.

In the area of computer software and software-based products, the need to share software source code may result in the disclosure of business plans that can be gleaned from the coding process. When a phone company releases its software code for interoperability purposes, that code discloses all the new functionality of the software, which is often sufficient for competitors to understand which new feature sets are being delivered.

Another form of independent discovery is through reverse engineering. Reverse engineering, the process of deconstructing a product, computer chip, or software, is a lawfully protected activity. Absent a contractual agreement not to reverse engineer, anyone can undertake to learn the secrets of a product by tearing it apart. The law considers reverse engineering beneficial to society, so it does not breach any good faith ethical norms to engage in this practice.

Because nondisclosure agreements rely on contractual obligations instead of trade secret law to limit the use of confidential information, it is important that independent disclosure be incorporated as a reason to terminate the nondisclosure agreement. While the risk may be small, no company wants to find itself as the only entity contractually precluded from information that is now freely available to the public. A sample nondisclosure agreement is provided in Appendix B.

6. *Relationship to Other Intellectual Property Laws.*

For trade secret protection to apply, the information must be secret. This axiomatic rule significantly limits the scope of trade secret protection. Information which is publicly available cannot be protected as a trade secret. For example, all information disclosed as part of a federal patent application is released publicly within eighteen months of the application or upon the grant of the patent. This information is therefore public and cannot be protected by trade secret laws.

Trade secrets and patents are generally considered alternative solutions to the problem of protecting new processes and other inventions that are not self-disclosing. The patent provides a public bargain in which the twenty years of patent protection is provided to the inventor in exchange for full disclosure of the patent. The public receives free, unlimited access to the invention when the patent expires, but it also gets immediate access to the science and techniques that went into the patent. Often, the patent provides vital information to other inventors about inventions and process unrelated to the patent holder's claim.

In contrast, trade secrets must be closely guarded. If the inventor is successful in guarding the secret, it can last indefinitely. The public may benefit from the invention, but it does not ever gain access to the science and techniques that gave rise to the invention. In his science fiction novel, *Friday*, noted author Robert Heinlein postulated that the richest company in the world developed its power because the inventor ignored advice to patent his inventions and instead began to carefully select loyal employees to launch his company.

The law does not favor patents over trade secrets, nor does it favor trade secrets over patents. The nature of the invention and the strategy of the company establishes which is the preferred solution. In addition, many economically valuable trade secrets are not ever patentable, so the tension exists only for that subset of inventions that can reasonably be protected by either patent or trade secret.

The tension with copyright is less severe. Copyright does not extend to ideas, methods, or processes. "In no case does copyright protection for an original work of authorship extend to any idea, procedure, process, system, method of operation, concept, principle, or discovery, regardless of the form in which it is described, explained, illustrated, or embodied in such work."[267] Copyright may cover other forms of trade secrets, however, so some modest overlap exists. Copyright law does not require that works be published or registered, so the easiest way to avoid tension between copyright and trade secret is not to register the work.

There are many documents which contain trade secrets, such as secure standardized academic tests (e.g. SAT, ACT, GRE, LSAT, etc.). For these and other copyrightable documents that contain trade secrets, the Copyright Office has provided special deposit regulations to protect them.[268] For software, in particular, there are often trade secrets in the coding or other processes which are not available to the public as users of the software but would be available to the copyright office when the source code for the software is deposited under the statutory requirements. To avoid this disclosure, the copyright office allows the source code to be deposited with the portions blacked out that contain the trade secrets, or otherwise avoid the disclosure of the trade secrets.[269]

Trademarks have little or nothing to do with trade secrets. Except for those rare situations in which the existence of the trade secret is incorporated into the trademarks and branding of a company, such as with KFC's secret recipe, the two disciplines do not overlap. Having said that, however, the strategies behind trademarking and branding are sometimes the most valuable trade secrets guarded by a company. This is particularly true since trademark priority is given to the company that first uses it in commerce. Trade secrets serve to protect the strategies that inform the brand development and maximize the trademarks.

---

[267] 17 U.S.C. § 102(b) (2018).

[268] *See* 37 C.F.R. §§ 202.19–202.20 (2018).

[269] *See Circular 61: Copyright Registration of Computer Programs*, U.S. COPYRIGHT OFFICE (revised Sept. 2017), http://www.copyright.gov/circs/circ61.pdf.

7.   *Federal Trade Secret Protection under the Economic Espionage Act.*

In 1996, Congress enacted the Economic Espionage Act to protect U.S. companies because "nearly $24 billion of corporate property was being stolen each year."[270] The first section of the law focused on international espionage, particularly that covering "evidence of foreign government sponsored or coordinated intelligence activity."[271]

Section 2 of the statute created a federal trade secret act with primarily criminal provisions. The law criminalizes the theft of trade secrets or conspiracy to commit theft of trade secrets, or receipt of stolen trade secrets. The federal law, however, has some requirements that are different than the DSTA or UTSA. To establish federal jurisdiction, the Economic Espionage Act, like the DSTA requires that the trade secret be related to a product placed in interstate or foreign commerce. Unique to the Espionage Act, there must also be an economic benefit to the thief, recipient or anyone other than the lawful owner, and there must be evidence to prove the thief knew the theft will injure the owner of the trade secret.[272]

---

[270] J. Michael Chamblee, Annotation, *Validity, Construction, and Application of Title I of Economic Espionage Act of 1996*, 177 A.L.R. Fed. 609, § 2 (2002) (*citing* HEFFERNAN & SWARTWOOD, TRENDS IN INTELLECTUAL PROPERTY LOSS 4, 15 (1996)).

[271] *Id.* (citations omitted).

[272] 18 U.S.C. § 1832(a) (2018). The full text of the Trade Secret Protection Provision of the Economic Espionage Act is as follow:

> (a) Whoever, with intent to convert a trade secret, that is related to or included in a product that is produced for or placed in interstate or foreign commerce, to the economic benefit of anyone other than the owner thereof, and intending or knowing that the offense will, injure any owner of that trade secret, knowingly—
>
> (1) steals, or without authorization appropriates, takes, carries away, or conceals, or by fraud, artifice, or deception obtains such information;
>
> (2) without authorization copies, duplicates, sketches, draws, photographs, downloads, uploads, alters, destroys, photocopies,

In addition to these additional elements of proof, the law is primarily limited to federal criminal prosecutions. The earlier civil provision allows the attorney general of the state to bring civil claims to stop or enjoin theft of trade secrets. Now that the DSTA is part of the federal law, the relationship of both the criminal and civil protections are very robust.

8. *Relationship to Federal Computer Anti-Fraud Statute.*

In the highly complex language of the Computer Fraud and Abuse Act (CFAA), a federal crime and civil claim was created for the unauthorized access to information, theft of information, or destruction of information on a person's or company's computer. The law has been amended since first written in 1984 to expand its scope to any computer theft or damage involving interstate commerce. This means any computer connected to the Internet or any criminal activities using the Internet or phone system is included within the jurisdiction of the federal law.

While trade secrets are not necessarily kept on computers, and the theft of trade secrets does not necessarily involve computers, the ubiquity of computers makes this aspect of information theft a new

---

replicates, transmits, delivers, sends, mails, communicates, or conveys such information;

(3) receives, buys, or possesses such information, knowing the same to have been stolen or appropriated, obtained, or converted without authorization;

(4) attempts to commit any offense described in paragraphs (1) through (3); or

(5) conspires with one or more other persons to commit any offense described in paragraphs (1) through (3), and one or more of such persons do any act to effect the object of the conspiracy, shall, except as provided in subsection (b), be fined under this title or imprisoned not more than 10 years, or both.

(b) Any organization that commits any offense described in subsection (a) shall be fined not more than $5,000,000.

Id.

federal crime and tort. Increasingly, it is hard to steal trade secrets without copying some of the information from the computers of the targeted company.

> Under the statute, "whoever . . . intentionally accesses a computer without authorization or exceeds authorized access, and thereby obtains . . . information from any protected computer . . . shall be punished [with fines or prison or both and] . . . any person who suffers damage or loss by reason of a violation of this section may maintain a civil action against the violator to obtain compensatory damages and injunctive relief or other equitable relief.[273]

The law was designed to stop computer hackers from breaking into computers to steal information or destroy the computer systems. But the law goes much further. It applies to anyone who accesses the computer without authorization or who exceeds authorization. In the definitions of the law, "the term 'exceeds authorized access' means to access a computer with authorization and to use such access to obtain or alter information in the computer that the accesser is not entitled so to obtain or alter."[274] This means that when an employee or other person obtains information from the computer to which that person is not entitled, the person has violated the CFAA and may be federally criminally and civilly liable.

This interpretation of the statute has already been applied in the context of trade secret thefts by former employees. There are many areas where the CFAA comes into play, such as stealing a co-worker's password to access information without authorization or otherwise manipulating systems to gain access in contravention of the permissions granted by the employer. Courts are inconsistent on the extent to which the CFAA applies to an employee gaining access to information for which there is a right to do so as an employee, but that employee is instead accessing the information to steal it for an unauthorized purpose. Since breaking into the computer system is the essence of a CFAA claim, these later cases will likely be dealt with under the DSTA.

---

[273] 18 U.S.C. § 1030 (2018).

[274] § 1030(e)(6).

Still, because of its broad sweep, the CFAA has grown into a powerful federal trade secret protection tool for interstate theft of trade secrets or other information stored on computers. Although some courts apply the law narrowly, others have been quite liberal in determining unauthorized access or access which exceeds authority. In most situations, the employees have signed confidentiality agreements or company personnel manuals that limit access to the company computers using language such as the following: *"Employees are authorized to use the Company's equipment, computers and computer network to the extent necessary to perform the Employee's duties on behalf of the company and for no other purposes."*

The net effect of these cases has been to create a powerful complement to trade secret protection that requires the use of a computer but avoids the need to prove secrecy or reasonable efforts to maintain the secret. Companies that use clear policies to control access to corporate information will have an important additional tool in managing and discouraging the theft of trade secrets and confidential information.

C.   Creating and Maintaining Trade Secrets.

1.   Create Trade Secrets as a Business Strategy First and Litigation Strategy Second.

The focus of this chapter on trade secret protection is to outline the state and federal laws that govern trade secrets. Those laws define the scope of trade secrets and the legal protection that will be available in the event that an enterprise's trade secrets are stolen by a competitor, lost to a computer hacker, or purloined by a current or former employee. But the more important lesson is how to go about developing valuable information that creates a competitive advantage and then securing that information in a manner that keeps the secrets from being stolen.

The practices of identifying documents protected as trade secrets, adding employee handbook provisions, insisting on contractual language for consultants and vendors, and taking the other reasonable and necessary steps to protect the right to sue for relief if the trade secrets are stolen are much more important as practice guidance. These steps help minimize the risk that trade secrets will fall into the hands of competitors or become available to the general public. As with any other area of risk management, the steps to prevent the harm are far more important than the right to bring a lawsuit to receive some partial compensation for that harm.

2.   *Originality and Secrecy.*

To create a trade secret, one must first create something that is not publicly known and is also economically valuable. This standard is far lower than the "new, useful, and nonobvious" standard of patent law, but it does differentiate trade secrets from the information and data that a company may prefer is not made public. Abstract ideas that are not sufficiently detailed so as to be protected as copyrightable expression may also be too vague to be protected as trade secrets.

Ideally, the precise documents and specimens that are to be treated as trade secrets should be marked as trade secrets. Although companies prefer not to have to meet this obligation, there is much to be gained from focusing trade secret protection on the "crown jewels" and not risking an overbroad policy that may be ignored by employees and therefore not sufficient for the important data.

For example, client lists are a species of information that is considered confidential by many companies but is often not protected by courts. Some courts suggest that the information is too readily obtained through market research. Other courts fear that the limitation on client lists would create an unreasonable burden on employees seeking new employment or to compete legitimately with their former employers.

3.   *Acquisition through Purchase or Licensing.*

In addition to protecting trade secrets created internally, it is very common for inventors and others to submit inventions, processes, and innovations for purchase. The seller of the trade secret must enter into an agreement with the prospective purchaser prior to any disclosure. These agreements typically provide the potential seller a time frame in which to evaluate the proffered item. In some instances, the agreement also provides the potential purchaser the opportunity to show that it already had access to the alleged secret information and has no need to purchase the information or invention from the seller. These agreements then provide that the prospective purchaser will not use the information without entering into an agreement with the seller. There is not an obligation to purchase unless the item has been evaluated.

Under such a nondisclosure agreement, the parties can determine the value for the trade secrets that are part of the transaction. The sales document should create an affirmative duty on the seller not to disclose the information to any third party and not to compete with the purchaser to the extent permitted by law. In economically significant transactions, the payments and continuing obligations can be drawn out over an extended period of time, so that the noncompetition period is tied to the continuing payments.

4.   *Termination of Trade Secrets.*

Trade secrets evaporate when the information becomes public or is no longer economically valuable. The mere declaration that information is a trade secret will not satisfy courts, so the underlying obligation to protect the information must be maintained. On the other hand, if the information remains nonpublic and economically valuable, trade secrets can last indefinitely.

Nondisclosure agreements are often drafted to limit the terms of those agreements to periods of five or seven years. Presumably, this is on the assumption that the inventions or processes disclosed will have been exploited during that period. In practice, however, a company that reviews an invention but does not purchase it may find it possesses valuable information that can be exploited once the agreement comes to an end, so some care should be taken about unintentionally undermining the value and length of these interests.

D.   Enforcement of Trade Secret Rights.

1.   *Prima   Facie   Case   for   Trade   Secret   Misappropriation.*

According to noted patent and trade secret expert Roger Milgrim, the following four elements must be proven by the plaintiff to establish the prima facie case in a trade secret misappropriation claim.

(1) Plaintiff is the owner of a trade secret. . . .

(2) Plaintiff disclosed the trade secret to defendant; or, defendant either procured unauthorized and wrongful access or wrongfully took the trade secret from plaintiff without plaintiff's authorization.

(3) Defendant was in a legal relation with reference to plaintiff as a result of which defendant's use or disclosure of the trade secret to plaintiff's detriment is wrongful.

(4) Defendant has used or disclosed (or will use or disclose) the trade secret to plaintiff's detriment; or, defendant, who knew or should have known of plaintiff's rights in the trade secret, used such secret to plaintiff's detriment.[275]

The first element of the prima facie case requiring that the plaintiff own the trade secret can be expanded somewhat. As one court recently explained, the "first element in a trade secret claim is that the plaintiff is the owner of a trade secret, or that the plaintiff has come to possess the trade secret, either by way of assignment, license, or some other means of conveyance from the trade-secrets owner or discoverer such that the owner no longer has a right to use the trade secret. . . ."[276] The plaintiff must be the exclusive holder of the trade secret, or else she must bring the actual licensor who owns the exclusive rights into the case as co-plaintiff.

Proof of the ownership of the trade secret will, in turn, relate back to evidence that the alleged information meets the trade secret definition. The information owned must be information kept reasonably confidential that is economically beneficial to the plaintiff. On the other hand, unauthorized public disclosure by the defendant cannot be the basis for claiming that there is no protection for the trade secret. This would create an injustice that the courts will not allow.

The second element illustrates the two types of trade secret cases. In one group of cases, the defendant had an affirmative duty to maintain the trade secret and then breached that duty. The defendants in that group are typically former employees, consultants, or parties with a contractual relationship with the trade secret owner. In the second group of cases, the defendant used espionage or otherwise wrongfully stole the trade secret.

---

[275] 4 ROGER M. MILGRIM & ERIC E. BENSIN, MILGRIM ON TRADE SECRETS § 15.01 (2018).

[276] DTM Research, L.L.C. v. AT&T Corp., 245 F.3d 327, 331 (4th Cir. 2001).

The third element reiterates that the taking was wrongful rather than a good faith public use of the trade secret, such as reverse engineering or bona fide research. And the fourth element alleges injury to the plaintiff.

2. *Defenses to Trade Secret Misappropriation Claim.*

Most of the defenses to a claim of trade secret misappropriation are more properly described as evidence intended to negate the prima facie claim of the plaintiff. In some settings these will be defenses while in others they will go to negate the element being proven by the plaintiff. For example, the defendant to a trade secret action will try a number of techniques to establish that the information involved is not a trade secret. It may assert that there is no economic value to the information; that the information is publicly available; that the plaintiff did not take reasonable steps to ever protect the information; or that the information was appropriately the property of the defendant. Each of these allegations attacks the sufficiency of the ownership of the trademark by plaintiff.

The second group of defenses will focus on the authority or propriety of the defendant in acquiring the information. The defendant will try to prove its legitimate actions in researching the information, reverse engineering, seeking public records, or complying with contractual duties. If the defendant did not exceed its authority or if it relied upon public information, then no misappropriation could have occurred. Of course, it is not sufficient to claim that the defendant "could have" reverse engineered or found the information publicly. If the defendant acted improperly, it is no defense that another party could have received the information while acting properly.

Other traditional common law defenses are also available, as with trademark cases. Claims of unclean hands, unreasonable delay (laches), or other equitable defenses are available in appropriate cases, but these tend not to be used if the conduct of the defendant was intentional theft of the information.

3. *Remedies.*

The primary relief sought is injunctive relief to stop the use of the trade secrets. Typically, this will be sought early in the process, to maintain the status quo pending the trial. If a court determines that a preliminary injunction can be granted, it necessarily has determined that victory is likely for the plaintiff and that the plaintiff will be harmed more by the continued misconduct of the defendant than the defendant will be harmed by a court order stopping the use of the trade secrets in question. Preliminary injunctions powerfully affect the outcome of cases. Often, trade secret cases settle after the court has ruled on the preliminary injunction.

When employees leave with critical knowledge, training, and know-how, the DTSA is somewhat less generous to the former employer seeking an injunction. The DTSA does not allow an injunction to "prevent a person from entering into an employment relationship, and that conditions placed on such employment shall be based on evidence of threatened misappropriation and not merely on the information the person knows. . . ."[277] Despite the federal balancing of the interests between employer and employee, the broader language available under some state laws may still result in courts issuing some broad injunctions to protect the inevitable disclosure of learned trade secrets.

In addition to injunctive relief, the plaintiff will seek economic compensation. The measure of damages under the DTSA and UTSA are very much like the measure of damages in copyright cases. The UTSA provides "[d]amages can include both the actual loss caused by misappropriation and the unjust enrichment caused by misappropriation that is not taken into account in computing actual loss."[278] Put another way, the plaintiff can receive the higher of either the money lost as a reasonable and provable consequence of the misappropriation of the trade secret or the provable net profits of the defendant that are attributable to the misappropriation. Courts may, instead, choose to calculate what a reasonable royalty rate would have been if the plaintiff had licensed the information to the defendant.

In extraordinary situations involving "willful and malicious misappropriation," the court may choose to double the award, under the damages provision of the UTSA with similar language in the DTSA. Finally, attorneys' fees may also be available if either party acted in bad faith, at the discretion of the court.

---

[277] 18 U.S.C. § 1836(b)(3)(A)(i)(I) (2018).

[278] UNIF. TRADE SECRETS ACT § 3(a) (UNIF. LAW COMM'N 1985).

E.   The International Implications of Trade Secret Protection.

The federal laws protecting U.S. companies from trade secret misappropriation clearly contemplate the protection in international trade. Other international treaties also recognize that trade secret protection is a part of national security and countries need to protect their economic interests through strong legislation.

Despite this, the evidentiary burden and impediments to protecting a company's trade secrets overseas are significant. The laws vary significantly from nation to nation and courts tend to defer to national interests to some degree. The problem is particularly acute in low cost manufacturing countries such as China, where the same companies serving as licensed manufacturing plants may be supplying identical goods to trademark counterfeiters and intellectual property pirates.

Appendices

A.   Charts: Overview of Intellectual Property.

1.   *Intellectual Property Reference Chart.*

Subject Matter

- *Utility Patents*: Inventions or discoveries of any new and useful process, act or method, machine, manufacture, or composition of matter, or any new and useful improvement thereof.

- *Copyrights*: Original works of authorship, including literary, dramatic, musical, artistic and certain other intellectual works.

- *Trademarks*: A word, phrase, symbol or design, or a combination of such, that identifies and distinguishes the source of the goods.

- *Trade Secrets*: A formula, pattern, compilation, program device, method, technique, or process, that: (i) derives economic value, being generally unknown and (ii) is subject to reasonable efforts to maintain the secrecy.

- *Publicity Rights*: Name, nickname, likeness, biography, voice and identity.

Method Acquired

- *Utility Patents*: Applied for by the inventor, joint inventors, or the enterprise to the PTO. The employer usually acquires through written employment agreement. In addition, an employee "employed to invent" does so for the benefit of the employer, who will own the patent.

- *Copyrights*: Automatically acquired upon fixation of the work (paper, disk, computer memory, sculpture, etc.).

- *Trademarks*: Through usage. ® May only be used after federal registration, but TM and SM may be used at any time.

- *Trade Secrets*: Initially, through usage, but maintained only through necessary steps to protect the secret.

- *Publicity Rights*: Varies by state. In most states, rights automatic, but some require actual use of rights in commerce.

Term

- *Utility Patents*: 20 years from the date on which the application for the patent was filed in the United States.

- *Copyrights*: Life of the author plus 70 years. Works-for-hire have a term of 95 years from publication or 120 years from creation, whichever is shorter.

- *Trademarks*: Indefinite, trademark will continue as long as usage continues.

- *Trade Secrets*: Indefinite, trade secret will continue so long as secret maintains economic value and secrecy.

- *Publicity Rights*: Throughout lifespan of person in all states where recognized. States differ on length of protection after death.

Time Needed to Acquire

- *Utility Patents*: 20 years from the date on which the application for the patent was filed in the United States. A patent application is generally published 18 months following the filing. The time for the issuance of the patent may be much longer.

- *Copyrights*: No waiting period. Registration with Copyright Office confers additional protections.

- *Trademarks*: May be acquired as early as 6 months prior to use in commerce, but generally acquired when mark is used in conjunction with the use of goods or services.

- *Trade Secrets*: No waiting period.

- *Publicity Rights*: No waiting period.

Renewals

- *Utility Patents*: Renewal not required but payment of "maintenance" fee is required. Maintenance fees are due at 3 ½, 7 ½ and 11 ½ years from the date the patent is granted.

- *Copyrights*: None required for works created beginning 1978; renewal required for works published before 1964.

- *Trademarks*: An Affidavit of Use ("Section 8 Affidavit") must be filed between the fifth and sixth year following initial registration, and within the year before the end of every ten-year period thereafter.

- *Trade Secrets*: Not applicable.

- *Publicity Rights*: Not applicable.

Federal Governmental Website

- *Utility Patents*: United States Patent and Trademark Office: www.uspto.gov.

- *Copyrights*: Copyright Office, a division of the Library of Congress: www.copyright.gov.

- *Trademarks*: United States Patent and Trademark Office: www.uspto.gov.

- *Trade Secrets*: Federal Government Office and Website: USPTO—Trade Secret Policy: https://www.uspto.gov/patents-getting-started/international-protection/trade-secret-policy.

- *Publicity Rights*: None (some similar protection under trademark law). State law protection only.

Applicable Law

- *Utility Patents*: U.S. Patent Act, 35 U.S.C. §1 et. sec.

- *Copyrights*: 1976 Copyright Act, 17 U.S.C. §101, et. sec.

- *Trademarks*: Trademark Act of 1946, 15 U.S.C. §1051, et. sec.

- *Trade Secrets*: Defend Trade Secrets Act and the Economic Espionage Act, 18 §§U.S.C. 1831-39.

- *Publicity Rights*: Examples of state law: Cal. Civ. Code §3344 (a) (West 2018); N.Y. Civ. Rights Law §§50-51 (McKinney 2018).

Transfer

- *Utility Patents*: Fully transferable, through a signed writing. Should be recorded with the PTO within three months of execution

- *Copyrights*: Fully transferable, exclusive transfer only in writing signed by transferring party. Registration of transfer helpful but not required.

- *Trademarks*: Assignable. Registration available through USPTO.

- *Trade Secrets*: Fully transferable. Care must be taken not to disclose the information before the transfer is complete.

- *Publicity Rights*: Owner of publicity rights may license use and transfer of licenses.

Property Excluded from Protection

- *Utility Patents*: Laws of nature; Physical phenomena; Abstract ideas; Works of authorship; Any machine, process that is not new or non-obvious.

- *Copyrights*: Ideas, procedures, methods, systems, processes, concepts, principles, discoveries, or devices, listings of ingredients or contents; and titles, names, short phrases, and slogans; typefaces; familiar symbols or designs.

- *Trademarks*: No protection for inventions, ideas, or products protected. Limited to protect the marks of goods or services. Trademarks do not prevent others from making the same goods or from selling the same goods or services under a different mark.

- *Trade Secrets*: Any publicly disclosed information; information without economic value; and information independently created.

- *Publicity Rights*: Does not extend to non-commercial use of name, likeness, etc. Cannot stop news sources or unauthorized biographies, etc.

2. **Copyright Timeline for Duration, Renewal & Termination.**

Duration

Works published before 1923 are in the public domain.

1. The work is in its renewal term on January 1, 1978, the 1976 Act (prior to the Sonny Bono Copyright Term Extension Act) gave the copyright proprietor an extended renewal term for 47 years (17 U.S.C. § 304(b)), which would have expired no later than December 31, 1997 (17 U.S.C. §305).

2. The Sonny Bono Copyright Term Extension Act would not operate to further extend this term for an additional 20 years because the work had fallen into the public domain before the effective date of the Sonny Bono Copyright Term Extension Act (October 27, 1998).

Works Published and Copyrighted Prior to January 1, 1978

1. 95 years from the time of publication.

2. The 95 years is comprised of two terms, an initial term of 28 years beginning at the date of first publication (17 U.S.C. § 304(a)), and additional term of 67 years (17 U.S.C. § 304(b)).

Works Created but not Published or Copyrighted prior to January 1, 1978

1. The 1976 Act creating federal copyright in unpublished works effectively ended the perpetual copyright in unpublished works.

2. §303(a) Copyright in a work created before January 1, 1978, but not theretofore in the public domain or copyrighted, subsists from January 1, 1978, endures for the longer of life+70, etc. or at least December 31, 2002.

3. If, however, such a work is published on or before December 31, 2002, the work will gain additional copyright protection which will not expire before December 31, 2047 (an additional 45 years).

Terminal Date of Copyright

All terms of copyright run to the end of the calendar year in which they would otherwise expire, so all copyrights end on December 31st of their final year. (17 U.S.C. § 304(5)).

Renewal

Works in their Renewal Term (Copyrighted Between 1923—1950 and Renewed Before January 1, 1978)

Under § 304(b), any copyright which had already been renewed (i.e. copyrighted and published between 1923-1950, and properly renewed) so that it was either registered or in its second term at any time between December 31, 1976 and December 31, 1977, received an automatic 19-year extension to its renewal term (for a second term of 47 years (extended to 67 years if the work still had copyright in 1998).

Works in their First Term at the time of the 1976 Act (Copyrighted Between January 1, 1950 and December 31, 1963) §304(A) (Superseded)

As enacted in 1976, § 304(a) required that any copyright in its first 28-year term on January 1, 1978 be renewed by the copyright owner at the end of its initial term in order to secure protection for a second term. If a copyright originally secured before January 1, 1964, was not renewed at the proper time, copyright protection expired at the end of the 28th calendar year of the copyright and could not be restored. (17 U.S.C. § 304(a) superseded).

If a valid renewal registration was made at the time, the person(s) entitled to renewal received a second, 47-year term (now 67) (up from 28 years under 1909 Act).

Works in their First Term at the Time of the 1976 Act (Copyrighted Between January 1, 1964 and December 31, 1977) §304(A) (Amended 1992)

1. The work is in its renewal term on January 1, 1978, the 1976 Act (*prior* to the Sonny Bono Copyright Term Extension Act) gave the copyright proprietor an extended renewal term for 47 years (17 U.S.C. § 304(b)), which would have expired no later than December 31, 1997 (17 U.S.C. §305).

2. The Sonny Bono Copyright Term Extension Act would not operate to further extend this term for an additional 20 years because the work had fallen into the public domain before the effective date of the Sonny Bono Copyright Term Extension Act (October 27, 1998).

Termination of Transfers

Work-Made-For-Hire has no Termination Rights

No termination rights exist. The employer or commissioning party is treated as the initial copyright owner, and the work cannot be divested by the employee.

The power to terminate is also unavailable to an employer or specially commissioning party who acquired copyright as a work-made-for-hire.

Terminations for Works Published and Grants Executed on or after January 1, 1923 but Before 1978 under §304(c)

Termination of the grant may be effected at any time during a period of five years beginning at the end of fifty-six years from the date copyright was originally secured, or beginning on January 1, 1978, whichever is later. (17 U.S.C. § 304(c)).

The notice shall state the effective date of the termination, which shall fall within the five-year period and the notice shall be served not less than two or more than ten years before that date.

Alternative Terminations for Works Published on or After January 1, 1923 but Before 1950 under §304(d) (Added by Sony Bono Copyright Extension Act)

The 20-year extension is subject to an additional termination right, if no termination right was previously exercised.

In the case of any copyright other than a work made for hire, in its renewal term on the effective date of the Sonny Bono Copyright Term Extension Act (October 27, 1998); if the prior termination rights expired unused; then termination of a grant may be effected at any time during a period of 5 years beginning at the end of 75 years from the date copyright was originally secured.

Terminations for Grants executed on or After January 1, 1978—§203(a)

The termination right may be exercised during a five-year period starting at the end of 35 years from the date of execution of the grant.

A derivative work made pursuant to the grant can still be exploited by the party which had its rights terminated, but no new derivative can be made after the new term begins. (E.g. films can be exhibited, but no remakes can be made.)

There is an exception if the grant was of a right of publication, in which case the five-year period begins at the earlier of 35 years after publication, or 40 years after the grant was made.

Effect of Other Agreements on Termination—§203(a)(5). Termination may be effected notwithstanding any agreement to the contrary, including an agreement to make any future grant or to make a will.

B.   Sample   Agreement: Trade   Secret Nondisclosure Agreement.

Sample nondisclosure agreement for submitting or reviewing a prototype.

Nondisclosure Agreement

This Agreement ("Agreement") is entered into as of the date written below, by and between _____ a(n) individual/corporation with offices located at _____ _____ ("Creator") and _____ a(n) individual/corporation with offices located at _____ _____ ("Recipient") with reference to the following facts:

Creator has developed specifications for a certain invention, process, or device ("Property") which Creator wishes to provide to Recipient for the purpose of developing a business relationship for the participation in the development or production of the Property.

Recipient has skills and experience relevant to the development of the Property and desires to engage in discussions which may lead to the participation in the creation or production of the Property.

In the course of discussions regarding the development of such Property information and specifications related to the Property shall be given to Recipient by Creator, and the parties wish to protect the proprietary nature of such information and recognize that no disclosure can be made without this Agreement.

NOW, THEREFORE, in consideration of the mutual covenants and agreements contained herein, Recipient and Creator agree as follows:

1. Confidentiality. Recipient shall not directly or indirectly, disclose, disseminate, publish, or use for its business advantage or for any other purpose, at any time during or after the term of this Agreement any information received from Creator deemed confidential by the other party ("Confidential Information") without the express written permission of Creator for a period of five (5) years following the date of receipt of Confidential Information.

a.   Definitions. For purposes of this Agreement, Confidential Information shall be defined as any information not generally known in the industry about Creator's ideas, concepts, products, designs, intellectual property, trade secrets, services, or any combination thereof, whether or not such information would be recognized as proprietary absent this Agreement, including but not limited to information related to the Property developed by Creator. In addition, Confidential Information also includes, without limitation, information relating to the parties' software, trade secrets, financial projections, customers, suppliers, employees, consultants, technologies, technical and business strategies, marketing and promotion strategies, and information either party is obligated to treat as confidential.

b.   Limitations. Notwithstanding any other provision of this Agreement, Recipient shall not be liable for disclosing, disseminating, publishing or using information which (i) was already known prior to the receipt of Confidential Information; (ii) is now or becomes public information through no wrongful act of the Recipient; (iii) is independently developed or acquired by Recipient without any use of Confidential Information in such development; or (iv) is required to be disclosed by law.

2. Documents and Materials. The documents and materials of Creator (including but not limited to all documents, inventions, processes, devices, data, reports, projections, records, notes, lists, specifications and designs) are furnished in accordance of this Agreement and shall remain the sole property of Creator. This information (collectively known as "Evaluation Material"), shall upon the termination of this Agreement be promptly returned to Creator, including all copies thereof which are in the possession or control of Recipient, its agents, and its representatives. No license under any trade secrets, copyrights, or other rights is granted by this Agreement or any disclosure of Confidential Information hereunder.

3. Term and Renewal. The term of this Agreement shall be one (1) year commencing as of the date hereof; provided however, that Paragraph 1 of this Agreement shall survive termination of this Agreement and shall remain in full force and effect for a period of five (5) years.

4. Miscellaneous.

a.   Further Documents. Each of the parties agrees to execute, acknowledge and deliver any and all further documents which may be required to carry into effect this Agreement and its respective obligations hereunder, all of which further documents shall be in accordance with and consistent with the terms of this Agreement.

b. <u>Resolution of Disputes; Attorneys' Fees</u>. The parties recognize that irreparable injury, as well as monetary damages may result as a result of a material breach of this Agreement. In the event of a breach of this Agreement, the prevailing party may be entitled to injunctive relief in addition to any remedies available at law. Such prevailing party shall also be entitled to reasonable attorneys' fees and related expenses incurred as a result of such breach.

c. <u>Headings</u>. Provision headings are solely for convenience and reference, and have no legal significance.

d. <u>Assignment</u>. Neither party may assign this Agreement without the written consent of the other party.

e. <u>Notices</u>. All notices, statements or other documents which either party shall desire to give to the other hereunder shall be in writing and shall be deemed given as when delivered personally or by telecopier, or 48 hours after deposit in the U.S. mail, postage prepaid and addressed to the recipient party at the address set forth in the opening paragraph of this Agreement, or at such address as either party hereto may designate from time to time in accordance with this Paragraph.

f. <u>Amendments</u>. This Agreement may be modified or amended only in a writing signed by both parties.

g. <u>Severability</u>. If any provision of this Agreement shall be held to be invalid or unenforceable for any reason, the remaining provisions shall continue to be valid and enforceable. If a court finds that any provision of this Agreement is invalid or unenforceable, but that by limiting such provision it would become valid and enforceable, then such provision shall be deemed to be written, construed, and enforced as so limited.

h. <u>Entire Agreement</u>. This Agreement contains the full and complete understanding between the parties hereto with reference to the within subject matter, supersedes all prior agreements and understandings, whether written or oral, pertaining thereto, and cannot be modified except by a written instrument signed by both of the parties hereto. Each of the parties acknowledges that no representation or promise not expressly contained in this Agreement has been made by the other or its agents or representatives.

IN WITNESS WHEREOF, the undersigned have executed this Agreement the day and year written below.

Date: _____

"Creator"

_____

By_____

Its_____

"Recipient"

(Company Name)

_____

By_____

Its_____

C. Sample Agreement: Website Content License Agreement.

This sample agreement is the type used when licensing the right to use another company's originally published content on the entrepreneur's website. The agreement includes provisions to cross-post the content in exchange for payments made by the website and advertising on the content provider's website.

WEBCASTER LLC COMMUNICATIONS COMPANY

PUBLICATION DISTRIBUTION AGREEMENT

This Agreement ("Agreement") is entered into as of this _____ day of _____, by and between WebCaster LLC, with offices located at [Address] ("WEBCASTER LLC" or "Company") and Newspapers Publishers, Inc., an Illinois corporation with offices at [Address] ("Publisher") with reference to the following facts:

WEBCASTER LLC provides an on-line, computer and multimedia sports entertainment and information services to the public ("Services"). WEBCASTER LLC desires to use, republish and distribute various full text sports articles, editorials, photographs and other sports related copy previously or currently published by Publisher.

Publisher is a corporation publishing and distributing newspapers, magazines, books and other content including ... (collectively, the "Newspapers"). Publisher desires to provide various full text articles, editorials, photographs and other copy to WEBCASTER LLC for its Services.

NOW, THEREFORE, in consideration of the mutual covenants and agreements contained herein, Publisher and WEBCASTER LLC agree as follows:

A. Publication Rights. Publisher hereby grants WEBCASTER LLC all rights necessary to republish and distribute all related content of the Newspapers to which Publisher (and its employees) are the author or exclusive copyright holder (the "Content"). Such rights include, but are not limited to all staff writers, columnists and photographers. The Content does not include any information or stories supplied to Publisher from an independent news source such as AP or UPI and no license to use such material is granted.

(1) The use of content shall be on a non-exclusive basis and shall be accompanied by a proper notice of copyright.

(2) Except as provided in this Agreement, all proprietary, copyright and literary rights to content shall remain the exclusive property of Publisher.

(3) Content shall be provided to WEBCASTER LLC on a daily basis in a manner technically satisfactory to WEBCASTER LLC and Publisher.

B. <u>Promotion</u>. In connection with content and services provided hereunder by Publisher, WEBCASTER LLC is hereby granted the non-exclusive right to use Publisher's name, trademark, the names, biographies, voices and likeness of Publisher's employees, and other rights of publicity for advertising and promoting its Services and Publisher's Content.

(1) Publisher shall provide, at its sole expense, advertising space of 12 column inches on a weekly basis on a location of the Newspapers to be mutually determined. Publisher shall provide artwork, design and layout for content supplied by WEBCASTER LLC.

(2) Throughout the term of this Agreement, including any extensions and renewals thereof, WEBCASTER LLC shall provide subscribers of the Newspapers a discount on the price of WEBCASTER LLC subscription of not less than one ($1.00) dollar off the regular monthly charge to promote readership of Publisher's Newspapers.

C <u>Compensation for Publisher Services</u>. Throughout the term of this Agreement, including any extensions and renewals thereof, as compensation for and in consideration of the services provided by Publisher, WEBCASTER LLC shall pay to Publisher the following amounts:

(1) A royalty of ten (10%) percent of the revenues received which are attributed to the total access time or use generated for content (less subscriber's free use and applicable credit card charge-offs); and

(2) A royalty of ten (10%) percent of the revenues received from the new subscribers (less subscriber's discount and applicable credit card charge-offs) to WEBCASTER LLC attributable to the advertisements in Publisher's Newspapers.

(3) <u>Prompt Payment</u>. WEBCASTER LLC shall, within fifteen (15) days of each fiscal quarter, prepare and furnish to Publisher a true, accurate and complete statement setting forth all royalties payable to Publisher, and pay to Publisher the aggregate amount of all royalties payable, calculated in accordance with this Paragraph.

(4)   <u>Account Records</u>. WEBCASTER LLC shall at all times, maintain accurate and complete records concerning each Account and shall make such records available to Publisher upon reasonable request. Such records shall be treated as confidential and shall not be provided to any third party other than Publisher's attorney or accountant.

D. <u>Term and Renewal</u>. The term of this Agreement shall be one (1) year commencing as of the date hereof, and provided neither party is in material breach of or in default under any term or provision hereof, this Agreement shall automatically renew for additional one (1) year periods thereafter, unless either party gives written notice of its election to terminate this Agreement not less than thirty (30) days prior to the expiration of the term.

E.   <u>Warranties and Representations of the Parties</u>. Each party to this Agreement hereby represents and warrants that it has the right and authority to enter into this Agreement and that it is not subject to any contract, agreement, judgment, statute, regulation or disability which might interfere with its full performance all of the covenants and conditions hereunder.

(1)   Each party agrees to indemnify the other and to hold the other harmless from and against any and all claims, action, cause of action, liabilities, damages, judgments, decrees, losses, costs and expenses, including reasonable attorneys' fees, arising out of any breach or alleged breach of any representations, warranties or agreements made by it hereunder.

(2)   Publisher represents and warrants that at all times throughout the term of this Agreement, nothing in content shall violate the copyright of any other party, nor shall it be defamatory or invade the privacy of any person. Publisher agrees to indemnify and hold WEBCASTER LLC harmless from any and all damages, causes of action, cost and expenses, including reasonable attorneys' fees, incurred by reason of Publisher's alleged breach of this paragraph.

F.   <u>Resolution of Disputes</u>. Any and all disputes hereunder shall be resolved by arbitration in accordance with the American Arbitration

Association of America ("AAA") under the rules then obtaining. Any party hereto electing to commence an action shall give written notice to the other party hereto of such election. The location for such arbitration shall be Los Angeles, California, subject to the convenience of the parties and any and all rights of discovery available pursuant to such arbitration shall be limited by the applicable arbitration provisions of the California Code of Civil Procedure. The award of such arbitrator may be confirmed or enforced in any court of competent jurisdiction. The costs and expenses of the arbitrator, including the attorneys' fees and costs of each of the parties, may be apportioned between the parties by such arbitrator.

G. Miscellaneous.

(1) No Obligation. Notwithstanding the rights granted herein, WEBCASTER LLC is under no obligation to utilize content as part of the Services of WEBCASTER LLC in any manner whatsoever, and failure to exercise any rights contained herein shall not constitute a breach of any covenant, express or implied.

(2) No Partnership or Joint Venture. Nothing in this Agreement shall be construed as creating a partnership, joint venture or employment relationship between the parties hereto, and each party is solely and exclusively responsible for its own debts and obligations.

(3) Further Documents. Each of the parties agrees to execute, acknowledge and deliver any and all further documents which may be required to carry into effect this Agreement and its respective obligations hereunder, all of which further documents shall be in accordance with and consistent with the terms of this Agreement.

(4) Confidentiality. The terms and conditions of this Agreement, and all technical specifications, subscriber information and related material are deemed trade secrets of WEBCASTER LLC and Publisher shall not disclose such trade secrets to any third party not directly associated with Publisher.

(5) Headings. Provision headings are solely for convenience and reference, and have no legal significance.

(6) Assignment. Neither party may assign this Agreement without the written consent of the other party.

(7) Governing Law. This Agreement shall be governed by and construed in accordance with the laws of the State of California applicable to agreements entered into and wholly performed therein.

(8) <u>Notices</u>. All notices, statements or other documents which either party shall desire to give to the other hereunder shall be in writing and shall be deemed given as when delivered personally or by telecopier, or 48 hours after deposit in the U.S. mail, postage prepaid and addressed to the recipient party at the address set forth in the opening paragraph of this Agreement, or at such address as either party hereto may designate from time to time in accordance with this Paragraph.

(9) <u>Amendments</u>. This Agreement may be modified or amended only in a writing signed by both parties.

(10) <u>Severability</u>. If any provision of this Agreement shall be held to be invalid or unenforceable for any reason, the remaining provisions shall continue to be valid and enforceable. If a court finds that any provision of this Agreement is invalid or unenforceable, but that by limiting such provision it would become valid and enforceable, then such provision shall be deemed to be written, construed, and enforced as so limited.

(11) <u>Entire Agreement</u>. This Agreement contains the full and complete understanding between the parties hereto with reference to the within subject matter, supersedes all prior agreements and understandings, whether written or oral, pertaining thereto, and cannot be modified except by a written instrument signed by both of the parties hereto. Each of the parties acknowledges that no representation or promise not expressly contained in this Agreement has been made by the other or its agents or representatives.

IN WITNESS WHEREOF, the undersigned have executed this Agreement the day and year first above written.

WEBCASTER LLC Communications Company

_____

[Name], Manager

"Publisher"

Newspapers Publishers, Inc.

_____

Its_____

D. Sample Agreement: Employment Agreement.

This sample agreement is the type used when employing key personnel. The agreement does not reflect any duties the employee would have as member-manager of an LLC, so that agreement would need to be modified to include those provisions and to adjust the termination provisions if the manager were also a member.

EMPLOYMENT AGREEMENT

THIS EMPLOYMENT AGREEMENT is entered into as of [Date] by and between WebCaster LLC, with offices located at [Address] ("Company") and _____ ("Employee").

1. Employment and Duties. Company hereby employs Employee as _____ of the Company on the terms and subject to the conditions contained in this Agreement. Employee shall be responsible for the duties described more fully in the attached job description in Appendix A (Job Description). Employee hereby accepts such employment and agrees to perform in good faith and to the best of Employee's ability all services which may be required of Employee hereunder and to be available to render services at all reasonable times and places in accordance with such reasonable directions, requests, rules and regulations made by the Company in connection with Employee's employment. Employee shall, during the term hereof, devote Employee's full time and energy to performing his duties. Employee shall be based at the Company's corporate offices. Employee understands, however, that Employee shall be required to travel to each of the Company's other facilities.

2. Employment Handbook. The policies of Company are set forth in an employee handbook ("Employee Handbook") governing the policies of Company which has been made available to Employee, and the receipt of which is hereby acknowledged. Employee understands that the terms of the Employee Handbook serve as additional obligations of Employee and failure to materially comply with the terms of the Employee Handbook shall be deemed a material breach hereunder. The parties further agree that Company has full authority to modify, repeal, restate and amend the Employee

532

Handbook at any time and Employee understands that all such modifications shall be binding on Employee. In the case of any conflict between this Agreement and the terms of the Employee Handbook, the terms specified in this Agreement shall take precedence over the terms of the Employee Handbook, to the minimum extent necessary to bring such provisions into compliance with this Agreement.

3. <u>Term of Employment</u>. The term of this Agreement shall commence as of the date hereof and shall terminate on _____, 20__, unless sooner terminated as provided herein.

4. <u>Compensation</u>. As full and complete compensation for Employee's services hereunder and all the rights granted hereunder by Employee to Company, Company shall pay Employee $_____ per month payable in accordance with Company's payroll practices for salaried employees, upon the condition that Employee fully and faithfully perform Employee's services hereunder in accordance with the terms and conditions of this Agreement. In addition, Employee shall be entitled to such bonuses as shall be determined by the Board of Directors of the Company in its sole and absolute discretion. The Company shall deduct and withhold from the compensation payable to Employee hereunder any and all amounts required to be deducted or withheld by the Company under the provisions of any statute, regulation, ordinance, or order and any and all amendments hereinafter enacted requiring the withholding or deducting from compensation payable to employees.

5. <u>Expense Reimbursement</u>. In addition, to the compensation hereinabove provided, Employee shall be reimbursed in a sum equal to the amount of all traveling, hotel, entertainment and other expenses properly and necessarily incurred by Employee in the discharge of Employee's duties hereunder, and Employee will supply the Company with vouchers, receipts and other details of such expenses upon the Company's request therefore.

6. <u>Death or Disability of Employee</u>. In the event of Employee's death or disability while in the employ of Company, this Agreement and the compensation due to Employee pursuant to Paragraph 3 hereof shall terminate upon the date of said death or disability and Company shall thereafter be required to make payments only to Employee or

Employee's estate, as the case may be, for all amounts due to Employee as compensation for the services rendered hereunder through the date of death or disability to the extent such amounts have accrued but have not been theretofore paid. If Employee shall recover from such disability prior to the expiration date of this Agreement set forth in Paragraph 2 hereof, this Agreement and Employee's employment hereunder shall be reinstated for the balance of term of this Agreement. Employee shall be deemed disabled if, Employee in the opinion of Company, is unable to substantially perform the services required of Employee hereunder for a period in excess of 60 consecutive days or 60 days during any 90 day period. In such event, Employee shall be deemed disabled as of such 60th day.

7. <u>Restrictive Covenant</u>. During the term of this Agreement, Employee shall (i) devote Employee's full time and energy solely and exclusively to the performance of Employee's duties described herein except during periods of illness or vacation periods; (ii) not directly or indirectly provide services to or through any company or firm except Company unless otherwise instructed by Company; (iii) not directly or indirectly own, manage, operate, join, control or participate in the ownership, management, operation or control of or be employed by or connected in any manner with any enterprise which is engaged in any business competitive with or similar to that of Company; and (iv) not render any services of any kind or character for Employee's own account or for any other person, firm or corporation without first obtaining the Company's consent in writing; provided, however, that Employee shall have the right to perform such incidental services as are necessary in connection with Employee's (a) private passive investments where Employee is not obligated or required to, and shall not in fact, devote any managerial efforts and provided such investments are not geographically competitive when made with the business of Company or (b) charitable or community activities, or in trade or professional organizations, upon the condition, however, that such incidental services do not interfere with the performance of Employee's services hereunder.

8. <u>Confidentiality</u>. Employee hereby acknowledges that during the term hereof, Company may, from time to time, disclose to Employee confidential information pertaining to the business and affairs of

Company and its clients, including but not limited to, any information not generally known in the industry about Company's ideas, concepts, products, designs, intellectual property, trade secrets, services, or any combination thereof, whether or not such information would be recognized as proprietary absent this Agreement, including but not limited to confidential information created by Employee whether in written form or embodied in tangible materials (including, without limitation, software, hardware, drafts, drawings, graphs, charts, spreadsheets, disks, tapes, prototypes, samples, letters, notes, memoranda or presentations) (Collectively, "Confidential Information"). Confidential Information shall also include customer lists and accounts and other similar items indicating the source of income of Company.

The parties acknowledge that all Confidential Information is the sole property of Company, that Employee shall take all steps necessary to maintain the confidence of Confidential Information by complying with Company security measures, marking documents as required, and restricting access to documents and data in Employee's possession. Employee shall not, at any time during or after the term of this Agreement, disclose to any third party or directly or indirectly make use of any such Confidential Information, All documents and data (whether written, printed or otherwise reproduced or recorded) containing or relating to any such Confidential Information, whether made or compiled by, or delivered or made available to, or otherwise obtained by Employee, shall be returned by Employee to Company at the time of the termination of this Agreement or upon any earlier request by Company, without Employee retaining any copies, notes or excerpts thereof.

9. <u>Restrictive Covenant Following Employment</u>. During a period of one year following the termination of this Agreement, Employee shall not accept employment, consulting services or otherwise engage in business with the direct competitors of Company listed on Appendix B or any direct or indirect competitor where Employee could reasonably utilize Confidential Information in a manner that is not generally known to the public.

10. <u>Ownership of Material and Ideas</u>. Employee agrees that all material, ideas, and inventions pertaining to the business of Company or of any client of Company, including but not limited to, all trade secrets,

patents and copyrights thereon and renewals and extensions thereof, and the names, addresses and telephone numbers of customers of Company, shall belong solely to Company.

11. <u>Fringe Benefits</u>. The Company shall provide to Employee throughout the term of this Agreement the benefits of any group life insurance plan, group medical insurance plan and other employee benefit plans available which the Company or its parent may adopt and for which Employee shall qualify as set forth in the Employee Handbook.

12. <u>Termination</u>. The Company may without notice terminate this Agreement and all of the Company's obligations hereunder for cause as such term is defined herein ("Cause"). For purposes hereof, Cause shall mean the Employee's conviction of a felony (which, through the lapse of time of otherwise is not subject to appeal) or material refusal, failure or neglect without proper cause to perform Employee's obligations under this Agreement or material breach of any of Employee's fiduciary obligations as an officer or member of the Board of Directors of Company. Upon termination for Cause, the Company shall thereafter be required to make payment to Employee only for amounts due to Employee as compensation for services rendered hereunder and not previously paid. In the event, Employee is terminated with Cause or without Cause, Employee is removed from the Employee's current position and not provided a comparable position during the term of his employment hereunder, the Company shall continue to be obligated to pay the balance of compensation otherwise payable to Employee without any obligation on Employee's part to mitigate and with Company having no right of offset in the event that Employee shall obtain other employment.

13. <u>Services Unique</u>. It is agreed that the services to be rendered by Employee hereunder are of a special, unique, unusual, extraordinary and intellectual character which gives them a peculiar value, the loss of which cannot be reasonably or adequately compensated in damages in an action at law and that a breach by Employee of any of the provisions contained herein will cause the Company irreparable injury and damage. Employee expressly agrees that the Company shall be entitled to injunctive or other equitable relief to prevent a breach thereof. Resort to any such equitable relief shall not be

construed as a waiver of any of the rights or remedies which the Company may have against Employee for damages or otherwise.

14. <u>Key Man Life Insurance</u>. During the term of this Agreement, the Company may at any time effect insurance on Employee's life and/or health in such amounts and in such form as the Company may in its sole discretion decide. Employee shall not have any interest in such insurance, but shall, if the Company requests, submit to such medical examinations, supply such information and execute such documents as may be required in connection with or so as to enable the Company to effect such insurance.

15. <u>Vacation</u>. Employee shall have the right during each one (1) year period of the term of this Agreement to take an aggregate of three (3) weeks of vacation, with pay, at such times mutually convenient to him and to the Corporation. Employee shall have the right, however, to accumulate his vacation from one period to the next period without the Company's consent.

16. <u>Applicable Law and Severability</u>. This document shall, in all respects, be governed by the laws of the State of California applicable to agreements executed and to be wholly performed within the State of California. Nothing contained herein shall be construed so as to require the commission of any act contrary to law, and wherever there is any conflict between any provision contained herein and any present or future statute, law, ordinance or regulation contrary to which the parties have no legal right to contract, the latter shall prevail but the provision of this document which is affected shall be curtailed and limited only to the extent necessary to bring it within the requirements of the law.

17. <u>Attorneys' Fees</u>. In the event any action be instituted by a party to enforce any of the terms and provisions contained herein, the prevailing party in such action shall be entitled to such reasonable attorneys' fees, costs and expenses as may be fixed by the Court.

18. <u>Modifications or Amendments</u>. No amendment, change or modification of this document shall be valid unless in writing and signed by all of the parties hereto.

19. <u>Successors and Assigns</u>. All of the terms and provisions contained herein shall inure to the benefit of and shall be binding upon the parties hereto and their respective heirs, personal representatives, successors and assigns.

20.   <u>Entire Agreement</u>. This document constitutes the entire understanding and agreement of the parties with respect to the subject matter of this Agreement, and any and all prior agreements, understandings or representations are hereby terminated and cancelled in their entirety and are of no further force or effect.

IN WITNESS WHEREOF, the parties hereto have duly executed this Agreement as of the day and year first above written.

WebCaster LLC,

a Minnesota Limited Liability Company

By: _____

"Company"

By: _____

"Employee"

E. Sample Agreement: Trademark License Agreement.

This sample agreement is the type used when licensing the right to use another company's trademark on the entrepreneur's goods.

TRADEMARK LICENSE AGREEMENT

THIS TRADEMARK LICENSE AGREEMENT (the "Agreement") is entered into this __th day of _____ by and between _____ ("Licensor") and _____ ("Licensee"), with reference to the following facts:

A. Licensor owns all intellectual property rights in the name and including but not limited to common law and federally registered trademarks, service marks and publicity rights in the names, characters, symbols, designs, likenesses and visual representations listed in attached Exhibit A and incorporated by reference, which intellectual property rights shall hereinafter be called collectively "Mark" or "Marks."

B. Licensee desires to utilize the Marks in connection with the sale of ___ more specifically described in paragraph 1.c. ("Licensed Articles"); and

C. Licensor desires to grant a license to Licensee permitting Licensee to cause such Licensed Articles to be manufactured and sold under one or more of the Marks and to sell such Licensed Articles as provided in this Agreement;

NOW, THEREFORE, in consideration of the mutual promises, covenants, and conditions herein contained, it is agreed as follows:

1. Grant of License.

   a. Licensor hereby grants to Licensee the exclusive right and license to use the Marks for sale upon and in connection with Licensed Articles manufactured by or at the direction of Licensee and distributed by Licensee for ultimate sale.

   b. Licensee shall use the license granted hereunder solely in connection with the design, development, manufacture, marketing, advertising, distribution and sale of the Licensed Articles.

2. <u>Term & Territory</u>.

    a.   The term of this Agreement shall be for ___ (___) years commencing as of as of the date hereof unless sooner terminated in accordance with the provisions hereof. This License shall be automatically renewed for a successive one (1) year period unless Licensor or Licensee gives the other party written notice of its intention not to renew the License at least ninety (90) days prior to the expiration date of the Agreement or any renewal thereof. Refusal to renew this License may be effected without cause.

    b.   The rights granted to Licensee hereunder may be exercised by Licensee in the United States including its territories, Canada and Mexico, (the "Territory").

3. <u>Exclusivity</u>.

    a. Licensee shall have the exclusive rights to exploit the Marks in the Licensed Products throughout the Territory.

    b. Nothing in this Agreement shall be construed to prevent Licensor from granting exclusive licenses to any other licensees for the use of the Marks on articles other than _____ and which are not directly competitive with the Licensed Articles.

4. <u>Royalty</u>.

    a.   Except as provided under section 4.2, Licensee agrees to pay Licensor an earned royalty of ten percent (10%) of the Net Sales Price (as defined below) on all Licensed Articles sold by Licensee under this Agreement.

    b.   The parties acknowledge that certain high-volume retail outlets, such as that offered by XYZ, Inc. require substantially lower profit margin than that traditionally available through department stores and other retail outlets. Licensee agrees to pay Licensor an earned royalty of three percent (3%) of the Net Sales Price earned from XYZ, Inc. and such other high-volume retail outlets as shall be mutually agreed upon by Licensor and Licensee.

c. The "Net Sales Price" shall be the invoiced price at which Licensed Articles are sold by Licensee, less any sales tax, less any cash discount stated on such invoice and actually taken by the Licensee's customer, and less any allowance to Licensee's customer for returned or rejected Licensed Articles, provided that such allowances relate to sales which were previously included in royalty calculations under this Agreement. The aforementioned deductions shall be the only subtractions from the invoice price allowed for purposes of computing royalties under this Agreement.

5. Statements and Payments.

a. On or before the fifteenth (15th) day of the first month of each calendar quarter, Licensee shall furnish to Licensor full and accurate quarterly statements, showing the number, description, and total Net Sales Prices of the Licensed Articles sold by the Licensee during the preceding calendar quarter. Licensee shall deliver simultaneously with such statements, a check to Licensor covering the royalties due thereon.

b. On or before the fifteenth (15th) day of the third month following the end of each Contract Year, Licensee shall furnish to Licensor a yearly statement certified by the Chief Financial Officer of Licensee showing gross shipments, net shipments, royalties due and royalties paid for the preceding contract year. If said yearly statement discloses that the amount of royalties actually paid during the period being reported was less than the amount required to be paid, including earned royalties, and interest on delinquent payments, Licensee shall pay any such difference with the statement. If said statement discloses the Licensee has actually paid royalties in excess of the amounts required to be paid, Licensee shall be given a credit for any such excess provided that no credit shall be earned where said excess is due to the fact that Licensee's earned royalties were less than said Minimum Guaranteed Royalties payable for that contract year. In the event of excess royalty payments during the final year of the Agreement, adjustments shall be made in cash rather than in the form of credit.

6. Quality Control, and Samples.

    a. All Licensed Products design and packaging shall be subject to Licensor approval, which approval shall not be unreasonably withheld.

    b. The Licensed Products, as well as all promotional, packaging, and advertising material relative thereto, shall include all appropriate legal notices as required by Licensor. The Licensed Products shall be of a high quality at least equal to comparable products previously manufactured and marketed by Licensee under its own trademarks.

    c. From time to time during the term hereof, or, whenever production is repeated, and/or upon Licensor's request, Licensee shall furnish a reasonable number of random samples of each Licensed Article to Licensor. All samples shall be provided free of cost to Licensor.

    d. If the quality of the Licensed Products falls below such quality, Licensee shall use its best efforts to restore such quality. In the event that Licensee has not taken appropriate steps to restore such quality within thirty (30) days after notification by Licensor, Licensor shall have the right to require that the Licensee cease using the Trademarks.

7. Protection of Marks.

    a. Licensee acknowledges Licensor's rights, title and interest in and to the Marks both at common law and under the Federal Trademark law and state statutes and will not, either directly or indirectly, at any time do any act or thing discrediting any part of such right, title or interest. Licensee agrees that its use of the Marks will inure entirely to the benefit of Licensor and that it will assist Licensor, to protect Licensor's rights in the Marks. Toward that end, upon Licensor's request, Licensee agrees to provide Licensor with two (2) specimens of any trademark used on Licensed Articles and whatever other documentation or information may be reasonably requested by Licensor for the purpose of registration of its Mark or Marks in the categories into which the Licensed Articles fall. Licensee shall mark each of the Licensed Articles with at least one Mark and shall apply trademark notice by affixing adjacent to Mark the federal registration symbol® ("R" in a circle) or a "TM" as may be appropriate.

b. Licensee recognizes that the ___ name and Licensor's associated marks are world famous and that, even if not registered in any country, the unauthorized use thereof would seriously dilute the distinctiveness of such name and the marks. Licensee shall immediately notify Licensor in writing of any infringements or imitations by others of the Marks of which it becomes aware.

c. Licensor agrees that licensor will, for the life of this agreement, maintain, protect and defend the registration of the trademarks and trade names described herein with the United States Patent and Trademark Office and with the State of ___ or other state at Licensor's discretion.

d. If licensor at any time fails to maintain, protect and defend licensor's rights to, and registration of, the trademarks and trade names described in this agreement against infringement or cancellation, licensee may then take such action and institute such proceedings in the name of licensor as may be necessary or appropriate to maintain, protect and defend any and all such trademarks and trade names. Licensee shall have the right to deduct any expenses incurred thereby from any royalties thereafter payable to licensor under the terms of this agreement. Licensor agrees at licensor's own expense to defend licensee in any legal proceeding arising out of licensee's use of licensor's trademarks or trade names pursuant to this agreement.

e. Throughout the term of this Agreement, Licensee agrees to comply with Licensor's "Standards for Vendors" and "Manufacture and Vendor Facility Agreement" which are set forth on Exhibit B (which are hereby incorporated by reference), and shall be subject to Licensor's audition procedures and restrictions on uses of the Marks as set forth therein. If Licensor's audit results in a finding that the policies are violated, Licensee shall have ninety (90) days to cure, either by conforming the practices to those required under the policies and this Agreement or by assigning the manufacturing to a sublicensee that complies with the terms of the policies and this Agreement.

The sole remedy for breach by Licensee of this section shall be termination of this Agreement or injunctive relief against Licensee and its sublicensees, or both, in the sole discretion of Licensor.

8. Representations and Warranties.

   a. Each party represents and warrants that (i) it has the legal right to enter into this Agreement and perform its obligations hereunder, and (ii) the performance of its obligations will not violate any applicable U.S. laws or regulations, or cause a breach of any agreements with any third parties.

   b. Each party represents that there is nothing known that will prevent, delay or otherwise interfere in any way whatsoever with any aspect of the performance either party's obligations under this Agreement.

   c. Each party represents that with respect to any copyrights, trademarks, patents, and rights of publicity utilized in performance under this Agreement, the party has the right to use and disclose the same in performing hereunder; that any rights furnished to the other party under this Agreement do not infringe any rights of any third party, including without limitation, any intellectual property, publicity, patent, copyright or trade secret rights.

   d. Licensor further represents and warrants that it has the right and power to grant the licenses granted herein, including without limitation the name ___ and the Marks, that there are no other agreements with any other party in conflict herewith, and that it has no actual knowledge that the Property and/or Trademark infringe any valid right of any third party.

   e. Licensee further represents and warrants that it (directly or through its sublicensees) shall be solely responsible for the manufacture, production, sale and distribution of the Licensed Products and will bear all related costs associated therewith.

9. Indemnification.

    a. Licensee will at all times indemnify, reimburse and hold harmless Licensor from all losses and expenses (including reasonable attorneys' fees) incurred in connection with any action, suit, or proceeding which arises out of (i) any actual or alleged design defect, manufacturing defect, breach of warranty, or any other product liability legal; (ii) the violation of any national, federal, state or local law, regulation, ruling, standard or directive or of any industry standard with respect to the Licensed Articles or to activities related thereto; or (iii) Licensee's violation or breach of any warranty, representation, agreement or obligation hereunder.

    b. Licensor will at all times indemnify, reimburse and hold harmless Licensor from all losses and expenses (including reasonable attorneys' fees) incurred in connection with any action, suit, or proceeding which arises out of (i) the use by Licensee of the Marks as authorized pursuant to this Agreement; (ii) the violation of any national, federal, state or local law, regulation, ruling, standard or directive or of any industry standard with respect to the Licensor's activities; or (iii) Licensor's violation or breach of any warranty, representation, agreement or obligation hereunder.

10. Insurance.

    a. Licensee shall acquire and maintain, throughout the term of this Agreement and at its own expense, insurance from an insurance company reasonably approved by Licensor, general liability insurance (including without limitation usual bodily injury and property damage aspects of product liability insurance, contractual liability coverage for all obligations assumed by Licensee hereunder including Licensee's obligations to indemnify Licensor).

    b. This insurance coverage shall be in a form satisfactory to Licensor and in an amount of Three Million Dollars ($3,000,000) combined single limit for bodily injury and property damage. Such insurance coverage shall be primary, not secondary, and shall name Licensor as an additional insured on the policy or policies. Upon request by Licensor, Licensee shall, within fifteen (15) days of such request, furnish to Licensor a certificate of Insurance as evidence of the insurance required hereunder, which certificate shall provide for ten (10) days prior written notice to Licensor in the event of cancellation or material change in such insurance.

11. Expiration, Termination & Disposal of Stock.

a. Upon termination or expiration of the license granted hereby, all rights granted to Licensee hereunder shall forthwith revert to Licensor, which shall be free to license to others the use of the Marks in the Territory, and Licensee will refrain from further use of the Marks or marks deemed by Licensor to be confusingly similar to the Marks, or any further reference to the Marks, direct or indirect, in connection with the operation of the Stores or the manufacture, sale or distribution of Licensee's products, except as provided in paragraph 10.

b. After expiration or termination of this Agreement, Licensee shall have no further right to manufacture, distribute, sell, exploit, or otherwise deal in any Licensed Articles which utilize the Marks except that Licensee may dispose of Licensed Articles which are on hand or in process at the time of expiration or termination so long as the disposal thereof is completed within a period of six (6) months thereafter in accordance with the terms of this Agreement.

12. Assignments, Transfers and Sublicenses.

a. Licensee shall not voluntarily or by operation of law, assign or transfer this Agreement or any of Licensee's rights or duties hereunder (except as specifically provided herein) or any interest of Licensee herein. Licensee may enter into a sublicense for the manufacture of Licensed Products, provided that such sublicense Licensee represents and warrants that it shall comply with Licensor's "Standards for Vendors" and "Manufacture and Vendor Facility Agreement," shall not have previously been found to have violated Licensor's standards, and shall be subject to Licensor's audition procedures and restrictions on uses of the Marks as set forth therein.

b. Licensor shall not voluntarily or by operation of law, assign or transfer this Agreement or any of Licensor's rights or duties hereunder (except as specifically provided herein) or any interest of Licensor herein; provided, however, that any transfer of any interest of Licensor under this Agreement to any entity in which the present owners or controlling shareholders of Licensor have voting control shall be deemed pre-approved under the condition that Licensor shall remain secondarily liable with respect to its obligations hereunder.

13. [Resolution of Disputes.

a. ANY AND ALL DISPUTES HEREUNDER SHALL BE RESOLVED BY ARBITRATION OR REFERENCE. ANY PARTY HERETO ELECTING TO COMMENCE AN ACTION SHALL GIVE WRITTEN NOTICE TO THE OTHER PARTY HERETO. THEREUPON, IF ARBITRATION IS SELECTED BY THE PARTY COMMENCING THE ACTION, THE CLAIM ("ARBITRATION MATTER") SHALL BE SETTLED BY ARBITRATION IN ACCORDANCE WITH THE THEN RULES OF THE AMERICAN ARBITRATION ASSOCIATION ("AAA").

b. The arbitrator or the referee shall diligently pursue determination of any Arbitration under consideration and shall render a decision within one hundred twenty (120) days after the arbitrator or referee is selected. The arbitrator may issue awards of compensatory damages, but shall have no authority to award indirect, incidental, consequential, special, exemplary or punitive damages. The arbitrator shall provide the parties with a written description of the reasons for any award or decision rendered. The determination of the arbitrator on all matters referred to it hereunder shall be final and binding on the parties hereto. The award of such arbitrator may be confirmed or enforced in any court of competent jurisdiction. The referee, arbitrator or its designee shall have full access to such records and physical facilities of the parties hereto as may be required. Each party shall pay for its own costs of arbitration.]

14. Additional Provisions.

a. Further Assurances. The parties hereto shall execute and deliver any and all additional documents and instruments and shall do any and all acts reasonably necessary to give effect to the provisions of this Agreement and the intent of the parties.

b. No Joint Venture. Nothing herein contained shall be construed to place the parties in the relationship of partners or joint venturers, and Licensee shall have no power to obligate or bind Licensor in any manner whatsoever.

c. No Waiver, Etc. None of the terms of this Agreement can be waived or modified except by an express agreement in writing signed by all parties. There are no representations, promises, warranties, covenants or undertakings other than those contained in this Agreement, which represents the entire understanding of the parties. The failure of either party hereto to enforce, or the delay by either party in enforcing, any of its rights under this Agreement shall not be deemed a continuing waiver or a modification thereof and either party may, within the time provided by applicable law, commence appropriate legal proceedings to enforce any or all of such rights. No person, firm, group or corporation other than Licensee or Licensor shall be deemed to have acquired any rights by reason of anything contained in this Agreement.

d. Entire Agreement, Amendments. This Agreement, and the Exhibits attached as a part hereof and incorporated by reference constitute the entire agreement between the parties hereto with respect to the subject matter hereof and supersedes all prior or contemporaneous written or oral agreements between them or any of their affiliates with respect to the subject matter hereof. No change, modification, alteration, amendment, agreement to discharge in whole or in part, abandonment or waiver of any of the terms and conditions of this Agreement shall be binding upon any party, unless same shall be made by written instrument signed and executed by the proper officers of each party, with the same formality as the execution of this Agreement.

e. Notices. Any notice or other communication given hereunder shall be in writing sent certified or registered mail, postage paid return receipt requested, or given in hand sent by a recognized national courier service next day delivery, to each respective party at its home office, or to such other addresses either party shall have theretofore designated by notice hereunder. Any such notice shall be deemed given one day after its sending, at the address listed on the Statement of Work.

f. Counterparts. This Agreement may be executed in one or more counterparts, all of which shall be considered one and the same agreement and shall become effective when one or more counterparts have been signed by each party and delivered to the others.

g. Governing Law. This Agreement shall be governed and construed in accordance with the laws of the State of New Hampshire applicable to agreements made and to be performed entirely within such State.

h. Section Headings. The section headings of this Agreement are for convenience of reference only and shall not be deemed to alter or affect any provision hereof.

i. Severability. If any provision of this Agreement shall be held or deemed to be or shall, in fact, be inoperative or unenforceable as applied in any particular case because it conflicts with any other provision or provisions hereof or any constitution or statute or rule of public policy, or for any other reason, such circumstances shall not have the effect of rendering the provision in question inoperative or unenforceable in any other case or circumstances, or of rendering any other provision or provisions herein contained invalid, inoperative, or unenforceable to any extent whatever. The invalidity of any one or more phrases, sentences, clauses, sections or subsections of this Agreement shall not affect the remaining portions of this Agreement.

IN WITNESS WHEREOF, the parties hereto have duly executed this Agreement as of the day and year first above written.

By: _____

"Licensor"

By: _____

"Licensee"

F. Sample Business Plan:—Business Plan for "Riders, LLC."

Business Plan for "Riders," a Limited Liability Company

1. Executive Summary

Riders, LLC ("Riders" or the "Company") will be formed as a retail sales company featuring individualized, custom, off-road racing cycles as well as bicycle accessories and consumer products. The company will feature the designs of racing specialist Terry Johnson, with business expertise from Guy Salazar and Jane Glenn. A principal investor in the company will be Java Spokes, a Delaware corporation, featuring a chain of upscale coffee houses, wholly owned by Guy Salazar. Each retail location of Riders will be contiguous with a Java Spokes outlet. The marketing will feature significant cross-promotional opportunities between the two ventures.

    a. Objectives

1. Begin retail operations in Laguna Beach, California before June 1, 2006.

2 Profitability by June 30, 2008.

3. Five retail locations by January 1, 2010.

    b. Mission

Riders provides premium custom designed off-road racing bicycles designed by Terry Johnson, first quality cycling parts and service and distinctive branded products, including shirts, sunglasses and riding helmets. The initial focus will be on the development of a retail outlet featuring the branded products. Cross-promotional marketing with Java Spokes will allow for placement of Riders products in retail stores throughout the country. The personal services of Terry Johnson will promote both companies and all product lines.

    c. Keys to Success

1. Pre-existing market identification with Terry Johnson.

2. Pre-existing market for premium cycles.

3. Cross-licensing opportunities with Java Rider to sell T-shirts, sunglasses and coffee items branded with the Riders designs.

4. Ability to sell through existing Java Spokes network of 27 retail outlets in Florida, California, Arizona and Nevada.

2. Business Activities: Product & Services

Riders is a start-up retail company featuring premium, custom-built off-road racing cycles designed by Terry Johnson. Johnson is a world-class off-road racer with three world titles. Through the name recognition of Johnson and the unique cross-licensing of merchandising with Riders principle investor, Java Spokes, the Company will gain access to a nationwide distribution channel while still in operation of its initial retail outlet.

- The name recognition and market recognition of the titles earned by Johnson provides significant credibility within the primary target audience.

- Each location will be adjacent to a Java Spokes outlet, a principal partner with Riders.

- The operations of each retail outlet will generate sufficient revenue from part sales and product sales (T-shirts, sunglasses and other brand merchandize) to generate positive net results.

- Web and related marketing will support the Terry Johnson designs, the Internet sales of goods and the locations of Java Spokes retail outlets. Java Spokes will cross-link and promote the Riders goods.

Each aspect of the business is intended to be self-sufficient in terms of costs and revenue. These components, described more fully below, augment each other by building market dominance in each of these niche markets.

a. Services to be Offered

- The company will begin with a single retail store in Laguna Beach, California.

- The company will offer premium cycle design and construction targeted at the premium sports market.

- The company will offer quality, guaranteed service and repair for premium cycles.

b. Product Description

- The company will sell top quality cycling equipment and accessories. As market dominance increases, the company will sell these products under its own brand name.

- The company will sell consumer products (T-shirts, sunglasses, Frisbee-style flying discs, etc.) under the company brand name to increase store traffic and brand awareness.

- The company will sell consumer products to Java Spokes for re-sale at all locations, other than those with a company retail outlet, to further promote brand awareness.

3. Market and Competitive Positioning

Riders is organized to take maximum advantage of the popularity of extreme sports and use the coffee-house market to reach older customers. Serving the 18-34 age market with a high quality core product line, an exclusive relationship with a premiere performer in the market and a strong distribution channel though the coffee-house marketplace provide a unique opportunity to enter the market and quickly dominate the field.

- The rise of "extreme" sports and the popularity of nontraditional athletics has continued unabated. Snowboarding has taken a place in the Olympic pantheon and BMX trick riding and dirt bikes have grown in viewership and popularity.

- A similar trend can be seen in the coffee house market. The availability of wireless Internet services has transformed these spaces into campus-like study halls and virtual libraries.

- Starbucks, the leader in the coffee house sector, has pushed their non-coffee related products to an older demographic with the launch of jazz CDs and similar items.

    a. Target Market

    The company will focus on selling custom-built bicycles to an affluent 18- to 34-year-old male target audience. All other products will be geared towards related markets, such as male teens.

    b. Competitive Comparison

- The cycle market is highly segmented with few companies selling in the premium market and none selling on a national level. Schwinn is the largest bicycle seller, but has little impact on the premium market. Although the discount market (sold through Walmart, K-Mart, Target, Sears and JCPenney) is highly competitive with low margins, no such market exists for premium cycles.

- The "cultural" sales of cutting-edge dangerous sports, the intersection of MTV, ESPN & ESPN2 sensibilities are visible in apparel industries. A similar trend exists in the coffee house phenomenon, best capitalized by Starbucks involving the next age group of consumers. Other national chains include Deidrichs, Java Spokes and Caribou Coffee. Very little differentiation exists between these companies, and as a result the market has become saturated. The strategic alliance between Riders and Java Spokes, a general partner of the company, serves to enhance the market dominance of each company in its segment with little direct competition or overlap.

- Sales of consumer products (T-shirts, sunglasses, Frisbee-style flying discs, etc.) have expanded in every market. These are high profit margin products which further increase brand dominance. In heavy tourist areas such as beach-front communities, the sales of these products tend to outpace other products on a sales-per-square-foot basis. These sales are enhanced by similar products (of other brands) sold in the same area.

c. Sales Literature & Advertising

The company will develop a distinctive trademark and brand look. The company will emphasize its marketing in cycling magazines and through sponsorship of Internet resources featuring the same market demographic as the company. The company will also utilize cooperative advertising with Java Spokes. Both companies will seek to develop sponsorships with additional leading athletes in the field. Over time, the Company will emphasize Johnson's role as a leading designer of competitive equipment, leveraging his fame as a competitor into success for the broader business.

d. Sourcing

Parts and brand-name products are available from a variety of sources, so the company will not be unduly constrained by difficulties in purchasing supplies.

e. Future Services

The costs of multiple locations will decrease the total cost of operation per store because the marketing costs and the brand-name products will remain substantially constant. Each location will be selected for high traffic from the local population, good tourist potential and proper market demographics. This should add to the company's net revenues. As a result, future expansion should include:

- Addition of retail outlets in locations such as Orlando, Phoenix, San Francisco, Tucson, Las Vegas, Boston, or Virginia Beach.

- Sponsorship of national competitions in off-road cycling and other cutting-edge high-risk sports.

- Addition of retail opportunities in locations not covered by Java Spokes.

- Addition of brand-name cycling products and accessories.

4. Strategy & Implementation

    a. Pricing Strategy

The company will be priced at the upper edge of what the market will bear, competing with other premium sales company. The pricing fits with the company's positioning to provide high-level products and services. Individual cycle designs will be based on an estimated hourly rate for the designers, led by Terry Johnson, with an anticipated range of $3,000 to $5,000 per cycle.

    b. Sales Forecast

The management will provide a monthly summary sales forecast.

    c. Strategic Alliances

The company will begin with a joint marketing agreement with Java Spokes. Terry Johnson will serve as a central personality for both companies to better integrate the joint marketing strategy. The company will also seek out strategic alliances with premium cycling manufactures for exclusive sales agreements, retail outlets (such as GAP or other premium retail clothiers) for sales of clothing products and appropriate media companies (MTV, ESPN2) for product placement and coverage.

5. Company Summary

    a. Company Ownership

Riders is a limited liability company. The current members are Terry Johnson, an individual, Java Spokes, a Delaware corporation, and Jane Glenn, an individual. The managers are Guy Salazar, Terry Johnson and Jane Glenn.

The Company anticipates selling membership interests equal to 45% of the ownership for non-manager members pursuant to the Riders LLC Limited Liability Company Operating Agreement ("Operating Agreement").

The partnership interests are as follows:

Java Spokes   20%

Terry Johnson   20%

Jane Glenn   15%

Held for sale   45%

b. Start-up Summary

Total start-up expense (including legal costs, logo design, stationery and related expenses) comes to $100,000. Start-up assets required include $100,000 in assets (store fixtures, etc.) and $50,000 in initial cash to handle the first purchase of inventory and allow for sales to generate positive cash flow. The details are included in Table 2-2.

c. Company Locations & Facilities

The company is currently in lease negotiations to acquire 8,000 square feet on Pacific Coast Highway. To reduce the cost of the retail space, the store-front space will be leased to Java Spokes, with access to Riders through the Java Spokes facility. Riders will be a sub-tenant of Java Spokes.

6. Management

a. Organizational Structure

The company is a general partnership with three key participants.

- Java Spokes, a Delaware corporation—provides capital, strategic planning and retail sales expertise. Guy Salazar, CEO of Java Spokes will act on behalf of the corporation.

- Terry Johnson -- world champion cyclist and top off-road cycle designer.

- Jane Glenn—C.P.A., expert business planner.

b. Management Team

Each of the three general partners will serve a significant role in managing the company. As the company grows, additional management will be added to expand the operations of the company.

- Terry Johnson will serve as CEO, responsible for day-to-day operations of the retail outlet and supervision of personnel. He will also act as company Spokesman and be available for participation in all marketing campaigns.

- Jane Glenn will serve as CFO, responsible for financial planning and operations.

- Guy Salazar (or his nominee) will provide the marketing and strategic planning services for the company.

c. Key Agreements

- Through a Joint Distribution Agreement between the company and Java Spokes, Java Spokes will provide retail marketing and strategic planning.

- Terry Johnson will appear in print and broadcast advertising for both the company and Java Spokes.

d. Personnel Plan

The retail outlet will include a cycle mechanic and sufficient counter staff to provide ongoing service, under the supervision of Johnson. Each additional retail outlet will be similarly staffed. Marketing does not require staff, because these services are outsourced to Java Spokes under the Joint Distribution Agreement.

e. Decision Making Process of Management

The decision making process of management is set forth in the Operating Agreement.

7. Key Risks and Risk Mitigation Strategy

The primary risk associated with the Company is the reliance on Terry Johnson for promotion and product development. Riders has attempted to mitigate this risk through an employment agreement which provides Johnson's services to Riders on an exclusive basis, includes financial incentives to align Johnson's interests with that of the Company and requires that Johnson indemnify the company for any material breach of his duty to the Company or his intentional misconduct or act of moral turpitude that brings Riders into disrepute. Key man insurance will also be carried to protect the Company in the event of an untimely death or the incapacity of Johnson.

A second risk is the reliance on performance by Java Spokes in the cross-licensing of the Company trademarks and sales of Riders branded goods. This risk has been mitigated through an express cross-licensing agreement which specifies the obligations of the parties and provides for a five-year minimum term and a one-year, post-contract noncompetition clause that prohibits Java Spokes from entering into a cross-licensing agreement with a BMX bike related manufacturer, distributor or retailer. Since the agreement has a similar prohibition, limiting Riders from entering into cross-licensing agreements for one year following the termination of the Java Spokes agreement in those markets where Java Spokes has retail operations, both parties must seek to maintain an effective arrangement.

A third risk is the inability to develop a strong reputation for business in custom bike design. Although this is a small part of the financial plan, success in this field will support the expansion in all other markets, particularly if these bikes are successful in competition. The Company may be compelled to provide competitive bikes at significant discount or for free to create a demand and presence in the field.

8. Financial Plan

The partnership will be formed using capital provided by Java Spokes and Jane Glenn and long-term debt provided by Java Spokes. Short-term debt will be sought though a commercial line of credit.

a. Balance Sheet

The partnership shall use capital provided by Java Spokes and Jane Glenn to start up the company. Terry Johnson will receive an equity interest in the partnership equal to his personal services for agreeing to serve as Spokesperson for the company and for Java Spokes.

In addition, Java Spokes will provide a long-term (ten-year) secured note for $_____ to provide adequate start-up capital and cash until the company achieves profitability.

The total Assets of the company (combination of equity and debt) is $350,000.

b. Equity Stakes

• Java Spokes ___%

- Jane Glenn ____%
- Terry Johnson ____%

c. Projected Income & Expense Report

...

G. Additional Resources: Reprinted Federal Governmental Materials.

As with other U.S. federal governmental works, the materials reprinted below are not protected by U.S. Copyright and reprinted without the need to obtain permission. Be aware, however, that works written by third parties for use by the U.S. government may be protected by copyright. The same statute does not automatically apply to the states. While the policy which bars the federal government from claiming or asserting copyright applies equally to individual states, the law barring copyright authorship does not extend to state governments and care must be taken when reproducing such materials.

1. Business Plan Basics from the United States Small Business Administration.

http://www.sba.gov/starting_business/planning/basic.html

Additional training programs and information is available from the U.S. Small Business Administration at:
http://www.sba.gov/training/courses.html#busplan.

Business Plan Basics

A business plan precisely defines your business, identifies your goals, and serves as your firm's resume. The basic components include a current and pro forma balance sheet, an income statement, and a cash flow analysis. It helps you allocate resources properly, handle unforeseen complications, and make good business decisions. Because it provides specific and organized information about your company and how you will repay borrowed money, a good business plan is a crucial part of any loan application. Additionally, it informs sales personnel, suppliers, and others about your operations and goals.

Plan Your Work

The importance of a comprehensive, thoughtful business plan cannot be overemphasized. Much hinges on it: outside funding, credit from suppliers, management of your operation and finances, promotion and marketing of your business, and achievement of your goals and objectives.

"The business plan is a necessity. If the person who wants to start a small business can't put a business plan together, he or she is in trouble," says Robert Krummer, Jr., chairman of First Business Bank in Los Angeles.

Despite the critical importance of a business plan, many entrepreneurs drag their feet when it comes to preparing a written document. They argue that their marketplace changes too fast for a business plan to be useful or that they just don't have enough time. But just as a builder won't begin construction without a blueprint, eager business owners shouldn't rush into new ventures without a business plan.

Before you begin writing your business plan, consider four core questions:

- What service or product does your business provide and what needs does it fill?

- Who are the potential customers for your product or service and why will they purchase it from you?

- How will you reach your potential customers?

- Where will you get the financial resources to start your business?

Writing the Plan

What goes in a business plan? The body can be divided into four distinct sections:

1) Description of the business

2) Marketing

3) Finances

4) Management

Addenda should include an executive summary, supporting documents, and financial projections.

Although there is no single formula for developing a business plan, some elements are common to all business plans. They are summarized in the following outline:

Elements of a Business Plan

1. Cover sheet

2. Statement of purpose

3. Table of contents

I. The Business

    A. Description of business

    B. Marketing

    C. Competition

    D. Operating procedures

    E. Personnel

    F. Business insurance

II. Financial Data

    A. Loan applications

    B. Capital equipment and supply list

    C. Balance sheet

    D. Breakeven analysis

    E. Pro-forma income projections (profit & loss statements)

- Three-year summary

- Detail by month, first year

- Detail by quarters, second and third years

- Assumptions upon which projections were based

    F. Pro-forma cash flow

III. Supporting Documents

- Tax returns of principals for last three years Personal financial statement (all banks have these forms)

- For franchised businesses, a copy of franchise contract and all supporting documents provided by the franchisor

- Copy of proposed lease or purchase agreement for building space

- Copy of licenses and other legal documents

- Copy of resumes of all principals

- Copies of letters of intent from suppliers, etc.

Sample Plans

One of the best ways to learn about writing a business plan is to study the plans of established businesses in your industry.

Review examples of real business plans. Those are available at http://www.bplans.com/sp/businessplans.cfm (a source outside of the U.S. Small Business Administration).

Using the Plan

A business plan is a tool with three basic purposes: communication, management, and planning.

As a communication tool, it is used to attract investment capital, secure loans, convince workers to hire on, and assist in attracting strategic business partners. The development of a comprehensive business plan shows whether or not a business has the potential to make a profit. It requires a realistic look at almost every phase of business and allows you to show that you have worked out all the problems and decided on potential alternatives before actually launching your business.

As a management tool, the business plan helps you track, monitor and evaluate your progress. The business plan is a living document that you will modify as you gain knowledge and experience. By using your business plan to establish timelines and milestones, you can gauge your progress and compare your projections to actual accomplishments.

As a planning tool, the business plan guides you through the various phases of your business. A thoughtful plan will help identify roadblocks and obstacles so that you can avoid them and establish alternatives. Many business owners share their business plans with their employees to foster a broader understanding of where the business is going.

2. Trademark FAQ (select answers from the Patent and Trademark Office).[279]

What is a trademark?

A trademark includes any word, name, symbol, or device, or any combination, used, or intended to be used, in commerce to identify and distinguish the goods of one manufacturer or seller from goods manufactured or sold by others, and to indicate the source of the goods. In short, a trademark is a brand name.

What is a service mark?

A service mark is any word, name, symbol, device, or any combination, used, or intended to be used, in commerce, to identify and distinguish the services of one provider from services provided by others, and to indicate the source of the services.

What is a certification mark?

A certification mark is any word, name, symbol, device, or any combination, used, or intended to be used, in commerce with the owner's permission by someone other than its owner, to certify regional or other geographic origin, material, mode of manufacture, quality, accuracy, or other characteristics of someone's goods or services, or that the work or labor on the goods or services was performed by members of a union or other organization.

What is a collective mark?

A collective mark is a trademark or service mark used, or intended to be used, in commerce, by the members of a cooperative, an association, or other collective group or organization, including a mark which indicates membership in a union, an association, or other organization.

---

[279] *See Trademark FAQs*, U.S. PATENT & TRADEMARK OFFICE, https://www.uspto.gov/learning-and-resources/trademark-faqs#type-browse-faqs (last visited June 30, 2018).

Do I have to register my trademark?

No, but federal registration has several advantages, including notice to the public of the registrant's claim of ownership of the mark, a legal presumption of ownership nationwide, and the exclusive right to use the mark on or in connection with the goods or services set forth in the registration.

What are the benefits of federal trademark registration?

1. Constructive notice nationwide of the trademark owner's claim.

2. Evidence of ownership of the trademark.

3. Jurisdiction of federal courts may be invoked.

4. Registration can be used as a basis for obtaining registration in foreign countries.

5. Registration may be filed with U.S. Customs Service to prevent importation of infringing foreign goods.

Do I have to be a U.S. Citizen to obtain a federal registration?

No. However, an applicant's citizenship must be set forth in the record. If an applicant is not a citizen of any country, then a statement to that effect is sufficient. If an applicant has dual citizenship, then the applicant must choose which citizenship will be printed in the Official Gazette and on the certificate of registration.

Where can I find trademark forms?

You can access forms through the Trademark Electronic Application System (TEAS), at http://www.uspto.gov/teas/index.html. TEAS can be used to file an application for registration of a mark, response to examining attorney's [Trademark] Office action, notice of change of address, amendment to allege use, statement of use, request for extension of time to file a statement of use, affidavit of continued use under 15 U.S.C. §1058, affidavit of incontestability under 15 U.S.C. §1065, combined affidavit under 15 U.S.C. §§1058 and 1065, or combined filing under 15 U.S.C. §§1058 and 1059. Additional forms may be available through the Trademark Assistance Center at 1-800-786-9199 (or 571-272-9250).

Where can I get basic trademark information?

The USPTO website at http://www.uspto.gov/main/trademarks.htm provides a wide variety of information about trademarks and offers electronic filing of trademark applications and other trademark documents. The Trademark Electronic Business Center contains all the information needed for the entire registration process. You can search the trademark database for conflicting marks using the Trademark Electronic Search System (TESS), at http://tess2.uspto.gov/bin/gate.exe?f=login&p_lang=english&p_d=trmk, file applications and other trademark documents online using the Trademark Electronic Application System (TEAS), at http://www.uspto.gov/teas/index.html, and check the status of applications and registrations through the Trademark Applications and Registrations Retrieval (TARR) database at http://tarr.uspto.gov.

For information about applying for a trademark, click **Basic Facts About Trademarks**. If you need answers to specific trademark questions, please contact the Trademark Assistance Center at 1-800-786-9199 (or 571-272-9250).

For patent information, please contact the Inventors Assistance Center at 1-800-786-9199. If you live in Northern Virginia, the number is (703) 308-4357.

Are there federal regulations governing the use of the designations "TM" or "SM" with trademarks?

No. Use of the symbols "TM" or "SM" (for trademark and service mark, respectively) may, however, be governed by local, state, or foreign laws and the laws of the pertinent jurisdiction must be consulted. These designations usually indicate that a party claims rights in the mark and are often used before a federal registration is issued.

When is it proper to use the federal registration symbol (the letter R enclosed within a circle -- ® -- with the mark?

The federal registration symbol may be used once the mark is actually registered in the U.S. Patent and Trademark Office. Even though an application is pending, the registration symbol may not be used before the mark has actually become registered. The federal registration symbol should only be used on goods or services that are the subject of the federal trademark registration. [Note: Several foreign countries use the letter R enclosed within a circle to indicate that a mark is registered in that country. Use of the symbol by the holder of a foreign registration may be proper.]

Do I need an attorney to file a trademark application?

No, although it may be desirable to employ an attorney who is familiar with trademark matters. An applicant must comply with all substantive and procedural requirements of the Trademark Act and Trademark Rules of Practice even if he or she is not represented by an attorney. The names of attorneys who specialize in trademark law may be found in the telephone yellow pages, or by contacting a local bar association. Trademark search firms are often listed in the yellow pages under the heading "Trademark Search Services" or "Patent and Trademark Search Services." The USPTO cannot aid in the selection of a search firm or an attorney.

3. Fair Use—Copyright Circular 102.[280]

One of the rights accorded to the owner of copyright is the right to reproduce or to authorize others to reproduce the work in copies or phonorecords. This right is subject to certain limitations found in sections 107 through 118 of the copyright act (title 17, U.S. Code). One of the more important limitations is the doctrine of "fair use." Although fair use was not mentioned in the previous copyright law, the doctrine has developed through a substantial number of court decisions over the years. This doctrine has been codified in section 107 of the copyright law.

Section 107 contains a list of the various purposes for which the reproduction of a particular work may be considered "fair," such as criticism, comment, news reporting, teaching, scholarship, and research.

---

[280] Circular 102 is no longer published by the Copyright Office. *See further* https://www.copyright.gov/fair-use/more-info.html.

Section 107 also sets out four factors to be considered in determining whether or not a particular use is fair:

1. the purpose and character of the use, including whether such use is of commercial nature or is for nonprofit educational purposes;
2. the nature of the copyrighted work;
3. amount and substantiality of the portion used in relation to the copyrighted work as a whole; and
4. the effect of the use upon the potential market for or value of the copyrighted work.

The distinction between "fair use" and infringement may be unclear and not easily defined. There is no specific number of words, lines, or notes that may safely be taken without permission. Acknowledging the source of the copyrighted material does not substitute for obtaining permission.

The 1961 *Report of the Register of Copyrights on the General Revision of the U.S. Copyright Law* cites examples of activities that courts have regarded as fair use: "quotation of excerpts in a review or criticism for purposes of illustration or comment; quotation of short passages in a scholarly or technical work, for illustration or clarification of the author's observations; use in a parody of some of the content of the work parodied; summary of an address or article, with brief quotations, in a news report; reproduction by a library of a portion of a work to replace part of a damaged copy; reproduction by a teacher or student of a small part of a work to illustrate a lesson; reproduction of a work in legislative or judicial proceedings or reports; incidental and fortuitous reproduction, in a newsreel or broadcast, of a work located in the scene of an event being reported."

Copyright protects the particular way an author has expressed himself; it does not extend to any ideas, systems, or factual information conveyed in the work. The safest course is always to get permission from the copyright owner before using copyrighted material. The Copyright Office cannot give this permission.

When it is impracticable to obtain permission, use of copyrighted material should be avoided unless the doctrine of "fair use" would clearly apply to the situation. The Copyright Office can neither determine if a certain use may be considered "fair" nor advise on possible copyright violations. If there is any doubt, it is advisable to consult an attorney.

FL-102, Revised December 2005

H. Regulations for Crowdfunding: A Small Entity Compliance Guide for Issuers

This summary of employment practices is reproduced and compiled from the *U.S. Securities and Exchange Commission* (SEC). Regulation Crowdfunding: A Small Entity Compliance Guide for Issuers first published May 13, 2016. As a government-authored work, the original work is not protected by copyright. The text may be found at https://www.sec.gov/info/smallbus/secg/rccomplianceguide-051316.htm.

1. Introduction

Under the Securities Act of 1933, the offer and sale of securities must be registered unless an exemption from registration is available. Title III of the Jumpstart Our Business Start-ups (JOBS) Act of 2012 added Securities Act Section 4(a)(6) that provides an exemption from registration for certain crowdfunding transactions.[2] In 2015, the Commission adopted Regulation Crowdfunding to implement the requirements of Title III.[3] Under the rules, eligible companies will be allowed to raise capital using Regulation Crowdfunding starting May 16, 2016.

2. Requirements **of** Regulation Crowdfunding

In order to rely on the Regulation Crowdfunding exemption, certain requirements must be met.

a. Maximum Offering Amount of $1 Million

A company issuing securities in reliance on Regulation Crowdfunding (an "issuer") is permitted to raise a maximum aggregate amount of $1 million in a 12-month period. In determining the amount that may be sold in a particular offering, an issuer should count:

- The amount it has already sold (including amounts sold by entities controlled by, or under common control with, the issuer, as well as any amounts sold by any predecessor of the issuer) in reliance on Regulation Crowdfunding during the 12-month period preceding the expected date of sale, plus

- The amount the issuer intends to raise in reliance on Regulation Crowdfunding in this offering.

- An issuer does not aggregate amounts sold in other exempt (non-crowdfunding) offerings during the preceding 12-month period for purposes of determining the amount that may be sold in a particular Regulation Crowdfunding offering.

b. Investors Subject to Limits

Individual investors are limited in the amounts they are allowed to invest in all Regulation Crowdfunding offerings over the course of a 12-month period:

- If either of an investor's annual income or net worth is less than $100,000, then the investor's investment limit is the greater of:

- $2,000 or 5 percent of the lesser of the investor's annual income or net worth.

- If both annual income and net worth are equal to or more than $100,000, then the investor's limit is 10 percent of the lesser of their annual income or net worth.

- During the 12-month period, the aggregate amount of securities sold to an investor through all Regulation Crowdfunding offerings may not exceed $100,000, regardless of the investor's annual income or net worth.

- Spouses are allowed to calculate their net worth and annual income jointly. This chart illustrates a few examples of the investment limits:

Investor Annual Income	Investor Net Worth	Calculation	Investment Limit[4]
$30,000	$105,000	Greater of $2,000 or 5% of $30,000 ($1,500)	$2,000
$150,000	$80,000	Greater of $2,000 or 5% of $80,000 ($4,000)	$4,000
$150,000	$100,000	10% of $100,000 ($10,000)	$10,000
$200,000	$900,000	10% of $200,000 ($20,000)	$20,000
$1,200,000	$2,000,000	10% of $1,200,000 ($120,000), subject to $100,000 cap	$100,000

c. Transactions Conducted Through an Intermediary

Each Regulation Crowdfunding offering must be exclusively conducted through one online platform. The intermediary operating the platform must be a broker-dealer or a funding portal that is registered with the SEC and FINRA.

Issuers may rely on the efforts of the intermediary to determine that the aggregate amount of securities purchased by an investor does not cause the investor to exceed the investment limits, so long as the issuer does not have knowledge that the investor would exceed the investment limits as a result of purchasing securities in the issuer's offering.

d. Eligibility

Certain companies are not eligible to use the Regulation Crowdfunding exemption. These include:

- Non-U.S. companies;

- Companies that already are Exchange Act reporting companies;

- Certain investment companies;

- Companies that are disqualified under Regulation Crowdfunding's disqualification rules;

- Companies that have failed to comply with the annual reporting requirements under Regulation Crowdfunding during the two years immediately preceding the filing of the offering statement; and

- Companies that have no specific business plan or have indicated their business plan is to engage in a merger or acquisition with an unidentified company or companies.

3. Disclosure by Issuers

a. Form C

Any issuer conducting a Regulation Crowdfunding offering must electronically file its offering statement on Form C through the Commission's Electronic Data Gathering, Analysis and Retrieval (EDGAR) system and with the intermediary facilitating the crowdfunding offering. A Form C cover page will be generated when the issuer provides information in XML-based fillable text boxes on the EDGAR system. Other required disclosure that is not requested in the XML text boxes must be filed as attachments to Form C. There is not a specific presentation format required for the attachments to Form C; however, the form does include an optional "Question and Answer" format that issuers may use to provide the disclosures that are required but not included in the XML portion.

b. Offering Statement Disclosure

The instructions to Form C indicate the information that an issuer must disclose, including:

- Information about officers, directors, and owners of 20 percent or more of the issuer;

- A description of the issuer's business and the use of proceeds from the offering;

- The price to the public of the securities or the method for determining the price;

- The target offering amount and the deadline to reach the target offering amount;

- Whether the issuer will accept investments in excess of the target offering amount;

- Certain related-party transactions; and

- A discussion of the issuer's financial condition and financial statements.

- The financial statements requirements are based on the amount offered and sold in reliance on Regulation Crowdfunding within the preceding 12-month period:

- For issuers offering $100,000 or less: Financial statements of the issuer and certain information from the issuer's federal income tax returns, both certified by the principal executive officer. If, however, financial statements of the issuer are available that have either been reviewed or audited by a public accountant that is independent of the issuer, the issuer must provide those financial statements instead and will not need to include the information reported on the federal income tax returns or the certification of the principal executive officer.

- Issuers offering more than $100,000 but not more than $500,000: Financial statements reviewed by a public accountant that is independent of the issuer. If, however, financial statements of the issuer are available that have been audited by a public accountant that is independent of the issuer, the issuer must provide those financial statements instead and will not need to include the reviewed financial statements.

- Issuers offering more than $500,000:

  - For first-time Regulation Crowdfunding issuers: Financial statements reviewed by a public accountant that is independent of the issuer, unless financial statements of the issuer are available that have been audited by an independent auditor.

- <u>For issuers that have previously sold securities in reliance on Regulation Crowdfunding</u>: Financial statements audited by a public accountant that is independent of the issuer.

c. Amendments to Offering Statement

For any offering that has not yet been completed or terminated, an issuer can file on Form C/A an amendment to its offering statement to disclose changes, additions or updates to information. An amendment is required for changes, additions or updates that are material, and in those required instances the issuer must reconfirm outstanding investment commitments within 5 business days, or the investor's commitment will be considered cancelled.

d. Progress Updates

An issuer must provide an update on its progress toward meeting the target offering amount within 5 business days after reaching 50% and 100% of its target offering amount. These updates will be filed on Form C-U. If the issuer will accept proceeds over the target offering amount, it also must file a final Form C-U reflecting the total amount of securities sold in the offering. If, however, the intermediary provides frequent updates on its platform regarding the progress of the issuer in meeting the target offering amount, then the issuer will need to file only a final Form C-U to disclose the total amount of securities sold in the offering.

e. Annual Reports

An issuer that sold securities in a Regulation Crowdfunding offering is required to provide an annual report on Form C-AR no later than 120 days after the end of its fiscal year. The report must be filed on EDGAR and posted on the issuer's website. The annual report requires information similar to what is required in the offering statement, although neither an audit nor a review of the financial statements is required. Issuers must comply with the annual reporting requirement until one of the following occurs:

(1) The issuer is required to file reports under Exchange Act Sections 13(a) or 15(d);

(2) The issuer has filed at least one annual report and has fewer than 300 holders of record;

(3) The issuer has filed at least three annual reports and has total assets that do not exceed $10 million;

(4) The issuer or another party purchases or repurchases all of the securities issued pursuant to Regulation Crowdfunding, including any payment in full of debt securities or any complete redemption of redeemable securities; or

(5) The issuer liquidates or dissolves in accordance with state law.

Any issuer terminating its annual reporting obligations is required to file notice on Form C-TR reporting that it will no longer provide annual reports pursuant to the requirements of Regulation Crowdfunding.

4. Limits on Advertising and Promoters

An issuer may not advertise the terms of a Regulation Crowdfunding offering except in a notice that directs investors to the intermediary's platform and includes no more than the following information:

- A statement that the issuer is conducting an offering pursuant to Section 4(a)(6) of the Securities Act, the name of the intermediary through which the offering is being conducted, and a link directing the potential investor to the intermediary's platform;

- The terms of the offering, which means the amount of securities offered, the nature of the securities, the price of the securities, and the closing date of the offering period; and

- Factual information about the legal identity and business location of the issuer, limited to the name of the issuer of the security, the address, phone number, and website of the issuer, the e-mail address of a representative of the issuer, and a brief description of the business of the issuer.

- Although advertising the terms of the offering off of the intermediary's platform is limited to a brief notice, an issuer may communicate with investors and potential investors about the terms of the offering through communication channels provided on the intermediary's platform. An issuer must identify itself as the issuer and persons acting on behalf of the issuer must identify their affiliation with the issuer in all communications on the intermediary's platform.

An issuer is allowed to compensate others to promote its crowdfunding offerings through communication channels provided by an intermediary, but only if the issuer takes reasonable steps to ensure that the promoter clearly discloses the compensation with each communication.

5. Restrictions on Resale

Securities purchased in a crowdfunding transaction generally cannot be resold for a period of one year, unless the securities are transferred:

- To the issuer of the securities;

- To an "accredited investor";

- As part of an offering registered with the Commission; or

- To a member of the family of the purchaser or the equivalent, to a trust controlled by the purchaser, to a trust created for the benefit of a member of the family of the purchaser or the equivalent, or in connection with the death or divorce of the purchaser or other similar circumstance.

6. Exemption from Section 12(g)

Section 12(g) of the Exchange Act requires an issuer with total assets of more than $10 million and a class of securities held of record by either 2,000 persons, or 500 persons who are not accredited investors, to register that class of securities with the Commission. However, securities issued pursuant to Regulation Crowdfunding are conditionally exempted from the record holder count under Section 12(g) if the following conditions are met:

- The issuer is current in its ongoing annual reports required pursuant to Regulation Crowdfunding;

- Has total assets as of the end of its last fiscal year of $25 million or less; and

- Has engaged the services of a transfer agent registered with the SEC.

As a result, Section 12(g) registration is required if an issuer has, on the last day of its fiscal year, total assets greater than $25 million and the class of equity securities is held by more than 2,000 persons, or 500 persons who are not accredited investors. In that circumstance, an issuer is granted a two-year transition period before it is required to register its class of securities pursuant to Section 12(g), so long as it timely files all of the annual reports required by Regulation Crowdfunding during such period.

An issuer seeking to exclude a person from the record holder count of Section 12(g) is responsible for demonstrating that the securities held by the person were initially issued in an offering made under Section 4(a)(6).

7. Bad Actor Disqualification

Rule 503 of Regulation Crowdfunding includes "bad actor" disqualification provisions that disqualify offerings if the issuer or other "covered persons" have experienced a disqualifying event, such as being convicted of, or subject to court or administrative sanctions for, securities fraud or other violations of specified laws.

a. Covered Persons

Understanding the categories of persons that are covered by Rule 503 is important because issuers are required to conduct a factual inquiry to determine whether any covered person has had a disqualifying event, and the existence of such an event will generally disqualify the offering from reliance on Regulation Crowdfunding.

"Covered persons" include:

- The issuer, including its predecessors and affiliated issuers;

- Directors, officers, general partners or managing members of the issuer;

- Beneficial owners of 20% or more of the issuer's outstanding voting equity securities, calculated on the basis of voting power;

- Promoters connected with the issuer in any capacity at time of sale; and

- Persons compensated for soliciting investors, including the general partners, directors, officers or managing members of any such solicitor.

b. Disqualifying Events

Under the final rule, disqualifying events include:

- Certain criminal convictions;

- Certain court injunctions and restraining orders;

- Certain final orders of certain state and federal regulators;

- Certain SEC disciplinary orders;

- Certain SEC cease-and-desist orders;

- Suspension or expulsion from membership in a self-regulatory organization (SRO), such as FINRA, or being barred from association with an SRO member;

- SEC stop orders and orders suspending the Regulation A exemption; and

- U.S. Postal Service false representation orders.

Many disqualifying events include a look-back period (for example, a court injunction that was issued within the last five years or a regulatory order that was issued within the last ten years). The look-back period is measured from the date of the disqualifying event—for example, the issuance of the injunction or regulatory order and not the date of the underlying conduct that led to the disqualifying event—to the date of the filing of an offering statement.

Disqualification will not arise as a result of disqualifying events relating to any conviction, order, judgment, decree, suspension, expulsion or bar that occurred before May 16, 2016, the effective date of Regulation Crowdfunding. Matters that existed before the effective date of Regulation Crowdfunding, are still within the relevant look-back period, and would otherwise be disqualifying are, however, required to be disclosed in the issuer's offering statement.

c. Exceptions and Waivers

Regulation Crowdfunding provides an exception from disqualification when the issuer is able to demonstrate that it did not know and, in the exercise of reasonable care, could not have known that a covered person with a disqualifying event participated in the offering.

The steps an issuer should take to exercise reasonable care will vary according to particular facts and circumstances. An instruction to the rule states that an issuer will not be able to establish that it has exercised reasonable care unless it has made, in light of the circumstances, factual inquiry into whether any disqualifications exist.

Disqualification will not arise if, before the filing of the offering statement, the court or regulatory authority that entered the relevant order, judgment or decree advises in writing—whether in the relevant judgment, order or decree or separately to the Commission or its staff—that disqualification under Regulation Crowdfunding should not arise as a consequence of such order, judgment or decree.

Regulation Crowdfunding also provides for the ability to seek waivers from disqualification by the Commission upon a showing of good cause that it is not necessary under the circumstances that the exemption be denied.

8. Other Resources

The adopting release Regulation Crowdfunding can be found on the SEC's website at http://www.sec.gov/rules/final/2015/33-9974.pdf.

Regulation Crowdfunding (17 CFR 227.100 et seq.) can be accessed through the "Corporation Finance" section of the SEC's website at http://www.sec.gov/divisions/corpfin/ecfrlinks.shtml.

You can also submit complaints or tips about possible securities laws violations on the SEC's questions and complaints page at http://www.sec.gov/complaint.shtml.

9. Contacting the SEC Staff

The SEC staff is happy to assist with questions regarding Regulation Crowdfunding. For issuer questions, you may contact the Division of Corporation Finance's Office of Small Business Policy using this online request form at or by telephone at (202) 551-3460. For intermediary questions, you may contact the Division of Trading and Markets, Office of Chief Counsel, at (202) 551-5777, or search for your answer in the Small Business Compliance Guide for Intermediaries.

[1] This guide was prepared by the staff of the U.S. Securities and Exchange Commission (the "Commission") as a "small entity

compliance guide" under Section 212 of the Small Business Regulatory Enforcement Fairness Act of 1996, as amended. The guide summarizes and explains the rules adopted by the SEC, but is not a substitute for any rule itself. Only the rule itself can provide complete and definitive information regarding its requirements.

[2] Crowdfunding is a relatively new and evolving method of using the Internet to raise capital to support a wide range of ideas and ventures. An entity or individual raising funds through crowdfunding typically seeks small individual contributions from a large number of people. Individuals interested in the crowdfunding campaign—members of the "crowd"—may share information about the project, cause, idea or business with each other and use the information to decide whether to fund the campaign based on the collective "wisdom of the crowd."

[3] The Regulation Crowdfunding adopting release is available at http://www.sec.gov/rules/final/2015/33-9974.pdf. The staff has also issued a small entity compliance guide concerning registration of funding portals, which is available at http://www.sec.gov/divisions/marketreg /tmcompliance/fpregistrationguide.htm.

[4] This "Investment Limit" column reflects the aggregate investment limit across all Regulation Crowdfunding offerings within a 12-month period.

I. First Edition Summary of Internet Business Models

Although dated, for entrepreneurs who have not considered the components of the Internet business structure, this chapter may be of helpful for those considering how the Internet developed and taxonomy the business models available. It has not been updated to reflect recent changes. Instead, it is a time capsule to the early days of Internet commerce.

The Internet and new technologies have revolutionized the manner in which information is made available to the public. For companies ranging from Internet-only enterprises to restaurants, there is a need to have some form of website presence, because many consumers no longer use telephone books or printed newspapers. Beyond the mere presence on the Internet, however, certain business models are built upon the Internet's unique capabilities. These provide a reference guide to the transformation of information-based businesses.

Although the Internet is described as the site for these business models, the model frequently has been extended to handheld Internet-enabled devices and cellular telephones. The Internet is merely the home base for the wireless communication services growing increasingly common.

These businesses were built around the various uses of the Internet. A recent study on Internet use found that for younger age groups, men and women use the Internet in roughly equal numbers. Some differences in the type of use were noted:

Compared with women, online men are more likely to use the Internet to: check the weather, get news, get do-it-yourself information, check for sports information, get political information, get financial information, do job-related research, download software, listen to music, rate a product/person/service through an online reputation system, download music files, use a webcam, and take a class.

Compared with men, online women are more likely to use the Internet to: send and receive email, get maps and directions, look for health and medical information, use web sites to get support for health or personal problems, and get religious information.[281]

The difference between genders suggests some variations in the services provided by web sites and Internet enterprises. Both genders tend to use the web as a research tool, though for different research goals. As of the 2005 date of the survey, men rely on the Internet as a media tool somewhat more than women.

1. *The Non-Business Model of Content Distribution.*

The most pervasive purpose of websites remains the promotion and marketing of all business activities, primarily those with only brick-and-mortar presences. Almost no business can afford to lose the communication opportunities provided by the Internet. The public increasingly turns to the Internet for its information. The marketing of a business on the Internet is not a business model for the Internet, but another way of communicating. Nonetheless, these sites provide a significant part of the web its content, often highly valuable and useful content that develops affinity between companies and their customers or provides a useful public service function.

The public and nonprofit sectors also embrace the public information aspect of the Internet. Government agencies at the state and federal level have increasingly used the Internet as an effective tool to provide public information. Laws, regulations and published reports on the web have been supplemented with an increasing amount of "how-to" information, FAQ's, and other public service content.

Educational and health institutions have used the Internet to publish or republish academic research, distribute helpful information and to extend the organization's resources to the widest possible audience. The services provided can be profoundly valuable to society. The commercial aspects of the Internet have diluted the presence of governmental, academic and nonprofit sites, but they have not diminished the usefulness of these sites, even if identification of authoritative information sources remains a challenge.

---

[281] Deborah Fallows, Pew Internet & American Life Project, *How Men and Women use the Internet*, ii (Dec. 28, 2005), *available at*
http://www.pewinternet.org/pdfs/PIP_Women_and_Men_online.pdf.

2. Web Portals and Traditional Media Sites.

Web portals are essential information aggregators, collecting content from various sources and organizing it in a useful manner for the subscriber. These sites are generally supported through advertising. Yahoo! was one of the early companies in the field and has remained a strong web presence in both the portal and search arenas.

Portals represented the first commercial success on the Internet. They used technology as a platform to extend traditional media into new space. Media companies such as Fox and Time Warner quickly moved to consolidate their presence and dominate the new medium.

Initially, it seemed that despite the ease with which one could create a website, the traditional media companies would use their portals to dominate the medium. Audience reach was quite limited for smaller companies. Unless the domain name was very intuitive, it was hard for the public to find unfamiliar content. Consolidation among portals arguably threatened to make the Internet look something like the radio spectrum, dominated by large central content producers with only small local competitors filling out the landscape. The rise of the search engines supplanted the need for the portal's Internet taxonomy and burst the bubble of the many media portal endeavors.

Today, specialized portals such as YouTube, iFilm, and atomfilms or podcasting portals provide content organizing services. Yahoo! and MyWay provide centralized home pages for news, games, e-mail and other advertising supported services. Further specialization will result in Spanish-language American portals and perhaps other portals focusing on language, ethnicity, political affiliation and religious preference.

3. Music, Video and Software Delivery Sites.

Napster.com led a revolution in music distribution. Napster was a peer-to-peer system that largely bypassed the direct download model of websites, but websites proliferated to support the peer-to-peer networks, providing the software and knowledge for millions of young music listeners to swap new music and steal commercial music. A series of lawsuits shuttered one peer-to-peer network after another, only to have the next technology update the platform and reset the litigation game board. Although the Supreme Court has removed any doubt that copying and distributing copyrighted music files and film files is illegal theft, an extremely large black market for such distribution remains.

Less well publicized, but structurally the same, peer-to-peer networks also swap illegally copied versions of software, motion pictures, pornography and literature. A second tier of businesses earn income promoting the services ancillary to the actual peer-to-peer networks, and like paraphernalia stores, operate marginally within the bounds of lawful conduct. These sites avoid promoting the illegal conduct while offering any and all services to facilitate the illegal conduct of their users.

4. Newspapers, News Centers and Publishers.

As discussed more fully above, newspapers and publishers are direct content creators that earn revenue through advertisements, and a handful require paid online subscriptions. These companies utilize content for print publications and exploit a second advertising market by making the information available online as well. They differ from portals because they are the source of the information.

Sites operated by news organizations like BBC, CNN and MSNBC are quite robust in their media formats, including radio (streaming broadcasts), video streams, text and photographs. The lines between print publishers and producers of content in other forms continues to shrink as regulations limiting cross-ownership of media weaken and the cost efficiencies of producing content in multiple formats increases.

The direct content providers remain the cornerstone of the commercial Internet. Without the constant creation of new content, the Internet would grow stale and tiresome. Over time, Internet economics will continue to pressure more newspapers out of the industry, and consolidation will begin. Unedited, self-published content cannot sustain the usefulness of the web. While there will always be the occasionally brilliant freelance writer, the process of fact-checking, editing and collaborating invariably generates more refined and more accurate information. The model of advertising-only financial support for these efforts may not be sustainable for long periods of time or for as many content providers as currently exist, and there will be a shake-out that ends this phase of the Internet.

The Internet giants of Google and Yahoo! are beginning to reconcile these competitive outlets for content and advertising, by cross-licensing the advertising revenue and content between the websites and the print publishers. This may be the first stages of a broad reorganization of the print industries as the Internet-based media giants consolidate the industry.

5. Game Sites.

At the conceptual opposite extreme from news publishers, gaming sites create highly popular locations for people to spend their time and money. Game sites range from online versions of board games and computer games to highly sophisticated role-playing virtual communities in which the participants live the lives of their characters in the literary fantasy world of the game designer. Both men and women spend considerable time participating in computer gaming, with 36-37% of the online community playing some games online.[282]

A close analog to the fantasy gaming sites are online gambling sites. Although generally illegal in most states, Internet gaming remains a significant pastime for approximately 4% of the online public.[283] Participants use off-shore accounts and other financial transactions to buy chips and play casino games and card games. The virtual casino is regulated through off-shore laws, if any. Both gaming sites and gambling sites provide a richness of content and interaction that cannot be matched with other media experiences. These effective virtual experiences have real financial consequences and social interactions that occasionally reach beyond the games.

6. Auction Sites.

Auction sites such as eBay provide the ultimate in disintermediation. The technology allows willing buyers and sellers to bid on goods shown through photographs on the site. Buyers and sellers are aligned, the information is made available, the transaction costs are low and the reputation systems provide a measure of self-policing. One vision of future retailing is that all goods will be sold in this fashion. But

---

[282] *Id.* at 40.

[283] *Id.*

consumers are often more interested in certainty and convenience than in the best price. This is demonstrated even on eBay. In many cases, vendors use eBay as a strip mall, with "buy-it-now" sales that essentially ignore the auction functions and instead rely on the consumer traffic to locate potential buyers.

Through the extensive use of reputation systems, the legitimacy of sellers is roughly evaluated. Despite the distance and the risks associated with purchasing goods sold by unknown individuals, auctions are extremely popular with collectors and shoppers.

7. Financial Services Sites.

Closely tied to eBay is PayPal, one of the most successful electronic, Internet-based financial services. PayPal, Cybercheck and Cyphermint are examples of financial services systems that use the ease of information transfer to conduct financial transactions without operating as traditional banks or credit card companies. They accept funds from credit cards or checking accounts and send information to vendors so that the credit card information is not provided to the potentially less trustworthy vendor. Antifraud technology may make the number of fraudulent transactions lower. Less regulatory protection for consumers makes the ability to refuse payment much harder than on credit cards. As a result, both the consumer and the vendor have certain benefit from these services.

These services allow for person-to-person payments that credit cards do not reach. These services also reduce nonpayment risks to vendors and increase the anonymity for the customer, providing legal benefits that some customers value. In addition, since Internet gambling sites, pornography sites and purveyors of questionable legal activity desire to avoid the consumer's protections afforded by credit cards, alternative financial services thrive on this use.

Traditional banking services, credit cards and brokerages also provide their services online. For many of these companies, their website is more convenient for their customers than in store transactions, and the cost of operating the website is substantially lower than the cost to staff hundreds or thousands of branch offices.

8. Online Learning and Education.

Distance education is perhaps one of the most profound changes wrought by the Internet. Through for-profit educators such as Argosy, University of Phoenix, DeVry, Cappella and others, hundreds of thousands of students have earned masters degrees as well as undergraduate degrees and doctoral degrees. Online education has become the fastest growing segment of the educational marketplace.

For undergraduates and other students seeking the transformative experience of leaving home and gaining independence, the online environment may be inappropriate and incapable of delivering the social network needed for personal growth. For the adult learner, particularly the part-time student who is integrating graduate education into a professional career, the online environment provides both the access to the education and the accountability of written work product that will engage the student.

Online educational content is perhaps the richest of content available on the Internet. Through books, lectures, video, audio and postings of fellow students, online students are exposed to the content that their brick-and-mortar counterparts read and hear. They use the Internet and e-mail to interact, and are often graded on the quality of their postings. Unlike traditional students who receive little or no feedback on their comments in class, written postings create much higher levels of personal responsibility. Each student can be required to participate in a manner that cannot practically occur in the lecture hall.

Recent elimination of restrictions to federal student loans will only accelerate the growth of this medium for life-long learning.

9. B2B Automated Corporate Suppliers.

The business-to-business model of business interaction relies on computers to eliminate almost all human mediation. These transactions link the goods producer directly to the retailer. For example, a food cannery can use tracking information to know the amount and type of each can of vegetables sold on a weekly, or even daily, basis. With previously negotiated prices, the grocery store chain can simply stock the shelves through standing orders. The grocery chain's computer informs the cannery's computers of the requests, and the orders are filled.

Process innovation eliminates confusion, processing steps and time. It also makes the relationship between buyer and seller stronger because of the embedded costs associated with changing the systems and assumptions. As a result, costs are reduced and stability is increased.

The same process works even better with parts suppliers to large manufacturers, such as Detroit automakers. The computers know the consumption rate of every nut and bolt, so the vendors know how many parts to ship and when to ship them. Again, the transactions are much smoother, and the significant costs of creating and tracking orders is eliminated.

10. Retail Vendors.[284]

Retail vendors range from operations, such as Amazon, that exist exclusively online, to retailers that put only a fraction of the regular goods online for shipment. The costs associated with shipping products directly to the purchaser's home may be offset by not having to ship from warehouse to store or to warehouse at all. The national and international reach of a website may also provide an opportunity for an otherwise local store to develop a national market.

Except for the shipping limitations and national reach opportunity, online retailing and traditional retailing are essentially the same. Both need customers to review the products, learn about their features, comparison shop and commit to the purchase. While price comparisons may be easier online, the ability to inspect the products is more difficult. Particularly for clothing and products sensitive to variations in texture or color, the inherent limitations of the computer screen remain something of a barrier. Nonetheless, generous return policies and good experiences have led increased numbers of consumers into online retail product transactions.

---

[284] Note: Convenience: Retail today seems to be all about convenience and this topic could be an interesting highlight. Companies like Instacart and Shipt are promising quick, cheap, customized delivery to their customers. Many retailers now offer curbside pick-up or in-store pick-up, and the new Amazon Go model promises no check lanes and extreme convenience for customers.

11. Search Engine Sites.

The search engine was the Internet's second revolution. It democratized the Internet in a way that the portal system never could. Through complex algorithms in the software used by Google, Alta Vista and others, the terms typed into the search box generate a list of hundreds or thousands of relevant websites. Because the user of the search engine is not too likely to look beyond the first two to four pages of hits, search placement has become critical in the success or failure of the website.

The first generation search engines essentially looked for the search's text on any Internet page. The more often the words appeared, the more relevant the page was presumed to be for the searcher. Savvy page designers quickly developed techniques to trick these search engines. Other search engines relied on indexes and websites submitted by their owners. The second generation search engines emphasized the connectedness of the pages with the words. A page is determined to be more relevant if a greater number of different pages are linked to that page. The content is evaluated by popularity. Marketing strategy then requires the page to be designed to make the content valuable to more third parties.

The search engine business has been dominated by Google, driving many former search companies out of the field. Google supplements its algorithm-derived search lists with paid links that appear on the top pages. These paid links allow advertisers to avoid creating complex, expensive content in order to be high on the list results.

Although the algorithms and indexes will continue to evolve, the amount of data and the number of websites will require some technology that will either search the Internet or index the websites used by each consumer and anticipate which sites are likely to be relevant.

12. Social Networks.

Social networks were among the earliest uses of the Internet and continue to operate in many forms. The communications tool created by the Internet, along with cellular phones and wireless handheld devices, have transformed the social interactions of the public. Many of the gaming sites include options to talk among participants through the computer game. Ten percent of men and seven percent of women use online dating services.[285] Millions more use chat rooms, websites, listserv and other online social networking services. In January 2006, for example, Marketwatch.com reported that "MySpace.com, a free social networking site focused on teenagers, now boasts 47.3 million subscribers, according to USA Today. And the site's adding 5 million registered users a month."[286] MySpace.com and its rival Facebook.com provide young adults the opportunity to create personal websites, create affinity groups and social networks.

The speed at which these communities have expanded suggests the potential of online social networks. Services may include e-mail, calendaring, photo sharing and blogging. Members rate music and media content, join fan clubs, and find ways to connect with one another. These communities may anticipate future political organizations and might be the source of new presidential candidates. The economic, political and social significance of these sites has not been analyzed but should not be understated.

Youtube.com was sold for a reported $1.65 billion in Google stock even though the company has no profitability and relies heavily on works posted to the site without the copyright holder's position. The popularity of the site and the legitimacy of Google as parent company together have the potential to reshape the business paradigm.

13. Business Process Outsourcing (BPO).

The globalization trend brought about by cheaper communications and shared Internet content has been most fully realized in the business known as Business Process Outsourcing (BPO). Outsourcing is the U.S. term for companies that divest themselves of salaried employees by contracting with other entities to provide those specific services. Outsourcing has long been a corporate strategy to reduce employee costs and avoid paying some categories of employees the same benefits

---

[285] Fallows, *supra* note 281, at 20.

[286] Frank Barnako, *Internet Daily: MySpace.com's Tops for Cyber Teens*, MARKETWATCH (Jan. 9, 2006), http://www.marketwatch.com/news/story/fast-growing-myspacecom-ranks-tops-cyber/story.aspx?guid=%7BF7FB24B6%2D2081%2D4B8B%2D9221%2D18DF529E50DB%7D.

available to other employees. Most often it is used to avoid paying the higher wages generally associated with union employees.

BPOs take this concept global. The business processes are often IT, data management and payroll. As it becomes more sophisticated, areas such as finance, legal and accounting are also being provided by service companies. The biggest change in recent years is that the source of these services has increasingly moved to India and other parts of Asia where sophisticated personnel are available at considerably lower prices. Companies offer these services, computer network management, software design and a host of other core business functions.

The amalgamation of the services available by BPOs, combined with the manufacturing services provided in other regions can result in the launch of large scale virtual companies. Senior executives would essentially oversee every aspect of the product design, development, manufacture, marketing, sales and distribution. The enterprise would merely coordinate these services through contracts, operating with little overhead and almost no employees. This structure would be the ultimate disintermediated entity, operating with nothing to make it real other than a business charter and the contracts it has signed.

J. Selected Bibliography.

The text includes a good deal of discussion regarding contract provisions; however, it does not contain actual form contracts. The number of contracts necessary would fill an entire second volume, and such forms are often used without properly consulting an attorney regarding the proper use of its content. For attorneys and others looking for examples of contracts, the following books should provide ample information.

1. Contracts & Form Agreement Books.

THE AMERICAN BAR ASSOCIATION, LEGAL GUIDE FOR SMALL BUSINESS (2d 3d. 2010).

FRED S. STEINGOLD, LEGAL GUIDE FOR STARTING & RUNNING A SMALL BUSINESS (Marcia Stewart ed., 15th ed. 2017).

LINDA PINSON, KEEPING THE BOOKS: BASIC RECORD KEEPING AND ACCOUNTING FOR THE SUCCESSFUL SMALL BUSINESS (6th ed. 2007).

TAD CRAWFORD, BUSINESS AND LEGAL FORMS FOR FINE ARTISTS (4th ed. 2014).

TAD CRAWFORD, BUSINESS AND LEGAL FORMS FOR PHOTOGRAPHERS (4th ed. 2009).

TAD CRAWFORD & EVA DOMAN BRUCK, BUSINESS AND LEGAL FORMS FOR GRAPHIC DESIGNERS (4th ed. 2013).

2. Nonlegal Reference Books.

CHRIS ANDERSON, THE LONG TAIL: WHY THE FUTURE OF BUSINESS IS SELLING LESS OF MORE (Hyperion 2008) (2006).

JIM C. COLLINS & JERRY I. PORRAS, BUILT TO LAST: SUCCESSFUL HABITS OF VISIONARY COMPANIES (HARPERCOLLINS 2002) (1994).

JULIE L. DAVIS & SUZANNE S. HARRISON, EDISON IN THE BOARDROOM: HOW LEADING COMPANIES REALIZE VALUE FROM THEIR INTELLECTUAL ASSETS (2001).

PATRICK H. SULLIVAN, PROFITING FROM INTELLECTUAL CAPITAL: EXTRACTING VALUE FROM INNOVATION (paperback ed. 2001).

PATRICK H. SULLIVAN, VALUE DRIVEN INTELLECTUAL CAPITAL: HOW TO CONVERT INTANGIBLE CORPORATE ASSETS INTO MARKET VALUE (2000).

PETER F. DRUCKER, INNOVATION AND ENTREPRENEURSHIP (HarperBusiness 1985).

PHILIP EVANS & THOMAS S. WURSTER, BLOWN TO BITS: HOW THE NEW ECONOMICS OF INFORMATION TRANSFORMS STRATEGY (2000).

SOREN HOUGAARD, THE BUSINESS IDEA: THE EARLY STAGES OF ENTREPRENEURSHIP (2005).

3. *Other law related books of interest.*

GORDON V. SMITH & RUSSELL L. PARR, VALUATION OF INTELLECTUAL PROPERTY AND INTANGIBLE ASSETS (3d ed. 2000).

ROBERT C. MEGANTZ, TECHNOLOGY MANAGEMENT: DEVELOPING AND IMPLEMENTING EFFECTIVE LICENSING PROGRAMS (2002).

WILLIAM J. WILHELM & JOSEPH D. DOWNING, INFORMATION MARKETS: WHAT BUSINESSES CAN LEARN FROM FINANCIAL INNOVATION (2001).

K. Web Bibliography and Primary Links.

1. Business Planning Websites and Other Resources.
Sample Business Plans:
http://www.bplans.com/sp/businessplans.cfm

Nolo.com:
www.nolo.com

BizFilings Toolkit:
https://www.bizfilings.com/toolkit

Better Business Bureau—Alerts & News:
https://www.bbb.org/washington-dc-eastern-pa/news-events/lists/scam-alerts/

Center for Business Planning:
http://www.businessplans.org

SBA—Small Business Startup Guide, starting your business:
www.sba.gov/starting_business/startup/guide.html

StartupJournal.com:
http://www.thestartupjournal.com/

Entrepreneur's SmallBizBooks:
https://smallbizbooks.com.cutestat.com/

Businessnation:
www.businessnation.com

IRS—Start-Up Business Information:
https://www.irs.gov/businesses/small-businesses-self-employed/starting-a-business

SBA—Finance Start-Up :
https://www.sba.gov/business-guide/plan-your-business/fund-your-business

The Small Business Start-Up Guide:
http://isquare.com/prologue.htm

Starting a SmallBusiness for an Entrepreneur:
www.bplans.com/st

State of Illinois Business Portal—Business Start-Up Guides:
https://www2.illinois.gov/business

Missouri Small Business Start-Up Kit:
https://www.slcl.org/content/missouri-small-business-start-kit

State of Colorado—Office of Economic Development:
https://choosecolorado.com/

StartupNation:
www.startupnation.com

Business 2.0: Bulletproof Startup:
money.cnn.com/magazines/business2/startups/index.html

Inc.com Starting a Business:
www.inc.com/guides/start_biz

SBA—Sources of Secondary Research
https://www.sba.gov/blogs/conducting-market-research-here-are-5-official-sources-free-data-can-help

ASAE Directory of Associations Online:
http://www.asaecenter.org/Directories/AssociationSearch.cfm

U.S. Library of Congress—Ask a Librarian:
http://www.loc.gov/rr/askalib

Bureau of Labor Statistics:
http://stats.bls.gov

Business Research Lab:
http://www.busreslab.com/evaluhd.htm

Center for Business Women's Research:
http://www.womensbusinessresearch.org

SBA—Economic Statistics & Research:
http://www.sba.gov/advo/research

Federal Data and Statistics:
https://www.usa.gov/statistics

Internet Public Library:
http://www.ipl.org/

FRANDATA Corporation:
www.frandata.com

FranchiseHelp, Inc.:
www.franchisehelp.com

CompuMark—Trademark Research and Protection:
http://www.compumark.com/trademark-searching/title-copyright-entertainment-services/us-copyright-search/

2. Academic Research on Small Business (Weblinks) Recommended by the SBA.

The following weblinks have been compiled by the Small Business Administration. The information has been abridged and renumbered for convenience:

Office of Advocacy Resources.
Office of Advocacy Resources: www.sba.gov/advo/research

The Small Business Economy: A Report to the President:
https://www.sba.gov/advocacy/small-business-economy

Small Business Quarterly Bulletins:
https://www.sba.gov/advocacy/small-business-quarterly-bulletins

Small Business Quarterly Lending Studies:
https://www.sba.gov/advocacy/quarterly-lending-bulletins

State and Territory Small Business Economic Profiles:
https://www.sba.gov/category/advocacy-navigation-structure/research-and-statistics/state-economic-profiles

Regulatory Research:
https://www.sba.gov/category/advocacy-navigation-structure/regulatory-policy_0

Research on Owner Demographics (women, minorities, veterans, etc.): https://www.sba.gov/advocacy/small-business-facts-and-infographics

Advocacy Working Paper Series:
www.sba.gov/advo/research/wkpapers.html

Chronological List of Other Advocacy Research Reports:
www.sba.gov/advo/research/chron.html

Small Business Journals.
Entrepreneurship Theory and Practice:
http://www.blackwellpublishing.com/journal.asp?ref=1042-2587

International Small Business Journal:
http://www.sagepub.com/journal.aspx?pid=306

Venture Capital: An International Journal of Entrepreneurial Finance:
https://www.tandfonline.com/loi/tvec20

Journal of Applied Management and Entrepreneurship:
https://www.questia.com/library/p62409/journal-of-applied-management-and-entrepreneurship

Journal of Entrepreneurial Finance and Business Ventures:
https://digitalcommons.pepperdine.edu/jef/

Journal of Business Venturing:
www.elsevier.com/wps/find/journaldescription.cws_home/505723/d
escription?navopenmenu=1

Journal of Small Business Management:
http://www.blackwellpublishing.com/journal.asp?ref=0047-2778

Small Business Economics:
www.kluweronline.com/issn/0921-898X/contents

Web-Based Resources.
Kauffman Entrepreneurial Research:
www.kauffman.org
Kauffman-RAND Center for Study of Small Business and
Regulation:
www.rand.org/icj/centers/small_business

National Bureau of Economic Research Working Paper Series:
www.nber.org/papers

National Women's Business Council:
www.nwbc.gov

Organization for Economic Co-operation and Development:
www.oecd.org

Research Papers in Economics:
http://econpapers.repec.org

Social Science Research Network:
www.ssrn.com

The World Bank's Doing Business Project:
www.doingbusiness.org

Data Sources.
U.S. Department of Commerce, Bureau of the Census
2012 Economic Census: https://www.census.gov/programs-surveys/economic-census/year.2012.html

2012 Economic Census (Survey of Business Owners): https://www.census.gov/library/publications/2012/econ/2012-sbo.html

American FactFinder: http://factfinder.census.gov
Nonemployer Statistics: https://www.census.gov/programs-surveys/nonemployer-statistics/data/datasets.html

Center for Economic Studies (CES) Data and Working Papers www.ces.census.gov.
CES Data is available at Research Data Centers for approved research proposals.

County Business Patterns: https://www.census.gov/programs-surveys/cbp.html

Survey of Income and Program Participation: https://www.census.gov/programs-surveys/sipp/library/publications.All.html/page/7.html

U.S. Department of Labor, Bureau of Labor Statistics
Business Employment Dynamics: www.bls.gov/bdm/home.htm
Current Population Survey: http://www.bls.gov/cps/home.htm

Federal Reserve Board
Federal Reserve Bulletin: https://www.federalreserve.gov/publications/bulletin.htm
Survey of Small Business Finances: www.federalreserve.gov/pubs/oss/oss3/nssbftoc.htm
Survey of Consumer Finances: www.federalreserve.gov/pubs/oss/oss2/scfindex.html

Senior Loan Officer Survey on Bank Lending Practices: www.federalreserve.gov/boarddocs/SnLoanSurvey

Internal Revenue Service—Statistics of Income Division: www.irs.gov/taxstats

Ewing Marion Kauffman Foundation—Kauffman Index of Entrepreneurial Activity: www.kauffman.org

National Federation of Independent Business—Small Business Economic Trends: https://www.nfib.com/surveys/small-business-economic-trends/

Small Business Polls: www.nfib.com

Other Longitudinal Databases
Global Entrepreneurship Monitor: www.gemconsortium.org
Panel Study on Entrepreneurial Dynamics: http://psed.isr.umich.edu/psed/home

3. Intellectual Property Websites.
United States Patent and Trademark Office
http://www.uspto.gov

United States Copyright Office
http://www.copyright.gov

WIPO-World Intellectual Property Organization
www.WIPO.Int

Intellectual Property Mall (Franklin Pierce Law Center)
https://law.unh.edu/franklin-pierce-center-intellectual-property

Professor Tom Field's The Practical and Legal Fundamentals of Intellectual Property
https://lsr.nellco.org/piercelaw_facseries/

American Intellectual Property Law Association

www.aipla.org

Legal Information Institute Cornell Law School
www.law.cornell.edu/topical.html

IPO—Intellectual Property Owners Association
www.ipo.org

Computer Crime and Intellectual Property Section (CCIPS) of the
Criminal Division of the US Department of Justice
www.cybercrime.gov

National Academies' Intellectual Property
http://sites.nationalacademies.org/pga/stl/ip/index.htm

Electronic Freedom Forum
www.eff.org

BitLaw
www.bitlaw.com

L. About the Author.

Jon M. Garon is dean of Nova Southeastern University Shepard Broad College of Law. Garon serves as chief academic officer for the law school, providing strategic leadership on programming, curriculum, enrollment management, marketing, and finance. He is a nationally recognized authority on technology law and intellectual property, particularly copyright law, entertainment and information privacy. A Minnesota native, he received his bachelor's degree from the University of Minnesota in 1985 and his juris doctor degree from Columbia University School of Law in 1988.

Prior to joining Nova Southeastern University in 2014, Dean Garon was the inaugural director of the Northern Kentucky University Salmon P. Chase College of Law, Law + Informatics Institute from 2011-2014. Garon served as dean and professor of law at Hamline University School of Law in St. Paul, Minnesota. He was professor of law from 2003 to 2011, dean of the Law School from 2003 to 2008 and Interim Dean of the Graduate School of Management from 2005 to 2006. Before Hamline, Garon taught Entertainment Law and Copyright at Franklin Pierce Law Center in Concord, New Hampshire and Western State College of Law in Orange County, California.

Dean Garon has held key leadership positions as past chair of both the American Bar Association's Law School Administration Committee and the Association of American Law Schools Section on Part-Time Legal Education. He also serves on the Test Development and Research committee for the Law School Admissions Council. His teaching and scholarship often focus on business innovation and structural change to media, education and content-based industries. He is the author of four books and numerous book chapters and articles, including

- The Entrepreneur's Intellectual Property & Business Handbook (Manegiere Publications 2018)

- Pop Culture Business Handbook for Cons and Festivals (Manegiere Publications 2017)

605

- The Independent Filmmaker's Law & Business Guide to Financing, Shooting, and Distributing Independent and Digital Films (A Cappella Books, 2d Ed. 2009)

- ENTERTAINMENT LAW & PRACTICE (2d Ed. 2014 Carolina Academic Press).

His publications can be found at the following:

- Amazon: https://www.amazon.com/default/e/B001JPCHA6

- SSRN: http://ssrn.com/author=378821

- BePress: https://works.bepress.com/jon_garon/

- Web: http://jongaron.com

Index

Table of Cases

Nike, Inc. v. "Just Did It" Enters., 6 F.3d 1225 (7th Cir. 1993)

Pacific Aerospace & Elec., Inc. v. Taylor, 295 F. Supp. 2d 1188 (E.D. Wash. 2003)

Peaches Entm't Corp. v. Entm't Repertoire Assocs., 62 F.3d 690 (5th Cir. 1995)

Price v. Hal Roach Studios, Inc., 400 F. Supp. 836 (S.D.N.Y. 1975)

Ralston Purina Co. v. Thomas J. Lipton, Inc., 341 F. Supp. 129 (S.D.N.Y. 1972)

Recording Indus. Ass'n of Am. v. Diamond Multimedia Sys., Inc., 180 F.3d 1072 (9th Cir. 1999)

Shurgard Storage Ctrs., Inc. v. Safeguard Self Storage, Inc., 119 F. Supp. 2d 1121 (W.D. Wash. 2000)

Sid & Marty Kofft Television Prod., Inc. v. McDonald's Corp., 562 F.2d 1157 (9th Cir. 1977)

Sony Corp. of Am. v. Universal City Studios, Inc., 464 U.S. 417 (1984)

V Secret Catalogue, Inc. v. Moseley, 605 F.3d 382 (6th Cir. 2010)

Wendt v. Host Int'l, Inc., 125 F.3d 806 (9th Cir. 1997)

Winters v. New York, 333 U.S. 507 (1948)

CPSIA information can be obtained
at www.ICGtesting.com
Printed in the USA
LVHW082319261121
704455LV00011B/720

9 781721 866533